“A Community of Peoples”

Harvard Museum of the Ancient Near East Publications

Harvard Semitic Studies

VOLUME 69

The titles published in this series are listed at *brill.com/hvss*

Daniel E. Fleming, Ethel and Irvin A. Edelman Professor of Hebrew and Judaic Studies, New York University.

WASHINGTON SQUARE PARK, OCTOBER 6, 2021. PHOTO COURTESY OF MICHAEL STAHL.

"A Community of Peoples"

Studies on Society and Politics in the Bible and Ancient Near East in Honor of Daniel E. Fleming

Edited by

Mahri Leonard-Fleckman
Lauren A.S. Monroe
Michael J. Stahl
Dylan R. Johnson

BRILL

LEIDEN | BOSTON

Cover illustration: Early Dynastic banquet scene, Lapis Lazuli. The Yale Babylonian Collection. Photograph by Klaus Wagensonner.

Library of Congress Cataloging-in-Publication Data

Names: Fleming, Daniel E., honouree. | Leonard-Fleckman, Mahri, editor. | Monroe, Lauren A. S., editor. | Stahl, Michael J., editor. | Johnson, Dylan R., 1988- editor.
Title: A community of peoples : studies on society and politics in the Bible and Ancient Near East in honor of Daniel E. Fleming / edited by Mahri Leonard-Fleckman, Lauren A.S. Monroe, Michael J. Stahl, Dylan R. Johnson.
Description: Leiden ; Boston : Brill, [2022] | Series: Harvard museum of the ancient near east publications | Includes bibliographical references and index.
Identifiers: LCCN 2022006163 (print) | LCCN 2022006164 (ebook) | ISBN 9789004511521 (hardback) | ISBN 9789004511538 (ebook)
Subjects: LCSH: Bible. Old Testament–Criticism, interpretation, etc. | Sociology, Biblical. | Politics in the Bible.
Classification: LCC BS1171.3 .C654 2022 (print) | LCC BS1171.3 (ebook) | DDC 221.6–dc23/eng/20220308
LC record available at https://lccn.loc.gov/2022006163
LC ebook record available at https://lccn.loc.gov/2022006164

Typeface for the Latin, Greek, and Cyrillic scripts: "Brill". See and download: brill.com/brill-typeface.

ISSN 0147-9342
ISBN 978-90-04-51152-1 (hardback)
ISBN 978-90-04-51153-8 (e-book)

This book is printed on acid-free paper and produced in a sustainable manner.

Contents

Abbreviations

A	(1) Louvre Tablet; or (2) Tablet in the collections of the Oriental Institute, University of Chicago
AbB	Altbabylonische Briefe in Umschrift und Übersetzung
ABC	Anchor Bible Commentary
ABD	*Anchor Bible Dictionary*. Edited by David N. Freedman. 6 vols. New Haven, CT: Yale University Press, 1992.
ABL	*Assyrian and Babylonian Letters Belonging to the Kouyunjik Collections of the British Museum*. Edited by Robert F. Harper. 14 vols. Chicago, IL: University of Chicago Press, 1892–1914.
ABS	Archaeology and Biblical Studies
acc.	Accusative case
ACS	Archaeology, Culture, and Society
AfOB	Archiv für Orientforschung: Beiheft
AHw	*Akkadisches Handwörterbuch*. Wolfram von Soden. 3 vols. Wiesbaden, 1965–1981.
AIL	Ancient Israel and Its Literature
AJA	*American Journal of Archaeology*
Akk.	Akkadian
AKT 6	*The Archive of the Šalim-Aššur Family*. Mogens Trolle Larsen. Vols. 1–4. Ankara Kültepe Tabletleri 6. Ankara: Türk Tarih Kurumu Basimevi, 2010–2016.
AlT	*The Alalakh Tablets*. D.J. Wiseman. Occasional Publications of the British Institute of Archaeology at Ankara 2. London: British Institute of Archaeology at Ankara, 1953.
AMD	Ancient Magic and Divination
ANEM	Ancient Near East Monographs
ANET	*Ancient Near Eastern Texts Relating to the Old Testament*. Edited by J.B. Pritchard. 3rd ed. Princeton, NJ: Princeton University Press, 1969.
AnOr	Analecta Orientalia
AnSt	*Anatolian Studies*
AO	Antiquités Orientales, museum siglum of the Louvre Museum
AOAT	Alter Orient und Altes Testament
AoF	*Altorientalische Forschungen*
AOS	American Oriental Society
ARM	Archives Royales de Mari
ARM 1	*Correspondance de Šamši-Addu et ses fils*. Edited by Georges Dossin. Paris: Imprimerie nationale, 1950.

ARM 2	*Lettre diverses*. Edited by Ch.-F. Jean. Paris: Imprimerie nationale, 1950.
ARM 5	*Correspondance Iasmaḫ-Addu*. Edited by Georges Dossin. Paris: Imprimerie nationale, 1952.
ARM 8	*Textes juridiques et administratifs*. Edited by Georges Boyer. Paris: Paul Geuthner, 1957.
ARM 10	*La correspondance féminine*. Edited by Georges Dossin. Paris: Paul Geuthner, 1967.
ARM 13	*Textes divers*. Edited by George Dossin, Jean Bottéro, and Maurice Birot. Paris: Paul Geuthner, 1964.
ARM 16/1	*Répertoire analytique des Archives royales de Mari (2e volume) des tomes I–XIV, XVIII et des textes divers hors collection: Première partie: noms propres*. Edited by Maurice Birot, Jean-Robert Kupper, and Olivier Rouault. Paris: Paul Geuthner, 1979.
ARM 26/1	*Archives épistolaire de Mari I/1*. Edited by Jean-Marie Durand. Paris: Éditions Recherche sur les Civilisations, 1988.
ARM 26/2	*Archives épistolaire de Mari I/2*. Edited by Dominique Charpin. Paris: Éditions Recherche sur les Civilisations, 1988.
ARM 28	*Lettres royales du temps de Zimri-Lim*. Edited by Jean-Robert Kupper. Paris: Éditions Recherche sur les Civilisations, 1998.
ARM 31	*La vaisselle de luxe des rois de Mari*. Edited by Michaël Guichard. Paris: Éditions Recherche sur les Civilisations, 2005.
ARM 33	*Les premières années du roi Zimrî-Lîm de Mari: Première partie*. Edited by Jean-Marie Durand. Boston, MA/Leuven/Paris: Peeters, 2019.
ARM 34	Not yet published
ARM 35	Not yet published
ArOr	*Archív orientální*
AS	Assyriological Studies
ASJ	*Acta Sumerologica*
ASJ 13	Tsukimoto, Akio. "Akkadian Tablets in the Hirayama Collection (II)." *ASJ* 13 (1991): 275–333.
ATA	Alttestamentliche Abhandlungen
ATANT	Abhandlungen zur Theologie des Alten und Neuen Testaments
AuOr	*Aula Orientalis*
AuOr 5	Arnaud, Daniel. "La Syrie du moyen-Euphrate sous le protectorate hittite: Contrats de droit privé." *AuOr* 5 (1987): 211–241.
AYBRL	Anchor Yale Bible Reference Library
BA	*Biblical Archaeologist*
BAH	Bibliothèque archéologique et historique
BaM	*Baghdader Mitteilungen*

BAR	*Biblical Archaeology Review*
BARB	*Bulletin de l'Académie Royale de Belgique*
BARIS	BAR (British Archaeological Reports) International Series
BASOR	*Bulletin of the American Schools of Oriental Research*
BCE	B.C.
BE	*The Babylonian Expedition of the University of Pennsylvania, Series A: Cuneiform Texts*. Philadelphia, PA: University of Pennsylvania, 1893–.
BE 6/2	*Babylonian Legal and Business Documents from the Time of the First Dynasty of Babylon: Chiefly from Nippur*. Arno Poebel. Philadelphia, PA: University of Pennsylvania, 1909.
BE	Biblische Enzyklopädie
BH	Biblical Hebrew
Bib	*Biblica*
BibInt	*Biblical Interpretation*
BibInt	Biblical Interpretation Series
BM	British Museum, museum sigla of the British Museum
BN	*Biblische Notizen*
Bo year/ …	Inventory numbers of Boğazköy tablets excavated from 1968 to the present
BO	*Bibliotheca Orientalis*
BRev	*Bible Review*
BRS	The Biblical Resource Series
BZAW	Beihefte zur Zeitschrift für die alttestamentliche Wissenschaft
c.	Common gender
ca.	Circa
CAD	*The Assyrian Dictionary of the Oriental Institute of the University of Chicago*. Edited by I.J. Gelb et al. 21 vols (A–Z). Chicago, IL: The Oriental Institute of the University of Chicago, 1956–2011.
CBQ	*Catholic Biblical Quarterly*
CBR	*Currents in Biblical Research*
CBS	Catalogue of the Babylonian Section, museum siglum of the Penn Museum of the University of Pennsylvania, Philadelphia
CE	A.D.
CHANE	Culture and History of the Ancient Near East
CHD	*The Hittite Dictionary of the Oriental Institute of the University of Chicago*. Edited by Hans G. Güterbock, Harry A. Hoffner Jr., and Theo P.J. van den Hout. Chicago, IL: The Oriental Institute of the University of Chicago, 1980–.
CIS	Copanhagen International Seminar
CLuw.	Cuneiform Luwian

cm.	Centimeter
CM	Cuneiform Monographs
col.	Column
COS	*The Context of Scripture*. Edited by W.W. Hallo. 4 vols. Leiden, 1997–.
Cowley	Cowley, Arthur E. *Aramaic Papyri of the Fifth Century B.C.* Oxford: Clarendon, 1923.
CRAI	Comptes rendus de l'Académie des inscriptions et belles-lettres
CRRAI	Comptus rendus des Recontres Assyriologiques Internationales
C-stem	Causative stem
CT	*Cuneiform Texts from Babylonian Tablets in the British Museum*
CTA	*Corpus des tablettes en cunéiformes alphabétiques découvertes à Ras Shamra-Ugarit de 1929 à 1939*. Edited by Andrée Herdner. Paris: Geuthner, 1963.
CTH	*Catalogue des textes hittites*. Emmanuel Laroche. Paris: Klincksieck, 1971.
CUSAS	Cornell University Studies in Assyriology and Sumerology
DAS	Documents d'archéologie syrienne
DCH	*Dictionary of Classical Hebrew*. Edited by David J.A. Clines. 9 vols. Sheffield: Sheffield Phoenix Press, 1993–2014.
DCLS	Deuterocanonical and Cognate Literature Studies
DDD	*Dictionary of Deities and Demons in the Bible*. Edited by Karel van der Toorn, Bob Becking, and Pieter W. van der Horst. 2nd rev. ed. Leiden: Brill, 1999.
Di	Inventory number for Ur-Utu archives excavated at Tell ed-Dër in Iraq by the Belgian Archaeological Expedition under the directorship of L. De Meyer
DN	Divine name(s)
D-stem	Verbal stem characterized by the optional doubling of the second radical
DNWSI	*Dictionary of the North-West Semitic Inscriptions*. Edited by Jacob Hoftijzer and Karel Jongeling. 2 vols. Leiden: Brill, 1995.
DULAT	*A Dictionary of the Ugaritic Language in the Alphabetic Tradition*. G. del Olmo Lete and J. Sanmartín. Translated by W.G.E. Watson. 2 vols. Leiden: Brill, 2004.
E	E source (hypothetical pentateuchal source)
ED	Early Dynastic
Emar (VI/3)	Arnaud, Daniel. *Recherches au pays d'Aštata, Emar VI/3: Textes sumériens et accadiens*. Paris: Editions Recherche sur les Civilsations, 1986.
EŞ	Eski Şark Eserleri Müzesi
ETCSL	Electronic Text Corpus of Sumerian Literature

FAT	Forschungen zum Alten Testament
FM	Florilegium marianum
FM 1	*Recueil d'études en l'honneur de Michel Fleury*. Edited by Jean-Marie Durand. Mémoires de NABU 1. Paris: SEPOA, 1992.
FM 2	*Recueil d'études à la mémoire de Maurice Birot*. Edited by Dominique Charpin and Jean-Marie Durand. Mémoires de NABU 3. Paris: SEPOA, 1994.
FM 3	*Recueil d'études à la mémoire de Marie-Thérèse Barrelet*. Edited by Dominique Charpin and Jean-Marie Durand. Mémoires de NABU 2. Paris: SEPOA, 1997.
FM 5	*Mari et le Proche-Orient à l'epoque amorrite: Essaie d'histoire politique*. Dominique Charpin and Nele Ziegler. Paris: SEPOA, 2003.
FM 6	*Recueil d'études à la mémoire d'André Parrot*. Edited by Dominique Charpin and Jean-Marie Durand. Paris: SEPOA, 2002.
FM 7	*Le culte d'Addu d'Alep et l'affaire d'Alahtum*. Jean-Marie Durand. Mémoires de NABU 8. Paris: Société pour l'étude du Proche-Orient Ancien, 2002.
FM 8	*Le culte des pierres et les monuments commémoratifs en Syrie amorrite*. Edited by Jean-Marie Durand. Mémoires de NABU 9. Paris: SEPOA, 2005.
FM 16	*L'agriculture irriguée au royaume de Mari: Essai d'histoire des techniques*. Edited by Hervé Reculeau. Mémoires de NABU 21. Paris: SEPOA, 2018.
FMA	*From the Mari Archives: An Anthology of Old Babylonian Letters*. Jack M. Sasson. University Park, PA: PSU Press, 2017.
FOTL	Forms of the Old Testament Literature
FRLANT	Forschungen zur Religion und Literatur des Alten und Neuen Testaments
Gilibert Zinjirli	*Syro-Hittite Monumental Art and the Archaeology of Performance: The Stone Reliefs at Carchemish and Zincirli in the Earlier First Millennium BCE*. Alessandra Gilibert. Berlin: de Gruyter, 2011.
GN	Geographical name(s)
G-stem	Grundstamm (basic stem)
HACL	History, Archaeology, and Culture of the Levant
HANE/M	History of the Ancient Near East/Monographs
HANE/S	History of the Ancient Near East/Studies
Haradum 2	*Haradum II: Les textes de la période paléo-babylonienne (Samsu-iluna—Ammi-ṣaduqa)*. Francis Joannès, Christine Kepinski-Lecomte, and Gudrun Colbow. Paris: Éditions Recherche sur les Civilisations, 2006.

HBM	Hebrew Bible Monographs
HdO	Handbuch der Orientalistik
HE	Hautes Études, siglum for tablets from the collections of the École Pratique des Hautes Études
Heb.	Hebrew
HeBAI	*Hebrew Bible and Ancient Israel*
HOS	Handbook of Oriental Studies
HEG	*Hethitisches etymologisches Glossar*. Johann Tischler. Edited by Günter Neumann and Erich Neu. 16 vols. Innsbrucker Beiträge zur Sprachwissenschaft 20. Innsbruck: Institut für Sprachwissenschaft der Universität Innsbruck, 1983–2016.
HFAC	*Hittite Fragments in American Collections*. Gary Beckmann and Harry A. Hoffner, Jr. Texts from the Babylonian Collection 2. New Haven, CT: Yale Babylonian Collection, 1982 = *JCS* 37/1 (1985): 1–60.
Hitt.	Hittite
HLuw.	Hieroglyphic Luwian
HSM	Harvard Semitic Monographs
HSS	Harvard Semitic Studies
HTR	*Harvard Theological Review*
HUCA	*Hebrew Union College Annual*
HW	*Hethitisches Wörterbuch*. J. Friedrich. Heidelberg: Winter, 1952–1954.
ICK	Inscriptions cunéiforms du Kultépé
IEJ	*Israel Exploration Journal*
IM	Iraq Museum, siglum of the Iraq Museum in Baghdad
IRT	Issues in Religion and Theology
JA	*Journal Asiatique*
JAA	*Journal of the American Academy of Religion*
JAJSup	Journal of Ancient Judaism Supplements
JANEH	*Journal of Ancient Near Eastern History*
JANES	*Journal of the Ancient Near Eastern Society*
JAOS	*Journal of the American Oriental Society*
JBL	*Journal of Biblical Literature*
JCS	*Journal of Cuneiform Studies*
JCS	Journal of Cuneiform Studies
JESHO	*Journal of the Economic and Social History of the Orient*
JNES	*Journal of Near Eastern Studies*
JRAS	*Journal of the Royal Asiatic Society*
JSJSup	Journal for the Study of Judaism Supplement Series
JSOT	*Journal for the Study of the Old Testament*
JSOTSup	Journal for the Study of the Old Testament: Supplement Series

JSS	*Journal of Semitic Studies*
KAI	*Kanaanäische und aramäische Inschriften*. Edited by Herbert Donner and Wolfgang Röllig. 2nd ed. Wiesbaden: Harrassowitz, 1966–1969.
KBo	*Keilschrifttexte aus Boghazköi*. 22 vols. Leipzig: Hinrichs, 1916–1923; Berlin: Gebr. Mann, 1954–.
KIM	Kültepe International Meetings
*KTU*³	*Die keilalphabetischen Texte aus Ugarit, Ras Ibn Hani und anderen Orten*. Edited by Manfried Dietrich, Oswald Loretz, and Joaquín Sanmartín. 3rd ed. AOAT 360/1. Münster: Ugarit-Verlag, 2014.
KUB	*Keilschrifturkunden aus Boghazköi*. Berlin: Akademie, 1921–.
LANE	Languages of the Ancient Near East
LAPO	Littératures anciennes du Proche-Orient
LAPO 16, 17, 18	*Documents épistolaires du palais de Mari*. J.-M. Durand. 3 vols. Paris: du Cerf, 1997–2000.
LAS	Leipziger Altorientalistische Studien
LBA	Late Bronze Age
LH	Laws of Hammurabi
LHBOTS	Library of Hebrew Bible/Old Testament Studies
Luw.	Luwian
LXX	Septuagint
m.	Meter
MARI	*Mari: Annales de recherches interdisciplinaires*
MB	(1) Middle Babylonian; or (2) Middle Bronze
MC	Mesopotamian Civilizations
MdB	Le Monde de la Bible
MEE	Materiali epigrafici de Ebla
MH	Middle Hittite
MHEO	Mesopotamian History and Environment, Occasional Publications
MIOF	*Mitteilungen des Instituts für Orientforschung*
MMA	Museum siglum of the Metropolitan Museum of Art, New York City
MRS	Mission de Ras Shamra
MT	Mas(s)oretic Text
MTT	Matériaux pour l'étude de la toponymie et de la topographie
MTT/1	*Les Toponymes paléo-babyloniens de la Haute-Mésopotamie*. Nele Ziegler and Anne-Isabelle Langlois. Paris: SEPOA, 2016.
MVS	Materiali per il vocabolario sumerico
NA	Neo-Assyrian
NABU	*Nouvelles assyriologiques breves et utilitaires*
NCB	New Century Bible
NEA	*Near Eastern Archaeology*

NH	New Hittite
NJPS	New Jewish Publication Society
NT	New Testament
NWS	Northwest Semitic
OB	Old Babylonian
OBO	Orbis biblicus et orientalis
OBO.SA	Orbis Biblicus et Orientalis, Series Archaeologica
obv.	Obverse
OECT	Oxford Editions of Cuneiform Texts
OECT 6	*Babylonian Penitential Psalms to Which Are Added Fragments of the Epic of Creation from Kish in the Eld Collection of the Ashmolean Museum Excavated by the Oxford-Field Museum Expedition.* Stephen Herbert Langdon. Paris: P. Geuthner, 1927.
OECT 8	*The Sayce and H. Weld Collection in the Ashmolean Museum: Sumerian Contracts from Nippur.* G.R. Hunter. London: Oxford University Press, 1930.
OI	Oriental Institute
OIP	Oriental Institute Publications
OIS	Oriental Institute Seminars
OLA	*Orientalia Lovaniensia Analecta*
OLA	Orientalia Lovaniensia Analecta
Or	*Orientalia*
ORA	Orientalische Religionen in der Antike
OTL	Old Testament Library
OTS	Old Testament Studies
PEQ	*Palestine Exploration Quarterly*
PIHANS	Publications de l'Institut historique-archéologique néerlandais de Stamboul
PIHANS 117	*The Royal Archives from Tell Leilan: Old Babylonian Letters and Treaties from the Lower Town Palace East.* Jesper Eidem et al. Leiden: Nederlands Institute voor het nabije Oosten, 2011.
PIPOAC	Publications de l'Institut du Proche-Orient ancien du Collège de France
pl.	Plural
PN	Personal name
PNF	Personal name (female)
PRU	*Le palais royal d'Ugarit: Mission de Ras Shamra.* Paris: Imprimerie nationale, 1956–.
PRU 6	*Le palais royal d'Ugarit, Vol. VI.* Mission de Ras Shamra 12. Paris: Imprimerie nationale/Librairie C. Klincksieck, 1970.

RA	*Revue d'assyriologie et d'archéologie orientale*
RAI	Rencontre assyriologique internationale
RB	*Revue biblique*
RC	*Religion Compass*
RE	*Texts from the Vicinity of Emar in the Collection of Jonathan Rosen.* Gary Beckman. HANE/M 2. Padova: Sargon, 1996
RelSoc	*Religion and Society*
RGTC	Répertoire géographique des textes cunéiformes
RGTC 6	*Die Orts- und Gewässernamen der hethitischen Texte.* G.F. del Monte and J. Tischler. Wiesbaden: Reichert, 1978.
RHA	*Revue hittite et asianique*
RIDA	*Revue internationale des droits de l'antiquité*
RIMA	The Royal Inscriptions of Mesopotamia, Assyrian Periods
RIMA 1	*Assyrian Rulers of the Third and Second Millennia BC (to 1115 BC).* A. Kirk Grayson. Toronto: University of Toronto Press, 1987.
RIMA 2	*Assyrian Rulers of the Early First Millennium BC (1114–859 BC).* A. Kirk Grayson. Toronto: University of Toronto Press, 1991.
RIME	The Royal Inscriptions of Mesopotamia, Early Periods
RINAP	Royal Inscriptions of the Neo-Assyrian Period
RlA	*Reallexikon der Assyriologie und vorderasiatischen Archäologie.* Edited by Erich Ebeling et al. 15 vols. Berlin: de Gruyter, 1928–.
RRBS	Recent Research in Biblical Studies
RSO	*Revista degli studi orientali*
S	*Ausgrabungen in Sendschirli v: Die Kleinfunde von Sendschirli.* Edited by Felix von Luschan. Mitteilungen aus den orientalischen Sammlungen 15. Berlin: de Gruyter, 1943.
SAA	State Archives of Assyria
SAA 1	*The Standard Babylonian Epic of Gilgamesh: Cuneiform text, Transliteration, Glossary, Indices and Sign List.* Simo Parpola. Helsinki: The Neo-Assyrian Text Corpus Project, 1997.
SAA 17	*The Babylonian correspondence of Sargon and Sennacherib.* Manfried Dietrich. Helsinki: Helsinki University Press, 2003.
SAAB	*State Archives of Assyria Bulletin*
SAAS	State Archives of Assyria Studies
SANER	Studies in Ancient Near Eastern Records
Sb	Object in the Louvre Museum
SBB	Stuttgarter biblische Beiträge
SBLABS	Society of Biblical Literature Academia Biblica Series
SBLDS	Society of Biblical Literature Dissertation Series
SBLMS	Society of Biblical Literature Monograph Series

SBLRBS	Society of Biblical Literature Resources for Biblical Study
SBLWAW	Society of Biblical Literature Writings from the Ancient World
SBT	Studien zu den Boğazköy-Texten
SCCNH	Studies on the Civilization and Culture of Nuzi and the Hurrians
Schwiderski BarRak	*Die alt- und reichsaramäischen Inschriften.* Dirk Schwiderski. Vol. 2. Berlin: de Gruyter, 2004.
ScrHier	Scripta Hierosolymitana
Sem	*Semitica*
sg.	Singular
ShA 1	*The Shemshara Archives, Vol. 1: The Letters.* Jesper Eidem and Jørgen Læssøe. Historisk-filosofiske Skrifter 23. Copenhagen: Royal Danish Academy of Sciences and Letters, 2001.
SHANE	Studies in the History of the Ancient Near East
SHCANE	Studies in the History and Culture of the Ancient Near East
SIA	Studia Instituti Anthropos
SJLA	Studies in Judaism in Late Antiquity
SMS	Syro-Mesopotamian Studies
ST	*Studia theologica*
STDJ	Studies on the Texts of the Desert of Judah
StEb	*Studi Eblaiti*
STT	*The Sultantepe Tablets.* Edited by O.R. Gurney, J.J. Finkelstein, and P. Hulin. 2 vols. Occasional Publications of the British Institute of Archaeology at Ankara 3 and 7. London: British Institute of Archaeology at Ankara, 1957 and 1964.
TADAE	*Textbook of Aramaic Documents from Ancient Egypt.* Bezalel Porten and Ada Yardeni. Vol. 1. Jerusalem: Hebrew University; Winona Lake, IN: Eisenbrauns, 1986.
TAPS	Transactions of the American Philosophical Society
TCS	Texts from Cuneiform Sources
TDOT	*Theological Dictionary of the Old Testament.* Edited by G. Johannes Botterweck and Helmer Ringgren. Translated by J.T. Willis, G.W. Bromiley, and D.E. Green. 17 vols. Grand Rapids, MI: Eerdmans, 1974–2021.
THeth	Texte der Hethiter
ThZ	*Theologische Zeitschrift*
TLB 4	*Briefe aus dem Leidener Sammlung* (*TLB IV*). Rintje Frankena. AbB 3. Leiden: Brill, 1968.
TM	Siglum of tablets from Tall Mardikh (Ebla)
TMH	Texte und Materialien der Frau Professor Hilprecht—Collection of Babylonian Antiquities im Eigentum der Universität Jena

TMH 10	*The Old Babylonian Administrative Texts in the Hilprecht Collection Jena*. Anne Goddeeris. With a contribution by Ursula Seidl. Wiesbaden: Harrassowitz Verlag, 2016.
Tropper B	*Die Inschriften von Zincirli: Neue Edition und vergleichende Grammatik des phönizischen, sam'alischen und aramäischen Textkorpus*. Josef Tropper. Münster: Ugarit-Verlag, 1993.
TSK	*Theologische Studien und Kritiken*
TSSI 2	*Textbook of Syrian Semitic Inscriptions, Volume II: Aramaic Inscriptions including Inscriptions in the Dialect of Zenjirli*. John C.L. Gibson. Oxford: Clarendon Press, 1975.
TTKY	Türk Tarih Kurumu yayınları
TTZ	*Trierer theologische Zeitschrift*
Ug. V	*Ugaritica V: Nouveaux textes accadiens, hourrites et ugaritiques des archives et bibliothèques privées d'Ugarit, commentaires des textes historiques*. Edited by J. Nougayrol, E. Laroche, C. Virolleaud, and C.F.A. Schaeffer. Vol. 1. Mission de Ras Shamra 16. Paris: Imprimerie nationale, 1968.
UF	*Ugarit-Forschungen*
UT	*Ugaritic Textbook*. Cyrus H. Gordon. AnOr 38. Rome: Pontifical Biblical Institute, 1965.
VA	Vorderasiatische Abteilung, museum siglum of the Vorderasiatisches Museum, Berlin
VS	Vorderasiatische Schriftdenkmäler der (Königlichen) Museen zu Berlin
VT	*Vetus Testamentum*
WAW	Writings from the Ancient World
WKZM	Wiener Zeitschrift für die Kunde des Morgenlandes
WMANT	Wissenschaftliche Monographien zum Alten und Neuen Testament
WO	*Die Welt des Orients*
WS	West Semitic
WVDOG	Wissenschaftliche Veröffentlichungen der Deutschen Orient-Gesellschaft
YOS	Yale Oriental Series, Babylonian Texts
YOS 7	*Records from Erech: Time of Cyrus and Cambyses (538–521 B.C.)*. Arch Tremayne. New Haven, CT: Yale University Press, 1925.
ZA	*Zeitschrift für Assyriologie*
ZABR	*Zeitschrift für altorientalische und biblische Rechtgeschichte*
ZAW	*Zeitschrift für die alttestamentliche Wissenschaft*
ZDPV	*Zeitschrift des deutschen Palästina-Vereins*
//	parallel passage or grammatical form
*	reconstructed form (grammatical or literary)

1

Introduction: "A Community of Peoples" (Gen 28:3)

Mahri Leonard-Fleckman, Lauren A.S. Monroe, and Michael J. Stahl

> I wanted to find in the past real bodies and living voices, and I knew that if I could not find these—the bodies having long moldered away and the voices fallen silent—I could at least seize upon those traces that seemed to be close to actual experience.[1]
>
> STEPHEN GREENBLATT, "Touch of the Real"

On the edge of a harbor in Connecticut sits a cottage bordered by gardens, looking out on the Long Island Sound. In a room flooded with light is a bookcase, an archive of cherished works. Some are written by Dan Fleming, to whom the archive belongs, and others by his former students and closest colleagues. These books, written over several decades, cover a wide range of topics in various academic fields, including Biblical, Ancient Near Eastern, and Jewish Studies. Without clear categorization by discipline or topic, they mingle comfortably on the shelves as a community of voices, held together by the personal relationships and shared intellectual questions that stand at the heart of Dan's distinguished career. Defying the artificial boundaries of traditional academic inquiry, this particular archive in Dan's house is a tangible expression of the social and interdisciplinary character of knowledge production in the modern academy. It reflects a history and the possibilities for history writing, both of which necessarily remain partial and incomplete.

The unfinished nature of the scholarly enterprise highlights an important facet of Dan's archive. Each book reflects Dan's commitment to asking fresh historical questions of old datasets in pursuit of what Sara Milstein in her contribution to this volume calls "New Ideas"—concepts and frameworks that push their respective fields in new, unexplored directions. Dan's scholarship

1 Stephen Greenblatt, "The Touch of the Real," in *The Fate of "Culture": Geertz and Beyond*, ed. Sherry B. Ortner (Berkeley, CA: University of California Press, 1999), 21.

 | DOI:10.1163/9789004511538_002

on ritual and social power at Late Bronze Emar, the interplay of collective and royal governance at Old Babylonian Mari, and Judah's appropriation of Israel's legacy during the Iron Age (to name just three examples) all illustrate how new, theoretically sophisticated paradigms—when grounded in the ancient data—can radically reshape our understanding of the peoples of antiquity. Yet, Dan's work does not claim to be the final word. Perhaps more than anything else, his mentorship of a new generation of scholars, whose books now populate his shelves, demonstrates the kind of intellectual curiosity and scholarly humility required to map out the frontiers of knowledge and reshape disciplines.

In his book *Making*, in a chapter entitled "Building a House," Tim Ingold observes of Chartres cathedral that despite its exterior magnificence and apparent harmony, it was, "the *ad hoc* accumulation of the work of many men [sic]."[2] Ingold muses that while the work was underway, no one could have predicted the final outcome, and that to this day "it remains unfinished." This reflection on the relationship between the cathedral's edifice and the underlying fluidity of its composition provides an apt metaphor for the archives of the ancient Near East, including the Hebrew Bible, which constitute the focus of Dan's scholarly life. In addition, and more intrinsic to the present context, it serves as a metaphor for a different "House of Dan," the *Bit-Dan*, to borrow an ancient convention.

For his former students, the *Bit-Dan* is the collective for whom he offers both an eponym and a point of departure. It is the imposing edifice he has created through his own *oeuvre*, as well as an intellectual space that many of his students at once inhabit and construct through our own research and writing. We travel on paths that Dan has blazed, but we take them in new directions, creating landscapes for which he drafted some of the earliest maps. It is also the "community of peoples" he has gathered around him, some of whose voices reverberate on the shelves of his Connecticut library, and many of which come together in this volume's chorus. Our title borrows the phrase "community of peoples" from Genesis 48:3, where an aged Jacob recounts to Joseph the blessing of El Shaddai who appeared to him at Luz, promising, "I will make you fruitful and multiply you, making you a community of peoples." Like Jacob's Israel, referred to elsewhere in the Bible as the *bet-Yaʿakov*, the *Bit-Dan* assembled in this volume is a diverse group that speaks in many voices, united in our connection to a single individual.

2 Tim Ingold, *Making: Anthropology, Archaeology, Art and Architecture* (New York/London: Routledge, 2013), 57.

In addition to our interest in evoking the community Dan has formed around him, who invigorate his scholarly life, our title also signals the communities and peoples whose voices Dan has amplified through his work. Dan is first and foremost a historian of the ancient Near East, with the Bible as one essential focus. Like the historian Carlo Ginzburg, he believes that the ideas and attitudes of a text's author(s) reveal worlds, flashes of which can be glimpsed through historiographic practice. Yet among the texts of the ancient Near East, the Bible is a particularly unruly source. As with Chartres cathedral, it is "a patchwork of irregularly disposed and imperfectly matched architectural elements," though with fewer anchors on which to secure the dates of its composition. It is a collaboration across time that can make it impossible to identify the "when" of its worlds. For some, this has led to an abandonment of the Bible altogether as a source for reconstructing the lived past. Not so for Dan, who has taught us to see glimpses of history sometimes where we least expect them. We would like to take this opportunity to articulate, for Dan, our own vision for participating in the historiographic work that he has started, and that in our hands too will remain unfinished.

Our vision is rooted in a fundamental hope and a desire to touch "real bodies" and "living voices," to borrow Stephen Greenblatt's words quoted above. We want to claim that the historical practice has utility, that if we listen carefully and pay attention we can detect the past's traces or traces of *pastness*, whispers of people and society coming to us through long chains of scribal composition, redaction, and transmission. And yet, that hope lives in tension with a simultaneous frustration, a sense of incompleteness that leaves us hungry and unsatisfied. We are not claiming (as some did and still do) that if we listen hard enough we will somehow hear a pure voice through the din of the past, that there is something akin to an unadulterated historical "kernel" or "core" that emerges in our work.[3] And yet, to feel the hunger for what we cannot know—for the voiceless characters and marginalized figures and nameless scribes—is ultimately more satisfying than taking the text at face value, or neglecting its historical dimensions, or claiming that the deep past is shut off to us and we must instead begin the process of interpretation from a later point in time.

History is therefore not a static word to us, but an active enterprise and an ongoing, devouring practice that leaves us wanting more. In this practice, there is and must always be a tension between trying to get the past "right" while

3 On "kernels" and "cores," see the discussion in Mahri Leonard-Fleckman, "All the גבול of Israel (1 Sam 27:1): Israel's 'Boundaries' in David's Wanderings," in *David in the Desert: Tradition and Redaction in the "History of David's Rise"*, ed. Hannes Bezzel and Reinhard G. Kratz (Boston, MA/Berlin: de Gruyter, 2021), 103–126.

recognizing that our work can only ever be partial and incomplete, that we are always "straining against the limits of the archive" while simultaneously acknowledging the impossibility of accurately representing what lies in the far distance behind us.[4] And yet we do not view the past as behind but instead always in front of us, a living history that calls us urgently forward, making demands on us to read responsibly; in other words, to read "for ethics" in light of our present realities.[5] The past is therefore not the past but "a position" that we take in the present.[6] As historians, then, we straddle time and space, conscious of our own subjectivity and situatedness, trying to do justice to what we can know in the long historical arc and through the integration of all methods at our disposal. For us, the past is living and dynamic, not hard and brittle and breath-less.

This collection of essays exemplifies our vision for reading and writing history. The community of scholars in this volume all participate in a dynamic historical enterprise, each one positioning themself somewhere along, or straddling, a Middle Eastern spatial continuum, and along a temporal trajectory from the Old Babylonian to the Persian periods. In their own way, each contributor attempts to touch a sliver of ancient history, whether a particular person or community, a text or visual image or scribal process. They do so through a diversity of methods and disciplines that include art history and visual studies; anthropological, archaeological, legal, literary and political tools; epigraphic, philological, and composition-historical approaches; myth, ritual, and religious studies; feminist, postcolonial, and spatial frameworks; and the lens of humor. None of these approaches stands on its own as an entrée to the past, but when brought together, they offer the possibilities for producing multivocal histories, Picasso-esque in both their fragmentation and evocation of human forms. There is a sensory element to all of these approaches. We feel the contours of texts, seek out seams, irregularities, and changes in texture. To compensate for our blindness, we touch, moving fingers across irregular surfaces, lingering to listen when we stumble on words or images that feel out of place, unexpected, discontinuous. The authors in this volume reach back into the ancient physical spaces of the Middle East—to the traces of people and communities, ritual and

4 Saidiya Hartman, "Venus in Two Acts," *Small Axe* 26 (2008): 14. In conversation with Hartman, and in relation to the continuous and unresolved unfolding of racism in the United States, Christina Sharpe describes this sense of incompleteness as "a form of *consciousness*" (italics hers) that she likens to staying in the hold of the ship on the Middle Passage (*In the Wake: On Blackness and Being* [Durham, NC/London: Duke University Press], 2016), 12–13.

5 Jane Gallop, "The Ethics of Reading," *Journal of Curriculum Theorizing* (2000): 17.

6 Michel-Rolph Trouillot, *Silencing the Past: Power and the Production of History*, 2nd rev. ed. (Boston, MA: Beacon Press, 2015), 15.

political processes—and draw them into the now, coloring stony landscapes into life, helping us to see and taste and touch the ancient world. Wissenschaft is personal.[7]

Like the bookshelf in Dan’s house, this collection is an archive and an expression of gratitude. Its authors are also a chorus of scribal voices in a stream of tradition, connecting past to present. Genesis 48:3 presents Jacob’s community of peoples, his Israel, as the living manifestation of the blessing of El Shaddai. Dan has treated each contributor to this volume as a blessing in his life. We offer this collection as a living manifestation of the community he has created.

Bibliography

Gallop, Jane. “The Ethics of Reading.” *Journal of Curriculum Theorizing* (2000): 7–17.

Greenblatt, Stephen. “The Touch of the Real.” Pages 14–29 in *The Fate of “Culture”: Geertz and Beyond*. Edited by Sherry B. Ortner. Berkeley, CA: University of California Press, 1999.

Hartman, Saidiya. “Venus in Two Acts.” *Small Axe* 26 (2008): 1–14.

Ingold, Tim. *Making: Anthropology, Archaeology, Art and Architecture*. New York, NY/London: Routledge, 2013.

Jonas, Hans. “Wissenschaft as Personal Experience.” *The Hastings Center Report* 32/4 (2002): 27–35.

Leonard-Fleckman, Mahri. “All the גבול of Israel (1Sam 27:1): Israel’s ‘Boundaries’ in David’s Wanderings.” Pages 103–126 in *David in the Desert: Tradition and Redaction in the “History of David’s Rise.”* Edited by Hannes Bezzel and Reinhard G. Kratz. Boston, MA/Berlin: de Gruyter, 2021.

Sharpe, Christina. *In the Wake: On Blackness and Being*. Durham, NC/London: Duke University Press, 2016.

Trouillot, Michel-Rolph. *Silencing the Past: Power and the Production of History*. 2nd rev. ed. Boston, MA: Beacon, 2015.

---

7 Hans Jonas, “Wissenschaft as Personal Experience,” *The Hastings Center Report* 32/4 (2002): 27–35.

2

La gestuelle de l'alliance à l'époque paléo-babylonienne: textes et images

Dominique Charpin

1 Introduction

C'est pour l'époque paléo-babylonienne que la documentation écrite a connu récemment le plus fort accroissement en ce qui concerne les modalités des alliances dans le Proche-Orient ancien[1]. De nombreuses lettres décrivent les négociations qui précédaient leur conclusion, puis les cérémonies lors desquelles les rois s'engageaient, que ce soit lors d'une réunion ou à distance. Depuis que Jean-Marie Durand a publié le premier "traité" conservé dans les archives de Mari[2], une dizaine d'autres a été publiée, provenant de Mari ou d'ailleurs[3]. Certains documents administratifs complètent les données des

1 Cette étude est publiée dans le cadre de ma participation comme *Fellow* au *Kollegforschergruppe* KFG 2615, *"Rethinking Oriental Despotism: Strategies of Governance and Modes of Participation in the Ancient Near East"* de la Freie Universität Berlin. Je remercie N. Ziegler pour son aide dans l'interprétation de la lettre ShA 1 71.

La présente contribution complète mes récentes études sur la conclusion des alliances: Dominique Charpin, "Guerre et paix dans le monde amorrite et post-amorrite," in *Krieg und Frieden im Alten Vorderasien: 52e Rencontre Assyriologique Internationale, Münster, 17.-21. Juli 2006*, ed. Hans Neumann et al., AOAT 401 (Münster: Ugarit-Verlag, 2014), 189-214; ma chronique sur "Les débuts des relations diplomatiques au Proche-Orient ancien," *RA* 110 (2016): 127-186; et en dernier lieu mon livre, *"Tu es de mon sang!" Les alliances dans le Proche-Orient ancien*, Docet omnia 4 (Paris: Les Belles Lettres/Collège de France, 2019).

2 Jean-Marie Durand, "Fragments rejoints pour une histoire élamite," in *Fragmenta Historiae Elamicae, Mélanges offerts à M.-J. Steve*, ed. L. De Meyer, H. Gasche, et Fr. Vallat (Paris: Éditions Recherche sur les Civilisations, 1986), 111-128. J'emploie le terme de "traité" avec des guillemets, car il ne s'agit pas à cette époque de textes définitifs contraignants, mais de propositions que les rois s'envoyaient lorsqu'ils ne pouvaient se rencontrer pour discuter les termes de leur serment: cf. Charpin, *Tu es de mon sang*, 97-102. J'omets par la suite les guillemets, mais la remarque est valable pour tous les traités évoqués dans cette contribution.

3 Pour les textes provenant de Kültepe, voir Klaas R. Veenhof, "New Mesopotamian Treaties from the Second Millennium BC from kārum Kanesh and Tell Leilan (Šehna)," *ZAR* 19 (2014): 23-58. Le "traité" le plus récemment publié, de provenance inconnue, contient le serment prêté par le roi d'Eshnunna Ibal-pi-El [I] au roi de Larsa Sin-iddinam et à celui d'Uruk Sin-

 | DOI:10.1163/9789004511538_003

lettres et des traités, permettant d'en préciser le contexte chronologique[4]. Les archives de Mari ont assurément livré le plus grand nombre de textes, mais elles ont été heureusement complétées par les découvertes épigraphiques effectuées sur d'autres sites, qu'elles soient contemporaines comme à Shemshara ou un peu plus tardives comme à Tell Leilan[5].

Mais la documentation textuelle n'est pas la seule à la disposition du chercheur en quête d'une histoire globale. Je voudrais ici montrer, à la fois tout l'intérêt qu'offre la confrontation des textes et des images, mais aussi les périls qui menacent un tel exercice[6]. Il ne s'agira pas ici de commenter un monument qui comporte à la fois une inscription et une représentation, comme la désormais fameuse stèle du roi d'Eshnunna Dadusha[7]; je souhaite ici mettre en rapport des gestes décrits dans des textes avec des représentations qu'on trouve sur divers supports. Je suis très heureux d'offrir cette étude à Daniel Fleming, auquel me lie une amitié qui remonte à près de trente ans[8] et dont les travaux

---

kashid, contre Sabium de Babylone et Ikun-pi-Sin de Nerebtum avec lesquels il s'engage à ne pas conclure une paix séparée (Michaël Guichard, "Un traité d'alliance entre Larsa, Uruk et Ešnunna contre Sabium de Babylone," *Sem* 56 [2014] : 9-34).

4 C'est le cas par exemple pour l'alliance conclue par Zimri-Lim avec le roi d'Eshnunna Ibal-pi-El II. Dominique Charpin, "Un traité entre Zimri-Lim de Mari et Ibâl-pî-El II d'Ešnunna," in *Marchands, Diplomates et Empereurs: Etudes sur la civilisation mésopotamienne offertes à Paul Garelli*, ed. D. Charpin et F. Joannès (Paris: Éditions Recherche sur les Civilisations, 1991), 162; et Dominique Charpin, *"Tu es de mon sang!"*, 213.

5 Les textes de Tell Leilan ont été publiés dans Jesper Eidem, *The Royal Archives from Tell Leilan: Old Babylonian Letters and Treaties from the Lower Town Palace East*, PIHANS 117 (Leiden: Nederlands Institute voor het nabije Oosten, 2011). Voir mes remarques dans Charpin, "Guerre et paix," 141-160 (lettres) et Charpin, "Les débuts," 148-186 (traités).

6 Cette contribution a fait l'objet d'un premier exposé lors d'un colloque organisé par L. Battini à Lyon en novembre 2016.

7 Voir en dernier lieu (avec bibliographie antérieure) Claudia Suter, "The Victory Stele of Dadusha of Eshnunna: A New Look at its Unusual Culminating Scene," *Ash-sharq* 2/2 (2018) : 1-29.

8 J'ai fait la connaissance personnelle de Daniel Fleming lors du Meeting de l'*American Oriental Society* organisé par Jack Sasson à Chapel Hill en avril 1993. Je l'ai revu à Paris lors du colloque sur "Les traditions amorrites et la Bible" organisé à l'École pratique des Hautes Études les 20 et 21 juin 1997 par Jean-Marie Durand, André Lemaire et moi-même (cf. Daniel Fleming, "Mari and the Possibilities of Biblical Memory," *RA* 92 [1998] : 41-78). Mais c'est surtout lors de l'année sabbatique qu'il a passée à Paris en 1997/98 (bénéficiant d'un *Senior Fulbright Fellowship*) que j'ai pu apprécier de près sa personnalité scientifique et humaine. J'ai encore très présente à l'esprit notre première rencontre en tête à tête en 1997. Après lui avoir montré les tablettes de Mari alors conservées dans les locaux de la rue de la Perle, je l'avais emmené dîner dans un restaurant rue des Archives (qui a disparu depuis) ; j'avais été très impressionné par ses efforts pour parler en français. Depuis, les occasions de rencontres ont été très nombreuses; je ferai un sort particulier à l'invitation que Daniel et Nancy firent chez eux le 24

sur Mari ont contribué à élargir le cercle trop étroit des savants intéressés par ces archives, qui comptent parmi les plus riches du monde antique[9].

2 Une lettre de Shemshara

Le point de départ de ma contribution se situe dans le Kurdistan irakien, à Tell Shemshara, l'antique Shusharra. Ce site a été fouillé par une équipe danoise en 1957-1958, ce qui a permis d'exhumer dans le palais environ 250 tablettes[10]. Il s'agit de documents administratifs[11] et de lettres[12], qui datent d'une période très restreinte du 18e siècle: le moment où le roi local, Kuwari, dut se soumettre à la grande puissance de l'époque, à savoir le Royaume de Haute-Mésopotamie de Samsi-Addu[13].

La lettre qui retiendra notre attention est malheureusement endommagée, de sorte que le début et la fin ont disparu. Une lacune au début de la tablette nous empêche de connaître le nom de l'expéditeur et du destinataire. On peut supposer qu'elle était adressée à Kuwari, le roi de Shusharra, comme beaucoup d'autres:

---

octobre 2015 à la suite du colloque que Daniel avait organisé à New York en l'honneur de Jack Sasson, ainsi qu'au séjour que Nele et moi avons effectué dans leur maison en avril 2018.

9 Outre la dizaine d'articles qu'il a consacrés à Mari depuis 1993, je pense en particulier à son livre sur ce qu'il a heureusement appelé la "gouvernance collective" (Daniel Fleming, *Democracy's Ancient Ancestors: Mari and Early Collective Governance* [Cambridge: Cambridge University Press], 2004) – sans parler de ses très nombreux travaux sur Emar ou sur la Bible.

10 Il y eut ensuite une mission irakienne en 1958-1959. Jesper Eidem et son équipe ont récemment repris la fouille de ce site. Deux tablettes supplémentaires ont été découvertes, en 2012 et 2013; elles sont encore inédites mais voir ce qui en est dit dans Jesper Eidem, "Back to Shemshara: NINO Excavations 2012-2015," in *Zagros Studies: Proceedings of the NINO Jubilee Conference and Other Research on the Zagros Region*, ed. Jesper Eidem, PIHANS 130 [Leyde/Leuven: Nederlands Institute voor het nabije Oosten, 2020], 180b-181.

11 Jesper Eidem, *The Shemshāra Archives 2: The Administrative Texts*, Historisk-filosofiske Skrifter 15 (Copenhagen: Munksgaard, 1992); les textes administratifs de Shemshara sont tous accessibles sur www.archibab.fr.

12 Jesper Eidem et Jørgen Læssøe, *The Shemshara Archives Vol. 1: The Letters*, Historisk-filosofiske Skrifter 23. (Copenhagen: Royal Danish Academy of Sciences and Letters, 2001) (ouvrage cité ci-dessous comme ShA 1); toutes ces lettres ont fait l'objet d'une réédition électronique par Nele Ziegler sur www.archibab.fr.

13 Pour le contexte historique, voir Dominique Charpin et Nele Ziegler, *Florilegium marianum v: Mari et le Proche-Orient à l'époque amorrite: essai d'histoire politique*, Mémoires de NABU 6 (Paris: SEPOA, 2003), 96 et 106.

> (...) 1′-3′ Tu m'as écrit à propos de Imdi-Addu, serviteur de S[amsi-Addu], qui a apporté à Endušše un présent-*tâmartum* d'argent (et) d'or ainsi que des marmites d'argent. 4′-6′ Cette information est véridique et j'ai entendu (la liste de) tout ce qu'il [lui] a apporté. L'argent, l'or ainsi que les marmites d'argent qu'il a fait porter, à cause de qui les a-t-il fait porter? 7′-8′ C'est à cause de toi qu'il les a fait porter! Il a envoyé ce message à Endušše: "9′ Moi et toi, nous nous sommes saisis fermement ensemble! 10′-12′ Je veux faire faire une représentation de toi et une représentation de moi en or, de sorte que l'un tienne la nuque de l'autre. 12′-15′ Je veux te donner ma fille et je veux te donner comme dot pour ma fille le pays de Shusharra et le pays de [...]" (cassure. Il ne reste pratiquement rien du revers)[14].

L'expéditeur se plaignait manifestement de ce que le grand Samsi-Addu ait fait une offre d'alliance en bonne et due forme au roi du Gutium, Endušše[15]. Imdi-Addu, envoyé par Samsi-Addu à Endušše, était porteur de présents, décrits comme *tâmartum*, en or et en argent, accompagnés par des marmites en argent. L'envoyé de Samsi-Addu était également chargé de transmettre un message, dont nous ne savons pas s'il était oral ou couché par écrit sur une tablette. Ce message comportait trois éléments: Samsi-Addu y faisait allusion à une rencontre avec Endušše, il voulait faire faire une représentation de leur accord et enfin il proposait de lui donner sa fille comme épouse, avec une dot. Ces trois points vont être examinés ci-dessous.

Samsi-Addu commençait par faire allusion à sa rencontre avec Endušše[16]. On sait que les alliances étaient alors réalisées de deux manières différen-

14 ShA 1 71: (...) (1′) [*ù aš-šu*]*m* ⸢^{I}*im-di*⸣-^{d}IŠKUR IR$_3$ ^{I}*sa*[*am-si*-^{d}IŠKUR] (2′) [*š*]*a ta*-⸢*ma*⸣-*ar-tam* KU$_3$.BABBAR KU$_3$.GI *ù ru*-[*uq-qa-at*] (3′) [K]Ù.BABBAR *a-na* ^{I}*in-du-úš-še ub-lu ta-aš-p*[*u-ra-am*] (4′) *a-wa-tum ši-i ki-na-at ù ma-li ub-l*[*u-šum*] (5′) *še-me-ku* KU$_3$.BABBAR KU$_3$.GI *ù ru-uq-qa-at* KU$_3$.[BABBAR] (6′) *ša ú-ša-bi-lu aš-šum ma-an-nim ú-ša-bi-i*[*l*] (7′) *aš-šu-mi-ka ú-ša-bi-il a-na en-du-úš*-[*še*] (8′) *ki-a-am iš-pu-ur um-ma*! *šu-ma-a* (9′) ⸢*a*⸣-*na-ku ù at-ta pu-ḫu-ur ni-iṣ-ṣa-b*[*i-it*] (10′) *ṣa-la-am-ka ù ṣa-al-mi ša* KU$_3$.GI (11′) *lu-še-pí-iš-ma a-ḫu-um ki-ša-ad a-ḫi-im* (12′) *li-ki-il* DUMU.MUNUS *ma-ar-ti* (13′) *lu-ud-di-na-ak-kum-ma a-na ša-ar-ra-k*[*u-ut*] (14′) DUMU.MUNUS-*ti-ia ma-a-at šu-šar-ra-a*^{ki} (15′) ⸢*lu-ud-di*⸣-*na-ak-kum ù ma-a-at* [...] (16′) (...). Cette citation correspond à l'intégralité de ce qui subsiste de la face de la tablette; du revers ne restent que quelques signes.

15 Voir Nele Ziegler, "Kakmum et le Gutium," in *Recherches en Haute-Mésopotamie* II*: Mission archéologique de Bash Tapa* (*campagnes 2012-2013*) *et les enjeux de la recherche dans la région d'Erbil*, ed. L. Marti, Ch. Nicolle, et K. Shawaly, Mémoires de NABU 17 (Paris: SEPOA, 2015), 23-36.

16 Jesper Eidem a lu la ligne 9′ comme ⸢*a*⸣-*na-ku ù at-ta pu-ḫu-ur-ni ú-za-bi*-[*il*] et traduit "our agreement is long overdue," sans commentaire. Cependant, *puḫrum* ne signifie pas

tes[17]. À l'époque paléo-babylonienne, contrairement à la période suivante, le problème n'était pas de savoir si une alliance était conclue entre pairs ou entre un roi de rang supérieur et un autre de rang inférieur, mais si l'alliance était conclue à distance ou en réunion. Lorsqu'il s'agissait d'une alliance conclue à distance, chaque roi envoyait à l'autre le texte des engagements qu'il souhaitait le voir souscrire. Le texte final comportait trois éléments: une liste de divinités par lesquelles le roi jurait, une série de clauses qu'il promettait de respecter et des malédictions en cas de parjure. Chacun de ces trois éléments était soumis à discussion. Quand un accord était trouvé, l'un des rois envoyait à son partenaire des délégués porteurs de symboles divins ainsi que le texte du serment qu'il devait prononcer. Le roi prêtait serment en pratiquant un geste symbolique nommé le "toucher de la gorge" (*lipit napištim*) : c'était une façon de mettre sa vie en jeu en cas de parjure. Une délégation symétrique partait ensuite dans la capitale de l'autre roi, où avait lieu une cérémonie analogue. La seconde façon de conclure une alliance s'effectuait lors d'une réunion. Les rois se mettaient directement d'accord sur le libellé du serment: de ce fait, aucun texte n'était mis par écrit. La cérémonie était accompagnée de l'immolation d'un ânon. Nous connaissons ce deuxième type d'alliances grâce aux lettres qui les décrivent ou qui en rappellent le souvenir. C'est à une alliance lors d'une rencontre que fait allusion Samsi-Addu dans la lettre retrouvée à Shemshara.

Passons immédiatement au troisième point: Samsi-Addu indique son intention de donner sa fille en mariage à Endušše, en lui offrant une dot. On a ici affaire à un mariage diplomatique consécutif à la conclusion d'une alliance comme on en connaît beaucoup à cette époque[18]. L'emploi du terme *šarra-*

"agreement." Par ailleurs, *zubbulum* signifie en principe "faire attendre quelqu'un" (avec une personne à l'accusatif) ; il n'est attesté avec le sens de "s'attarder" que pour une personne ou une maladie, et ce sens est l'inverse de "être en retard" (qui se dit *uḫḫurum*). La restitution et la traduction ne sont donc pas sûres (la photo de la tablette qui figure sur la jaquette du livre Eidem et Læssøe 2001 laisse malheureusement dans l'ombre la fin de la ligne). Læssøe avait traduit "Hvad mig selv og dig angår, er vort forbund etableret," soit "En ce qui me concerne et en ce qui te concerne, notre alliance est établie" (Jørgen Læssøe, *Det Første Assyriske Imperium* [Copenhagen: Københavns Universitet, 1966], 105). Le *CAD* a transcrit *pu-ḫu-ur ni-iṣ-ṣa-bi-*[*it*] et traduit "You and I quarreled together" (*P*: 501b). Vu le contexte, cette traduction me semble à modifier: *ṣabātum Gt* signifie aussi "einander umfassen, festhalten" (*AHw* 3:1069a). Quoi qu'il en soit du sens de la l. 9′, le sens général de cet extrait reste le même: il y a ici dans tous les cas allusion à une alliance conclue lors d'une rencontre.

17 Cf. en dernier lieu Charpin, *"Tu es de mon sang!"*, 47-73.

18 Charpin, *"Tu es de mon sang!"*, 216-234 (avec bibliographie antérieure).

katum pour "dot," qui avait gêné Eidem, ne pose en réalité pas de problème[19]. Ce qui est en revanche à ma connaissance sans parallèle, c'est la nature de la dot prévue par Samsi-Addu: deux pays vassaux! Il faut ici bien sûr prendre des précautions, car c'est l'auteur de la lettre qui donne cette information. Or le fait que Samsi-Addu puisse ainsi disposer du pays de Shusharra devrait avoir provoqué la colère de Kuwari, qui était souverain de ce pays, d'où une légitime suspicion de l'historien contemporain: l'affaire pourrait avoir été tout simplement inventée par l'expéditeur de la lettre pour pousser Kuwari à se révolter contre Samsi-Addu, mais on ignore son identité.

Le deuxième point du message de Samsi-Addu est celui qui retiendra le plus longtemps notre attention: Samsi-Addu souhaitait faire faire une représentation de la conclusion de son alliance avec Endušše. Cette mention de la fabrication d'une représentation des deux rois est sans parallèle. Elle a manifestement troublé l'éditeur du texte, Eidem, qui a traduit: "10′ I will have a statue of you and a statue of me made in gold, and brother shall embrace brother."[20]

Il a commenté ce passage en avouant ne pas comprendre comment deux statues pouvaient s'embrasser:

> The diplomatic gesture of producing gold statues (– or one statue with both kings embracing?) is not otherwise attested in this period, but of course reminiscent of practices mentioned in the letters from Amarna etc[21].

19 ShA 1, p. 148: "Forms *šarrākum/šarrakūtum* (from *šarākum*) are found in texts from especially Alalah to denote a special class of people (see *CAD* Š/II 68f.), but *šarrakūtum* here seems to be the (royal?) equivalent of *šeriktum* 'marriage prestation' (*CAD* S/III: 103f.)." Le terme *šarrakûtum* a échappé aussi bien au *CAD* qu'au *AHw*; il figurait pourtant déjà dans ARM 8 87:6 (où G. Boyer l'avait, il est vrai, pris pour un nom de personne, lisant: 2 MUNUS.MEŠ *ša Ra-ka-tu-um*, alors qu'il faut comprendre 2 MUNUS.MEŠ *ša-ra-ka-tu ša* PNF); cf. déjà D. Charpin, "Données nouvelles sur la région du Petit Zab au XVIIIe siècle av. J.-C.," *RA* 98 (2004): 175. Cette lecture a été depuis confirmée par Haradum 2 113: 4, où une esclave est décrite comme (4) *šar-ra-ka-tum ša* munus [...] (5) DUMU.MUNUS dEN.ZU-*gim-la-an-ni* "dot de dame [...], fille de Sin-gimlanni"; F. Joannès a traduit "cadeau de mariage (*širiktu*)" sans commentaire (Francis Joannès, Christine Kepinski-Lecomte, et Gudrun Colbow, *Haradum II: Les textes de la période paléo-babylonienne* (*Samsu-iluna – Ammi-ṣaduqa*) [Paris: Éditions Recherche sur les Civilisations, 2006], 154).

20 La traduction de Læssøe était semblable: "I will have a statue of yourself and a statue of myself made in gold, and one brother shall embrace the other" (*People of Ancient Assyria: Their Inscriptions and Correspondence* [London: Routledge & Keagan Paul, 1963], 155).

21 ShA 1, p. 148. Laessoe avait traduit: "Jeg vil lade fremstille et billede af dig og af mig i guld, hvor den ene broder skal omfavne den anden," soit "Je ferai faire une image de toi et de

Cependant, *ṣalmum* signifie de façon large "représentation." Il peut s'agir de "statues" dans bien des cas. Mais ce peut être aussi une figure sur une stèle, comme celle qui est ainsi décrite dans une lettre de Mari:

> Au dessus d'une estrade(?) élevée(?), à gauche, (il y a) une figure (*ṣalmum*) d'Amurrum portant une arme-*gamlum*; devant lui, la figure de mon seigneur en orant (*kâribum*). Au dessus des figures, (il y a) un disque solaire et un croissant lunaire[22].

Clairement, *ṣalmum* ne désigne pas ici des statues, mais des figures représentées sur une stèle. Je propose donc de traduire la lettre de Shemshara ainsi:

> 12′ Je veux faire faire une représentation de toi (*ṣalamka*) et une représentation de moi (*ṣalmî*) en or, de sorte que l'un tienne la nuque de l'autre (*aḫum kišad aḫim lîkil*).

Il s'agit bien d'une "embrassade," dans l'un des sens que ce mot possède en français[23].

3 Des parallèles iconographiques

Quel est ce geste qui consiste à se tenir la nuque?

3.1 *Un bassin d'Ebla*

On pense aussitôt à une découverte faite dans le temple N d'Ebla, d'époque paléo-babylonienne (Figure 2.1). Il s'agit d'un bassin en calcaire de 75 cm. de haut, dont la face antérieure est perdue, mais la face postérieure est entièrement conservée. Quand on voit cette image, on reconnaît aussitôt le geste de deux hommes qui s'étreignent. Au premier plan, le personnage de gauche serre avec sa main droite le poignet gauche de son homologue; il passe sa main

---

moi en or, un frère embrassant l'autre" (Læssøe, *Assyriske Imperium*, 105). Le CAD a ainsi traduit: "and one should hold the other in an embrace" (*K*: 447b).

22 FM 8 38: (19) *e-li* ⟨*pa-*⟩*ra-ki š*[*a*]*-qí-*[*im šu-me-l*]*am ṣa-la-am* ᵈMAR.TU (20) *ga-am-la-am na-š*[*i*]*-i* (21) *i-na pa-ni-šu ṣa-la-am be-lí-ia ka-ri-bu* (22) *e-le-nu-um ṣa-al-mi-*[*im*] (23) [*š*]*a-am-šu ù ás-qa-ru.* Voir le commentaire de Dominique Charpin ("Textes et images: le cas de deux stèles paléo-babyloniennes," *NABU* [2005]: 95) et tout récemment Michaël Guichard ("Les statues divines et royales à Mari d'après les textes," *JA* 307 [2019]: 4).

23 Voir https://www.cnrtl.fr/definition/embrassade.

FIGURE 2.1 *Bassin lustral du temple N à Ebla* (TM.72.N.468; musée archéologique d'Alep)
PAOLO MATTHIAE, COPYRIGHT MISSIONE ARCHEOLOGICA ITALIANA IN SIRIA

gauche autour du cou du personnage qui lui fait face, lequel passe sa main droite autour du cou de son homologue. C'est sans doute la raison pour laquelle cette image a été choisie par Amanda Podany comme illustration de son ouvrage sur les relations internationales[24]. Mais il faut faire attention: l'image reproduite Fig. 2.1, extraite d'un livre de Paolo Matthiae, est en fait un montage qui ne donne qu'une partie de la scène. Cela a trompé Bertrand Lafont, qui a commenté la lettre de Shemshara en ces termes:

> L'un des intérêts de cette lettre, fort précieuse à plus d'un titre, est qu'elle peut être mise en relation avec une représentation figurée très proche de celle que Samsî-Addu décrit: il s'agit du bas-relief sculpté sur le "bassin rituel" d'Ebla (TM.72.N.468), qui est plus ou moins contemporain de cette lettre (…) On y voit deux dignitaires barbus (sans doute des rois) qui s'embrassent, la main de l'un étant levée vers la bouche de l'autre. Ce geste d'alliance, qui est donc désormais attesté d'Ebla à Shemshâra, serait-il à mettre en relation avec le geste du *lipit napištim* (ci-dessus § III/2 et n. 269)[25]?

Ce commentaire appelle deux remarques: d'une part, comme nous allons le voir, la scène ne se limite pas à deux personnages. Par ailleurs, je ne crois pas que la main d'un roi soit levée vers la bouche de l'autre: le problème du sculpteur consistait à représenter la main qui passe derrière le cou de l'autre[26]. Enfin, et surtout, cette scène n'a aucun rapport avec le geste du *lipit napištim*. Comme je l'ai déjà indiqué, ce rite était effectué lorsqu'une alliance était conclue *à distance*: il y aurait donc là une contradiction.

Une photo complète de la face postérieure de ce bassin (Figure 2.2) a été commentée par Matthiae en ces termes:

> La face postérieure, intégralement conservée, était décorée avec une scène de fonctionnaires représentés en train de s'embrasser et de se placer aux côtés d'une plante sacrée, selon une représentation symbol-

24 Amanda H. Podany, *Brotherhood of Kings: How International Relations Shaped the Ancient Near East*. New York, NY/Oxford: Oxford University Press, 2010.

25 Bertrand Lafont, "Relations internationales, alliances et diplomatie au temps des royaumes amorrites," in *Mari, Ébla et les Hourrites: dix ans de travaux. Actes du colloque international (Paris, mai 1993). Deuxième partie*, ed. Jean-Marie Durand et Dominique Charpin, Amurru 2 (Paris: Éditions Recherche sur les Civilisations, 2001), 313 n. 415.

26 Le geste des deux rois est identique; le sculpteur a réussi à montrer la main droite du roi situé à droite posée sur l'épaule droite du roi situé à gauche, mais pas l'inverse.

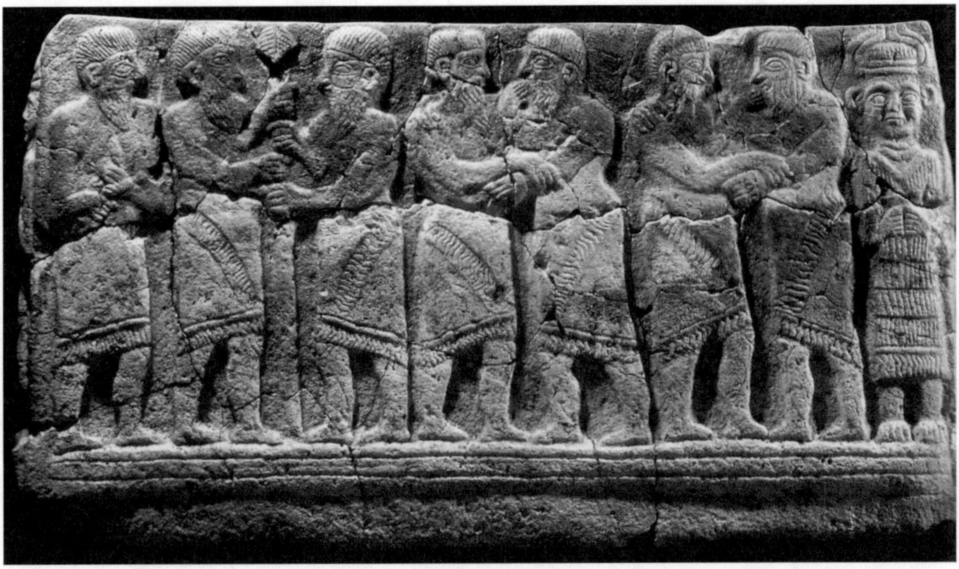

FIGURE 2.2 *Bassin lustral du temple N à Ebla: vue d'ensemble*
PAOLO MATTHIAE, COPYRIGHT MISSIONE ARCHEOLOGICA ITALIANA IN SIRIA

ique rare qui devait faire allusion à la prestation des serments qui accompagnaient la conclusion de l'alliance[27].

S'agit-il vraiment de fonctionnaires, ou a-t-on affaire à une alliance conclue entre plusieurs rois? On peut citer en ce sens une déclaration de Hammurabi de Babylone à Abi-mekim, qui lui avait été envoyé par le roi de Mari Zimri-Lim. Abi-mekim rendit compte de sa mission en ces termes:

> 3 L'expédition de mon seigneur va bien. Je suis arrivé à Babylone et 4 j'ai transmis à Hammurabi le message que mon seigneur m'avait confié; 5 il s'est beau[coup ré]joui et il a déclaré: "6 C'est vraiment sur l'injonction d'un dieu que Zimri-Lim m'a envoyé ces mots. 7 Depuis que moi-même, Zimri-Lim et Yarim-Lim nous avons fait alliance 8 et que nous nous sommes pris par la main l'un l'autre (*qa-tam a-na qa-tim ti-iṣ-bu-ta-nu*), (ni)

27 Paolo Matthiae: "La faccia posteriore, integralmente conservata, era decorata con scene di funzionari raffigurati nell'atto di abbracciarsi e affiancati a una pianta sacra, secundo una rara rappresentazione simbolica che deve alludere alla ratifica dei giuramenti che accompagnavano la stipula dell'accordo" (*La storia dell'arte dell'Oriente Antico: Gli stati territoriali 2100-1600 a.C* [Milan: Electa, 2000], 193).

> adversaire (ni) ennemi [9] ne peut rien faire [10] et nous arracherons du cœur du pays la griffe de cet ennemi." [11] Hammurabi a dit cela et bien d'autres choses[28].

L'expression "se prendre par la main" est-elle une allusion à la gestuelle de l'alliance? Il semblerait bien, à première lecture[29]. Cependant, le contexte est celui de la guerre contre les Elamites. Or cette alliance des trois rois d'Alep (Yarim-Lim), Mari (Zimri-Lim) et Babylone (Hammurabi), que nous connaissons par de nombreux textes, n'a pas été conclue en réunion, mais à distance: il s'agit donc d'une façon de dire. La question qui se pose est de savoir si métaphoriquement, Hammurabi n'utilise pas une expression désignant un geste qui était réellement effectué lors de la conclusion d'une alliance en réunion. Si l'on rapproche ce passage du bassin d'Ebla, on serait tenté de le penser.

Il en va de même pour un autre geste symbolique, qui consistait à nouer la frange du vêtement des deux rois. Une lettre expédiée à Zimri-Lim par son émissaire auprès du roi d'Eshnunna Ibal-pi-El rappelle ainsi l'objet de la mission:

> [17] À présent, mon seigneur [20] a envoyé [18] chez son père ses dieux, [17] les grandes "armes" (*kakkî rabûtim*) et nous ses serviteurs, [18] pour faire procéder à l'engagement (lit. "pour faire toucher la gorge" *napištam šulputum*) [19-20] et pour nouer la frange (*sissiktam kaṣârum*) du père et du fils pour toujours[30].

Une expression semblable se retrouve dans la bouche même de Hammurabi, alors qu'il s'adressait à Zimri-Lim par l'intermédiaire de son envoyé et envisageait la conclusion d'une alliance: "Une frange éternelle sera nouée entre

---

28 ARM 26/2 468: (3) KASKAL *be-lí-ia ša-al-ma-at a-na* KA$_2$.DINGIR.RA^{ki} *ak-šu-ud-ma* (4) *[te$_4$-m]a-am ša be-lí ú-wa-e-ra-an-ni a-na ḫa-am-mu-ra-bi ad-di-in-ma* (5) *ma-[di-iš iḫ]-du ù ki-a-am iq-⸢bi⸣ um-ma šu-ú-ma* (6) *a-wa-a-tim an-né-e-tim i-na qí-bí-it* DINGIR*-lim-ma zi-im-ri-li-[im iš-p]u-ur-ši-na-ti* (7) *ù iš-tu a-na-ku zi-im-ri-li-im ù ia-ri-im-li-im ta-a[l-l]a-nu-ma* (8) *qa-tam a-na qa-tim ti-iṣ-bu-ta-nu le-em-nu-um ù a-ia-bu-um* (9) *mi-im-ma e-pé-ša-am ú-ul [i-l]e-i [ù ṣú]-pu-ur* LU$_2$.KUR$_2$ *ša-a-tu* (10) *i-na li-ib-bi ma-a-tim ni-na-as-sà-a[ḫ an-n]é-e-tim ù ma-da-tim-ma* (11) *ᴵḫa-am-mu-ra-bi id-bu-ub-ma a-na zi-im a-wa-ti-šu ša i-na ḫa-di-šu id-bu-bu*. Pour la l. 7, cf. Erica Reiner, "Supplement to Chicago Assyrian Dictionary T (Volume 18)," *JNES* 66 (2007): 50.

29 Et elle rappelle l'expression *puḫur niṣṣabit* de ShA 1 71:9′.

30 A.3354+: (17) *i-na-an-na be-lí* DINGIR.MEŠ*-šu* ^{giš}TUKUL.MEŠ *ra-bu-tim ù* IR$_3$.MEŠ*-šu ne-e-ti* (18) *a-na ṣe-er a-bi-šu a-na na-pí-iš-tim šu-ul-pu-tim* (19) *ù sí-sí-ik-ti a-bi-im ù ma-ri-im* (20) *⸢a⸣-na da-re-e-tim ra-ka-si-im iṭ-ru-da-an-né-e-ti* (texte cité dans Charpin, "Un traité," 163).

nous."[31] Là encore, il s'agit d'une métaphore, mais qui repose sans doute sur des gestes symboliques réellement pratiqués quand les rois se rencontraient[32].

Le bassin d'Ebla a fait l'objet de deux études récentes de Matthiae, qui y voit représentée une alliance entre les rois d'Alep et d'Ebla du temps de Yarim-Lim I[er33]. Matthiae a malheureusement suivi Lafont dans l'interprétation du geste comme celui du *lipit napištim*[34]. Le bassin d'Ebla représente peut-être une scène de conclusion d'alliance, sans que cela soit certain et mon but n'est pas de fournir un commentaire de l'ensemble de la scène qui s'y trouve représentée (et dont seule une partie a survécu); il me paraît sûr en tout cas qu'on y voit figuré un double geste consistant à passer une main derrière la nuque de son partenaire et à saisir son autre main de l'autre[35]. On peut donc penser que Samsi-Addu avait une représentation de ce genre en vue lorsqu'il envoya son message au roi Endušše.

---

31 ARM 26/2 449: 55 [*ù*] *sí-sí-ik-tum da-ri-tum bi-ri-ni ik-ka-aṣ-ṣa-ar.*

32 Voir encore FM 7 22: (10) *um-ma šu-ma da-am-qí-iš* (11) *a-ḫi-i ṣa-bi a-na* KA$_2$.DINGIR.RA/[ki] (R.12) *iṭ-ru-ud* (13) *ù sí-sí-ik-ti* (14) *it-ti* LÚ KA$_2$.DINGIR.RA[ki] (15) *a-ḫi ir-ku-ús* "(10) C'est très bien que (11) mon frère (12) ait envoyé (11) ma troupe à Babylone (13) et que (15) mon frère ait noué (13) ma frange (14) à (celle de) l'Homme de Babylone." Il s'agit ici d'une alliance tripartite: le propos émane du roi d'Alep Hammurabi, qui se félicite que le roi de Mari ("mon frère") l'ait allié avec celui de Babylone. Aucun des trois rois ne se trouvait alors auprès d'un des deux autres: les alliances ont été conclues à distance, donc la façon dont le geste est évoqué relève forcément de la métaphore.

33 Paolo Matthiae, "The Old Syrian Temple N's Carved Basin and the Relation between Aleppo and Ebla," *StEb* 4 (2018) : 109-138; Matthiae, "Again on the Limestone Carved Basin of Temple N of Ebla," *StEb* 5 (2019) : 207-212. Le deuxième article fait allusion à un manuscrit préliminaire de la présente étude, que je lui avais envoyé en mars 2019.

34 Encore dans Matthiae ("Limestone Carved Basin," 210 n. 10), où il cite côte à côte Lafont ("Relations internationales") et Charpin (*"Tu es de mon sang!"*), sans se rendre compte apparemment de la divergence entre ces deux auteurs. Malheureusement, P. Matthiae a mal compris ce que j'ai écrit, lorsqu'il indique: "The *lipît napištim / napištam lapātum* was accomplished by representatives of the kings in their absence" ("Limestone Carved Basin," 210 n. 12). En réalité, lorsque l'alliance était conclue à distance, chacun des rois procédait au rite du *lipit napištim* en présence d'un ou plusieurs représentants de son homologue: c'était chaque roi qui, séparément, touchait sa propre gorge. Le texte PIHANS 117 54 est particulièrement clair à cet égard et il a l'intérêt de situer la scène à Alep (cf. plus bas).

35 Pour Matthiae, les deux personnages lèvent une main vers la bouche ou la gorge de leur partenaire. Il parle de la représentation de "couples of characters embracing each other and raising a hand at the mouth or throat of the partner" ("Limestone Carved Basin," 208). Je ne suis pas persuadé par cette description; mais si tel est bien le cas, c'est une raison de plus pour dissocier cette scène du rite du *lipit napištim*, car lors de celui-ci c'est chaque roi qui touche *sa propre gorge*.

3.2 *Un sceau-cylindre de la collection de Clercq*

La glyptique nous offre un autre document qui me paraît encore plus probant. Il s'agit d'un sceau-cylindre de la collection de Clercq, qui a été versé au dossier des alliances par Pierre Amiet (Figure 2.3); mais personne à ma connaissance n'a encore fait le rapprochement entre ce sceau-cylindre et la lettre de Shemshara. Or c'est manifestement cette image qui ressemble le plus à la description que donne Samsi-Addu dans la lettre ShA 1 71: d'une façon cette fois non ambiguë, on y voit deux rois qui se passent le bras derrière la nuque.

Amiet avait commenté: "Les deux rois s'embrassent aussi affectueusement que des époux."[36] Jean-Georges Heintz est revenu sur cette interprétation, qui ne lui semble pas pertinente:

> En effet, la comparaison "affectueuse" nous semble ici aussi erronée que la métaphore conjugale qu'elle introduit, car la corrélation des deux dossiers, textuel et iconographique, leur co-occurrence géographique et chronologique, nous incitent à voir ici plutôt une représentation du rituel de "toucher la gorge" (*lipit napištim*) – tel qu'il est mentionné dans les textes de Mari, notamment: la partie centrale de la scène, par la posture "hiératique" des deux personnages, placés à distance et en antagonisme symétrique par rapport à l'axe central dont la partie supérieure est occupée par le symbole stellaire, nous semble devoir être interprétée en ce sens, ce qui confirme l'insertion du motif dans la thématique globale – rendue par les textes et par les représentations – de l'alliance en domaine syro-mésopotamien à l'époque babylonienne ancienne[37].

Ce commentaire me semble à corriger sur deux points. D'abord, et une nouvelle fois, parce que le rite du *lipit napištim* ne se pratiquait que lors d'une alliance conclue à distance. Une lettre de Tell Leilan récemment publiée le confirme:

---

36 Pierre Amiet, "Alliance des hommes, alliance des dieux dans l'iconographie orientale," in *Collectanea Orientalia: Histoire, arts de l'espace et industrie de la terre. Etudes offertes en hommage à Agnès Spycket*, ed. Hermann Gasche et Barthel Hrouda, Civilisations du Proche-Orient Série I Archéologie et Environnement 3 (Paris/Neuchâtel: Recherches et Publications, 1996), 3 n. 25.

37 Jean-Georges Heintz, *Prophétisme et alliance: Des Archives royales de Mari à la Bible hébraïque. Recueil d'études édité par Stephan Lauber avec Othmar Keel et Hans Ulrich Steymans. Mit einem Vorwort von Manfred Weippert*, OBO 271 (Fribourg: Academic Press; Göttingen: Vandenhoeck & Ruprecht, 2015), 318 (reproduisant une étude de 1997).

FIGURE 2.3 *Sceau-cylindre De Clercq n° 390-ter*
DESSIN PAR PIERRE AMIET ("ALLIANCE DES HOMMES," 5 FIG. 3)

> (1-2) Dis à Till-Abnu: ainsi (parle) Halu-rabi, ton frère. (3) J'ai entendu (lire) ta tablette que tu m'as fait porter. (4-13) Relativement à (ta décision de) ne pas aller à Alep que tu m'as écrite: puisque tu n'iras pas à Alep en personne et que tu n'auras pas d'entrevue avec le roi, qu'un serviteur à toi de confiance prenne la tête de tes troupes-*piḫrum* et qu'il vienne avec moi à Alep. (14-20) Et à Alep, que le roi s'engage (lit. frappe sa *napištum*) par égard pour toi, que ton serviteur le voie, qu'il te rapporte que le roi s'est engagé (lit. a frappé sa *napištum*) par égard pour toi et que ton cœur s'apaise. (21-24) Et une fois que je serai revenu d'Alep, viens et aie une entrevue avec moi, afin que je te donne des nouvelles du roi[38].

Comment comprendre l'insistance sur le fait que l'envoyé de Till-Abnu devra rapporter qu'il a bien vu le geste du *lipit napištim* ? On pourrait dire bien sûr que le geste aurait eu lieu de toute façon, même si Till-Abnu s'était déplacé: c'est ce qu'a fait Eidem, qui en conclut que, contrairement à ce que j'avais proposé, il n'y a pas d'opposition entre deux rituels, l'immolation d'un ânon lorsque les

38 PIHANS 117 54: ⸢*a*⸣-*na ti-la-ab-nu-ú qí-bí-ma* (2) [*u*]*m-ma ḫa-lu-ra-bi a-ḫu-k*[*a-a-ma*] (3) *ṭup-pa-ka ša tu-ša-bi-lam eš-*[*me*] (4) *a*[*š-šum l*]*a a-la-ki-ka a-na* ^{uru}*ḫa-la-ab*^{ki} (5) *ša ta-a*[*š-p*]*u-ra-am* (6) *iš-tu a-na* [^{ur}]^{u}*ḫa-la-a*[*b*^{ki}] (7) *at-ta la ta-al-la-k*[*a-am-ma*] (8) *it-ti* LUGAL *la ta-an-na-am-ma-ru* (9) 1 IR$_3$-*ka tak-lam* (T.10) *pa-an* ERIN$_2$.MEŠ *pí-iḫ-ri-ka* (11) *li-iṣ-ba-tam-ma* (12) *it-ti-ia a-na* ^{uru}*ḫa-la-ab*^{ki} (R.13) *li-il-li-*{x}*ik* (14) ⸢*ù i*⸣-*na* ^{uru}*ḫ*[*a-l*]*a-ab*^{ki} (15) *aš-*⸢*šu-mì*⸣-*ka* LUGA[L *n*]*a-pí-iš*$_7$-*t*[*a-šu*] (16) [*l*]*i-il-*{pu}*p*[*u-ut*] (17) ⸢*ù*⸣ IR$_3$-*ka li-mu-u*[*r-šu-ma*] (18) [*š*]*a aš-šu-mì-ka* LU[GAL *na-pí-iš*$_7$*-ta-šu*] (19) ⸢*il*⸣-*pu-tu li-te-er-*⸢*ra-ak-kum-ma*⸣ (20) ⸢*li*⸣-*ib-ba-ka li-nu-uḫ* (21) *ù i-nu-ma iš-tu* ^{uru}*ḫa-la-ab*^{ki} (22) *ak-ta-áš-dam al-kam-ma* (T.23) [*i*]*t-ti-ia na-an-me-er* (24) *ù ṭe*$_4$-*em* LUGAL *lu-ud-bu-ba-/ak-kum.*

rois se rencontraient et le geste du *lipit napištim* lorsque l'alliance était conclue à distance[39]. Personnellement, je suis au contraire frappé par l'insistance de l'auteur de la lettre dans la description de la façon dont l'alliance sera conclue: elle me semble due au fait que Till-Abnu ne sera finalement pas présent.

J'ai un autre élément de désaccord avec Heintz dans l'interprétation du sceau De Clercq n° 390-ter: le rapprochement entre mariage et alliance suggéré par Amiet n'a rien de saugrenu. Cela se voit d'abord dans la gestuelle: la conclusion du mariage comme celle de l'alliance se faisait en nouant la frange des vêtements des deux parties[40]. L'expression est selon les cas *sissiktam kaṣârum* ou *sissiktam rakâsum*[41]. C'est ainsi que deux envoyés mariotes écrivent à Zimri-Lim pour signifier que le roi de Babylone est disposé à conclure une alliance: "Hammurabi est prêt à de bonnes relations et à nouer la frange."[42]

Inversement, lorsque deux époux se séparaient, on disait qu'ils coupaient la frange (*sissiktam batâqum*)[43]: ils mettaient ainsi fin à l'accord qui les liait. Ce geste est également connu en contexte diplomatique: "Coupe la frange (de l'habit) et fais ainsi connaître ton hostilité."[44]

---

39 Eidem, *Royal Archives from Tell Leilan*, 327.

40 Pour les mariages, on ne connaît que le geste inverse, lors d'un divorce, qui consiste à couper la frange (*sissiktam batâqum*). Cette expresssion étant également utilisée en matière diplomatique (Charpin, "Guerre et paix," 197-198), il est clair que le geste consistant à "nouer la frange" lors des alliances est analogue à celui qui devait être pratiqué lors des mariages.

41 Voir les références réunies par Lafont, "Relations internationales," 259. Mais je ne partage pas son interprétation, qui voit dans ces expressions la marque d'une alliance inégalitaire (Lafont, "Relations internationales," 258 n. 195). Ce n'est vrai que pour *sissiktam kullum* (ou encore *qaran ṣubâtim kullum / ṣabâtum*) et leur inverse (*sissiktam wuššurum*).

42 ARM 26/2 450: (17) ^{I}*ḫa-am-mu-ra-bi a-na dam-qa-tim* (18) *ù sí-sí-ik-tim ka-ṣa-ri-im* (19) *qa-qa-as-sú uk-ti-il*. Pour le contexte historique, voir Charpin et Ziegler, *Florilegium marianum V*, 202. Pour d'autres exemples, voir ci-dessus notes 28 à 30.

43 Jacob J. Finkelstein, "Cutting the *sissiktu* in Divorce Proceedings," *WO* 8 (1976): 236-240. Voir depuis Raymond Westbrook, *Old Babylonian Marriage Law*, AfOB 23 (Horn: Verlag Ferdinand Berger & Söhne, 1988), 69-71. Comme souvent, la symbolique n'est explicitée que dans un texte tardif, en l'occurrence dans le *Dream-book*: dans ce contexte, on coupe la frange du vêtement de façon que les mauvais présages apportés par les rêves s'éloignent du rêveur (citation dans le *CAD* S 322b § a 2'; voir désormais Sally A.L. Butler, *Mesopotamian Conceptions of Dreams and Dream Rituals*, AOAT 258 [Münster: Ugarit-Verlag, 1998], 314-317, col. ii 10-13: "Just as this hem was cut off from my garment, and cannot return to my garment, because it was cut off—(so may) the evil of this dream (…) not reach me!").

44 ARM 26/2 313: 12 [*sí-s*]*í-ik-tam bu-tu-uq-ma nu-ku-ur-ta-k*([*a šu*]*-te*$_9$*-di-ma*). J'avais pensé en éditant le texte que le passage faisait allusion au divorce de Ḫaya-Sumu et Kiru (Dominique Charpin et al., *Archives Royales de Mari 26: Archives épistolaire de Mari I/2* [Paris:

Le deuxième point où mariage et alliance sont comparables concerne la formule relative aux relations communes. Dès le plus ancien "traité" connu, le serment d'un roi élamite s'alliant à Naram-Sin d'Akkad, on trouve comme engagement d'avoir mêmes amis et mêmes ennemis: "L'ennemi de Naram-Sin est aussi mon ennemi, l'ami de Naram-Sin est aussi mon ami."[45]

On retrouve la même formule dans des textes des archives de Mari. Il s'agit d'abord de l'engagement de rois lors de la conclusion d'une alliance avec Zimri-Lim:

> [10] Les rois se sont levés et ont parlé ainsi: [11] "Nous sommes en paix avec qui est en paix avec notre seigneur Zimri-Lim [12] et nous sommes en guerre avec l'ennemi de notre seigneur. Notre situation [13] est entre les mains de notre seigneur: que notre seigneur [14] fasse [13] ce qui lui plaît!" [14] Voilà ce qu'ils ont dit[46].

On trouve aussi cette formule à l'impératif dans le serment que Hammurabi de Babylone souhaite faire jurer par Atamrum:

> Sois hostile [avec mes ennemis] [et sois en bons termes] avec mes amis[47].

Une telle formule ne se retrouve pas entre mari et femme dans la conclusion du mariage. Elle est en revanche très proche de celle qu'on trouve dans certains

Éditions Recherche sur les Civilisations, 1988], 75 note a). Mais une nouvelle interprétation de nature politique en a été proposée, qui me paraît convaincante (Michaël Guichard, "Violation du serment et casuistique à Mari," *Méditerranées* 10-11 [1996] : 81). Pour *nukurtam wuddûm* "faire connaître son hostilité, déclarer la guerre," voir aussi ARM 26/1 217: 30′.

45 Walther Hinz, "Elams Vertrag mit Naram-Sîn von Akkad," ZA 58 (1967) : 91 et 93: iii 10-17. Comme Hinz l'a remarqué, ce passage avait été compris par Scheil dès 1911 ("Elams Vertrag," 75). La formule est au cœur des traités d'alliance au Bronze Moyen comme au Bronze Récent; voir respectivement Charpin ("Guerre et paix," 213) et Mario Liverani (*Prestige and Interest: International Relations in the Near East, ca. 1600-1100 B.C.*, HANE/S 1 [Padova: Sargon, 1990], 180 et n. 5). Pour une nouvelle traduction et interprétation du "traité de Naram-Sin," voir Bejamin R. Foster, *The Age of Agade: Inventing Empire in Ancient Mesopotamia* (New York, NY/London: Routledge, 2016), 172-173.

46 Inédit A.484 (cité dans Charpin, "Guerre et paix," 213) : (10) *it-b[u]-⸢ú⸣-ma* LUGAL.MEŠ *ke-em iq-bu-ú ⸢um⸣-ma-mi* (11) *sa-li-ma-at zi-im-ri-li-im be-el-ni sa-al-ma-nu* (12) *ù na-ki-ir be-lí-ni*$_5$ *na-ak-ra-nu te*$_4$*-em-ni* (13) *i-na qa-at be-lí-[ne] ⸢ù⸣ be-el-[ni] ša e-li-šu ṭà-bu* (14) *li-pu-úš an-ni-tam i[q-b]u-ú.*

47 ARM 26/2 372: (58)... [... *it-ti na-ak-ri-ia*] (59) *lu-ú na-ak-ra-a-ta it-ti sa-li-mi-ia* [*lu-ú sa-al-ma-a-ta*]. Les restitutions sont assurées par le parallélisme du passage.

contrats de mariage, lorsqu'un homme prend une deuxième épouse: on dit que la deuxième épouse doit s'aligner sur la conduite de l'épouse principale[48]. La formule la plus fréquente est:

> Elle (l'épouse secondaire) haïra celui qu'elle (l'épouse principale) hait (*zenîša izenni*) et elle sera en paix avec qui elle est en paix (*salâmiša isallim*)[49].

Ces similitudes entre serments d'alliance et mariage (ou adoption) montrent bien le caractère profondément personnel des engagements entre rois au Bronze Moyen.

La conclusion me semble sans équivoque: le cylindre de Clercq 390-ter représente le geste de deux rois qui se passent le bras derrière la nuque, marquant leur unité consécutive à la conclusion de leur alliance.

3.3 *La description textuelle d'une embrassade?*

Pour finir, je voudrais citer un dernier texte, qui pourrait bien décrire le même geste ou un geste voisin. Il s'agit de l'alliance conclue entre Atamrum d'Andarig et Asqur-Addu de Karana, telle qu'elle fut décrite à Zimri-Lim par son représentant à Andarig, le général Yasim-El:

> [61] L'ânon [62] fut mis à mort. Chacun fit prêter par l'autre le serment par le dieu et [63] ils se tinrent pour la coupe. Une fois qu'ils se furent embrassés? (*garâšum*) et qu'ils eurent bu à la coupe, [64] ils s'offrirent un présent l'un à l'autre, puis Asqur-Addu [65] repartit [64] dans son pays [65] et Atamrum repartit pour Andarig[50].

---

48 Ce point a déjà été noté par Samuel Greengus, "Redefining 'Inchoate Marriage' in Old Babylonian Contexts," in *Riches Hidden in Secret Places: Ancient Near Eastern Studies in Memory of Thorkild Jacobsen*, ed. Tzvi Abusch (Winona Lake, IN: Eisenbrauns, 2002), 123-139. Il y cite ARM 26/2 372 (*itti nakrīya lū nakrāta itti salāmiya lū salmāta*) et indique: "Similar phrases proclaiming sororal solidarity are found in OB marriage documents involving co-wives who become adoptive sisters" (p. 135 n. 42). On peut ajouter que c'est la même chose en ce qui concerne l'adoption d'un enfant: cf. ARM 8 1, où l'on précise l'attitude du fils adoptif vis-à-vis de ses parents adoptifs: "il partagera leurs joies et souffrira leurs peines" (4) *da-ma-qí-šu-nu i-da-mi-iq* (5) *li-mi-ni-šu-nu i-le-mi-in*.

49 Westbrook, *Old Babylonian Marriage Law*, 109.

50 ARM 26/2 404: (61)… ANŠE *ḫa-a-ru-um* (62) *iq-qa-ṭì-il a-ḫu-um a-ḫa-a*[*m*] *ni-*[*iš*] DINGIR-*lim* [*ú*]-*ša-àz-ki-ir*{*ir*}-*ma* (63) *a-na ka-si-im úš-bu iš-tu ig-ru-šu ù ka-sa-am iš-*[*tu*]-*ú* (64) *a-ḫu-um a-na a-ḫi-im qí-iš-tam iš-ši-ma ás-qùr-*dIŠKUR *a-na ma-a-ti-šu* (65) *ú-ra-am-mi ù a-tam-rum a-na li-ib-bi* [*an*]-*da-ri-ig*ki *ú-ra-am-mi*.

Le verbe *iG/Q-ru-šu* a fait l'objet de nombreuses conjectures. Francis Joannès avait reconnu ici le verbe de mouvement *garâšum* employé en hendiadys avec *šatûm* et traduit "ils s'installèrent (près) de la coupe,"[51] mais Durand a mis en évidence deux sens possibles du verbe *garâšum*[52]. C'est le deuxième sens qu'a retenu Eidem, proposant avec prudence de comprendre qu'on aurait découpé la viande de l'ânon pour en extraire le sang bu dans la coupe[53]. Cela n'a guère de sens: on n'a pas besoin de découper une carcasse pour saigner un animal mis à mort, comme le montrent les abattages *casher* ou *halal*. Par ailleurs, un texte encore inédit montre le sort réservé à un ânon dans le cadre du rituel de la conclusion d'une alliance: on ne touchait pas à sa carcasse. Il s'agit d'une lettre du chef sim'alite Hali-hadun au roi de Mari Zimri-Lim à un moment

51 Francis Joannès avait traduit le passage ainsi: "(60-61) Après qu'ils se furent concertés et eurent fait alliance, l'ânon d'alliance (62) fut immolé; ils se prêtèrent mutuellement serment par le dieu et (63) ils s'installèrent (près) de la coupe" et commenté en note: "J.-M. Durand me signale que le même verbe *garâšum* se retrouve dans la lettre A.607 (cf. Jean-Marie Durand, "Problèmes d'eau et d'irrigation au royaume de Mari," in *Les techniques et les pratiques hydro-agricoles traditionnelles en domaine irrigué: Approche pluridisciplinaire des modes de culture avant la motorisation en Syrie, Actes du colloque de Damas, 27 juin-1er juillet 1987*, ed. B. Geyer, BAH 136 [Paris: Paul Geuthner, 1990]), en hendyadis[sic] avec *etêqum*. On a donc considéré ici que les deux verbes *garâšum* + *šâtum* sont à prendre comme un ensemble, avec le sens de 'aller boire'" (Joannès dans Charpin et al., *Archives Royales*, 263 note r).

52 "Il existe d'autre part à Mari un verbe *garâšum* qui, employé absolument, signifie 'aller par un raccourci,' 'couper par lui,' comme le montre A.607: 16: 'Sur sa route, mon Seigneur devra couper par NG' (*kîma etêqim-ma, bêlî ina* NG, *li-iG-ru-úš*). Il faut comprendre ici l'expression avec *harrânam* sous-entendu. Le sens propre de GRŠ avec un PN devrait donc être à Mari 'couper qu'un d'un lieu,' 'l'empêcher d'y avoir accès.' Ce verbe est, d'autre part, attesté lexicalement sous la forme KUD = *ga-ra-šu* et, à époque récente, pour signifier 'découper' de la viande. Il est attesté aussi, avec le même sens, sous sa forme emphatique *gurrušum*, dès l'époque paléobabylonienne (TLB 4 11: 28, 'débiter des régimes de dattes pour en faire des rations'). Les graphies babyloniennes montrent clairement que le verbe est *garâšum* non *qarâšum*! La décision de *AHw*, p. 903a, et de *CAD* Q 128, de ranger le verbe sous *qarâšum* est peu satisfaisante" (Jean-Marie Durand, *Les Documents épistolaires du palais de Mari, Vol. II*, LAPO 17 [Paris: Éditions du Cerf, 1998], 645). L'inédit A.607 est devenu FM 16 14 (cf. Hervé Reculeau, *Florilegium marianum XVI: L'agriculture irriguée au royaume de Mari. Essai d'histoire des techniques*, Mémoires de NABU 21 [Paris: SEPOA, 2018], 342-343).

53 Son commentaire est le suivant: "The Akkadian IK-*ru-šu* leaves us a choice between two very rare verbs: the editor's *garāšum* "approach" or *qarāšum* "to carve meat" (*CAD* Q 128). If the latter choice is correct a reference to the slaughtered donkey should be involved and the substance drunk from the cup may have been its blood(?)" (PIHANS 117: 313 n. 43). Il faut ici souligner le fait que lorsqu'il est question de sang dans les alliances, c'est toujours celui des rois auquel il est fait allusion (Charpin, *"Tu es de mon sang!"*, 74-78).

où le roi Sibkuna-Addu s'était rangé du côté de Zimri-Lim, au contraire des autres rois du Zalmaqum:

> [8] Du fait que, à l'heure actuelle, [9] Sibkuna-Addu [10] parle franchement [9] à mon seigneur et aux Bédouins (Sim'alites) [10-11] et qu'il ne cesse de m'envoyer des messages amicaux, à présent, sans aucun doute[54] [12] les rois, ses frères, l'ont blamé, [13] en ces termes: "Pourquoi t'es-tu dépêché de [14] tuer les ânons [13] avec Zimri-Lim [14] et les Sim'alites [14] et leur parles-tu franchement?" [16] Voilà ce qu'ils lui ont dit et il a envoyé un message [17] en ces termes: "Les ânons que nous avions tués [18] ne puaient pas encore [18] et vous êtes venus [20] attaquer [19] le troupeau des Yaminites [19] à l'intérieur du Zalmaqum. (…)."[55]

Je ne m'attarderai pas ici à commenter le contexte politique. Je retiens seulement que pour indiquer la proximité temporelle d'une action consécutive à la conclusion d'une alliance, Sibkuna-Addu indique: "Les ânons que nous avions tués ne puaient pas encore." Cela signifie qu'après l'immolation des ânons lors de la conclusion d'une alliance, les caracasses des bêtes étaient laissées sur place: il n'est donc guère vraisemblable qu'elles aient été découpées. Ce sens de *garâšum* n'est donc pas à retenir dans le contexte de ARM 26/2 404.

Cependant, le verbe *garâšum* apparaît parfois dans des contextes sexuels: Brigitte Groneberg avait proposé la traduction "avoir des relations sexuelles,"[56] mais le sens est plutôt "embrasser" – et embrasser ne se dit pas seulement dans un registre sexuel. Or on a vu la proximité qui existe parfois entre le vocabulaire

---

54 Ici, la particule modale *minde* ne peut signifier "peut-être" ni même "vraisemblablement" (cf. l. 16); voir Nathan Wasserman, *Most Probably: Epistemic Modality in Old Babylonian*, LANE 3 (Winona Lake, IN: Eisenbrauns, 2012), 43-63.

55 A.1208: (8) (…) *ù ša [an]-na-nu-um* (9) *ˡsi-ib-ku-na-ᵈ*IŠKUR *it-ti be-lí-ia ù ḫa-na.*MEŠ (10) *i-ša-ri-iš i-da-ab-bu-bu ù a-wa-tim dam-qa-tim-ma* (11) *iš-ta-na-ap-pa-ra-am i-[na-a]n-na mi-id-di* (12) [LU]GAL.MEŠ *aḫ-ḫu-šu i-na a-wa-tim ú-ri-ru-šu* (13) *um-ma-a-mi a-na mi-nim ta-aḫ-mu-ṭam-ma it-ti zi-im-ri-li-im*(14) [*ù* DUMU *si-i*]*m-a-al* ANŠE *ḫa-a-ri ta-aq-tu-ul* (15) *ù i-ša-ri-iš it-ti-šu-nu ta-da-ab-bu-ub* (16) *an-né-e-tim id-bu-bu-šum-ma ki-a-am iš-pu-ra-am* (17) *um-ma šu-ma a-di-ni* AN̊Š[E *ḫa*]*-a-ru ša ni-iq-tu-lu* (18) *ú-ul i-bi-šu ù ta-al-li-ka-nim-ma* (19) *i-na bi-ri-it za-al-ma-qí-im na-wi-a-am ša* DUMU *ia-mi-na* (20) *ta-aš-ḫi-i-ṭà.* Je remercie J.-M. Durand qui m'a permis de citer ce texte avant sa parution dans ARM 35. À la l. 18, reconnaître une forme du verbe *epêšum* ne donne pas un sens satisfaisant; or *ba'âšum* "puer" se dit précisément à propos de viande avariée dans FM 2 84: 15.

56 Voir les textes réunis dans Brigette Groneberg, "Abriss eines thematischen Vergleichs zwischen CT 15, 5-6 und CTA 24 = UT 77," *UF* 6 (1974): 66 n. 4.

de l'alliance et celui du mariage. Il me semble donc que le texte ARM 26/2 404 pourrait décrire le geste de l'embrassade consécutif à la prestation du serment d'alliance.

On notera enfin que dans la description de Yasim-El, le geste de l'embrassade est suivi par le fait de boire à la même coupe; il se pourrait bien que de telles scènes soient également représentées, comme sur des terres cuites qui ont été réunies par Dominique Beyer[57].

4 Conclusion

Des actes aussi importants que les alliances ont donc laissé de nombreuses traces dans les textes, où différents gestes sont décrits: les rois engageaient toute leur personne et le signifiaient par tout leur corps. Il est possible d'en trouver des échos dans l'iconographie, même si les rapprochements doivent être effectués avec prudence[58]. C'est surtout le geste consistant à s'embrasser en passant la main derrière le cou de son partenaire qui nous est documenté par l'image, sans qu'on puisse établir si cela est dû au hasard des découvertes.

Bibliographie

Amiet, Pierre. "Alliance des hommes, alliance des dieux dans l'iconographie orientale." Pages 1-6 in *Collectanea Orientalia: Histoire, arts de l'espace et industrie de la terre. Etudes offertes en hommage à Agnès Spycket.* Edited by Hermann Gasche and Barthel Hrouda. Civilisations du Proche-Orient Série I Archéologie et Environnement 3. Paris/Neuchâtel: Recherches et Publications, 1996.

Attinger, Pascal, Antoine Cavigneaux, Catherine Mittermayer, Mirko Novàk, ed. *Text and Image: Proceedings of the 61e Rencontre Assyriologique Internationale, Geneva and Bern, 22–26 June 2015.* OBO SA 40. Leuven/Paris/Bristol: Peeters, 2018.

Beyer, Dominique. "A propos d'une terre cuite de Sfiré." Pages 21-26 in *Collectanea Orientalia: Histoire, arts de l'espace et industrie de la terre. Etudes offertes en hommage*

57 Dominique Beyer, "A propos d'une terre cuite de Sfiré," in *Collectanea Orientalia: Histoire, arts de l'espace et industrie de la terre. Etudes offertes en hommage à Agnès Spycket*, ed. H. Gasche et B. Hrouda, Civilisations du Proche-Orient Série I Archéologie et Environnement 3 (Paris/Neuchâtel: Recherches et publications, 1996), 21-26 (fig. 1-4).

58 Pour d'autres approches, voir notamment les contributions réunies dans Attinger et al. (ed.), *Text and Image: Proceedings of the 61e Rencontre Assyriologique Internationale, Geneva and Bern, 22–26 June 2015*, OBO SA 40 (Leuven/Paris/Bristol: Peeters, 2018).

à Agnès Spycket. Edited by Hermann Gasche and Barthel Hrouda. Civilisations du Proche-Orient Série I Archéologie et Environnement 3. Paris/Neuchâtel: Recherches et publications, 1996.

Boyer, Georges. *Archives Royales de Mari VIII: Textes juridiques et administratifs*. Paris: Paul Geuthner, 1957.

Butler, Sally A.L. *Mesopotamian Conceptions of Dreams and Dream Rituals*. AOAT 258. Münster: Ugarit-Verlag, 1998.

Charpin, Dominique. "Un traité entre Zimri-Lim de Mari et Ibâl-pî-El II d'Ešnunna." Pages 139-166 in *Marchands, Diplomates et Empereurs: Etudes sur la civilisation mésopotamienne offertes à Paul Garelli*. Edited by Dominique Charpin and F. Joannès. Paris: Éditions Recherche sur les Civilisations, 1991.

Charpin, Dominique. "Données nouvelles sur la région du Petit Zab au XVIIIe siècle av. J.-C." *RA* 98 (2004): 151-178.

Charpin, Dominique. "Textes et images: le cas de deux stèles paléo-babyloniennes." *NABU* (2005): 95.

Charpin, Dominique. "Guerre et paix dans le monde amorrite et post-amorrite." Pages 189-214 in *Krieg und Frieden im Alten Vorderasien: 52e Rencontre Assyriologique Internationale, Münster, 17.-21. Juli 2006*. Edited by Hans Neumann, Reinhard Dittmann, Susanne Paulus, Georg Neumann, and Anais Schuster-Brandis. AOAT 401. Münster, Ugarit-Verlag, 2014.

Charpin, Dominique. "Les débuts des relations diplomatiques au Proche-Orient ancien." *RA* 110 (2016): 127-186.

Charpin, Dominique. *"Tu es de mon sang!" Les alliances dans le Proche-Orient ancien*. Docet omnia 4. Paris: Les Belles Lettres/Collège de France, 2019.

Charpin, Dominique, Jean-Marie Durand, Francis Joannès, Sylvie Lackenbacher, and Bertrand Lafont. *Archives Royales de Mari 26: Archives épistolaire de Mari I/2*. Paris: Éditions Recherche sur les Civilisations, 1988.

Charpin, Dominique, and Jean-Marie Durand, ed. *Florilegium marianum II: Recueil d'études à la mémoire de Maurice Birot*. Mémoires de NABU 3. Paris: SEPOA, 1994.

Charpin, Dominique, and Nele Ziegler. *Florilegium marianum V. Mari et le Proche-Orient à l'époque amorrite: essai d'histoire politique*. Mémoires de NABU 6. Paris: SEPOA, 2003.

Durand, Jean-Marie. "Fragments rejoints pour une histoire élamite." Pages 111-128 in *Fragmenta Historiae Elamicae: Mélanges offerts à M.-J. Steve*. Edited by L. De Meyer, H. Gasche, and Fr. Vallat. Paris: Éditions Recherche sur les Civilisations, 1986.

Durand, Jean-Marie. "Problèmes d'eau et d'irrigation au royaume de Mari." Pages 101-142 in *Les techniques et les pratiques hydro-agricoles traditionnelles en domaine irrigué: Approche pluridisciplinaire des modes de culture avant la motorisation en Syrie, Actes du colloque de Damas, 27 juin-1er juillet 1987*. Edited by B. Geyer. BAH 136. Paris: Paul Geuthner, 1990.

Durand, Jean-Marie. *Les Documents épistolaires du palais de Mari, Vol. II*. LAPO 17. Paris: Éditions du Cerf, 1998.

Durand, Jean-Marie. *Florilegium marianum VIII: Le Culte des pierres et les monuments commémoratifs en Syrie amorrite*. Mémoires de NABU 9. Paris: SEPOA, 2005.

Eidem, Jesper. *The Shemshāra Archives 2 : The Administrative Texts*. Historisk-filosofiske Skrifter 15. Copenhagen: Munksgaard, 1992.

Eidem, Jesper. "Back to Shemshara: NINO Excavations 2012-2015." Pages 157-195 in *Zagros Studies: Proceedings of the NINO Jubilee Conference and Other Research on the Zagros Region*. Edited by Jesper Eidem. PIHANS 130. Leyde/Leuven: Nederlands Institute voor het nabije Oosten, 2020.

Eidem, Jesper, and Jørgen Læssøe. *The Shemshara Archives Vol. 1 : The Letters*. Historisk-filosofiske Skrifter 23. Copenhagen: Royal Danish Academy of Sciences and Letters, 2001.

Eidem, Jesper, Lauren Ristvet, and Harvey Weiss. *The Royal Archives from Tell Leilan: Old Babylonian Letters and Treaties from the Lower Town Palace East*. PIHANS 117. Leiden: Nederlands Institute voor het nabije Oosten, 2011.

Finkelstein, Jacob J. "Cutting the *sissiktu* in Divorce Proceedings." *WO* 8 (1976) : 236-240.

Fleming, Daniel E. "Mari and the Possibilities of Biblical Memory." *RA* 92 (1998) : 41-78.

Fleming, Daniel E. *Democracy's Ancient Ancestors: Mari and Early Collective Governance*. Cambridge: Cambridge University Press, 2004.

Foster, Benjamin R. *The Age of Agade: Inventing Empire in Ancient Mesopotamia*. New York, NY/London: Routledge, 2016.

Frankena, Rintje. *Briefe aus dem Leidener Sammlung: TLB IV*. AbB 3. Leyde: Brill, 1968.

Greengus, Samuel. "Redefining 'Inchoate Marriage' in Old Babylonian Contexts." Pages 123-139 in *Riches Hidden in Secret Places: Ancient Near Eastern Studies in Memory of Thorkild Jacobsen*. Edited by Tzvi Abusch. Winona Lake, IN : Eisenbrauns, 2002.

Groneberg, Brigette. "Abriss eines thematischen Vergleichs zwischen CT 15, 5-6 und CTA 24 = UT 77." *UF* 6 (1974) : 65-68.

Guichard, Michaël. "Violation du serment et casuistique à Mari." *Méditerranées* 10-11 (1996) : 71-84.

Guichard, Michaël. "Un traité d'alliance entre Larsa, Uruk et Ešnunna contre Sabium de Babylone." *Sem* 56 (2014) : 9-34.

Guichard, Michaël. "Les statues divines et royales à Mari d'après les textes." *JA* 307 (2019) : 1-56.

Heintz, Jean-Georges. *Prophétisme et alliance: Des Archives royales de Mari à la Bible hébraïque. Recueil d'études édité par Stephan Lauber avec Othmar Keel et Hans Ulrich Steymans. Mit einem Vorwort von Manfred Weippert*. OBO 271. Fribourg: Academic Press; Göttingen: Vandenhoeck & Ruprecht, 2015.

Hinz, Walther. "Elams Vertrag mit Naram-Sîn von Akkad." *ZA* 58 (1967) : 66-96.

Joannès, Francis, Christine Kepinski-Lecomte, and Gudrun Colbow. *Haradum II: Les textes de la période paléo-babylonienne (Samsu-iluna – Ammi-ṣaduqa)*. Paris: Éditions Recherche sur les Civilisations, 2006.

Læssøe, Jørgen. *People of Ancient Assyria: Their Inscriptions and Correspondence.* London: Routledge & Keagan Paul, 1963.

Læssøe, Jørgen. *Det Første Assyriske Imperium.* Copenhagen: Københavns Universitet, 1966.

Lafont, Bertrand. "Relations internationales, alliances et diplomatie au temps des royaumes amorrites." Pages 213-328 in *Mari, Ébla et les Hourrites: dix ans de travaux: Actes du colloque international (Paris, mai 1993). Deuxième partie.* Edited by Jean-Marie Durand and Dominique Charpin. Amurru 2. Paris: Éditions Recherche sur les Civilisations, 2001.

Liverani, Mario. *Prestige and Interest: International Relations in the Near East, ca. 1600-1100 B.C.* HANE/S 1. Padova: Sargon, 1990.

Matthiae, Paolo. *Aux origines de la Syrie: Ebla retrouvée.* Découvertes Gallimard. Paris: Gallimard, 1996.

Matthiae, Paolo. *La storia dell'arte dell'Oriente Antico: Gli stati territoriali 2100-1600 a.C.* Milan: Electa, 2000.

Matthiae, Paolo. "The Old Syrian Temple N's Carved Basin and the Relation between Aleppo and Ebla." *StEb* 4 (2018): 109-138.

Matthiae, Paolo. "Again on the Limestone Carved Basin of Temple N of Ebla." *StEb* 5 (2019): 207-212.

Matthiae, Paolo, Frances Pinnock, and Gabriella Scandone Matthiae. *Ebla: Alle origini della civiltà urbana: Trent'anni di scavi in Siria dell'Università di Roma "La Sapienza".* Milan: Electa, 1995.

Podany, Amanda H. *Brotherhood of Kings: How International Relations Shaped the Ancient Near East.* New York, NY/Oxford: Oxford University Press, 2010.

Reculeau, Hervé. *Florilegium marianum XVI: L'agriculture irriguée au royaume de Mari. Essai d'histoire des techniques.* Mémoires de NABU 21. Paris: SEPOA, 2018.

Reiner, Erica. "Supplement to Chicago Assyrian Dictionary T (Volume 18)." *JNES* 66 (2007): 47-61.

Suter, Claudia. "The Victory Stele of Dadusha of Eshnunna: A New Look at its Unusual Culminating Scene." *Ash-sharq* 2/2 (2018): 1-29.

Veenhof, Klaas R. "New Mesopotamian Treaties from the Second Millennium BC from kārum Kanesh and Tell Leilan (Šehna)." *ZAR* 19 (2014): 23-58.

Wasserman, Nathan. *Most Probably: Epistemic Modality in Old Babylonian.* LANE 3. Winona Lake, IN: Eisenbrauns, 2012.

Westbrook, Raymond. *Old Babylonian Marriage Law.* AfOB 23. Horn: Verlag Ferdinand Berger & Söhne, 1988.

Ziegler, Nele. "Kakmum et le Gutium." Pages 23-36 in *Recherches en Haute-Mésopota-*

mie II: Mission archéologique de Bash Tapa (campagnes 2012-2013) et les enjeux de la recherche dans la région d'Erbil. Edited by L. Marti, Ch. Nicolle, and K. Shawaly. Mémoires de NABU 17. Paris: SEPOA, 2015.

3

Commensality and Kinship: Exodus 24 and the Emar *Zukru* Festival

Jessie DeGrado

In Exodus 24:3–8 + 11bβ–15 (Exodus 24*), the Israelites ratify divine legislation from the mountain of God through a covenantal ceremony. Enacted before twelve standing stones corresponding to the tribes of Israel, the rite includes an unusual step: the application of sacrificial blood to the assembled community. William Robertson Smith saw the peculiarities of this rite as emblematic of early Israelite worship—a primitive past in which kinship was constituted through bloody sacrifice.[1] In the past century, scholarship has moved away from the social evolutionary assumptions undergirding Smith's work. Nonetheless, the application of blood to the people in Exodus 24 remains a puzzle as it is otherwise unparalleled in biblical rituals. This paper analyzes the covenantal ceremony of Exodus 24* in the light of an overlooked parallel in the *zukru* festival at Emar (Emar 373+:34–37). The Emar ritual shares three significant features with the story of Exodus 24*: (1) the establishment of standing stones; (2) sacrifice and blood manipulation performed outside the confines of city structures; and (3) a communal feast. Drawing on additional data from Mari (A.981 and A.2226), I argue that the biblical text reflects details that conform to known ritual praxis from the ancient Levant. These rites, unknown to Smith in the late nineteenth century, do, in fact, constitute and strengthen kinship ties through commensality and the manipulation of blood. Such practices are not, however, restricted to nonmonarchic societies, as the texts from Mari and Emar demonstrate. Rather than reflecting details from a hoary past, Exodus 24* combines elements from disparate rituals that operate at multiple levels of society (both royal and kin-based) in order to imagine Israel at the moment of its founding.

1 Exodus 24:3–8 in the Reconstruction of Israel's History

Exodus 24 narrates a covenant ceremony performed at the foot of the mountain of God. Within the pentateuchal text, the covenant represents the moment

1 William Robertson Smith, *Lectures on the Religion of the Semites* (London: Adam & Charles Black, 1889), 300–301.

 | DOI:10.1163/9789004511538_004

at which the Israelites, freed from bondage in Egypt, are constituted as a people in preparation for their entry into the Promised Land. Within this chapter, a short passage (vv. 3–8) presents a unique sacrificial ritual of blood manipulation performed by lay Israelites to ratify their covenant with Yahweh. This ritual was central to late nineteenth- and early twentieth-century approaches to biblical ritual and the historical origins of Israel. For Smith, for example, the sacrificial ceremony in Exodus 24 confirmed his theory of commensality as the motivating factor behind sacrifice.[2] Smith argued that the ritual narrated in Exodus 24:3–8 was employed to constitute and consolidate kinship between the people of Israel and their deity.

Smith's theory of sacrifice had a significant impact on Julius Wellhausen, who developed his own evolutionary approach to Israelite religion in conversation with his colleague and friend.[3] Wellhausen posited that Israelite sacrifice developed from small kin-based festivals like that of Exodus 24 into abstract and (in his view) stultified cultic worship. Wellhausen's contemporaries were similarly drawn to the unique features of the rite. The lay officiants and unusual application of blood were seen as indicative of a premonarchic date for the pericope itself (or a tradition underlying it).[4] And for Martin Noth, the scene represented the earliest stages of the development of an Israelite amphicty-

2 Smith, *Lectures*, 300–301.

3 Wellhausen's most famous work on Israelite religion (*Prolegomena to the History of Israel*, trans. J. Sutherland Black and Allan Menzies [Edinburgh: Adam & Charles Black, 1885]) was published several years before the initial publication of Smith's, *Lectures on the Religion of the Semites*. Nonetheless, Wellhausen engages Smith's earlier work in his *Prolegomena* (93 n. 1, 274), and Smith was one of the initial supporters of Wellhausen's hypotheses. Wellhausen later published an entry on Israel in *Encyclopaedia Britannica* at the behest of Robertson Smith, and his discussion of how Yahweh evolved from the tribal god of Israel to the mysterious and transcendental god of the universe proceeds directly from Smith's work (reprinted in Wellhausen, *Prolegomena*, 429–548, esp. 435–438). For additional discussion of the relationship between Smith and Wellhausen, see Gary A. Anderson and Saul M. Olyan, "Preface," in *Priesthood and Cult in Ancient Israel*, ed. Gary A. Anderson and Saul M. Olyan, JSOTSup 125 (Sheffield: Sheffield Academic Press, 1991), 7–10; Bernhard Maier, *William Robertson Smith: His Life, His Work, and His Times*, FAT 67 (Tübingen: Mohr Siebeck, 2009), 207–210; and Steven Weitzman, *The Origin of the Jews: The Quest for Roots in a Rootless Age* (Princeton, NJ: Princeton University Press, 2017), 112–113.

4 So, e.g., Carl Steuernagel, "Der jehovistische Bericht über den Bundesschluss am Sinai," *TSK* 72 (1899): 319–350. This view continued to have adherents through the mid-to-late twentieth century and is accepted in modified form by Lothar Perlitt (*Bundestheologie im Alten Testament*, WMANT 36 [Neukirchen-Vluyn: Neukirchener Verlag, 1969], 190–203) and Erich Zenger (*Die Sinaitheophanie: Untersuchungen zum jahwistischen und elohistischen Geschichtswerk* [Würzburg: Echter, 1971], 75–76), who maintain that the divine covenant has been inserted into an earlier sacrificial ritual.

ony.[5] This short pericope thus had an outsized impact on late nineteenth- and early twentieth-century reconstructions of Israel's earliest history.

Over the past half century, of course, many of the presuppositions underlying these analyses have been challenged. Scholarship has moved beyond credulous readings of the pentateuchal narratives as reflecting ancient Israel's premonarchic past.[6] Equally significant, the evolutionary paradigms of Smith and Wellhausen rely on an assumption of linear development from kinship-based societies to monarchy. More recent works by scholars including Daniel Fleming and Norman Yoffee, discussed in more detail below, have shown this schematization to be problematic.[7]

In response to these developments, compositional and ritual studies approaches to Exodus 24:3–8 have diverged. Recent studies of the ritual actions in Exodus 24 have tended to eschew more substantive compositional analysis. Ronald Hendel and Theodore Lewis, for example, confine their analyses to these five verses, focusing on parallels in texts drawn from Mesopotamia and the Levant.[8] Thus, while they shed light on the logic underlying the ritual actions, they do not discuss the role that Exodus 24:3–8 plays within its larger compositional context or in Israelian and/or Judean historiography.[9] Compositional studies, by contrast, often bypass analysis of the ritual entirely.[10] When

5 Martin Noth, *The History of Israel*, 2nd ed. (New York, NY: Harper & Row, 1958), 128.

6 Instrumental here were Thomas L. Thompson, *The Historicity of the Patriarchal Narratives: The Quest for the Historical Abraham* (Berlin: de Gruyter, 1974); and John Van Seters, *Abraham in History and Tradition* (New Haven, CT: Yale University Press, 1975); Van Seters, *In Search of History: Historiography in the Ancient World and the Origins of Biblical History* (New Haven, CT: Yale University Press, 1983).

7 Daniel E. Fleming, *Democracy's Ancient Ancestors: Mari and Early Collective Governance* (Cambridge: Cambridge University Press, 2004); Norman Yoffee, *Myths of the Archaic State: Evolution of the Earliest Cities, States, and Civilizations* (Cambridge: Cambridge University Press, 2005).

8 Ronald S. Hendel, "Sacrifice as a Cultural System: The Ritual Symbolism of Exodus 24,3–8," *ZAW* 101 (1989): 366–390; Theodore J. Lewis, "Covenant and Blood Rituals: Understanding Exodus 24:3–8 in Its Ancient Near Eastern Context," in *Confronting the Past: Archaeological and Historical Essays on Ancient Israel in Honor of William G. Dever*, ed. Seymour Gitin, J. Edward Wright, and J.P. Dessel (Winona Lake, IN: Eisenbrauns, 2006), 341–350.

9 I adopt the terminology *Israelian* to denote the political entity of Israel due to the inherent ambiguity of the term *Israelite*. When discussing the characters in the story of Exodus 24*, however, I use the term Israelite since the story is not necessarily referring to the political origins of the Israelian (as opposed to Judean) state (on which see section 4 below). For further discussion see H.L. Ginsberg, *The Israelian Heritage of Judaism* (New York, NY: Jewish Theological Seminary of America, 1982), 1–2.

10 This is characteristic of both neodocumentary approaches (so Baden, Stackert) and more redaction-critical works (so, e.g., Blum and Schmid). See Erhard Blum, *Studien zur Kom-*

the role of commensality and kinship is taken up, it is frequently only to question whether the text preserves any "authentic" or "ancient" memories for premonarchic Israel. For example, Konrad Schmid, who dates the passage to the exilic or postexilic period, remarks of the ritual, "It must at present remain a matter of speculation whether behind the Sinai tradition, which in any case is literarily late, some older and even pre-state memories … lie hidden."[11]

Schmid's evaluation of the passage relies implicitly on an opposition between the political systems of kinship and kingship—an unexamined holdover from the evolutionary paradigm of Wellhausen and Smith.[12] In my own analysis of Exodus 24:3–8 + 11bβ–15, I will consider how epigraphic finds from Emar and Mari can contribute to our understanding of this passage, not as a vestigial reflection of premonarchic ritual but as a narrative representation of ritual that draws on kinship rites present throughout Israelian and Judean history. The analysis comes in three parts. First, I delimit the textual unit and its relationship to other source material in the book of Exodus. I argue here that the text of Exodus 24*, which describes the covenant ritual enacted by Moses

---

position des Pentateuch (Berlin: de Gruyter, 1990), 92–99; Joel S. Baden, *The Composition of the Pentateuch: Renewing the Documentary Hypothesis* (New Haven, CT: Yale University Press, 2012), 117–118; Konrad Schmid, *The Old Testament: A Literary History*, trans. Linda M. Maloney (Minneapolis, MN: Fortress Press, 2012), 126; Jeffrey Stackert, *A Prophet Like Moses: Prophecy, Law, and Israelite Religion* (Oxford: Oxford University Press, 2014), 75–82. Two recent exceptions to this trend are Simeon Chavel, "A Kingdom of Priests and Its Earthen Altars in Exodus 19–24," *VT* 65 (2015): 169–222; and Samuel L. Boyd, "Applied Ritual: The Application of Blood and Oil on Bodies in the Pentateuchal Sources," *BibInt* 29 (2021): 120–147.

11 Konrad Schmid, *The Old Testament*, 126.

12 This issue is not unique to Schmid's work. Wellhausen's periodization of Israelite history has resulted in a tendency to view much legal material in the Bible as exilic or postexilic and therefore irrelevant to a reconstruction of Israelian and Judean history in the period of the monarchies. Thus, Kratz argues that the ritual ceremony of Exodus 24 belongs to the postexilic period because it relies on the lawgiving, and "the original character of pre-exilic Israelite religion … was not yet dominated by the law" (Reinhard G. Kratz, *The Composition of the Narrative Books of the Old Testament*, trans. John Bowden [London: T&T Clark, 2005], 139). There are two significant difficulties with this argument. First, although the covenant ceremony is certainly associated with a theophany and the receipt of divine instruction, it is possible that the legal material of the Covenant Code is a later interpolation (similarly the reference to וְאֵת כָּל־הַמִּשְׁפָּטִים in 24:3), as Chavel has argued ("A Kingdom of Priests," 189 n. 54). Even more important, however, is the fact that the tendency to view all legal material as late relied implicitly on an anti-Jewish (and, to a lesser degree, anti-Catholic) bias in its original formulation; although contemporary scholars do not share Wellhausen's prejudices, "they perpetuate," as Stackert puts it, "an overly simplistic and tainted view of degenerative development in Israelite religion from early prophetic religion to legalism in the post-exilic period and beyond" (*A Prophet Like Moses*, 71).

and the Israelites, originally concluded with the description of feasting (Exodus 24:11bβ) and Moses's receipt of a divinely crafted copy of the Covenant Code (Exodus 24:12–15). The full set of ritual actions, including sacrifice, blood manipulation, and communal feasting at the site of standing stones, is compared to the *zukru* ritual at Emar in the second section of the paper.[13] Drawing also on kin-based rituals attested in texts from Mari, I argue that Exodus 24:3–8 + 11bβ contains elements of ritual praxis that constitute and reinforce bonds of kinship in creating an alliance. As Fleming has compellingly shown, however, there is no reason to restrict these types of rituals to a premonarchic period. Instead, I argue in the final section of this paper that the author of the biblical text drew on kin-based ritual practice that persisted throughout the Iron Age in order to imagine Israel's mythic past.

2 Delimiting the Passage: Exodus 24:3–8 + 11bβ–15

The composite nature of Exodus 24 has long been recognized by scholars who take a variety of compositional approaches to the Pentateuch.[14] The narrative difficulties are already apparent in the first several verses of the chapter, which concludes Yahweh's delivery of the Covenant Code (Exodus 20–23). In Exodus 24:1–2, the deity instructs Moses to ascend the mountain with Aaron, Nadav, Abihu, and seventy elders. The instruction is puzzling, since Moses is already atop the mountain. Furthermore, in verse 3, Moses gives no indication of having heard the instructions. Instead, he gathers all the people and gives a full

13 Although this connection has not been explored fully, both Exodus 24:3–8 and the *zukru* ritual are adduced together already in Fleming's discussion of biblical anointing practices (Daniel E. Fleming, "The Biblical Tradition of Anointing Priests," *JBL* 117 [1998]: 401–414, here 410). Mark Smith likewise notes the potential relevance of the Emar *zukru* texts as a parallel to the type of ritual described in Exodus 24 (Mark S. Smith, *God in Translation: Deities in Cross-Cultural Discourse in the Biblical World* [Grand Rapids, MI: Eerdmans, 2008], 59–60 n. 102).

14 So, e.g., August Dillmann, *Die Bücher Exodus und Leviticus* (Leipzig: S. Hirzel, 1897), 284–285; Otto Eissfeldt, *Hexateuch-Synopse: Die Erzählung der fünf Bücher Mose und des Buches Josua mit dem Anfange des Richterbuches* (Leipzig: Hinrichs, 1922), 151*–152*; Martin Noth, *Exodus: A Commentary*, OTL (Philadelphia, PA: Westminster, 1962), 194; Dennis J. McCarthy, *Treaty and Covenant: A Study in Form in the Ancient Oriental Documents and in the Old Testament* (Rome: Pontifical Biblical Institute, 1963), 253–254; E.W. Nicholson, "The Covenant Ritual in Exodus XXIV 3–8," *VT* 32 (1982): 74; Baruch Schwartz, "What Really Happened at Mount Sinai? Four Biblical Answers to One Question," *BRev* 13 (1997): 20–30, 46; Baden, *Composition*, 117–118. The analysis presented here largely follows the analysis presented in Schwartz, "What Really Happened?," with the exception of the treatment of 11bβ.

report of Yahweh's speech. That Moses here refers to the preceding legal material rather than the summons in verses 1–2 is widely recognized.[15] The narrator refers to Yahweh's words and laws (אֵת כָּל־דִּבְרֵי יְהוָה וְאֵת כָּל־הַמִּשְׁפָּטִים), and the people respond with their assent. The story continues uninterrupted through verse 8 with a description of the covenant ceremony, including the sacrifice of well-being offerings (שְׁלָמִים).

If we attempt to read straight through the chapter, continuing in verse 9, the story becomes muddled. Moses leaves abruptly and without fanfare. Accompanied by Aaron, Nadab, Abihu, and the seventy elders, he ascends the mountain and experiences a theophany. This scene, described in verses 9–11bα, clearly picks up on the command in verses 1–2 and is intrusive to the description of the covenant ceremony. In addition, the assembled elders' response to the theophany in 11bβ is rather surprising in its current context—they respond to the deity's sublime appearance by holding an impromptu picnic (וַיֹּאכְלוּ וַיִּשְׁתּוּ).[16]

Given the clear evidence for the juxtaposition of source material here, one wonders whether the feasting might belong originally to the description of the covenant conducted in verses 3–8.[17] In addition to the extensive evidence for feasting as a component of covenant ceremonies,[18] the presentation of well-

---

15 In addition to the sources in n. 14 above, see the extensive discussion in Dale Patrick, "The Covenant Code Source," *VT* 27 (1977): 145–157, here 145–147, and, more recently, Chavel, "Kingdom of Priests," 190–194.

16 Scholars who understand 11bβ to follow directly on verses 9–11bα must explain the feast as part of the experience of theophany, despite a lack of parallels for this phenomenon. Propp, who sees only one source in Exodus 24:1–15, argues that the meal is intended to communicate the elders' subservience to Yahweh. However, he quickly returns to the covenant context in describing the meal, despite the trip up the mountain that intervenes. See William Propp, *Exodus: A New Translation with Introduction and Commentary*, AB 2A (New York, NY: Doubleday, 2006), 297. The strained connection between theophany and feast is also evident in Noth's analysis (*Exodus*, 194). He likewise identifies the eating and drinking of verse 11bβ as part of a covenant ceremony, despite the fact a covenant is never mentioned in his posited source (Exodus 24:1, 9–11).

17 Suggested already in Baden, *Composition*, 118; Chavel, "Kingdom of Priests," 190 n. 58; and followed by Boyd, "Applied Ritual," 124. As Chavel observes, a connection between the feasting and covenant ceremony was noted already by medieval commentators including Ibn Ezra.

18 For a general overview, see the discussion in Baruch A. Levine, *In the Presence of the Lord: A Study of Cult and Some Cultic Terms in Ancient Israel*, SJLA 5 (Leiden: Brill, 1974), 35–41; and JoAnn Scurlock, "Animal Sacrifice in Ancient Mesopotamian Religion," in *A History of the Animal World in the Ancient Near East*, ed. Billy Jean Collins, HOS 64 (Leiden: Brill, 2002), 399–400. The use of sacrifice to conclude covenants is especially common in Levantine sources (Moshe Weinfeld, "Covenant Making in Anatolia and Mesopotamia," *JANES* 22 [1992]: 135–139). Ritualized consumption in the context of treaties, however, appears also in Mesopotamian sources of the first millennium (Lewis, "Covenant and Blood Ritu-

being offerings (שְׁלָמִים) in verse 8 primes the reader to expect a celebration—well-being offerings entail the sacrifice of only offal, with the remainder of the meat consumed by the offerer.[19] In sum, the feasting that seems an odd response to theophany can be readily understood in the context of the covenant ceremony.

There is another reason to see a compositional seam at 24:11bβ. Verse 12 opens with Yahweh summoning Moses to ascend the mountain (וַיֹּאמֶר יְהוָה אֶל־מֹשֶׁה עֲלֵה אֵלַי הָהָרָה וֶהְיֵה־שָׁם), where he will receive a copy of the laws that they have just ratified (וְאֶתְּנָה לְךָ אֶת־לֻחֹת הָאֶבֶן וְהַתּוֹרָה וְהַמִּצְוָה אֲשֶׁר כָּתַבְתִּי לְהוֹרֹתָם). In verses 13–15a, Moses obeys the command and ascends the mountain to receive this divinely crafted copy of the laws.[20] But, according to verses 9–11bα, Moses is already atop the mountain. Again, the contradiction can be alleviated by disentangling the two juxtaposed sources and assigning verses 11bβ–15a to the covenant ceremony. The full narrative of the covenant ceremony and receipt of divinely crafted legal tablets thus appears as follows:

als," 342). Interestingly, both Lewis ("Covenant and Blood Rituals," 342) and Smith (*God in Translation*, 58–60) adduce examples of feasting in Assyrian texts when discussing Exodus 24:3–8 despite not including 11bβ (the description of feasting itself) in their treatment of the scene.

19 On the connection between the well-being offering and feasting in the Hebrew Bible, see Levine, *In the Presence of the Lord*, 35–41; and Liane M. Feldman, *The Story of Sacrifice: Ritual and Narrative in the Priestly Source*, FAT 141 (Tübingen: Mohr Siebeck, 2020), 113–114. Further discussion of iconographic and archaeological evidence for sacrificial feasts in the Levant in particular is surveyed in Jessie DeGrado, "An Infelicitous Feast: Ritualized Consumption and Divine Rejection in Amos 6.1–7," *JSOT* 45 (2020): 178–197, here 187–189.

20 The idea that the Israelites would swear on a temporary copy of the law and receive a display copy later likely draws on broader practices associated with international treaties and loyalty oaths. The practice is already attested in the Old Babylonian period (Dominique Charpin, *Writing, Law, and Kingship in Old Babylonian Mesopotamia*, trans. Jane Marie Todd [Chicago, IL: The University of Chicago Press, 2010], 109). Similarly, in the Neo-Assyrian period it is possible to distinguish between archival copies of *adê*–texts and display copies, which are larger, sealed, and rotate along the vertical axis rather than the usual horizontal rotation (Karen Radner, "Assyrische *ṭuppi adê* als Vorbild für Deuteronomium 28,20–44?," in *Die deuteronomistischen Geschichtswerke: Redaktions- und religionsgeschichtliche Perspektiven zur "Deuteronomismus"—Diskussion in Tora und Vorderen Propheten*, ed. Markus Witte et al., BZAW 365 [Berlin: de Gruyter, 2006], 373–374; Jacob Lauinger, "Neo-Assyrian Scribes, Esarhaddon's Succession Treaty, and the Dynamics of Textual Mass Production," in *Text and Contexts: The Circulation and Transmission of Cuneiform Texts in Social Space*, ed. Paul Delnero and Jacob Lauinger, SANER 9 [Berlin: de Gruyter, 2015], 287). A letter from Sargon's correspondence (SAA 1 76 = ABL 90) indicates that display copies (*ṭuppi adê*) of treaties could also be erected for a short time in order to administer the *adê* and subsequently returned to the Assyrian capital (noted already in Simo Parpola, "Neo-Assyrian Treaties from the Royal Archives of Nineveh," *JCS* 39 [1987]: 161–189, here 161 n. 5).

3 וַיָּבֹא מֹשֶׁה וַיְסַפֵּר לָעָם אֵת כָּל־דִּבְרֵי יְהוָה וְאֵת כָּל־הַמִּשְׁפָּטִים וַיַּעַן כָּל־הָעָם קוֹל אֶחָד
וַיֹּאמְרוּ כָּל־הַדְּבָרִים אֲשֶׁר־דִּבֶּר יְהוָה נַעֲשֶׂה׃ 4 וַיִּכְתֹּב מֹשֶׁה אֵת כָּל־דִּבְרֵי יְהוָה וַיַּשְׁכֵּם
בַּבֹּקֶר וַיִּבֶן מִזְבֵּחַ תַּחַת הָהָר וּשְׁתֵּים עֶשְׂרֵה מַצֵּבָה לִשְׁנֵים עָשָׂר שִׁבְטֵי יִשְׂרָאֵל׃ 5 וַיִּשְׁלַח
אֶת־נַעֲרֵי בְּנֵי יִשְׂרָאֵל וַיַּעֲלוּ עֹלֹת וַיִּזְבְּחוּ זְבָחִים שְׁלָמִים לַיהוָה פָּרִים׃ 6 וַיִּקַּח מֹשֶׁה חֲצִי הַדָּם
וַיָּשֶׂם בָּאַגָּנֹת וַחֲצִי הַדָּם זָרַק עַל־הַמִּזְבֵּחַ׃ 7 וַיִּקַּח סֵפֶר הַבְּרִית וַיִּקְרָא בְּאָזְנֵי הָעָם וַיֹּאמְרוּ
כֹּל אֲשֶׁר־דִּבֶּר יְהוָה נַעֲשֶׂה וְנִשְׁמָע׃ 8 וַיִּקַּח מֹשֶׁה אֶת־הַדָּם וַיִּזְרֹק עַל־הָעָם וַיֹּאמֶר הִנֵּה
דַם־הַבְּרִית אֲשֶׁר כָּרַת יְהוָה עִמָּכֶם עַל כָּל־הַדְּבָרִים הָאֵלֶּה׃ 11* וַיֹּאכְלוּ וַיִּשְׁתּוּ׃ 12 וַיֹּאמֶר
יְהוָה אֶל־מֹשֶׁה עֲלֵה אֵלַי הָהָרָה וֶהְיֵה־שָׁם וְאֶתְּנָה לְךָ אֶת־לֻחֹת הָאֶבֶן וְהַתּוֹרָה וְהַמִּצְוָה
אֲשֶׁר כָּתַבְתִּי לְהוֹרֹתָם׃ 13 וַיָּקָם מֹשֶׁה וִיהוֹשֻׁעַ מְשָׁרְתוֹ וַיַּעַל מֹשֶׁה אֶל־הַר הָאֱלֹהִים׃ 14
וְאֶל־הַזְּקֵנִים אָמַר שְׁבוּ־לָנוּ בָזֶה עַד אֲשֶׁר־נָשׁוּב אֲלֵיכֶם וְהִנֵּה אַהֲרֹן וְחוּר עִמָּכֶם מִי־בַעַל
דְּבָרִים יִגַּשׁ אֲלֵהֶם׃ 15* וַיַּעַל מֹשֶׁה אֶל־הָהָר

3 Moses went and told the people all the words of Yahweh and all the laws. And the people responded together: "Everything that Yahweh has said we shall do!"

4 Then Moses wrote all down all the words of Yahweh. He arose early in the morning and set up an altar beneath the mountain as well as twelve standing sones for the twelve tribes of Israel. 5 He sent the youths of Israel, and they sent up burnt offerings and sacrificed cattle as well-being offerings for Yahweh. 6 Then Moses took half of the blood and put it into basins; the other half he sprinkled on the altar. 7 Moses took the book of the covenant and read it to the people. They replied, "Everything that Yahweh has said we shall do and obey!"

8 Moses took the blood and sprinkled it over the people, saying, "Here is the blood of the covenant which Yahweh has established with you based on all of these matters."

11 So they ate and drank. 12 Then Yahweh said to Moses, "Come up the mountain to me and stay here so I can give you stone tablets, the teaching and the law which I have written to instruct them."

13 Moses and his attendant Joshua arose, and Moses ascended the Mountain of God. 14 As for the elders, he had instructed them, "Stay here until we return to you. Aaron and Hur are with you. Whoever has an issue should go to them." 15 So Moses went up the mountain.

For those like myself who subscribe to the Neo-Documentary hypothesis, the narrative sequence here is identified with the longer Elohistic source (E).[21]

21 Schwartz, "What Really Happened?"; Baden, *Composition*, 118; Stackert, *A Prophet Like Moses*, 74–82; Chavel, "A Kingdom of Priests," 172; Boyd, "Applied Ritual," 123–124.

However, the recognition that these verses form a complete and coherent narrative unit does not require accepting a documentarian approach. For example, noting narrative continuities between portions of Exodus 19, 20–23, and 24, Dale Patrick proposed identifying a "Covenant Code Source" that includes the passage we have just demarcated.[22] Taken as a whole, this textual unit opens with Yahweh's invitation to a covenant and theophany (19:2b–9a, 16*[23]–17, 19),[24] includes the legal material of 20–23,[25] and concludes with the covenant ceremony outlined above.

3 Constituting Kinship: The Evidence from Emar and Mari

The covenant ceremony of Exodus 24* contains a coherent set of ritual actions. These consist of the establishment of standing stones, sacrificial offering and the manipulation of blood, and communal feasting. The application of blood to lay people outside the confines of a sanctuary is unique in the biblical record.[26] A comparable practice does appear, however, in the *zukru* festival at Emar,[27] where blood is applied to a series of standing stones that have been established outside the city. Like the ritual in Exodus 24*, the *zukru* festival includes feast-

22 Patrick, "Covenant Code Source," 145–146. See Blum's identification of both Exodus 19:3b–8 and 24:3–8 with his KD source (*Studien*, 92–93, 98–99) and, similarly, Wright's argument for a Covenant Code Narrative (David P. Wright, *Inventing God's Law: How the Covenant Code of the Bible Used and Revised the Laws of Hammurabi* [Oxford: Oxford University Press, 2009], 335–341).

23 The majority of the verse after the initial temporal clause: וַיְהִי קֹלֹת וּבְרָקִים וְעָנָן כָּבֵד עַל־הָהָר וְקֹל שֹׁפָר חָזָק מְאֹד וַיֶּחֱרַד כָּל־הָעָם אֲשֶׁר בַּמַּחֲנֶה.

24 This follows the Neo-Documentarian identification of Elohistic material in chapter 19 (so Schwartz, "What Really Happened?," 24–25). It is also possible that some of verse 18 belongs to this account (see Wright, *Inventing God's Law*, 338; Chavel, "Kingdom of Priests," 189 n. 54).

25 I am sympathetic to Chavel's ("Kingdom of Priests," 172 n. 7) argument that much of the legal material (20:1–17 and 21:1–23:19) is an interpolation into a much shorter set of laws focused on proper worship (20:22–26) (following the versification of chapter 20 in *BHS*, which combines two distinct traditions of cantillation preserved in the Leningrad Codex [on which see Chavel, "Kingdom of Priests," 170 n. 2]). For the alternate perspective, see Wright, *Inventing God's Law*, 335–336.

26 For a recent discussion of the application of blood and oil to humans in the pentateuchal texts, see Boyd, "Applied Ritual."

27 Edited by Daniel E. Fleming, *Time at Emar: The Cultic Calendar and the Rituals from the Diviner's Archive* (Winona Lake, IN: Eisenbrauns, 2000). The texts have recently been reedited in John Tracy Thames, *The Politics of Ritual Change: The* zukru *Festival in the Political History of Late Bronze Age Emar*, HSM 65 (Leiden: Brill, 2020).

ing at the site of the standing stones.[28] Despite the chronological gap between the Late Bronze Age texts from Emar and the composition of Exodus 24* in the first millennium, a comparison of the texts will allow us to better reconstruct the type of ritual envisaged by the biblical authors.[29]

The *zukru* festival first came to light through salvage excavations conducted at the North Syrian site of Tell Meskeneh-Qadimeh between 1970 and 1976, prompted by the building of the Tabqa Dam in 1973. Subsequent excavations were undertaken by a Syrian team in 1992–1995 and a joint Syrian-German team from 1996–2002.[30] In the course of the initial French excavations, archaeologists uncovered a textual archive in a building dubbed "Temple M_1" by Jean-Claude Margueron.[31] The archival texts, written in Akkadian, describe the provisioning and proceedings of local festivals, unknown from Mesopotamian sources. Of these, the most prominent is the annual *zukru* festival. Its importance can be seen in the epigraphic record, as it is the only calendar-based ritual to be preserved in multiple exemplars (Emar 373+, 375+). The *zukru* is also the most expensive local rite, requiring 50 calves and 700 lambs. Nonetheless, the copies are fragmentary, and the better known, more elaborate version of the ritual, intended to be performed every seven years, is recorded on Emar 373+.[32]

The seven-day ritual begins with a procession of the city's entire divine populace (in the form of statues) from the temples to an area outside of the city walls where standing stones have been set up. The town's population follows the divine procession to the ritual arena where an elaborate sacrificial feast is

---

28 As Fleming (*Time at Emar*, 68) notes, an administrative text from Ebla (TM.75.6.1376 = *MEE* 2 48 rev. ix 6–viii 1) also mentions a "feast of the steles" (nidba$_2$ na-ru$_2$). The text is edited in G. Pettinato and F. Pomponio, *Testi amministrativi della biblioteca L. 2769*, MEE 2 (Naples: Istituto universitario orientale), 317.

29 My approach here builds on the foundational work Fleming has done in using second-millennium evidence, not to reconstruct a premonarchic history of Israel and Judah, but to explore configurations of religious practice in the context of collaborative politics that may have persisted across centuries (so, e.g., Daniel E. Fleming, *The Legacy of Israel in Judah's Bible: History, Politics, and the Reinscribing of Tradition* [Cambridge: Cambridge University Press, 2012], 119).

30 An overview of excavations can be found in Fleming, *Time at Emar*, 1–12, and Thames, *Politics of Ritual Change*, 5–6.

31 On the function of the building, see the discussion in Fleming, *Time at Emar*, 4–5, and Matthew Rutz, *Bodies of Knowledge in Ancient Mesopotamia: The Diviners of Late Bronze Age Emar and Their Tablet Collection*, AMD 9 (Leiden: Brill, 2013), 303–308.

32 A less elaborate annual version of the *zukru* appears on the more fragmentary Emar 375+, which is quoted below. For an overview of the *zukru* texts, see Fleming, *Time at Emar*, 48–49. The manuscript evidence is discussed in detail in Thames, *Politics of Ritual Change*, 16–21 (Emar 375+) and 84–88 (Emar 373+).

then carried out. The participation of the entire populace in a state-sponsored ritual sets the *zukru* apart from other festivals at Emar and from festivals and sacrificial rituals known from Mesopotamia.[33] Like the sacrificial ritual imagined in Exodus 24*, we have here a festival that sets the collective populace rather than royal or priestly actors at its conceptual center.

The most significant point of comparison for Exodus 24* comes in the description of feasting conducted at the site of the upright stones. Although a similar practice was likely observed in the less elaborate annual *zukru* observance (Emar 375+:14–17),[34] the best-preserved description comes from the festival text describing the celebration in year six of the seven-year cycle (Emar 373+ i:34–37):[35]

> *ki-i-me-e* KU$_2$ NAG NA$_4$.MEŠ *gab*$_2$*-ba*$_2$ *iš-tu* I$_3$.MEŠ *u*$_3$ UŠ$_2$.MEŠ *i-ṭar-ru-u*
> UDU.U$_8$ 2 *ta-pal* NINDA.GUR$_4$.RA.MEŠ *pa-pa-si*$_2$ 1 ^{dug}*ḫu-par*$_2$ *ša* LUGAL *a-na pa-ni*
> KA$_2$.GAL *ša qa-ab-li ku-ba-da a-na gab*$_2$*-bi* DINGIR.MEŠ DU$_3$ 1 UDU.U$_8$ *ša-a-ši*
> *a-na gab*$_2$*-bi* DINGIR.MEŠ *i-qa-al-lu-u*$_2$ NINDA.MEŠ KAŠ.MEŠ[36] UZU *i-na* URU *e-el-*⸢*lu*⸣

> When they eat and drink, they rub all the stones with oil and blood. They do homage to all the gods with an ewe, two pairs of porridge-bread loaves, and one *ḫuppar*-vessel[37] from the king before the Central Gate. They burn that one sheep for all the gods. The bread, the beer, and the meat will go up into the city.

Here, we can note the close connection of sacrifice and feasting before standing stones. In addition, the rite features an extremely unusual use of blood. While the anointing of stones or statues with oil is well known across the ancient Mid-

33 See the overview of the festival text (Emar 373+) in Fleming, *Time at Emar*, 39–54.

34 The most recent edition of these lines, incorporating new manuscript evidence, can be found in Thames, *Politics of Ritual Change*, 24.

35 The recent edition of Thames (*Politics of Ritual Change*, 90) does not significantly differ from that of Fleming (*Time at Emar*, 370). I take Fleming's edition as my point of departure and comment on any divergences in the notes below.

36 I retain Fleming's reading of KAŠ over Thames's suggested reading of AMAR (*Politics of Ritual Change*, 115). Although Thames's suggestion makes good contextual sense, the presence of beer at a festival is not surprising (even if it has not been explicitly mentioned), and his reading is based on copies rather than visual autopsy of the tablet.

37 On the identification of the *ḫuppar*, see Thames (*Politics of Ritual Change*, 202–203).

dle East and appears in other rituals at Emar,[38] the use of blood in anointing stones is otherwise unique.[39] In other rituals from Emar, individual standing stones are identified with specific deities. This has led Fleming to suggest that the anointing of the stones constitutes a part of the preparation for the god Dagan's passage between the stones.[40] The combination of feasting, sacrifice, and blood manipulation may thus be understood as both constituting the community and indexing Dagan's presence. In other words, the ritual both consolidates ties between the assembled populace and brings them into contact with the deity.[41]

A similar logic underlies the ritual of Exodus 24*, which imagines Israel at the moment of its founding. Like the *zukru* at Emar, the ritual described in the biblical text focuses on the participation of the entire populace and includes sacrifice and feasting before standing stones. There is, however, a significant difference in how the stones themselves seem to be conceptualized. In verse 4, the altar is the locus of divine presence whereas the stones are allocated to the twelve assembled tribes (וַיִּבֶן מִזְבֵּחַ תַּחַת הָהָר וּשְׁתֵּים עֶשְׂרֵה מַצֵּבָה לִשְׁנֵים עָשָׂר שִׁבְטֵי יִשְׂרָאֵל). The blood is then divided, with half applied to the altar and the other half gathered in basins and sprinkled on the assembled people. The image of blood splattered on lay Israelites is so unique that Ginsberg has argued that

38 Fleming ("Anointing," 405–407) provides a brief overview of the practices of anointing in the ancient Middle East. For an overview of *sikkānu*-stones in Bronze Age Syria with extensive secondary literature cited, see Daniel E. Fleming, *The Installation of Baal's High Priestess at Emar: A Window on Ancient Syrian Religion*, HSS 42 (Atlanta, GA: Scholars Press, 1992), 76–79, and Fleming, *Time at Emar*, 84–87. More recent in-depth treatments include Jean-Marie Durand, *Le culte des pierres et les monuments commémoratifs en Syrie amorrite*, FM 8 (Paris: SEPOA, 2005); Patrick Michel, *Le culte des pierres à Emar à l'époque Hittite*, OBO 266 (Fribourg: Academic, 2014).

39 The closest parallel outside the Hebrew Bible would seem to be the use of blood to purify a newly minted divine statue in KUB 29.4 iv 38–40 = *CTH* 481. See the discussion in Gary Beckman, "Blood in Hittite Ritual," *JCS* 63 (2011): 95–102, here 101, and Theodore J. Lewis, *The Origin and Character of God: Ancient Israelite Religion Through the Lens of Divinity* (Oxford: Oxford University Press, 2020), 135.

40 Fleming, *Time at Emar*, 82–84. Similarly, see the discussion in Michel, *Le culte des pierres*, 14. Biblical authors may similarly have seen the anointing of standing stones as a practice that facilitates divine presence, as Gen 28:18–22 suggests. For further discussion of the biblical passage, see Lewis, *Origin and Character of God*, 135.

41 Fleming notes as well how Dagan's titles *abumma*, "the veritable father," and *bēl bukāri*, "lord of the offspring," invoke his position as father of the pantheon, thus also organizing the pantheon under the rubric of kinship (*Time at Emar*, 89–93). Fleming does not normalize the noun *bu-ka-ri*, but the cuneiform orthography and the vocalization of the Hebrew lexeme בְּכֹר point to a shared nominal base of **qutāl*. For a differing interpretation of both titles, see Thames, *Politics of Ritual Change*, 144–150.

the blood must have been applied to the stones (which he believes represent the twelve tribes) rather than the people themselves.[42] Without this application, Ginsberg argues, the standing stones themselves play no role in the ceremony.

On the surface, Ginsberg's suggestion offers a tantalizing parallel to the Emar *zukru* as it would posit the same ritual action. There are, however, significant issues. First, verse 8 does not state that the blood was applied to the twelve tribes (each of which was allotted a stone) but to the people (העם). Thus, it does not seem to be a self-evident conclusion that the blood was applied to the standing stones. In addition, the ritual function of the stones is not entirely clear in this passage. If Ginsberg is correct that they are intended to represent the tribes of Israel, then their function is certainly different than that of the *sikkānu*-stones, which index divine presence in much the same way that the altar does in Exodus 24:4.[43] In this case, the stones might function to commemorate the pact made between the twelve tribes and the deity, rather than being the locus of Yahweh's presence.[44] Alternatively, we might understand the standing stones in a function more analogous to the *sikkānu*-stones at Emar, despite the lack of blood application. The *lamed* in verse 4 (וּשְׁתֵּים עֶשְׂרֵה מַצֵּבָה לִשְׁנֵים עָשָׂר שִׁבְטֵי יִשְׂרָאֵל) could simply indicate that the stones are for each of the tribes (i.e., a dative of advantage)—and not that they directly represent them. In this case, we might understand the stones as concretizing Yahweh's presence in concert with the altar—essentially, acting as lightning rods for the deity's attention.[45] Under either interpretation, we see here a ritual that uses blood manipulation to consolidate kinship ties and mediate divine presence in a way that is conceptually similar to the logic of the *zukru* ritual, even as it differs in some of the actions taken.

---

42 Ginsberg, *The Israelian Heritage*, 45–46.

43 For further discussion of the interrelated functions of standing stones in the southern Levant, which might include commemoration as well as indexing divine presence, see Elizabeth Bloch-Smith, "Will the Real *Massebot* Please Stand Up: Cases of Real and Mistakenly Identified Standing Stones in Ancient Israel," in *Text, Artifact, and Image: Revealing Ancient Israelite Religion*, ed. Gary Beckman and Theodore J. Lewis (Providence, RI: Brown University, 2006), 78; and, more recently, Lewis, *Origin and Character of God*, 121, 169–172.

44 This is similar to the use of twelve standing stones to commemorate the crossing of the Jordan in Joshua 4:1–10 (thanks to Michael Stahl for calling my attention to this parallel).

45 This would be more similar to the use of standing stones to represent or presence deities at Emar. It also finds a parallel in Jacob's theophany at Bethel (Gen 28: 17–19, 22a), in which the stone both instigates and commemorates the divine vision. I am not aware of any examples in which multiple standing stones were used in a single ritual to index the presence of just one deity, which may lend credence to the first interpretation.

There is a second difference between the *zukru* and the narrativized biblical ritual worth considering. Whereas the *zukru* is integrated into the festival calendar, the biblical rite is imagined as a one-time event at Israel's founding. Consequently, the unique features of the biblical rite may not reflect one specific underlying ritual like the *zukru*; rather, we might see it as an imagined ceremony that combines elements of repeated kin-based rituals with practices common to covenant-making.[46]

The potential connection between Exodus 24* and treaty-making ceremonies has already been explored in previous studies. Lewis, for example, notes the practice of donkey sacrifice at Mari as a means to unite two tribes or potentially transfer an individual's allegiance from one tribe to another.[47] In a famous example, elders from the town of Dabish, affiliated with the Yaminite tribe, write to king Zimri-Lim of Mari and request to join the Simʾalites (A.981:39–41a):[48]

> *a-na li-ib-bi* DUMU *si-i*[*m-a*]*-al*
> *i-na ni-ha-di-i i n*[*i-r*]*u-ub-ma* ANŠE *ha-a-ri*
> *i ni-iq-tu-ul*
>
> Let us enter into the Simʾalite tribe, among the Niḫadû, and slaughter a donkey.

46 This is not to say that covenant and kinship are fundamentally at odds, a position that Abusch compellingly disputes in his treatment of this text (I. Tzvi Abusch, "Blood in Israel and Mesopotamia," in *Emanuel: Studies in the Hebrew Bible, the Septuagint, and the Dead Sea Scrolls in Honor of Emanuel Tov*, ed. Shalom M. Paul et al. [Leiden: Brill, 2003], 675–684, here 676–677). Rather, I would argue that we can explore how this text draws on complementary aspects of occasional treaty-making rituals with the types of practices that we have observed in the context of calendrical rituals focused on consolidating the preexisting relationship between people and their gods.

47 Lewis, "Covenant and Blood Rituals," 347. For an overview of Mari texts that refer to slaughtering a donkey in the context of treaty negotiations, see Kenneth Way, *Donkeys in the Biblical World: Ceremony and Symbol*, HACL 2 (Winona Lake, IN: Eisenbrauns, 2011), 74.

48 Although the text is frequently cited, it has not yet been subject to a full edition. Lines 32–52 only are edited in Jean-Marie Durand, "Unité et diversités au Proche-Orient à l'époque amorrite," in *La circulation des biens, des personnes et des idées dans le Proche-Orient ancien*, ed. Dominique Charpin and Francis Joannès, CRRAI 38 (Paris: Éditions Recherche sur les Civilisations, 1992), 117–118. For further discussion of the text, see Fleming, *Democracy's Ancient Ancestors*, 97–99; Adam Miglio, *Tribe and State: The Dynamics of International Politics and the Reign of Zimri-Lim*, Gorgias Studies in the Ancient Near East 8 (Piscataway, NJ: Gorgias, 2014), 144–154.

The slaughter of a donkey thus provides a means of consolidating kinship between the town of Dabish and members of the Simʾalite tribe.[49]

In certain cases, the phrase *ḫayyāram qatālum*, "to kill a donkey," may simply be a formulaic way of expressing that a treaty has been concluded.[50] However, other texts make clear that the formula derives from actual practice. For example, several letters reflect Zimri-Lim's preference for the use of the donkey as a sacrificial animal for sealing treaties.[51] In one instance, an official reports emphatically that he had personally purchased a donkey to seal an alliance (A.2226:11–16):[52]

> [*um-ma-m*]*i* UZ$_3$ ⸢*u*$_3$⸣ *me*$_2$*-ra-nam a-na* [*za-ka-r*]*i-ni*
> [*i ni-i*]*q-tu-u*[*l*] *u*$_3$ *a-na-ku u*$_2$*-ul* [*am-gu-ur*]
> [*um-ma a-n*]*a-ku-ma iš-tu pa-na a-di wa-*[*ar-ka*]
> [*ma-ti*]-⸢*ma*⸣ *be-el-ni* ^{I}*Zi-im-r*[*i-li-im*]
> [U]Z$_3$ [*u*$_2$]*-lu-ma me*$_2$*-ra-nam a-na* [*za-ka-ri-im u*$_2$*-ul iq-tu-ul*]
> *a-na-ku* ANŠE *a-na* KUG.BABBAR *a-ša-*[*am*]

> [They sai]d, "Let us slay a goat and a puppy for our [treat]y." But I myself did not agree. I [said], [at no point wha]tsoever, past or fu[ture], would our lord Zimr[i-Lim slay] a [go]at or a puppy [to make a treaty]. So I myself purchased a donkey with silver.

The focus on obtaining the proper animals demonstrates here that ritualized slaughter was an essential component of constituting alliances at Mari.[53]

---

49 In light of the continuing relationship between Dabish and Yarim-Lim, leader of the Yaminite Yaḫrurû tribe, Fleming suggests that the ceremony in A.981 might not indicate a binary tribal transfer from Yaminite to Simʾalite but rather reflects "a forging of a tribal brotherhood between neighbors" (*Democracy's Ancient Ancestors*, 253 n. 80).

50 So, e.g., Abraham Malamat, "A Note on the Ritual of Treaty Making in Mari and the Bible," *IEJ* 45 (1995): 226–229, here 227.

51 Charpin has argued that the killing of the donkey does not properly constitute a sacrifice since it is conducted to seal an alliance rather than for the express purpose of offering the animal to a deity. However, the two options need not be mutually exclusive, and we lack texts describing the ritual itself. In the absence of further evidence, I thus consider it reasonable to understand the practice within the broader context of animal sacrifice. For further discussion, see Dominique Charpin, *« Tu es de mon sang »: Les alliances dans le Proche-Orient ancien*, Docet omnia (Paris: Les Belles Lettres, 2019), Chapter 2 par. 8 (online edition, available at https://books.openedition.org/lesbelleslettres/300).

52 Edited as text no. 7 in Dominique Charpin, "Un souverain éphémère en Ida-Maraṣ: Išme-Addu d'Ašnakkum," *MARI* 7 (1993): 165–191.

53 Charpin has suggested that slaughter of a donkey was the special prerogative of kings,

Although these texts do not provide details of ritual, they provide useful context for the treaty background invoked in Exodus 24*.

4 Kinship and Kingship as Operative Paradigms in Exodus 24*

The narrativized ritual at the mountain of God preserves two features known from second-millennium Syrian cuneiform sources: the use of sacrifice to seal political alliances and practices of commensality and blood manipulation as a means of uniting a population. This suggests that the author of the covenant ceremony in Exodus 24* was conversant in the rituals associated with the world of decentralized "collaborative politics," to use Fleming's terminology.[54] Thus, even if the steps of the ritual were constructed to suit the narrative—something I consider likely—the literary imagining still engages interpretations of kinship and sacrifice that are deeply rooted in Levantine political practices.

I am not, however, suggesting that Exodus 24* preserves a memory of a premonarchic kinship system. As Fleming has shown, kinship and kingship are not diametrically opposed modes of organizing society.[55] In fact, the elaborate form of the *zukru* festival discussed above certainly required the considerable resources of the palace, despite the conspicuous absence of the king himself in the festivities, which emphasize the population as a collective.[56] Similarly, Zimri-Lim himself ruled through a combination of top-down bureaucracy and flexible negotiations with tribal leaders.[57] Thus, while Exodus 24* draws on a tradition of decentralized politics in presenting the imagined origins of a collective Israel, there is no reason to see the text itself as somehow preserving a premonarchic past.[58]

How, then, do we situate Exodus 24* in the history of Israel and Judah? Fleming has argued that the two kingdoms had different political origins that

---

which would explain the official's insistence on obtaining a donkey here (Charpin, *« Tu es de mon sang »*, Chapter 2 par. 11 [online edition]). This may be the case, but I prefer to imagine that there is another reason for the official's horror: perhaps he and Zimri-Lim, like Dan Fleming and myself, were dog lovers and simply could not countenance the thought of harming man's best friend.

54 See especially Fleming, *Legacy of Israel*, 179–192 for a discussion of collaborative politics in ancient Israel.

55 Fleming, *Democracy's Ancient Ancestors*.

56 Fleming, *Time at Emar*, 56–57.

57 Fleming, *Democracy's Ancient Ancestors*, 25.

58 Similarly, see the conclusion of Chavel, "A Kingdom of Priests," 197–200.

resulted in different ways of imagining the past. In Fleming's analysis, Israel emerged through the consolidation of peoples in the southern Levant who maintained a tradition of decentralized power. In imagining their collective origins, scribes from Israel thus made use of kinship as an organizing paradigm. By contrast, Fleming argues that Judah emerged as a small monarchy centered at Jerusalem in which rulers authorized themselves with reference to the House of David rather than in terms of collective leadership. The imagined tribal origins thus entered Judah only through identification with a greater Israel.[59]

Given its deep engagement with kinship as a mode of political organization, this text may belong alongside other texts treated by Fleming as part of Israel's legacy in Judah's Bible. Within the Neo-Documentary framework, such a possibility is especially interesting given other indications that E reflects an Israelian perspective.[60] In addition, Chavel has noted resonances between the image of lay Israelites sacrificing at earthen altars in Exodus 19*–24* and the critique leveled at priests and royalty in the books of Amos and Hosea, themselves largely products of Israelian scribes.[61] He sees in the narrative a critique of centralized royal power that is quite consistent with Fleming's understanding of Israel's tradition of collective governance.

The text does, however, exhibit several features that are often taken to be indicative of a post-720 dating, particularly among scholars who adhere to redaction-critical models: the central presence of legal material to the narrative and the reliance on a twelve-tribe schema.[62] Underlying both concerns is the supposition that we can identify the moment of a text's composition based on thematic content. As Sommer has argued, however, the fact that an idea likely had salience in a particular historical setting does not necessitate its com-

59 Fleming, *Legacy of Israel*, 25–30.

60 So, e.g., Alan W. Jenks, *The Elohist and North Israelite Traditions* (Atlanta, GA: Scholars Press, 1977), though I do not necessarily agree with all aspects of his source analysis or dating conclusions.

61 Chavel, "Kingdom of Priests," 199–201.

62 Studies that date the pericope based on the presence of legal material are cited in n. 12 above. On the potential development of a twelve-tribe schema in post-720 Judah, see, e.g., Christoph Levin, "Das System der zwölf Stämme Israels," in *Congress Volume: Paris 1992*, ed. John A. Emerton, VTSup 61 [Leiden: Brill, 1995], 163–178, here esp. 172; Jean-Daniel Macchi, *Israël et ses tribus selon Genèse 49*, OBO 171 (Göttingen: Vandenhoeck & Ruprecht, 1999), 272–273. Weingart has recently argued that Judah came to see itself as part of a broader tribal heritage shared with Israel prior to the fall of Samaria in 720. She does, however, locate the idealized number of twelve tribes in a Judean context. See Kristen Weingart, "'All These are the Twelve Tribes of Israel': The Origins of Israel's Kinship Identity," *NEA* 82 (2019): 24–31, here esp. 31.

position in that period.[63] This is especially the case for arguments about the prevalence of law in exilic or postexilic contexts given the reliance of such a model on implicitly antisemitic conceptualizations of Judaism as fundamentally legalistic.[64]

The second question, that of the origin of a twelve-tribe schema, requires more consideration because it not only depends on thematic considerations but also potentially engages an underlying sociopolitical reality. In this case, recent analyses clearly show the fluidity of tribal lists in texts such as Genesis 49, Judges 5, and Deuteronomy 33.[65] Yet, the fact that there was never a stable twelve-tribe Israelian association does not obviate the possibility that the symbolic number was used to represent an idealized past or to accommodate new affiliations. In other words, the same pressure to include new groups that is seen as an impetus for the Judean development of the twelve-tribe system[66] could have been obtained already at some point in Israel's history. Thus, I do not think we can differentiate between an idea that was developed in the waning years of the Israelian monarchy and later adopted in Judah, seeking to claim a spot in Israel's history, and one that emerged independently in Judah after the fall of Samaria.[67]

Given the critique of pseudo-historicism just advanced, I find it prudent to leave open the precise date and location of the text's composition. One potential scenario is suggested by Chavel's analysis of Exodus 19*–24*. Perhaps, he suggests, the author resents "the metals and manpower appropriated and sent off to imperial powers by native kings aiming to maintain local hegemony."[68] This broader ideological concern could have emerged in the later years of an Israelian kingdom. In this scenario, the focus on the kingdom's origins may be a way of creatively reimagining the people's unity, composed at a time when the institution of monarchy itself was under threat. As Tiglath-pileser III began to reorganize kingdoms of the southern Levant as Assyrian provinces—a fate that befell Israel's rival and ally Damascus in 734 BCE—the long tradition of kin-based politics may have emerged as an especially appealing alternative to kingship.

Alternatively, the text may have been composed in Judah after the fall of Samaria. This would make it one of the relatively rarer texts that evince col-

63 Sommer, "Pseudo-historicism," 104.

64 See n. 12 above.

65 See n. 62 above.

66 So, e.g., Fleming, *Legacy of Israel*, 77 n. 12.

67 Alternatively, of course, one might see the specific number twelve as a editorial insertion since nothing in the ritual itself requires the presence of a specific number of tribes.

68 Chavel, "Kingdom of Priests," 200.

lective political action in Judah. In this case, the text may reflect an earlier tradition appropriated from Israel, but this is not the only possibility. As Fleming notes, "collective activity as such does not distinguish Israel from Judah; rather, it is the dependence of the collective on the political center that sets Judah apart."[69] This, too, is a useful warning against pseudo-historicism: since kin-based structures did exist in Judah, it is entirely possible that an author drew on extant ritual praxis to imagine the origins of a collective Israel to which Judah belonged. As in the first scenario considered above, such a decision may have been in part influenced by displays of Assyrian might: i.e., the choice to imagine Israel's (and hence Judah's) origins in a kin-based ceremony provided a way of defining Yahweh's relationship to collective Israel regardless of the unstable political situation.

5 By Way of Conclusion

This paper has explored one small way in which the ritual texts from Emar can contribute to our understanding of the Hebrew Bible and the history of Israel and Judah, a fitting subject to honor Dan Fleming. Along the way, we have seen how the covenantal narrative of Exodus 19*–24* engages ritual practices tied to the practice of collaborative governance. This allowed us to uncover another text with many of the same features as those surveyed by Fleming under the rubric of Israel's legacy in Judah's Bible. Finally, the text selected for analysis demonstrates the power of imagination and shows how commensality can become an enduring foundation for kinship—the building blocks of what we now call chosen family. I thus offer this paper to Dan not only in appreciation of his scholarship but in gratitude for a bond formed over many years of shared meals.

Bibliography

Abusch, I. Tzvi. "Blood in Israel and Mesopotamia." Pages 675–684 in *Emanuel: Studies in the Hebrew Bible, the Septuagint, and the Dead Sea Scrolls in Honor of Emanuel Tov*. Edited by Shalom M. Paul, Robert A. Kraft, Eva Ben-David, Lawrence H. Schiffman, and Weston W. Fields. Leiden: Brill, 2003.

69 Fleming, *Legacy of Israel*, 45.

Anderson, Gary A., and Saul M. Olyan. "Preface." Pages 7–10 in *Priesthood and Cult in Ancient Israel*. Edited by Gary A. Anderson and Saul M. Olyan. JSOTSup 125. Sheffield: Sheffield Academic Press, 1991.

Baden, Joel S. *The Composition of the Pentateuch: Renewing the Documentary Hypothesis*. New Haven, CT: Yale University Press, 2012.

Beckman, Gary. "Blood in Hittite Ritual." *JCS* 63 (2011): 95–102.

Bloch-Smith, Elizabeth. "Will the Real *Massebot* Please Stand Up: Cases of Real and Mistakenly Identified Standing Stones in Ancient Israel." Pages 64–79 in *Text, Artifact, and Image: Revealing Ancient Israelite Religion*. Edited by Gary Beckman and Theodore J. Lewis. Providence, RI: Brown University, 2006.

Blum, Erhard. *Studien zur Komposition des Pentateuch*. Berlin: de Gruyter, 1990.

Boyd, Samuel L. "Applied Ritual: The Application of Blood and Oil on Bodies in the Pentateuchal Sources." *BibInt* 29 (2021): 120–147.

Charpin, Dominique. "Un souverain éphémère en Ida-Maraṣ: Išme-Addu d' Ašnakkum." *MARI* 7 (1993): 165–191.

Charpin, Dominique. *Writing, Law, and Kingship in Old Babylonian Mesopotamia*. Translated by Jane Marie Todd. Chicago, IL: The University of Chicago Press, 2010.

Charpin, Dominique. *« Tu es de mon sang »: Les alliances dans le Proche-Orient ancien*. Docet omnia. Paris: Les Belles Lettres, 2019.

Chavel, Simeon. "A Kingdom of Priests and Its Earthen Altars in Exodus 19–24." *VT* 65 (2015): 169–222.

DeGrado, Jessie. "An Infelicitous Feast: Ritualized Consumption and Divine Rejection in Amos 6.1–7." *JSOT* 45 (2020): 178–197.

Dillmann, August. *Die Bücher Exodus und Leviticus*. Leipzig: S. Hirzel, 1897.

Durand, Jean-Marie. "Unité et diversités au Proche-Orient à l' époque amorrite." Pages 97–128 in *La circulation des biens, des personnes et des idées dans le Proche-Orient ancien*. Edited by Dominique Charpin and Francis Joannès. CRRAI 38. Paris: Éditions Recherche sur les Civilisations, 1992.

Durand, Jean-Marie. *Le culte des pierres et les monuments commémoratifs en Syrie amorrite*. FM 8. Paris: SEPOA, 2005.

Eissfeldt, Otto. *Hexateuch-Synopse: Die Erzählung der fünf Bücher Mose und des Buches Josua mit dem Anfange des Richterbuches*. Leipzig: Hinrichs, 1922.

Feldman, Liane M. *The Story of Sacrifice: Ritual and Narrative in the Priestly Source*. FAT 141. Tübingen: Mohr Siebeck, 2020.

Fleming, Daniel E. *The Installation of Baal's High Priestess at Emar: A Window on Ancient Syrian Religion*. HSS 42. Atlanta, GA: Scholars Press, 1992.

Fleming, Daniel E. "The Biblical Tradition of Anointing Priests." *JBL* 117 (1998): 401–414.

Fleming, Daniel E. *Time at Emar: The Cultic Calendar and the Rituals from the Diviner's Archive*. Winona Lake, IN: Eisenbrauns, 2000.

Fleming, Daniel E. *Democracy's Ancient Ancestors: Mari and Early Collective Governance*. Cambridge: Cambridge University Press, 2004.

Fleming, Daniel E. *The Legacy of Israel in Judah's Bible: History, Politics, and the Reinscribing of Tradition*. Cambridge: Cambridge University Press, 2012.

Ginsberg, H.L. *The Israelian Heritage of Judaism*. New York, NY: Jewish Theological Seminary of America, 1982.

Hendel, Ronald S. "Sacrifice as a Cultural System: The Ritual Symbolism of Exodus 24,3–8." *ZAW* 101 (1989): 366–390.

Jenks, Alan W. *The Elohist and North Israelite Traditions*. Atlanta, GA: Scholars Press, 1977.

Kratz, Reinhard G. *The Composition of the Narrative Books of the Old Testament*. Translated by John Bowden. London: T&T Clark, 2005.

Levin, Christoph. "Das System der zwölf Stämme Israels." Pages 163–178 in *Congress Volume: Paris 1992*. Edited by John A. Emerton. VTSup 61. Leiden: Brill, 1995.

Levine, Baruch A. *In the Presence of the Lord: A Study of Cult and Some Cultic Terms in Ancient Israel*. SJLA 5. Leiden: Brill, 1974.

Lewis, Theodore J. "Covenant and Blood Rituals: Understanding Exodus 24:3–8 in Its Ancient Near Eastern Context." Pages 341–350 in *Confronting the Past: Archaeological and Historical Essays on Ancient Israel in Honor of William G. Dever*. Edited by Seymour Gitin, J. Edward Wright, and J.P. Dessel. Winona Lake, IN: Eisenbrauns, 2006.

Lewis, Theodore J. *The Origin and Character of God: Ancient Israelite Religion Through the Lens of Divinity*. Oxford: Oxford University Press, 2020.

Macchi, Jean-Daniel. *Israël et ses tribus selon Genèse 49*. OBO 171. Göttingen: Vandenhoeck & Ruprecht, 1999.

Maier, Bernhard. *William Robertson Smith: His Life, His Work, and His Times*. FAT 67. Tübingen: Mohr Siebeck, 2009.

Malamat, Abraham. "A Note on the Ritual of Treaty Making in Mari and the Bible." *IEJ* 45 (1995): 226–229.

McCarthy, Dennis J. *Treaty and Covenant: A Study in Form in the Ancient Oriental Documents and in the Old Testament*. Rome: Pontifical Biblical Institute, 1963.

Michel, Patrick. *Le culte des pierres à Emar à l'époque Hittite*. OBO 266. Fribourg: Academic, 2014.

Miglio, Adam. *Tribe and State: The Dynamics of International Politics and the Reign of Zimri-Lim*. Gorgias Studies in the Ancient Near East 8. Piscataway, NJ: Gorgias, 2014.

Nicholson, E.W. "The Covenant Ritual in Exodus XXIV 3–8." *VT* 32 (1982): 74–86.

Noth, Martin. *The History of Israel*. 2nd ed. New York, NY: Harper & Row, 1958.

Noth, Martin. *Exodus: A Commentary*. Translated by J.S. Bowden. OTL. Philadelphia, PA: Westminster, 1962.

Parpola, Simo. "Neo-Assyrian Treaties from the Royal Archives of Nineveh." *JCS* 39 (1987): 161–189.

Patrick, Dale. "The Covenant Code Source." *VT* 27 (1977): 145–157.

Pettinato, Giovanni, and Francesco Pomponio. *Testi amministrativi della biblioteca L. 2769*. MEE 2. Naples: Istituto universitario orientale, 1980.

Perlitt, Lothar. *Bundestheologie im Alten Testament*. WMANT 36. Neukirchen-Vluyn: Neukirchener Verlag, 1969.

Propp, William. *Exodus 19–40: A New Translation with Introduction and Commentary*. AB 2A. New York, NY: Doubleday, 2006.

Radner, Karen. "Assyrische *ṭuppi adê* als Vorbild für Deuteronomium 28,20–44?" Pages 351–378 in *Die deuteronomistischen Geschichtswerke: Redaktions- und religionsgeschichtliche Perspektiven zur "Deuteronomismus"—Diskussion in Tora und Vorderen Propheten*. Edited by Markus Witte, Konrad Schmid, Doris Prechel, and Jan Christian Gertz. BZAW 365. Berlin: de Gruyter, 2006.

Rutz, Matthew. *Bodies of Knowledge in Ancient Mesopotamia: The Diviners of Late Bronze Age Emar and Their Tablet Collection*. AMD 9. Leiden: Brill, 2013.

Schwartz, Baruch. "What Really Happened at Mount Sinai? Four Biblical Answers to One Question." *BRev* 13 (1997): 20–30, 46.

Scurlock, JoAnn. "Animal Sacrifice in Ancient Mesopotamian Religion." Pages 389–403 in *A History of the Animal World in the Ancient Near East*. Edited by Billy Jean Collins. HOS 64. Leiden: Brill, 2002.

Sommer, Benjamin. "Dating Pentateuchal Texts and the Perils of Pseudo-Historicism." Pages 85–108 in *The Pentateuch: International Perspectives on Current Research*. Edited by Thomas B. Dozeman, Konrad Schmid, and Baruch J. Schwartz. FAT 78. Tübingen: Mohr Siebeck, 2011.

Smith, Mark S. *God in Translation: Deities in Cross-Cultural Discourse in the Biblical World*. Grand Rapids, MI: Eerdmans, 2008.

Smith, William Robertson. *Lectures on the Religion of the Semites. Fundamental Institutions. First Series*. London: Adam & Charles Black, 1889.

Stackert, Jeffrey. *A Prophet Like Moses: Prophecy, Law, and Israelite Religion*. Oxford: Oxford University Press, 2014.

Steuernagel, Carl. "Der jehovistische Bericht über den Bundesschluss am Sinai." *TSK* 72 (1899): 319–350.

Thames, John Tracy, Jr. *The Politics of Ritual Change: The* zukru *Festival in the Political History of Late Bronze Age Emar*. HSM 65. Leiden: Brill, 2020.

Thompson, Thomas L. *The Historicity of the Patriarchal Narratives: The Quest for the Historical Abraham*. Berlin: de Gruyter, 1974.

Van Seters, John. *Abraham in History and Tradition*. New Haven, CT: Yale University Press, 1975.

Van Seters, John. *In Search of History: Historiography in the Ancient World and the Origins of Biblical History*. New Haven, CT: Yale University Press, 1983.

Way, Kenneth. *Donkeys in the Biblical World: Ceremony and Symbol.* HACL 2. Winona Lake, IN: Eisenbrauns, 2011.

Weinfeld, Moshe. "Covenant Making in Anatolia and Mesopotamia." *JANES* 22 (1993): 135–139.

Weingart, Kristen. "'All These are the Twelve Tribes of Israel': The Origins of Israel's Kinship Identity." *NEA* 82 (2019): 24–31.

Weitzman, Steven. *The Origin of the Jews: The Quest for Roots in a Rootless Age.* Princeton, NJ: Princeton University Press, 2017.

Wellhausen, Julius. *Prolegomena to the History of Israel.* Translated by J. Sutherland Black and Allan Menzies. Edinburgh: Adam & Charles Black, 1885.

Wright, David P. *Inventing God's Law: How the Covenant Code of the Bible Used and Revised the Laws of Hammurabi.* Oxford: Oxford University Press, 2009.

Yoffee, Norman. *Myths of the Archaic State: Evolution of the Earliest Cities, States, and Civilizations.* Cambridge: Cambridge University Press, 2005.

Zenger, Erich. *Die Sinaitheophanie: Untersuchungen zum jahwistischen und elohistischen Geschichtswerk.* Würzburg: Echter, 1971.

4

"Do You Hear the People Sing?" At the Interface of Prophecy and Music in Chronicles

Julie B. Deluty

It is a joy to join friends and colleagues in honoring Dan Fleming with a volume that underscores his work on "people" and their changing sociopolitical identities. My contribution began in a doctoral course with Dan in Fall 2011 on the books of Chronicles at New York University. In his singularly masterful way in seminars, Dan challenged me to refine the details and scope of inquiry. I have turned back to Dan's initial questions about terminology, history, and historiography in preparing this piece. Years ago, I was fortunate to have met Dan in my freshman year of college in 2003 when I enrolled in his MAP Ancient Israel class. Both as an undergraduate and then graduate student at NYU, Dan taught me that biblical texts can always be read anew while thinking carefully about larger social and political categories. This perspective continues to influence my own work. Thank you, Dan, for introducing me to the ever-rich world of biblical studies. I can hardly believe that it has been nineteen years; my gratitude is boundless.

In keeping with the current volume's theme on "people," this paper examines the Chronicler's re-formalization of the prophet's role by the Davidic king via the social unit of Levitical singers.[1] Not only does the mode of prophecy change in Chronicles from speech to song, but David is invoked to legitimize the role of the singers as prophets by designating them as *nəbîʾîm*, "prophets." The notion of prophecy in this postexilic text is not only imagined as communication from the divine to the people through a royal envoy like Gad. Rather, it also comprises the liturgical response of the prophet back to Yahweh in the temple context. Chronicles institutionalizes prophecy through the First Temple cultic link to David with one key change: the *nābîʾ* is reconceived to separate the king from the populace, while the prophetic response on behalf of the people now is directed back to Yahweh by singing praise. Though far removed from the context of the acclaimed song of *Les Misérables*, we do in fact "hear the people sing."

1 An earlier version of this study was presented at the 2018 SBL conference in Denver, CO.

 | DOI:10.1163/9789004511538_005

1 Introduction

In the Hebrew Bible, Chronicles is the only place where prophecy is linked to the Levitical singers, one group of temple personnel institutionalized by David through Gad, the king's "seer" (1 Chr 21:9; 29:29; 2 Chr 29:25). An initial analogy with Gad is created when the collective of Levitical singers is given the title of *ḥōzeh*, "seer," in 2 Chr 29:30 and 35:15. However, the Chronicler then differentiates the singers from Gad through the primary label, *nābîʾ*. Gad is not called a *nābîʾ* in 1 Chr 29:29 and 2 Chr 29:25, contrary to his title in 1 Sam 22:5 and 2 Sam 24:11. While scholars have noted that the work of the singers is termed prophetic, the analogy with Gad has not been addressed.[2] The Chronicler's recasting of the non-Levite Gad and the Levitical singers expands the function of prophecy in a monarchy—namely, to invoke the divine and to communicate on behalf of the people, not the king. The books of Chronicles purport to describe the institution of prophecy as central to the first Jerusalem temple, but they modify its representation and function to suit the different political and religious realities of the Second Temple period.

The Chronicler ascribes a central place to the cultic personnel in the Jerusalem temple, even though they are not central to his social world.[3] These individuals, from among the priests and the Levites, carry out cultic activities and

2 See especially David Petersen, *Late Israelite Prophecy: Studies in Deutero-Prophetic Literature and in Chronicles*, SBLMS 23 (Missoula, MT: Scholars Press, 1977), 55–96; H.G.M. Williamson, *1 and 2 Chronicles*, NBC (Grand Rapids, MI: Eerdmans, 1982), 72–73, 165–169; Sara Japhet, *The Ideology of the Book of Chronicles and Its Place in Biblical Thought* (Winona Lake, IN: Eisenbrauns, 2009), 178–181, 185–186; Raymond Jacques Tournay, *Seeing and Hearing God with the Psalms: The Prophetic Liturgy of the Second Temple in Jerusalem*, JSOTSup 118 (Sheffield: JSOT Press, 1991), 34–68; John W. Kleinig, *The Lord's Song: The Basis, Function and Significance of Choral Music in Chronicles*, JSOTSup 156 (Sheffield: JSOT Press, 1993); William M. Schniedewind, *The Word of God in Transition: From Prophet to Exegete in the Second Temple Period*, JSOTSup 197 (Sheffield: JSOT Press, 1995), 31–129; Schniedewind, "Prophets and Prophecy in the Books of Chronicles," in *The Chronicler as Historian*, 204–224; Gary N. Knoppers, *1 Chronicles 10–29*, AB 12A (New York, NY: Doubleday, 2004), 843–860.

3 On the temple in Persian Yehud, see especially Peter R. Bedford, *Temple Restoration in Early Achaemenid Persia*, JSJSup 65 (Leiden: Brill, 2001). Bedford argues that the Jerusalem temple cult became part of the Persian imperial framework during the Chronicler's time. Cf. Louis Jonker, "Who Constitutes Society? Yehud's Self-Understanding in the Late Persian Era as Reflected in the Books of Chronicles," *JBL* 127 (2008): 703–726. Jonker argues that "it is very clear that the identity of the Chronicler's community is closely associated with the southern kingdom of the preexilic era. Not only does the monarchic line of the southern kingdom form the plot line of the Chronicler's history (established by the omission of the northern voices), but the cultic values associated with the southern kingdom are also presented as the norm" ("Who Constitutes Society," 714–715).

sometimes serve as judges.[4] The link between the Second Temple and prophecy is striking, especially since the question of prophecy as an institution in the Chronicler's day remains debated.[5] As Gary Knoppers notes, "the importance of public music and singing should not be downplayed in the Chronicler's history. In the reigns of later kings, levitical choirs are an essential part of the Chronicler's cult, appearing some thirty times in his history."[6] While the association between singing and prophecy is not an innovation of Chronicles, the book reimagines the prophetic activity of a collective unit that communicates with God through music.[7]

2 Gad and the Levitical Singers

Prior to Chronicles, the Bible presents groups of prophets linked to royal courts, but these are never located in a temple or given cult-related titles. After establishing an analogy between the intermediary position of Gad and the Levitical singers, the Chronicler distinguishes the role of a specific group.[8] The figure of

---

4 On the history of the Yehudite priesthood, see Gary N. Knoppers, "*Hierodules*, Priests, or Janitors? The Levites in Chronicles and the History of the Israelite Priesthood," *JBL* 118 (1999): 49–72. Cf. Antti Laato, "The Levitical Genealogies in 1 Chronicles 5–6 and the Formation of Levitical Ideology in Post-Exilic Judah," *JSOT* 62 (1994): 77–99; Rüdiger Lux, "Der zweite Tempel von Jerusalem—ein persisches oder prophetisches Projekt?," in *Das Alte Testament—ein Geschichtsbuch? Geschichtsschreibung oder Geschichtsüberlieferung im antiken Israel*, ed. U. Becker and J. van Oorschot (Leipzig: Evangelisches Verlagsanstalt, 2005), 145–172.

5 For an effective survey on the transformation of prophecy in the postexilic period, see Schniedewind, *The Word of God in Transition*, 12–22. Cf. Isaac Kalimi, "The Date of the Book of Chronicles," in *God's Word for Our World. Volume I: Biblical Studies in Honor of Simon John De Vries*, ed. J. Harold Ellens et al., JSOTSup 388 (London: T&T Clark, 2004), 347–371.

6 Knoppers, "*Hierodules*, Priests, or Janitors?," 68. Cf. Kleinig, *The Lord's Song*; Harry V. van Rooy, "Prophet and Society in the Persian Period According to Chronicles," in *Second Temple Studies 2: Temple and Community in the Persian Period*, ed. T. Eskenazi, and K. Richards, JSOTSup 175 (Sheffield: Sheffield Academic Press, 1994), 163–179.

7 For an interesting ancient Near Eastern comparison, see *FM* 3 2:61 for the only link between music and prophecy in the Mari archives. Cf. Jean-Marie Durand and Michel Guichard, "Les rituels de Mari," in *Florilegium marianum III: Recueil d'études à la mémoire de Marie-Thérèse Barrelet*, ed. D. Charpin and J.-M. Durand, Mémoires de NABU 4, Supplément à NABU no. 2 (Paris: SEPOA, 1997), 19–78. As Nele Ziegler also notes, music helps provoke a trance by the *muḫḫûm* (lines ii 21′, 27′). See Ziegler, *Les musiciens et la musique d'après les archives de Mari*, Mémoires de NABU 10 = Florilegium Marianum IX (Paris: Société pour l'Étude du Proche-Orient Ancien, 2007).

8 See Steven Schweitzer, *Reading Utopia in Chronicles*, LHBOTS 442 (New York, NY: T&T Clark, 2007), 160–173.

Gad, called "the seer of David" in 2 Sam 24:11; 1 Chr 21:9, and "the visionary of the king" in 1 Chr 29:29; 2 Chr 29:25, is central to the organization of temple worship. He announces the future locale of the temple in 2 Samuel 24 and 1 Chronicles 21. As the designated *ḥōzeh* between Yahweh and the king, Gad issues a harsh rebuke to David after David goes against the divine will and takes a census in 1 Chronicles 21. This defines Gad as the one who brings divine messages not to the people, but to the king. Gad tells David to choose one of the following as his punishment: a three year famine, three months in flight from an adversary, or three days at the mercy of Yahweh's wrath. David picks the last option and cedes to the divine. He takes responsibility and acknowledges his fault over and against the rest of the people in conducting the census. Taken on its own, 1 Chronicles 21 signals Gad's "messenger" role vis-à-vis David and provokes the anticipated response of repentance by the king, not the people at large.

The divine warning as spoken by Gad is averted through David's obeisance to Yahweh, who in turn desists before his angel destroys Jerusalem. Consequently, Yahweh instructs Gad to tell David to set up an altar that will foreshadow the construction of the temple. This altar ultimately serves as the medium for the king to thank Yahweh for not destroying his people ("Then on that day David first appointed the singing of praises to the LORD by Asaph and his kindred," 1 Chr 16:7). Gad oversees the transfer of the ark to Jerusalem, the very place where David then will appoint Asaph to serve as *nābîʾ*.

In this way, the assigned role that the Levitical singers play in the temple cult by approaching Yahweh mirrors the role that Gad plays. Yahweh designates Gad to be David's *ḥōzeh* and then David institutionalizes the function of the singers as intermediaries between Yahweh and the people. A circle of communication is established: Yahweh transmits his command to Gad, David's seer, and Gad conveys the message to David, who then appoints the Levitical singers. They act as prophets and speak to Yahweh on behalf of the people. However, unlike 2 Sam 24:11, Gad is not called a *nābîʾ* in Chronicles and the Chronicler instead applies the title to the Levitical singers.[9] He reinterprets the communication by distancing the people from the king, who alone is culpable in 1 Chronicles 21. In the organization of the temple complex, David initiates worship at the altar in order to legitimize the people's response back to Yahweh.[10] David "assigns" (*nātan*; 1 Chr 16:7) and "separates out" (*wayyabdēl*; 1 Chr

9 In 2 Chr 18:7–11, 17, Micaiah son of Imlah and all the prophets on the threshing floor at the gate of Samaria are also described as prophesying: *mitnabbēʾ*, *mitnabbəʾîm*. Cf. 2 Chr 20:37, where Eliezer son of Dodavahu of Mareshah prophesies against Jehoshaphat.

10 Cf. Knoppers, *1 Chronicles 10–29*, 856–860; John W. Wright, "The Legacy of David in Chronicles: The Narrative Function of 1 Chronicles 23–27," *JBL* 110 (1991), 229–242.

25:1) a group tied to the Psalms collection in order to anchor active communication and make prophecy accessible to the people. In doing so, the Levitical singers redefine the traditional role of a prophet and formalize prophetic invocation of a specified group in a cultic context.[11]

3 The Leaders of the Levitical Singers Who Prophesy

The singers are first named in 1 Chr 15:16–24 in connection with the transfer of the ark to Jerusalem. They are identified as kinsmen of the Levites and instructed to sing and play musical instruments.[12] Subsequently in 1 Chr 16:4–7, the Asaphites, from the lineage of Asaph son of Berechiah (cf. 15:17), minister before the ark in Jerusalem and offer a psalm of thanksgiving. This hymn of praise associates three tasks with individuals separated out from among the Levites: "He [David] appointed before the ark of Yahweh from among the Levites to lead—to invoke, to thank, and to praise Yahweh, God of Israel" (ויתן לפני ארון יהוה מן הלוים משרתים ולהזכיר ולהודות ולהלל ליהוה אלהי ישראל; 1 Chr 16:4).

Why would this group among the Levites be distinguished for the purpose of extoling Yahweh and be entrusted "to give thanks to Yahweh [and] to call upon his name" (1 Chr 16:8)? The act of singing praise and glorifying divine past deeds is governed by the root נבא. In 1 Chr 25:1–3, the title *nābîʾ* for the Levitical singers goes back to David's organization of the group. David separates out the families of the designated Levitical singers, whose task with musical instruments is deemed prophetic according to the *Qere* of the MT, LXX, Targum, and Vulgate. For textual-critical reasons, the *Qere* reading of the *niphal* plural participle *hannibbəʾîm* is preferable to the *Ketiv* nominal plural form *hannəbîʾîm*.[13] Not only does David appoint Asaph, Heman, and Jeduthun to prophesy through song, but he also further defines the nature of their prophecy.[14] According to the

11 See Ralph W. Klein, *1 Chronicles*, Hermeneia (Minneapolis, MN: Fortress, 2006), 348–351.

12 Following H. Gese, Schniedewind notes the four stages of the singers' history (see Schniedewind, *The Word of God in Transition*, 164): (1) After the return from exile, the singers are called "sons of Asaph" (Ezra 2:41; Neh 7:44); (2) during the time of Nehemiah, the Levitical singers are viewed as Levites and divided into two groups: the sons of Asaph and the sons of Jeduthun (cf. Neh 11:3–19; 1 Chr 9:1–18); (3) the Levitical singers are further organized into three groups: Asaph, Heman, and Jeduthun (cf. 1 Chr 16:4–12; 2 Chr 5:12; 29:13–14; 35:15); (4) Ethan replaces Jeduthun as one of the singers in 1 Chr 6:31–48 and 15:16–22.

13 See Knoppers, *Prophets, Priests, and Promises*, 181.

14 Cf. Schniedewind, *The Word of God in Transition*, 170–188. He maintains that the emphasis should be placed on a connection between divine inspiration and the creation of music. However, the prophetic activity of the Levitical singers does not solely involve

Qere of v. 1: ויבדל דויד ושרי הצבא לעבדה לבני אסף והימן וידותון הנבאים בכנרות בנבלים ובמצלתים ויהי מספרם אנשי מלאכה לעבדתם; "David set apart the sons of Asaph, Heman, and Jeduthun for service, those prophesying to the accompaniment of lyres, harps, and cymbals."

The *Qere niphal* participial reading *hannibbəʾîm* bolsters the importance of Davidic authority in appointing the singers.[15] They are defined by their behavior, which is to prophesy through song. These individuals serve as prophets at the hand of the king through their invocation and exaltation of the divine: "the one prophesying, by way of thanking and praising Yahweh" (*hannibbāʾ ʿal-hōdôt wəhallēl layhwh*; v. 3).

By linking the work of one group of temple personnel to prophecy, the act of singing and playing instruments within the cult is identified as prophetic.[16] This ascribed role of the singers denotes a collective intermediary function that approaches Yahweh. For the Chronicler, the singers are part of the hierarchy of the Jerusalem temple who are depicted as representatives of the people. The singers do not relay divine rebuke or admonishment to the king, as exemplified by an individual prophet such as Gad. By contrast, they actively minister praise in front of the ark, and their association with prophecy in Chronicles is localized within the larger narrative of the transfer of the ark to Jerusalem. To this end, the voice of the Levitical singers is also conveyed through the title *ḥōzeh*. In 2 Chr 29:30, Hezekiah and the officers order the Levites to praise Yahweh in the words of David and "Asaph, the seer": *ləhallēl layhwh bədibrê dāwîd wəʾāsāp haḥōzê*. Here this second title for Asaph reaffirms the appointed task of acting as a *nābîʾ* and actively mediating for the people.[17] Within the confines of the cult, the Levitical singers, as named through their eponymous ancestor, are set apart.

---

the performance of music in the temple. Schniedewind notes the distinction between the *Qere*, "those who prophesy," and the *Ketiv*, "the prophets." Ultimately, however, the verb is denominative and underlines the act of prophesying with the use of musical instruments. The LXX and Targum of 25:1 reflect the *Qere* reading of the MT, that is, prophecy under the influence of the divine spirit. Cf. Knoppers, *1 Chronicles 10–29*, 844–853.

15 The Davidic origin of the Levitical singers is reflected in 2 Chr 8:14; 23:18; 29:20, 25; 35:15. Cf. Joseph Blenkinsopp, *A History of Prophecy in Israel: From the Settlement in the Land to the Hellenistic Period* (Philadelphia, PA: Westminster, 1983), 254–255.

16 Cf. Japhet, *I and II Chronicles*, 440–441. She argues: "It seems that this term [prophecy] is meant to ascribe to the Temple music a special significance as the most elevated function of the cult, rather than indicate the continuation of an earlier phenomena."

17 Elsewhere Asaph is called *ḥōzê* in 2 Chr 33:18; 35:15, and Jeduthun is called *ḥōzê* in 2 Chr 35:15.

The prophetic activity of the singers illustrates the bidirectional nature of transmitting a message between Yahweh and the people at a time when the Psalter receives central attention in temple prayer.[18] With the exile of the people and reconstruction of the temple, the Chronicler reconfigures the image of prophecy from the books of Samuel and Kings so that the Levitical singers assert cultic leadership in the postexilic context.[19] However, the larger question concerns the association of the specific use of *nābîʾ* with the temple.[20] To what extent does the schema of the Levitical singers reflect real practice during the Second Temple period versus the literary imagination of Chronicles? Indeed, there is a link between the role of the prophet and the temple singers, though the exact nature of the connection remains in question.[21]

Biblical scholars have recognized the association between some prophets and the temple cult.[22] For Lester Grabbe, a cult prophet should be narrowly defined as "a member of the temple personnel who acts (at least sometimes) in the temple as a prophet. This might be in the regular liturgy or service, but it might also simply be to give formal prophecies now and then, perhaps addressed to the king or the administration."[23] The category of "cult

18 Contrast G. Knoppers, "Democratizing Revelation? Prophets, Seers and Visionaries in Chronicles," in *Prophecy and Prophets in Ancient Israel: Proceedings of the Oxford Old Testament Seminar*, LHBOTS 531 (New York, NY: T&T Clark, 2010), 400.

19 See H.F. van Rooy, "Prophet and Society in the Persian Period according to Chronicles," in *Second Temple Studies 2: Temple and Community in the Persian Period*, ed. T.C. Eskenazi and K.H. Richards, JSOTSup 175 (Sheffield: Sheffield Academic Press, 1994), 163–179. Cf. Petersen, *Late Israelite Prophecy*, 56, 85; Robert P. Carroll, *When Prophecy Failed: Reactions and Responses to Failure in Old Testament Prophetic Traditions* (London: SCM Press, 1979), esp. 204–205.

20 See Lester L. Grabbe, "Cultic Prophecy *Déjà vu*," in *Prophecy and Its Cultic Dimensions*, ed. Lena-Sofia Tiemeyer, JAJSup 31 (Göttingen: Vandenhoeck & Ruprecht, 2019), 39–49. I thank Professor Grabbe for first sharing the article with me before publication. Cf. Grabbe, "Prophets in the Chronicler," 297–310.

21 By way of a classical Greek analogy, Stephen Geller remarks that "The tension [between prophets and poets] was perceptible to the Greeks. To be sure, they ascribed divine inspiration to both prophets and poets. The muse inspired the latter as Apollo did his Pythian oracle." See Stephen A. Geller, "Were the Prophets Poets?," *Prooftexts* 3 (1983): 211.

22 See Sigmund Mowinckel, *Psalmenstudien: III. Kultprophetie und prophetische Psalmen*, Skrifter utgit av Videnskapsselskapets i Kristiania I: Hist.-Filos. Klasse (Oslo: Dybwad, 1922); Mowinckel, "Cult and Prophecy," in *Prophecy in Israel: Search for Identity*, trans. James L. Schaaf, IRT 10 (Philadelphia, PA: Fortress, 1987), 74–98. Cf. W.H. Bellinger, Jr., *Psalmody and Prophecy*, JSOTSup 27 (Sheffield: JSOT Press, 1984), 9–21; Aubrey R. Johnson, *The Cult Prophet in Israel*, 2nd ed. (Cardiff: University of Wales, 1962); John W. Hilber, *Cultic Prophecy in the Psalms*, BZAW 352 (New York, NY/Berlin: de Gruyter, 2005); Grabbe, "Cultic Prophecy *Déjà vu*," 39–49.

23 Grabbe, "Cultic Prophecy *Déjà vu*," 40.

prophet" locates the main social setting for the prophet's behavior in the temple context—not anywhere else.[24] Grabbe questions whether "the former cult prophets … have been assimilated into the Levites and temple singers."[25] When it comes to the books of Chronicles, David appoints the sons of Asaph, Heman, and Jeduthun to "prophesy with lyres, harps, and cymbals" (1 Chr 25:1). The references to the Levitical singers as *ḥōzeh* all are associated with the making of music, unlike the use of this term for Gad.[26] In 2 Chr 29:25, the Levites are located in the temple with musical instruments "by the command of David." They then "sing the song of Yahweh" in v. 27. Additionally, the singers carry out their tasks according to the "command of David" in 2 Chr 35:15.[27]

Reflecting on the place of monarchic Israel in the development of biblical prophecy, David Petersen argues that the "correlation between monarchy and prophecy is not accidental, but constitutes the critical clue to the locus of classical Israelite prophecy, its connection with the political institution of monarchy."[28] He focuses his attention on 1 Chr 25:1–6, 2 Chr 20:14–17, and 2 Chr 34:30, the three focal points of any link between prophecy and the Levitical singers. In an innovative way, the Chronicler has reformulated the older, established notion of prophetic invocation of a collective group in a defined, cultic locale. Through the category of the singers, that invocation has been institutionalized within the postexilic setting of the Jerusalem temple.[29] The singers are cast in the role of monarchic-period prophets who in turn may perform ritual music (1 Chr 25:1–8; 2 Chr 35:25) as a collective unit (cf. 2 Kgs 23:2).[30]

24 For an overview of prophetic views on cult and worship, see Göran Eidevall, *Sacrificial Rhetoric in the Prophetic Literature of the Hebrew Bible* (Lewiston, NY: Edwin Mellen Press, 2012), 5–30. Cf. Martti Nissinen, *Ancient Prophecy: Near Eastern, Biblical, and Greek Perspectives* (Oxford: Oxford University Press, 2018), 201–256.

25 Grabbe, "Cultic Prophecy *Déjà vu*," 45.

26 As previously noted, the LXX supports the participial reading of the *Qere*. In the LXX translation of 1 Chr 25:1–6, the verb, *nbʾ*, is translated as "making musical sounds," underscoring a change in the understanding of prophecy.

27 See Schniedewind, *The Word of God in Transition*, esp. 172–173.

28 Petersen, *Late Israelite Prophecy*, 2.

29 To situate the book of Chronicles in the late Persian period, see Ralph W. Klein, *1 Chronicles: A Commentary*, Hermeneia (Minneapolis, MN: Fortress, 2005), 13–16; Gary N. Knoppers, *1 Chronicles 1–9: A New Translation with Introduction and Commentary*, AB 12 (New York: Doubleday, 2003), 101–117; Sarah Japhet, *I and II Chronicles*, OTL (London: SCM, 1993), 23–28.

30 This does not mean that a line of continuity exists between old cultic prophets and the Levitical singers. Such a claim is argued in A. Johnson, *The Cultic Prophet in Ancient Israel*, 66–75. Nevertheless, the cult remains of primary concern for postexilic prophets like Haggai and Zechariah, and is central to the Chronicler's worldview and to the role of a prophet. Grabbe argues that "texts in Chronicles and in Ezra–Nehemiah cannot just be dismissed

Moreover, Knoppers argues that the Levitical singers represent "temporary spokespersons of the deity" for the Chronicler.[31]

4 Prophecy as Active Invocation of Yahweh

According to the Chronicler, mediation through singing serves as a means to institutionalize the interaction with Yahweh as a key component of the cult. By labeling this activity as prophecy, the Chronicler has legitimized the bidirectional focus of communication that now also enables the people to interact with Yahweh. Drawing on an established biblical model for prophetic behavior of a group linked to a cultic structure, the response affirms allegiance to Yahweh. The Chronicler asserts a link between the category of singers and the task of a prophet to mediate between humanity and the divine. However, the direction of group prophecy in Chronicles as approach *to* Yahweh marks a contrast to the pattern of an individual prophet as a messenger *from* Yahweh.

Though the etymological meaning of the word *nābîʾ* remains contested, there is a biblical precedent that denotes the act of calling on Yahweh through direct communication. The denominative usage of the verb נבא suggests the role of the *nābîʾ*, as is reflected in narrative settings elsewhere.[32] One notes the type of invocation by a group versus an individual, which is localized also in a cultic context. Outside of Chronicles, examples of a unit of prophets who call on Yahweh from a shrine or similar locale provide a certain framework for evaluating the prophecy. However, it is these very passages in Samuel and Kings that echo the specific function of the Levitical singers, which are then set aside in the composition of Chronicles.

For example, in 1 Sam 10:5–13 Saul encounters a group of prophets who descend from a high place preceded by musical instruments (*ḥebel nəbîʾîm yōrədîm mēhabbāmâ*). Through the root נבא they invoke Yahweh in praise. This band of prophets is a specified group that descends from the *bāmāh*, a physical structure in the Yahwistic cult and a recognized site at which to conduct sacrifices. Similarly, the behavior of the seventy elders who are stationed around

---

but must be accepted as a reflection on the later temple situation, perhaps in the Persian period." See Grabbe, "Cultic Prophecy *Déjà vu*," 45.

31 Gary N. Knoppers, *Prophets, Priests, and Promises: Essays on the Deuteronomistic History, Chronicles, and Ezra–Nehemiah*, ed. C.M. Maier and H.G.M. Williamson, VTSup 186 (Leiden: Brill, 2021), 174. Cf. Knoppers, "Democratizing Revelation?," 391–409.

32 For example, in Gen 20:4–18, Abimelech of Gerar pleads with the *nābîʾ*, Abraham, to intercede on his behalf and save him.

the Tent of Meeting by Moses in Num 11:25–27 is delimited—*wayyitnabbəʾû*, "and they prophesied."[33] The elders resemble a cult group in the camp setting that stands outside the Tent of Meeting, but which operates in the capacity of prophets of the people and thereby helps Moses govern in the wilderness.[34] As a third marker of a group's active approach to a deity, the prophets of Baal represent a collective unit of divine emissaries in 1 Kgs 18:25–29. These *nəbîʾê habbaʿal* also call upon the deity within a defined sacred space, here the altar on Mount Carmel. Though Elijah rebukes the worship of Baal in the official Israelite cult, the very condemnation itself reflects the function of this religious group, namely to mediate with Baal. Like the prophets of the *bāmāh* and the elders at the Tent of Meeting, this account shows the prophetic act of speaking or calling out to a deity, and does not suggest the one-directional relay of a divine message or the prayer of an individual prophet to one person.

These conceptual divisions between a collective group of prophets and an individual prophet, and between a defined cultic place or an alternate space, provide a context to frame the etymological debate surrounding the verb נבא. Scholars have posited that the title *nābîʾ* is likely related to the Akkadian cognate *nabû*, meaning "to call or announce." The discussion over the passive or active meaning of this verb, as well as the interpretation of the noun *nābîʾ* as "one who is named by God," is debated. Notably, John Huehnergard maintains the general view of Hebrew *nābîʾ* in the passive sense. By contrast, Daniel Fleming argues for the active interpretation of the root grounded in two Akkadian cognates from Bronze Age Syria, *nābû* and *munabbiātu*, so that *nābîʾ* designates a spokesman who calls out to the divine.[35]

---

33 With respect to Saul's ecstatic state when David plays the lyre in 1 Sam 18:10–11, Martti Nissinen writes: "*hitnabbēʾ* does certainly not imply any kind of transmission of divine messages or other intermediary functions but expressly indicates unusual behavior, leaving the reader struggling with the semantic problem of how to relate this kind of 'prophesying' to prophesying in general" ("Prophecy and Ecstasy," 186–187). Nissinen notes that the accompaniment of music with Saul's frenzy may be compared to musicians in Old Babylonian Mari who react to the behavior of prophets. See Nissinen, *Ancient Prophecy: Near Eastern, Biblical, and Greek Perspectives*, 176–178, 186–191.

34 Steven McKenzie argues that texts such as 1 Sam 10:5 that include instruments may provide the background for the designation of the Levitical singers' task as prophecy. However, he notes that in Chronicles, "the singing or prophecy was a permanent feature of temple worship and neither an isolated phenomenon nor ecstatic experience," *1–2 Chronicles*, Abingdon Old Testament Commentaries (Nashville, TN: Abingdon Press, 2004), 196.

35 See Daniel E. Fleming, "The Etymological Origins of the Hebrew *nābîʾ*: The One Who Invokes God," *CBQ* 55 (1993): 217–224. According to Fleming, two Syrian nouns, *nābû* and *munabbiātu*, offer a framework for comparison since they provide cognates to the Hebrew *nābîʾ*. He argues that these terms "are best understood as designating those who call on or

According to Fleming, this human summoning of the deity does not consist in the delivery of a message to an individual such as that of Gad to David. Quite the contrary, for the Chronicler, the utterance of words of praise by a group in itself connotes the prophecy within the physical walls of the Jerusalem temple setting. Through the persona of Asaph, one of the heads of the singers, the idea of prophecy as active invocation is transformed and thereby yields a response—the people's exaltation of the divine. Moreover, the older idea of prophecy as an approach to God in prayer like Elisha or Elijah is revocalized as an oral offering of praise that conveys the voice of the people.[36]

5 Asaph and the Chronicler's Innovation

The Chronicler repeatedly uses two verbs to identify how the singers Asaph, Heman, and Jeduthun are said to prophesy: "to thank," *ləhôdôt*, and "to praise," *ləhallēl*, Yahweh. Only one time does the Chronicler associate the function of the Levitical singers with a different verb: "to invoke," *ləhazkîr*, in 1 Chr 16:4. Through invocation, the people are reminded of God, but the Levites also call out to Yahweh and remind Yahweh of his steadfast relationship with his people. This would support the view that the divine is the object of the oft-recurring verbs "to praise" and "to thank." While part of the designated occupation involves music in the royal setting, the use of the verb נבא does not necessitate that the singers are considered "'inspired royal musicians.'"[37]

In association with the Jerusalem temple, the only legitimate cultic locale in the Chronicler's milieu, Asaph is said to prophesy in his capacity as a member of the Levitical singers. Identified in the genealogical line of Gershon, Asaph is the administrative head of the Levitical group in Jerusalem who is associated with sounding the cymbals (cf. 1 Chr 15:17–24). The Asaph who praised Yahweh in the Psalter (Psalms 50, 73–83) is remembered for his simultaneous

---

invoke the gods, an active etymology from the same verbal root" (221). Cf. Fleming, "*nābû* and *munabbiātu*: Two New Syrian Religious Personnel," 217–224; Jonathan Stökl, *Prophecy in the Ancient Near East: A Philological and Sociological Comparison*, CHANE 56 (Leiden: Brill, 2012), 161–167.

36 The potential link between prophecy and music is reflected in 2 Kings 3 when Elisha asks for music to help generate his prophetic oracle in v. 15. See also 1 Sam 10:5; Ex 15:20.

37 By contrast, Schniedewind argues: "[These] contexts in which the title *ḥozeh* is applied to Asaph, Heman and Jeduthun indicate that they were the royal musicians. Their music, as indicated by the use of the verb 'to prophesy' (√נבא), was probably considered as inspired by the Chronicler and his contemporaries. We might call them 'inspired royal musicians.'" See *The Word of God in Transition*, 172–173.

relationship with the divine, the human king, and the people. Through David's formalization of the temple and subsequent demarcation of the singers, the Chronicler has taken part in a "larger interpretative prophetic tradition"[38] of this three-part relationship. The Chronicler harks back to the tradition-history of Asaph in order to contextualize David's relationship with Asaph, but then he reframes Asaph's current prophetic role: to administer the people's praise to Yahweh.[39]

Consequently, the centralized temple and its nucleus around the ark become the locale where the Levitical singers utter a new message of adulation back to the divine. Moreover, Hezekiah authorizes the use of psalms for the purposes of praising Yahweh (cf. 2 Chr 29:30).[40] By initially associating the prophetic function of Asaph with Gad, who transmitted Yahweh's instruction for the organization of music in the temple, these psalms take on a prophetic nature.[41] As Adele Berlin explains, "whether or not the construct was invested for that purpose, the Chronicler uses David-as-psalmist in his legitimization and promotion of Second Temple psalmody."[42] For the Chronicler, the ascription of the psalms to David goes hand in hand with the role of David in the temple, "reshap[ing the link] according to [the Chronicler's] own agenda, in which David is the designer of the Temple and its cultus."[43] The application of the Psalter's tradition of David and Asaph therefore is reinterpreted in the later context of Chronicles.

In turn, the royal institution in Chronicles governs the systematization of the temple personnel. This act draws on the period of the monarchy and the actual First Temple, which provides a model to situate the category of Levitical singers as those who call upon Yahweh. With David's establishment of the temple, the

38 Knoppers, "Democratizing Revelation?," 405; cf. Schniedewind, "Prophets and Prophecy in the Books of Chronicles," 222.

39 The tradition-historical analysis of Asaph extends beyond the scope of this paper. For scholarship, see Harry Nasuti, *Tradition History and the Psalms of Asaph*, SBLDS 88 (Atlanta, GA: Scholars Press, 1988); Michael Goulder, *The Psalms of Asaph and the Pentateuch: Studies in the Psalter, III*, JSOTSup 233 (Sheffield: Sheffield Academic Press, 1996).

40 Tournay argues that the Levitical singers are the heirs of the prophets (cf. 1 Chr 15, 25; 2 Chr 20). See Tournay, *Seeing and Hearing God with the Psalms*. Cf. H.N. Wallace, "What Chronicles Has to Say about Psalms," in *The Chronicler as Author: Studies in Text and Texture*, ed. M.P. Graham and S.L. McKenzie, JSOTSup 263 (Sheffield: Sheffield Academic Press, 1999), 267–291.

41 Regarding the use of psalmody in Chronicles, see Adele Berlin, "Psalms in the Book of Chronicles," in *Shai le-Sara Japhet: Studies in the Bible, Its Exegesis and Its Language*, ed. M. Bar-Asher, D. Dom-Shiloni, E. Tov, and N. Wazana (Jerusalem: Bialik Institute, 2007), 21–36.

42 Berlin, "Psalms in the Book of Chronicles," 25.

43 Berlin, "Psalms in the Book of Chronicles," 25.

installation of the singers before the divine ark grants legitimacy to their communicative role. It should be noted that the ark itself is never depicted as part of the Second Temple structure.

According to the Chronicler's narrative chronology, the monarchic setting is pivotal to the retelling of history, contrary to Deuteronomistic or Priestly literature.[44] Singers as a class are not mentioned in Deuteronomy within the regulations concerning judges, priests, prophets, and kings in Deut 16:18–18:22. Rather, through the figure of David, Chronicles remembers the monarchy for elevating one group of Levites to oversee temple music (1 Chr 6:16). While the author of Chronicles does not directly expound on the origin of this separate body affiliated with the ark, he does elevate the status of the monarchic administration in "the divinely authorized incorporation of the Tabernacle in the Temple."[45]

The sons of Asaph, Heman, and Jeduthun, who are commanded to sing temple hymns, serve with musical instruments in 1 Chr 25:1. Berlin notes that "time after time Chronicles links the Temple hymnology with divine inspiration and divine command."[46] For present purposes, the Levitical singers are directly attached to David, who inspired the composition of the psalms. In the reestablishment of the Judahite monarchy, this is clearly established. According to 2 Chr 29:30, "King Hezekiah and the officers told the Levites to praise Yahweh with the words of David and Asaph the seer." These "words of David and Asaph" may be understood as the psalms, which are deemed authoritative praises to Yahweh.[47] The performance of psalmody by cult professionals is carefully constructed by the Chronicler, and serves a central role in the organization of the personnel.[48]

By establishing the category of the Levitical singers, the Chronicler thus imbues the professional group with a function that is grounded in its connection to David, the purported "psalmist of Israel" (2 Sam 23:1).[49] Such an association serves to justify the new role of the singers within the temple sanctum, at

44 See esp. Matthew Lynch, *Monotheism and Institutions in the Book of Chronicles: Temple, Priesthood, and Kingship in Post-Exilic Perspective*, FAT 2/64 (Tübingen: Mohr Siebeck, 2014), 209–234.

45 Knoppers, "Democratizing Revelation?," 429.

46 Berlin, "Psalms in the Book of Chronicles," 30.

47 For the understanding of "the words of David and Asaph" as the Psalms, see Berlin, 30; Japhet, *I & II Chronicles*, 929; Wallace, "What Chronicles Has to Say about Psalms," 287–289; Kleinig, *The Lord's Song*, 61–62.

48 Japhet, *I & II Chronicles*, 504.

49 For a discussion of the relationship between David and the Psalms within Chronicles, see Kirsten Nielsen, "Whose Song of Praise? Reflections on the Purpose of the Psalm in

the same time that it acts as a literary marker in the text.[50] Now that the singers are linked to the monarchy, they are separated out for the specific function of prophesying (cf. 1 Chronicles 25) on behalf of the populace. The paradigm of active invocation of Yahweh by a collective group in a cultic locale is upheld and is institutionalized in the Chronicler's narrative. The Chronicler has portrayed a history of prophecy in the First Temple period through the attribution of Jerusalem cultic practice to David.[51]

The reformulation of prophecy grants the singers their authority in the temple through this link to David. It does not appear intended as an exact program for the present but rather as a history of the past monarchy.[52] According to Chronicles, David the musician separates out the Levitical singers for temple worship.[53] Music is central to the representation of the Second Temple in the books of Chronicles, where the Levitical singers legitimize cultic practice. The class of Levitical singers, as primarily designated through the names of the three eponymous heads, Asaph, Heman, and Jeduthun, has redefined the role of prophet with echoes of earlier divine invocation by prophetic groups. Indeed "the Chronicler and his redactors have gone to great trouble to argue that the

---

1 Chronicles 16," in *The Chronicler as Author: Studies in Text and Texture*, ed. M.P. Graham and S.L. McKenzie, JSOTSup 263 (Sheffield: Sheffield Academic Press, 1999), 327–336.

50 Alex Jassen states that "priests and the temple represent one of the new spaces in which prophecy can thrive." See Alex P. Jassen, "Prophecy and Priests in the Second Temple Period," in *Prophecy and Its Cultic Dimensions*, ed. Lena-Sofia Tiemeyer, JAJSup 31 (Göttingen: Vandenhoeck & Ruprecht, 2019), 87.

51 Later, in a Psalms scroll from Qumran, King David the musician (11Q5 XXVIII, 4 [= LXX Ps 151:2]) is described as composing "through prophecy" (*nəbûʾâ*). He is said to be under the influence of "a discerning and enlightened spirit" from God (11Q5 XXVII, 4, 11; cf. 2 Sam 23:2). See further Alex P. Jassen, "The Prophets in the Dead Sea Scrolls," in *The Oxford Handbook of the Prophets*, ed. Carolyn J. Sharp (New York, NY: Oxford University Press, 2016), 353–372.

52 This does not deny the fact that "[the author of Chronicles] validate[s] contemporary sacerdotal arrangements and aspirations by recourse to nature precedents in Israel's past." See Knoppers, *1 Chronicles*, 797.

53 In biblical scholarship, a case has been made for three traditions about David: David the poet, David the musician, and David the psalmist. Chronicles presents the tradition of David as psalmist, as reflected in 2 Chr 23:18. See especially Alan M. Cooper, "The Life and Times of King David According to the Book of Psalms," in *The Poet and the Historian: Essays in Literary and Historical Biblical Criticism*, ed. R.E. Friedman (Chico, CA: Scholars Press, 1983), 117–131. Cooper notes that "inferring David's liturgical activity from stories about his mastery of the harp (1 Sam 16:16–23), his composition of dirges (2 Sam 1:17; 3:33) and other poems (2 Sam 22 f.), and his invention of musical instruments (Amos 6:5; Neh 12:36; 1 Chr 23:5; 2 Chr 7:6, etc.) *is exactly what the Chronicler wants us to do*" (126–127; italics in the original).

Levitical singers of Israel's past were really prophets."[54] In this creation of an idealized past, the singers' occupation illuminates the bidirectional notion of prophecy that now transmits praise back to Yahweh and gives voice to the people.

Bibliography

Amit, Yairah. "The Role of Prophecy and Prophets in the Chronicler's World." Pages 80–101 in *Prophets, Prophecy, and Prophetic Texts in Second Temple Judaism*. Edited by Michael H. Floyd and Robert D. Haak. OTS 427. London: T&T Clark, 2006.

Bedford, Peter R. *Temple Restoration in Early Achaemenid Persia*. JSJSup 65. Leiden: Brill, 2001.

Bellinger, Jr., W.H. *Psalmody and Prophecy*. JSOTSup 27. Sheffield: JSOT Press, 1984.

Berlin, Adele. "Psalms in the Book of Chronicles." Pages 21–36 in *Shai le-Sara Japhet: Studies in the Bible, Its Exegesis and Its Language*. Edited by Michal Bar-Asher, Dalit Rom-Shiloni, Emanuel Tov, and Nili Wazana. Jerusalem: Bialik Institute, 2007.

Blenkinsopp, Joseph. *A History of Prophecy in Israel: From the Settlement in the Land to the Hellenistic Period*. Philadelphia, PA: Westminster, 1983.

Carroll, Robert P. *When Prophecy Failed: Reactions and Responses to Failure in Old Testament Prophetic Traditions*. London: SCM Press, 1979.

Cooper, Alan M. "The Life and Times of King David According to the Book of Psalms." Pages 117–131 in *The Poet and the Historian: Essays in Literary and Historical Biblical Criticism*. Edited by Robert E. Friedman. Chico, CA: Scholars Press, 1983.

Durand, Jean-Marie, and Michel Guichard. "Les rituels de Mari." Pages 19–78 in *Florilegium marianum III: Recueil d'études à la mémoire de Marie-Thérèse Barrelet*. Edited by Dominique Charpin and Jean-Marie Durand. Mémoires de NABU 4. Supplément à NABU no. 2. Paris: SEPOA, 1997.

Eidevall, Göran. *Sacrificial Rhetoric in the Prophetic Literature of the Hebrew Bible*. Lewiston, NY: Edwin Mellen Press, 2012.

Fleming, Daniel E. "The Etymological Origins of the Hebrew *nābîʾ*: The One Who Invokes God." *CBQ* 55 (1993): 217–224.

Fleming, Daniel E. "*nābû* and *munabbiātu*: Two New Syrian Religious Personnel." *JAOS* 113 (1993): 175–183.

Geller, Stephen A. "Were the Prophets Poets?" *Prooftexts* 3 (1983): 211–221.

54 See Petersen, *Late Israelite Prophecy*, 87. Cf. Schniedewind, 177 n. 43. As Schniedewind notes, "outside of the heads of the Levitical singers the Chronicler evinces no knowledge or understanding of the institution of cult prophecy."

Goulder, Michael. *The Psalms of Asaph and the Pentateuch: Studies in the Psalter, III*. JSOTSup 233. Sheffield: Sheffield Academic Press, 1996.

Grabbe, Lester. L. "Prophets in the Chronicler: The Books of 1 and 2 Chronicles and Ezra–Nehemiah." Pages 297–310 *Enemies and Friends of the State: Ancient Prophecy in Context*. Edited by Christopher A. Rollston. University Park, PA: Eisenbrauns, 2018.

Grabbe, Lester L. "Cultic Prophecy *Déjà vu*." Pages 39–49 in *Prophecy and Its Cultic Dimensions*. Edited by Lena-Sofia Tiemeyer. JAJSup 31. Göttingen: Vandenhoeck & Ruprecht, 2019.

Hilber, John W. *Cultic Prophecy in the Psalms*. BZAW 352. Berlin: de Gruyter, 2005.

Japhet, Sara. *I and II Chronicles*. OTL. Louisville, KY: Westminster John Knox, 1993.

Japhet, Sara. *The Ideology of the Book of Chronicles and Its Place in Biblical Thought*. Winona Lake, IN: Eisenbrauns, 2009.

Jassen, Alex P. "The Prophets in the Dead Sea Scrolls." Pages 353–372 in *The Oxford Handbook of the Prophets*. Edited by Carolyn J. Sharp. New York, NY: Oxford University Press, 2016.

Jassen, Alex P. "Prophecy and Priests in the Second Temple Period." Pages 63–88 in *Prophecy and Its Cultic Dimensions*. Edited by Lena-Sofia Tiemeyer. JAJSup 31. Göttingen: Vandenhoeck & Ruprecht, 2019.

Johnson, Aubrey R. *The Cult Prophet in Israel*. 2nd ed. Cardiff: University of Wales, 1962.

Jonker, Louis. "Who Constitutes Society? Yehud's Self-Understanding in the Late Persian Era as Reflected in the Books of Chronicles." *JBL* 127 (2008): 703–726.

Kalimi, Isaac. "The Date of the Book of Chronicles." Pages 347–371 in *God's Word for Our World, Volume 1: Biblical Studies in Honor of Simon John De Vries*. Edited by J.H. Ellens, D.L. Ellens, R.P. Knierim, and I. Kalimi. JSOTSup 388. London: T&T Clark, 2004.

Klein, Ralph W. *1 Chronicles: A Commentary*. Hermeneia. Minneapolis, MN: Fortress, 2005.

Kleinig, John W. *The Lord's Song: The Basis, Function and Significance of Choral Music in Chronicles*. JSOTSup 156. Sheffield: JSOT Press, 1993.

Knoppers, Gary N. "*Hierodules*, Priests, or Janitors? The Levites in Chronicles and the History of the Israelite Priesthood." *JBL* 118 (1999): 49–72.

Knoppers, Gary N. *1 Chronicles 1–9: A New Translation with Introduction and Commentary*. AB 12. New York, NY: Doubleday, 2003.

Knoppers, Gary N. *1 Chronicles 10–29: A New Translation with Introduction and Commentary*. AB 12A. New York, NY: Doubleday, 2004.

Knoppers, Gary N. "Democratizing Revelation? Prophets, Seers and Visionaries in Chronicles." Pages 391–409 in *Prophecy and Prophets in Ancient Israel: Proceedings of the Oxford Old Testament Seminar*. Edited by John Day. LHBOTS 531. New York, NY: T&T Clark, 2010.

Knoppers, Gary N. *Prophets, Priests, and Promises: Essays on the Deuteronomistic History, Chronicles, and Ezra–Nehemiah*. Edited by Christl M. Maier and Hugh G.M. Williamson. VTSup 186. Leiden: Brill, 2021.

Laato, Antti. "The Levitical Genealogies in 1 Chronicles 5–6 and the Formation of Levitical Ideology in Post-Exilic Judah." *JSOT* 62 (1994): 77–99.

Lux, Rüdiger. "Der zweite Tempel von Jerusalem—ein persisches oder prophetisches Projekt?" Pages 145–172 in *Das Alte Testament—ein Geschichtsbuch? Geschichtsschreibung oder Geschichtsüberlieferung im antiken Israel.* Edited by Uwe Becker and Jürgen van Oorschot. Leipzig: Evangelisches Verlagsanstalt, 2005.

Lynch, Matthew. *Monotheism and Institutions in the Book of Chronicles: Temple, Priesthood, and Kingship in Post-Exilic Perspective*, FAT 2/64. Tübingen: Mohr Siebeck, 2014.

McKenzie, Steven L. *1–2 Chronicles*. Abingdon Old Testament Commentaries. Nashville, TN: Abingdon Press, 2004.

Mowinckel, Sigmund. *Psalmenstudien: III. Kultprophetie und prophetische Psalmen.* Skrifter utgit av Videnskapsselskapets i Kristiania I: Hist.-Filos. Klasse. Oslo: Dybwad, 1922.

Mowinckel, Sigmund. "Cult and Prophecy." Pages 74–98 in *Prophecy in Israel: Search for Identity*. Translated by James L. Schaaf. IRT 10. Philadelphia, PA: Fortress, 1987.

Nasuti, Harry. *Tradition History and the Psalms of Asaph.* SBLDS 88. Atlanta, GA: Scholars Press, 1988.

Nielsen, Kirsten. "Whose Song of Praise? Reflections on the Purpose of the Psalm in 1 Chronicles 16." Pages 327–336 in *The Chronicler as Author: Studies in Text and Texture.* Edited by M. Patrick Graham and Steven L. McKenzie. JSOTSup 263. Sheffield: Sheffield Academic Press, 1999.

Nissinen, Martti. *Ancient Prophecy: Near Eastern, Biblical, and Greek Perspectives.* Oxford: Oxford University Press, 2018.

Petersen, David. *Late Israelite Prophecy: Studies in Deutero-Prophetic Literature and in Chronicles.* SBLMS 23. Missoula, MT: Scholars Press, 1977.

Schniedewind, William M. *The Word of God in Transition: From Prophet to Exegete in the Second Temple Period.* JSOTSup 197. Sheffield: JSOT Press, 1995.

Schniedewind, William M. "Prophets and Prophecy in the Books of Chronicles." Pages 204–224 in *The Chronicler as Historian.* Edited by M. Patrick Graham, Kenneth G. Hoglund, and Steven L. McKenzie. JSOTSup 238. Sheffield, Sheffield Academic Press, 1997.

Schweitzer, Steven. *Reading Utopia in Chronicles.* LHBOTS 442. New York, NY: T&T Clark, 2007.

Tournay, Raymond Jacques. *Seeing and Hearing God with the Psalms: The Prophetic Liturgy of the Second Temple in Jerusalem.* JSOTSup 118. Sheffield: JSOT Press, 1991.

van Rooy, H.F. "Prophet and Society in the Persian Period According to Chronicles." Pages 163–179 in *Second Temple Studies 2: Temple and Community in the Persian*

Period. Edited by Tamara Cohn Eskenazi and K.H. Richards. JSOTSup 175. Sheffield: Sheffield Academic Press, 1994.

Wallace, Howard N. "What Chronicles Has to Say about Psalms." Pages 267–291 in *The Chronicler as Author: Studies in Text and Texture*. Edited by M. Patrick Graham and Steven L. McKenzie. JSOTSup 263. Sheffield: Sheffield Academic Press, 1999.

Warhurst, Amber K. "What Was Prophetic for the Chronicler?" Pages 165–182 in *What Was Authoritative for Chronicles?* Edited by Ehud Ben Zvi and Diana V. Edelman. Winona Lake, IN: Eisenbrauns, 2011.

Williamson, H.G.M. *1 and 2 Chronicles*. NCB. Grand Rapids, MI: Eerdmans, 1982.

Wright, John W. "The Legacy of David in Chronicles: The Narrative Function of 1 Chronicles 23–27." *JBL* 110 (1991): 229–242.

Ziegler, Nele. *Les musiciens et la musique d'après les archives de Mari*. Mémoires de NABU 10 = Florilegium Marianum IX. Paris: Société pour l'Étude du Proche-Orient Ancien, 2007.

5

L'aînesse au Proche-Orient ancien: Droit du premier-né ou choix du père?

Sophie Démare-Lafont

Les études sur le droit biblique ont été longtemps centrées sur les parties législatives de la Torah, pour déterminer leurs caractères spécifiques par rapport aux textes normatifs cunéiformes[1] ou au contraire leur appartenance à une culture juridique orientale commune[2]. On aurait tort cependant de négliger les parties narratives de la Bible, où sont mises en scène des situations qui illustrent la profondeur sociologique du droit et apportent de précieuses informations sur la vie juridique[3]. Même si les messages théologiques y occupent une place importante, la lecture juridique des faits et des comportements qui y sont décrits ouvre des pistes de recherche souvent fécondes, notamment dans une perspective comparatiste.

Les plus célèbres de ces récits font partie de l'imaginaire collectif de l'Occident chrétien, qui les a insérés dans un discours moralisant en associant souvent un personnage à une vertu ou un défaut. Tel est le cas d'Ésaü, incarnation du "bon sauvage," sorte d'homme des bois velu et rustique, habile à la chasse mais peu éduqué, qui accepte de brader son droit d'aînesse en échange d'un modeste plat de lentilles[4]. La disproportion entre l'ampleur de la perte et le caractère dérisoire et trivial du gain, que la sagesse populaire résume dans

1 Par exemple, Moshe Greenberg, "Some Postulates of Biblical Criminal Law," in *Studies in Bible and Jewish Religion: Yehezkel Kaufmann Jubilee Volume*, ed. Menahem Haran (Jerusalem: Magnes Press, 1960), 5-28; et Greenberg, "More Reflections on Biblical Criminal Law," in *Studies in Bible*, ed. Sara Japhet, Scripta Hierosolymitana 31 (Jerusalem: Magnes Press, 1986), 1-17.

2 Raymond Westbrook, "Biblical and Cuneiform Law Codes," *RB* 92 (1985): 247-265; et Westbrook, "Cuneiform Law Codes and the Origins of Legislation," *ZA* 79 (1989): 201-222.

3 Le commentaire juridique comparé des parties narratives de la Bible, d'abord accepté puis beaucoup critiqué, a connu un regain d'intérêt (cf. Mark W. Chavalas, "Assyriology and Biblical Studies: A Century and a Half of Tension," in *Mesopotamia and the Bible: Comparative Explorations*, ed. Mark W. Chavalas and K. Lawson Younger, Jr., JSOTSup 341 [New York, NY/London: Sheffield Academic Press, 2002], 21-67) et continue à produire des résultats stimulants (cf. récemment Dylan R. Johnson, *Sovereign Authority and the Elaboration of Law in the Bible and the Ancient Near East*, FAT 2 Reihe 122 [Tübingen: Mohr Siebeck, 2020]).

4 À certains égards, Ésaü ressemble à Enkidu, le rival de Gilgamesh, qui vit dans la steppe et

 | DOI:10.1163/9789004511538_006

l'expression "Perdre son âme pour un bol de soupe," fige Ésaü dans le rôle du primitif inculte, dont les actes sont guidés par la gloutonnerie et non par la raison.

Comme toujours, la situation est en réalité plus complexe et doit être replacée dans son contexte à la fois narratif et juridique. En renonçant à l'aînesse, Ésaü accomplit le destin annoncé à sa mère pendant sa grossesse. Rébecca apprend en effet en même temps qu'elle porte des jumeaux et que "le plus grand (*rab*) obéira au plus petit (*ṣāʿîr*)" (Gen 25:23). Les relations tumultueuses entre Ésaü et son frère Jacob s'inscrivent dans ce propos téléologique[5] mais présentent aussi des aspects juridiques qui méritent d'être explorés à la lumière des sources cunéiformes.

C'est un grand plaisir d'offrir les réflexions qui suivent à Daniel Fleming, bibliste et assyriologue renommé, qui plus est francophone et francophile, en hommage à sa riche et belle carrière académique mais aussi à notre longue et solide amitié.

1 Isaac, Ésaü et Jacob.

L'histoire d'Ésaü et Jacob s'organise en trois temps. Le premier est celui de la cession par Ésaü de son droit d'aînesse (*bəkôrâ*) à Jacob. Revenant bredouille et affamé de la chasse, Ésaü trouve son frère occupé à cuisiner quelques légumes pour son repas et se rue sur la nourriture en jurant, sur les instances de Jacob, qu'il lui laissera son privilège en échange (Gen 25:27-34).

La seconde étape se place plusieurs années plus tard. Alors qu'Isaac est devenu aveugle et qu'il se sent mourir, il donne sans le savoir sa bénédiction à Jacob. Découvrant trop tard la supercherie, Ésaü veut se venger et attend la mort imminente d'Isaac pour éliminer son frère, lequel s'enfuit sur les conseils de Rébecca (Gen 27:1-40).

L'épilogue de cette longue rivalité intervient vingt ans après, lors des retrouvailles et de la réconciliation des deux ennemis (Gen 33:1-17). Refusant dans un geste apparemment magnanime le cadeau (*minḥâ*; Gen 33:10) offert par Jacob,

---

agit sans calcul, au gré de ses seuls besoins immédiats. Cf. Gregory Mobley, "The Wild Man in the Bible and the Ancient near East," *JBL* 116 (1997): 217-233.

5 La portée de cette prophétie, qui retrace les origines de la rivalité entre Israël et Édom, et plus largement l'interprétation du cycle de Jacob sur les origines d'Israël, ont été abondamment étudiées; cf. en dernier lieu Benedikt Hensel, ed., *The History of the Jacob Cycle (Genesis 25–35)*, Archaeology and Bible 4 (Tübingen: Mohr Siebeck, 2021). On se bornera à traiter ici les aspects juridiques de l'histoire de Jacob et Ésaü, en prenant le récit dans sa forme finale sans aborder les questions liées à sa composition littéraire.

Ésaü obtient la restitution de la "donation/bénédiction" (*bərākâ*) (Gen 33:11), qui lui permet de reprendre, au moins symboliquement, la place dont il avait été privé[6].

Le terme "aîné" (*bəkôr*) n'est jamais utilisé dans ces trois passages, et celui d'"aînesse" (*bəkôrâ*) apparaît seulement dans l'épisode de la vente à Jacob (Gen 25:31-34; Gen 27:36). Ailleurs, Ésaü est appelé le "grand" (*rab*, Gen 25:23; *gādol* Gen 27:1, 15, 42), une donnée objective marquant l'antériorité de sa naissance par rapport à Jacob. La primogéniture, simple fait biologique, est ainsi distinguée de l'aînesse, statut juridique composé d'obligations et d'avantages patrimoniaux. Mais ce statut est-il un droit opposable pour le premier-né ou un choix laissé à l'appréciation du chef de famille[7]? Dans le premier cas, l'aîné ne peut être dépossédé de ses prérogatives par ses frères ou par son père, et il peut aussi renoncer à son rang. Dans le second cas, l'autorité paternelle est assez large pour inclure la capacité de désigner arbitrairement un aîné contre l'ordre naturel des naissances. Derrière cette alternative, deux conceptions de la famille se laissent apercevoir, l'une individualiste et l'autre patriarcale.

S'ajoute à ce tableau la circonstance particulière de la gémellité des deux frères, attestée une autre fois dans la Bible à propos de Tamar, belle-fille de Juda (Gen 38:27), et plus fréquemment dans les sources cunéiformes, principalement la littérature de présages[8]. Du point de vue du droit, l'arrivée de jumeaux dans une famille peut avoir une incidence sur la dévolution successorale si elle

---

6 Sur la proximité phonétique des deux termes "premier-né" (*bəkôr*) et "donation/bénédiction" (*bərākâ*), cf. en dernier lieu Kyu Seop Kim, *The Firstborn Son in Ancient Judaism and Early Christianity: A Study of Primogeniture and Christology*, BibInt 171 (Boston, MA/Leiden: Brill, 2019), 65-69, avec la bibliographie antérieure.

7 Sur cette question, cf. Eryl W. Davies, "The Inheritance of the First-Born in Israel and the Ancient Near East," *JSS* 38/2 (1993): 175-179; Gershon Brin, *Studies in Biblical Law from the Hebrew Bible to the Dead Sea Scrolls*, JSOTSup 176 (Sheffield: Sheffield Academic Press, 1994), 251-263.

8 Les naissances multiples sont mentionnées notamment dans la série *šumma izbu* (cf. Erle Leichty, *The Omen Series* šumma izbu, TCS 4 [Locust Valley/New York, NY: J.J. Augustin, 1970], 39) et dans les diagnostics médicaux (cf. JoAnn Scurlock, *Sourcebook for Ancient Mesopotamian Medicine*, WAW 36 [Atlanta, GA: SBL Press, 2014], 251-252). Je remercie Annie Attia qui m'a communiqué ces références. Cf. aussi pour Mari la lettre ARM 10 26 envoyée par la reine Shibtu à son mari Zimri-Lim pour lui annoncer la naissance de jumeaux, et une liste de personnes attribuées comme butin, incluant deux jumelles (FM 2 72.ii:63 // FM 2 73.ii:66 et le commentaire de Nele Ziegler, "Jumelles d'Admatum," *NABU* [1999/3]: 73 no. 73); cf. aussi Nele Ziegler, "Les enfants du palais," *Ktèma* 22 (1997): 45-57. Pour Ebla, cf. Marco Bonechi, "Of Cucumbers and Twins in the Ebla Palace G Texts," in *A Oriente del Delta: Scritti sull'Egitto ed il Vicino Oriente antico in onore di Gabriella Scandone Matthiae*, ed. Agnese Vacca, Sara Pizzimenti, and Maria Gabriella Micale, Contributi e Materiali di Archeologia orientale 18 (Roma: Scienze e Lettere, 2018), 91-107.

est organisée selon le rang de naissance. Déterminer qui a été conçu en premier était et reste scientifiquement impossible. Certains médecins français du XVIIIe s. affirmaient que celui qui sort du corps de la mère en dernier s'est installé en premier au fond de l'utérus[9]. Les juristes de la même époque, peu convaincus par cette allégation, se demandaient plutôt à quel moment précis se situe la naissance et raisonnaient à partir du passage de la Bible qui décrit la venue au monde des jumeaux de Tamar et Juda: Zérah sort d'abord une main et la sage-femme lui attache un fil écarlate au poignet pour marquer son antériorité, mais Pérèṣ passe devant lui et naît en premier (Gen 38:28-30). Dans le récit qui nous occupe, le narrateur précise que Jacob arrive en second, tenant Ésaü par le talon (Gen 25:26; cf. aussi Os 12:3), ce qui évoque une lutte similaire entre les deux frères sans que l'on sache si Jacob a été doublé par Ésaü ou a voulu le retenir. Pour la doctrine juridique, le simple fait de paraître, même partiellement – comme Zérah – ne suffit pas à désigner le premier-né, il faut qu'il ait vu la lumière, autrement dit qu'il soit entièrement sorti du ventre de la mère[10]. La gémellité est ainsi alignée sur la règle générale, fondée sur l'ordre chronologique de naissance des enfants. L'objectif est de faire coïncider la primogéniture, élément de fait, avec l'aînesse, notion de droit[11], et d'éviter ainsi les contestations lors de la division du patrimoine familial.

La même finalité se retrouve dans les sources de l'Antiquité orientale. L'aîné, lorsque les textes permettent de l'identifier, est le plus âgé des fils. Ce statut ne lui confère pas toujours un avantage successoral, les coutumes étant parfois égalitaires, et son privilège peut varier selon les régions et les types de biens hérités[12]. Les pratiques décrites dans la Bible (Num 27:1-11; Deut 21:15-17) rejoignent celles de certaines villes mésopotamiennes, avec une transmission en ligne descendante masculine et une part double pour l'aîné[13]. Le Deutéro-

9 Cf. Pierre-Louis Boyer, "Primogéniture et gémellité: Le droit d'aînesse dans son ordre naturel," *Revue historique de droit français et étranger* 89/4 (2011): 514 n. 4. Cette croyance n'a pas totalement disparu aujourd'hui.

10 *Primogenitus est, qui prior in lucem editus est* "L'aîné est celui qui est venu à la lumière le premier." Cf. Boyer, "Primogéniture," 517 n. 12 et 522 n. 37. On relèvera avec intérêt que la Bible est invoquée comme argument d'autorité pour justifier une règle somme toute arbitraire, "parce qu'il faut une décision, vraie ou fausse" comme le souligne Diderot (*L'Encyclopédie* t. 9 v° Jumeaux, 57).

11 Cette distinction est reprise aux jurisconsultes romains, en particulier Ulpien (Digeste 1, 5, 16).

12 Cf. Raymond Westbrook, "The Character of Ancient Near Eastern Law," in *A History of Ancient Near Eastern Law*, ed. Raymond Westbrook, HdO 72/1 (Boston, MA/Leiden: Brill, 2003): 56-62.

13 Tel est le cas à Larsa ou encore à Mari à l'époque paléo-babylonienne. Cf. Josef Klíma, "La position économique, sociale et juridique de l'enfant d'après les sources cunéiformes de

nome envisage l'hypothèse où le chef de famille aurait des enfants de deux lits différents et souhaiterait favoriser le fils de sa seconde épouse au motif qu'il déteste la première. La loi le lui interdit, réservant le droit d'aînesse (*bəkorâ*) au "premier fruit de sa force" (*rēʾšît ʾōnô*, Deut 21:17). Le premier-né aurait donc vocation, par principe, à être l'aîné, ce qui signifie qu'Ésaü avait de par sa naissance un droit acquis à ce statut.

Toutefois, ce que prohibe le texte deutéronomique est la faveur accordée arbitrairement à une épouse et non pas directement à un enfant[14]. Et de fait, les récits des patriarches fournissent plusieurs exemples d'ultimogéniture, le cadet ou le benjamin recevant les prérogatives qui auraient dû revenir au plus âgé: outre Jacob substitué à Ésaü, Isaac supplante Ismaël (Gen 21:10-14; 25:5), Juda remplace Ruben (Gen 49:3-4; 1 Chr 5:1-2) et Ephraïm est désigné à la place de Manassé (Gen 48:8-20). Il est vrai que souvent, le changement est lié à des circonstances spécifiques: Ésaü est écarté grâce aux manœuvres de Jacob puis de sa mère (Gen 25:27-34 et 27:1-40); Ismaël est le fils d'une concubine d'Abraham (Gen 16:15) alors qu'Isaac est celui de Sarah (Gen 21:2), l'épouse en titre; quant à Ruben, il a défié l'autorité paternelle en couchant avec Bilha, la concubine d'Isaac (Gen 35:22).

En revanche, aucun motif similaire n'explique l'éviction de Manassé[15], ni la préférence de certains pères pour leurs cadets, comme Hossa vis-à-vis de Shimri (1 Chr 26:10-11). L'arbitraire est encore plus visible lorsqu'il s'agit de désigner l'héritier au trône: contredisant l'interdit posé par le Deutéronome, Roboam institue Abiya, le fils de sa seconde épouse (2 Chr 11:22) et David choisit Salomon, le fils de Bethsabée, plutôt qu'Adonias (1 Kgs 1:29-30, 35). Même si le titre d'aîné est constamment évité au profit d'un vocabulaire plus neutre évoquant l'autorité du leader (*rōʾš*, "chef"), le puîné reçoit des prérogatives habituellement confiées à l'aîné, et ce par l'effet de la seule volonté du père.

Ces contradictions sont encore compliquées, dans l'histoire de Jacob et Ésaü, par deux anomalies juridiques. La première tient à la cession du droit d'aînesse, mentionnée dans la première partie du récit. Les commentaires se sont surtout concentrés sur la désinvolture d'Ésaü, qui le rend indigne des responsabilités que lui confère son rang de premier-né. Mais sur le plan juridique,

---

Mari," *ArOr* 42 (1974): 232-244 et Marcelo Rede, "Famille et transmission du patrimoine à Larsa: Une approche anthropologique," in *La famille dans le Proche-Orient ancien: Réalités, symbolismes et images: Proceedings of the 55th Rencontre Assyriologique Internationale, Paris 6-9 July 2009*, ed. Lionel Marti (Winona Lake, IN: Eisenbrauns, 2014), 317-340. Pour Num 27:1-11, cf. Johnson, *Sovereign Authority*, 217-265.

14 Westbrook, "Character," 59-60.

15 Gerhard von Rad, *Genesis*, 3rd ed. (London: John Knox Press, 1972), 415-416 y voit un acte de la volonté divine et non de la décision de Jacob.

cette initiative est étonnante et même inédite. La seconde curiosité réside dans le fait que la tromperie imaginée par Rébecca et accomplie par Jacob n'invalide pas la bénédiction donnée par Isaac. Or, l'erreur sur la personne, consécutive à une manipulation évidente, aurait dû conduire à l'annulation de sa décision.

C'est donc une situation doublement atypique qui est racontée ici, comme si les rédacteurs avaient voulu concilier les deux aspects de l'aînesse, à la fois droit d'Ésaü, puisqu'il peut le vendre, et choix d'Isaac puisqu'il peut l'attribuer au cadet, fût-ce sur un malentendu[16].

2 L'aînesse comme droit du premier-né

L'acte d'Ésaü est sans parallèle, non seulement dans la Bible mais encore dans l'ensemble de la documentation orientale antique. La description de la Genèse insiste sur la nature contractuelle de l'accord conclu entre les frères, en particulier à travers le serment que Jacob exige de son jumeau pour sceller la vente (Gen 25:31-33)[17]. Le prix, un modeste plat de lentilles, rappelle la petite somme d'argent parfois remise aux membres de la famille du vendeur mésopotamien pour qu'ils abandonnent leur droit de rachat[18]. Mais il n'est pas certain qu'Ésaü ait voulu céder ce droit, au vu du motif qu'il invoque pour justifier l'aliénation. L'expression emphatique "Je marche à la mort!" (Gen 25:32) peut dénoter la rudesse du personnage, plus préoccupé par l'appel de son estomac que par les intérêts supérieurs de son statut[19]. Mais on pourrait aussi la comprendre comme une référence à une période de disette, qui est toujours, au Proche-Orient ancien, un motif légitime de révision ou d'annulation des

16 La double dépossession d'Ésaü a été comprise comme un outil narratif permettant d'unifier un récit d'origine composite; cf. Jean-Pierre Sonnet, "L'analyse narrative des récits bibliques," in *Manuel d'exégèse de l'Ancien Testament*, ed. Michaela Bauks et Christophe Nihan, MdB 61 (Genève: Labor et Fides, 2008), 50-53.

17 Cf. Isaac Mendelsohn, "On the Preferential Status of the Eldest Son," *BASOR* 156 (1959): 39 n. 6; Richard Hiers, "Transfer of Property by Inheritance and Bequest in Biblical Law and Tradition," *Journal of Law and Religion* 10 (1993): 145.

18 Cette pratique est attestée dans les ventes archaïques de Fara (Ignace Gelb, Piotr Steinkeller, and Robert Whiting, *Earliest Land Tenure Systems in the Near East: Ancient Kudurrus*, OIP 104 [Chicago, IL: The Oriental Institute of the University of Chicago, 1991], 222-224) et les contrats paléo-babyloniens tardifs (Dominique Charpin, "Les formulaires des contrats de Mari à l'époque amorrite: Entre tradition babylonienne et innovation," in *Trois millénaires de formulaires juridiques*, ed. Sophie Démare-Lafont and André Lemaire, Hautes Études Orientales – Moyen et Proche-Orient 48 [Genève: Droz, 2010], 28-29).

19 Cf. par exemple Thomas Brodie, *Genesis as Dialogue: A Literary, Historical, and Theological Commentary* (Oxford: Oxford University Press, 2001), 300-301.

contrats conclus sous la contrainte[20]. Même si cette circonstance est mentionnée après (Gen 26:1 "Il y eut une famine dans le pays") et non pendant le récit de la vente, elle pourrait être à l'arrière-plan de l'épisode entier.

Ésaü aurait donc agi non pas pour assouvir son appétit féroce de chasseur mais sous la pression d'une crise frumentaire et dans l'espoir de récupérer plus tard le privilège vendu par nécessité. L'objectif du narrateur serait de montrer qu'il est licite, quoique moralement discutable, de disposer du droit d'aînesse dans un contexte de détresse. La cession effectuée par Ésaü représenterait ainsi une exception et non pas une règle, ce qui expliquerait son caractère isolé.

Un coup d'œil vers les partages successoraux d'époque paléo-babylonienne soutient cette conclusion[21]. L'aliénation par l'aîné de sa part préférentielle, s'il en a une, n'est jamais explicitement attestée. Il arrive que des compensations financières soient versées au moment de la division du patrimoine, mais elles visent à équilibrer les lots des héritiers en tenant compte de l'emplacement ou de la qualité des biens fonciers attribués. Elles ne sont donc pas toujours payées par le premier-né, et, lorsqu'il est possible de vérifier, ne correspondent pas à l'avantage qu'il a reçu.

Une question plus délicate est celle de la renonciation, qui est aussi une façon de disposer de la part préférentielle, à titre gratuit cette fois et non plus contre un prix. Les sources mésopotamiennes n'y font pas référence directement, mais certaines pratiques paléo-babyloniennes en sont peut-être des attestations implicites. Par exemple à Nippur, région où l'inégalité prédomine habituellement, il arrive que les descendants reçoivent des lots équivalents alors même que l'aîné est nommément indiqué[22]. Peut-être a-t-il renoncé à la coutume locale pour favoriser ses propres intérêts ou ceux de sa famille. À Ur, où la primogéniture est moins fréquente, un partage entre deux frères favorise aussi le plus âgé mais il doit payer un dédommagement au cadet pour compenser cet avantage[23]. Par le jeu des arrangements, les deux héritiers se retrouvent

---

20 Cf. Raymond Westbrook, "The Price Factor in the Redemption of Land," *RIDA* 32 (1985): 97-127 et Westbrook, "Social Justice and Creative Jurisprudence in Late Bronze Age Syria," *JESHO* 43 (2001): 22-43.

21 Je remercie Jules Jallet-Martini pour les informations qu'ils m'a communiquées, issues de sa thèse en cours sur le droit successoral au deuxième millénaire avant n.è.

22 Par exemple OECT 8 17 et 18 (Archibab T25328). Les partages égalitaires sans indication de l'aîné sont plus nombreux (par exemple TMH 10 18, 19 [Archibab T23289, T23290, T23314, T23319]; BE 6/2 44 [Archibab T10225]).

23 HE 316 et HE 317 (tablette et enveloppe; Archibab T17775). Ce document appartient à une archive de marchands d'Ur qui ont migré à Larsa, où il a peut-être été retrouvé (cf. Walter Farber, "Imgur-Sîn und seine beiden Söhne: Eine (nicht ganz) neue altbabylonische Erbteilungsurkunde aus Ur, gefunden wahrscheinlich in Larsa," in *Studies Presented to Robert*

quasiment à égalité, ce qui était probablement leur intention et laisse supposer que l'aîné a abandonné son privilège sans contrepartie financière apparente et sans le déclarer formellement.

Reste à comprendre la cause de telles renonciations. L'impérieuse nécessité de ne pas mourir de faim est assurément un motif recevable, qui n'est cependant attesté que dans le cas d'Ésaü, et de manière allusive. Une autre raison, peut-être plus répandue, tient à la lourdeur de la charge qui inclut la conduite des affaires familiales et cultuelles[24], et surtout une responsabilité à l'égard des dettes du défunt. Ce dernier point est mentionné dans un procès de Sippar au XVIIe s. avant n.è. où quatre frères sont assignés par une créancière de leur père. Trois d'entre eux refusent de payer et se tournent vers l'aîné en lui disant: "Ce n'est pas à nous de donner l'argent! C'est à toi que notre père a donné sa part, alors c'est à toi de payer l'argent."[25]

Un marqueur juridique de cette obligation réside dans la possession du ou des sceaux du père, habituellement remis à l'aîné. Lorsque celui-ci décède à son tour, c'est le cadet qui le(s) récupère et devient l'interlocuteur des créanciers comme le montre une autre tablette de Sippar concernant la famille d'un haut dignitaire militaire[26]. Ici, la primogéniture est clairement un caractère "naturel" lié à l'ordre de naissance plutôt qu'un droit, le plus jeune recevant la qualité juridique du plus âgé lorsqu'il meurt.

Dans le milieu des marchands paléo-assyriens, le passif de la succession est plutôt réglé selon un principe de solidarité entre les héritiers, qui permet aux fournisseurs et partenaires commerciaux de s'adresser à n'importe quel fils du défunt pour réclamer le paiement de la dette[27]. Mais il arrive qu'un héritier refuse cette solution, ce qui provoque des complications en chaîne illustrées

---

Biggs June 4, 2004, ed. Martha Roth, Walter Farber, Matthew W. Stolper, and Paula von Bechtolsheim, AS 27 [Chicago, IL: The Oriental Institute of the University of Chicago, 2007], 65-66). On observera que le texte utilise les expressions "grand frère" (ŠEŠ GU.LA l. 11) et "petit frère" (ŠEŠ TUR l. 24), à la place des formes habituelles "frère aîné" (ŠEŠ GAL) et "son frère" (ŠEŠ.A.NI). Ce choix terminologique insiste sur la primogéniture, donnée biologique, plutôt que sur l'aînesse, notion juridique.

24 Cf. par exemple l'expression "invoquer les morts et les dieux" dans certains testaments d'Emar (Karel van der Toorn, *Family Religion in Babylonia, Syria, and Israel: Continuity and Change in the Forms of Religious Life*, SHCANE 7 [Leiden: Brill, 1996], 55-58).

25 Di 1784 ll. 15′-18′; cf. Caroline Janssen, "Inanna-mansum et ses fils: Relation d'une succession turbulente dans les archives d'Ur-Utu," *RA* 86/1 (1992): 35-36. Ce texte appartient au dossier d'Ur-Utu, dont on reparlera plus loin.

26 Franz Van Koppen, "Redeeming a Father's Seal," in *Mining the Archives: Festschrift for Christopher Walker on the Occasion of His 60th Birthday*, ed. Cornelia Wunsch (Dresden: ISLET, 2002), 147-176.

27 Cf. par exemple ICK 1 12b, cité par *CAD* M 312a *māru*.

dans un petit dossier concernant un certain Ali-ahum[28]: en décidant de se dissocier de ses frères, il fait peser toute la charge du passif sur l'aîné ce qui donne lieu à une procédure judiciaire pour essayer de trouver une issue satisfaisante.

Au total, en l'état actuel des sources, l'existence d'un véritable droit au profit du premier fils n'est pas clairement établie. Ce sont plutôt des obligations qui lui incombent, dont le poids pourrait expliquer certaines renonciations implicites après la mort du père. Si donc Ésaü a cédé à Jacob une prérogative qui ne lui appartient pas, la vente n'a aucune valeur juridique et n'est pas opposable à Isaac. Il faut maintenant se demander si le chef de famille peut de son côté disposer de l'aînesse pour l'attribuer à l'un de ses enfants.

3 L'aînesse comme choix du chef de famille

Les informations sont ici plus nombreuses mais leur interprétation n'est pas toujours aisée. La désignation de l'aîné par le père est comprise tantôt comme un acte exceptionnel lié à des événements particuliers[29], tantôt au contraire comme un aspect ordinaire de l'exercice de l'autorité paternelle[30]. Parmi les exemples bibliques habituellement cités, ceux d'Abraham donnant tous ses biens à Isaac (Gen 25:5) et de Jacob destituant Ruben (Gen 49:3-4, 10) ne sont pas des expressions de l'arbitraire paternel puisque, comme on l'a vu, le choix d'Abraham se porte sur le fils de son épouse légitime et celui de Jacob sanctionne une faute. La préférence accordée à Ephraïm plutôt qu'à Manassé (Gen 48:8-20) ressemble en revanche à une décision discrétionnaire de Jacob. La complexité de ces situations tient souvent à un environnement familial qu'on dirait aujourd'hui "recomposé" et qui suscite des rivalités entre épouses et entre enfants de plusieurs lits.

Les sources paléo-babyloniennes montrent comment les parents tentent de prévenir ces conflits en redéfinissant le rang des héritiers lors d'une adoption ou d'un remariage. Certains contrats contiennent ainsi une clause garantissant à l'adopté qu'il conservera sa position à la tête de la fratrie, même si d'autres enfants viennent à naître[31]. Cette place lui permet d'accéder en priorité à un

---

28 Mogens T. Larsen, *Ankara Kültepe Tabletleri 6a: The Archive of the Šalim-Aššur Family, Vol. 1: The First Two Generations*, TTKY 6/33d-a. (Ankara: Türk Tarih Kurumu Basımevi, 2010), 229.

29 Davies, "Inheritance," 177.

30 Ephraim Neufeld, *Ancient Hebrew Marriage Laws* (London: Longmans, Green & Co, 1944), 261-262; Ze'ev Falk, "Testate Succession in Jewish Laws," *JJS* 12 (1961): 72-73.

31 Cf. par exemple VS 8 127 (Archibab T4658) ll. 9-12 (Sippar): "Bunene-abi et Hušutum

bien successoral très convoité: la fonction paternelle. Ce point est explicitement évoqué dans un document de Nippur[32] où une femme seule, sans doute veuve, confère à un homme la qualité d'aîné et la charge de prêtre-*nešakkum*, ainsi que les biens qui s'y rattachent. En échange, l'adopté s'engage à entretenir l'adoptante et à compenser ses frères (les enfants de l'adoptante) pour l'avantage qu'il a reçu. Quoique juridiquement, le texte s'apparente à une vente viagère, il se présente formellement comme une adoption[33], motivée par le fait que les autres enfants sont inaptes ou trop jeunes pour exercer le sacerdoce.

L'enjeu de telles stratégies est donc de modifier l'ordre naturel des descendants pour préserver le patrimoine familial. L'aînesse apparaît alors comme un statut que le chef de famille peut certes octroyer, mais sous certaines conditions et non pas de manière arbitraire.

Il existe pourtant deux contre-exemples dans lesquels sa volonté discrétionnaire semble à première vue reconnue. Le premier concerne Abraham, qui "donna tout ce qu'il possédait à Isaac" (Gen 25:5). Une telle expression paraît renvoyer à une forme de primogéniture accordant à l'aîné non pas un supplément de biens mais leur totalité[34]. Cette pratique, attestée en Égypte ancienne[35], revient à faire du premier-né (ou décidé tel) le "seul-né,"[36] qui recueille toute la succession et pourvoit aux besoins de sa mère et de ses frères et sœurs[37]. Une telle conception de l'hérédité repose sur l'indivision du patrimoine, géré par l'aîné en remplacement du père défunt jusqu'à ce que les descendants décident de se séparer. L'objectif est de prolonger le plus longtemps possible la copropriété familiale, ce qui correspond bien à l'esprit des sociétés orientales antiques.

---

auraient-ils dix fils, c'est Shamash-apili qui est leur frère aîné." La formule inverse est attestée dans certains textes d'époque postérieure (Nuzi, Assur).

32 TMH 10 2 (Archibab T523253).

33 Ce type de contrat est bien connu à Nuzi; cf. Brigitte Lion, "Les adoptions d'hommes à Nuzi (XIVe s. av. J.-C.)," *Revue historique de droit français et étranger* 82/4 (2004): 537-576 et Josué Justel, "Verkaufsadoption," *RlA* 14 (2016): 549-550.

34 Andreas Eherharter, *Das Ehe- und Familienrecht der Hebräer mit Rücksicht auf die ethnologische Forschung*, ATA 5/1-2 (Münster: Aschendorff, 1914), 180; Ze'ev Falk, *Hebrew Law in Biblical Times: An Introduction* (Jerusalem: Wahrmann Books, 1964), 165-166.

35 Sandra Lippert, *Einführung in die altägyptische Rechtsgeschichte*, 2nd ed., Einführung und Quellentexte zur Ägyptologie 5 (Berlin: LIT Verlag, 2012), 16-17.

36 Pour reprendre une expression de Ralph E. Giesey, *The Juristic Basis of Dynastic Right to the French Throne*, TAPS 51/5 (Philadelphia, PA: American Philosophical Society, 1961), 8-9 à propos de la succession au trône dans l'ancien droit français.

37 C'est avec ce sens de "fils unique" que l'Église catholique interprète la référence à Jésus comme "fils premier-né" (Luke 2:7).

Mais Abraham peut-il vraiment donner tout son patrimoine à un seul enfant? Il a été observé à juste titre qu'Isaac n'est pas le seul héritier puisque ses demi-frères, issus de concubines, reçoivent eux aussi une gratification avant d'être envoyés vers l'orient (Gen 25:6). Isaac est dès lors dans la position d'un légataire universel, récupérant tout ce qui reste après la distribution des legs particuliers aux enfants des concubines[38], ce qui inclut non seulement les actifs mais aussi les dettes éventuelles. Juridiquement, l'acte d'Abraham tient à la fois du testament et de la donation: il réserve à Isaac l'essentiel de ce qu'il possède et remet de son vivant aux autres fils des biens spécifiques grâce auxquels ils peuvent aller s'établir ailleurs[39]. En dépit de sa formulation large, Gen 25:5 ne reflète donc pas la capacité du chef de famille à déshériter complètement ses enfants mais lui permet seulement de désigner un aîné en le faisant légataire universel, qu'il soit ou non le plus âgé.

Une situation très similaire est décrite dans une tablette paléo-babylonienne tirée des archives d'Ur-Utu, Grand Lamentateur de la déesse Annunitum de Sippar. Dans cette lettre sans adresse[40], il reconstitue l'histoire de ses démêlés avec ses trois frères à propos de la succession de leur père Inanna-mansum.

Celui-ci refuse de transmettre sa charge de son vivant, ce que rappelle le début du texte: "Comme mon seigneur le sait, Inanna-mansum notre père refusa de son vivant de partager la part."[41] Du point de vue d'Ur-Utu, la fonction paternelle est une part successorale, celle qui est manifestement au centre des querelles, et qui inclut une maison et les objets qui s'y trouvent. Sous la pression de l'un de ses fils, Inanna-mansum finit par désigner Ur-Utu pour succéder à sa fonction après sa mort: "À eux (les trois autres fils) je ne laisserai pas la part. Ur-Utu est mon fils, celui qui de moi a reçu mon sceptre. C'est à

---

38 En ce sens, Reuven Yaron, *Gifts in Contemplation of Death in Jewish and Roman law* (Oxford: Clarendon Press, 1960), 4-5.

39 Le droit français connaît ce type de répartition mixte du patrimoine sous le nom de donation-partage (art. 1076ss Code civil).

40 Di 1194 (Archibab T22209); cf. l'*editio princeps* de Janssen, "Inanna-mansum" et les études de Luc Dekiere, "La généalogie d'Ur-Utu, gala-mah à Sippar-Amnânum," in *Cinquante-deux réflexions sur le Proche-Orient ancien offertes en hommage à Léon De Meyer*, ed. Herman Gasche, Michel Tanret, Caroline Janssen, and Ann Degraeve, MHEO 2 (Leuven: Peeters, 1994), 125-141; Lucile Barberon, "Quand la mère est une religieuse: Le cas d'Ilša-hegalli d'après les archives d'Ur-Utu," *NABU* (2005/4): 12-13 no. 89; Michel Tanret, "Learned, Rich, Famous, and Unhappy: Ur-Utu of Sippar," in *The Oxford Handbook of Cuneiform Culture*, ed. Karen Radner and Eleanor Robson (Oxford: Oxford University Press, 2011), 270-287; Lucile Barberon, *Les religieuses et le culte de Marduk dans le royaume de Babylone*, Archibab 1, Mémoires de NABU 14 (Paris: SEPOA, 2012), 226-227.

41 Di 1194 ll. 1-3 *ki-ma be-lí i-du-ú*, ^{Id}INANNA.MA.AN.SUM *a-bu-ni i-na ba-al-ṭú-ti-šu, a-na* ḪA.LA *za-zi-im ú-ul im-gu-ur*.

lui que je donnerai tout."[42] Cette déclaration, comme celle d'Abraham, paraît exclure tous les autres descendants masculins, ce que la suite de la lettre et le reste du dossier contredisent puisqu'un partage a bien eu lieu après la mort d'Inanna-mansum, déclenchant un âpre conflit familial[43]. En réalité, personne n'est déshérité; seul le choix du père est remis en question par les fils évincés, dont l'attitude est d'ailleurs empreinte d'une certaine mauvaise foi: ils tentent en effet de priver Ur-Utu de sa part préférentielle par diverses manœuvres[44] mais s'empressent aussi de lui rappeler que, en tant qu'aîné, il doit payer seul les dettes paternelles[45].

On observera au passage que Sippar est une ville de coutume égalitaire, ce qui pourrait expliquer la résistance des enfants face à la volonté de leur père de recourir au principe de l'aînesse. Il est difficile de savoir sur quel critère repose la décision d'Inanna-mansum. La stérilité statutaire de son épouse le conduit à adopter ou à recourir à des concubines pour trois de ses fils[46] mais rien n'est dit sur l'origine et le rang du quatrième, Ur-Utu[47]. La compétition entre eux laisse supposer que le père n'a pas suivi la chronologie des arrivées dans la famille, préférant tenir compte des capacités ou des compétences de chacun. Ur-Utu est ainsi un aîné "fait" et non pas "né." En recevant le sceptre, il accède non seulement à la fonction paternelle[48] mais aussi à la tête de la fratrie. De la même manière, après la faute de Ruben, Jacob remet le sceptre à Juda (Gen 49:10), ce qui lui donne une position de leader incontesté dans la famille (Gen 49:8) alors même qu'il est le quatrième dans l'ordre des naissances et que Ruben reste le premier-né (*bəkôr* Gen 49:3).

L'expression "donner tout" utilisée par Abraham et Inanna-mansum renvoie donc au caractère indivisible de l'aînesse. La distribuer entre plusieurs détenteurs risquerait de fragiliser la cohésion de la famille et de ses biens. Le père

---

42 ll. 16-17 ḪA.LA *ú-ul a-za-ás-su-nu-ši-im* ⌜UR.^{d}UTU⌝ *ma-ri, ša ḫa-aṭ-ṭi im-ḫu-ra-an-ni šu-*⌜*ú*⌝*-ma ú-ga-am-ma-ar*.

43 Janssen, "Inanna-mansum," 34, 39; Tanret, "Learned," 273-274.

44 Cf. Janssen, "Inanna-mansum," 36-39.

45 Di 1784 ll. 15′-18′ : "Ce n'est pas à nous de donner l'argent! C'est à toi que notre père a donné sa part, alors c'est à toi de payer l'argent." Cf. *supra* n. 25.

46 Barberon, "Quand la mère," et *Religieuses*, 226-227; Tanret, "Learned," 273.

47 Tanret, "Learned," 273 pense qu'il est l'aîné; Barberon, *Religieuses*, 227 suggère plutôt qu'il a été adopté lui aussi.

48 Janssen, "Inanna-mansum," 36. Inversement, "briser le sceptre" revient à interrompre la continuité du lignage ou de la dynastie, comme le montrent les occurrences mésopotamiennes de cette expression; cf. Dominique Charpin, "Le sceptre de l'héritier," *NABU* (1994/1) : 8 no. 8, à quoi on ajoutera la malédiction de l'épilogue du Code de Hammurabi contre celui qui porterait atteinte à la stèle, dont le sceptre sera brisé par le grand dieu Anu (xlix 50-51).

peut ainsi choisir l'aîné, mais ses motifs ne peuvent être totalement arbitraires même s'ils sont susceptibles d'être contestés après sa mort.

4 Aînesse et tromperie

Un dernier point attire l'attention dans le récit de Jacob et Ésaü. Il porte sur la validité de la bénédiction d'Isaac, accordée à la suite d'une manipulation (Gen 27:1-40). Sentant sa mort venir, Isaac demande à Ésaü, son "fils aîné" (Gen 27:1) de lui rapporter du gibier pour préparer son dernier repas. Profitant de l'absence de son frère, et sur les instances de Rébecca, Jacob se fait passer pour Ésaü et apporte à son père les plats cuisinés par sa mère. La tromperie fonctionne, malgré les doutes d'Isaac qui s'étonne du retour si rapide d'Ésaü et ne reconnaît pas sa voix (Gen 27:20, 22), mais finit quand même par bénir celui qu'il croit être son premier-né. Le contrat antérieur entre les deux frères n'a donc pas réalisé le transfert de l'aînesse sur Jacob, qui doit recevoir le privilège directement de son père. Curieusement, le mensonge, facilité par la cécité et le grand âge d'Isaac, n'est pas un motif recevable d'annulation de la décision (Gen 27:37). Accorder la même bénédiction une seconde fois, comme le demande Ésaü (Gen 27:38), reviendrait à partager l'aînesse, qui justement est indivisible comme on vient de le voir.

L'argument de l'altération de la volonté est rarement évoqué dans les sources juridiques du Proche-Orient ancien[49], et il est d'autant plus intéressant de le trouver au centre d'un litige successoral de Mari récemment publié. Il s'agit d'une lettre[50] dans laquelle le gouverneur Sumu-Hadu rend compte à Zimri-Lim de l'avancement du dossier judiciaire que le roi lui a confié et qui oppose les frères d'un certain Rip'i-lim à ses descendants. Sumu-Hadu a fait venir l'emblème d'Itur-Mer pour que les demandeurs fassent leur déclaration sous serment. Malgré les lacunes du texte et le caractère parfois elliptique des

---

49 Il est visé indirectement dans les malédictions des traités d'alliance ou des codes de lois, contre celui qui violerait son propre engagement en faisant agir un tiers pour échapper au châtiment divin. Cf. par exemple l'épilogue du Code de Hammurabi xlix 36-38 *aššum errētim šināti šaniamma uštāḫiz* "par peur de ces malédictions, il fait faire par un autre." Il a été suggéré également que l'expression *ina bulṭišu*, littéralement "de son vivant," qui figure dans certains testaments d'Emar, signifie "sain de corps et d'esprit" (Daniel Arnaud, *Recherches au Pays d'Aštata*, Emar VI/3 [Paris: ERC, 1986], 23 no. 15 et *passim*) et renvoie ainsi au plein discernement du testateur.

50 ARM 33 98 (Archibab T23790), publié par Jean-Marie Durand, *Les premières années du roi Zimrî-Lîm de Mari: Première partie*, ARM 33 (Boston, MA/Leuven/Paris: Peeters, 2019).

propos des parties, on peut reconstituer les étapes de l'histoire familiale et les enjeux du conflit de la manière suivante.

Dagan-teri se marie une première fois et donne naissance à Abierah, dont la filiation légitime est établie[51]. Elle est ensuite abandonnée par son mari pendant dix ans, au cours desquels deux autres fils voient le jour, Ushtashni-el et Dagan-pilah, qui sont dits "enfantés pour la rue,"[52] c'est-à-dire hors mariage. À son retour, le mari reprend chez lui sa femme et son fils et accueille les deux autres garçons[53]. On ignore combien de temps dure cette situation, qui prend fin vraisemblablement avec le veuvage de Dagan-teri ou sa répudiation. Elle revient alors "dans sa maison (à elle),"[54] c'est-à-dire dans sa propre famille, et épouse Rip'i-lim qui vient manifestement habiter chez elle. Ces deux éléments ne sont pas explicitement indiqués mais doivent être présumés pour la cohérence du récit. Les secondes noces et la cohabitation au domicile de la femme étaient certainement fréquentes mais sont peu traitées par le droit[55], qui n'y attache pas l'importance reconnue à la première union. C'est dans le cadre de cette seconde union que Dagan-teri accouche de Samsera et Ummi-Nikkal "pour la deuxième fois,"[56] une formulation qui fait écho à la naissance d'Abierah, le premier fils. Rip'i-lim est donc le second mari et le père de Samsera et Ummi-Nikkal.

Au total, Dagan-teri a eu cinq enfants, dont deux hors mariage: Ushtashni-el et Dagan-pilah. Elle craint qu'ils ne soient vendus comme esclaves (ll. 29-32), peut-être parce qu'elle-même était en servitude temporaire lorsqu'ils sont nés. Pour garantir leur intégration dans son nouveau ménage, elle demande à Rip'i-lim de les adopter et d'attribuer à Abierah, le plus âgé de toute la fratrie, le

51 L. 14 *a-na mu-ti-ša pa-né-em ú-li-id* "elle a enfanté (Abierah) pour son premier mari/pour son mari en premier." Quelle que soit la traduction, la phrase souligne que l'enfant est né dans le mariage.

52 L. 17 *a-na sú-qí-im ú-⟨li⟩-id*. Dagan-teri n'est pas considérée comme adultère car la longue absence de son conjoint et le manque de ressources laissent présumer la dissolution du mariage. Cf. Code de Hammurabi § 134.

53 Le droit babylonien autorise le mari à reprendre son épouse lorsqu'il s'est absenté pour un motif légitime (obligation de service, captivité; cf. § 29 Lois d'Eshnunna). Les enfants nés d'un second lit suivent leur père (§ 135 Code de Hammurabi; § 45 tabl. A Lois assyriennes), lorsqu'il peut être identifié, ce qui n'est pas le cas ici. Sur l'absence en droit mésopotamien, cf. Sophie Démare-Lafont, "L'absence dans les droits cunéiformes," in *Le monde de l'itinérance en Méditerranée, de l'Antiquité à l'époque moderne: Procédures de contrôle et d'identification*, ed. Claudia Moatti, Wolfgang Kaiser, and Christophe Pébarthe, Etudes 22 (Pessac: Ausonius Editions, 2009), 275-305.

54 L. 23 [*i*]*š-tu a-na* É-*ša i-tu-ru* "depuis qu'elle est revenue dans sa (fém.) maison."

55 Cf. par exemple §§ 28 et 35 tabl. A des Lois assyriennes.

56 L. 26 2-⌜*šu*⌝ *ú*-[*li*]-*id*.

statut d'aîné. Rip'i-lim fait une déclaration solennelle en ce sens et établit un document scellé (ll. 35-40).

Il est rare que la décision d'un chef de famille soit attaquée en justice de son vivant, c'est pourquoi le litige a dû survenir après le décès de Rip'i-lim. Les demandeurs invoquent l'absence de discernement du mari défunt, qui aurait été victime d'une épouse manipulatrice et enjôleuse. Le texte utilise le terme *suppûm* (l. 35) qui désigne la "prière" mais aussi la "séduction."[57] En incluant les trois enfants de sa femme parmi ses héritiers et en réservant l'aînesse au plus âgé, Rip'i-lim aurait cédé aux manœuvres malhonnêtes de Dagan-teri. À force de suppliques et de cajoleries, elle aurait réussi à influencer la volonté d'un mari qu'on suppose aveuglé par l'amour ou la sénilité. Soucieux de garder les biens familiaux dans leur lignage, les frères de Rip'i-lim tentent donc de faire annuler ce qu'ils considèrent comme un abus de confiance. Il est malheureux que la lacune du texte nous empêche de connaître la suite de l'affaire. La lettre s'achève par une mise en garde concernant l'envoi des témoins au roi, qui pourrait se révéler difficile pour certains d'entre eux. Sumu-hadu demande peut-être de cette manière détournée l'autorisation de rendre la sentence lui-même.

Si le dol est incertain dans l'affaire de Ri'pi-lim, il est clairement avéré dans l'histoire d'Isaac, qui accorde sa bénédiction par erreur à Jacob. Que se serait-il passé si Ésaü, au lieu de vouloir tuer Jacob, était allé trouver les juges en invoquant l'indisponibilité du droit d'aînesse et l'erreur sur la personne? Les récits des patriarches n'envisagent pas ce genre d'issue judiciaire pour régler les conflits familiaux, qui relèvent plutôt de la vengeance personnelle. Tel est bien le projet d'Ésaü, qui attend la mort de son père pour agir et donne ainsi à Jacob l'occasion de s'enfuir. La séparation des deux frères rétablit une forme d'équilibre, chacun pouvant se considérer comme l'aîné ou le "seul-né," ce qui ouvre la voie à la réconciliation finale.

Bibliographie

Arnaud, Daniel. *Recherches au Pays d'Aštata*. Emar VI/3. Paris: ERC, 1986.

Barberon, Lucile. "Quand la mère est une religieuse: Le cas d'Ilša-hegalli d'après les archives d'Ur-Utu." *NABU* (2005/4): 12-13 no. 89.

57 Antoine Cavigneaux, "Prier et séduire," in *Dans le laboratoire de l'historien des religions: Mélanges offerts à Philippe Borgeaud*, ed. Francesca Prescendi and Youri Volokhine, Religions en perspective 24 (Genève: Labor et fides, 2011), 496-503.

Barberon, Lucile. *Les religieuses et le culte de Marduk dans le royaume de Babylone*. Archibab 1. Mémoires de NABU 14. Paris: SEPOA, 2012.

Bonechi, Marco. "Of Cucumbers and Twins in the Ebla Palace G Texts." Pages 91-107 in *A Oriente del Delta: Scritti sul'Egitto ed il Vicino Oriente antico in onore di Gabriella Scandone Matthiae*. Edited by Agnese Vacca, Sara Pizzimenti, and Maria Gabriella Micale. Contributi e Materiali di Archeologia orientale 18. Roma: Scienze e Lettere, 2018.

Brin, Gershon. *Studies in Biblical Law from the Hebrew Bible to the Dead Sea Scrolls*. JSOTSup 176. Sheffield: Sheffield Academic Press, 1994.

Brodie, Thomas L. *Genesis as Dialogue: A Literary, Historical, and Theological Commentary*. Oxford: Oxford University Press, 2001.

Boyer, Pierre-Louis. "Primogéniture et gémellité: Le droit d'aînesse dans son ordre naturel." *Revue historique de droit français et étranger* 89/4 (2011): 515-541.

Cavigneaux, Antoine. "Prier et séduire." Pages 496-503 in *Dans le laboratoire de l'historien des religions: Mélanges offerts à Philippe Borgeaud*. Edited by Francesca Prescendi and Youri Volokhine. Religions en perspective 24. Genève: Labor et fides, 2011.

Charpin, Dominique. "Le sceptre de l'héritier." *NABU* (1994/1): 8 no. 8.

Charpin, Dominique. "Les formulaires des contrats de Mari à l'époque amorrite: Entre tradition babylonienne et innovation." Pages 13-42 in *Trois millénaires de formulaires juridiques*. Edited by Sophie Démare-Lafont and André Lemaire. Hautes Études Orientales – Moyen et Proche-Orient 48. Genève: Droz, 2010.

Chavalas, Mark W. "Assyriology and Biblical Studies: A Century and a Half of Tension." Pages 21-67 in *Mesopotamia and the Bible: Comparative Explorations*. Edited by Mark W. Chavalas and K. Lawson Younger, Jr. JSOTSup 341. New York, NY/London: Sheffield Academic Press, 2002.

Davies, Eryl W. "The Inheritance of the First-Born in Israel and the Ancient Near East." *JSS* 38/2 (1993): 175-191.

Dekiere, Luc. "La généalogie d'Ur-Utu, gala-mah à Sippar-Amnânum." Pages 125-141 in *Cinquante-deux réflexions sur le Proche-Orient ancien offertes en hommage à Léon De Meyer*. Edited by Herman Gasche, Michel Tanret, Caroline Janssen, and Ann Degraeve. MHEO 2. Leuven: Peeters, 1994.

Démare-Lafont, Sophie. "L'absence dans les droits cunéiformes." Pages 275-305 in *Le monde de l'itinérance en Méditerranée, de l'Antiquité à l'époque moderne: Procédures de contrôle et d'identification*. Edited by Claudia Moatti, Wolfgang Kaiser, and Christophe Pébarthe. Etudes 22. Pessac: Ausonius Editions, 2009.

Durand, Jean-Marie. *Les premières années du roi Zimrî-Lîm de Mari: Première partie*. ARM 33. Boston, MA/Leuven/Paris: Peeters, 2019.

Eherharter, Andreas. *Das Ehe- und Familienrecht der Hebräer mit Rücksicht auf die ethnologische Forschung*. ATA 5/1-2. Münster: Aschendorff, 1914.

Falk, Ze'ev W. "Testate Succession in Jewish Laws." *JJS* 12 (1961): 67-77.

Falk, Ze'ev W. *Hebrew Law in Biblical Times: An Introduction*. Jerusalem: Wahrmann Books, 1964.

Farber, Walter. "Imgur-Sîn und seine beiden Söhne: Eine (nicht ganz) neue altbabylonische Erbteilungsurkunde aus Ur, gefunden wahrscheinlich in Larsa." Pages 65-79 in *Studies Presented to Robert Biggs June 4, 2004*. Edited by Martha Roth, Walter Farber, Matthew W. Stolper, and Paula von Bechtolsheim. AS 27. Chicago, IL: The Oriental Institute of the University of Chicago, 2007.

Gelb, Ignace J., Piotr Steinkeller, and Robert M. Whiting. *Earliest Land Tenure Systems in the Near East: Ancient Kudurrus*. OIP 104. Chicago, IL: The Oriental Institute of the University of Chicago, 1991.

Giesey, Ralph E. *The Juristic Basis of Dynastic Right to the French Throne*. TAPS 51/5. Philadelphia, PA: American Philosophical Society, 1961.

Greenberg, Moshe. "Some Postulates of Biblical Criminal Law." Pages 5-28 in *Studies in Bible and Jewish Religion: Yehezkel Kaufmann Jubilee Volume*. Edited by Menahem Haran. Jerusalem: Magnes Press, 1960.

Greenberg, Moshe. "More Reflections on Biblical Criminal Law." Pages 1-17 in *Studies in Bible*. Edited by Sara Japhet. Scripta Hierosolymitana 31. Jerusalem: Magnes Press, 1986.

Hensel, Benedikt, ed. *The History of the Jacob Cycle* (*Genesis 25-35*). Archaeology and Bible 4. Tübingen: Mohr Siebeck, 2021.

Hiers, Richard H. "Transfer of Property by Inheritance and Bequest in Biblical Law and Tradition." *Journal of Law and Religion* 10 (1993): 121-155.

Janssen, Caroline. "Inanna-mansum et ses fils: Relation d'une succession turbulent dans les archives d'Ur-Utu." *RA* 86/1 (1992): 19-52.

Johnson, Dylan R. *Sovereign Authority and the Elaboration of Law in the Bible and the Ancient Near East*. FAT 2/122. Tübingen: Mohr Siebeck, 2020.

Justel, Josué. "Verkaufsadoption." *RlA* 14 (2016): 549-550.

Kim, Kyu Seop. *The Firstborn Son in Ancient Judaism and Early Christianity: A Study of Primogeniture and Christology*. BibInt 171. Leiden/Boston: Brill, 2019.

Klíma, Josef. "La position économique, sociale et juridique de l'enfant d'après les sources cunéiformes de Mari." *ArOr* 42 (1974): 232-244.

Larsen, Mogens T. *Ankara Kültepe Tabletleri 6a: The Archive of the Šalim-Aššur Family, Vol. 1: The First Two Generations*. TTKY 6/33d-a. Ankara: Türk Tarih Kurumu Basimevi, 2010.

Leichty, Erle. *The Omen Series* šumma izbu. TCS 4. Locust Valley/New York, NY: J.J. Augustin, 1970.

Lion, Brigitte. "Les adoptions d'hommes à Nuzi (XIVe s. av. J.-C.)." *Revue historique de droit français et étranger* 82/4 (2004): 537-576.

Lippert, Sandra. *Einführung in die altägyptische Rechtsgeschichte: Einführung und Quellentexte zur Ägyptologie 5*. 2nd ed. Berlin: LIT Verlag, 2012.

Mendelsohn, I. "On the Preferential Status of the Eldest Son." *BASOR* 156 (1959): 38-40.

Neufeld, Ephraim. *Ancient Hebrew Marriage Laws*. London: Longmans, Green & Co, 1944.

Rad, Gerhard von. *Genesis*. 3rd ed. London: John Knox Press, 1972.

Rede, Marcelo. "Famille et transmission du patrimoine à Larsa: Une approche anthropologique." Pages 317-340 in *La famille dans le Proche-Orient ancien: Réalités, symbolismes et images. Proceedings of the 55th Rencontre Assyriologique Internationale, Paris 6-9 July 2009*. Edited by Lionel Marti. Winona Lake, IN: Eisenbrauns, 2014.

Scurlock, JoAnn. *Sourcebook for Ancient Mesopotamian Medicine*. WAW 36. Atlanta, GA: SBL Press, 2014.

Sonnet, Jean-Pierre. "L'analyse narrative des récits bibliques." Pages 49-94 in *Manuel d'exégèse de l'Ancien Testament*. Edited by Michaela Bauks and Christophe Nihan. MdB 61. Genève: Labor et Fides, 2008.

Tanret, Michel. "Learned, Rich, Famous, and Unhappy: Ur-Utu of Sippar." Pages 270-287 in *The Oxford Handbook of Cuneiform Culture*. Edited by Karen Radner and Eleanor Robson. Oxford: Oxford University Press, 2011.

Van der Toorn, Karel. *Family Religion in Babylonia, Syria, and Israel: Continuity and Change in the Forms of Religious Life*. SHCANE 7. Leiden: Brill, 1996.

Van Koppen, Franz. "Redeeming a Father's Seal." Pages 147-176 in *Mining the Archives: Festschrift for Christopher Walker on the Occasion of His 60th Birthday*. Edited by Cornelia Wunsch. Dresden: ISLET, 2002.

Vaux, Roland de. *Les institutions de l'Ancien Testament, Vol. 1: Le nomadisme et ses survivances, institutions familiales, institutions civiles*. Paris: Le Cerf, 1958.

Westbrook, Raymond. "The Price Factor in the Redemption of Land." *RIDA* 32 (1985): 97-127.

Westbrook, Raymond. "Biblical and Cuneiform Law Codes." *RB* 92 (1985): 247-265.

Westbrook, Raymond. "Cuneiform Law Codes and the Origins of Legislation." *ZA* 79 (1989): 201-222.

Westbrook, Raymond. "Social Justice and Creative Jurisprudence in Late Bronze Age Syria." *JESHO* 43 (2001): 22-43.

Westbrook, Raymond. "The Character of Ancient Near Eastern Law." Pages 1-90 in *A History of Ancient Near Eastern Law*. Edited by Raymond Westbrook. HdO 72/1. Boston, MA/Leiden: Brill, 2003.

Yaron, Reuven. *Gifts in Contemplation of Death in Jewish and Roman Law*. Oxford: Clarendon Press, 1960.

Ziegler, Nele. "Les enfants du palais." *Ktèma* 22 (1997): 45-57.

Ziegler, Nele. "Jumelles d'Admatum." *NABU* (1999/3): 73 no. 73.

6

The Southwest of the Near East According to Mari: The Example of Qaṭna

Jean-Marie Durand

The interest (and disadvantage) of Mari's documents is that they are totally unique.[1] Generally written in grammatically correct Akkadian—accounting for what must be considered simple misspellings—these texts were nonetheless produced by people who were not native Akkadian speakers. At best, they practiced a type of diglossia that mediated between Akkadian and their own Semitic dialect. In any case, these scribes had an undeniable propensity to "Akkadianize" their writings as much as possible, which is apparent not only with proper names,[2] but also with place names.[3]

Above all, Mariote scribes speak of events that have no overlaps in the documentation of other sites, while simultaneously providing important information on places that are otherwise documented only in later periods. For example, Georges Dossin wrote numerous interesting articles on references to several western Near Eastern sites in the Mari archives, including Aleppo, Qaṭna, and Ugarit—not to mention the biblical land of Canaan—that previously were known only from texts dating to much later periods.[4] Today, with the continuation of archaeological excavations at the site of Mari (Tell Hariri), numerous tells have been gradually identified with sites mentioned in the Mari texts. Usually, these sites are either older (third millennium BCE) or later (middle of the second millennium BCE) than the best-attested period of the royal

1 I thank the editors of this volume for correcting the English of this contribution.

2 One of the most obvious cases is "Bunu-Eshtar" versus "Bina-Eshtar" (Binashtar).

3 Ilum-malik is also known as Ilum-muluk, but in ARM 35 (A.3857) Maggabum is found instead of the toponym Na(g)gibum, thus revealing the true name of the place.

4 Georges Dossin, "Aplaḫanda, roi de Carkémiš," *RA* 35 (1938): 115–121; Dossin, "Iamḫad et Qatanum," *RA* 36 (1939): 46–54; Dossin, "Message d'Hammurapi, roi d'Alep," in *Ugaritica I: Etudes relatives aux découvertes de Ras Shamra*, ed. Claude F.-A. Schaeffer et al., MRS 3 (Paris: Librairie Orientaliste Paul Guethner, 1939), 16–17; Dossin, "Une mention de Hattuša dans une lettre de Mari," *RHA* 5 (1939): 69–76; Dossin, "Le royaume d'Alep au XVIIIe siècle avant notre ère," *BARB* 38 (1952): 229–239; Dossin, "Le royaume de Qatna au XVIIIe siècle avant notre ère," *BARB* 40 (1954): 417–425; Dossin, "Kengen, pays de Canaan," *RSO* 32 (1957): 35–39.

 | DOI:10.1163/9789004511538_007

archives of Mari during the reign of Zimri-Lim. These sites include, for example, important cities such as Urkish (Tell Mozan) and Mardaman (Bassetki). Meanwhile, although excavations at the site of Tell Mohammed-Diyab (most probably ancient Azamhul) produced a splendid text from the Middle Assyrian period, the eponym was unknown.

Documentation from the kingdoms of Mari's vassals (when it exists) also provides scarce evidence about the reign of Zimri-Lim, including Terqa (Tell Ašhara), which includes evidence dating to Zimri-Lim's reign yet does not speak of international affairs, as well as evidence that comes from a more recent period (the Ḫana period). The epigraphic finds of Tell Bi'a (ancient Tuttul), in turn, date earlier than Zimri-Lim's reign. In the Upper Jezirah, the well-documented sites contemporary with the Mari archives, such as Shubat-Enlil (Tell Mozan) or Ashnakkum (Chagar-Bazar), have not yielded texts connected to or documenting his reign, though many still remain unpublished.

Letters of Zimri-Lim have been found at Tell Rimah (ancient Qaṭṭara), though this remains the exception.[5] To the west and north of Mari, excavations of the great urban centers of Ebla, Aleppo, Ugarit, Qaṭna, Hazor, and Carchemish have only yielded written documentation subsequent to the Mari period. On the eastern side, excavations of the great metropolises of Babylon, Eshnunna, and Larsa have produced no state archives with information that could overlap with what is known from Mari. The documentation found in his capital at Mari is, for the moment, the only witness to the reign of Zimri-Lim. This material offers a remarkably rich picture of events that are supposed to have occurred during his reign, but unfortunately without corroboration from other historical sources. Hopefully, when archaeological excavations reach the Old Babylonian levels of sites on the Balih river or in Syria in general, archaeologists will uncover the great urban centers of Ṭûr-'Abdîn and the region of Sindjar, which may help fill out the picture of Mari during Zimri-Lim's reign. Undoubtedly, our understanding of the "metropolis of the Middle Euphrates" will then require readjustment.

What complicates the historical approach to this period, apart from the uniqueness of the documentation, is the fact that the servants of Hammurabi of Babylon had the opportunity to read the Mari archives and remove any texts that concerned diplomatic relations between Mari and Babylon, leaving only those tablets that concerned the internal administration of the kingdom and

5 See Dominique Charpin and Jean-Marie Durand, "Le nom antique de Tell Rīmah," *RA* 81 (1987): 125–146.

some vassals in the north. Thus, missing are not only the letters sent by the Mari chancellery, but also the responses or initiatives of the most important rulers of the time. In this way, a great deal of critically important information on international relations during the Old Babylonian period was concealed and remains so today. While the governors' letters provide information on the management of the palace stocks or on legal actions, they are obscure in their details and difficult to locate chronologically.

Rediscovering these hidden events is an essential undertaking for the historian today, which is only possible by interpreting the surviving documents. Indeed, these documents occasionally refer to events that must have made the headlines in their time, but which nowadays often appear only as fleeting allusions.[6] So here, in honor of a scholar who was able to link the documents from the banks of the Euphrates to those found in the west, I would like to address the western site of Qaṭna—an important monarchy of its time—from the perspective of the Mari archives. The Mari archives are at present the only source concerning this important metropolis, which has as of yet only yielded Middle Babylonian documentation.

Despite the vast desert of Palmyra between them, Qaṭna had contact with the regions in the east in general, and with the banks of the Euphrates in particular. Even if one can suppose that Qaṭna normally looked westward through the "Gap of Homs," and that the Orontes valley was its natural access to the northern regions, several roads linked it to the east. Thus, the great king of Ekallatum, Samsi-Addu, spoke of the three roads leading to Qaṭna from the Middle Euphrates:[7]

– ARM 5 15 (LAPO 17.722) envisaged Mari's sheep, as well as those of the Bedouins, taken to the rich pastures controlled by Qaṭna. This assumes that there were enough watering wells on the route to provide regular water for the flocks.
– A letter from the minister of Carchemish, ARM 26 530, attests to direct links between Qaṭna and Carchemish; according to this letter, the merchant Nabi-Sîn proposed to go to Qaṭna to administer an oath about a sum of money due to him. This merchant planned to travel down the Euphrates to Abattum (Tell Thadayin), where one of the three routes to Qaṭna opens out, without having to take the Orontes valley, which would have meant making a long diversion via Aleppo.

---

6 Thus in ARM 26/2 452, the allusion to the fact that it was the emperor of Elam who gave Ḫît to Mari. See the commentary in ARM 34 (not yet published) in this regard.

7 See Jean-Marie Durand, "Documents pour l'histoire du royaume de Haute-Mésopotamie, I/C, les trois routes de l'Euphrate à Qatna à travers le désert," *MARI* 5 (1987): 159–167.

- Išhî-Addu, king of Qaṭna, believed his daughter, queen of Mari, could return home to honor her gods, which implies that the trip could be made safely, if not comfortably. In making this trip, the queen of Mari likely returned along the same route that had once led her to her husband, for it is unlikely that she would have passed through Aleppo, which was then in conflict with her father-in-law, Samsi-Addu. Once she became the wife of Zimri-Lim, she must have taken this route again in a palanquin (*nubalum*).[8]

Going to Qatna was not the same extraordinary feat as that which required Samsi-Addu to send his armies into the west.[9] This route toward the west had already been taken by Yaḫdun-Lim, when he had pursued his enemies from the Mār yamīna,[10] who had led him to the shores of the Mediterranean Sea and to places where he had been able to cut the wood necessary for the construction of a temple for the sun god, Shamash, in Mari.[11] The links between the Bedouins of the Euphrates to the west are obvious. For example:

- Samsi-Addu spoke of the strong relationship between the Rabbaeans and the kingdom of Aleppo and asked Yasmaḫ-Addu to take this into account when making his census.[12] Under Zimri-Lim, Dâdî-hadun, the king of the Rabbaeans, was often in Aleppo, where he was a useful intermediary for Mari's interests in many ways. At the end of the conflict between the Mār yamīna and the king of Mari, Dâdî-hadun took refuge between the Lebanon and Anti-Lebanon mountains.[13] No doubt he had chosen this region either because it was his, or because it was outside the control of the kings of Aleppo and/or Qaṭna, who had then sided with Zimri-Lim.

---

8 See ARM 33 315.

9 This expedition gave rise to an important group of tablets, still unpublished for the most part, which is to be edited by Dominique Charpin and Jean-Marie Durand (cf. Dominique Charpin, *Florilegium Marianum 5: Mari et le proche-Orient à l'époque amorrite: Essai d'histoire politique* [Paris: Société pour l'étude du Proche-Orient Ancien, 2003], 224).

10 In ARM 33, 34, and 35, the term "Mār yamīna" was used instead of the ordinary "Benjaminite" to respect what the Akkadian scribes wrote, in view of the "evolved" form *marmûm*. Similarly, I use "Mār sim'al" instead of "Ben simal(ite)."

11 See Georges Dossin, "L'inscription de fondation de Iaḫdun-Lim, roi de Mari," *Syria* 32 (1955): 1–28, col. ii.

12 See ARM 1 6 (LAPO 17.641).

13 See the letter of the *mer'ûm* Ibal-pi-El (ARM 35.A.48:31–34): "Dâdî-hadun does not cease to write to me to (establish) an agreement of non-aggression. Now when my lord ⟨had routed⟩ his people, out of fear these men settled in Sarôn and Lebanon" (*da-di-ḫa-du-un a-na sa-li-mi-im iš-ta-na-ap-pa-ra-am, ù i-nu-ma be-lí ṣa-ab ra-ma-⟨ni-šu ú-ka⟩-ni-šu-ma,* LÚ-*me-eš šu-nu ad-ru-ma sa-ri-ia-an, ù la-ab-na-a sa-ak-nu*).

- When the Mariote forces that had gone west under Samsi-Addu entered Kinaḫnum (Canaan), they found the ruined town of Yariha,[14] a name closely resembling that of the Yariḫ tribe and which may have been the place from which the latter had originated.
- Samsi-Addu emphasized the Uprapaeans' intimate knowledge of the desert roads (of Palmyra).[15] The Uprapaeans were led by King Lâ(y)ûm, king of Samanum, one of the three Mār yamīna tribes against which Yahdun-Lim fought. According to Samsi-Addu, the Uprapaeans used to cross the desert with their herds, and undoubtedly Yaḫdun-Lim had arrived on the Mediterranean coast in pursuit of them.[16]

---

14 See N. Ziegler, MTT/1, 409 (not yet published).

15 "Since there are Uprapaeans who have experience (*âtammurû*) of these roads, send these people who have experience of these roads so that they may know well what to expect regarding the water resources of these roads" (ARM 1.85$^+$:21–25).

16 In the Yaḫdun-Lim Inscription, passage iv 4 in particular has yet to be fully understood. It states: *ù ki-ša-ad pu-ra-tim ig-mu-ur-ma*. In his edition Dossin translated: "He then completely repaired the banks of the Euphrates." In RIME 4.5.8.2, 607, the translation—"he controlled the banks of the Euphrates"—is better but still inaccurate. The expression is in fact reminiscent of ARM 34.A.925$^+$:37: *ù* ID$_2$.DA *ú-ga-am-ma-ra-kum* = "Then I will give you the whole river!" See commentary ad loc. in ARM 34. In this case, it refers to the divinity's gift of the totality (*gummurum*) of the river, for the key city Saggâratum remained in the kingdom and, in exchange, Mishlan was given to the tribe of Yaḫrur. This passage in the Yaḫdun-Lim Inscription thus alludes to the fact that he fully annexed the kingdom of Samanum to the kingdom of Mari, which later allowed for the construction of the Citadel of Yaḫdun-Lim (Dûr-Yaḫdun-Lim) and the digging of the Ishîm-Yaḫdun-Lim canal. The king of Mari, on the other hand, assumed the kingship of Tuttul, which was considered a territory outside the kingdom. As far as the Rabbaeans were concerned, it was necessary to take account of the power represented by Aleppo. Therefore, a matrimonial alliance with Abattum had to be established through the marriage of Hadnî-Addu (perhaps Yaḫdun-Lim's eldest son) to Addu-dûrî (the daughter of Ayalu, king of Abattum).

From then on, the question of who "Kaṣûri-halâ" was, king of the mysterious "Haman" (a city unattested elsewhere) arises. *CAD* U 117b translated iii 28–29 *um-ma-at ḫa-na, ša a-bu-ú ḫa-na ka-lu-šu-nu i-pu-šu-šu* by "mainstay of the Ḫana tribe which all the leaders of Ḫana had built." *Ummatum* actually represents a human community and, as *epēšum* with *ālum* means "to fortify," not "to build," it should probably be understood as "confederal center (Hammân from √ḪMM, "to gather") of the Bedouins to the fortification of which all the Bedouin clan leaders (*abbû*) had contributed." This might be the intertribal center on the Balih that preceded Ahhunâ (√HÛN). For the proper name *Ka=ṣuri=ḫala* ("The brother of my mother is as my rock"), see the still unpublished examples *ka-ṣú-ra-ḫa-lu*, M.5716, *ka-ṣú-ri*-AN, M.6501 rev. ii, and the shortened name *ka-ṣú-rum* M.6916.

The country by the Sea (ii 22 *ma-ta-am ša ki-ša-ad a-a-ab-b*[*a*]), on which Yahdun-Lim imposed a perpetual tribute (ii 26 *bi-il-ta-am ka-ia-an-ta-am*), could be in the region of Hazor (see ARM 34), where a fragment of a letter from Samsi-Addu was found, claiming what looks like a tribute, after his capture of Mari from the Mār sim'al dynasty. See Dominique Charpin and Nele Ziegler, "Une lettre de Samsî-Addu découverte à Hazor?" *NABU* (2004/4): 84.

The diplomatic life of Qaṭna fluctuated, and its evolution is not well understood. Its king, Išhî-Addu, was a contemporary of the RHM[17] and a reliable ally of Samsi-Addu of Ekallatum. He gave his daughter in marriage to Yasmaḫ-Addu, who was son of Samsi-Addu, the king of Mari at that time. It was their joint military conflicts against Aleppo that cemented the friendship between Išhî-Addu and Samsi-Addu. By contrast, Išhî-Addu's successor, Amut-pâ-ila,[18] was the contemporary of Zimri-Lim and, from the beginning of his reign, a trusted ally—although the king of Mari participated in the downfall of the political order centered on the RHM. Zimri-Lim sent people to Qaṭna[19] and Amut-pî-ila, in exchange for goodwill, sent him soldiers to fight against the Mār yamīna. The king of Qaṭna made presents to his "brother"[20] of Mari during his great tour to the Mediterranean.[21] Later on he was solicited by Aplahanda, king of Carchemish, against Elam.[22] However, he is the one who told the emperor of Elam that the land was given to him,[23] thus dissociating himself from his allies, Aleppo and Mari.[24]

The circuit that the Mār yamīna king of Samanum, Samsi-Addu, made during his exile provides further insight into the diplomatic life of Qaṭna. First, he sought refuge in Qaṭna. Possibly, Samsi-Addu had traveled from somewhere

---

17 RHM = "Royaume de Haute-Mésopotamie" (Kingdom of Upper Mesopotamia). This acronym designates the territories grouped under the authority of the great king of Ekallatum, Samsi-Addu.

18 This name (much discussed, see Herbert B. Huffmon, *Amorite Personal Names in the Mari Texts* [Baltimore, MD: Johns Hopkins University Press, 1965], 167) has several spellings: *a-mu-ut-pí*-AN (ARM 16/1, 26/1, 28, 30, 31), *a-mu-ut-pí-i-la* (ARM 16/1, FM 7), [*a-mu-ut*]-*pa*-AN (ARM 28 14:3). The variants show that AN = *ila*, genitive in -*a* of *ilum*. The PN has as theonym the "Word-of-God" (see *OLA* 162/1, 657–658), where the construct state of *pûm* seems to have been *pâ*. The namesake king of Shuduhum also has this form in *pâ*. The written form *pî* may represent the contraction of /-a-i-/ and be interpreted as /*pê*/ or be an Akkadianization. For the first part of the PN, Benno Landsberger was probably right to link it to √ʾ*MT*, since there is no obligation to read the UT sign of the PN with a /*d*/ as is traditionally done, but it must be a verbal form (*amut*), "happens to be true," rather than a noun ("truth") corresponding to Hebrew *ʾĕmet* or Ugaritic *ʾimt*.

19 See ARM 33 306–307.

20 This is how Zimri-Lim calls Amut-pâ-ila in a preserved correspondence letter, ARM 33 15:4, and in the copy of another letter in ARM 26 25 (33 136):13.

21 See ARM 31 61:11; 159:7; 164:19.

22 See A.715, letter from Ishtarān-nāṣir, published by Georges Dossin in "Aplaḫanda, roi de Carkémiš," *RA* 35 (1938): 115–121; and cited in "Iamḫad et Qatanum," *RA* 36 (1939): 46–54 (= LAPO 16.346).

23 A.266, published in *MARI* 6, p. 40 and n. 7 = *LAPO* 16.298.

24 This is probably due to the fact that there was a new king in Aleppo, where Hammurabi had replaced his father Yarim-Lim.

close to the kingdom of Qaṭna, or from a place that was part of the kingdom, and had found refuge there, though it is unclear from where the Uprapaeans whom he led came. That Išhî-Addu's successor commanded him to resume his wandering based on the orders of the king of Aleppo demonstrates that, in addition to a change of policy in Qaṭna, relations between Aleppo and Qaṭna had changed dramatically after the death of Išhî-Addu.[25] In fact, Samsi-Addu had to withdraw to Carchemish[26] and accompany Ḫardum and Yaggiḫ-Addu to Serdâ.[27]

The date of Išhî-Addu's death is not explicitly stated in any Mari text, though it likely occurred when Yasmaḫ-Addu disappeared and Zimri-Lim rose to power.[28] However, it is unclear how important the kingdom of Qaṭna was from the perspective of Mari; given that Išhî-Addu's death concerned Yasmaḫ-Addu's father-in-law as well as Zimri-Lim, it is perplexing that his disappearance did not attract more attention. In fact, it must have occurred at a very troubled time in Mari's history, especially when the western part of the RHM had to deal with the incursions of Bedouin bands or when Zimri-Lim came to power. Several texts show that it was necessary for Yasmaḫ-Addu to fight against the bands that invaded the kingdom of the Euphrates at least the year before the decisive arrival of the Mār yamīna and Mār sim'al tribes.[29] Zimri-Lim's accession to the throne does not seem to have been easy, since he had to change the name of his father.[30] Thus, at that time, the dramatic events that took place within the kingdom of Mari must have overshadowed external developments.

However, there is one case that deserves to be mentioned, concerning two white horses that the king of Qaṭna sent to Ishme-Dagan, King of Ekallatum.[31] The Mari archives preserve a furious missive from Išhî-Addu (ARM 5 20 = LAPO 16.256), who considered that such animals deserved much more than the twenty minas of tin that he had received as a counter-gift—he considered their value to be six hundred shekels[32] (i.e., ten minas) of silver.[33] Two remarks are

25 The fact is indicated by FM 7 8:50–54.

26 See FM 7 7:47.

27 See FM 7 6, 8 and the commentary in ARM 34.

28 See J.-R. Kupper, ARM 28 15 n. 18.

29 Samples can be found in *MARI* 5, 210 ff. where ARM 2 45 and 5 2 are discussed.

30 See Dominique Charpin and Jean-Marie Durand, "La prise du pouvoir par Zimrî-Lîm," *MARI* 4 (1985): 336–337.

31 See ARM 33 84–86.

32 The king of Qaṭna expresses himself in the western way, using multiples of the basic unit of the shekel rather than converting these into minas, which was the "Sumero-Akkadian" way of describing quantities of metal.

33 Which equates to one hundred tin minas, not twenty. The white horse was rare at the time and seems to have originated in the west; see J.-M. Durand and M. Guichard, "Noms

necessary: first, these horses never made it to Ekallatum and Ishme-Dagan, as Zimri-Lim found them in the Mari palace, according to a letter found there.[34] The horses had therefore been kept by Ishme-Dagan's brother, Yasmaḫ-Addu, as well as Išhî-Addu's letter of recrimination. Second, even if Išhî-Addu had said to Ishme-Dagan, "You behave like a sovereign king, you," he nevertheless refers to him as his brother, just as he does for Yasmaḫ-Addu. His irony may show that Ishme-Dagan had not yet replaced Samsi-Addu.

If the horses were not sent to Ekallatum, it is certainly because relations between Mari and the central region of the RHM had been severed. This is understandable if Bannum, who commanded the Mār sim'al of Numhâ and Yamutbal, had become a dissident during the time when the RHM was under attack from the Mār yamīna. Likely, the two white horses represented a consignment for Ishme-Dagan's coronation. Nevertheless, it is not obligatory to suppose that Samsi-Addu was dead at that point in time, for he could have had his son Ishme-Dagan proclaimed king during his lifetime to ensure a smooth succession. The death of the great king may have occurred only after the proclamation of Ishme-Dagan's kingship, and the sending of the two white horses contemporary with the cessation of relations between Mari and Ekallatum.[35]

In the west, if the king of Aleppo could have ordered King Amut-pâ-ila of Qaṭna to chase the Mār yamīna king Samsi-Addu from his kingdom, then Išhî-Addu must have died in the period between the rupture of relations between Mari and Ekallatum and the flight of the king of Samanum. These latter events occurred during the conflict between Zimri-Lim and the Mār yamīna kings, following Zimri-Lim's capture of Kahat—events dating to the very beginning of his reign. Given that relations were not good between the kings of Qaṭna and

d'équidés dans les textes de Mari," *Sem* 54 (2012): 9–18. According to ARM 35 (A.606), the price of a horse (of luxury, since it is connected to the coronation of a Mār yamīna king) was ten tin minas: *ša-ni-tam* 10 *ma-na* AN.NA *a-na* ANŠE.KUR.RA *ša-mi-im ḫa-aš-ḫa-ku* = "in addition, I need ten tin minas for a horse purchase" [ll. 17–19]. Ishme-Dagan, who in fact paid "the normal price" for such an animal, had not taken into account that white horses were more valuable. The price of a tin mina in Mari is normally six silver shekels. What Ishme-Dagan sent was therefore only four hundred shekels of silver, or two thirds of the expected sum: six minas and forty shekels (two thirds of a mina), whereas Išhî-Addu expected ten minas, i.e. three minas, one third more. Ishme-Dagan, who reigned in Ekallatum, controlled the tin trade that passed through Assur. There we find the need that the Near Eastern western dynasts felt to receive supplies of tin, a metal that became more and more essential at the time. The issue weighed heavily in the relations between Aleppo and Mari, according to A.1153 (= ARM 33 14) and ARM 35 (A.606) 53–54.

34 ARM 10 147 (ARM 33 26).

35 For the death of the great king, see the considerations in FM 5 136–138.

Aleppo at the time of Samsi-Addu, the fact that the king of Qatna received an order from the king of Aleppo suggests that the political balance had shifted in the west and a new order had been established there.

In fact, a text that Dossin quoted long ago (A.164 [= ARM 33 138]) describes how Amut-pâ-ila came to Aleppo to establish a pact of friendship (*awâtum damqâtum*), sanctioned by an oath (*nīš ilim*) and an alliance (*riksātum*). As is often the case at Mari, the event is described from the perspective of a third party to the actual pact. In another Mari letter, Dâdî-hadun wants to make peace with the king of Mari—praising Yarim-Lim's leniency in preferring an alliance pact with the king of Qaṭna to sacking the enemy city—suggesting that the king of Mari should show the same leniency toward the Rabbaeans. The letter reads as follows:

> *He established light over his country*. Returned Amut-pâ-ila ... to Yarim-Lim. (Yarim-Lim) had taken by arms the various cities that his father (Išhî-Addu) had fortified *on his border* and left (them) to him. They put in the ground the matters that angered them, and they established friendship between them. Now, on that day when god came to Yarim-Lim's aid, why did he not say this: "He who has ill-treated me, on the day when god gave him to me, I want to do with him as I please?" For if he had pursued (the fugitives), nothing would have prevented the capture of Qaṭna. You, this you know.[36]

So it is possible that at the end of Išhî-Addu's reign, there were problems with Qatna's succession to the throne,[37] which Amut-pâ-ila won thanks to the military intervention of the king of Aleppo. The beginning of the text is not preserved perfectly, but the meaning of Dâdî-hadun's account is to show that Zimri-Lim is an example of royal leniency, to which the king of Mari is encouraged to conform. At the time of his intervention, Yarim-Lim would have taken control of the fortresses that Išhî-Addu had installed on his border with

36 *ù nu-ra-am a-n[a ma-ti-šu iš-ku-un* (?)], ⸢*i*⸣°*-tu-úr-ma* ᴵ *a-[mu-ut-pí-i-la], a-na ia-ri-im-l[i-im* ...] 30 *a-la-ne-e ša [a-bu-šu i-na pa-ṭì-šu], i-pu-šu i-na* GIŠ-TUKUL *[iṣ-ba-at-ma]* 32 *[ú-wa]-aš-še-er-šum a-wa-tim le-em-né-tim, [i-n]a qa-qa-ri-i[m i]š-ku-un-ma* 34 *a-wa-tim dam-qa-[ti]m bi-ri-šu-nu iš-ku-nu,* ⸢*ù*⸣? *i-na* u_4*-mi-šu i-nu-ma* AN*-lum tap-pu-/ut* 36 ᴵ *ia-ri-im-li-im il-li-ku, a-na mi-nim ki-a-am la iq-bi an-ni-a-am* 38 *ša le-mu-tam i-pu-ša-an-ni, i-nu-ma* AN*-lum id-di-na-aš-šu* 40 *ša e-pé-ši-ia lu-pu-us*$_x$(UŠ$_2$)*-su ù šum-ma-an, i-ra-da-dam ṣa-ba-at qa-ṭà-nim*[ki] 42 *mi-im-ma-an ú-ul ik-la at-ta a-wa-tim, ši-na-ti ti-de* (ARM 35/A.102:27–41).

37 "To establish the light," if the text is correctly restored, would refer to the act of *mišārum*, attested in the west in Aleppo, as shown in the texts published in FM 7.

Yamhad. It would have been up to him to march on Qaṭna and take control of it, putting an end to the existence of a dangerous rival, which he did not do.

The difficulties that Amut-pâ-ila encountered on his way to becoming king after Išhî-Addu explain why Zimri-Lim considered, and even carried out, a military expedition to Qaṭna. Dam-hurāṣi's momentary return to her former residence may have been motivated not only by attending ceremonies in honor of her father,[38] but also by providing a kind of legitimization to the new king who was perhaps her brother. In return for this military support, Amut-pâ-ila later sent troops to support Zimri-Lim's effort in the conflict with the Mār yamīna. By contrast, the king of Eshnunna may have held the opposite opinion: refusing to recognize the new king of Qaṭna, considering him an impostor.[39] ARM 28 14 (ARM 33 137) shows that both the kings of Qaṭna and Aleppo were under hostility from the king of Eshnunna. These events were of great political importance, but today nothing remains of the epistolary exchanges between Qaṭna and Mari that they must have generated, and which would have shed decisive light on them.

Bibliography

Charpin, Dominique, and Nele Ziegler. *Florilegium Marianum 5: Mari et le proche-Orient à l'époque amorrite: Essai d'histoire politique*. Paris: Société pour l'étude du Proche-Orient Ancien, 2003.

Charpin, Dominique, and Jean-Marie Durand. "La prise du pouvoir par Zimrî-Lîm." *MARI* 4 (1985): 293–343.

Charpin, Dominique, and Jean-Marie Durand. "Le nom antique de Tell Rīmah." *RA* 81 (1987): 125–146.

Charpin, Dominique, and Nele Ziegler. "Une lettre de Samsî-Addu découverte à Hazor?" *NABU* (2004/4): 84.

Dossin, Georges. "Aplaḫanda, roi de Carkémiš." *RA* 35 (1938): 115–121.

Dossin, Georges. "Iamḫad et Qatanum." *RA* 36 (1939): 46–54.

Dossin, Georges. "Message d'Hammurapi, roi d'Alep." Pages 16–17 in *Ugaritica I: Études relatives aux découvertes de Ras Shamra*. Edited by Claude F.-A. Schaeffer. MRS 3. Paris: Librairie Orientaliste Paul Guethner, 1939.

Dossin, Georges. "Une mention de Hattuša dans une lettre de Mari." *RHA* 5 (1939): 69–76.

Dossin, Georges. "Le royaume d'Alep au XVIIIe siècle avant notre ère." *BARB* 38 (1952): 229–239.

38 For such ceremonies in the west, see for Aleppo, FM 7 45:3–5.

39 See ARM 33 307–308.

Dossin, Georges. "Le royaume de Qatna au XVIIIe siècle avant notre ère." *BARB* 40 (1954): 417–425.

Dossin, Georges. "L'inscription de fondation de Iaḫdun-Lim, roi de Mari." *Syria* 32 (1955): 1–28.

Dossin, Georges. "Kengen, pays de Canaan." *RSO* 32 (1957): 35–39.

Durand, Jean-Marie. "Documents pour l'histoire du royaume de Haute-Mésopotamie, I/C, les trois routes de l'Euphrate à Qatna à travers le désert." *MARI* 5 (1987): 159–167.

Durand, Jean-Marie, and Michaël Guichard. "Noms d'équidés dans les textes de Mari." *Sem* 54 (2012): 9–18.

Huffmon, Herbert. *Amorite Personal Names in the Mari Texts: A Structural and Lexical Study*. Baltimore, MD: Johns Hopkins University Press, 1965.

Kupper, Jean-Robert. *Lettres royales du temps de Zimri-Lim*. ARM 28. Paris: ERC, 1998.

Ziegler, Nele. *Les toponymes paléo-babyloniens de la Haute-Mésopotamie*. Paris: SÉPOA, 2016.

7

tapariya- and *tapariyalli-*: Local Leaders and Local Agency in the Hittite Period and Its Aftermath

N. İlgi Gerçek and Lorenzo d'Alfonso

Recent research in ancient history and archaeology has increasingly highlighted the agency of small-scale, local, and peripheral groups or polities in social transformation across various spatial and temporal scales.[*,1] Agency-based approaches have been employed fruitfully in research on Late Bronze and Iron Age Anatolia and northern Syria on a number of diverse, yet interconnected topics such as borderlands, identity formation, collapse, resilience, resistance, and the overall processes of state-formation and imperialism.[2]

* The paper is the result of a fruitful collaboration between N.İ. Gerçek and L. d'Alfonso. For the sake of the Italian evaluation of academic output, N.İ. Gerçek is responsible for the part dealing with the Hittite empire, and L. d'Alfonso is responsible for the part dealing with the post-Hittite period.

1 Geoff Emberling, "Counternarratives: The Archaeology of the Long Term and the Large Scale," in *Social Theory in Archaeology and Ancient History: The Present, Past, and Future of Counternarratives*, ed. Geoff Emberling (Cambridge: Cambridge University Press, 2016), 4; Lorenzo d'Alfonso and Karen Rubinson, "Borders and Archaeology," in *Borders in Archaeology: Anatolia and the South Caucasus ca. 3500–500 BCE*, ed. Lorenzo d'Alfonso and Karen Rubinson (Leuven/Paris/Bristol, CT: Peeters, 2021), 20–21. Focusing on the local and small scale does not necessarily exclude engaging with large-scale and long-term research questions, as can be observed in the work of Norman Yoffee (*Myths of the Archaic State: Evolution of the Earliest Cities, States, and Civilizations* [Cambridge: Cambridge University Press, 2005]), and in scholarship he has influenced or inspired, such as some of the essays collected in Geoff Emberling, ed., *Social Theory in Archaeology and Ancient History: The Present, Past, and Future of Counternarratives* (Cambridge: Cambridge University Press, 2016). On agency and collective action approaches to collapse and resilience, see Ronald Faulseit, "Collapse, Resilience, and Transformation in Complex Societies: Modeling Trends and Understanding Diversity," in *Beyond Collapse: Archaeological Perspectives on Resilience, Revitalization, and Transformation on Complex Societies*, ed. Ronald Faulseit (Carbondale, IL: Southern Illinois University Press, 2016), 17–19; see also the other contributions in the same volume.

2 See, for instance, Lorenzo d'Alfonso, "An Age of Experimentation: New Thoughts on the Multiple Outcomes following the Fall of the Hittite Empire after the Results of the Excavations at Niğde-Kınık Höyük (South Cappadocia)," in *Anatolia between the 13th and the 12th Century BCE*, ed. Stefano de Martino and Elena Devecchi (Firenze: LoGismo, 2020), 95–116; d'Alfonso, "Reorganization vs. Resilience in Early Iron Age Monumental Art of Central Anatolia," in *talugaeš witteš: Ancient Near Eastern Studies Presented to Stefano de Martino on the Occasion of*

 | DOI:10.1163/9789004511538_008

These studies arguably mark a break from tradition, inasmuch as research on sociopolitical structure and social transformation in Hittite (Late Bronze Age) Anatolia has typically focused on the state (i.e., its king and administrative apparatus), at the expense of much else.[3]

This paper will explore the agency and long-term resilience of local communities, their institutions, and representatives in Hittite and post-Hittite Anatolia and northern Syria. As a case study, we will focus on the term *tapariya-* and related words that connote command, authority, and sovereignty, particularly the title *tapariyalli-*. Attested in the cuneiform sources of the Hittite Empire, the term *tapariya-* has the general meaning "to rule, to order, to govern, to decide." The term *tapariya-* and other words related to it have typically been understood to imply central, official, and royal command. It has been suggested, for instance, that *tapariya-* in specific contexts has the derived meaning of a provincial administrative district established by royal command,[4] or that

---

His 65th Birthday, ed. Michele Cammarosano et al., Kasion 2 (Münster: Zaphon, 2020), 81–101; Claudia Glatz, "Empire as Network: Spheres of Material Interaction in Late Bronze Age Anatolia," *JAA* 28 (2009): 127–141; Glatz, *The Making of Empire in Bronze Age Anatolia: Hittite Sovereign Practice, Resistance, and Negotiation* (Cambridge: Cambridge University Press, 2020). Local, peripheral, and non-state agency have also been themes explored in various contributions to the panel "Interdisciplinary Approaches to Collapse, Resilience, and Resistance in the Ancient Near East," organized by L. d'Alfonso, T. Hartnell, and N. Highcock at the ASOR Annual Meeting 2020.

3 See Eva von Dassow "The Public and the State," in *Organization, Representation, and Symbols of Power in the Ancient Near East*, ed. Gernot Wilhelm (Winona Lake, IN: Eisenbrauns, 2012), 171–190, for a critique of state-centered modern narratives of ancient Near Eastern societies. In Hittitology, the almost exclusive focus on king and state has as much to do with the nature of the extant sources as it has with their interpretation; while it is true that the entirety of the Hittite textual record has been produced by and for the state, it is also true (and methodologically problematic) that there has been little effort to balance out the state-centered narratives.

4 The interpretation of *tapariya-* as "district" (e.g., in Alfonso Archi, "A Seal Impression from El-Qiṭār/Til-Abnu (Syria)," *AnSt* 43 [1993]: 205) goes back to Johannes Friedrich, *Hethitisches Wörterbuch: Kurzgefasste kritische Sammlung der Deutungen hethitischer Wörter, 1.–4. Lieferung* (Heidelberg: Carl Winter Universitätsverlag, 1952), 211 and *HEG* T.D/1:118–119, especially the latter's translation of *tapariya-* in KUB 26.1 iii 34 as "Herrschaftsgebiet." The substantive *tapariya-* is attested in the Anatolian hieroglyphic script on a seal impression from el-Qiṭār, seemingly dating to the thirteenth century BCE: *ti-la-pa-nu*(-)*tà-pá+ra/i-i*(*a*) URBS. Archi ("Seal Impression," 205) suggests that *ti-la-pa-nu*(-)*tà-pá+ra/i-i*(*a*) may be a compound place name modified by URBS "city," comprising the two elements *ti-la-pa-nu* "Til-Abnu" and *tà-pá+ra/i-i*(*a*) "district." He suggests that the administrative term *tapariya-* referring to a Hittite-controlled district may have come to form a place name. For a similar hypothesis, namely, that the geographic term Tabala, used in Assyrian sources to indicate central Anatolia, derives from *tapariya-*, see Lorenzo d'Alfonso, "Tabal, an 'Out-Group Definition' in the 1st Millennium BC," in *Leggo! Studies Presented to Frederick Mario Fales on the Occasion of His*

its derivative *tapariyalli-* denotes a governor appointed by royal command.[5] The first half of our paper will challenge this view through a reexamination of the terms *tapariyalli-, tapariya-* (noun and verb), and *tapar-* (verb), suggesting that some uses of *tapariya-* and *tapar-* refer to local authority and government, and that *tapariyalli-* is better understood as the representative of a local community rather than an appointee of the Hittite court in the periphery. This interpretation of *tapariya-* and *tapariyalli-* leads to a new understanding of the agency of local communities and their representatives not only during the Hittite period, but also and especially during the post-Hittite period, which will be the topic of the second half of our paper. While the terms related to *tapariya-* occur in Luwian Hieroglyphic texts in both southern Anatolia and northern Syria, *tapariyalli-* is the only nonroyal, official title that occurs both in Hittite and post-Hittite sources in south-central Anatolia. In our discussion of the post-Hittite period, we contrast the agency of the *tapariyalli-* as representatives of local communities in the post-Hittite sociopolitical landscape of south-central Anatolia to the top-down dynastic continuity represented by the Upper Euphrates courts of Carchemish and Malatya, which were very influential in defining authority and its representation in the Iron Age Syro-Hittite city-states.

Our reason for focusing on *tapariya-* (and connected terms) is twofold. First, it allows us to investigate small-scale and peripheral agents over the long term (from ca. 1450 to 700 BCE), and thereby to inquire into the nature of political agency and resilience within the context of the Hittite imperial process and its aftermath. Second, it permits us to instigate a discussion on the language of power and authority in Hittite and post-Hittite Anatolia.[6] This focus on widening our understanding of power institutions in pre-Classical Anatolia is strongly indebted to the lifelong contribution of Dan Fleming to unveiling

---

65th Birthday, ed. Giovanni Battista Lanfranchi et al. (Wiesbaden: Harrassowitz, 2012), contra Federico Giusfredi et al., "On the Origin and Meaning of the Assyrian Toponym Tabal," forthcoming.

5 See, for instance, Itamar Singer's (*Hittite Prayers* [Atlanta, GA: Society of Biblical Literature, 2002], 12, 40) translation of *tapariyalli-* as "governor" in *CTH* 375, the Prayer of Arnuwanda and Ašmunikal (see below), and his suggestion that these governors may have been present as audience at the time when the prayer was recited.

6 For a brief discussion of *tapar-* and *tapariyalli-* in relation to other terms that denote command and authority, see Emmanuel Laroche, "Pouvoir central et pouvoir local en Anatolie Hittite," in *Les pouvoirs locaux en Mesopotamie et dans les régions adjacentes: Actes du Colloque organisé par l'Institut des Hautes Études de Belgique, 28 et 29 janvier 1980*, ed. André Finet (Bruxelles: Institut des Hautes Études de Belgique, 1989), 142–143.

modalities and expressions of sociopolitical organization in ancient western Asia beyond palatial monarchy. It is a great pleasure to participate in this volume in his honor.

1 *tapariya-* and Related Terms in Hittite Sources

In modern scholarship, the Hittite (Hitt.) verb *tapar(r)iya-*, the Cuneiform Luwian (CLuw.) verb *tapar-*, and their various derivatives in Hitt., CLuw., and Hieroglyphic Luwian (HLuw.), have come under scrutiny mainly because of their putative connection to the Hittite personal name and royal title *Labarna/Tabarna*—a connection we will not pursue in the present discussion.[7] CLuw. *tapar-* may have been the origin of the following forms in CLuw., Hitt., and HLuw.: CLuw. *taprammaḫit-* (n.), *taparamman-* (adj.); Hitt. *tapar(r)iya-*, *tapariya-* (c.), [LÚ]*tapariyalli-*; HLuw. verb *tapariya-*, noun *tapariya-*, *tapara/ita-*, *taparaḫit-*, *tapariyala/i-* (c.), *tapariyala-*. The first among these words to enter the Hittite textual record is the title [LÚ]*tapariyalli-*, which will be the center and starting point of our discussion.

1.1 [LÚ]tapariyalli- *"Leader, (Local) Ruler"*

The title [LÚ]*tapariyalli-*[8] is documented predominantly in Middle Hittite (MH) texts and has traditionally been translated "commander" or "governor." All but two attestations of the title come from the prayer of the royal couple Arnuwanda and Ašmunikal (*CTH* 375). This well-known prayer addressing the Sun-goddess of Arinna describes the conflicts between the Hittite state and the groups called Kaška in the central Black Sea region.[9] The composition describes

7 H. Craig Melchert ("Prehistory," in *The Luwians*, ed. H. Craig Melchert [Leiden, Boston: Brill, 2003], 19) suggests that Hitt. *tapariya-* and CLuw. *tapar-* are cognates. Alwin Kloekhorst (*Etymological Dictionary of the Hittite Inherited Lexicon* [Leiden, Boston: Brill, 2008], 830–831) argues against their connection. For a summary of the earlier literature, see *CHD L–N* 43, s.v. "*labarna-*."

8 The noun *tapariyalli-* is a derivative of the stem *tapariya-* with the Luw. suffix *-alli*. According to Kloekhorst (*Etymological Dictionary*, 830) it derives from the verbal stem, whereas Harry A. Hoffner and H. Craig Melchert (*A Grammar of the Hittite Language* [Winona Lake, IN: Eisenbrauns, 2008], 55) note that this suffix forms nouns or adjectives from nouns. For most of the occurrences of *tapariyalli-*, see Franca Pecchioli-Daddi, *Mestieri, professioni e dignità nell'Anatolia ittita* (Roma: Edizioni dell'Ateneo, 1982), 437.

9 For the Kaška, see Einar von Schuler, *Die Kaškäer: Ein Beitrag zur Ethnographie des alten Kleinasien* (Berlin: Walter de Gruyter, 1965); Claudia Glatz and Roger Matthews, "Anthropology of a Frontier Zone: Hittite-Kaska Relations in Late Bronze Age North-Central Anatolia,"

in some detail how the Kaška who had previously been placed under oath took control of various cult centers in the northern peripheries of Hittite territory, taking away their personnel and valuables. Some manuscripts of this composition incorporate lists of the towns and their *tapariyalleš* (pl.), "leaders."[10] The lists have the following structure: URU-*aš ḫūmanza* $^{\text{LÚ.MEŠ}}$*tapariyallešš=a* PN$_1$ PN$_2$, "^{URU}GN, the entire town and *tapariyalleš* PN$_1$ (and) PN$_2$."[11] The *tapariyalleš* listed in various versions of the prayer appear to be the local authorities who had taken oaths as representatives of their towns and who later entered into conflict with the Hittite state.[12]

The title ^{LÚ}*tapariyalli-* is found in yet another composition attributed to Arnuwanda I, known as the Indictment of Madduwatta (*CTH* 147). In this document, ^{LÚ}*tapariyalli-* seems to refer to the local ruler of Pitašša, a town and territory west of Hatti.

> But later, I, My Majesty, brought infantry and chariotry out of the land of Šalpa and [out of the land of ... But] Madduwatta caused the *tapariyalli*-m[an[13] of] the land of Pitašša [and] the elders of Pitašša to swear an oath

BASOR 339 (2005): 47–65; Paul Zimansky, "The Lattimore Model and Hatti's Kaska Frontier," in *Settlement and Society: Essays Dedicated to Robert McCormick Adams*, ed. Elizabeth C. Stone (Los Angeles, CA: Cotsen Institute of Archaeology, 2007), 157–173; Carlo Corti, "The North: Hanhana, Hattena, Ištahara, Hakpiš, Nerik, Zalpuwa, Tummana, Pala and the Hulana River Land," in *Hittite Landscape and Geography*, ed. Mark Weeden and Lee Ullmann (Leiden: Brill, 2017), 219–238.

10 While it is possible that all versions of the composition originally included a list of towns and their *tapariyalleš*, this section is only found in the following, which includes both MH and NH manuscripts: KUB 53.10+ (*CTH* 375.1.B), KBo 51.17+ (*CTH* 375.1.C), KUB 48.107+ (*CTH* 375.3.A) and KBo 58.5 (*CTH* 375.3.B), KBo 52.15a(+) (*CTH* 375.6), KBo 57.17 (*CTH* 375.9), KBo 55.20 (*CTH* 375.10), HFAC 72 (*CTH* 375.16), KBo 58.246 (*CTH* 375.17).

11 Some Kaška PNs appear with what have been called "onomastic epithets," for which see *CHD P* 263, s.v. "*piggapilu*." Some fragments such as KBo 52.15a (*CTH* 375.6), Bo 7768 (*CTH* 375.7), and KBo 52,15b (*CTH* 375.8) display a slightly different structure: ^{URU}GN *QADU* $^{\text{LÚ.MEŠ}}$*tapariyallit* "the town GN with the *tapariyalli*-men." Though the instrumental form *tapariyallit* does not distinguish number, the determinative LÚ.MEŠ is clearly plural.

12 This can be observed in KBo 53.10 (*CTH* 375.4.A) and KBo 55.18 (*CTH* 375.4.B), where the list of *tapariyalleš* directly follows the narrative of the offences of the Kaška. Cf. Singer, *Hittite Prayers*, 12, 40 (see note 5 above).

13 Since *tapariyalli-* is written with a singular determinative ($^{\text{⸢LÚ⸣}}$*ta-pa-ri-ya-al-⸢li⸣-[iš]*), we interpret this instance of the term as singular; cf. *CHD L–N* 225, s.v. *mi(ya)ḫu(wa)nt-* 3a; Gary Beckman et al., *The Ahhiyawa Texts* (Atlanta, GA: Society of Biblical Literature, 2011), 88–89, where this particular attestation is treated as plural. Because the ending of this word is broken, we have opted to use the more cautious form "*tapariyalli*-man" rather than the expected sg. form **tapariyalliš*.

> against [My Majesty], and led [them astray, (saying)]: "Be mine! Occupy [the lands of his Majesty]! Attack Hatti!" Then they proceeded [to attack the lands of My Majesty], and they burned down fortified cities.[14]

Excluding the New Hittite (NH) manuscripts of the above-mentioned prayer of Arnuwanda and Ašmunikal (*CTH* 375), the only evidence of the continued use of LÚ*tapariyalli-* in NH documentation is a broken attestation from what appears to be a NH letter fragment (KBo 18.32), where it seems to refer to Kaška men: LÚ.MEŠ*da-pa-r*[*i-* ...].[15]

The Kaška *tapariyalleš* and the *tapariyalli*-man of Pitašša (along with the elders of Pitašša) all seem to be individuals with both military and political authority, not only leading their towns' forces but taking oaths as representatives of their communities. Individuals bearing the title *tapariyalli-* seem to have operated in the peripheries of the Hittite heartland from the north(east) to the (south)west. The observation that the term *tapariyalli-* is not encountered elsewhere in the rich corpus of Hittite administrative documents, and that Hittite texts use various other terms and descriptions to refer to local authorities and leaders in other contexts,[16] suggest that *tapariyalli-* was likely a local term adopted by the Hittite administration, rather vice versa.[17] That the

---

14 KUB 14.1 (*CTH* 147) rev. 38–40: 38 ⸢*a-ap*⸣*-pa-ma-kán* dUTU-*ŠI IŠ*-⸢*TU*⸣ KUR URU*Šal-pa Ù I*[*Š-TU* KUR URU ...]*-ša* ÉRIN.MEŠ ANŠE.KUR.RA.ḪI.A *ar-ḫa ú-wa-te-nu-un* m*Ma-ad-du-wa-at-t*[*a-aš-ma A-NA* dUTU-*ŠI*] 39 [*ŠA*] KUR URU*Pí-i-ta-aš-ša* ⸢LÚ⸣*ta-pa-ri-ya-al-*⸢*li*⸣-[*iš Ù* LÚ.MEŠ]⸢ŠU⸣.GI URU*Pí-i-ta-aš-ša-ya me-na-aḫ-ḫa-an-ta li-in-ga-nu-uš-*⸢*ki*⸣-[*it nu-uš pár-ra-an-ta*] 40 *ti-it-nu-ut am-me-el-wa-az e-eš-tén nu-wa-za-kán š*[*A*? dUTU-*ŠI* KUR.KUR-*TI*]*M e-eš-du-ma-at* KUR URU*Ḫa-at-ti-ma-wa wa-al-aḫ-te-en nu ú-e-*[*er ŠA* dUTU-*ŠI* KUR.KUR-*TIM wa-al-ḫi-ir*] 41 ⸢*nu*⸣ URU.DIDLI.ḪI.A BÀD *ar-ḫa wa-aḫ-nu-ir*. Restoration and translation follow Beckman et al., *Ahhiyawa Texts*, 88–90, with some modifications.

15 KBo 18.32 (*CTH* 209) lower edge l. 10′. As was already noted by Albertine Hagenbuchner (*Die Korrespondenz der Hethiter: 2. Teil, Die Briefe mit Transkription, Übersetzung und Kommentar*, THeth 16 [Heidelberg: Carl Winter Universitätsverlag 1989], 124–125), the personal names that are mentioned in this letter are similar to Kaška names.

16 In the treaties with Kaška groups (*CTH* 137–140), the leaders who take the oath as representatives of their troops are not called *tapariyalleš*, but "men of GN" (LÚ.[MEŠ] URUGN), who sometimes appear with "onomastic epithets" like the *tapariyalleš*. There are, in addition to *tapariyalli-*, other terms that refer to local authority figures or institutions, such as LÚ.MEŠ GAL "greats" (KBo 14.9 ii 15, for which see note 18 below), LÚ(.MEŠ)DUGUD "dignitary, commander" (CTH 260), and descriptive expressions such as *peran ḫuwai-* "to run before," referring to commanders of town troops (KBo 50.64[+]).

17 The use of a Hittite-Luwian title among the Kaška is not controversial or unexpected, since the Kaška appear to have been a composed of linguistically, culturally, and possibly ethnically diverse groups. See von Schuler, *Kaškäer*, 90; Itamar Singer, "Who Were the Kaška?," *Phasis* 10 (2007): 173–177, for the use of Luwian personal and divine names among the Kaška.

title *tapariyalli-* denoted local and at times non-state and non-Hittite authority becomes apparent when we look into the meaning and use of related terms.

1.2 tapar(r)iya- (*Hitt.*) *"to Command, to Order, to Authorize"*

The Hitt. verb *tapar(r)iya-* is found exclusively in NH documentation. The subject of the verb *tapar(r)iya-* could be the Hittite king, the gods, or more significantly for the present discussion, the ruler of another polity or a local authority figure. We may distinguish the following uses:

1.2.1 "To Order or Authorize (Something)"

The earliest attestation of the verb *tapar(r)iya-* comes from the Extensive Annals of Muršili II. In this composition, the verb *tapar(r)iya-* is used in reference to local leaders in the peripheries of Hatti who incite a rebellion:

> [… who (was) Pendumli] and who (was) Pizumuri, men of the Daḫara River, were in Atḫulišša. And [furthermore] those Kaška who had come forth [and] were in Hatti *ordered* a rebellion: let us start (lit. "do") a [rebellion] and go back to Kaška land.[18]

Later in the same text:

> I then went t[o At[ḫuli]šša. Pendumli and Pizzumuri, who were "greats" of Atḫulišša, *had ordered* a rebellion.[19]

In both of these passages, Pendumli and Pi(z)zumuri appear as Kaška leaders ("greats") from Atḫulišša, who possessed the authority to order a rebellion.

We find the verb *tapar(r)iya-* in two later texts, in which it refers to the act of ordering an (evil) undertaking by a king. In the Bronze Tablet (*CTH* 106.I.1, the treaty between Tudḫaliya IV and Kurunta of Tarḫuntašša), future rulers of Hatti are cautioned against ordering the destruction of Tarḫuntašša:

---

18 KBo 14.20 + KUB 34.33 (*CTH* 61.II) i 14 […]x *ku-iš* ^{m}*Pí-zu-mu-ri-iš-ša* LÚ.MEŠ ^{ÍD}*Da-ḫa-ra* 15 […] ⌜*e*⌝*-šir na-at I-NA* ^{URU}*At-ḫu-liš-ša e-šir* 16 […]*-ya ku-i-*⌜*e*⌝-[eš LÚ$^{?}$ ^{UR}]^{U}*Ga-aš-ga*$^{ḪI.A}$ *pa-ra-a ú-wa-an-te-eš e-šir* 18 […] *I-NA* ^{KUR}*Ḫat-ti* ⌜*e*⌝*-šir nu a-pu-u-uš-ša* BAL *da-pár-ri-ya-e-er* 19 [BAL*-w*]*a i-ya-u-e-ni n*[*u-w*]*a I-NA* ^{URU}*Ga-aš-ga* EGIR*-pa pa-a-i-u-e-ni.*

19 KBo 14.19 (*CTH* 61.II) ii 15: *nam-ma pa-ra-a* ⌜*I*⌝-[*NA* ^{URU}]*At-*[*ḫu-li-i*]*š-ša pa-a-u-un nu* ^{m}*Pe-en-du-um-li-iš* 16 ^{m}*Pí-iz-zu-mu-ri-iš-*[*š*]*a ku-it* [LÚ].⌜MEŠ⌝ GAL ^{URU}*At-ḫu-li-iš-ša* 17 BAL *da-pár-ri-ya-an ḫar-kir*. We interpret the verbal form *daparriyan ḫarkir* as an analytic perfect construction with the neuter nom.-acc. participle plus the auxiliary verb *ḫar(k)-*.

> The Sun-goddess of Arinna and the Storm-god of Hatti shall take away the kingship of Hatti from … whoever takes away kingship from the progeny of Kurunta, or diminishes it, or *orders* its destruction.[20]

Similarly, in the treaty between Šuppiluliuma II and Talmi-Teššup of Carchemish, the latter is warned against "ordering evil" for the Hittite king or his progeny:

> If you *order* evil for Šuppiluliuma or for the child(ren) of Šuppiluliuma beneath the Sun-god of Heaven, may the Thousand Gods of the oath and the heat of the Sun-god destroy you at that moment. If you *order* it at night, beneath the Moon-god, may the Moon-god and his mace destroy ⟨you⟩, [together] with your wife, your children, your descendants, your land, [and …].[21]

1.2.2 "To Appoint a Successor"

The verb *tapar(r)i̯ya-* is used twice to refer to the act of appointing a successor. In the treaty between Muwatalli and Alakšandu of Wiluša (*CTH* 76), Muwatalli refers to Alakšandu's successor as "your son, whom you *appoint* for kingship."[22] Similarly, in the Bronze Tablet, the verb *tapar(r)i̯ya-* is used to refer to Tudḫaliya's appointment as successor:

> At that time, my father had not yet *appointed* me for kingship.[23]

1.2.3 "To Command Someone"

In the Bronze Tablet we find a clause that gives Kurunta the sole authority to appoint his successor:

---

20 Bo 86/299 iii 71–77: 71 *ku-iš-ma-kán A-NA* NUMUN ^{md}LAMMA *ŠA* KUR ^{URUd}U-*ta-aš-ša* LUGAL-*iz-na-tar* 72 *ar-ḫa da-a-i na-aš-ma-at te-ep-nu-zi na-aš-ma-at ḫar-ga-an-na* 73 *ta-pár-ri-ya-iz-zi* 75 … *a-pé-e-da-ni-ma-kán* 76 ^{d}UTU ^{URU}*A-ri-in-na* ^{d}U ^{URU}*Ḫa-at-ti-ya* 77 LUGAL-*iz-na-tar ar-ḫa da-an-du.*

21 KUB 26.25+ (*CTH* 122.2) ii 8′–14′: 8′ *ma-a-an ŠA* ^{m}KÙ.PÚ-*ma* ḪUL-*lu na-aš-šu ŠA* DUMU ^{m}*Šu-up-pí-lu-l*[*i-u-ma*] 9′ ḪUL-*lu* GAM ^{d}UTU AN-*E ta-pár-ri-ya-ši a-pé-da-ni-ták-kán* 10′ *me-ḫu-ni LI-IM* DINGIR.MEŠ *MA-MIT* ^{d}UTU-*aš wa-an-te-em-ma-aš* 11′ *ḫar-ni-en-kán-du ma-a-an-at* GE$_6$-*za-ma ŠA-PAL* ^{d}XXX 12′ *ta-pár-ri-ya-ši* ^{d}XXX *-aš-ša*⟨*-ták-kán*⟩ *a-pé-el :ḫa-at-tal-li-ša* 13′ [*QA-D*]*U* DAM-*KA* DUMU.MEŠ-*KA* NUMUN-*KA* KUR-*KA* 14′ [o o] x x ⸢*kat-ta*⸣ *ḫar-ni-ik-du.*

22 KUB 21.1+ (*CTH* 76.A) i 65: [DUMU]-*KA-ma ku-in* LUGAL-*iz-na-an-ni zi-ik ta-pár-ri-ya-š*[*i.*

23 Bo 86/299 ii 36–37: 36 *am-mu-uk-ma a-pé-e-da-ni me-e-ḫu-ni* LUGAL-*iz-na-ni na-ú-i ta-pár-ri-ya-an* 37 *ḫar-ta.*

> Whichever son Kurunta approves, whether he is the son of that woman or of another woman, whichever son Kurunta has in mind, and whichever son Kurunta approves, he shall install him in kingship in Tarḫuntašša. No one shall *command* Kurunta in this matter.[24]

It is established in this passage that the authority to appoint a successor is Kurunta's alone, and that no one should possess the authority to *command* him in this matter.

1.2.4 "To Order, To Command" (with Divine Subject, with or without Direct Obj.)

In a number of cases, the subject of the verb *tapar(r)i̯ya-* is divine.[25] The commands of the gods may be revealed through an oracular investigation, as we see in the example below from the Instructions for Priests and Temple Personnel:

> They will conduct an oracular investigation concerning you (pl.), and they will do to you as the gods, your lords, *command* concerning you.[26]

Similarly, in a fragment from a votive text, we come across the following exhortation to the Ishtar of Lawazantiya to command or arrange a matter for the better:

---

24 Bo 86/299 ii 90–94: 90 *ku-in-za im-ma* DUMU-*an* ^{md}LAMMA *ma-la-a-iz-zi ma-a-na-aš a-pé-el* 91 *ŠA* MUNUS-*TI* DUMU-*aš ma-a-na-aš ta-me-e-el ku-e-el-qa* MUNUS-*aš* DUMU-*aš* 92 *nu ku-iš* DUMU-aš *A-NA* ^{md}LAMMA ZI-*an-za ku-in-za* DUMU-*an* ^{md}LAMMA-*aš ma-la-iz-zi* 93 *nu I-NA* KUR ^{URUd}U-*ta-aš-ša* LUGAL-*iz-na-ni a-pu-u-un ti-it-ta-nu-ud-du* 94 ^{md}LAMMA-*an ke-e-da-ni me-mi-ya-ni le-e ku-iš-ki ta-pár-ri-ya-iz-zi.*

25 Beside the examples cited here, there are a few fragmentary occurrences of the verb *tapar(r)i̯ya-* with a divine subject, such as KBo 13.101 i 3, 4 (*CTH* 435.1, a ritual for the elimination of an unfavorable omen), and KUB 46.13 iv 8 (*CTH* 635, a fragment of Festival for Zippalanda and Mt. Daḫa). KUB 2.2 ii 48 (*CTH* 725, an OH Hittite-Hattic bilingual) presents a more difficult case where the verb appears in 1pl. pres.: *ma-a-na-at ta-pa-ri-ya-u-e-ni-ma la-ba-ar-na-aš* LUGAL-*wa-aš* É-*ir*, "when we *ordered/appointed* it the abode of the Labarna, the king." Manuscript B (KBo 51.216 ii 4′) has a 3pl. verb form here (]-*ya-e-er*), based on which Giulia Torri and Carlo Corti ("CTH 725," last modified August 16, 2011, https://www.hethport.uni-wuerzburg.de/txhet_besrit/intro.php?xst=CTH%20725&prgr=§%201&lg=IT&ed=G.%20Torri%20-%20C.%20Corti) suggest emending *tapari̯yaueni* "we command" to *tapari̯yaēr* "they commanded." If correct, the subject of the *tapari̯yaēr* would be the gods (DINGIR.MEŠ), attested in the previous paragraph in Hittite (KUB 2.2. ii 43).

26 KUB 13.4 (*CTH* 264.A) iv 8–9: 8 … *nu-uš-ma-aš a-ri-an-zi nu-uš-ma-aš* DINGIR.MEŠ EN.MEŠ-*K*[(*U-NU*)] 9 *ma-aḫ-ḫa-an ta-pa-ri-ya-an-zi nu-uš-ma-aš* *QA-TAM-MA* *i-en-zi.*

The matter of the towns *Šapla* which His Majesty knows and wh[ich ...] *command* that matter! You, Ishtar of Lawazantiya, take care of that matter well.[27]

1.3 tapar- (*Luw.*) *"to Reign, to Rule, to Govern, to Command"*

The Luw. verb *tapar-* is also found exclusively in NH documentation, though more frequently and with a slightly wider semantic range than Hitt. *tapar(r)iya-*.[28] Like its Hitt. counterpart, the Luw. *tapar-* can have as its subject the Hittite king, queen, crown prince, or a deity, as well as a ruler or local authority in another polity or territory.

1.3.1 "To Reign, to Rule" (with or without Direct Obj.)

Like the Hitt. verb *tapar(r)iya-*, the earliest instances of the Luw. *tapar-* come from the Extensive Annals and the Ten-Year Annals of Muršili II and have local authorities as subject. The following two excerpts from the Extensive Annals and the Ten-Year Annals of Muršili II demonstrate, on the one hand, the close connection between the verb *tapar-* and a specific type of authority, namely, kingship, and on the other, they point to the contrast between *tapar-* "to rule" and *maniyaḫḫ-* "to administer, govern."[29] The first excerpt concerns a certain Aparru, "the man of Kalašma," to whom Muršili II had given the land of Kalašma to govern:

27 KBo 8.63 (*CTH* 590) i 9′–11′: 9′ ^{d}UTU-*ŠI ku-in me-mi-an ŠA* ^{URU}*Šap-la I-DI nu ku-*[*in*]$^{?}$10′ *a-pu-u-un me-mi-an*:⸢*ta*⸣*-pár-ri-ya-i* ^{d}IŠTAR ^{URU}*La-*⸢*a*⸣*-*[*u-wa-za-an-ti-ya* 11′ ⸢SIG$_5$-*in*⸣ *aš-ša-nu-ši*. Kloekhorst (*Etymological Glossary*, 830) interprets *taparriyai* as a 2sg. imperative form, whereas Johan de Roos (*Hittite Votive Texts* [Leiden: Nederlands Instituut voor het Nabije Oosten 2007], 135 n. 283) takes it as a dative sg. form of a substantive *taparriya-*. Note, however, that the dative sg. form documented elsewhere is *tapariya* (KBo 40.13 obv. 10) or *taparriya* (KUB 26.1 iii 34). Hoffner and Melchert (*Grammar*, 202 n. 102) interpret this as a Luwian *-ḫi* verb in the 3sg. present, later altered to Hittite *taparriyaizzi*.

28 For attestations (with or without gloss marks) see H. Craig Melchert, *Cuneiform Luvian Lexicon* (Chapel Hill, NC: self-pub., 1993), 207. There are a few instances in fragmentary contexts. KUB 31.136 (*CTH* 386.2) iii 11–12: 11 [...]-⸢*an*⸣ LUGAL ^{MUNUS}⸢*ta-wa*⸣*-na-an-* [...] 12 [... *zi*]*-ik ta-pár-ši* "the king [and] *tawanan*[*na* ...] you rule"; in this prayer for the Storm-god of Nerik, the verb is 2sg. pres. and it is not clear whether the accusative forms on l. 11 are the direct objects. KUB 21.38 (*CTH* 176) obv. 36′: *an-da ta-pár-ri-ya-i* "command!"; this 2sg. imp. act. form in this letter from queen Puduḫepa to Rameses II, appears to be an injunction from the former to the latter. KBo 6.3 (*CTH* 572) l. 14: GIM-*an ta-pár-ti* "just as you command"; the verb likely has the deity as subject.

29 Cf. Laroche, "Pouvoir central," 142–143.

> I gave him the land of Kalašma to administer. I [th]en made him swear an oath. And he became arrogant and became hostile [toward m]e. He [unit]ed the land of Kalašma and he *ruled* it like a king.[30]

It is clear from this passage that Aparru did not administer (*maniyaḫḫ-*) in the manner desired by the Hittite king, but, uniting the territory of Kalašma, *ruled* it like a king.

The second excerpt concerns Piḫḫuniya, a Kaška leader who defies tradition and begins to *reign* like a king:

> Furthermore, Piḫḫuniya did not *reign* in the Kaška manner. Suddenly, when there was no *command* (see the noun *tapariya-* below) of one in Kaška (land), said Piḫḫuniya *reigned* like a king.[31]

1.3.2 "To Rule, to Govern (a Place or Institution)," "to Command and Army"

The verb *tapar-* is employed several times with the meaning "to rule" or "to govern" a town, territory, or institution. For instance, in a prayer of Muršili II concerning the banishment of the Tawananna, the verb *tapar-* is used with the Tawananna as subject and the "palace and the land of Hatti" as direct obj.:

> Just as [she *ruled*] the [pala]ce and the land of Hatti at the time of my father, she *ruled* [them] just the same [then, too].[32]

---

30 KBo 16.17 (*CTH* 61.II.10) iii 26–31: 26 *nu-uš-ši* KUR ^{URU}*Ka-la-a-aš-ma* 27 *ma-ni-ya-aḫ-ḫu-u-wa-an-zi pí-iḫ-ḫu-un* 28 [*na*]*m-ma-an li-in-ga-nu-nu-un na-aš šu-ul-le-e-et* 29 [*nu-m*]*u ku-u-ru-ur-ri-aḫ-ta nu-za-kán* KUR ^{URU}*Ka-la-a-aš-ma* 30 [1-*e-e*]*t-ta ne-ya-at na-at* LUGAL-*u-e-ez-na-aš* 31 *i-*⸢*wa-ar*⸣ ⸢*ta*⸣*-pa-ar-ta*.

31 KBo 3.4 (*CTH* 61.I.A) iii 73–76: 73 *nam-ma* ^{m}*Pí-iḫ-ḫu-ni-ya-aš* *Ú-UL ŠA* ^{URU}*Ga-aš-ga i-wa-ar :ta-pa-ar-ta* 74 *ḫu-u-da-ak ma-aḫ-ḫa-an I-NA* ^{URU}*Ga-aš-ga Ú-UL ŠA* 1-*EN ta-pa-ri-ya-aš* 75 *e-eš-ta a-ši-ma* ^{m}*Pí-iḫ-ḫu-ni-ya-aš ŠA* LUGAL-*UT-TIM i-wa-ar* 76 *ta-pa-ar-ta*. The same events are also narrated in the Extensive Annals of Muršili II (KUB 14.17 [*CTH* 61.II] ii 34–36), for which see *CHD Š* 335, s.v. "*šia-*."

32 KUB 14.4 (*CTH* 70.1.A) i 7′–8′: 7′ [É.LUG]AL *Ù* KUR ^{URU}*Ḫa-at-ti A-NA PA-NI A-BI-YA ma-aḫ-ḫa-an* 8′ [*ta-pa-ar-ta a-pí-ya-ya-at*] *QA-TAM-MA-pát ta-pa-ar-ta*. See also the similar lines 11′–12′: 11′ [*A-NA PA-NI A-BI-YA Ù A-NA-PA-N*]*I ŠEŠ-YA ma-aḫ-ḫa-an ta-pa-ar-ta a-pí-ya-ya-at* 12′ [*QA-TAM-MA-pát ta-pa-ar-ta*] "Just as she *ruled* the palace and the land of Hatti [in the time of my father and in the ti]me of my brother, she [*ruled*] them [just the same] then, too." Restoration and translation follow Jared L. Miller, "Mursili II's Prayer Concerning the Misdeeds and the Outstanding of Tawananna," in *Proceedings of the Eighth International Congress of Hittitology: Warsaw, September 5–9, 2011*, ed. Piotr Taracha (Warsaw: Widawnictwo Agade, 2014), 518–519 n. 7, 523–524, with modifications.

The verb *tapar-* appears several times in the Apology of Hattušili III, with either Hattušili III or his successor Tudḫaliya IV as subject. In the first example below, Hattušili III describes how his brother Muwatalli II had established him as ruler of the Upper Land. Note again the intentional contrast between the verbs *tapar-* "to rule" with king Hattušili III as subject and *maniyaḫḫ-* "to govern" with Arma-Tarḫunta (Hattušili's rival and court opponent) as subject:

> He gave me the Upper Land to administer and I *ruled* the Upper Land. But before me, Arma-Tarḫunta, son of Zida, used to govern it.[33]

Later on in this composition, the same verb is used with the army and chariotry as direct obj.:

> He placed the entire army (and) chariotry of Hatti in my hand and I myself *commanded* the entire army and chariotry of Hatti.[34]

The examples cited above demonstrate that the Luw. verb *tapar-* had a meaning distinct from *maniyaḫḫ-* "to administer, govern, show"; in all clear contexts *tapar-* denotes an action performed by an autonomous, sovereign authority.

1.4 ***The Substantive*** **tapariya- (*c.*) "*(Royal) Order, Ruling, Command; Rule, Reign*"**

The substantive *tapariya-* also appears only in NH texts and most commonly denotes a royal order or command; in all clear contexts this command is issued by the highest authority, i.e., the (Hittite) king. Four occurrences of *tapariya-* date to the reign of Hattušili III, three of which come from the same composition, namely, the prayer of Hattušili III and Puduḫepa to the Sun–

33 KUB 1.1 (*CTH* 81.1) i 26–28: 26 KUR UGU-*ya-mu ma-ni-ya-aḫ-ḫa-an-ni pé-eš-ta* 27 *nu* KUR UGU-*TI :ta-pár-ḫa pé-ra-an-ma-at-mu* ^{m}XXX-^{d}U-*aš* 28 DUMU ^{m}*Zi-da-a ma-ni-ya-aḫ-ḫi-iš-ki-it.*

34 KUB. 1.1 (*CTH* 81.1) i 65–67: 65 … *nu-mu-kán* KARAŠ ANŠE.KUR.RA.MEŠ 66 *ŠA* KUR ^{URU}*Ḫa-at-ti ḫu-u-ma-an-da-an* ŠU-*i da-a-iš nu* KARAŠ 67 ANŠE.KUR.RA.MEŠ *ŠA* KUR ^{URU}*Ḫa-at-ti ḫu-u-ma-an-da-an am-mu-uk :ta-par-ḫa.* This statement is repeated in ii 72–74. See also ii 57–61, wherein Hattušili III relates the towns and troops he *commanded* (*taparḫa*). In the Extensive Annals of Muršili II, too, the infinitive of the verb *tapar-* denotes "to command an army." KUB 19.29 (*CTH* 61.II.1): *nu-wa-za* DUMU-*aš ku-i*[*š zi-ik*] [*nu-w*]*a-ra-an-kán ta-pa-ru-na ku-wa-pí pa-i-ši* "And you who are but a child, where/when will you go to *command* them?" The object of the infinitive is the 3sg. acc. enclitic pronoun *-an*, which likely refers to the troops and chariots that are mentioned earlier in the text.

goddess of Arinna (*CTH* 383).[35] The word turns up twice in the same paragraph concerning the transfer of the gods from Ḫattuša to Tarḫuntašša by Muwatalli:

> [...] I was [in no way involved in the] *command* concerning the removal of the deities, I was compelled, he was my lord. The removal of the deities was not a desire of mine, and I was worried by that [command]. He t[ook] the silver and the gold of all deities, but I was in no way involved in any *command* concerning whose silver and gold he gave to which god.[36]

In this passage *tapariya-* is clearly the command formulated by a supreme authority concerning a given task or office (i.e., *tapariya-* + genitive "*command* concerning something"). The construct *tapariya anda eš-* "to be in/party to a command" does not necessarily imply taking part in performing the command, but rather, playing an active role in the formulation of the command. Hattušili clearly affirms that he took part in the removal of the gods, but he had no part in the conception of the plan; he performed it because it was his lord's command.

The third example occurs in the following passage of the prayer, better understood thanks to a join made by Itamar Singer:[37]

> I myself was not involved in the affair of the ruin of the son of Danu-ḫepa. I indeed passed judgment over him; he was *genzu* to me, but nobody was ruined by the word (or) *command* of my mouth.[38]

35 See Dietrich Sürenhagen, "Zwei Gebete Ḫattušilis und der Puduḫepa: Textliche und literaturhistorische Untersuchungen," *AoF* 8 (1981): 83–168 and more recently Singer, *Hittite Prayers*, 97–101.

36 KUB 14.7 (*CTH* 383.1) obv. i 6′–15′: 6′ [...] 7′ *ta-pa-ri-ya* DINGIR.MEŠ-*aš ar-n*[*u-um-ma-aš* *Ú-UL ku-it-ki an-da*] 8′ ⌜*e*⌝-*šu-un* ⌜GÉŠPU⌝-*ah-hu-u-wa-aš* ⌜*e*⌝-[*šu-un*] 9′ EN-*YA*-*aš-mu e-eš-ta* DINGIR.MEŠ-*aš-ma-*[*m*]*u* ⌜*ar*⌝-*n*[*u-um-mar*] 10′ *Ú-UL* ZI-*an-za e-eš-ta a-pí-e-da-ni*[*-ya ta-pa-ri-ya*] 11′ *pí-ra-an ú-e-ri-te-iš-ša-*[*a*]*n-za e-šu-u*[*n*] 12′ KÙ.BABBAR-*ya* GUŠKIN *ŠA* DINGIR.MEŠ *hu-ma-an-da-aš d*[*a*-x x x] 13′ *nu ku-el-la* KÙ.BABBAR GUŠKIN *ku-e-da-ni* 14′ *A-NA* DINGIR-*LIM pí-iš-ki-it nu-za-kán a-pí-e-*⌜*da*⌝-[*ni-ya*] 15′ *ta-pa-ri-ya Ú-UL ku-it-ki an-da* [*e-šu-un*].

37 Itamar Singer, "Danuhepa and Kurunta," in *Anatolia Antica: Scritti in ricordo di Fiorella Imparati*, ed. Stefano de Martino and Franca Pecchioli-Daddi (Firenze: LoGisma, 2002), 739–751.

38 KUB 21.19 (*CTH* 383.1) obv. ii 4–10: 3 ... *am-mu-uk-ma-za-kán* 4 *a-pí-e-da-ni ŠA* ^{m}*Da-nu-ḫé-pa* DUMU-*ŠU* 6 *ḫar-ga-na-aš me-mi-ni an-da Ú-UL e-šu-un* 7 *še-er-ši im-ma ḫa-an-ne-iš-ki-nu-un* 8 *ge-en-zu-ya-*⌜*aš*⌝-*mu e-eš-ta am-me-el-ma* KAxUD-*aš* 9 *me-mi-ya-ni-it ta-pa-ri-ya-az Ú-UL* 10 *ku-iš-ki ḫar-ak-ta*.

In this passage Hattušili exculpates himself from the ruin of Danu-ḫepa's son in the presence of the Sun-goddess of Arinna, emphasizing that said son of Danu-ḫepa did not come to ruin by Hattušili's word or command.

The fourth occurrence dating to Hattušili III is found in an oracular inquiry concerning military campaign strategy (*CTH* 561). The paragraphs leading up to the lines quoted below establish that an official named Temeti was tasked with the invasion of the places Taptena and Ḫuršama while the Great King was on a military campaign against Assyria (KUB 5.1 iii 77–83), and that the town Nerik was troubled by Kaška. The relevant passage inquires the results of a military action assigned to an official named Temeti while the Great King being on a campaign against the Assyrians and the city of Nerik was under threat, likely from the Kaška.

> If the *taparriya-* as (it was assigned) to Temeti is disapproved by the deity, (the result of the inquiry) shall be not positive ... (It is) not positive.[39]

In this context *tapariya-* might have the meaning "district," but it more likely refers to the military command assigned to the official Temeti.

In Tudḫaliya IV's instructions for lords, princes, and courtiers we find *tapariya-* once again as a specific *command* issued by the Hittite king for specific officials. In this case, the command concerns foreign affairs:

> Or, when I send you chiefs, together with sons of the king and lords to a foreign mission under a *command*, you may not twist the word of the king. It shall be placed under oath.[40]

The substantive *tapariya-* is further found in a treaty fragment, which seems to concern a *command* sent to (?) Carchemish: "you sent a *command* [to? Ca]rchemish."[41] We come across the substantive *tapariya-* in some administra-

---

39 KUB 5.1 (*CTH* 561) iii 93–94: 93 *i-wa-ar* ^{m}*Te-me-it-ti ta-pár-ri-aš IŠ-TU* DINGIR-*LIM mar-ki-an-za* NU.SIG$_5$-*du* 94 ... NU.SIG$_5$. See *CHD L–N* 189, s.v. "*markiya-*" 1a2′; Ahmet Ünal, *Ḫattušili III: Teil 1, Ḫattušili bis zu seiner Thronbesteigung*, THeth 3 (Heidelberg: Carl Winter Universitätsverlag, 1974), 78 ff.; Richard H. Beal, "Seeking Divine Approval for Campaign Strategy—KUB 5.1 + KUB 52.65," *Ktema* 24 (1999): 51–54.

40 KUB 26.1 (*CTH* 255.2.A) iii 32–36: 32 *na-aš-ma šu-um-ma-aš ku-it* LÚ.MEŠ SAG x[x x] 33 *IT-TI* DUMU.MEŠ LUGAL *BE-LU*.ḪI.A *A-NA* INIM *a-ra-aḫ-ze-na-aš* 4 *ta-pár-ri-ya* GAM-*an u-i-iš-ke-mi* 35 *nu-kán* INIM LUGAL *le-e wa-aḫ-nu-ut-te-ni* 36 GAM *NI-ÌŠ* DINGIR-*LÌ-at* GAR-*ru*.

41 KBo 40.13 (*CTH* 212.12) 4′–8′: 4′ KUR *Ka*]*r-qa-maš ta-pár-ri-an TÀŠ-PUR* 5′ [...]-*e-da-ni ma-an-qa* 6′ [...]x *ša-li-i-ik* 7′ [... *da*]-*pí-an ar-ḫa tár-na-aš* 8′ [...]x PAP-*nu-ut*. On the spelling KUR *kar-qa-maš* see *RGTC* 6: 181, where this fragment is not cited.

tive letters as well, though unfortunately in very fragmentary contexts that do not reveal much about the noun's use and semantic sphere.[42]

The second-millennium evidence collected here demonstrates that *tapariyalli-* and related terms denoted not only royal, central, or Hittite authority, but local authority, often wielded against the Hittite state. Based on the chronological distribution and geographical relevance of the term *tapariyalli-*, along with the observation that the earliest occurrences of both Hitt. *tapar(r)iya-* and Luw. *tapar-* in compositions dating to Muršili II refer to local agents in the peripheries of Hatti, we may tentatively suggest that *tapariya-* and related terms were appropriated by the Hittite state from local, peripheral agents and introduced into the Hittite lexicon of power.

2 *tapariya-* and Related Terms in the Post-Hittite Hieroglyphic Luwian Sources

A decade ago, F. Giusfredi put together a detailed treatment of the occurrences of *tapariya-* and its cognates in Hieroglyphic Luwian; we have no substantial changes to his treatment.[43] We will instead revise the interpretation of the uses of *tapariya-* and its derivatives based on a more nuanced understanding of *tapariyalli-* and the derivative *tapariyalla-* within the Hieroglyphic Luwian sources of the post-Hittite period.

2.1 tapariyalli- *"Leader, Local Ruler"*

To those listed by Giusfredi, we may add the occurrence in SULTANHAN §48. The passage below from Maraş is the earliest and the better preserved. It is dated to the late ninth century on solid synchronisms with Assyrian campaigns in the region and internal paleographic analysis.[44] The title *tapariyalli-* refers here to the ancestors of king Halparuntiya:

42 E.g., KBo 18.88 (*CTH* 209) rev. 16′–17′: 16′ [...]x-*an-wa* ᵐ*Tal-*⌜*mi*⌝*-la-aš* 17′ [... *t*]*a-pa-ri-ya-an*; the rest of the letter mentions, merchants, the land of Kinaḫḫawa, and ^ÉRIN.MEŠ^*ŠUTI*, see Hagenbuchner, *Korrespondenz*, 143–144. Two attestations of the sign sequence TA-PÁR-RI in KBo 18.48, a letter from the king to prince Hešni, have been interpreted by Hagenbuchner (*Korrespondenz*, 8–12), followed by Harry A. Hoffner (*Letters from the Hittite Kingdom* [Atlanta, GA: Society of Biblical Literature, 2009], 332–334), as the Akkadian verb *barû(m)*. Since Hagenbuchner notes that the use of the Akkadian verb is "singular," we may perhaps interpret TA-PÁR-RI as a form of *tapar-*: KBo 18.48 obv. 11–12 GIM-*an* UDU-*un ta-pár-ri-*[...] "when [...] order [...] a sheep," i.e., the king orders (the performance) of extispicy.

43 Federico Giusfredi, *Sources for a Socio-Economic History of the Neo-Hittite States*, THeth 28 (Heidelberg: Universitätsverlag Winter 2010), 104–107.

44 J. David Hawkins, *Corpus of the Hieroglyphic Luwian Inscriptions, Vol. 1: Inscriptions of the*

> I am the *tarwani*-Halparuntiya, king of the Land of Gurgum, son of Larama, the *tapariyalli-*, grandson of Halparuntiya, the hero, great-grandson of the *warpali*-Muwatalli, great-great-grandson of the *tarwani*-Halparuntiya, great-great-great-grandson of Muwizi, the hero, offspring of Larama, the *tapariyalli-*.[45]

The use of the title by the founder of the lineage, Larama, is worthy of comment. We may suggest that this genealogy represents the passage of a lineage from a local rulership or governorship into a more broadly accepted sacred kingship defined by regional, territorial control and divine sanction.[46]

The SULTANHAN example, dating to the second part of the eighth century BCE, is part of a fragmentary and not entirely understood passage:

> Whoever desires this name, whether a woman of xxx bring it away, or it is a *tapariyalli-*, or a king, …[47]

On the one hand, this passage indicates the existence of local rulers titled *tapariyalli-* at a time when kingship was established north of the Taurus; on the other, it suggests an opposition between the *tapariyalli-* as local ruler and king, likely also a hierarchical differentiation among them.

Contrary to the title *tarwani-*, whose earliest attestations are from the Syro-Hittite region south of the Taurus, *tapariyalli-* occurs only once south of the Taurus, and likely at a later stage than the examples from the Anatolian Plateau.[48] In the fragmentary context of JISR EL-HADID Fr. 3, *tapariyalinzi* (nom. pl.) appear as a group of local rulers who had some form of agency in the process of the definition of monarchic power of the author to which the inscription apparently refers.[49]

Differently from second-millennium sources, Hieroglyphic Luwian texts of the first millennium BCE demonstrate the existence of a verb *tapariyalla-*,

---

Iron Age (New York, NY/Berlin: de Gruyter, 2000), 262; Lorenzo d'Alfonso and Annick Payne, "The Paleography of Anatolian Hieroglyphic Stone Inscriptions," *JCS* 68 (2016): 116.

45 MARAŞ 1, 1–3: Hawkins, *Corpus*, 216–265.

46 Lorenzo d'Alfonso, "City-States, Canton States, Monarchy and Aristocracy: The Political Landscape of the Early Iron Age in Central Anatolia within the Context of the Eastern Mediterranean (11th–9th Century BCE)," forthcoming.

47 SULTANHAN 46–49: our translation, based upon Hawkins, *Corpus*, 467, 471–472; and Ilya Yakubovic, "SULTANHAN," Provisional Annotation of the Hieroglyphic Luwian Corpus, accessed July 15, 2021, https://www.ediana.gwi.uni-muenchen.de/corpus.php.

48 For a late dating of JISR EL-HADID Fr. 1–3, see d'Alfonso and Payne, "Paleography," 118.

49 Hawkins, *Corpus*, 378–380.

derived from *tapariyalli-* possibly through a denominative suffix *-a-*.[50] Whether the verb has a transitive-causative or an intransitive meaning is still unclear.[51] The occurrence in the KARABURUN inscription seems to require an intransitive meaning:

> Sipis was the king, and Sipis son of Niyas was *tapariyalli-*.[52]

The second occurrence of the verb in the KULULU 4 inscription has traditionally been assigned a causative meaning:

> I was dear to my lords, and they made me *tapariyalli-*, and I was the Overseer of the house in the house of the lord(s).[53]

However, this translation is based on the presumption that the *tapariyalli-* were appointed by the central authorities. A different translation is also possible:

> I was dear to my lords, and they were *tapariyalli-* to me, and I was the Overseer of the house in the house of the lord.[54]

Depending on the value assigned to the verb in the second clause, *tapariyalli-* can be understood as a position assigned to an individual by a superior (royal?) authority, or a powerful figure (chief) emerging from internal dynamics within local communities. While it is not inconceivable that a locally defined office was at times imposed top-down by regional authorities, the interpretation of the passage as well as the appointment of the office in the post-Hittite period should better remain open.

2.2 taparahit *"Local Authority, Rulership"*

The noun *taparahit* is documented only once, but the passage is very meaningful for the understanding of the nature of the office of *tapariyalli-* in the post-Hittite period. Once again, the passage comes from Gurgum, the land which offers the most detailed information on the *tapariyalli-*. The only instance of

---

50 H. Craig Melchert, "Language," in *The Luwians*, ed. H. Craig Melchert (Boston, MA/Leiden: Brill, 2003), 199.

51 Giusfredi, *Sources*, 105–106; Ilya Yakubovic, "KARABURUN," Provisional Annotation of the Hieroglyphic Luwian Corpus, accessed July 15, 2021, https://www.ediana.gwi.uni-muenchen.de/corpus.php.

52 KARABURUN § 2–3.

53 KULULU 4 § 6–7.

54 KULULU 4 § 6–7.

the abstract noun *taparahit* comes from the inscription MARAŞ 4. The inscription can be considered as a celebration of the elevation of the local dynasty of Gurgum from rulership (chiefdom) to kingship, under Halparuntiya son of Mu(wa)talli in the mid-ninth century BCE. In this case, the development of monarchic power can be interpreted as a case of secondary political development due to the impact of the Assyrian expansion in the region:

> I (am) Halparuntiya the *tarwani-*, the Gurgumean king, son of Muwatalli, the *tarwani-* ... To my father and grandfather there was *taparahit*, but it did not belong to either (my) father nor (my) grandfather. In fact, I, Halparuntiya, son of Muwatalli, great-grandson of Muwizi, "allowed it to myself." I exalted (my) father, grand-father, great-grandfather and forefather ... and thereby I exalted my image for myself. But I came forth, (and) [I seated] myself on my throne ...[55]

In this passage *taparahit* is the political power exercised within a community and the dative vs. genitive construction in §§ 8–9 is indicative of the difference between the exercise of power (my father and my grandfather had/used power) and authority, that is, the legitimate control of power (power was not of my father or my grandfather). This form of power named *taparahit* evolves when Halparuntiya produces images of himself (a motif that recalls *ṣalam šarrūtīya*, namely, the definition of the royal stele by Assyrian kings), and takes his seat on the throne. This also goes with the adoption of the title REX-tis, "king," not previously used in the dynasty, as implied in this passage and shown by the MARAŞ 8 stele.

This post-Hittite trajectory toward monarchic power is profoundly different than the one of the neighboring Syro-Hittite states on the Upper Euphrates valley. There, monarchic power does not emerge from dynamics within the local communities, but from the preservation of dynastic power based on Hittite Great Kings' blood as well as divine support and legitimation, represented by the scene of the king libating to the Storm-god.[56]

55 MARAŞ 4 §§ 1, 8–11, 15–17.

56 Federico Manuelli and Lucia Mori, "The King at the Gate: Monumental Fortifications and the rise of Local Elites at Arslantepe at the end of the 2nd millennium BCE," *Origini* 39 (2016): 209–242; d'Alfonso, "Reorganization vs. Resilience"; d'Alfonso, forthcoming.

3 Conclusions

Though Hittite and post-Hittite written sources predominantly express the views and interests of central, monarchic, and imperial power, the evidence presented in the foregoing discussion demonstrates that local authorities and institutions in the political landscape of second- and early first-millennium Anatolia and northern Syria not only can be traced in the textual record, but that their careful consideration may allow us to reconstruct the local, often peripheral counterparts to royal cores in the mostly centrally produced power narratives from the Hittite and post-Hittite periods. Councils of elders and other collective institutions representative of village and city communities are known to have been part of the political landscape both in Anatolia and in Syria, particularly before the end of the Palatial Age. Dan Fleming's enormous contribution to the sociopolitical history of the ancient Near East has been to shed light on the peculiar development and great importance of these collective institutions, and their interconnection with kingship in the societies of the Middle Euphrates in the second millennium BCE and in the early first-millennium biblical world. In this paper we have focused on a particular type of local office, that of the *tapariyalli-*, whose significance and resilience may be observed through its continued documentation from the mid-fifteenth to the eighth century BCE. The second-millennium sources suggest that *tapariyalli-* denoted local authority, and that *tapariya-* and its derivatives could similarly denote the command and authority wielded by local agents. As suggested above, the chronological and geographical distribution of *tapariyalli-* and related terms suggest that they may have been adopted by the Hittite state during the process of its territorial expansion and consolidation, which had gathered momentum in the mid-fifteenth century BCE.

The sources for the post-Hittite period are less clear, but they seem to demonstrate that *tapariyalli-* was an office that continued to exist in Anatolia and was adopted in the south of the Taurus only at a much later stage. Within Anatolia, the significance of the office of *tapariyalli-* in the transition from the Hittite to the post-Hittite period can best be understood through the political developments in the Land of Gurgum. Here, by the turn of the second millennium, a powerful local family rose to prominence among the population of a river valley in the region of Kahramanmaraş and was assigned and/or claimed the office of *tapariyalli-*, thus wielding power within their community (*taparahit*). The adoption of the Anatolian Hieroglyphic script, the Luwian language, and monumental art dates to this specific period and is representative of the definition of canton states at this early stage in southern Anatolia west of the Euphrates. Kingship in Gurgum follows the earlier stage of a power derived from dynamics within the local community, and developed in connection with superregional military confrontation, the definition of royal insignia (such as the statue or the throne), and the impact of Assyrian expansionism of the mid-ninth century. While kingship in other areas of the post-Hittite world derived directly from the Hittite legacy (e.g., Malatya and Carchemish), or was an evolution of dynamics already present in the territory (e.g., the Syro-Hittite world), local societies in the Taurus region and in Cappadocia might well have maintained the administrative and territorial organization of the Late Bronze Age. When the Hittite empire collapsed, the survival of the Hittite legacy was possible thanks to the activity of local *tapariyalli*-s, who reorganized their canton polities by selecting elements of the former Hittite period and building them into a new society with new worldviews, cults, and economies.

Bibliography

Archi, Alfonso. "A Seal Impression from El-Qiṭār/Til-Abnu (Syria)." *AnSt* 43 (1993): 203–206.

Beal, Richard H. "Seeking Divine Approval for Campaign Strategy—KUB 5.1 + KUB 52.65." *Ktema* 24 (1999): 51–54.

Beckman, Gary M., Trevor R. Bryce, and Eric H. Cline. *The Ahhiyawa Texts*. Atlanta, GA: Society of Biblical Literature, 2011.

Corti, Carlo. "The North: Hanhana, Hattena, Ištahara, Hakpiš, Nerik, Zalpuwa, Tummana, Pala and the Hulana River Land." Pages 219–238 in *Hittite Landscape and Geography*. Edited by Mark Weeden and Lee Ullmann. Leiden: Brill, 2017.

d'Alfonso, Lorenzo. "Tabal, an 'Out-Group Definition' in the 1st Millennium BC." Pages 73–94 in *Leggo! Studies Presented to Frederick Mario Fales on the Occasion of His 65th Birthday*. Edited by Giovanni Battista Lanfranchi, Daniele Morandi Bonacossi, Cinzia Pappi, and Simonetta Ponchia. Wiesbaden: Harrassowitz, 2012.

d'Alfonso, Lorenzo. "An Age of Experimentation: New Thoughts on the Multiple Outcomes following the Fall of the Hittite Empire after the Results of the Excavations at Niğde-Kınık Höyük (South Cappadocia)." Pages 95–116 in *Anatolia between the 13th and the 12th Century BCE*. Edited by Stefano de Martino and Elena Devecchi. Firenze: LoGismo, 2020.

d'Alfonso, Lorenzo. "Reorganization vs. Resilience in Early Iron Age Monumental Art of Central Anatolia." Pages 81–101 in *talugaeš witteš: Ancient Near Eastern Studies Presented to Stefano de Martino on the Occasion of his 65th Birthday*. Kasion 2. Edited by Michele Cammarosano, Elena Devecchi, and Maurizio Viano. Münster: Zaphon, 2020.

d'Alfonso, Lorenzo. "City-States, Canton States, Monarchy and Aristocracy: The Political Landscape of the Early Iron Age in Central Anatolia within the Context of the Eastern Mediterranean (11th–9th Century BCE)." Forthcoming.

d'Alfonso, Lorenzo, and Annick Payne. "The Paleography of Anatolian Hieroglyphic Stone Inscriptions." *JCS* 68 (2016): 107–127.

d'Alfonso, Lorenzo, and Karen Rubinson. "Borders and Archaeology." Pages 3–35 in *Borders in Archaeology: Anatolia and the South Caucasus ca. 3500–500 BCE*. Edited by Lorenzo d'Alfonso and Karen Rubinson. Leuven/Paris/Bristol, CT: Peeters, 2021.

Emberling, Geoff. "Counternarratives: The Archaeology of the Long Term and the Large Scale." Pages 3–16 in *Social Theory in Archaeology and Ancient History: The Present, Past, and Future of Counternarratives*. Edited by Geoff Emberling. Cambridge: Cambridge University Press, 2016.

Emberling, Geoff, ed. *Social Theory in Archaeology and Ancient History: The Present, Past, and Future of Counternarratives*. Cambridge: Cambridge University Press, 2016.

Faulseit, Ronald. "Collapse, Resilience, and Transformation in Complex Societies: Modeling Trends and Understanding Diversity." Pages 43–69 in *Beyond Collapse: Archaeological Perspectives on Resilience, Revitalization, and Transformation on Complex Societies*. Edited by Ronald Faulseit. Carbondale, IL: Southern Illinois University Press, 2016.

Faulseit, Ronald, ed. *Beyond Collapse: Archaeological Perspectives on Resilience, Revitalization, and Transformation on Complex Societies*. Carbondale, IL: Southern Illinois University Press, 2016.

Friedrich, Johannes. *Hethitisches Wörterbuch: Kurzgefasste kritische Sammlung der Deutungen hethitischer Wörter. 1.–4. Lieferung*. Heidelberg: Carl Winter Universitätsverlag, 1952.

Giusfredi, Federico. *Sources for a Socio-Economic History of the Neo-Hittite States*. THeth 28. Heidelberg: Universitätsverlag Winter, 2010.

Giusfredi, Federico, Valerio Pisaniello, and Alfredo Rizza. "On the Origin and Meaning of the Assyrian Toponym Tabal." Forthcoming.

Glatz, Claudia. "Empire as Network: Spheres of Material Interaction in Late Bronze Age Anatolia." *JAA* 28 (2009): 127–141.

Glatz, Claudia. *The Making of Empire in Bronze Age Anatolia: Hittite Sovereign Practice, Resistance, and Negotiation*. Cambridge: Cambridge University Press, 2020.

Glatz, Claudia, and Roger Matthews. "Anthropology of a Frontier Zone: Hittite-Kaska Relations in Late Bronze Age North-Central Anatolia." *BASOR* 339 (2005): 47–65.

Hagenbuchner, Albertine. *Die Korrespondenz der Hethiter: 2. Teil, Die Briefe mit Transkription, Übersetzung und Kommentar*. THeth 16. Heidelberg: Carl Winter Universitätsverlag, 1989.

Hawkins, J. David. *Corpus of the Hieroglyphic Luwian Inscriptions: Vol. 1, Inscriptions of the Iron Age*. New York, NY/Berlin: de Gruyter, 2000.

Hoffner, Harry. A., and H. Craig Melchert. *A Grammar of the Hittite Language*. Winona Lake, IN: Eisenbrauns, 2008.

Hoffner, Harry A. *Letters from the Hittite Kingdom*. Atlanta, GA: Society of Biblical Literature, 2009.

Kloekhorst, Alwin. *Etymological Dictionary of the Hittite Inherited Lexicon*. Boston, MA/Leiden: Brill, 2008.

Laroche, Emmanuel. "Pouvoir central et pouvoir local en Anatolie hittite." Pages 138–143 in *Les pouvoirs locaux en Mesopotamie et dans les régions adjacentes: Actes du Colloque organisé par l'Institut des Hautes Études de Belgique, 28 et 29 janvier 1980*. Edited by André Finet. Bruxelles: Institut des Hautes Études de Belgique, 1989.

Manuelli, Federico, and Lucia Mori. "The King at the Gate: Monumental Fortifications and the rise of Local Elites at Arslantepe at the end of the 2nd millennium BCE." *Origini* 39 (2016): 209–242.

Melchert, H. Craig. *Cuneiform Luvian Lexicon*. Chapel Hill, NC: self-published, 1993.

Melchert, H. Craig. "Prehistory." Pages 8–26 in *The Luwians*. Edited by H. Craig Melchert. Boston, MA/Leiden: Brill, 2003.

Melchert, H. Craig. "Language." Pages 170–210 in *The Luwians*. Edited by H. Craig Melchert. Boston, MA/Leiden: Brill, 2003.

Miller, Jared. L. "Mursili II's Prayer Concerning the Misdeeds and the Outstanding of Tawananna." Pages 516–557 in *Proceedings of the Eighth International Congress of Hittitology: Warsaw, September 5–9, 2011*. Edited by Piotr Taracha. Warsaw: Widawnictwo Agade, 2014.

Pecchioli-Daddi, Franca. *Mestieri, professioni e dignità nell'Anatolia ittita*. Roma: Edizioni dell'Ateneo, 1982.

de Roos, Johan. *Hittite Votive Texts*. Leiden: Nederlands Instituut voor het Nabije Oosten, 2007.

Singer, Itamar. *Hittite Prayers*. Atlanta, GA: Society of Biblical Literature, 2002.

Singer, Itamar. "Danuhepa and Kurunta." Pages 739–751 in *Anatolia Antica: Scritti in ricordo di Fiorella Imparati*. Edited by Stefano de Martino and Franca Pecchioli-Daddi. 2 vols. Firenze: LoGisma, 2002.

Singer, Itamar. "Who Were the Kaška?" *Phasis* 10 (2007): 166–178.

Sürenhagen, Dietrich. "Zwei Gebete Ḫattušilis und der Puduḫepa: Textliche und literaturhistorische Untersuchungen." *AoF* 8 (1981): 83–168.

Tischler, Johann. *Hethitisches Etymologisches Glossar*. Innsbruck: Institut für Sprachen und Literaturen, 1983–2016.

Torri, Giulia, and Carlo Corti, ed. "CTH 725." Last modified August 16, 2011. https://www.hethport.uni-wuerzburg.de/txhet_besrit/intro.php?xst=CTH%20725&prgr=§%201&lg=IT&ed=G.%20Torri%20-%20C.%20Corti.

Ünal, Ahmet. *Ḫattušili III: Teil 1, Ḫattušili bis zu seiner Thronbesteigung*. THeth 3. Heidelberg: Carl Winter Universitätsverlag, 1974.

von Dassow, Eva. "The Public and the State." Pages 171–190 in *Organization, Representation, and Symbols of Power in the Ancient Near East*. Edited by Gernot Wilhelm. Winona Lake, IN: Eisenbrauns, 2012.

von Schuler, Einar. *Die Kaškäer: Ein Beitrag zur Ethnographie des alten Kleinasien*. Berlin: Walter de Gruyter, 1965.

Yakubovich, Ilya. "KARABURUN." Provisional Annotation of the Hieroglyphic Luwian Corpus. Accessed July 15, 2021. https://www.ediana.gwi.uni-muenchen.de/corpus.php.

Yakubovich, Ilya. "SULTANHAN." Provisional Annotation of the Hieroglyphic Luwian Corpus. Accessed July 15, 2021. https://www.ediana.gwi.uni-muenchen.de/corpus.php.

Yoffee, Norman. *Myths of the Archaic State: Evolution of the Earliest Cities, States, and Civilizations*. Cambridge: Cambridge University Press, 2005.

Zimansky, Paul. "The Lattimore Model and Hatti's Kaska Frontier." Pages 157–173 in *Settlement and Society: Essays Dedicated to Robert McCormick Adams*. Edited by Elizabeth C. Stone. Los Angeles, CA: Cotsen Institute of Archaeology, 2007.

8

A Man of Both Assur and Kanesh: The Case of the Merchant Ḫabdu-mālik

Nancy Highcock

1 Introduction

Toward the end of Zimri-Lim's reign, documents associated with the official Iddin-Numushda, more commonly known as Iddiyatum, were kept in Room 24 of the Mari palace archives.[1] These documents, consisting mostly of letters and brief administrative notes, comprised Iddin-Numushda's working archive, and thus provide a glimpse into the personal matters and professional activities of a "private" individual, albeit one closely connected to the king and often at his service.[2] Iddin-Numushda was not only a *wakil tamkārī*, or "Chief of Merchants,"[3] but he also belonged to the king's inner circle. He was one of the king's notables (*wedûtum*) who participated in diplomatic missions and advised the king on happenings in the city of Karana.[4] Although a powerful public official with access to the palace archives, the two letters (A.2881 and ARM 13 101) that inspire this article concern a more private relationship forged between Iddin-Numushda and an Old Assyrian merchant named Ḫabdu-mālik. The two

---

1 It is with great pleasure that I offer this contribution to Dan Fleming. His work on the people and their places of the second millennium BCE has added much richness and depth to our greater understanding of Syro-Mesopotamian sociopolitical history, and this contribution stems from our many illuminating conversations as he guided me through my dissertation research. Dan's work on the complex identities of those peopling the Mari Archives has inspired much of my own work on the men and women of Assur. I have not only benefitted intellectually from his curiosity, wisdom, and support but have also been guided by his people-first approach in nurturing my own relationships with colleagues and students.

2 Jean-Marie Durand, "Une alliance matrimoniale entre un marchand assyrien de Kanesh et un marchand mariote," in *Veenhof Anniversary Volume: Studies Presented to Klaas R. Veenhof on the Occasion of his Sixty-fifth Birthday*, ed. W.H. van Soldt, J.G. Dercksen, N.J.C. Kouwenberg, and Th.J.H. Krispijn (Leiden: NINO, 2001), 148; Ilya Arkhipov, "Chroniques Bibliographiques 19: The 'Treasure Archive' of Puzriš-Dagan from a Mari Perspective," *RA* 111 (2017): 148.

3 Dominique Charpin, "Iddiyatum et Iddin-Numusda," *NABU* 59 (1989): 38.

4 Durand, "Une alliance matrimoniale," 119 n. 4; Wolfgang Heimpel, *Letters to the Kings of Mari: A New Translation, with Historical Introduction, Notes, and Commentary* (Winona Lake, IN: Eisenbrauns, 2003), 394–404.

 | DOI:10.1163/9789004511538_009

letters, written by Ḫabdu-mālik to his counterpart in Mari, only provide half of the correspondence, of course, but their very existence, as well as the way in which Ḫabdu-mālik describes himself and Iddin Numushda, sheds light on the dynamic nature of mercantile networks and professional identity. Furthermore, Ḫabdu-mālik does not appear in any of the contemporary Old Assyrian sources, and thus these documents found at Mari are particularly illuminating with regard to not only an otherwise unknown personality, but also provides a late Old Assyrian view of a notable from Mari.

The vast majority of textual sources concerning the Old Assyrian mercantile network and life in Assur and Anatolia during the early second millennium BCE date to the *kārum* Level II period (ca. 1974–1832 BCE), and within that evidence there are only scattered references to Assyrian contacts with the wider world beyond the Anatolian-Assur axis. Textual sources dating to the Level II *kārum* period only rarely mention non-Anatolian cities and their citizens, and Mari is no exception.[5] A preexisting trade or diplomatic connection between the two cities is perhaps indicated by the presence of a seal of the *šakkanakkum* of Mari Iṣi-Dagan (ca. 2000 BCE), discovered beneath the floor of the Ishtar Temple E 2 in Assur,[6] but the bulk of recorded evidence for any ties between these two polities comes from the Mari archives dating to the reign of Shamshi-Adad, roughly coinciding with the beginning of the Level Ib *kārum* period (ca. 1831–1718 BCE).[7]

5 See Nancy Highcock, "Community Across Distance: The Forging of Identity Between Aššur and Kaneš" (Ph.D. diss., New York University, 2018), 99–100 for a general overview of the cities and groups mentioned in the Old Assyrian sources.

6 Jürgen Bär, *Die älteren Ischtar-Tempel in Assur*, WVDOG 105 (Wiesbaden: Harrassowitz, 2003).

7 For a brief overview of these sources, see Klaas R. Veenhof, "The Old Assyrian Period," in *Mesopotamia: The Old Assyrian Period*, OBO 160/5, ed. Klaas R. Veenhof and Jesper Eidem (Fribourg: Academic Press; Göttingen: Vandenhoek & Ruprecht, 2008), 140–146. For a thorough analysis of Assur and its people in the Mari archives, see Dominique Charpin and Jean-Marie Durand, "Aššur l'avant Assyrie," *MARI* 8 (1997): 367–392; and Nele Ziegler, "Ein Bittbrief eines Händlers," in *Festschrift für Hans Hirsch zum 65. Geburtstag gewidmet von seinen Freunden, Kollegen und Schülern*, ed. Arne A. Ambros and Markus Kohbach, WKZM 86 (Wien: Institut für Orientalistik, 1996), 479–488; and Ziegler, "Le Royaume d'Ekallâtum et son horizon géopolotique," in *Recueil d'études à la mémoire d'André Parrot*, ed. Dominique Charpin and Jean-Marie Durand, FM 6 (Paris: SEPOA, 2002), 211–274. Ziegler recounts a letter written by an unknown person in Carchemish to Zimri-Lim that hints at interaction between Assyrian merchants in Anatolia and Mari residents ("Ein Bittbrief," 480–482). The unknown writer promises to bring his lord various luxury goods from the cities of Kanesh, Ḫattuša, and Ḫarsamna—the first being a known location of a concentrated population of Assyrians during this period. Gojko Barjamovic (*A Historical Geography of Anatolia in the Old Assyrian Colony Period* [Copenhagen: Museum Tusculanum Press, 2011], 8–9 n. 38) also notes that Zimri-Lim's attempts to enter into trade with the king of Kanesh failed and that Anatolian goods found their way to Mari through Carchemish. See also Dominique Charpin, "Die

Evidence from the Mari archives, including a text referencing a caravan of 300 donkeys travelling to Kanesh, as well as the appearances of four new *kārums* during Level Ib, show that trade was still flourishing despite the smaller number of Assyrian mercantile documents produced during this latter period.[8] This evidence of course stems from a different sociopolitical situation than that of the earlier Old Assyrian heyday, and reflects Mari's view of Assyrians more directly than it does an Assyrian view of Mari's citizens. The existence of two letters dating to the reign of Zimri-Lim and written by an Assyrian merchant therefore offer an exciting opportunity for better understanding the Assyrians' conception of their wider network during this relatively late period.

Previous scholars have discussed both letters in detail, with Jean-Marie Durand in particular demonstrating their importance for understanding trade contacts between Mari and regions further afield.[9] Building upon Dominique Charpin's earlier conclusion that Iddin-Numushda and Iddiyatum are one and the same, Durand has shown that ARM 13 101 is the follow-up letter to the initial text A.2881 also sent by Ḫabdu-mālik.[10] As both letters have been transliterated, translated, and commented upon previously, only a brief summary of their contents is provided here.[11] The following analysis will then focus on the Assyrian perspective gained from the letters.

In the initial letter A.2881, Ḫabdu-mālik writes to the Mariote "Chief of the Merchants" Iddin-Numushda in order to enter into a personal business relationship that is to be materialized not only through the exchange of luxury items including textiles listed along with the equivalent silver value, but also through the marriage of their children. As part of his attempt to convince

Beziehungen zwischen Anatolien und der syro-mesopotamischen Welt in der altbabylonischen Zeit," in *Hattuša-Bogazköy: Das Hethitherreich im Spannungsfeld des Alten Orients*, ed. Gernot Wilhem (Wiesbaden: Colloquien der Deutschen Orient-Gesellschaft, 2008), 105–106.

8 Gojko Barjamovic, Thomas Hertel, and Mogens Trolle Larsen, *Ups and Downs at Kanesh: Chronology, History and Society in the Old Assyrian Period* (Leiden: NINO, 2012), 77. They note that the largest caravan attested during the Level II period consisted of 34 donkeys (*AKT* 6, 143–145). The caravan of 300 donkeys (ARM 26 432:1, 3–7) dates to REL 204 and may be a one-time occurrence.

9 Durand, "Une alliance matrimoniale"; see also Veenhof, "The Old Assyrian Period," 60 for a brief discussion of A.2881 and its listing of luxury trade items.

10 Charpin, "Iddiyatum et Iddin-Numusda," 39; Durand, "Une alliance matrimoniale," 119–120 and see n. 4 for his discussion of Lafont's previous argument that the recipients of these two letters were different men.

11 For full transliteration, translation, and commentary, see Durand, "Une alliance matrimoniale," 121–126.

Iddin-Numushda of his proposition, Ḫabdu-mālik situates them both on an equal social plane by calling him "my brother" and stating: "Lui, dans la ville de Mari, et moi, dans la ville d'Aššur (et) la ville de Kanesh, (nous sommes) des gens de renom" (^{6} *um-ma a-na-ku-ma šu-ú ina* URU ⌜*Ma-r*⌝*i*^{ki} ^{7} *ù a-na-ku ina* URU^{ki} *A-šur*$_{x}$ ⌜^{ki}⌝ ^{8} *i-na* URU *Ka-ni-iš*^{ki} LÚ *šu-mi*).[12] In the following letter ARM 13 101, the deal has not yet been finalized and Ḫabdu-mālik again implores Iddin-Numushda to consider his offer, although this time he refers to himself as "your son" in his opening salutation.[13] Durand has interpreted this change as indicating an acceptance of the Mariote "Chief of Merchants" as the Assyrian's superior—perhaps as established in the missing interim reply from Iddin-Numushda to Ḫabdu-mālik. Veenhof, on the other hand, has argued that this obsequiousness is only due to Ḫabdu-mālik's urgency in formalizing their partnership and not to a real or perceived power differential between the two men.[14]

In either case, it is entirely possible that Ḫabdu-mālik was himself a "Chief of Merchants," as this title was in use in Assur by this period. The title UGULA.DAM.GAR$_3$ is not known from the Old Assyrian archives dating to either *kārum* Level II or Ib, but it appears in the Old Babylonian letters AbB 8 15 and ARM 26 342. AbB 8 15 dates to the reign of Shamshi-Adad I and refers to a chief merchant in the service of that king. It may indicate a new official position established either by Shamshi-Adad or the merchants themselves to mitigate the new king's disruption of long-established trading relationships by providing a regular functionary to mediate between the merchants and the king.[15] This position was then continued during the rule of Zimri-Lim,[16] and ARM 26 342, written during the reign of Ishme-Dagan, specifically refers to an Assyrian official. In this letter, the general Yamṣûm recounts the use by the chief merchant of the Assyrians (UGULA.DAM.GAR$_3$ ^{d}*A-šur*^{ki}) of Assyrian donkeys to transport grain from Karana to Ekallatum and the Assyrian takeover of trading interests in Karana—a bold action that indicates certain Assyrian merchants continued to hold great power after the supposed heyday of the Assyrian-Anatolian trade.

The "Chief of the Merchants" was a longstanding position in southern Mesopotamia, as evidenced by archives dating to the Ur III Period, and it is well

12 Durand, "Une alliance matrimoniale," 123–124. A.2881: 6′–8′.

13 Durand, "Une alliance matrimoniale," 126. ARM 13 1010:2′.

14 Veenhof, "The Old Assyrian Period," 60, n. 243.

15 Veenhof, "The Old Assyrian Period," 141.

16 Charpin and Durand, *Aššur l'avant Assyrie*, 373–374; Dominique Charpin and Nele Ziegler, *Mari et le Proche-Orient à l'epoque amorrite: Essaie d'histoire politique*, FM 5 (Paris: SEPOA, 2003), 236.

attested at other Old Babylonian period cities such as Sippar.[17] At Sippar, the "Chief of the Merchants" acts mainly in judicial and administrative contexts, and in the late Old Babylonian period this official is closely tied to royal authority, often describing himself in seal inscriptions as a servant of the king.[18] One such figure, Ilshu-ibni, for whom three different seal impressions are known, was responsible, along with the *kārum*, for provisioning fortresses with grain and other supplies, and the Shamash Temple with sheep.[19] These civic roles led Rivkah Harris to conclude that the persons holding this title are rarely associated with trading activity, and that the "Chief of the Merchants" cannot be assumed to be a merchant.[20] However, unlike the private merchants' archives from Kanesh, or even our two letters from Ḫabdu-mālik to Iddin-Numushda at Mari, the available Old Babylonian data was produced in official legal and administrative contexts. The fact that during the late Old Babylonian period one of the chief administrators of the city is still named as the "Chief of the Merchants" at least suggests that merchants were elite agents within the city's social infrastructure and were indeed, "men of great fame," as Ḫabdu-mālik claims, regardless of their day-to-day involvement in actual trading.

The "Chiefs of the Merchants" not only possessed prestige and power within their own cities, acting as agents of the king or representatives of civic decision-making bodies, but also were able to manifest that agency across political and cultural borders, forging new networks and drawing upon their learned knowledge of faraway peoples and places. More generally, a merchant's professional activities and necessitated high levels of mobility and social acumen, and thus

17 See Steven Garfinkle, *Entrepreneurs and Enterprise in Early Mesopotamia: A Study of Three Archives from the Third Dynasty of Ur (2112–2004)* (Bethesda, MD: CDL Press, 2012) for his analysis of the archive of Tūram-ilī, a "Chief of the Merchants" from Iri-sağrig.

18 Rivkah Harris, *Ancient Sippar: A Demographic Study of an Old-Babylonian City (1894–1595)*, PIHANS 36 (Leiden: NINO, 1975), 71–76, 257. For seal impressions describing merchants thusly, see Douglas Frayne, *Old Babylonian Period (2003–1595 B.C.): Early Periods*, RIME 4 (Toronto: University of Toronto Press, 1990), 417, no. 2013; 410, no. 2007.

19 Seth Richardson, *Texts from the Late Old Babylonian Period* (Boston, MA: ASOR), 15–17. Caroline Janssen, "Samsu-iluna and the Hungry Naditums," in *Mesopotamian History and Environment: Northern Akkad Project Reports* 5, ed. L. de Meyer and H. Gasche (Ghent: University of Ghent, 1991), 3–39, shows that the iimportance of this role is again reflected in later school copies of a letter where the king Shamshu-iluna writes to the *kārum* of Sippar and the "Chief of the Merchants" about the impoverished conditions of the *nadītu*-women. This suggests that the economic concerns of both the *gagûm* and *kārum* were intertwined and that the merchants possessed the wealth and authority to effect social measures within the city.

20 Harris, *Ancient Sippar*, 73.

they could forge new and innovative networks of communication and connection beyond those of official diplomatic or economic channels. Ḫabdu-mālik's description of himself and his Mariote colleague may be an ingratiating boast, but it also hints at these networks and how merchants conceived of their place in a multicultural and highly interconnected world.

2 Alternative Mercantile Networks

Ḫabdu-mālik's exaltation of his and Iddin-Numushda's own importance is thus of twofold importance. By reaching out to a powerful notable in another city, he is attempting to create a new trading relationship that operates on a personal level, outside of official treaties sanctioned by the central authorities or governing body of the merchant collective, i.e., the *kārum*. Secondly, his description of himself as a man of both Assur and Kanesh speaks to the type of expansive community that the Assyrian merchants generated and maintained across great distances, as well as how some of these men and women may have perceived themselves as belonging to multiple places across time and space—a true cosmopolitan elite.

The Assyrian merchant community continued to regulate trade between themselves and polities abroad as demonstrated by the fact that three of the four extant Old Assyrian trade treaties date to the *kārum* Level Ib period. These treaties, conducted between the "City" (Assur) and the foreign rulers of Kanesh and Ḫaḫḫum in Anatolia and Apum in Syria—all postdate Shamshi-Adad's reign, much as our two Mari letters do. They have been discussed at length with regard to their actors, stipulations, and wider implications for socio-political relationships during the mid-eighteenth century BCE.[21] The treaties provide a general set of ground-rules for interaction between the Assyrian merchants and foreign polities. However, there were many different types of business and personal relationships that occurred between Assyrians and others within these

21 Jesper Eidem, "An Old Assyrian Treaty from Tell Leilan," in *Marchands, dilpomates et empereurs: Études sur la civilisation Mésopotamienne offertes à Paul Garelli*, ed. Dominique Charpin and F. Joannès (Paris: Éditions Recherche sur les Civilisations, 1991), 185–207; Eidem, *The Royal Archives from Tell Leilan: Old Babylonian Letters and Treaters from the Lower Town Palace East*, PIHANS 117 (Leiden: NINO, 2011); Veenhof, "The Old Assyrian Period," 183–218; Klaas R. Veenhof, "New Mesopotamian Treaties from the Early Second Millennium BC from the *Kārum* Kanesh and Tell Leilan (Šehna)," *ZAR* 19 (2013): 23–57; Cahit Günbattı, "Two Treaty Texts Found at Kültepe," in *Assyria and Beyond: Studies Presented to Mogens Trolle Larsen*, ed. by Jan Gerrit Dercksen, PIHANS 100 (Leiden: NINO, 2004); Highcock, "Community Across Distance," 259–297.

cities and the many other settlements where Assyrian merchants lived and worked. As demonstrated by the numerous mixed Assyrian-Anatolian families and business interactions, the professional was often, if not always, personal. Outside of Anatolia, however, there is far less concrete evidence concerning the types of personal connections that the Assyrian merchants could forge with their foreign counterparts: this is why the correspondence between Ḫabdu-mālik and Iddin-Numushda is so valuable. Not only do the letters reveal an Assyrian reaching out to a Mariote he considers his business equal, but he proposes to merge not only their trade interests, but also their families through the marriage of their children.

Texts from private houses in the important trading center of Sippar shine another spotlight on how marriage could potentially aid in furthering business interests abroad. As mentioned, Sippar was home to a civic administration in which men with the title of "Chief of Merchants" played a significant role. Furthermore, there is substantial evidence that merchants from Sippar also lived and worked in *kārum* communities at cities such as Mari and Susa. Sippar's position on the Middle Euphrates encouraged its role as a mediator between the south and the northwest; the city is listed as a stop on an itinerary between Larsa and Emar.[22] It is not surprising, then, that a small number of cuneiform sources in Old Assyrian ductus from Sippar mention Sippar and its merchants along with "proper" Assyrian names and invocations of the god.[23] This evidence does not substantiate the presence of an Assyrian *kārum* in Sippar. Indeed, it is clear from the textual record that Assyrians did not generally travel south but received people and goods in Assur. Rather, these texts demonstrate that smaller networks between individual merchants could exist alongside the one regulated by "The City" (Assur).

One particular letter in this group (BM 97188), first analyzed by Christopher Walker, lists fourteen different loans, the first of which names the issuer as a certain Warad-Sin. Four of the loans are made to people with distinctly Assyrian names. One of the loans is dated to the *limmum* (or Assyrian year-eponym) and uses the "weight of the City Hall" (NA4 É *a-lim*); another also uses such a weight.[24] Walker surmised that the references to Assyrian institutions signified that these loan transactions occurred in Assur and that Warad-Sin

---

22 Christopher Walker, "Some Assyrians at Sippar in the Old Babylonian Period," *Anatolian Studies* 30 (1980): 15.

23 Farouk H.N. al-Rawi and Stephanie Dalley, *Old Babylonian Texts from Private Houses at Abu Habbah Ancient Sippar*, Edubba 7 (London: Nabu Publications, 2000); see also Walker, "Some Assyrians at Sippar," 15–16 and the references therein.

24 Walker, "Some Assyrians at Sippar," 17.

was an institutional official with authority over foreign trade.[25] In 1991, Klaas Veenhof published two related commercial texts listing shipments (BM 97079) and shipments and loans (BM 96968) which, when compared to the known correspondence of Warad-Sin, deepened our understanding of this relationship between Sippar and Assur. Veenhof demonstrated that Warad-Sin was the writer/speaker of all these texts and was most likely acting not in an institutional capacity, but as a private merchant and successful moneylender. Furthermore, related correspondence between Warad-Sin and his daughter in Assur, as well as the fact that many of the shipments were coming *to* Sippar, led Veenhof to conclude that Warad-Sin was himself an Assyrian. Rather than running his trading activities from Assur, he had settled down with a second wife in Sippar for a period of at least ten years across the reigns of Hammurabi and Samsi-iluna (ca. 1750–1740 BCE).[26] However, there does not appear to be enough evidence to confirm this scenario, and the texts may instead reflect loans where purchases were made in Assur on credit. In this second interpretation, Warad-Sin does not embody evidence for Assyrian merchants settling in a Babylonian city, but rather shows how business contacts developed alongside kinship relationships such as marriage. In either case, such a network would reflect the work of a well-connected individual as opposed to the official collective endeavour demonstrated in the roughly contemporary treaties and bulk of the Assyrian evidence dating back to the *kārum* Level II period.

In addition to the personal business letters of merchants such as Ḫabdu-mālik and Warad-Sin, more official correspondence also hints at the types of independent and fluid trade activities that could take place alongside more centrally organized interregional exchange. One Late Babylonian text concerning trade between Sippar and Babylon demonstrates that much of the cross-regional trade of this period may have skirted around official procedures and routes.

25 Walker, "Some Assyrians at Sippar," 17; Klaas R. Veenhof, "Assyrian Commercial Activities in Old Babylonian Sippar—Some New Evidence," in *Marchands, dilpomates et empereurs: Études sur la civilisation Mésopotamienne offertes à Paul Garelli*, ed. Dominique Charpin and F. Joannès (Paris: Éditions Recherche sur les Civilisations, 1991), 287.

26 Veenhof, "Assyrian Commercial Treaties," 298. Veenhof writes (p. 301): "One might venture the conclusion that Warad-Sin was originally an Assyrian trader, with regular contacts with Northern Babylonia, who eventually settled in Sippar, where he acquired his own *bīt naptārim*, from which he organized the import and sale of products for which there was a local demand. Though based in Sippar, he must have travelled regularly, since the letters of his wife were written from Sippar when he was away."

> Speak to my master: thus says Shami-rabi. As my master knows, since at the time of Hammurapi the brickwork of Baṣu has been laid, we live in the post of Baṣu. With regard to boats going up and going downstream, a merchant who has a passport (lit. *ṭuppi šarrim* = tablet of the king) we examine and let pass, a merchant who has no passport we send back to Babylon. Now since the house of Anatum and Rish-Shamash has been established at Babylon, everyone from Emar and Halab (?) has been allowed to pass me and I could not examine any boat in their hands.[27]

In this letter, Shami-rabi of Sippar is describing two different scenarios of merchant mobility. In general, merchants travelling up and down the Euphrates River must stop at the control station located at Baṣu, possibly north of Sippar, in order to present their proof of royal permission. In another, the two houses (É) of Anatum and Rish-shamash have been given permission to pass through the control-point unchecked. These two merchant firms are probably from Emar and Halab (Aleppo) and have established trading posts at Babylon. The freedom with which merchants from the northwest Euphrates could travel to and from Babylon seems surprising when juxtaposed with the Babylonian merchants sent back to their city for lacking the appropriate permission. However, when read in tandem with the other texts discussed above, the flexibility and operational diversity inherent to these trade networks makes more sense. This text dates to after the time of Hammurabi, who extended his Babylonian kingdom as far north as Mari. Therefore, the region including both Babylon and Baṣu fell under the same political control. A possible interpretation is that the merchants from Emar and Halab, as true outsiders, were granted special access with no need of royal decree: their foreignness provided them with the ability to operate outside of Babylonian control. It is possible these men were operating independently, or at least outside of the regulated networks controlled by official treaties and agreements.

Jan Gerrit Dercksen has postulated that such alternative networks, at least in the Old Assyrian case, may have proliferated in the post Shamshi-Adad era. In addition to the letters between Ḫabdu-mālik and Iddin-Numushda, there is further evidence from Mari that ca. 1770 BCE envoys from the *kārum*s of Kanesh and Urshu may have traveled to Mari on trading missions. The envoys in question bear Babylonian and Assyrian names, and so Dercksen has argued that

27 *CT* 2 20; see Wilhelmus F. Leemans, *Foreign Trade in the Old Babylonian Period: As Revealed by Texts from Southern Mesopotamia* (Leiden: E.J. Brill, 1960), 105–106 (discussed on 108, no. 16).

they represent Assyrians operating beyond the normative trade relations.[28] That such relationships appear in these non-Anatolian contexts after the death of Shamshi-Adad may indicate that the earlier regulated network had broken down, and that Assyrian *kārums* in Anatolia were able to act independently. As Dercksen points out, this hypothesis fits very well with the overtures of Ḫabdu-mālik—another Assyrian merchant looking to forge direct trade connections beyond the Anatolia-Assur axis. The letters A.2881 and ARM 13 101 thus indicate a possible transformation in the types of trade networks in which Assyrian merchants engaged, during the mid-eighteenth century BCE. This is not to say that such personal side ventures were unknown in the earlier period of Old Assyrian trade: it is well known that the Old Assyrian merchant firms were generally trading in a private capacity. This customary trading independence perhaps developed into new, previously unexplored or off-limit connections as sociopolitical circumstances changed, in this case with Mari.

3 A Man of Assur and Kanesh

Despite Ḫabdu-mālik's branching out into new trade opportunities, he still regards himself as both a "man of the city of Assur" and a "man of the city of Kanesh." This identity is deeply tied to the longstanding trade relationship between Assur and Anatolia but the way that it is formulated is important: he is a man who identifies with two places at once! Of course, he cannot physically be in both places simultaneously, but that is how he conceptually describes himself as an Assyrian to this foreign merchant: a man of both Assur and Kanesh. Furthermore, identifying himself with the city of Kanesh, and not the *kārum* Kanesh is unusual, and may again speak to how the Assyrian merchants viewed themselves in in this late stage of the Old Assyrian mercantile network. Previous studies of the *kārum* Kanesh Level II texts and Level Ib treaties have examined the collective identity of Assyrians at Kanesh and other Anatolian settlements, arguing that the Assyrian community was spread over distance; that despite the intercultural or third culture community forged at Kanesh and elsewhere, there was still a strong Assyrian identity that extended across Anatolian-Mesopotamian cultural and political borders.[29]

28 Jan Gerrit Dercksen, "Assyrian *kārum* envoys in Mari," *NABU* 78 (2014): 127–128.

29 Highcock, "Community Across Distance," and Nancy Highcock, "Assyrians Abroad: Expanding Borders through Mobile Identities in the Middle Bronze Age," *JANEH* 4 (2017): 61–93.

In those records, men and women from the city-state of Assur could designate themselves as a "son" or "daughter" of Assur (DUMU.MEŠ/*mēr'a, mēr'at Aššur*), in contrast to the etic designation *aš-šu-ri* or LÚ.MEŠ *aš-šu-ri* in the records from Mari. The emic formula probably denotes independent and property-holding free citizens of the city, sometimes also referred to as *awīlum/awīltum* in the texts, as opposed to slaves (*wardum/amtum*) who comprised the other sector of Assyrian society.[30] Thomas Hertel argues that as free citizens, the concept of *mēr'a/mēr'at Aššur* was tied not only to their geographical origins, but to their religious and ethnic origins as well. Hertel himself acknowledges that this designation is rare and always occurs with a "legal emphasis," though legal boundaries can certainly align with cultural boundaries, particularly in the Old Assyrian case where the term is often used to differentiate Assyrians from Anatolians.[31]

This legal boundary is normally that of the *kārum*—the merchant community living abroad. In early second-millennium Mesopotamia, the *kārum* became a major feature of the urban landscape and the merchants residing there organized themselves and exercised a degree of autonomy within the broader political networks of the city.[32] References to the *kārum* Sippar in Mari and in Mishlan or to the "street of the men of Isin" in Sippar indicate that merchants often set up communities in foreign towns and that, though the term *kārum* often retained a spatial dimension, it also represented the community—the people—that resided there. The *kārum* sent and received letters, issued legal decisions, and met with foreign authorities. It was a body of people physically living apart from the population of their home city that could still exercise their rights abroad as members of the *kārum* of their home city.

The Old Assyrian merchants, however, used the term *kārum only* in the latter sense, losing the semblances of its original meaning as a physical quay/harbour and instead defining it as a political community, "distinguished from the local inhabitants not by walls, but by jurisdiction."[33] In Anatolia, there were no merchant "harbours" located on navigable waterways; the Assyrians adopted the

30 Klaas R. Veenhof, "Old Assyrian Period," in *A History of Ancient Near Eastern Law*, ed. Raymond Westbrook, HOS 1 (Leiden: Brill), 447.

31 Thomas Hertel, *Old Assyrian Legal Practices: Law and Dispute in the Ancient Near East*, PIHANS 123 (Leiden: NINO, 2013), 22 n. 174, 33.

32 Mogens Trolle Larsen, *Ancient Kanesh: A Merchant Colony in Bronze Age Anatolia* (New York, NY: Cambridge University Press, 2015), 149 citing texts found in Leemans, "Foreign Trade," 106–107 and Harris, "Ancient Sippar," 11.

33 Gökçe Bike Yazicioğlu-Santamaria, "Locals, Immigrants, and Marriage Ties at Kültepe: Results of Strontium Isotope Analysis on Human Teeth from Lower Town Graves," in *Move-*

term solely to mean the merchant community that settled and traveled among the local inhabitants. It is telling that unlike their southern counterparts, the Old Assyrian merchants did not refer to the portion of their population abroad as the *kārum* Assur residing in GN—e.g., *kārum Aššur ša ina Kaneš wašbu*—but rather as the *kārums* Kanesh, Durhamit, Ḫaḫḫum, etc. The members of these *kārums* were undoubtedly Assyrian citizens residing in those Anatolian polities, but the semantic difference between the Old Babylonian and Old Assyrian use of this term denotes a conceptually different "political and commercial pattern" in the Assyrian community.[34] Although the *kārum* was a body of people living physically apart from the population of Assur, it still operated under the jurisdiction of its mother city. At the same time, the *kārum* integrated itself, through professional and personal relationships, into a local community that was different from its own with regard to language, law, politics, and social and religious practice.

Ḫabdu-mālik describing himself as a man of the *city* of Kanesh speaks not only of his flexible identity as a mobile, cosmopolitan long-distance merchant, but also of his sense of himself as a fully active member of two different societies. This is not only a case of a community across distance but of an individual who is personally invested in two different places. In his study of collective governance during the Mari period, Daniel Fleming's overarching framework for studying the civic and tribal identities of his subjects incorporated "the social phenomenon that stands at the center of archaeological study of the ancient world: the town as hamlet, as village, as city; as political, military, or symbolic center."[35] Towns and cities are not just built spaces, but socially charged places. The distinction is crucial, as historians and archaeologists alike have often conceived of this ubiquitous term—Akkadian *ālum*—largely as a physical entity located in a particular time and place, and less as a population. Indeed, as Fleming as demonstrated, for the Mari landscape, these non-social approaches do not fit the extant evidence:

> When we search for all of the institutions or stock terminologies defined by the "town" we find only towns in action as bodies of people. Kings could

---

ment, Resources, Interaction: Proceedings of the 2nd Kültepe International Meeting, Kültepe, 26–30 July 2015: Studies Dedicated to Klaas Veenhof, ed. Fikri Kulakoğlu and Gojko Barjamovic, Subartu 39/KIM 2 (Turnhout: Brepols, 2017), 77.

34 Larsen, *Ancient Kanesh*, 149.

35 Daniel E. Fleming, *Democracy's Ancient Ancestors: Mari and Early Collective Governance* (Cambridge: Cambridge University Press, 2004), 170.

> not build their governments without contending with what must have been a preexisting landscape of towns, and these towns were defined in deeply collective terms.[36]

By aligning himself with the city of Kanesh, Ḫabdu-mālik designates himself as part of the Kanesh collective identity. He describes himself as a notable person in a wider population in both places, independent of the Assyrian *kārum* collective but very much a part of the Kaneshite collective. Whether this is an accurate portrayal of his position in both societies or not, he represents himself as the most effective kind of merchant: not simply a mobile individual able to code-switch or integrate when the context calls, but a man able to be part of both cities at once.

4 Conclusion

The texts A.2881 and ARM 13 101 illustrate the tensions inherent in merchant mobility during the Middle Bronze Age. They were at once agents of the state, bound by trade treaties and tied to the economic interests of the king, while also potentially independent agents capable of working beyond diplomatic controls. Merchants could not only move across established political and cultural borders, but they could potentially become fully integrated members of foreign cities. Their freedom of movement depended on the current political climate and the agendas of the central authorities, but they retained agency in matters of trade that could not be curtailed fully by changing political fortunes. Ḫabdu-mālik seized upon an opportunity to create a new trading partnership and expand his economic prospects, perhaps at a time when the traditional trading relationships between Assur and Kanesh were being disrupted or transformed in other ways. At the same time, he clearly thrived in a world in which the political, legal, and even social borders between Assur and Kanesh were blurred, to the extent that he was no longer an Assyrian travelling or living in Kanesh but a man who lived as both an Assyrian and Kaneshite. These two letters from Mari thus not only offer a tantalizing glimpse of a powerful elite during the reign of Zimri-Lim, but also illuminate the fading days of the Assyrian trade network during the late Old Assyrian period.

36 Fleming, *Democracy's Ancient Ancestors*, 171.

Bibliography

al-Rawi, Farouk H.N., and Stephanie Dalley. *Old Babylonian Texts from Private Houses at Abu Habbah Ancient Sippar*. Edubba 7. London: Nabu Publications, 2000.

Arkhipov, Ilya. "Chroniques Bibliographiques 19: The 'Treasure Archive' of Puzriš-Dagan from a Mari Perspective." *RA* 111 (2017): 147–154.

Bär, Jürgen. *Die älteren Ischtar-Tempel in Assur*. WVDOG 105. Wiesbaden: Harrassowitz, 2003.

Barjamovic, Gojko. *A Historical Geography of Anatolia in the Old Assyrian Colony Period*. Copenhagen: Museum Tusculanum Press, 2011.

Barjamovic, Gojko, Thomas Hertel, and Mogens Trolle Larsen. *Ups and Downs at Kanesh: Chronology, History and Society in the Old Assyrian Period*. Leiden: NINO, 2012.

Charpin, Dominique. "Iddiyatum et Iddin-Numusda." *NABU* 59 (1989): 38.

Charpin, Dominique. "Die Beziehungen zwischen Anatolien und der syro-mesopotamischen Welt in der altbabylonischen Zeit." Pages 95–108 in *Hattuša-Bogazköy: Das Hethitherreich im Spannungsfeld des Alten Orients*. Edited by Gernot Wilhem. Wiesbaden: Colloquien der Deutschen Orient-Gesellschaft, 2008.

Charpin, Dominique, and Jean-Marie Durand. "Assur l'avant Assyrie." *MARI* 8 (1997): 367–392.

Charpin, Dominique, and Nele Ziegler. *Mari et le Proche-Orient à l'epoque amorrite: Essaie d'histoire politique*. FM 5. Paris: SEPOA, 2003.

Dercksen, Jan Gerrit. "Assyrian *kārum* envoys in Mari." *NABU* 78 (2014): 127–128.

Durand, Jean-Marie. "Une alliance matrimoniale entre un marchand assyrien de Kanesh et un marchand mariote." Pages 119–132 in *Veenhof Anniversary Volume: Studies Presented to Klaas R. Veenhof on the Occasion of his Sixty-fifth Birthday*. Edited by van W.H. Soldt, Jan Gerritt Dercksen, N.J.C. Kouwenberg, and Th.J.H. Krispijn. PIHANS 89. Leiden: NINO, 2001.

Eidem, Jesper. "An Old Assyrian Treaty from Tell Leilan." Pages 185–207 in *Marchands, dilpomates et empereurs: Études sur la civilisation Mésopotamienne offertes à Paul Garelli*. Edited by Dominique Charpin and F. Joannès. Paris: Éditions Recherche sur les Civilisations, 1991.

Eidem, Jesper. *The Royal Archives from Tell Leilan: Old Babylonian Letters and Treaties from the Lower Town Palace East*. PIHANS 117. Leiden: NINO, 2011.

Fleming, Daniel E. *Democracy's Ancient Ancestors: Mari and Early Collective Governance*. Cambridge: Cambridge University Press, 2004.

Frayne, Douglas. *Old Babylonian Period (2003–1595 B.C.): Early Periods*. RIME 4. Toronto: University of Toronto Press, 1990.

Garfinkle, Steven. *Entrepreneurs and Enterprise in Early Mesopotamia: A Study of Three Archives from the Third Dynasty of Ur (2112–2004)*. Bethesda, MD: CDL Press, 2012.

Günbattı, Cahit. "Two Treaty Texts Found at Kültepe." Pages 249–268 in *Assyria and Beyond: Studies Presented to Mogens Trolle Larsen*. Edited by Jan Gerrit Dercksen. PIHANS 100. Leiden: NINO, 2004.

Harris, Rivkah. *Ancient Sippar: A Demographic Study of an Old-Babylonian City (1894–1595)*. PIHANS 36. Leiden: NINO, 1975.

Heimpel, Wolfgang. *Letters to the Kings of Mari: A New Translation, with Historical Introduction, Notes, and Commentary*. Winona Lake, IN: Eisenbrauns, 2003.

Hertel, Thomas. *Old Assyrian Legal Practices: Law and Dispute in the Ancient Near East*. PIHANS 123. Leiden: NINO, 2013.

Highcock, Nancy. "Assyrians Abroad: Expanding Borders through Mobile Identities in the Middle Bronze Age." *JANEH* 4 (2017): 61–93.

Highcock, Nancy. "Community Across Distance: The Forging of Identity Between Aššur and Kaneš." Ph.D. diss., New York University, 2018.

Janssen, Caroline. "Samsu-iluna and the Hungry Naditums." Pages 3–39 in *Mesopotamian History and Environment: Northern Akkad Project Reports 5*. Edited by L. de Meyer and H. Gasche. Ghent: University of Ghent, 1991.

Larsen, Mogens Trolle. *Ancient Kanesh: A Merchant Colony in Bronze Age Anatolia*. New York, NY: Cambridge University Press, 2015.

Leemans, Wilhelmus F. *Foreign Trade in the Old Babylonian Period: As Revealed by Texts from Southern Mesopotamia*. Leiden: E.J. Brill, 1960.

Richardson, Seth. *Texts from the Late Old Babylonian Period*. Boston, MA: ASOR, 2010.

Veenhof, Klaas R. "Assyrian Commercial Activities in Old Babylonian Sippar—Some New Evidence." Pages 287–303 in *Marchands, dilpomates et empereurs: Études sur la civilisation Mésopotamienne offertes à Paul Garelli*. Edited by Dominique Charpin and F. Joannès. Paris: Éditions Recherche sur les Civilisations, 1991.

Veenhof, Klaas R. "Old Assyrian Period." Pages 431–482 in *A History of Ancient Near Eastern Law*. Edited by Raymond Westbrook. HOS 1. Leiden: Brill, 2003.

Veenhof, Klaas R. "The Old Assyrian Period." Pages 13–264 in *Mesopotamia: The Old Assyrian Period*. Edited by Klaas R. Veenhof and Jesper Eidem. OBO 160/5. Fribourg: Academic Press; Göttingen: Vandenhoek & Ruprecht, 2008.

Veenhof, Klaas R. "New Mesopotamian Treaties from the Early Second Millennium BC from the *Kārum* Kanesh and Tell Leilan (Šehna)." *ZAR* 19 (2013): 23–57.

Walker, Christopher. "Some Assyrians at Sippar in the Old Babylonian Period." *Anatolian Studies* 30 (1980): 15–22.

Yazıcıoğlu-Santamaria, Gökçe Bike. "Locals, Immigrants, and Marriage Ties at Kültepe: Results of Strontium Isotope Analysis on Human Teeth from Lower Town Graves." Pages 63–84 in *Movement, Resources, Interaction: Proceedings of the 2nd Kültepe International Meeting, Kültepe, 26–30 July 2015: Studies Dedicated to Klaas Veenhof*. Edited by Fikri Kulakoğlu and Gojko Barjamovic. Subartu 39/KIM 2. Turnhout: Brepols, 2017.

Ziegler, Nele. "Ein Bittbrief eines Händlers." Pages 479–488 in *Festschrift für Hans Hirsch zum 65. Geburtstag gewidmet von seinen Freunden, Kollegen und Schülern*. Edited by Arne A. Ambros and Markus Kohbach. WKZM 86. Wien: Institut für Orientalistik, 1996.

Ziegler, Nele. "Le Royaume d'Ekallâtum et son horizon géopolitique." Pages 211–274 in *Recueil d'études à la mémoire d'André Parrot*. Edited by Dominique Charpin and Jean-Marie Durand. FM 6. Paris: SEPOA, 2002.

9

City Dwellers and Backcountry Folk: Ritual Interactions between Mobile Peoples and Urban Centers in Late Bronze Age Syria

Dylan R. Johnson

In his work on the Mari archives, Daniel Fleming outlined two "modes" by which ancient Near Eastern scribes described social identity: one was by place, especially in relation to a settlement, and the other was by names that "transcend[ed] the boundaries of settled polities."[1] Individuals could claim both social identities simultaneously and deploy them for different purposes.[2] Middle Bronze Age (MBA) Mari revealed that dichotomies like tribe and state, nomad and city-dweller, pastoralist and farmer were too reductive, often conflating subsistence strategies, settlement patterns, and social organization into a single monolithic category defined in opposition to the urbanized state. Far from hostile outsiders, mobile peoples were fundamental components of the Mari kingdom and shared a common social identity with urban dwellers—an identity that both groups maintained across space and time.[3]

The current article returns to the cuneiform archive that first captured Fleming's academic interest, Late Bronze Age (LBA) Emar, evaluating it according to the two modes of social identity that he defined at Mari. This study is divided into two parts: the first section compares and contrasts Assyrian, Hittite, and Emarite depictions of mobile peoples in the Middle Euphrates, reeval-

1 Daniel Fleming, *Democracy's Ancient Ancestors: Mari and Early Collective Governance* (Cambridge: Cambridge University Press, 2004), 28.

2 The ability to negotiate different social identities defined the reign of Zimri-Lim, who assumed kingship over the settled people of Mari (the so-called *Aḫ-Purratim*) through the political and military strength of his tribal kin (the Sim'alites). This was reflected in his titulary as "king of Mari and the *māt Ḫana*" (Dominique Charpin and Jean-Marie Durand, "'Fils de Sim'al': Les origines tribales des rois de Mari," *RA* 80 [1986]: 230–231).

3 This is what the sociologist Anthony Giddens deemed "distanciation," describing how physical and temporal separation of populations need not necessarily result in fragmentation (*A Contemporary Critique of Historical Materialism*, vol. 1 of *Power, Property and the State* [Berkeley, CA: University of California Press, 1981], 90–108). See also Anne Porter, "Beyond Dimorphism: Ideologies and Materialities of Kinship as Time-Space Distanciation," in *Nomads, Tribes, and the State in the Ancient Near East: Cross-disciplinary Perspectives*, ed. Jeffery Szuchman, OIS 5 (Chicago, IL: Oriental Institute of the University of Chicago, 2009), 201–225.

 | DOI:10.1163/9789004511538_010

uating the traditional dimorphic model for nomadic-sedentary interactions. The second section focuses on three Emar rituals that celebrate the interchange between summer and fall—the rites of Zarātu (Emar 446) and two forms of the *zukru* ritual (Emar 373+/Emar 375+). These rituals show how the inhabitants of Emar not only carved out a space for mobile peoples within their urban framework, but also how they laid claim to an alternative social identity for themselves. This identity was embedded in the physical landscape, it was imagined to predate the town and its administrative organs, and most importantly, it was an identity that they shared with mobile peoples.

1 Depictions of Mobile Peoples in Late Bronze Age Syria

To understand how the inhabitants of Emar used ritual to incorporate both urban and nonurban stakeholders in the city, a brief foray into the complex sociopolitical landscape of Emar and its environs is necessary. MBA Emar, more commonly spelled Imar, and the region of Yamḫad represented the northwestern terminus of the Yaminite territorial "range" (*nigḫum*).[4] During this period, mobile peoples operated throughout the Fertile Crescent, with clear political and social ties to sedentary populations.[5] By the LBA, however, the archives of Emar depict a largely urban-centered world, where social identity was defined almost exclusively in association with towns.[6] Unlike contemporary Ugarit

4 In a letter sent to Zimri-Lim (A.2730), the Sim'alite *merḫûm* Ibâl-El reminds the king of the pastoral range of the Yaminites and Sim'alites: "The land of Yamḫad, the land of Qaṭna, and the land of Amurrû is the pastoral range (*ni-ig-ḫu-um*) of the Yaminites. In that land, the Yaminites sate themselves with grain and tend flocks (in) their pastures. Since the (parting$^{?}$) of ways (*ù iš-tu da-ar-ka-tim*), the pastoral range of the Ḫana (= Sim'alites) has been Ida-Maraṣ." For treatments of this text, see ARM 26/2, pp. 32–34; Jean-Marie Durand, "Peuplement et sociétés à l'époque amorrite: les clans bensim'alites," in *Amurru 3: Nomades et sédentaires dans le Proche-Orient ancien*, ed. Christophe Nicolle, CRRAI 46 (Paris: Éditions de recherche, 2004), 120–121; Fleming, *Democracy*, 29; Sasson, *From the Mari Archives: An Anthology of Old Babylonian Letters*. (Winona Lake, IN: Eisenbrauns, 2015), 145–146; "A.2730: Lettre de Ibal-El à son seigneur (= Zimri-Lim)," www.archibab.fr.

5 An OB letter from the site of Emar mentions the *sutû* ($^{\text{lú.meš}}$*su-ti-i*^{ki}) (Emar 536:26–27) (Jean-Marie Durand, "La cité-état d'Imâr à l'époque des rois de Mari," *MARI* 6 [1990]: 90). The fifteenth-century BCE Idrimi Inscription mentions both *sutû* pastoralists (ERIN.MEŠ *su-tu-ú*^{ki}) in the desert regions near Emar (*i-na ma-at ḫu-ri-ib-te*^{ki}) and the *'apiru* (ERIN.MEŠ ^{lú}SA.GAZ) in the town of Amiya, situated in the land of Canaan (*i-na ma-at ki-in-a-nim*^{ki})—perhaps just south of Tripoli, Lebanon.

6 For individuals identified by towns at Emar, see the helpful index in Sophie Démare-Lafont and Daniel Fleming, "Emar Chronology and Scribal Streams: Cosmopolitanism and Legal Diversity," *RA* 109 (2015): 75–76.

and Amarna, the abundant documentation from Emar makes almost no reference to mobile peoples like the *sutû* or the *ʿapiru*. Previous interpreters like Gary Beckman surmised that "wider groupings of kin seem to be vestigial in thirteenth-century Emariote society. No particular designations for clans or tribes are to be found in the documents, comparable to the Beni Yamina and Beni Simʾal of the Mari archives."[7] Jean-Marie Durand similarly emphasized how dramatically the social structures of LBA Emar differed from those of the Mari period, while cautioning that the perceived absence of mobile populations at Emar was the result of their obscurity in the documentation, not their departure from this region.[8] Like Ugarit and the southern Levant, the mobile populations of the Middle Euphrates were often affiliated with urban centers, though not necessarily defined by them.[9] The inhabitants of Emar set aside important places for mobile peoples within their urban frameworks, but the terms they used to describe them differed from those used elsewhere.

The inherent difficulties with identifying mobile peoples in the Emar archives began with the initial publications of the corpus in the 1980s. Both Daniel Arnaud and John Huehnergard identified a social group, known as the "*liʾmu* of the field(s)" ($^{\text{[diš]}}$*li-im* A.ŠA$_3$$^{\text{[meš/ḫi.a]}}$),[10] which seemed to describe a mobile component of Emar's population.[11] Interpreting the writing of *li-im* as

---

7 Gary Beckman, "Family Values on the Middle Euphrates in the Thirteenth Century BCE," in *Emar: The History, Religion, and Culture of a Syrian Town in the Late Bronze Age*, ed. Mark Chavalas (Bethesda, MD: CDL, 1996), 59.

8 Jean-Marie Durand observed that, "les anciennes structures bédouines (grands rassemblements tribaux à économie surtout pastorale) sont remplacées dans notre documentation par des groupements familiaux plus réduits (clans villageois) autour d'intérêts fonciers précis. Je ne dis pas que l'ancien ordre a disparu, mais ce n'est pas celui que nous documentent les villages euphratiques" ("1 *lîm* a-šà = «même de loin», à Emar," *NABU* [2004]: 24).

9 Brendon C. Benz, *The Land Before the Kingdom of Israel: A History of the Southern Levant and the People who Populated It*, HACL 7 (Winona Lake, IN: Eisenbrauns, 2016), 136.

10 Found in the nonrepudiation clause of twelve legal documents, the expression appears in both scribal streams at Emar: the earlier Syrian/Conventional style (S/C) and the later Syro-Hittite/Free-Format documents (SH/FF) (Daniel Arnaud, "Les textes d'Emar et la chronologie de la fin du bronze recent," *Syria* 52 [1975]: 87–92; Daniel Fleming and Sophie Démare-Lafont, "Tablet Terminology at Emar: 'Conventional' and 'Free Format'," *AuOr* 27 [2009]: 19–26). Most of these texts are testaments (*ASJ* 13 24; *ASJ* 13 27; Emar 30; 80; 180; 185; 213; RE 15; 39; 57), though there is also an adoption contract (*AuOr* 5 14) and a manumission contract (RE 66).

11 Daniel Arnaud translated *li-im* A.ŠA$_3$.(MEŠ/ḪI.A) as, "le(s) voisin(s) du/des champ(s)" (*Recherches au pays d'Aštata, Emar VI/3: Textes sumériens et accadiens* [Paris: Éditions Recherche sur les Civilsations, 1986], 42, 89). Following Arnaud, John Huehnergard hesitantly rendered the expression "*people*$^{(?)}$ of the field" ("Five Tablets from the Vicinity of

the West Semitic word *li'mu*, "tribe/clan/people," this entity seemed to recall the old Yaminite tribal divisions of the Mari period.[12] Almost immediately after these first publications, however, Durand tried to dissuade interpreters from viewing the social landscape of Emar through the lens of Mari in a simplistic way. He demonstrated that the expression $^{(\text{diš})}$*li-im* A.ŠA$_3$$^{(\text{meš/ḫi.a})}$ had nothing to do with people, but rather, represented an idiomatic legal construction, "même de loin (= aucunement)," that emphasized the impossibility for certain individuals to file a legal claim.[13] Yet despite Durand's objections, scholars continued to use the Emar evidence to describe and understand the social landscape of LBA Syria with terms borrowed from earlier periods.[14]

In reality, the social identities of mobile peoples in LBA Syria anticipate categories and terminology that would come to describe Arameans of the first millennium BCE. Middle Assyrian kings recorded their frequent encounters with *sutû* and *aḫlamû*-Arameans in the Jezirah, but these exonyms (especially the latter) stem from an Assyro-Babylonian frame of reference not necessarily

---

Emar," *RA* 77 [1983]: 21 n. 13). See also Eugene Pentiuc, *West Semitic Vocabulary in the Akkadian Texts from Emar*, HSS 49 (Winona Lake, IN: Eisenbrauns, 2001), 110–111.

12 *AHw* 1:554a, mng. 2; *CAD* L 198a, mng. C. On the *li'mum* at Mari, see Daniel Fleming, "The Sim'alite *gayum* and the Yaminite *li'mum* in the Mari Archives," in Nicolle, *Amurru 3*, 209–210. Although the West Semitic term *li'mu* is attested at Emar (Emar 373:156–157; 378:14–15), it is written with the distinctive MB *aleph*-sign (i.e., *li-'i-mi*) (Stefano Seminara, *L'accadico di Emar*, MVS 6 [Rome: Università Degli Studi di Roma « La Sapienza » Dipartimento di Studie Orientali, 1998], 155–158).

13 Jean-Marie Durand, review of *Recherches au Pays d'Aštata, Emar VI, Textes sumériens et accadiens, vol. 1, 2 et 3* by Daniel Arnaud, *RA* 83 (1989): 180–181; Durand, "1 *lîm* a-šà = « même de loin », à Emar," *NABU* (2004): 24; Durand, "Quelques textes sur le statut de la femme à Émar," *Sem* 55 (2013): 33 n. 28. See also William Hallo, "Love and Marriage in Ashtata," in *Sex and Gender in the Ancient Near East: Proceedings of the 47th Rencontre Assyriolgique Internationale, Helsinki, July 2–6, 2001*, ed. Simo Parpola and Robert M. Whiting, CRRAI 47 (Helsinki: Neo-Assyrian Text Corpus Project, 2002), 206–211. Durand convincingly demonstrated that this nonrepudiation formula originally meant "(within) a thousand fields," derived from the literal sense of the verbs *qerēbu* and *šanāqu*, "to approach/arrive at a locality," used in some Emar documents to describe the initiation of legal claims (RAI 47 1:29–31 [SH/FF]; RE 15:18–21 [S/C]; Emar 80:30 [SH/FF]; 180:19–20 [S/C]; 185:20–21 [S/C]).

14 For instance, Richard Beale identified a Hittite military contingent known as the LU$_2$.MEŠ *LĪM ṢĒRI*, a semi-autonomous military unit with troops drawn from regions on the fringes of the empire, taking the designation as Akkadian, *li'm ṣēri*, "clansmen of the countryside" (*The Organization of the Hittite Military*, THeth 20 [Heidelberg: Carl Winter Universitätsverlag, 1992], 103 n. 380). Beckman connected this Hittite group to Emar's *li-im* A.ŠA$_3$, viewing the kinship term *li'mu* as a vestige of the Mari era ("Family Values," 59). However, the Hittite *LĪM ṢĒRI* most likely refers to a "troop (of one thousand men) of the steppe," who may have come from the fringes of the empire but were not clearly a kin-based entity (see n. 38 below).

shared by scribes in the Middle Euphrates. The divergent depictions of mobile peoples in Emarite and Assyrian texts relate to shifting scribal conventions in Assyrian annalistic writing, not to incursions of *aḫlamû*-Arameans. In the inscriptions of King Adad-nirari I (1307–1275 BCE), for instance, the *aḫlamû* are listed alongside other vanquished populations like the *sutû* and the *Iūru*.[15] The term *aḫlamû* derives from an Amorite tribal group that resided in the vicinity of Old Babylonian (OB) Suḫum, evidently a primary point of reference for mobile peoples encountered by the Assyrians.[16] Beginning in the reign Adad-nirari I, Assyrian scribes essentially replaced the word *sutû* with *aḫlamû* until the time of Sargon II (722–705 BCE), when *sutû* was revived as an archaic ethnicon for Arameans.[17] While the name *aḫlamû* may have been an accurate means to describe mobile peoples near LBA Suḫu, the Assyrians used the term to refer to any mobile group they encountered throughout Syria, describing a diverse assortment of social entities in monolithic terms amenable to their rhetorical needs—but it was not an accurate depiction of the social diversity of the region.

The terms *sutû* and *aḫlamû* represent generic designations of "steppe people" who were neither exclusively mobile pastoralist (though many were), nor ethnically homogenous.[18] Though defined in terms of their mobility, these LBA populations lived in towns and had deep historical connections to settled populations throughout the Fertile Crescent. Tiglath-pileser I (1114–1076 BCE) used the ethnicon "*aḫlamû*-Arameans" ($^{[\text{kur}]}$*Aḫlamê*/*î* ^{kur}*Armayya*^{meš}) to describe mobile groups he plundered from the land of Suḫu to Carchemish, also mentioning that he destroyed "six of their towns at the foot of Mount Bishri" (6 URU.MEŠ-*šu-nu ša* GIR$_3$ ^{kur}*bé-eš-ri*).[19] Middle Assyrian kings encountered pop-

15 A.0.76.1, line 23 (A. Kirk Grayson, *Assyrian Rulers of the Third and Second Millennia BC [to 1115 BC]*, RIMA 1 [Toronto: University of Toronto Press, 1987], 132).

16 This group appears in one OB letter (AbB 13 60:32–42), where they are associated with the mobile Ḫana of that region (Michael P. Streck, *Die Amurriter, die onomastische Forschung, Orthographie und Phonologie, Nominalmorphologie*, vol. 1 of *Das amurritische Onomastikon der altbabylonischen Zeit*, AOAT 271 [Münster: Ugarit-Verlag, 2000], 28). In a letter found at LBA Emar, the *aḫlamû* still seem to reside in the vicinity of Suḫu (Emar 263).

17 John A. Brinkman, *A Political History of Post-Kassite Babylonia: 1158–722 B.C.*, AnOr 43 (Rome: Biblical Pontifical Institute, 1968), 285 n. 1844.

18 Brinkman, *Political History*, 287; Hélène Sader, "History," in *The Arameans in Ancient Syria*, ed. Herbert Niehr, HdO 106 (Leiden: Brill, 2014), 18–20; K. Lawson Younger, Jr., *A Political History of the Arameans: From Their Origins to the End of Their Polities*, ABS 13. (Atlanta, GA: SBL, 2016), 80–94.

19 A.0.87.1, v. 59 (A. Kirk Grayson, *Assyrian Rulers of the Early First Millennium BC (1114–859 BC)*, RIMA 2 [Toronto: University of Toronto Press, 1991], 23); A.0.87.2, line 29

ulations of *aḫlamû* as far west as the Lebanese mountains and along the length of the Euphrates River basin—locating them at Babylon, Suḫu, Tuttul, Jebel Bishri, Palmyra, and the land of Hatti.[20] There is no fixed name for this vast territorial range: Tukulti-Ninurta I (1243–1207 BCE) described a region known as the "*aḫlamû*-mountains" (*šadān aḫlamî*),[21] Tiglath-pileser I referred to the *aḫlamû* of "the Aramean land" (KUR *Armayyu*), and Assur-bēl-kala (1074–1056 BCE) described the *šiddu aḫlamî*, "(river) bank of the *aḫlamû*."[22] The geography depicted in the Middle Assyrian inscriptions is ideologically loaded and littered with hyperbole,[23] but the association of mobile peoples with the physical landscape and urban settlements suggests that their living patterns transcended political boundaries and were not reducible to a strict dichotomy between town-dweller and nomad.

Although the Assyrians located *aḫlamû*-Arameans throughout the Middle Euphrates, the term *aḫlamû* appears in just one letter found at Emar (Emar 263) describing two men from the region of Suḫu—the same site associated with the *aḫlamû* in the OB period.[24] The term *aḫlamû* is attested at Emar in the form of personal names, but it did not describe people living in the town's

(RIMA 2:34). Younger understood these towns and the steppe as the two poles of the nomadic economy ("Tiglath-Pileser I and the Initial Conflicts of the Assyrians with the Arameans," in *Wandering Arameans: Arameans Outside Syria: Textual and Archaeological Perspectives*, ed. Angelika Berlejung, Aren M. Maeir, and Andreas Schüle, LAS 5 [Wiesbaden: Harrassowitz Verlag, 2017], 203–204). In any "tribal" group, a segment of the population resided in towns while another operated in the steppe. Individuals fluidly moved between these two subsistence patterns (two poles of a broader continuum) based on seasonal changes and social exigencies (Michael P. Streck, "Zwischen Weide, Dorf und Stadt: Sozio-ökonomische Strukturen des ammurischen Nomadismus am Mittleren Euphrat," *BaM* 33 [2002]: 168).

20 Frederick Mario Fales, "The Djezireh in Neo-Assyrian Sources," in *The Syrian Jezira: Cultural Heritage and Interrelations*, ed. Michel Al-Maqdissi et al., DAS I (Damascus: Ministère de la Culture à Damas, 1996), 182; Younger, *Arameans*, 85–86.

21 A.0.78.23, line 70 (RIMA 1:273).

22 A.0.89.6, line 14 (RIMA 2:98); A.0.89.9, line 9 (RIMA 2:107).

23 Younger, "Tiglath-Pileser I," 203.

24 On the social and political identity of the *aḫlamû*, see Brinkman, *Political History*, 267–288; Sader, "History," 18–21; Streck, *Amurriter*, 334–335; Younger, *Arameans*, 80–88; Ron Zadok, "Elements of Aramean Pre-history," in *Ah Assyria …: Studies in Assyrian History and Ancient Near Eastern Historiography presented to Hayim Tadmor*, ed. Mordechai Cogan and Israel Eph'al, ScrHier 33 (Jerusalem: Magnes Press, 1991), 104–117. On this term at Emar, see Murray Adamthwaite, "Ethnic Movements in the Thirteenth Century B.C. as Discernible from the Emar Texts," in *Cultural Interaction in the Ancient Near East: Papers Read at a Symposium Held at the University of Melbourne, Department of Classics and Archaeology, 29–30 September 1994* (Leuven: Peeters, 1996), 93.

immediate hinterland.[25] In fact, the scribes of Emar almost never referred to mobile groups by any collective term, with the rare exception of a thirteenth- or fourteenth-century BCE administrative document from the nearby site of Ekalte. This fragmentary text identifies a man named Yashur-Dagan as a "leader of the *sutû*" (GAL $^{\text{lú.meš}}$*su-ti-e*),[26] who receives an undisclosed quantity of silver and stored grain (*kurā'u*) from two "sons of the town (of Ekalte)" (DUMU.MEŠ *ša a-li*).[27] Yashur-Dagan's important social status in relation to these inhabitants of Ekalte may be construed from the payment/tribute set "before" (*pānu*) him and the seal impression that immediately follows his name on the tablet. In contrast to the two "townsmen" who pay Yashur-Dagan, four individuals—perhaps including Yashur-Dagan himself—are called "tribal leaders (from) across the Euphrates" (4 *na-sí-ku e-bi-ir ša* ^{d}ID.DINGIR-*la*).[28] The origin of these tribal leaders "across the Euphrates" could describe any part of the vast territorial swath of the Jezirah, the region over which the Assyrians exercised only marginal control.[29] In the first millennium BCE, the title *nasīku* becomes the highest social rank among Aramean chieftains who oversaw tribes, towns, lands, and even rivers.[30] In southern Mesopotamia, the title first appears in the inscriptions of Assurnaṣirpal II (883–859 BCE),[31] but a Syrian/Conventional administrative text from LBA Emar refers to an unnamed "tribal leader" (^{lú}*na-sí-ku*) who had seized the sons of two different men.[32] Yashur-Dagan's position

25 Several Emarites bore the personal names ^{m}*Aḫlamû* or the feminine ^{f}*Aḫlamîtu* (Regine Pruzsinsky, *Die Personennamen der Texte aus Emar*, SCCNH 13 [Bethesda, MD: CDL, 2003], 103).

26 Ekalte 34, obv. line 7 (Walter Mayer, *Tall-Munbāqa—Ekalte II: Die Texte* [Saarbrücken: Saarbrücker Druckerei und Verlag, 2001], 105). Mayer read this word as *na-sí-qú*, "Arbeitspflichtige," recognizing it as an antithetical parallel to the DUMU.MEŠ *ša a-li*, but nonetheless arguing that it could hardly designate a sheikh. Given the reference to Sutean nomads, the attestation of the ^{lú}*na-sí-ku* at Emar, and the interchangeability of the titles GAL and *nasīku* among Aramean leaders of the first millennium BCE, I see no reason to doubt that the title *nasīku* referred to a leader of some kind of mobile population in this text.

27 Mayer took *kurā'u* as "Mietarbeiter," based on Aramaic *kara'a* "vermieten" (*Ekalte*, 38, 163). However, Akkadian *kurû* (= GUR$_7$), "pile of stored barley" (*CAD* K 226a) makes more sense in construct with a "tower/agricultural estate" (AN.ZA.⟨GAR$_3$⟩ = *dimtu*).

28 This would refer to the Jezirah, where Tiglath-pileser I would confront *aḫlamû* nomads (Younger, "Tiglath-Pileser I," 202).

29 Younger, "Tiglath-Pileser I," 198–199.

30 *AHw* 2:754a; *CAD* N/2 27a. See Brinkman, *Political History*, 274–275; Frederick Mario Fales, "Moving Around Babylon: On the Aramean and Chaldean Presence in Southern Mesopotamia," in *Babylon: Wissenskultur in Orient und Okzident*, ed. Eva Cancik-Kirschbaum, Margarete van Ess, and Joachim Marzahn (Berlin: de Gruyter, 2011), 94.

31 A.0.101.1, ii.24; iii.35 (RIMA 2:203); A.0.101.17, ii.78 (RIMA 2:244).

32 RE 95:5.

as the GAL of the *sutû* and a *nasīku* of peoples in the Jezirah corresponds to the titles that Aramean leaders in these same regions would bear a few centuries later.[33] In contrast to the Assyrians' hostile view of these mobile groups, however, the evidence from Ekalte and Emar suggests a more intimate knowledge of who these people were. The inscriptions of Middle Assyrian kings treat mobile peoples in broad demographic strokes, whereas they appear as individuals with specific interests in the Emar and Ekalte archives.

There is a similar dissonance between Assyrian descriptions of mobile populations in the service of the Hittite army and how the Hittites themselves characterized such groups. Assyrian kings like Shalmaneser I (1263–1234 BCE) claimed to have confronted "Hittite and *aḫlamite* troops" (*ummān ḫattî u aḫlamî*) while Tiglath-pileser I encountered the *aḫlamû* in the land of Hatti.[34] The Hittites, by contrast, never referred to any population as *aḫlamû*,[35] but rather, distinguished those mobile groups in the empire's service (LU_2.MEŠ *LI-IM ṢE-RI*) from those that were not (e.g., *ʿapiru* or *sutû*).[36] In an Old Hittite treaty (ca. 1750–1500 BCE), a group of *ʿapiru* prepare to join the ranks of Hittite palace guards (DUMU.MEŠ É.GAL) and an enigmatic group known as the "men of the *LĪM ṢĒRI*" (LU_2.MEŠ *LI-IM ṢE-RI*).[37] The men of the *LĪM ṢĒRI*, probably referring to the "troop (of one thousand men) of the steppe," consisted of semi-autonomous military units from regions on the fringes of the empire.[38] The late

33 Younger, *Arameans*, 56, 688, 731.

34 Shalmaneser I (A.0.77.1, line 61 [RIMA 1:184]); Tiglath-pileser I (A.0.87.2, lines, 29–30 [RIMA 2:37]).

35 The only Hittite reference to the *aḫlamû* appears in a thirteenth-century BCE letter from King Hattušili III to the Babylonian King Kadashman-Enlil II ("Letter from Ḫattušili III of Ḫatti to Kadašman-Enlil II of Babylon," trans. Harry A. Hoffner, Jr. [*COS* 3.31:52]). The Hittite scribe only uses the term *aḫlamû* in reference to groups the Babylonians had complained about in a previous message.

36 Like the rulers of other urban centers throughout the Levant, the Hittites recruited groups like the *ʿapiru* and the *sutû* to achieve their military ambitions. For mobile peoples that had been in their service for centuries, the Hittites used the term LU_2.MEŠ *LI-IM ṢE-RI* (Beale, *Hittite Military*, 104–112).

37 *CTH* 27 (= KBO 9.73+), obv. lines 9–11 (Heinrich Otten, "Zwei althethitische Belege zu den Ḫapiru (SA.GAZ)," *ZA* 52 [1957]: 220–222). For all references to this group and their leaders, see Franca Pecchioli Daddi, *Mestieri, professioni e dignità nell'Anatolia ittita* (Rome: Edizioni dell'Ateneo, 1982), 470–473.

38 The use of the Akkadogram *ṢĒRI*, rather than Hittite *gim*(*ma*)*ra-* "steppe/grassland/open field" (*HW* 109b), may suggest a Semitic-speaking origin of these figures (Beale, *Hittite Military*, 103 n. 380). In contrast to Beale, who took the writing *LI-IM* as WS *liʾmu* ("tribe/clan/people"), *LI-IM* is the standard writing for the number one thousand, commonly used as a term for a military troop. A Neo-Assyrian letter to King Sargon II mentions the loyal Aramean Puqūdu tribe, Aramean leaders ([lú]*nasīkū*) in various towns, and a mil-

sixteenth-century Edict of Telipinu identifies the leader of this military group as the "chief of the overseers of the *LĪM ṢĒRI*" (GAL $^{\text{lú.meš}}$UGULA *LI-IM ṢE-RI*),[39] evidently a figure wielding considerable influence within the Hittite administrative hierarchy.[40] The identification of these troops with the "steppe" (*ṢĒRI*) points to a social identity not bound to a particular town or ethnicity, but by the spaces that these individuals occupied.[41] More than just nomadic mercenaries to the Hittites, the people of the steppe were an integral component of Hittite society throughout all major periods of the empire, even participating in state-sponsored rituals like the KI.LAM festival at the imperial capital of Ḫattuša.[42]

What emerges from this comparison of Assyrian, Hittite, and Emarite sources is that social identity—and the social identity of mobile populations in particular—was very much a matter of perspective. The obscurity of mobile peoples in the Emar archives is ironically the result of their familiarity to the town's inhabitants, who identified individuals rather than larger demographic populations in their documents. The traditional dimorphic model of nomadic-sedentary interaction, which largely conflates social organization (tribe, chiefdom, state) with social identity, best aligns with the Assyrians' mischaracterization of mobile Syrian populations as *aḫlamû*-Arameans, an exonym only meaningful to the Assyrians themselves.[43] The following section explores the benefits of using ritual to access self-defined social identity, opening new avenues of historical research.

---

itary official bearing the title ^{lú}GAL 1 *li-im* (SAA 17 152 [= ABL 774], rev. line 7). The same convention can be found in Hebrew as well, where אלף, "one thousand/military unit/clan," often refers to units of this size (e.g., "the commanders of the [units of] thousands [שרי האלפים]" [Num 31:14]).

39 Edict of Telipinu (*CTH* 19 ii.71); Treaty of Tudḫaliya IV and Karunta of Tarḫuntašša (*CTH* 106.A.1 [= Bo 86/299] iv.35). These two texts illustrate the chronological range of the term in Hittite sources. Individuals bearing the title UGULA *li-im* appear in the Late Bronze Age archives of Alalaḫ (AlT 172:38; 222:26) and at Ugarit (*PRU* 6 52; *Ug.* V 52).

40 In the witness list of the late thirteenth-century BCE Treaty of Tudḫaliya IV and Karunta of Tarḫuntašša, a GAL UGULA *LI-IM*^{MEŠ} named Alalimu is listed after the Hittite crown princes but before a number of vassal kings.

41 Assyrian kings would similarly designate populations of both *aḫlamû*-Arameans (ERIM.MEŠ EDIN ^{kur}*Aḫ-la-me-e* ^{kur}*Ar-ma-a-ia*^{meš}) (A.0.99.2, line 33 [RIMA 2:149]) and *sutû* (^{lú}*Su-te-e* ERIM.MEŠ EDIN) as "troops/people of the steppe" ([Grant Frame, *The Royal Inscriptions of Sargon II, King of Assyria (721–705 BC)*, RINAP 2 (Winona Lake, IN: Eisenbrauns, 2021), 73 (1:266)]).

42 Sponsored and attended by the Hittite king at his capital, the people of the steppe carried enigmatic *aliyazenuš karkidanduš* ritual objects in the KI.LAM festival (Itamar Singer, *The Hittite KI.LAM Festival*, 2 vols., SBT 27 [Wiesbaden: Harrassowitz, 1983], 1:57, 60, 94).

43 Michael B. Rowton, "Urban Autonomy in a Nomadic Environment," *JNES* 32 (1973): 202–204.

2 Social (Re)integration in the Emar Rituals

Like the Hittites, the inhabitants of Emar used ritual to maintain social ties with mobile peoples and locate the gods of the town in a broader regional pantheon. But beyond this, the inhabitants of Emar felt that they had a shared historical identity with these mobile peoples, one invoked through the use of sacred space and ritual movement. The integration of Emar and its cult in the broader region plays out through three specific rituals: the *Text for Six Months*, which delineated the sacrificial rites for the month of Zarātu (Emar 446); the annual *zukru* ritual (Emar 375+); and the seven-year *zukru* festival (Emar 373+). All three rituals associated a litany of cultic rites with the fifteenth of Zarātu, which Fleming labeled "the crown of Emar's ritual calendar."[44] The month of Zarātu marked the seasonal interchange between the hot, dry summer months and the rainy winter season. Deriving from the Semitic root √*ḏrʿ*, "to sow/seed," the rituals of Zarātu were predominantly associated with agricultural activities sponsored by various urban social groups.[45] But the autumn also marked the transformation of the backcountry from arid desert to fertile steppe, a time when mobile populations prepared to depart for winter pastures.[46] These rituals offered an important mechanism for mobile and settled peoples with a shared social identity to create moments and spaces for (re)integration, maintaining shared identities across space and time.

In Emar's oldest ritual text, the *Text for Six Months* (Emar 446), social (re)integration involved ritual movement in and out of the city and the participation

44 Daniel Fleming, *Time at Emar: The Cultic Calendar and the Rituals from the Diviner's Archive*, CM 11 (Winona Lake, IN: Eisenbrauns, 2000), 160.

45 The timing of the month of Zarātu in the late summer through autumn is probably parallel to the month (or two months) known as *yrḥw zrʿ* in the tenth-century BCE Gezer Calendar (*KAI* 182.1–2).

46 During the Mari period, the region between Imar and Tuttul was the summer range of the Yaminite Rabbaeans, which they departed during the winter for the Jezirah (Michael Astour, *The Rabbaeans: A Tribal Society on the Euphrates from Yahdun-Lim to Julius Caesar*, SMS 2/2 [Malibu: Undena, 1978], 3; Streck, "Zwischen Weide, Dorf und Stadt," 163–164). For the effects of climatic patterns on the movement of Syrian peoples, see Jean Sapin, "La géographie humaine de la Syrie-Palestine au deuxième millénaire avant J.C. comme voie de recherche historique," *JESHO* 24 (1981): 18–19; Sapin, "La géographie humaine de la Syrie-Palestine au deuxième millénaire avant J.C. comme voie de recherche historique," *JESHO* 25/1 (1982): 1–49; Sapin, "La géographie humaine de la Syrie-Palestine au deuxième millénaire avant J.C. comme voie de recherche historique," *JESHO* 25/2 (1982): 113–186; Streck, "Zwischen Weide, Dorf und Stadt," 158–168.

of both sedentary and mobile peoples in a cultic meal.[47] The cultic activities for the month of Zarātu centered on Dagan (head of the regional pantheon) as the "lord of the seed" (*be-el* NUMUM^{meš}), the city god ^{d}NIN.URTA, and various other deities.[48] Most ritual activities took place at city gates, with the various offerings culminating in the diviner's (MAŠ$_2$.ŠU.GID$_2$.GID$_2$) symbolic scattering of seed (NUMUN) before planting (*e-ri-ši*) could begin. Among other themes, the ritual integrated Emar's mobile population through the participation of a social authority known as the "leader of the people of the steppe" (^{lú}GAL LU$_2$.MEŠ EDIN). Michael Rowton has argued that tribal and parasocial leaders functioned as the link between mobile and urban society, as their privileged position enabled them movement between these two worlds.[49] Rowton's focus was integration on the elite social level, which does occur in the rituals of Zarātu. Yet, there was also a corporate component to these rites, as the ritual participants were identified as the whole populace (LU$_2$.MEŠ *ga-ma-ru*). These ritual actors would process and arrive at the "great gate" (KA$_2$.GAL), perhaps a main ceremonial city gate,[50] where they would provide the diviner and this leader of the people of the steppe with offerings that the latter would consume in a ritualized meal (Emar 446:24–29). By describing the ritual participants as "the entire populace" (LU$_2$.MEŠ *ga-ma-ru*), the rituals of Zarātu cast a broader net than social identities defined by the town (URU^{ki}), theoretically allowing them to incorporate a population defined by their association with the steppe as well.

The significance of the seasonal interchange as a moment for reintegrating the urban and the nonurban is not unique to Emar, but also appears in ritu-

---

47 Fleming noted that the *Text for Six Months* (Emar 446) and the annual *zukru* (Emar 375) are the only ritual texts composed in the Conventional/Syrian style, suggesting that they draw from earlier local custom (*Time at Emar*, 109–113). See also John Tracey Thames, Jr., *The Politics of Ritual Change: The* zukru *Festival in the Political History of Late Bronze Age Emar*, HSM 65 (Boston, MA/Leiden: Brill, 2020), 284.

48 In a parallel calendar used at Emar, the month of Zarātu was known as SAG.MU, "head of the year" (Fleming, *Time at Emar*, 121).

49 Michael B. Rowton, "Dimorphic Structure and the Tribal Elite," in *Al-Bāḥiṯ: Festschrift Joseph Henninger zum 70. Geburtstag am 12. Mai 1976*, ed. Franz Josef Thiel, SIA 28 (St. Augustin bei Bonn: Anthropos-Instituts, 1976), 219–257; Rowton, "Dimorphic Structure and the Parasocial Element," *JNES* 36 (1977): 191–192.

50 The KA$_2$.GAL in the rituals for Zarātu may correspond to the central "Great Gate of Battle" (KA$_2$.GAL *qa-ab-li*) mentioned in the *zukru* rituals (Fleming, *Time at Emar*, 93). Mori considered generic references to a KA$_2$.GAL in the Emar tablets an indication that one gate (she counted a total of six) was more monumental and ceremonially important than the others ("The City Gates at Emar: Reconsidering the Use of the Sumerograms KÁ.GAL and KÁ in Tablets Found at Meskené Qadime," *Quaderni di Vicino Oriente* 5 [2010]: 261).

als at contemporary Ḫattuša, Ugarit, and later in Israel/Judah.[51] These parallels provide some helpful insight into why rituals defined by and marking the agricultural cycle are concern with mobile peoples. Most illuminating in this regard is the Ugaritic text known as *The Feast of the Goodly Gods* (KTU³ 1.23), a unique blend of mythic narrative and ritual report.[52] The text begins with an invitation for the "goodly gods" (*ilm nʿmm*)—voracious deities who reside in the barren desert (*mdbr*)—to join the urban pantheon (Ilu, Athiratu/Raḥmay, and the *nġr mdrʿ*) for a feast in a place called "the sown" (*mdrʿ*).[53] This feast occurs in the late summer/early autumn—expressed in the mythic register as the waning influence of Môtu—when summer fruits were harvested, winter crops were sown, and the barren desert (*mdbr*) transformed into fertile steppe (*šd*).[54] This is the connection between agricultural rites marking the fall interchange and rites celebrating social (re)integration with mobile peoples. In both the ritual and mythic registers, (re)integration occurred through reciprocal movement of people and deities between urban and rural spaces. First, the urban pantheon and human rulers of the city (i.e., the king and queen of Ugarit) entered the steppe (*šd*) for a "hunt" (*ṣwd*);[55] later, the goodly gods and the human "enter-

51 For the Hittite rituals, see Alfonso Archi, "Fêtes de printemps et d'automne et réintégration rituelle d'images du culte dans l'Anatolie hittite," *UF* 5 (1973): 24. An autumnal integration ritual may be preserved in the elliptical reference to Gaʿal son of Ebed in Judg 9:26–27 (see Mark S. Smith, *The Rituals and Myths of the Feast of the Goodly Gods of KTU/CAT 1.23: Royal Constructions of Opposition, Intersection, Integration, and Domination*, SBLRBS 51 [Atlanta, GA: Society of Biblical Literature, 2006], 51). Gaʿal and his kin are said to "enter" (עבר) the built urban environment of Shechem during the grape harvest (late summer), only to leave it again and hold a הלולים-ritual feast in the "house of their god(s)" (בית אלהיהם) that is located in "the field/steppe" (השדה). Priestly tradition associates the הלולים with a first fruits offering (harvested in the early fall) dedicated to Yahweh (Lev 19:24).

52 Smith, *Goodly Gods*, 151.

53 Based on the same Semitic root as Emar's month of Zarātu and the *yrḥw zrʿ* of the Gezer calendar, the sown represents a "shared space" that brings the urban pantheon outside the typical cultic locales of the temple and palace and draws the goodly gods from the desert/steppe (Smith, *Goodly Gods*, 107).

54 The reference to "pruning" (*zmr*) Môtu (ll. 19–20) is probably an allusion to the first fruits gathered in the early fall (Smith, *Goodly Gods*, 63). This parallels the first fruit offerings in Emar 446 (*bu-kà-ra-tu*$_4$) and in biblical tradition (הלולים).

55 In the mythic register, both Athiratu/Raḥmay and the goodly gods are said to "hunt" (*ṣd*) in the "steppe" (*šd*). Smith tentatively connects this myth to one aspect of the ritual procurement of game meat for a feast, brought in by the enigmatic "enterers" (Smith, *Goodly Gods*, 21, 60–61). However, he cautions against any "simple correspondence of myth and ritual," as KTU³ 1.23 combines two separate hunting myths (*Goodly Gods*, 61). On the place of hunting in the economic relations of sedentary and mobile populations, see Streck, "Zwischen Weide, Dorf und Stadt," 167, 172.

ers" (*ʿrbm*) are granted access to the bounty of the sown (*mdrʿ*).[56] Previous interpreters explained the social metaphor of the *Goodly Gods* in terms of the disinheritance and exile of kin: the heads of the urban pantheon banished their children to subsist like the *ʿapiru* on the fringes of the desert.[57] Yet, neither the sown nor the steppe are granted priority in this text: each space has something to offer the other. Recognizing that the *Feast of the Goodly Gods* offers a uniquely Ugaritic form of a fall (re)integration ritual, it nonetheless affirms that social identity is deeply tied to cultic space and that ritual movement communicates something about social relationships.

The *Feast of the Goodly Gods* offers a model for interpreting the use of cultic space and ritual movement in the two other Emar ritual texts at the center of this study (Emar 373+/Emar 375+). Both rituals (re)define the local rites on the fifteenth of Zarātu as a *zukru* that the inhabitants of Emar "give" (*nadānu*) to Dagan.[58] First appearing in the Mari period, the *zukrum* was a ritual that a leader of the Yaminite Yariḫu tribe in the environs of Aleppo gave (*nadānum*) to the regional god Addu.[59] With no clear ties to the seasonal calendar, what

---

56 Previous interpreters saw the *ʿrbm* as a type of cultic personnel, akin to the Akkadian *ērib bīti* (CAD E 290a). Yet, such officials appear nowhere else in the Ugaritic archives ("Dawn and Dusk," trans. Dennis Pardee [COS 1.87:276 n. 12]; Smith, *Goodly Gods*, 38). More plausibly, Smith (*Goodly Gods*, 61) connected these figures with their cultic role in this text, where they "process with goodly sacrifice" (*hlkm bdbḥ nʿmt* [ll. 26–27]). Another possibility, based on the Emar parallels, is that these enterers are mobile peoples invited to join the elites of urban society for a ritualized feast.

57 Schloen characterized subsistence in the desert in negative terms of loss and banishment ("The Exile of Disinherited Kin in KTU 1.12 and KTU 1.23," *JNES* 52 [1993]: 209–220). This misses the many positive depictions of the steppe as a space offering its own bounty and appeal to settled peoples and their gods.

58 The annual *zukru* represented an older local ritual (Fleming, *Time at Emar*, 152), which was vastly expanded under Hittite sponsorship from Carchemish into a "festival" (EZEN) observed once every seven years (Thames, *Ritual Change*, 303–306). The older and more fragmentary Emar 446 does not include the term *zukru*, though Fleming cautiously identified the ritual for Zarātu as "rites affiliated with the *zukru*" (*Time at Emar*, 152). Accepting Fleming's identification of the month as that of Zarātu, Thames considered it "better to view [the ritual activities] as preexisting calendrical rites that helped to give the *zukru* ritual its shape as it developed into the ritual complex recorded in Emar 375+ and, eventually, 373+" (*The Politics of Ritual Change*, 82). Surprisingly, the seven-year *zukru* festival bears the strongest similarities with the earlier rites of Zarātu, listing cultic participants known as the "seven sowers of the palace" (7 LU_2.MEŠ *zi-ir-ra-ti ša* E_2.GAL-*lì*) and Dagan's epithet, ^{d}KUR EN *bu-ka-ri*, probably referring to the "first fruits offering" (*bu-kà-ra-tu*$_4$) in Emar 446 (Thames, *Ritual Change*, 149–150).

59 Evidence for this rite comes from a single letter sent to Zimri-Lim (A.1121+A.2731). See Jean-Marie Durand, *Le culte d'Addu d'Alep et l'affaire d'Alahtum*, FM 7, Mémoires de NABU 8

connected the Yaminite and Emarite *zukru(m)*s was not the date of their performances, but rather their dedication to two regional gods with shrines at more than one urban center: Dagan of the Middle Euphrates and Addu in the Aleppo Plateau. Fleming points to another possible connection: the performance of the *zukrum* by a Yaminite tribe and Emar's legacy as an important Yaminite center during the Mari period.[60] Whether or not the rites observed on the fifteenth of Zarātu at Emar were always known by the cultic term *zukru*, the veneration of the regional deity Dagan at the *sikkānu*-stones outside the city gates and the participation of the ^{lú}GAL LU_2.MEŠ EDIN evoked Syrian cultic traditions that were in some senses older than public rites connected to the temples of the town.[61] Defining these rites as a *zukru* invoked this connection to the nonurban cultic past more explicitly.

Despite the association of the *zukru(m)* with mobile peoples in the MBA, many aspects of the annual *zukru* at Emar were thoroughly town centered. In contrast to the whole populace (LU_2.MEŠ *ga-ma-ru*) that participated in the ritual for Zarātu (Emar 446), participants in the annual *zukru* (Emar 375) included the personified city (^{uru}*E-mar*^{ki}), the people of Emar (*ni-šu-ú* ^{uru}*E-mar*^{ki}), and citizens and leaders of the town (DUMU.MEŠ *ù* GAL.ḪI.A *ša* URU^{ki}). The descriptions of participants changed again in the seven-year *zukru*, which included "the people and the gods" (UN.MEŠ *ù* DINGIR.MES), or "the citizens of the land of Emar" (DUMU.MEŠ ^{kur}*E-mar*)—the latter potentially including a larger segment of the population than those defined by the city alone (^{uru}*E-mar*^{ki}).

What the old ritual of Zarātu achieved through the integration of mobile and sedentary ritual participants, the annual and seven-year *zukru*s achieved through ritual movement. Fleming observed that the veneration of Emar's deities with the regional god Dagan at the *sikkānu*-stones evoked other modes of worship "not bound to urban forms."[62] Just as these offerings and feasts outside the town reconnected the people and gods of Emar with sacred spaces in

(Paris: Société pour l'étude du Proche-Orient Ancien, 2002), 137–140; Fleming, *Time at Emar*, 113–121; Lafont, "Le roi de Mari et les prophètes du dieu Adad," *RA* 78 (1984): 7–18. Fleming argued that the term *zukru* refers to the "invocation" of a deity (*Time at Emar*, 113–126). For the other etymological possibilities, see Thames, *Ritual Change*, 223–225.

60 Fleming, *Time at Emar*, 114, 121.

61 Fleming, *Time at Emar*, 98–99. The *zukru* rituals exhibit a double tendency to place Emar in religious and cultural continuity with older Syrian traditions and incorporate new cultic forms through Hittite influence (Patrick M. Michel, *Le culte des pierres à Emar à l'époque hittite* [Fribourg: Academic Press; Göttingen: Vandenhoeck & Ruprecht, 2014], 269–274).

62 Fleming, *Time at Emar*, 91.

the countryside,[63] the "return" (*târu*) to the city reintegrated all participants (urban and nonurban) into the sacred space within the town. In the processional return to Emar, the city god ^{d}NIN.URTA rode in a cart with Dagan that was pulled to the Great Gate of Battle (KA$_2$.GAL *qabli*), where a *kudabu*-offering was performed. As a liminal space between urban and nonurban space, this gate was an important locus for social (re)integration. In the earlier ritual for Zarātu, it was at the gate—perhaps even the same gate—that the leader of the people of the steppe consumed his sacred feast.[64] These rites of social integration could explain the name of one of Emar's city gates, the "gate of the Sarta clan" (KA$_2$ *li-ʾi-mi sar-ta*) and the divinized tribe ^{d}*li-iʾ-mi sar-ta*, which both appear only in the seven-year *zukru* (Emar 373:156–157).[65] The term *li-iʾ-mi* recalls the first-order tribal division of Mari's Yaminite coalition (the *liʾmum*).[66] Despite this tantalizing allusion, there is no evidence that any inhabitant of Emar was a *mār liʾm sarta*, or that tribal affiliations at Emar operated anything like they did in the early second millennium BCE. Nonetheless, the reference to this divinized tribe alongside other deities scattered across the Middle Euphrates and Jezirah (the storm-god of Mount Basalamaʾa, various Baliḫ-river deities, and an old writing for the Storm-god of Emar [^{d}IM EN *I-mar*]) evoked the historical connections between Emar and the surrounding landscape.

Participation in local rituals marked stakeholders in the community and was an expression of community identity. The ritual meal shared by the town's diviner and the leader of the people of the steppe in the rites of Zarātu (Emar 446:29) offered the clearest evidence for the ritual (re)integration of mobile populations at Emar. In the annual *zukru* ritual (Emar 375), the boundaries between town and countryside were made porous through the procession of the inhabitants of Emar (^{uru}*E-mar*^{ki}) to the feast outside the city, attended by Dagan and ^{d}NIN.URTA.[67] As the biblical and Ugaritic parallels illustrate, the fall

---

63 On the identity of the gate of the *sikkānu*-stones as the confluence of a river, see Jean-Marie Durand and Lionel Marti, "Chroniques du Moyen Euphrate 2: Relectures des documents d'Ekalte, Emar et Tuttul," *RA* 97 (2003): 144–145; Mori, "City Gates," 262.

64 Mori, "City Gates," 261. See also n. 50 above.

65 This deity also appears in a god-list (Emar 378:14–15) that begins with ^{d}EN *bu-ka-ri*, suggesting this text was connected to the seven-year *zukru* (see n. 54 above).

66 Fleming, "The Simʾalite *gayum*," 209–210.

67 Daniel Fleming, "The Rituals from Emar: Evolution of an Indigenous Tradition in Second-Millennium Syria," in *New Horizons in the Study of Ancient Syria*, ed. Mark W. Chavalas and John L. Hayes (Malibu: Undena, 1992), 59; Fleming, "The Emar Festivals: City Unity and Syrian Identity under Hittite Hegemony," in Chavalas, *Emar*, 85.

interchange was an auspicious time for the (re)integration of urban and nonurban peoples and their deities, evoked through the participation of mobile peoples or the observance of rites apart from the cultic institutions of the town.

3 Conclusion

In recent decades, scholars have made great progress unpacking the unique, town-based social structures of Emar and how they interacted with the Hittite administrative hierarchy. Yet, the relationship between Emar's inhabitants and mobile peoples in the broader regional landscape remains poorly understood. As a primary witness to the transition from the Amorite tribal groups of the Mari period to the Aramean kingdoms of the first millennium BCE, this aspect of Emar's history is an important topic in need of further study. The Middle Assyrian royal annals attest to mobile peoples operating in the vicinity of Emar during the LBA. However, the description of these groups as *aḫlamû*—Arameans stems from a skewed southern Mesopotamian perception of the region's social geography. In the local documentation from Emar, Ekalte, and Hatti, such groups are deemed the "people of the steppe" (LU$_2$.MEŠ EDIN) or *sutû*, whose leaders (the [lú]GAL or [lú]*nasīku*) point toward social categories used by later Aramean tribes. There is no sign that these mobile groups were considered outsiders to urban centers; quite the contrary, the inhabitants of settled polities believed themselves to have a shared social identity with these populations.

The agricultural cycle offered an opportunity for social (re)integration; it marked auspicious moments when the inhabitants of Emar would invoke and evoke their current and historical ties to the broader physical and social landscape. Social (re)integration ensured that physical and temporal separation of populations need not necessarily result in their fragmentation. Through cultic meals and ritual processions, the inhabitants of Emar not only carved out a space for mobile peoples within their urban framework, but also laid claim to an alternative social identity for themselves. This identity was remembered through old tribal names like the *li'mu sarta*, archaic titles of the city god of Emar, a Yaminite tribal custom known as the *zukru*, and rituals performed at cultic stones in the countryside. But this identity was not just a half-forgotten memory of Emar's tribal past. It was a way for the inhabitants of Emar to identify with mobile groups who still occupied the Middle Euphrates, to lay claim to a common historical descent and a shared social identity embedded in the physical landscape and the worship of the deities who occupied it.

Bibliography

Adamthwaite, Murray. "Ethnic Movements in the Thirteenth Century B.C. as Discernible from the Emar Texts." Pages 91–112 in *Cultural Interaction in the Ancient Near East: Papers Read at a Symposium Held at the University of Melbourne, Department of Classics and Archaeology, 29–30 September 1994*. Leuven: Peeters, 1996.

Archi, Alfonso. "Fêtes de printemps et d'automne et réintégration rituelle d'images du culte dans l'Anatolie hittite." *UF* 5 (1973): 7–27.

Arnaud, Daniel. "Les textes d'Emar et la chronologie de la fin du bronze récent." *Syria* 52 (1975): 87–92.

Arnaud, Daniel. *Recherches au pays d'Aštata, Emar VI/3: Textes sumériens et accadiens, textes*. Paris: Editions Recherche sur les Civilsations, 1986.

Astour, Michael. *The Rabbaeans: A Tribal Society on the Euphrates from Yahdun-Lim to Julius Caesar*. SMS 2/2. Malibu: Undena, 1978.

Beale, Richard. *The Organization of the Hittite Military*. THeth 20. Heidelberg: Carl Winter Universitätsverlag, 1992.

Beckman, Gary. "Family Values on the Middle Euphrates in the Thirteenth Century BCE." Pages 57–79 in *Emar: The History, Religion, and Culture of a Syrian Town in the Late Bronze Age*. Edited by Mark Chavalas. Bethesda, MD: CDL, 1996.

Benz, Brendon C. *The Land Before the Kingdom of Israel: A History of the Southern Levant and the People who Populated It*. HACL 7. Winona Lake, IN: Eisenbrauns, 2016.

Brinkman, John A. *A Political History of Post-Kassite Babylonia: 1158–722 B.C.* AnOr 43. Rome: Biblical Pontifical Institute, 1968.

Charpin, Dominique, and Jean-Marie Durand. "'Fils de Sim'al': Les origines tribales des rois de Mari." *RA* 80 (1986): 141–183.

Daddi, Franca Pecchioli. *Mestieri, professioni e dignità nell'Anatolia ittita*. Rome: Edizioni dell'Ateneo, 1982.

Démare-Lafont, Sophie, and Daniel Fleming. "Emar Chronology and Scribal Streams: Cosmopolitanism and Legal Diversity." *RA* 109 (2015): 45–77.

Durand, Jean-Marie. Review of *Recherches au Pays d'Aštata, Emar VI, Textes sumériens et accadiens, vol. 1, 2 et 3*, by Daniel Arnaud. *RA* 83 (1989): 163–191.

Durand, Jean-Marie. "La cité-état d'Imâr à l'époque des rois de Mari." *MARI* 6 (1990): 39–92.

Durand, Jean-Marie. *Le culte d'Addu d'Alep et l'affaire d'Alahtum*. FM 7. Mémoires de N.A.B.U. 8. Paris: Société pour l'étude du Proche-Orient Ancien, 2002.

Durand, Jean-Marie. "1 *lîm* a-šà = « même de loin », à Emar." *NABU* (2004): 24.

Durand, Jean-Marie. "Peuplement et sociétés à l'époque amorrite: les clans bensim'alites." Pages 111–197 in *Amurru 3: Nomades et sédentaires dans le Proche-Orient ancien*. Edited by Christophe Nicolle. CRRAI 46. Paris: Éditions de recherche, 2004.

Durand, Jean-Marie. "Quelques textes sur le statut de la femme à Émar." *Sem* 55 (2013): 25–60.

Durand, Jean-Marie, and Lionel Marti. "Chroniques du Moyen Euphrate 2: Relectures des documents d' Ekalte, Emar et Tuttul." *RA* 97 (2003): 144–145.

Fales, Frederick Mario. "The Djezireh in Neo-Assyrian Sources." Pages 181–199 in *The Syrian Jezira: Cultural Heritage and Interrelations*. Edited by Michel Al-Maqdissi, Maamoun Abdul Karim, Amr Al-Azm, and Moussa Dib Al-Khoury. DAS I. Damascus: Ministère de la Culture à Damas, 1996.

Fales, Frederick Mario. "Moving Around Babylon: On the Aramean and Chaldean Presence in Southern Mesopotamia." Pages 91–112 in *Babylon: Wissenskultur in Orient und Okzident*. Edited by Eva Cancik-Kirschbaum, Margarete van Ess, and Joachim Marzahn. Berlin: de Gruyter, 2011.

Fleming, Daniel. "The Rituals from Emar: Evolution of an Indigenous Tradition in Second-Millennium Syria." Pages 51–61 in *New Horizons in the Study of Ancient Syria*. Edited by Mark W. Chavalas and John L. Hayes. Malibu: Undena, 1992.

Fleming, Daniel. "The Emar Festivals: City Unity and Syrian Identity under Hittite Hegemony." Pages 81–121 in *Emar: The History, Religion, and Culture of a Syrian Town in the Late Bronze Age*. Edited by Mark W. Chavalas. Bethesda, MD: CDL Press, 1996.

Fleming, Daniel. *Time at Emar: The Cultic Calendar and the Rituals from the Diviner's Archive*. CM 11. Winona Lake, IN: Eisenbrauns, 2000.

Fleming, Daniel. *Democracy's Ancient Ancestors: Mari and Early Collective Governance*. Cambridge: Cambridge University Press, 2004.

Fleming, Daniel. "The Sim'alite *gayum* and the Yaminite *li'mum* in the Mari Archives." Pages 199–212 in *Amurru 3: Nomades et sédentaires dans le Proche-Orient ancien*. Edited by Christophe Nicolle. CRRAI 46. Paris: Éditions de recherche, 2004.

Fleming, Daniel, and Sophie Démare-Lafont. "Tablet Terminology at Emar: 'Conventional' and 'Free Format'." *AuOr* 27 (2009): 19–26.

Frame, Grant. *The Royal Inscriptions of Sargon II, King of Assyria (721–705 BC)*. RINAP 2. Winona Lake, IN: Eisenbrauns, 2021.

Giddens, Anthony. *A Contemporary Critique of Historical Materialism*. Vol. 1 of *Power, Property and the State*. Berkeley, CA: University of California Press, 1981.

Grayson, A. Kirk. *Assyrian Rulers of the Third and Second Millennia BC (to 1115 BC)*. RIMA 1. Toronto: University of Toronto Press, 1987.

Grayson, A. Kirk. *Assyrian Rulers of the Early First Millennium BC I (1114–859 BC)*. RIMA 2. Toronto: University of Toronto Press, 1991.

Hallo, William. "Love and Marriage in Ashtata." Pages 203–216 in *Sex and Gender in the Ancient Near East: Proceedings of the 47th Rencontre Assyriolgique Internationale, Helsinki, July 2–6, 2001*. Edited by Simo Parpola and Robert M. Whiting. CRRAI 47. Helsinki: Neo-Assyrian Text Corpus Project, 2002.

Huehnergard, John. "Five Tablets from the Vicinity of Emar." *RA* 77 (1983): 11–43.

Lafont, Bertrand. "Le roi de Mari et les prophètes du dieu Adad." *RA* 78 (1984): 7–18.

Mayer, Walter. *Tall-Munbāqa—Ekalte II: Die Texte*. Saarbrücken: Saarbrücker Druckerei und Verlag, 2001.

Michel, Patrick M. *Le culte des pierres à Emar à l'époque hittite*. Fribourg: Academic Press; Göttingen: Vandenhoeck & Ruprecht, 2014.

Mori, Lucia. "The City Gates at Emar: Reconsidering the Use of the Sumerograms ká.gal and ká in Tablets Found at Meskené Qadime." *Quaderni di Vicino Oriente* 5 (2010): 249–268.

Otten, Heinrich. "Zwei althethitische Belege zu den Ḫapiru (SA.GAZ)." *ZA* 52 (1957): 216–223.

Pardee, Dennis. "Dawn and Dusk." Pages 274–283 in *Context of Scripture 1: Canonical Compositions from the Biblical World*. Leiden: Brill, 1997.

Pentiuc, Eugene. *West Semitic Vocabulary in the Akkadian Texts from Emar*. HSS 49. Winona Lake, IN: Eisenbrauns, 2001.

Porter, Anne. "Beyond Dimorphism: Ideologies and Materialities of Kinship as Time-Space Distanciation." Pages 201–225 in *Nomads, Tribes, and the State in the Ancient Near East: Cross-disciplinary Perspectives*. Edited by Jeffery Szuchman. OIS 5. Chicago, IL: Oriental Institute of the University of Chicago, 2009.

Pruzsinsky, Regine. *Die Personennamen der Texte aus Emar*. SCCNH 13. Bethesda, MD: CDL, 2003.

Rowton, Michael B. "Urban Autonomy in a Nomadic Environment." *JNES* 32 (1973): 201–215.

Rowton, Michael B. "Dimorphic Structure and the Tribal Elite." Pages 219–257 in *Al-Bāḥiṯ: Festschrift Joseph Henninger zum 70. Geburtstag am 12. Mai 1976*. Edited by Franz Josef Thiel. SIA 28. St. Augustin bei Bonn: Anthropos-Instituts, 1976.

Rowton, Michael B. "Dimorphic Structure and the Parasocial Element." *JNES* 36 (1977): 181–198.

Sader, Hélène. "History." Pages 11–36 in *The Arameans in Ancient Syria*. Edited by Herbert Niehr. HdO 106. Leiden: Brill, 2014.

Seminara, Stefano. *L'accadico di Emar*. MVS 6. Rome: Università Degli Studi di Roma « La Sapienza » Dipartimento di Studie Orientali, 1998.

Sapin, Jean. "La géographie humaine de la Syrie-Palestine au deuxième millénaire avant J.C. comme voie de recherche historique." *JESHO* 24 (1981): 1–62.

Sapin, Jean. "La géographie humaine de la Syrie-Palestine au deuxième millénaire avant J.C. comme voie de recherche historique." *JESHO* 25/1 (1982): 1–49.

Sapin, Jean. "La géographie humaine de la Syrie-Palestine au deuxième millénaire avant J.C. comme voie de recherche historique." *JESHO* 25/2 (1982): 113–186.

Sasson, Jack M. *From the Mari Archives: An Anthology of Old Babylonian Letters*. Winona Lake, IN: Eisenbrauns, 2015.

Schloen, David J. "The Exile of Disinherited Kin in KTU 1.12 and KTU 1.23." *JNES* 52 (1993): 209–220.

Singer, Itamar. *The Hittite KI.LAM Festival*. 2 vols. SBT 27. Wiesbaden: Harrassowitz, 1983.

Smith, Mark S. *The Rituals and Myths of the Feast of the Goodly Gods of KTU/CAT 1.23: Royal Constructions of Opposition, Intersection, Integration, and Domination*. SBLRBS 51. Atlanta, GA: Society of Biblical Literature, 2006.

Streck, Michael P. *Die Amurriter, die onomastische Forschung, Orthographie und Phonologie, Nominalmorphologie*. Vol. 1 of *Das amurritische Onomastikon der altbabylonischen Zeit*. AOAT 271. Münster: Ugarit-Verlag, 2000.

Streck, Michael P. "Zwischen Weide, Dorf und Stadt: Sozio-ökonomische Strukturen des ammurischen Nomadismus am Mittleren Euphrat." *BaM* 33 (2002): 155–209.

Thames, John Tracy, Jr. *The Politics of Ritual Change: The* zukru *Festival in the Political History of Late Bronze Age Emar*. HSM 65. Boston, MA/Leiden: Brill, 2020.

Younger, K. Lawson, Jr. *A Political History of the Arameans: From Their Origins to the End of Their Polities*. ABS 13. Atlanta, GA: SBL, 2016.

Younger, K. Lawson, Jr. "Tiglath-Pileser I and the Initial Conflicts of the Assyrians with the Arameans." Pages 195–228 in *Wandering Arameans: Arameans Outside Syria: Textual and Archaeological Perspectives*. Edited by Angelika Berlejung, Aren M. Maeir, and Andreas Schüle. LAS 5. Wiesbaden: Harrassowitz Verlag, 2017.

Zadok, Ron. "Elements of Aramean Pre-history." Pages 104–117 in *Ah Assyria …: Studies in Assyrian History and Ancient Near Eastern Historiography presented to Hayim Tadmor*. Edited by Mordechai Cogan and Israel Ephʿal. ScrHier 33. Jerusalem: Magnes Press, 1991.

10

A Head of Hammurabi? Thoughts on Royal Representations and the Legacies of Kings

Elizabeth Knott

In the collection of the Musée du Louvre there exists an exceptional work of art that was found during excavations of Susa at the beginning of the twentieth century. This artwork is a statue of a king, made of diorite or another black stone.[1] Once, the statue would have been a half-human sized full-body portrayal, with the king shown in a seated or standing position.[2] All that remains, however, is the uninscribed head and neck of the ruler. Although the identity of the ruler is unknown, the statue fragment has long been associated with the Babylonian king Hammurabi (ca. 1792–1750 BCE),[3] whose famous "Laws of Hammurabi" (LH) stele was also found at Susa. Thus, the statue is known today as "Tête royale dite 'tête de Hammurabi'" or "Head of a Ruler" (Sb 95).

"Head of a Ruler" has been singled out in modern scholarship as a uniquely important representation of a Mesopotamian king due to the unusual manner in which the face of the ruler is carved (Fig. 10.1). With puffy eyelids, sagging undereye folds, and sunken cheeks, the statue head appears to show a ruler at an advanced age.[4] Portrayals of aged kings are almost unknown from

1 Scholars have shown that it can be difficult to differentiate between types of hard black stone. See, e.g., Karen Leslie, "Examination and Tentative Identification of Some Black Stone Objects," *ZA* 92 (2002): 296–300; and Julian Reade, "Early Monuments in Gulf Stone at the British Museum, with Observations on Some Gudea Statues and the Location of Agade," *ZA* 92 (2002): 258–295. Both the statue head and the Laws of Hammurabi (LH) stele are said to be made of diorite, but questions have been raised about the material of the latter in, e.g., Tallay Ornan, "Unfinished Business: The Relief on the Hammurabi Louvre Stele Revisited," *JCS* 71 (2019): 85–109.

2 The head bears many of the traditional markings of kingship—including the thick and wide brimmed cap that covers nearly all of the man's hair, as well as the finely carved arching eyebrows, curling hair, and twisted beard—and is, undoubtedly, a depiction of a king-like figure. Further evidence for royal production may come from the very material of the statue head and its fineness of carving.

3 All dates follow Marc Van de Mieroop, *A History of the Ancient Near East ca. 3000–323 BC.*, 2nd ed. (Malden, MA: Blackwell, 2007).

4 Eyes of royal statues may be deeply carved to show a king's attentiveness, but I know of no other examples of royal representations with sagging skin beneath the eyes and cheekbones.

 | DOI:10.1163/9789004511538_011

Mesopotamia, and "Head of a Ruler" stands at odds with what we know of Mesopotamian cultural attitudes toward kingship. The statue head is therefore often described as a marvel and an enigma.[5]

At the center of much scholarship on "Head of a Ruler" lies the supposition that the puffy eyelids, sagging undereye folds, and sunken cheeks of the statue capture the actual appearance of a real historical figure. Scholars have described the statue head as a uniquely "naturalistic" representation of a king—i.e., a successful copy from life. Such characterizations draw the artwork into discussions of likeness and portraiture, with several important, and so far unrecognized, consequences. First, the identification of the head as a possible portrait of a king prompts searches for the identity of the figure, with scholars repeatedly turning to the best-known king of the early second millennium BCE: Hammurabi of Babylon.[6] Association of "Head of a Ruler" with Hammurabi appears in introductions to Mesopotamian visual arts (from Henri Frankfort's popular survey to Zainab Bahrani's recent overview)[7] as well as

---

Note that many physical characteristics associated with age can also be associated with deprivation and strain. They may also be interpreted as manifestations of an individual's inner character, the ethos of a particular time in history, and even as political messages. To help avoid introducing modern biases, I work under the premise that the physical qualities shown in the statue head represent the face of an older man, and that Mesopotamian attitudes toward aging and kingship should stand at the forefront of analysis. For a similar discussion of the significance of the portrayal of age in Egyptian statuary, see Lisa Saladino Haney, *Visualizing Coregency: An Exploration of the Link between Royal Image and Co-Rule during the Reign of Senwosret III and Amenemhet III* (Boston, MA/Leiden: Brill, 2020), 137–175.

5 See, e.g., Frankfort's identification of the sculpture as "the greatest surviving work of art of the Old Babylonian period" (Henri Frankfort, *The Art and Architecture of the Ancient Orient*, 5th ed. [New Haven, CT/London: Yale University Press, 1954 (1996)], 119); and Harper's comment on the statue as "a remarkable expression of character and strength" (Prudence O. Harper, "Head of a Ruler," in *The Royal City of Susa: Ancient Near Eastern Treasures in the Louvre*, ed. Prudence O. Harper, Joan Aruz, and Françoise Tallon. [New York, NY: Metropolitan Museum of Art, 1992], 175). Text on an earlier version of the Louvre's website (accessed May 2021) described the work as "an astonishing mix of conventional features and realism."

6 The attribution of "Head of a Ruler" to Hammurabi comes, I suspect, from the legacy of the modern rediscovery of the ancient Near East, and the way in which Hammurabi became the epitome of Old Babylonian kingship in modern scholarship.

7 Frankfort (*The Art and Architecture of the Ancient Orient*, 119) neatly equates what is, in his mind, the "greatest surviving work of the period" with the "greatest figure of the age" (i.e., Hammurabi). Anton Moortgat (*The Art of Ancient Mesopotamia: The Classical Art of the Near East* [New York, NY/London: Phaidon, 1969], 90 and Fig. 222) and André Parrot (*Sumer: The Dawn of Art* [New York, NY: Golden Press, 1961], 306–307) also explicitly connect the monument to Hammurabi. Zainab Bahrani (*Mesopotamia: Ancient Art and Architecture* [London: Thames & Hudson, 2017], 180) introduces the statue as a possible representation of Hammurabi.

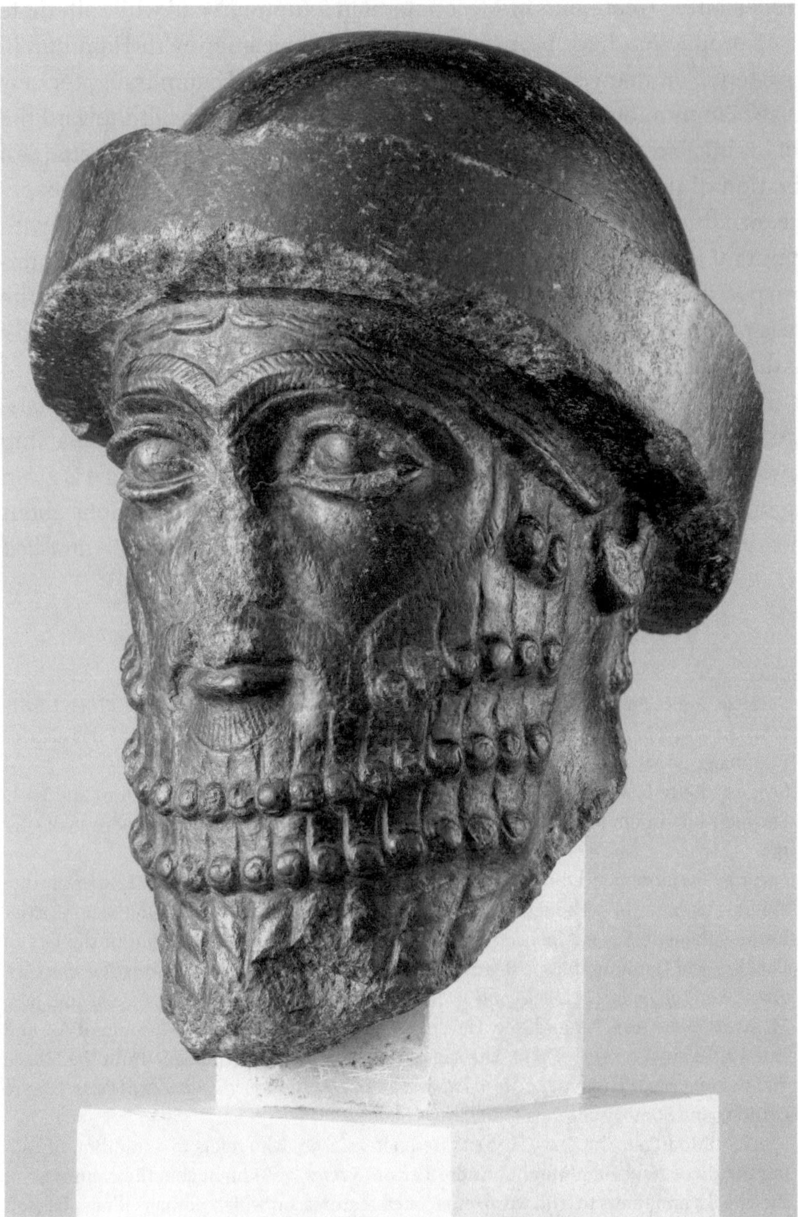

FIGURE 10.1 Three-quarters view of "Head of a Ruler" found during excavations at Susa. Musée du Louvre, Sb 95. H. 15.2 cm; W. 9.70 cm; D. 11 cm (c) MUSÉE DU LOUVRE, DIST. RMN-GRAND PALAIS. PHOTO: RAPHAËL CHIPAULT

more specialized treatments of Mesopotamian sculpture;[8] and while alternate dates of production have been proposed,[9] the association with Hammurabi is persistent.[10] In many cases, the figure is identified as Hammurabi precisely because Hammurabi was a long-lived king who suffered ill-health toward the end of his life.[11] In other instances, the gaunt face of the ruler is interpreted as a celebration of those qualities that we often associate with age, such as experience, erudition, and wisdom.[12] Yet the equation of "Head of a Ruler" with Hammurabi is far from certain. Moreover, the association restricts our interpretive possibilities, focusing on *who* the statue represents rather than *why* the figure is portrayed at an advanced age. Second, discussion of the statue head's naturalism has the (unintended) consequence of valuing the artistic ability to copy from life over other forms of signification and artistic intent. By emphasizing (and even celebrating) the creation of a naturalistic work of art, scholarship gives way to a teleological narrative of art history, where little credence is given to the importance of the artwork in its own time and place. Questions about the possible meanings of the artist's portrayal of an aged king remain unasked

8 See, e.g., Agnès Spycket, *La statuaire du Proche-Orient ancien* (Leiden and Köln: E.J. Brill, 1981), 245–246; Béatrice André-Salvini, *Le code de Hammurabi* (Paris: Réunion des musées nationaux, 2003), 17–18.

9 See, e.g., Betty L. Schlossman, "Portraiture in Mesopotamia in the Late Third and Early Second Millennium B.C., Part II: The Early Second Millennium," *AfO* 28 (1981/1982): 154–159.

10 See, e.g., the aforementioned title for the object on the Louvre's website ("Tête royale dite tête de Hammurabi"). Though described as the "diorite head of a ruler" in the 2008 exhibition catalogue *Beyond Babylon*, the statue is illustrated in a discussion of the city of Babylon and Hammurabi; see Béatrice André-Salvini, "Babylon," in *Beyond Babylon: Art, Trade, and Diplomacy in the Second Millennium B.C.*, ed. Joan Aruz, Kim Benzel, and Jean M. Evans (New York, NY and New Haven, CT/London: Metropolitan Museum of Art and Yale University Press, 2008), 18. The same is true for a recent catalogue from the Musée du Louvre. Ariane Thomas, *La Mésopotamie au Louvre: de Sumer à Babylone* (Paris: Louvre éditions and Somogy éditions d'art, 2016), 66–67.

11 See, e.g., Moortgat, *The Art of Ancient Mesopotamia*, 90, who refers to a tradition of calling the piece "Old Ḫammurabi." André Parrot (*Sumer*, 306) highlights the gauntness of the cheeks and refers to "the worn, emaciated features, on which perhaps illness has left its mark, of a Hammurabi well advanced in years." Spycket (*La statuaire*, 245–246) notes that the face of aged man with emaciated figures could well be Hammurabi, as he was particularly long-lived.

12 Moortgat (*The Art of Ancient Mesopotamia*, 90) describes the facial features as being "lined by work and spiritual grief." An exhibition on the Code of Hammurabi described the figure portrayed in the statue head (Hammurabi) as exuding "la maîtrise que donne l'expérience d'une vie longue et remplie." See André-Salvini, *Le code de Hammurabi*, 17–18.

and unexplored. Such approaches help an unfamiliar audience appreciate the magnetism of Mesopotamia, but they do little to draw us closer to the beliefs and practices of Mesopotamian peoples.

The present paper invites us to consider "Head of a Ruler" in relationship to cultural attitudes toward aging and kingship. It does so by revisiting the dating of the statue head in order to fix the artwork in a chronological framework that is not constrained by the identification with Hammurabi; by reconsidering the goals of royal representation in light of scholarship on Mesopotamian portraiture; and by discussing changing political conditions that may have impacted ideals of kingship.[13] The contribution is dedicated with thanks and fondness to Dan Fleming—an exceptional teacher, whose research on the ancient Near East reshapes our understanding of the peoples of Mesopotamia.[14]

1 Aging and Kingship in Mesopotamia

Age—universally experienced, yet culturally defined—is fundamental to the human condition. While the vocabulary and parameters used to measure age are culturally contingent, our lives are all defined by the passage through time. For some, growing older is a marker of increased experience, wisdom, and stability. For others, it is anathema to the exuberance and vitality associated with

---

13 I would like to thank Melissa Eppihimer, Mahri Leonard-Fleckman, and Michael Stahl for comments on the initial draft; Agnete W. Lassen and Klaus Wagensonner for conversations about the works of art under discussion; and Helen Gries and Ariane Thomas for assistance with images. All errors remain my own.

14 It has not escaped my notice that discussions of aging and likeness may hit close to home, and I beg forgiveness for any apparent connection of these topics to the aforementioned scholar, who is celebrating his 65th birthday and who is known on NYU's campus for his likeness to Van Gogh's self-portrait. To Dan: the inspiration for this research came from the idea that the attribution of this artwork to Hammurabi oversimplifies the history of the Old Babylonian period and the legacy of its kings. My thanks to you for opening up the world of the early second millennium BCE and its complexities by way of Mari, without which I may have never given the present statue further thought. In particular, our conversations about Samsi-Addu over the years have led me to wonder about the extent to which this king of Upper Mesopotamia may have served as a kind of royal role model for Hammurabi. I had initially hoped to discuss the legacy of Mari's kings for the rulers who followed in their footsteps (a much more fitting piece for my deeply appreciated advisor!), but I got stuck on this particular statue, its treatment in modern scholarship, and its possible relationship to the legacies of earlier kings. Here again, I thank you for indulging my wonderings and my wanderings, always seeing the potential in different directions of research.

youth. In Mesopotamia, old age was—so far as we can tell—antithetical to celebrations of kingship. Textual and visual records of Mesopotamia have little to say about aged rulers (or even the process of aging more generally).[15] One list of the infirmaries of old age appears on the stele of Adad-guppi, the long-lived mother of the Babylonian king Nabonidus (555–539 BCE). While the text on this stele does not, in fact, name the infirmaries experienced by older adults, it does describe the 104-year-old mother of the king as having keen eyesight, excellent hearing, perfect hands and feet, good diction, and healthy digestion—alluding to the ailments of old age.[16] Adad-guppi's age-defying good health highlights the emphasis placed on the youthful qualities of royals. The kind of physical qualities that would characterize age—failing eyesight, shrinking bones, bent posture, or weathered skin—are rigorously ignored and even denied. This rejection of physical imperfections (including those brought about by age) is part of a broader Mesopotamian tradition of royal representations in textual and visual sources that celebrate the king's physical perfection, strength, and success in battle. The famous *Gilgamesh Epic*, for example, highlights the heroics of youthful kings.[17] Similarly, in a study of Hammurabi's fragmentary inscriptions, Marc Van de Mieroop notes that the emphasis lies squarely on the ruler's vigor and prowess in battle—and not on the longevity of his reign or his wisdom.[18] Positive traits that may come with time (e.g., experience, wisdom) are never explicitly related to age in royal texts.[19] In visual representations,

15 Physical signs of aging were clearly understood to mark the passage of time. The verb *eṭēlu*, "to grow up," for example, is also used to mean "to grow a beard." See Rivkah Harris, *Gender and Aging in Mesopotamia: The Gilgamesh Epic and Other Ancient Literature* (Norman, OK: University of Oklahoma Press, 2000), 23–24. Yet once we approach the later part of life, we find relatively few indicators of what the peoples of Mesopotamia thought about aging.

16 Harris, *Gender and Aging*, 54–55. For a recent translation, see Sarah C. Melville, "The Autobiography of Adad-Guppi," in *The Ancient Near East: Historical Sources in Translation*, ed. Mark Chavalas (Malden, MA/Oxford: Blackwell, 2006), 389–393.

17 If he must one day die, Gilgamesh says to Enkidu, it should be at a young age and in battle against Huwawa, so that he ensures his enduring fame. For this statement on the Yale tablet of the Old Babylonian *Gilgamesh Epic*, see Andrew R. George, *The Babylonian Gilgamesh Epic: Introduction, Critical Edition and Cuneiform Text* (New York, NY/Oxford: Oxford University Press, 2003), 200–220. I focus here on the remains of the earlier version of this epic, rather than the longer text of the Standard Babylonian Version, which refers to the ruler's strife and weariness but was developed long after the time that "Head of a Ruler" was created.

18 Marc Van de Mieroop, "Hammurabi's Self-presentation," *Or* 80/4 (2011): 305–338.

19 This may be particularly striking for the LH stele, which is imagined to have been created toward the end of Hammurabi's life. Although the text celebrates his many conquests and

rulers are strong and well-formed men, attentive worshipers of the gods, and active figures in battle.[20] These references highlight the uniqueness of "Head of a Ruler" and offer some explanation for scholarly reactions to the work of art as an exceptional royal representation.

Interpretations of culturally defined attitudes toward age in Mesopotamia are, of course, complicated by the nature of the surviving records—how well textual records track potential shifts in cultural outlooks over time, across space, or according to individual circumstances—in addition to our ability to translate, characterize, and classify the various remains. In addition to showing little interest in physiological changes, Mesopotamian written sources categorize age in different ways.[21] Various sources provide contrasting perspectives: while the gods are thought to reward the pious with long life, old age can also be a kind of curse on those who have lost favor.[22] Idiomatic expressions are not easily interpreted, as in the case of the verb *labārum*, "to last, endure"—

---

the stability of his rule, and proclaims him the king of justice, there is no outright correlation between the experience of his advanced years and his wisdom. As noted by Harris, wisdom is not the exclusive property of the old, but it is commonly associated with age (Harris, *Gender and Aging*, 63). Literary descriptions of the older generation of gods refer to their expert counsel, but also depict the senior deities as slower to act and less directly connected to those whom they rule. Harris refers to this divide between generations as a contrast between "active mastery" and "passive mastery," moving from "aggressive competitive behavior" to "apathy and immobility" (Harris, *Gender and Aging*, 59).

20 Victory steles, like that of Naram-Sin, epitomize this kind of royal representation, often portraying a physically powerful ruler in the process of subduing enemies; see Irene J. Winter, "Sex, Rhetoric, and the Public Monument: The Alluring Body of Naram-Sîn of Agade," in *Sexuality in Ancient Art: Near East, Greece, and Italy*, ed. Natalie B. Kampen and Bettina Bergmann (New York, NY/Cambridge: Cambridge University Press, 1996), 11–26.

21 Some texts juxtapose the young (Sumerian TUR.MEŠ; Akkadian *ṣiḫrum*) and the old (Sumerian GAL.MEŠ; Akkadian *rabûm*); others use a tripartite division of old men and women, adult men and women, and children (Harris, *Gender and Aging*, 6). The Akkadian noun *eṭlum* (Sumerian GURUŠ) is used for able-bodied men and can include both young and mature adults. Elsewhere, *batūlu* is used for adolescent men (Harris, *Gender and Aging*, 23). See further Joan Goodnick Westenholz and Ilona Zsolnay, "Categorizing Men and Masculinity in Sumer," in *Being a Man: Negotiating Ancient Constructs of Masculinity*, ed. Ilona Zsolnay (Milton: Taylor & Francis, 2016), 12–41.

22 Harris, *Gender and Aging*, 54, 59. It may be that the variety of views expressed in the texts reflects the different realities that various sectors of society could face in growing older. More optimistic outlooks may come from those who were in a position to enjoy certain comforts, or from those whose professional position and place in society may have advanced with age. For example, see Harris, *Gender and Aging*, 28–31, on a seventh-century BCE text known as STT 400, with a "pro-old-age bias" that Harris believes was written by a scribe who perhaps saw a link between longevity and creativity.

generally used to express wishes for a ruler's long life, but also appearing in the expression *labīrūtu alākum*, "to become dilapidated."[23] Two scholars can read the same text or image differently, suggesting that our own modern biases play some role in the identification of stereotypes and characteristics associated with age.[24] Moving between our own cultural and individual perspectives on aging and kingship to those of the peoples of ancient Mesopotamia will never be straightforward, and it may not be possible to identify an overarching Mesopotamian cultural attitude toward aging.

When it comes to the visual representation of rulers, we have almost no evidence for any kind of physical characteristics of aging in Mesopotamian arts. Conditions affecting old age (including reductions of size, alterations of posture, loss of hair, and wrinkling of skin) are almost entirely absent from the visual record. Rivkah Harris suggests that "the appearance of gray hair was *the* distinguishing sign of old age," yet statues made of dark stone, like "Head of a Ruler," show the beard and hair of rulers with the black luster of youth, and would have had to be painted to indicate any sign of aging.[25] While future scientific analysis of paint residues on reliefs and sculptures may produce new insights, no statues with white-painted hair have been observed thus far. In fact, only one exception to the rule of black-haired kings—found on a fragmentary wall painting from Mari—is known to me.[26] This painting shows a male figure

23 Used for both humans and buildings, the verb is also known in the D-stem (*lubburum*), meaning "to last a long time," or "to live to an old age." See Harris, *Gender and Aging*, 51 for initial comments, and *CAD* L 13–16; *AHw* 1:522–523.

24 One good example of this kind of contrast is the scholarly discussion of Marduk in the *Erra Epic*: while Jeremy Black and Anthony Green characterize the god as a "bumbling and old incompetent," Ben Foster has argued that the text portrays the god as "remote and all-wise" (see Harris, *Gender and Aging*, 61, with references). Note that Harris herself seems to take contradicting interpretations of Mesopotamian attitudes toward aging; while suggesting that most Mesopotamians wished for a long life, she states that "old age is certainly not the desideratum" (Harris, *Gender and Aging in Mesopotamia*, 30).

25 Harris (*Gender and Aging*, 51 with references) notes the existence of recipes for hair coloring. Supposing that the use of hair dye was prevalent among the elite, it is possible that the juxtaposition of weathered skin and shiny black hair seen on "Head of Ruler" approximates the reality of an older king's look.

26 The painting was once fixed to the wall in Room 132, an open shrine for the goddess Ishtar that lay alongside Courtyard 131. See André Parrot, "Les peintures du palais de Mari," *Syria* 18/4 (1937) : 325–354; and André Parrot, *Le palais: Peintures murals* (Paris: Librarie orientaliste Paul Geuthner, 1958) for reconstructions of this multiregister composition, as well as Béatrice Muller, "Contextes techniques et historiques des peintures murales du Grand Palais Royal de Mari: Une mise au point," in *Tracing Technoscapes: The Production of Bronze*

with a long white beard who stands as a worshiper on a platform before the god Sin. Though the dress of this figure is unusual, his position within the scene and skull cap would suggest that he is a ruler.[27] The Mari wall painting with the old king is dated to the beginning of the second millennium BCE, around the time that "Head of a Ruler" is thought to have been created. Yet while the wall painting uses a white beard to signify age, "Head of a Ruler" appears to use the skin of the face to portray the king at an older age. The contrasts between these early second millennium BCE artworks is provocative and highlights the importance of a reevaluation of cultural attitudes toward age and kingship at this time.

2 Dating "Head of a Ruler"

Rather than linking the exceptional "Head of a Ruler" with an outstanding figure in history (i.e., Hammurabi), we can use the evidence at hand to define a chronological horizon for the statue head, and then explore the possible resonances of the artwork with cultural attitudes toward kingship at that time. Archaeological evidence, the rendering of the royal beard, and the naturalism of the statue have all been used to date the artwork. While gaps in the archaeological evidence preclude dating, recent discussions of the stylistic development of royal beards may offer new inroads. I find the use of naturalism as a criterion for dating unsatisfying and suggest that the entire approach to the historical contextualization of the statue head needs to shift.

Found in the early twentieth century during French-led excavations of Susa directed by Jacques de Morgan, the statue head's find spot on the *acropole* of Susa was not carefully recorded.[28] The statue may have been one of those monuments that was taken from the Mesopotamian heartland by the Elamite ruler Shutruk-Nahhunte I in ca. 1158 BCE. If so, its existence at Susa is secondary, and knowledge of the original location of the monument (presumably one of the

---

Age Wall Paintings in the Eastern Mediterranean, ed. Johannes Jungfleisch and Constance von Rüden (Leiden: Sidestone Press, 2018) for a recent overview of the Mari wall paintings with bibliography.

27 The scene unusually reverses the clothing of the deity and approaching (royal) figure: Sin wears the kind of garment typically associated with kingship, while the royal figure wears the dress of a god. Unlike the male figure, the god's beard is black.

28 For notes on the recovery of "Head of a Ruler" during de Morgan's excavations of Susa, see Spycket, *La statuaire*, 245, FN 101.

cities of the Mesopotamian heartland) is lost. Yet the identification of "Head of a Ruler" as a Mesopotamian monument is uncertain, as the "Mesopotamian" monuments found by Morgan's excavations at Susa were unearthed in various states of preservation and were not all found in the same location.[29] Several of the presumed Mesopotamian monuments bear inscriptions that directly identify them as booty, but many, including the "Head of a Ruler," do not have surviving inscriptions and could have arrived at Susa by way of gift or exchange, or could even be local productions.[30]

In the absence of archaeological and inscriptional evidence for the dating of the statue head, scholars have turned to visual comparisons.[31] The thick, wide brimmed cap of the ruler, for example, is of a type known beginning in the late third millennium BCE and continuing through the second millennium BCE.[32] The ruler's beard, rendered in a bipartite fashion, with curls of the chin laid out in a grid-like fashion and tendrils of twisted hair shown in vertical rows with diagonal crosshatches, offers another line of evidence for stylistic dating.[33]

---

29 See Prudence O. Harper, "Mesopotamian Monuments Found at Susa," in *The Royal City of Susa: Ancient Near Eastern Treasures in the Louvre*, ed. Prudence O. Harper, Joan Aruz, and Françoise Tallon (New York, NY: Metropolitan Museum of Art, 1992), 159–162 for an introduction to these monuments.

30 Harper ("Mesopotamian Monuments Found at Susa," 159) suggests that the statue head could be a portrayal of a prince or king of Susa made by a local craftsperson versed in Mesopotamian-style sculpture. If so, she thinks that one goal of local production was to replicate the kinds of artworks being produced in Mesopotamia.

31 For publications of "Head of a Ruler," see Bahrani, *Mesopotamia*, 180–181; Thomas, *La Mésopotamie au Louvre*, 66–67; André-Salvini, "Babylon," 18; André-Salvini, *Le code de Hammurabi*, 17–18; Harper, "Head of a Ruler," 175–176; Schlossman, "Portraiture in Mesopotamia, Part II," 154–159; Spycket, *La statuaire*, 245–246; Moortgat, *The Art of Ancient Mesopotamia*, 90 and Fig. 222; Parrot, *Sumer*, 306–307; Frankfort, *The Art and Architecture of the Ancient Orient*, 119. For a closer look at stylistic parallels, see Appendix. Future research could consider the materials and size of the statue head. If indeed the statue was made of diorite, we might begin to situate the work of art in time by looking at those rulers which had access to the stone, and the possibility of reuse of earlier diorite monuments. These considerations lie beyond the scope of the present paper but could help balance discussions of dating that are based on the style of carving.

32 Examples can be found in depictions of Ur III rulers and Hammurabi on the LH stele.

33 Long and elaborate beards carrying connotations of maturity, status, virility, and prowess are another standard element of royal representations. On definitions of masculinity in a royal context, see Winter, "Sex, Rhetoric, and the Public Monument"; Claudia E. Suter, "The Royal Body and Masculinity in Early Mesopotamia," in *Menschenbilder und Körperkonzepte im Alten Israel, in Ägypten und im Alten Orient*, ed. Angelika Berlejung, Jan Dietrich, and Joachim F. Quack (Tübingen: Mohr Siebeck, 2012), 433–458; Claudia E. Suter, "Kings and Queens: Representation and Reality," in *The Sumerian World*, ed. Harriet Crawford (Hoboken, NJ: Taylor & Francis, 2013), 201–226.

Articulation of royal beards—both in the treatment of the overall beard (either as a whole or in a bipartite fashion, distinguishing between hair on the face and hair on the chest) and in the markings used to represent the texture and styling of the beard on the face and chest (in particular, layers of the beard extending down the chest can be defined horizontally or vertically)—varies over time.[34] Early representations show a horizontal definition of the beard (applied to the hair of both the face and chest), but beginning in the late third millennium BCE, rulers are shown with bipartite beards like that of "Head of a Ruler."[35]

Variations within the larger tradition of bipartite beards have encouraged the creation of more refined typologies with mixed results.[36] Betty Schlossman, for example, examines the styles of royal beards in her study of Mesopotamian portraiture from the late third and early second millennium BCE.[37] Rejecting the longstanding association of "Head of a Ruler" with Hammurabi, she dates the statue head to the reign of Hammurabi's ancestor, Sumulael (1880–1845 BCE).[38] Schlossman's primary argument for the earlier dating is based on contrasts between the articulation of the beard on the statue and on the LH stele, where Hammurabi is shown with an incised horizontally defined chest beard.[39] Tallay Ornan, however, now argues that the horizontally defined beards of both Hammurabi and Shamash on the LH stele are the result of a later reworking of the monument by Elamite artists.[40] Ornan's interpretation

---

34 See further Ornan, "Unfinished Business." I use Ornan's terminology.

35 Examples of the bipartite beard can be seen in two- and three-dimensional representations in both stone and terracotta. See the Appendix for some examples in stone and metal. In terracotta, we have the statue of a god found at Ur (BM 122934) as well as perhaps a standing male figure found at Kish (Louvre AO 10405). The horizontally defined beard does not entirely disappear, however, and can be seen on the LH stele. See further discussion below.

36 Preliminary comparison of the conventional features like the bipartite beard with a grid-like facial beard and a vertically defined chest beard across a group of royal representations in two and three dimensions shows the difficulty of stylistic analysis. See Appendix.

37 Betty L. Schlossman, "Portraiture in Mesopotamia in the Late Third and Early Second Millennium B.C., Part I: The Late Third Millennium," *AfO* 26 (1978/1979): 56–77; Schlossman, "Portraiture in Mesopotamia, Part II."

38 Schlossman, "Portraiture in Mesopotamia, Part II," 156. Harper, "Head of a Ruler," 176, follows this attribution. Schlossman appears to cite Sumulael in order to keep the association with Babylon, while providing the piece an earlier date.

39 Schlossman, "Portraiture in Mesopotamia, Part II," 156.

40 Ornan, "Unfinished Business." As noted by Ornan ("Unfinished Business," 97–98), the surface of the chest beards of Hammurabi and Shamash lie at a lower plane than the face beards, suggesting that these may have been carved down at a later date.

makes Schlossman's use of the LH stele as an anchor for dating less compelling and reopens the question of dating beard styles from the early second millennium BCE.[41]

Schlossman and Ornan's research exemplifies one problem with stylistic analysis: the emergence of new data and interpretations. Other challenges include the treatment of different materials across two- and three-dimensional representations, and the existence of regional styles. Many royal representations from the late third and early second millennium BCE are missing inscriptions, lack archaeological provenience, or were found in a secondary location, further confounding the study of royal beards. These challenges become increasingly evident in the comparison of "Head of a Ruler" with two other royal statues that feature the bipartite beard: the statue of the Mari ruler Puzur-Ishtar (ca. 2030 BCE) found at Babylon and in the collection of the Vorderasiatisches Museum (VA 8748) and a head from Tello provisionally dated to the early Akkadian period (ca. 2340–2200 BCE) in the collection of the Musée du Louvre (AO 14). The statue of Puzur-Ishtar shows a face beard with large flat spiral curls that line up with tightly coiled tendrils of the chest beard (Fig. 10.2); the Tello head features long and thin spiral curls that are more deeply carved (Fig. 10.3). The tight and deeply carved spiral curls of "Head of a Ruler" (Fig. 10.4) could suggest that the statue head is located close in time to the early Tello head, but the similarity could also be explained by regional styles or the later emulation of Akkadian period artworks.[42] A single line of comparison, in other words, does not warrant a full equation of styles and periods of production.[43]

In my own perusal of royal representations from the late third and early second millennium BCE, a two-dimensional limestone relief from Sippar in the collection of the British Museum (BM 22454 / 1882,0714.999) emerged as a possibly noteworthy correlate for "Head of a Ruler."[44] The fragmentary relief shows a ruler in a thick wide-brimmed cap facing two inscription panels. Both "Head of a Ruler" and the figure shown here wear a thick cap resting over the ears and are

41 Ornan ("Unfinished Business," 95) does not directly discuss "Head of a Ruler," but notes that the long bipartite beard was the only kind of beard shown in the Old Babylonian period.

42 On the citation of Akkadian imagery in later artworks, see Melissa Eppihimer, *Exemplars of Kingship: Art, Tradition, and the Legacy of the Akkadians* (New York, NY: Oxford University Press, 2019).

43 Indeed, the distinctive loosely twisted and roughly carved tendrils on the chest beard of "Head of a Ruler" have been used to suggest a later period of production. Schlossman, "Portraiture in Mesopotamia, Part II," 155–159.

44 See Appendix. Further analysis of the two artworks is needed.

FIGURE 10.2 Frontal view of Head of Statue of Puzur-Ishtar originally from Mari but found at Babylon. Vorderasiatisches Museum, Berlin. VA 8748. H. ca. 30 cm. (Body of Statue in the collection of Eski Şark Eserleri Müzesi EŞ 7814)
(C) STAATLICHE MUSEEN ZU BERLIN—VORDERASIATISCHES MUSEUM. PHOTO: OLAF M. TEẞMER

FIGURE 10.3 Frontal view of Head of a Bearded Male found at Tello. Musée du Louvre, AO 14. H. 12 cm

FIGURE 10.4 Frontal view of "Head of a Ruler." Musée du Louvre, Sb 95
(C) MUSÉE DU LOUVRE, DIST. RMN-GRAND PALAIS. PHOTO: RAPHAËL CHIPAULT

shown with a diagonal beard line that follows the contours of the cheek, a thin, downward curving mouth, and a bipartite beard with a vertically defined tendrils running down the chest (Figs. 10.5, 10.6). According to the text inscribed in two panels on the limestone relief, a protective figure (^{d}LAMMA) was dedicated by Itur-ashdum to the goddess Ashratum for the life of Hammurabi.[45] This inscription would appear to suggest that the figure on the relief is Hammurabi, and many scholars have followed this identification, noting similarities to the representation of Hammurabi on the LH stele.[46] In fact, the main contrast between the limestone relief and the LH stele is the rendering of the ruler's beard—a contrast that is eliminated by Ornan's proposal to see the beard on the LH stele as a later reworking.[47] I would therefore tentatively suggest that the limestone relief may match the earlier rendering of the beard on the famous LH stele. If so, both reliefs could support the dating of "Head of a Ruler" to the reign of Hammurabi.

While the evidence offered by such features as the ruler's skull cap and the articulation of the bipartite beard may help determine a dating horizon for "Head of a Ruler," I find no compelling parallels for those naturalistic features associated with the depiction of age. Nevertheless, many scholars have used the puffy eyelids, sagging undereye folds, and sunken cheeks of the sculpture as a starting point for the investigation of a date and place of production. By characterizing these features as the result of a naturalistic turn in the arts of Mesopotamia, scholars are able to identify other naturalistic royal represen-

---

45 For the text and its translation, see Douglas Frayne, *The Old Babylonian Period (2003–1595 B.C.)*, RIME 4 (Toronto: University of Toronto Press, 1990), 359–360 (RIME 4.3.6.2001). Given that the *kispum* ritual from Mari refers to the *lamassātu* of Sargon and Naram-Sin (see reference below), I wonder whether the term ^{d}LAMMA could refer to the ruler shown on the left. Alternatively, it may be that a representation of a Lamma-goddess appeared on the now-lost right-hand side of the relief. The existence of a second figure could be suggested by the curved shape of the top of the relief, as well as the gap between the two inscription panels which may leave room for part of a second abraded figure. My thanks to Klaus Wagensonner for discussing the image and inscription with me.

46 See, e.g., Ornan, "Unfinished Business," 91, who identifies the relief as an image of Hammurabi, but notes parallels with other royal representations. The webpage of the British Museum also defines the figure as Hammurabi; see https://www.britishmuseum.org/collection/object/W_1882-0714-993. Schlossman ("Portraiture in Mesopotamia, Part II," 168) follows Eva Strommenger in wondering whether this could be a representation of Itur-ashdum. She notes slight differences in the fringe of the garment, the beard pattern, and the overall execution.

47 Ornan, "Unfinished Business." Contrast in the rendering of the beard seems to be what pushes Schlossman away from an identification of the figure on the limestone relief as Hammurabi. Schlossman, "Portraiture in Mesopotamia, Part II," 168.

FIGURE 10.5 Limestone Relief from Sippar dedicated by the high official Itur-Ashdum and sometimes thought to show Hammurabi. The British Museum, 1882,0714.993. H. of figure ca. 15.2 cm

tations as stylistic parallels for "Head of a Ruler." Edith Porada, for example, observed that statues of the Egyptian rulers Senwosret III and Amenemhet III in the nineteenth century BCE show aging visages of kings.[48] Statuary of Senwosret III, in particular, shares several features with "Head of a Ruler," including

48 Edith Porada, "Review of Henri Frankfort, *The Birth of Civilization in the Near East* and *The Art and Architecture of the Ancient Orient*," *Art Bulletin* 38 (1956): 123. For a recent review of the statuary of the Middle Kingdom period co-regents, see Saladino Haney, *Visualizing Coregency*, with further references. Porada's observation has been repeated in several treatments of the statue and used to help define a dating horizon for "Head of a Ruler."

FIGURE 10.6 Side view of "Head of a Ruler." Musée du Louvre, Sb 95

heavy eyelids and slackened skin.[49] Two copper heads in the collections of the Metropolitan Museum of Art (47.100.80) and the Cincinnati Museum of Art (1958.520) have also been cited as parallels for "Head of a Ruler."[50] The larger and better-preserved Met head (Fig. 10.7), dated to ca. 2300–2000 BCE, is described as having individualistic features—including large ears, heavy-lidded eyes, a rounded nose, and a full mouth.[51] The smaller Cincinnati head seems to similarly show large ears, heavy-lidded or closed eyes, a rounded nose, and a full mouth, but has been less fully published.[52]

Parallels seen between the Egyptian statues or two copper heads and "Head of a Ruler" do not, in my opinion, offer solid grounds for the dating of "Head of a Ruler." The statues of Senwosret III share only an interest in the rendering of heavy eyes and slackened skin.[53] These features are so fundamental to the representation of age that they could easily cooccur in separate artistic traditions and should not be relied upon for the identification of any kind of

49 The emphasis on age in these statues is further achieved through the ruler's furrowed brow and downturned long mouth.

50 For Schlossman, "Head of a Ruler" and the Met head represent a response to both Akkadian heritage and the naturalistic tendencies of early Ur III period art. She sees the Met head sharing with "Head of a Ruler" a style that combines "soft yet distinctive pattern joined to a naturalistic countenance" and finds parallels in the ways in which the moustache is shaped and the border between the face and beard is defined. Schlossman, "Portraiture in Mesopotamia, Part II," 158. Harper ("Head of a Ruler," 176) treats both statues, as well as the Cincinnati head, as evidence for "impressionistic and naturalistic sculptural styles" of the late third and early second millennium BCE. Both heads are among the earliest examples of large-scale metal works. Neither the Met head nor the Cincinnati head has a clear provenance, though they were reported to have been found together near Hamadan in Iran—a region to the north of Susa and well into the Zagros Mountains; see Harper, "Head of a Ruler," 175–176; also Oscar Muscarella, *Bronze and Iron: Ancient Near Eastern Artifacts in the Metropolitan Museum of Art* (New York, NY: The Metropolitan Museum of Art, 1988), 368–374. Melissa Eppihimer (personal communication) finds the association with Iran suspect and believes that any interpretation of the heads must derive from the heads themselves. My thanks to Melissa for discussing her research with me.

51 Schlossman ("Portraiture in Mesopotamia, Part II," 154–159) first drew attention to the Met head as a parallel for "Head of a Ruler" in her survey of portraiture. She seems to imagine the artwork as a later representation of an Akkadian period ruler. Schlossman, "Portraiture in Mesopotamia, Part II," 157.

52 Though executed in a different style from the Met head, Harper finds that the Cincinnati head, with the depressions under the eyes, modeled cheeks, and realistic line of the beard across the cheek "displays some of the same naturalistic features." Harper, "Head of a Ruler," 176.

53 An entirely different constellation of features is joined to these images and there is little reason to believe that they would have been viewed or experienced in the same way as "Head of a Ruler."

FIGURE 10.7 Frontal view of Copper Alloy Head of a Ruler. Metropolitan Museum of Art. MMA 47.100.80. H. 34.3 cm

cross-cultural exchange or concomitant artistic development.[54] The two copper heads, by contrast, have full rounded cheeks and their observed naturalistic features (the protruding ears and full mouth) are not to be found on the statue head. The only thing that unites these heads is their supposed deviance from a norm of royal representation. Not only do the parallels between all of these objects do nothing to refine the date of "Head of a Ruler," they also do nothing to explain the possible local appeal of the statue in Mesopotamia.

3 Reconsidering the Goals of Royal Representations

For decades, the uniqueness of the "Head of the Ruler" has been described in relationship to questions of likeness, naturalism, and portraiture.[55] Portraiture may be used to refer to the physiognomic representation of an individual, the capture of an individual's state of mind or mode of action, or even an expression of an individual's morals.[56] The term often carries Western expectations of art that prioritize an artist's ability to capture likeness. By celebrating "Head of a Ruler" as a naturalistic artwork or portrait, scholars are therefore identifying

54 Comparison with "Head of a Ruler" assumes forms of cross-cultural reference (borrowing, imitation, etc.) that require further analysis of the mechanics of exchanges of ideas, forms, and techniques of carving across long distances. Bahrani (*Mesopotamia*, 181) suggests that evidence for the kind of cultural contacts that would lead to the imitation of an apparently Egyptian style of royal representation in a single work of art has yet to be identified.

55 Without referring to the statue as a portrait, Frankfort (*The Art and Architecture of the Ancient Orient*, 119) highlighted the "impressionistic" qualities of the face, observing that "The sculptor's interest in physical substance has led him to an almost impressionistic rendering of the face." Parrot (*Sumer*, 306) referred to the sculpture as "one of the most moving" works of portraiture in the art history of the region. Moortgat (*The Art of Ancient Mesopotamia*, 90) describes the piece as "half a picture of a king and half a portrait." Schlossman ("Portraiture in Mesopotamia, Part II," 158–159) focused on the "naturalistic countenance" of the statue head in her treatment of Mesopotamian portraiture. Harper ("Head of a Ruler," 175–176) went so far as to associate the "impressionistic" and "naturalistic" sculpture style of the head in relationship to a particular ethos, writing: "Although hardly a portrait in our sense of the word, the head conveys a feeling of mood and personality that is distinctive and largely absent from the art of southern Mesopotamia and Syria in the late third and early second millennia B.C." Even recently, Bahrani (*Mesopotamia*, 181) characterized the head as showing an "interest in the naturalistic representation of age." These treatments classify the statue head's features as resulting from efforts to create a naturalistic work of art—or portrait of the king.

56 The term portraiture has a long history of scholarship and can be defined in slightly different ways. For the purposes of this paper, I follow the discussions of representation and portraiture by Irene Winter. See below.

successful copying from life as an advanced state of artistic thinking and production. In addition to carrying teleological attitudes toward art and culture, this approach fails to engage with the possible significance of "Head of a Ruler" for ancient audiences.

To better approach possible ancient understandings of the statue head, we can turn to the work of Irene Winter, who has sought to redefine portraiture from a Mesopotamian perspective. Winter argues that the goal of royal portraiture in Mesopotamia is to encapsulate the qualities of kingship that rulers should strive to meet.[57] A successful portrait facilitates recognition; it may or may not achieve resemblance.[58] Since the 1980s, Winter has defined what she refers to as the "signature elements" in royal representations and their correlation with the lexicon of kingship in various periods. In her well-known study of Gudea's statuary, for example, she observes how visual attributes of the king parallel his epithets: the exposed musculature of his right arm as a metaphor for (divinely endowed) strength, the broad face and visible ears as a correlate for wisdom, and so on.[59] She likewise notes correspondences between textually ascribed qualities of kingship and royal representations in her discussions of the visual program of Assurnaṣirpal II; and her treatment of the Stele of Naram-

57 See, e.g., Irene J. Winter, "Royal Rhetoric and the Development of Historical Narrative in Neo-Assyrian Reliefs," *Visual Communication* 7 (1981): 2–38; Winter, "Review of A. Spycket, *La statuaire du proche-orient*," JCS 36/1 (1984): 102–114; Winter, "The Body of the Able Ruler: Toward an Understanding of the Statues of Gudea," in *Dumu-É-dub-ba-a: Studies in Honor of Å.W. Sjöberg*, ed. Hermann Behrens Darlene Loding, and Martha T. Roth (Philadelphia, PA: The University Museum, 1989), 573–583; Winter, "Sex, Rhetoric, and the Public Monument," 11–26; Winter, "Art in Empire: The Royal Image and the Visual Dimensions of Assyrian Ideology," in *Assyria 1995: Proceedings of the 10th Anniversary Symposium of the Neo-Assyrian Text Corpus Project, Helsinki, September 7–11,1995*, ed. Simo Parpola and Robert M. Whiting (Helsinki: Neo-Assyrian Text Corpus Project, 1997), 359–381; Winter, "The Affective Properties of Styles: An Inquiry into Analytical Process and the Inscription of Meaning in Art History," in *Picturing Science, Producing Art*, ed. Peter Galison and Caroline A. Jones (Hoboken, NJ: Taylor & Francis, 1998), 55–77; Winter, "What/When Is a Portrait? Royal Images of the Ancient Near East," *Proceedings of the American Philosophical Society* 153/3 (2009): 254–270. Her studies critically address not just the evidence from the first millennium BCE, but the earlier Akkadian and Ur III periods, offering insight into the production of royal images at a time before "Head of a Ruler" was made. For recent reviews of these topics in relationship to Mesopotamian art, see Claudia E. Suter, "Statuary and Reliefs," in *A Companion to Ancient Near Eastern Art*, ed. Ann C. Gunter (Hoboken, NJ: Wiley Blackwell, 2019), 395–396 and Dominik Bonatz and Marlies Heinz, "Representation," in Gunter, *Companion to Ancient Near Eastern Art*, 385–410.

58 Winter, "What/When Is a Portrait?," 267.

59 See Winter, "The Body of the Able Ruler," 156–159 for further discussion.

Sin similarly focuses on how the articulation of the ruler—his dress, form, pose, and placement in the larger scene—underline his right to rule and divinity.[60] In each case, the ideal qualities of the king are brought out in both textual and visual representations so that the ruler is "coded for leadership."[61] She therefore concludes that Mesopotamian portrayals of kings are images of *kingship*—"the portrait of *a* king" rather than "a portrait of *the* king."

Following Winter's lead, we might approach "Head of a Ruler" as a representation of *kingship* rather than a representation of a king. If Mesopotamian representations of rulers are semiotic (i.e., meant to convey cultural ideals of kingship) and not mimetic, then the puffy eyelids, sagging undereye folds, and sunken cheeks may not just represent the physiognomy of an aged king. Instead, they would be indicators that the very ideals of kingship were shifting—or at least open to experimentation—at the time that the statue was made. The results of this change in perspective can be quite stunning: instead of seeking a place or time when Mesopotamian artists were more successful or more interested in capturing resemblance (relying on other naturalistic works of art to date the Susa statue head), we could look for those moments in which ideals of kingship may have come to embrace the qualities of age.

4 Historical Context

While Mesopotamian attitudes toward aging may be generally characterized as negative, Mesopotamian culture is by no means static or unchanging. Indeed, ideals of kingship could take different forms across time and space.[62] Similarly, attitudes toward aging—particularly when it comes to the figure of the

60 For the visual program of Assurnaṣirpal II, see Winter, "Royal Rhetoric"; for the syntax of the throne room reliefs, Winter, "Art in Empire"; and for the modelling of the ruler's body, Winter, "Art in Empire." For the Stele of Naram-Sin, see Winter, "Sex, Rhetoric, and the Public Monument."

61 Winter, "What/When Is a Portrait?," 262.

62 On changing ideals of kingship, and in particular the notion of divine kingship, see the articles in Nicole Brisch, ed., *Religion and Power: Divine Kingship in the Ancient World and Beyond* (Chicago, IL: The Oriental Institute of the University of Chicago, 2008), especially: Piotr Michalowski, "The Mortal Kings of Ur: A Short Century of Divine Rule in Ancient Mesopotamia," 33–46; Irene J. Winter, "Touched by the Gods: Visual Evidence for the Divine Status of Rulers in the Ancient Near East," 75–101; as well as Nicole Brisch, "Of Gods and Kings: Divine Kingship in Ancient Mesopotamia," *RC* 7/2 (2013): 37–46; Tallay Ornan, "A Silent Message: Godlike Kings in Mesopotamian Art," in *Critical Approaches to Ancient Near Eastern Art*, ed. Brian Brown and Marian H. Feldman (Berlin: de Gruyter, 2013), 569–595 (with references).

TABLE 10.1 Table showing longest-reigning kings of the late third and early second millennium BCE

Ruler	Period of rule	Years
Sargon of Akkad	2334–2279 BCE	55
Naram-Sin of Akkad	2254–2218 BCE	36
Šulgi of Ur	2094–2047 BCE	47
Ishbi-Erra of Isin	2017–1985 BCE	32
Samium of Larsa	1976–1942 BCE	34
Sumulael of Babylon	1880–1845 BCE	35
Ipiq-Adad II of Eshnunna	1862?–1818? BCE	44
Rim-Sin I of Larsa	1822–1763 BCE	59
Shamshi-Adad of Ekallatum / Assur	1808?–1776 BCE	32
Hammurabi of Babylon	1792–1750 BCE	42
Samsuiluna of Babylon	1749–1712 BCE	37
Ammiditana of Babylon	1683–1647 BCE	36

Regnal years following Van de Mieroop 2007 [2004]

king—might also shift at a particular historical moment or in a given situation. To better appreciate "Head of a Ruler," I therefore suggest that we look at the political world of the early second millennium BCE and explore the possible historical and social settings that may have yielded such a surprising work of art.[63] While the dating of the statue head remains open and it is possible that the artwork belongs to the late third millennium BCE, parallels with the limestone relief described above suggest that "Head of a Ruler" may be best situated in the early second millennium BCE.

In my own examination of "Head of a Ruler," I have begun to wonder whether the realities of the early second millennium BCE altered earlier perspectives on the ideals of kingship in relationship to age. The early second millennium BCE has long been characterized as an age of competing kings in which the suzerainty achieved by the earlier rulers of the Akkadian and Ur III periods was no longer possible. It was also a time that saw a number of long-reigning kings (Table 10.1). Hammurabi may be the most famous king of the early second millennium BCE in our own history books, but he was not the only ruler to

63 See Marc Van de Mieroop, "The Reign of Rim-Sin," *RA* 87 (1993): 47–69, for a similar perspective.

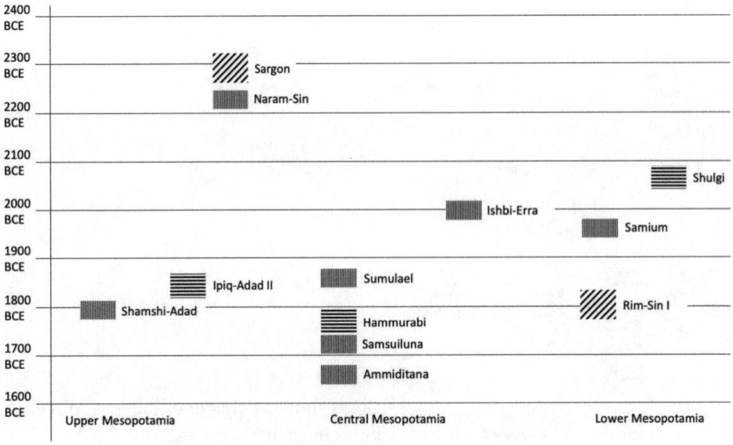

FIGURE 10.8 Chart showing long-reigning kings according to location and period

reach a venerable age.[64] Rim-Sin I reigned from ca. 1822–1763 BCE—a whopping fifty-nine years. Further north, Samsi-Addu is thought to have been an older king when he first came to power in Ekallatum and Assur, and he may have quite old at the time of his death.[65] Tracking the long-reigning kings of the late third and early second millennium BCE, we see a drastic increase in the frequency of old kings around the late nineteenth and eighteenth centuries BCE (Figs. 10.8, 10.9). I propose that the increasing prevalence of older kings (resulting from the coexistence of many kingdoms and many kings) helped shift in attitudes toward aging and kingship, facilitating the creation of a statue that shows an aged ruler.[66] Such a proposal should not be startling, as the portrayal

64 While it is rarely possible to establish the exact age of the rulers of Mesopotamia, we have fairly strong data for the lengths of their reigns. At thirty years of rule, many kings may have begun to go gray, and at fifty or more years, we must assume that the signs of aging could not be hidden entirely. Of course, a ruler who reigned for even ten years may have achieved old age (one thinks of the modern-day Prince Charles of England). Yet, while we cannot be sure that a short regnal period corresponds to an early death, we can be relatively certain that a long regnal period corresponds to a ruler's move away from a youthful physique.

65 According to the Mari Eponym Chronicle, Samsi-Addu was born during the eponym of Dadiya. Nele Ziegler, "Šamšī-Adad I," *RlA* 11 (2006–2008): 632. This would put him around the age of seventy at the time of his death.

66 I do not mean to imply that the early second millennium BCE saw a drastic change in cultural attitudes toward age and kingship that are somehow missing from the majority of our records; rather, I wish to suggest that new political realities opened the door to new experimentations.

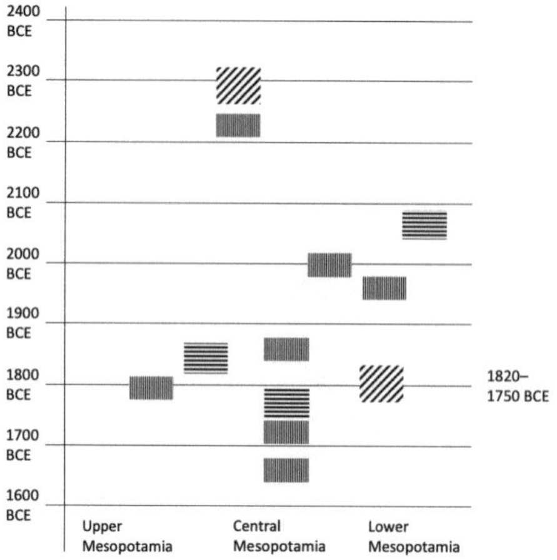

FIGURE 10.9
Chart showing cluster of long-reigning kings in ca. 1820–1750 BCE

of older rulers in Egypt at this time can also be seen as a result of changing political circumstances and ideologies.[67]

I offer a couple of possible scenarios in which the representation of an aged king may have become, thanks to political circumstances, particularly appealing. First, a king of the early second millennium BCE may have been inspired to show himself at an advanced age in order to allude to his superiority in relationship to other contemporary kings.[68] We can guess that the representation of age signified divine blessing, experience, and success, and furthermore marked a status that not all kings achieved.[69] Both Rim-Sin I and Samsi-Addu were long-lived and highly successful kings, and it is tempting to link "Head of a Ruler" with their reigns or legacies. Hammurabi, too, was a long-lived and highly suc-

67 Lisa Saladino Haney, for example, argues that statuary from this period was created to support the practice of co-regency, especially during the long (almost twenty year) co-reign of Senwosret III and Amenemhat III in the nineteenth century BCE. Saladino Haney, *Visualizing Coregency*. Saladino Haney's explanation of Middle Egyptian statuary as a dynamic response to contemporary political realities matches my approach to the Mesopotamian evidence.

68 For claims of superiority that involve an assertion of royal divinity, see Jack Sasson, "King Hammurabi of Babylon," in *Civilizations of the Ancient Near East*, ed. Jack Sasson (New York, NY: Scribners, 1995), 913; Jack Sasson, "Mari Theomorphism: Intimation of Sacrality in the Royal Correspondence," in u_4-du_{11}-ga-ni sá mu-ni-ib-du_{11}: *Ancient Near Eastern Studies in Memory of Blahosla Hruška*, ed. Ludek Vacín (Dresden: Islet, 2011), 195–212; and Van de Mieroop, "The Reign of Rim-Sin," 67, with references.

69 Harris notes that rulers regularly saw long-life as a sign of divine favor. Thus, in certain contexts, the representation of age may signal closeness to the divine world. Harris, *Gender and Aging*, 31 with references.

cessful king. Yet Rim-Sin I and Samsi-Addu were established rulers at the time that Hammurabi came to power and, to a certain extent, Hammurabi would have "grown up" in their shadows. Thus, if "Head of a Ruler" is indeed a depiction of Hammurabi, we might imagine that the acknowledgement of old age and its positive correlations were perhaps inspired or at least made possible by figures like Rim-Sin I and Samsi-Addu.

Second, I wonder whether the existence of periods of co-rule in Mesopotamia at this time encouraged the use of age as a visual marker to distinguish the senior ruler, as it did in Egypt.[70] Rim-Sin I shared power with a brother prior to becoming king, Samsi-Addu set up his two sons as local rulers beneath him, and Hammurabi's son Samsi-iluna began to take over responsibilities of ruler prior to his father's death.[71] Several artworks of the early second millennium BCE are thought to show father and son, but these works are unfortunately piecemeal and it is not always clear how the faces of the two figures are distinguished.[72] If the Mari wall painting from Sanctuary 132 discussed above shows a ruler and his heir, then there is some evidence for the use of hair color (and thus age) to distinguish a senior king. Traditions of power-sharing and power transfer may

70 The possible use of age to distinguish two rulers acting together draws us back to Porada's initial observation of the parallels between "Head of a Ruler" and the statuary of Senwosret III. In this case, however, the shared representation of age across Egypt and Mesopotamia would not come about as a result of transmission of artistic forms or a rise in naturalistic inclinations; instead, it would be the result of similar changes in political circumstances. It would be possible to imagine some level of cross-cultural communication between Egypt and Mesopotamia that drew the two traditions more closely together—but not necessary.

71 On Rim-Sin, see Van de Mieroop, "The Reign of Rim-Sin," 50–51; on Samsi-Addu see Pierre Villard, "Shamshi-Adad and Sons: The Rise and Fall of an Upper Mesopotamian Empire," in *Civilizations of the Ancient Near East*, ed. Jack Sasson (New York, NY: Scribners, 1995), 874–875; on Hammurabi, see Sasson, "King Hammurabi of Babylon," 911; Marc Van de Mieroop, *King Hammurabi* (Malden, MA/Oxford: Blackwell, 2005), 121; Dominique Charpin, *Hammu-rabi de Babylone* (Paris: Presses Universitaires de France, 2003), 104. For further discussion of this phenomenon, see Dominique Charpin, "Histoire politique du proche-orient amorrite (2002–1595)," in *Mesopotamien: Die altbabylonische Zeit*, ed. Dominique Charpin, Dietz Otto Edzard, and Marten Stol (Fribourg: Academic Press; Göttingen: Vandenhoeck & Ruprecht, 2004), 257.

72 The wall painting found in Room 132, discussed below, is sometimes interpreted as a portrayal of a ruler and son. Jean-Claude Margueron, *Mari, métropole de l'Euphrate* (Paris: Picard, 2004), 409. On the Dadusha Stele, see Eppihimer, *Exemplars of Kingship*, 80. Similarly, several scholars have suggested that works in the Old Babylonian period could have been created posthumously by a son for a father, including the monument of Dadusha and the statue of Puzur-Ishtar. See Eppihimer, *Exemplars of Kingship*, 80 and 119–120 with references. Although these examples do not show two rulers together, they may be part of the representation practices that responded to transfers of power within a dynasty.

offer one enticing and plausible backstory for the creation of "Head of a Ruler," and would benefit from further research.

5 Conclusions

Study of "Head of a Ruler" is made challenging by multiple factors: the interpretation of certain facial features as a depiction of age; the absence of any clear definitive expression of the qualities (positive or negative) of longevity in a king; and our own modern biases regarding age and artistic intent. The loss of archaeological context and the body of the statue (its pose, dress, and inscription) further limit the strength of any interpretive proposal. For these reasons, "Head of a Ruler" will continue to defy interpretation and may stand as an unusual royal representation for decades to come. Inquiries into the significance of the statue head, however, help shift our focus from the sensationalism of a naturalistic portrait of a famous king to the historical realities that underline the creation of an exceptional artwork.

Specifically, I find that the stylistic examination of "Head of a Ruler" does not preclude the identification of the statue head with Hammurabi—though nor does it guarantee its association with Babylon's famous ruler. I argue that, regardless of the statue head's attribution, we should understand the artwork as a response to and participant in contemporary ideas of kingship. Focus on the naturalism of the statue head does not critically contend with Mesopotamian notions of portraiture and does little to situate the work of art in time and space. The very existence of this unusual statue would seem to suggest that there were select contexts in which the old age of a ruler may have been appropriately highlighted. Perhaps age became a marker of success and divine favor among kings—a visual cue that a ruler could call upon toward the end of his reign. Or perhaps age helped distinguish the senior member of royal family, particularly during periods of co-rule and transition. By expanding the directions of our inquiries, we can begin to appreciate "Head of a Ruler" not as a stand-alone art object, but as part of a larger cultural whole that may be richer than we have so far imagined.

Appendix: Comparing "Head of a Ruler"

Stylistic analyses of "Head of a Ruler" have often focused on select features and qualities of the statue head—including the figure's headdress, the rendering of the hair and the style of the beard, and the naturalism of the face—to date and describe the otherwise enigmatic work of art. To test these analyses, the appendix compares "Head of a Ruler" with select representations of kings from the late third and early second millennium BCE, considering both conventional and unconventional features of the head.[73] Table 10.2 uses conventional features of "Head of a Ruler" as the basis for comparison with other artworks; Table 10.3 uses unconventional features. What emerges from these comparisons is a sense of which artworks may offer the best parallels for "Head of a Ruler."[74]

List of Artworks

Statues

Assur Statue

Statue of Male Figure from Assur. Dated to Akkadian period (ca. 2334–2154 BCE) or later. Iraq Museum (head) and Vorderasiatisches Museum (body). IM 89000 and VA 2147.

Tello Head

Head of a Bearded Male from Tello. Dated to early Akkadian period (ca. 2340–2200 BCE). Musée du Louvre. AO 14.

Bismaya Head

Head of a Bearded Man from Bismaya. Dated to Ur III period (ca. 2112–2004 BCE). Oriental Institute. OI A173.

Ishtup-Ilum

Statue of Ishtup-Ilum. Dated to ca. 2125 BCE. Aleppo National Museum. M 800.[75]

---

73 Because of the travel restrictions of the global pandemic, my analysis has been based on photographs of the artworks and should be considered provisional. Fuller analysis requires in-person investigation of the selected objects and could additionally consider glyptic arts, terra cottas, and more from the late third and early second millennium BCE. While comparison of the features of "Head of a Ruler" with contemporary royal representations offers a useful measure of earlier analyses, future study of the dating of the statue head could also consider what features it lacks. My thanks to Melissa Eppihimer for this observation.

74 Interestingly, the Met Head, previously cited as a similarly naturalistic work of art, does not share any of the unconventional (i.e., naturalistic) features of "Head of a Ruler." The two-dimensional limestone relief, however, emerges as a possible parallel worthy of further analysis.

75 Dates for Mari Shakkanakku rulers follow Margueron, *Mari, métropole de l'Euphrate*, 328.

Ur-Ningirsu

Statue of Ur-Ningirsu. Dated to reign of Ur-Ningirsu (ca. 2080 BCE). Vorderasiatisches Museum. VA 8970.

Puzur-Ishtar

Statue of Puzur-Ishtar. Dated to ca. 2030 BCE. Vorderasiatisches Museum (head) and Eski Şark Eserleri Müzesi (body). VA 8748 and EŞ 7814.[76]

Head of a Ruler

Head of a Ruler. Dated to 20th–18th centuries BCE. Musée du Louvre. Sb 95.

Metal Sculptures

Iraq Head

Copper Alloy Head of a Ruler, often identified as Sargon or Naram-Sin. Dated to Akkadian Period (ca. 2334–2154 BCE). Iraq Museum. IM 11331.

Met Head

Copper Alloy Head of a Ruler. Dated to ca. 2300–2000 BCE. Metropolitan Museum of Art. MMA 47.100.80.

Reliefs

Ur-Namma Stele

Fragment of Ur-Namma Stele. Dated to reign of Ur-Namma (ca. 2112–2095). Penn Museum. CBS 16676.14.

Darband-i Gawr

Rock Relief at Darband-i Gawr. Tentatively dated to Ur III period (ca. 2112–2004 BCE). Located south of Sulaimaniyah, Iraq.[77]

---

76 Margueron, *Mari, métropole de l'Euphrate*, 328.

77 For images and discussions of these rock reliefs, see Eppihimer, *Exemplars of Kingship*, 57–65 (black and white photographs); J. Nicholas Postgate and Michael Roaf, "The Shaikan Relief," *Al-Rafidan* 18 (1997): 151 (drawings); and Robert Rollinger, "The Relief at Bisitun and Its Ancient Near Eastern Setting: Contextualizing the Visual Vocabulary of Darius' Triumph Over Gaumata," in *Diwan: Studies in the History and Culture of the Ancient Near East and the Eastern Mediterranean. Festschrift für Josef Wisehöfer zum 65. Geburtstag*, ed. C. Binder et al. (Duisberg: Wellem, 2016), 5–51. For location, see map in Postgate and Roaf, "The Shaikan Relief," 144.

Annubanini

Rock Relief of Annubanini at Sarpol-i Zohab. Dated to ca. 2000 BCE. Located south of the Darband-i Gawr Rock Relief near the Iran-Iraq border, Iran.[78]

Limestone Relief

Limestone Relief from Sippar sometimes thought to depict Hammurabi. Tentatively dated to reign of Hammurabi (ca. 1792–1750 BCE). British Museum. BM 22454.

Laws of Hammurabi Stele

Laws of Hammurabi Stele. Dated to reign of Hammurabi (ca. 1792–1750 BCE) with possible later reworking. Musée du Louvre. Sb 8.

Conventional Features of "Head of a Ruler" (Table 1)

1. Brim of the cap is thick and protrudes over the forehead
2. Ears rest partially underneath the cap
3. Hair appears on the forehead underneath the cap in carefully combed waves
4. Hair appears on the nape of the neck beneath the cap in curling locks
5. Line of the beard is cut diagonally across the side of the face in a wavy S-shaped curve that follows the cheek
6. Beard is separated from the face by a thin line
7. Line separating the beard and face has vertical hatching
8. Bipartite beard is shown in a grid-like fashion on the face and as vertical tendrils on the chest
9. Thin spiral curves are used to represent facial beard
10. Twists of the chest beard are shown through diagonal lines
11. Moustache surrounds the mouth on top and sides of the lips
12. Mouth is narrow
13. Mouth has the impression of curving downward
14. Hair beneath the mouth is distinguished from the beard as an arc with a series of vertical lines

Unconventional Features of "Head of a Ruler" (Table 2)

1. Vertical crease in forehead
2. Lower eyelids sag
3. Puffy eyelids thicken at the outer corners of the eyes
4. Undereye fold
5. Sunken cheeks

78 See references in n. 77.

TABLE 10.2 Comparison of conventional features

Relief or statue	1	2	3	4	5	6	7	8	9	10	11	12	13	14
Assur Statue	N	N	Y	?	N	N	N	Y	N	?	?	Y	?	?
Tello Head[79]	n/a	n/a	n/a	?	Y	Y	?	Y	Y	Y	?	N	N	N
Bismaya Head	N	N	N	?	Y	N	N	N	N	N	Y	Y	Y	?
Ishtup-Ilum	N	N	N	?	N	N	N	N	N	N	Y	N	Y	N
Ur-Ningirsu	Y	Y	?	?	Y	N	N	N	Y	Y	n/a	Y	n/a	n/a
Puzur-Ishtar[80]	N	N	N	?	N	Y	N	Y	N	Y	N	Y	?	?
Head of a Ruler	Y	Y	Y	Y	Y	Y	Y	Y	Y	Y	Y	Y	Y	Y
Iraq Head[81]	N	N	Y	Y	Y	N	N	Y	N	Y	N	N	N	N
Met Head[82]	N	N	Y	?	Y	Y	Y	Y	N	N	Y	N	Y	Y
Ur-Namma Stele	N	Y	?	?	N	?	?	Y	N	Y	?	Y	?	?
Darband-i Gawr	Y	Y	N	Y	N	?	?	Y	Y	N	?	N	N	?
Annubanini	Y	Y	Y	?	N	N	N	Y	Y	N	?	Y	Y	?
Limestone Relief	Y	Y	?	?	Y	Y	?	Y	Y	N	?	Y	Y	?
Laws of Hammurabi Stele	Y	Y	?	?	N	N	N	N	N	N	?	Y	Y	?

?—requires first-hand visual analysis
n/a—too broken to determine

79 The facial hair is much more deeply carved than that of "Head of a Ruler" and the hair below the mouth, while defined by vertical lines, is triangular in shape.

80 Small spiral curls appear along the extreme sides of his forehead, leading toward the ear. The curls of the facial beard are thick and flat, not unlike those on the Assur head. The diagonal lines on the chest beard are much finer than the other examples.

81 The headdress and hairstyle of the male are entirely different from that of "Head of a Ruler" though they share some similarities in the articulation of the hair. The curve of the beard is less dramatic, and the hair below the lip is triangular in shape.

82 Faint traces of wavy hair are visible above the bridge of the nose. The beard is separate

TABLE 10.3 Comparison of unconventional features

Relief or statue	1	2	3	4	5
Assur Statue	?	Y	?	?	N
Tello Head	n/a	N	n/a	N	N
Bismaya Head	N	N	Y	N	N
Ishtup-Ilum	N	Y	N	Y	N
Ur-Ningirsu	N	Y	Y	N	N
Puzur-Ishtar	N	Y	N	Y	N
Head of a Ruler	Y	Y	Y	Y	Y
Iraq Head[a]	Y	N	N	N	N
Met Head[b]	?	N	N	N	N
Ur-Namma Stele	n/a	Y	n/a	N	N
Darband-i Gawr	n/a	N	n/a	N	N
Annubanini	n/a	N	n/a	N	N
Limestone Relief	n/a	Y	n/a	?	?
Laws of Hammurabi Stele	n/a	Y	n/a	?	N

a Two horizontal waves above the bridge of the nose are visible.
b There may be lines across the bridge of the nose.
?—requires first-hand visual analysis
n/a—too broken to determine

Bibliography

André-Salvini, Béatrice. *Le code de Hammurabi.* Paris: Réunion des musées nationaux, 2003.

André-Salvini, Béatrice. "Babylon." Pages 18–20 in *Beyond Babylon: Art, Trade, and Diplomacy in the Second Millennium B.C.* Edited by Joan Aruz, Kim Benzel, and Jean M. Evans. New York, NY: Metropolitan Museum of Art; New Haven, CT/London: Yale University Press.

Bahrani, Zainab. *Mesopotamia: Ancient Art and Architecture.* London: Thames & Hudson, 2017.

Bonatz, Dominik, and Marlies Heinz. "Representation." Pages 233–260 in *A Companion*

from the face by two thin lines with vertical hatching. The curls of the face beard are defined by diagonal lines and terminate in spirals, while the chest beard is depicted with wavy lines. Different from the "Head of a Ruler," the hair beneath the mouth extends to the corner of the lips and meets the moustache.

to Ancient Near Eastern Art. Edited by Ann C. Gunter. Hoboken, NJ: Wiley Blackwell, 2019.

Brisch, Nicole, ed. *Religion and Power: Divine Kingship in the Ancient World and Beyond*. OIS 4. Chicago, IL: The Oriental Institute of the University of Chicago, 2008.

Brisch, Nicole. "Of Gods and Kings: Divine Kingship in Ancient Mesopotamia." *RC* 7/2 (2013): 37–46.

Charpin, Dominique. *Hammu-rabi de Babylone*. Paris: Presses Universitaires de France, 2003.

Charpin, Dominique. "Histoire politique du proche-orient amorrite (2002–1595)." Pages 25–480 in *Mesopotamien: Die altbabylonische Zeit*. Edited by Dominique Charpin, Dietz Otto Edzard, and Marten Stol. Fribourg: Academic Press; Göttingen: Vandenhoeck & Ruprecht, 2004.

Eppihimer, Melissa. *Exemplars of Kingship: Art, Tradition, and the Legacy of the Akkadians*. New York, NY: Oxford University Press, 2019.

Frankfort, Henri. *The Art and Architecture of the Ancient Orient*. 5th ed. New Haven, CT/London: Yale University Press, 1954 [1996].

Frayne, Douglas. *The Old Babylonian Period (2003–1595 B.C.)*. RIME 4. Toronto: University of Toronto Press, 1990.

Gates, Marie-Henriette. "The Palace of Zimri-Lim at Mari." *BA* 47/2 (1984): 70–87.

George, Andrew R. *The Babylonian Gilgamesh Epic: Introduction, Critical Edition and Cuneiform Text*. Vol. 1. New York, NY/Oxford: Oxford University Press, 2003.

Harper, Prudence O. "Head of a Ruler." Pages 175–176 in *The Royal City of Susa: Ancient Near Eastern Treasures in the Louvre*. Edited by Prudence O. Harper, Joan Aruz, and Françoise Tallon. New York, NY: Metropolitan Museum of Art, 1992.

Harper, Prudence O. "Mesopotamian Monuments Found at Susa." Pages 159–162 in *The Royal City of Susa: Ancient Near Eastern Treasures in the Louvre*. Edited by Prudence O. Harper, Joan Aruz, and Françoise Tallon. New York, NY: Metropolitan Museum of Art, 1992.

Harris, Rivkah. *Gender and Aging in Mesopotamia: The Gilgamesh Epic and Other Ancient Literature*. Norman, OK: University of Oklahoma Press, 2000.

Leslie, Karen. "Examination and Tentative Identification of Some Black Stone Objects." *ZA* 92 (2002): 296–300.

Margueron, Jean-Claude. *Mari, métropole de l'Euphrate*. Paris: Picard, 2004.

Melville, Sarah C. "The Autobiography of Adad-Guppi." Pages 389–393 in *The Ancient Near East: Historical Sources in Translation*. Edited by M. Chavalas. Malden, MA/Oxford: Blackwell, 2006.

Michalowski, Piotr. "The Mortal Kings of Ur: A Short Century of Divine Rule in Ancient Mesopotamia." Pages 33–46 in *Religion and Power: Divine Kingship in the Ancient World and Beyond*. Edited by Nicole M. Brisch. Chicago, IL: The Oriental Institute of the University of Chicago, 2008.

Moortgat, Anton. *The Art of Ancient Mesopotamia: The Classical Art of the Near East.* New York, NY/London: Phaidon, 1969.

Muller, Béatrice. "Contextes techniques et historiques des peintures murales du Grand Palais Royal de Mari: Une mise au point." Pages 41–84 in *Tracing Technoscapes: The Production of Bronze Age Wall Paintings in the Eastern Mediterranean.* Edited by Johannes Jungfleisch and Constance von Rüden. Leiden: Sidestone Press, 2018.

Muscarella, Oscar. *Bronze and Iron: Ancient Near Eastern Artifacts in the Metropolitan Museum of Art.* New York, NY: The Metropolitan Museum of Art, 1988.

Ornan, Tallay. "A Silent Message: Godlike Kings in Mesopotamian Art." Pages 569–595 in *Critical Approaches to Ancient Near Eastern Art.* Edited by Brian A. Brown and Marian H. Feldman. Berlin: de Gruyter, 2013.

Ornan, Tallay. "Unfinished Business: The Relief on the Hammurabi Louvre Stele Revisited." *JCS* 71 (2019): 85–109.

Parrot, André. "Les Peintures du Palais de Mari." *Syria* 18/4 (1937): 325–354.

Parrot, André. *Le Palais: Peintures murals.* Mission archéologique de Mari. Vol. 2. Paris: Librarie orientaliste Paul Geuthner, 1958.

Parrot, André. *Sumer: The Dawn of Art.* Translated by Stuart Gilbert and James Emmons. New York, NY: Golden Press, 1961.

Porada, Edith. "Review of Henri Frankfort, *The Birth of Civilization in the Near East* and *The Art and Architecture of the Ancient Orient.*" *Art Bulletin* 38 (1956): 121–124.

Postgate, J. Nicholas, and Michael Roaf. "The Shaikan Relief." *Al-Rafidan* 18 (1997): 143–156.

Reade, Julian. "Early Monuments in Gulf Stone at the British Museum, with Observations on Some Gudea Statues and the Location of Agade." *ZA* 92 (2002): 258–295.

Rollinger, Robert. "The Relief at Bisitun and Its Ancient Near Eastern Setting: Contextualizing the Visual Vocabulary of Darius' Triumph Over Gaumata." Pages 5–51 in *Diwan: Studies in the History and Culture of the Ancient Near East and the Eastern Mediterranean. Festschrift für Josef Wisehöfer zum 65. Geburtstag.* Edited by Carsten Binder, Henning Börm, Andreas Luther, and Josef Wiesehöfer. Duisberg: Wellem, 2016.

Saladino Haney, Lisa. *Visualizing Coregency: An Exploration of the Link between Royal Image and Co-Rule during the Reign of Senwosret III and Amenemhet III.* Boston, MA/Leiden: Brill, 2020.

Sasson, Jack. "King Hammurabi of Babylon." Pages 901–915 in *Civilizations of the Ancient Near East.* Edited by Jack Sasson. New York, NY: Scribners, 1995.

Sasson, Jack. "Mari Theomorphism: Intimation of Sacrality in the Royal Correspondence." Pages 195–212 in u$_4$-du$_{11}$-ga-ni sá mu-ni-ib-du$_{11}$: *Ancient Near Eastern Studies in Memory of Blahosla Hruška.* Edited by Ludek Vacín. Dresden: Islet, 2011.

Schlossman, Betty L. "Portraiture in Mesopotamia in the Late Third and Early Second Millennium B.C., Part I: The Late Third Millennium." *AfO* 26 (1978/1979): 56–77.

Schlossman, Betty L. "Portraiture in Mesopotamia in the Late Third and Early Second Millennium B.C., Part II: The Early Second Millennium." *AfO* 28 (1981/1982): 143–170.

Spycket, Agnès. *La statuaire du Proche-Orient ancien*. Leiden and Köln: E.J. Brill, 1981.

Suter, Claudia E. "The Royal Body and Masculinity in Early Mesopotamia." Pages 433–458 in *Menschenbilder und Körperkonzepte im Alten Israel, in Ägypten und im Alten Orient*. Edited by Angelika Berlejung, Jan Dietrich, and Joachim F. Quack. Tübingen: Mohr Siebeck, 2012.

Suter, Claudia E. "Kings and Queens: Representation and Reality." Pages 201–226 in *The Sumerian World*. Edited by Harriet Crawford. Hoboken, NJ: Taylor & Francis, 2013.

Suter, Claudia E. "Statuary and Reliefs." Pages 385–410 in *A Companion to Ancient Near Eastern Art*. Edited by Ann C. Gunter. Hoboken, NJ: Wiley Blackwell, 2019.

Thomas, Ariane. *La Mésopotamie au Louvre: de Sumer à Babylone*. Paris: Louvre éditions and Somogy éditions d'art, 2016.

Van de Mieroop, Marc. "The Reign of Rim-Sin." *RA* 87 (1993): 47–69.

Van de Mieroop, Marc. *King Hammurabi*. Malden, MA/Oxford: Blackwell, 2005.

Van de Mieroop, Marc. *A History of the Ancient Near East ca. 3000–323 BC*. 2nd ed. Malden, MA: Blackwell, 2007.

Van de Mieroop, Marc. "Hammurabi's Self-presentation." *Or* 80/4 (2011): 305–338.

Villard, Pierre. "Shamshi-Adad and Sons: The Rise and Fall of an Upper Mesopotamian Empire." Pages 873–883 in *Civilizations of the Ancient Near East*. Edited by Jack Sasson. New York, NY: Scribners, 1995.

Westenholz, Joan Goodnick, and Ilona Zsolnay. "Categorizing Men and Masculinity in Sumer." Pages 12–41 in *Being a Man: Negotiating Ancient Constructs of Masculinity*. Edited by Ilona Zsolnay. Milton: Taylor & Francis, 2016.

Winter, Irene J. "Royal Rhetoric and the Development of Historical Narrative in Neo-Assyrian Reliefs." *Visual Communication* 7 (1981): 2–38.

Winter, Irene J. "Review of A. Spycket, *La statuaire du proche-orient*." *JCS* 36/1 (1984): 102–114.

Winter, Irene J. "The Body of the Able Ruler: Toward an Understanding of the Statues of Gudea." Pages 573–583 in *Dumu-É-dub-ba-a: Studies in Honor of Åke W. Sjöberg*. Edited by Hermann Behrens Darlene Loding, and Martha T. Roth. Philadelphia, PA: The University Museum, 1989.

Winter, Irene J. "Sex, Rhetoric, and the Public Monument: The Alluring Body of Naram-Sîn of Agade." Pages 11–26 in *Sexuality in Ancient Art: Near East, Greece, and Italy*. Edited by Natalie B. Kampen and Bettina Bergmann. New York, NY/Cambridge: Cambridge University Press, 1996.

Winter, Irene J. "Art in Empire: The Royal Image and the Visual Dimensions of Assyrian Ideology." Pages 359–381 in *Assyria 1995: Proceedings of the 10th Anniversary Symposium of the Neo-Assyrian Text Corpus Project, Helsinki, September 7–11, 1995*. Edited by Simo Parpola and Robert M. Whiting. Helsinki: Neo-Assyrian Text Corpus Project, 1997.

Winter, Irene J. "The Affective Properties of Styles: An Inquiry into Analytical Process and the Inscription of Meaning in Art History." Pages 55–77 in *Picturing Science, Producing Art*. Edited by Peter Galison and Caroline A. Jones. Hoboken, NJ: Taylor & Francis, 1998.
Winter, Irene J. "Touched by the Gods: Visual Evidence for the Divine Status of Rulers in the Ancient Near East." Pages 75–101 in *Religion and Power: Divine Kingship in the Ancient World and Beyond*. Edited by Nicole Brisch. Chicago, IL: The Oriental Institute of the University of Chicago, 2008.
Winter, Irene J. "What/When Is a Portrait? Royal Images of the Ancient Near East." *Proceedings of the American Philosophical Society* 153/3 (2009): 254–270.
Ziegler, Nele. "Šamšī-Adad I." *RlA* 11 (2006–2008): 632–635.

11

La conclusion des alliances diplomatiques au temps des rois de Mari: un dossier qui reste ouvert

Bertrand Lafont

Grâce à leur heureuse initiative, les éditeurs du présent ouvrage m'offrent l'occasion, et je les en remercie, de célébrer une amitié de près de trente ans: Dan et moi avons fait connaissance en avril 1993, à Chapel Hill, lors du meeting de l'AOS accueilli cette année-là par Jack Sasson.* Au fil des ans et de sa production scientifique, j'ai toujours beaucoup admiré, encore plus que les passerelles qu'il n'a cessé de jeter entre études bibliques et assyriologiques, la démarche profondément "historienne" qu'il privilégie en permanence et dont je me sens proche.

Alors même qu'il terminait son livre sur les institutions de Mari[1], je venais pour ma part d'achever et de publier un article de synthèse sur "les relations internationales à l'époque amorrite."[2] Comment oublier alors les longues discussions que nous avons eues sur ces sujets, soit dans sa maison du Connecticut qui fait face à Long Island, soit dans les environs de Paris où je réside? En témoignage de ma fidèle amitié et en hommage à ses travaux, je propose de revenir précisément ici à ce thème des "relations internationales."

Comme on le sait, les recherches de ces trente dernières années ont fourni quantité d'informations nouvelles sur la conclusion des alliances à l'époque amorrite, dans le premier tiers du IIe millénaire avant notre ère. Un ouvrage récent[3] a proposé de faire le point sur cette question, montrant que le serment

---

* Cet article a été préparé indépendamment de celui que propose ici-même D. Charpin, dont j'ai découvert après coup qu'il traitait des mêmes problématiques mais avec une approche et des conclusions très différentes.

1 Daniel Fleming, *Democracy's Ancient Ancestors: Mari and Early Collective Governance* (Cambridge: Cambridge University Press), 2004.

2 Bertrand Lafont, "Relations internationales, alliances et diplomatie au temps des royaumes amorrites: Essai de synthèse," in *Mari, Ebla et les Hourrites, dix ans de travaux*, ed. J.-M. Durand and D. Charpin, Amurru 2 (Paris: Éditions Recherche sur les Civilisations, 2001), 213-328.

3 Dominique Charpin, *"Tu es de mon sang": Les alliances dans le Proche-Orient ancien* (Paris: Collège de France – Les Belles Lettres, 2019), livre qui reprend en partie et vient en complément de son article "Chroniques bibliographiques 18: Les débuts des relations diplomatiques au Proche-Orient ancien," *RA* 110 (2016) : 127-186, et spécialement 180-186, § 4.6 "La conclusion des traités." Voir aussi Charpin, "Les alliances au Proche-Orient ancien, entre diplomatie et religion," *Annuaire du Collège de France* 116 (2018) : 229-242.

 | DOI:10.1163/9789004511538_012

prêté sous couvert et en présence des divinités (*nīš ilī*) était au cœur même des procédures de conclusion de ces alliances, mais qu'il pouvait être accompagné de plusieurs rituels différents. C'est à partir des années 1988-1990, à travers la publication de nouvelles pièces de correspondance et de plusieurs textes de "traité" des archives de Mari, qu'ont commencé à être précisément décrites et mises en ordre les procédures utilisées pour s'allier[4]. Mais il y a eu du neuf depuis lors. Notamment avec la publication en 2011 des textes provenant de Tell Leilan, qu'a fait connaître Jesper Eidem[5] et qui permettent sans doute de pousser les réflexions encore un peu plus loin. Le dossier est complexe et foisonnant et je m'en tiendrai ici à trois éléments.

1 Se toucher la gorge (*napištam lapātum*) ou sacrifier un ânon (*ḫayāram qaṭālum*)

Deux rituels d'alliance, on le sait, sont désormais bien documentés et ont été clairement décrits: celui dit du "toucher de gorge" (*lipit napištim*) d'un côté et celui où il s'agit de sacrifier un ou plusieurs ânon(s) (*ḫayāram qaṭālum*) de l'autre. Selon Dominique Charpin, le premier protocole était utilisé pour les alliances conclues *à distance* par deux rois qui ne se rencontrent pas et le second pour les alliances conclues par deux rois *en réunion*, les deux manières étant exclusives l'une de l'autre.

Une lettre de Tell Leilan (PIHANS 117 54)[6] ne manque cependant pas d'intriguer à ce propos. Elle évoque une rencontre qui était prévue entre les rois d'Alep et d'Apum. Le second ayant annulé au dernier moment son déplacement jusqu'à Alep, on lui suggère l'envoi d'un émissaire:

> [6] Puisque toi tu n'iras pas à Alep et que tu n'auras pas d'entrevue avec le roi, que l'un de tes serviteurs de confiance prenne la tête de la troupe de tes soldats-*piḫrum* et qu'il vienne avec moi à Alep. Et à Alep que le roi "se

4 Voir notamment, Dominique Charpin, *Archives Épistolaires de Mari I/2*, ARM 26/2 (Paris: Éditions Recherche sur les Civilisations, 1988), 139-205, spécialement chapitre 3. À compléter par Charpin, "Une alliance contre l'Elam et le rituel du *lipit napištim*," in *Contribution à l'histoire de l'Iran: Mélanges offerts à Jean Perrot*, ed. F. Vallat (Paris: Éditions Recherche sur les Civilisations, 1990), 109-118.

5 Jesper Eidem, *The Royal Archives from Tell Leilan: Old Babylonian Letters and Treaties from the Lower Town Palace East*, PIHANS 117 (Leiden: Brill, 2011).

6 Cf. Eidem, *Royal Archives*, 122-123 et 327 D, et Charpin, *Chroniques bibliographiques*, 181-182, repris dans *"Tu es de mon sang,"* 72-73.

touche la gorge" pour toi. Que ton serviteur le voie et qu'il te rapporte que le roi "s'est touché la gorge" pour toi (afin) que ton cœur soit rassuré[7].

À lire et comprendre au plus simple cette lettre, il est donc conseillé au roi d'Apum d'envoyer l'un de ses serviteurs à Alep à l'occasion de la cérémonie du "toucher de gorge" (*lipit napištim*) à laquelle il aurait dû participer en personne, avant sa soudaine renonciation. Cet émissaire pourra alors témoigner que le rituel d'alliance a été correctement accompli par le roi d'Alep et il pourra revenir pour rassurer son maître.

Sans que cela soit une certitude, il semble bien que la cérémonie entre les souverains d'Alep et d'Apum, avec le rituel du "toucher de gorge," aurait donc dû se dérouler *en présence* des deux acteurs, avant que l'un d'eux ne fasse défaut. Les nombreux autres exemples disponibles qui évoquent ce rite[8] insistent tous, quoi qu'il en soit, sur l'engagement de *deux* partenaires l'un envers l'autre, même s'il est clair que ces textes documentent le plus souvent une procédure qui était en effet réalisée à distance, comme ce fut finalement le cas ici. Cela ne doit cependant pas étonner: c'est précisément lorsque l'un des protagonistes ne pouvait être physiquement présent à la cérémonie qu'il était nécessaire d'écrire des lettres rapportant l'événement. Lorsque la rencontre entre deux rois était effective et que le rituel était accompli en présence l'un de l'autre et devant témoins, l'utilité d'un rapport était évidemment bien moindre.

Mentionnons aussi la lettre PIHANS 117 75 qui semble montrer que les rois Till-Abnu d'Apum et Yamṣi-Hatnu de Kahat se sont personnellement rencontrés lorsqu'ils ont entériné l'accord passé entre eux[9]. Une lettre comme ARM 28 40 pour sa part, qui concerne une alliance conclue entre Zimri-Lim de Mari et Yawi-Ila de Talhayum, montre bien la concomitance du *lipit napištim* et du serment solennel *nīš ilī*[10]. Si les deux rois ne pouvaient pas se rencontrer, la cérémonie se déroulait une fois chez l'un, une fois chez l'autre, de façon symétrique. Elle associait quoi qu'il en soit une gestuelle ritualisée (toucher de

7 *iš-tu a-na* [^{ur}]^{u}*ḫa-la-a*[*b*^{ki}] *at-ta la ta-al-la-k*[*a-am-ma*] *it-ti* LUGAL *la ta-an-na-am-ma-ru* 1 IR$_3$-*ka ta-ak-la-am pa-an* ERIN$_2$.MEŠ *pí-iḫ-ri-ka li-iṣ-ba-tam-ma it-ti-ia a-na* ^{uru}*ḫa-la-ab*^{ki} *li-il-li-ik ù i-na* ^{uru}*ḫ*[*a-l*]*a-ab*^{ki} *aš-šu-mì-ka* LUGA[L *n*]*a-pí-iš*$_7$*-t*[*a-šu l*]*i-il-p*[*u-ut*] *ù* IR$_3$-*ka li-mu-u*[*r-šu-ma š*]*a aš-šu-mì-ka* LU[GAL *na-pí-iš*$_7$*-ta-šu*] *il-pu-tu li-te-er-ra-ak-kum-ma li-ib-ba-ka li-nu-uḫ*.

8 Cf. Lafont, *Relations internationales*, 271-274, liste B.

9 C'est ce que propose Eidem, *Royal Archives*, 326, en lien avec le traité LT3 et un texte administratif, *contra* Charpin, *Chroniques bibliographiques*, 181.

10 L. 15′: "Je prononcerai le serment par les dieux pour mon seigneur et (il faudra) alors que mon seigneur pareillement 'touche sa gorge' pour moi son serviteur."

gorge) et un engagement verbal (serment) au cours d'une même cérémonie qui scellait l'alliance entre les deux partenaires. Cela est manifeste également dans ce que rapporte l'importante lettre ARM 26/2 372[11] concernant l'alliance entre les rois de Babylone et d'Eshnunna, dans laquelle sont associés trois éléments fondamentaux pour le bon déroulement de la procédure: le geste (*lipit napištim*), la parole (*nīš ilī*) et l'écrit (*ṭuppum*, voir ci-après).

Quant à la signification de l'action consistant à se "toucher la gorge," une abondante exégèse existe à son sujet[12]. Elle a souvent été interprétée comme une mimique d'auto-malédiction en cas de rupture du pacte: le jureur aurait signifié par ce geste qu'il engageait sa propre vie[13] dans la conclusion de l'accord et dans son respect. Cependant, comme on le verra, des explications alternatives sont sans doute à envisager.

Un autre point mérite de retenir l'attention: l'idée que la rencontre physique de deux rois décidés à s'allier pouvait être d'usage courant dans le monde amorrite est renforcée par ce que montre l'iconographie contemporaine qui met en scène les gestes dont on peut supposer qu'ils sont ceux qui étaient accomplis à cette occasion. Cela a déjà été remarqué[14]: dans la glyptique ou la statuaire de cette époque (fig. 11.1 et 11.2)[15], on dispose de plusieurs pièces représentant deux partenaires face à face, s'affichant dans une scénographie généralement interprétée comme une "embrassade." Cependant, est-il vraiment certain que l'on ait affaire ici à un tel geste d'étreinte? Car c'est bien leurs *gorges* respectives que semblent *toucher* les protagonistes dans ces scènes figurées: cela pourrait-il être mis en relation avec ce que nous disent les textes? Nous aurons à revenir plus loin sur cette question.

En définitive, il est particulièrement intéressant de voir que le rituel du *lipit napištim* est désormais bien attesté, non seulement dans la documentation de

---

11 Commentée par Charpin, *"Tu es de mon sang,"* 97-99.

12 Depuis l'article de Joan Margaret Munn-Rankin, "Diplomacy in Western Asia in the Early Second Millennium B.C.," *Iraq* 18 (1956): 89-90. Voir aussi Lafont, *Relations internationales*, 275, ainsi que Charpin, *"Tu es de mon sang,"* 72, et "Les alliances au Proche-Orient ancien," 232: "le geste signifie que l'on met sa vie en jeu en cas de parjure."

13 Puisqu'il s'agit là du sens premier de *napištum*: "vie, souffle de vie," et par extension "gorge" (voir *CAD* N/2 296).

14 Je me permets de renvoyer à mon article *Relations internationales*, 283 n. 269, et 313 n. 415.

15 Dominique Beyer, "Deux nouveaux sceaux de style syrien provenant de Mari," *MARI* 8 (1997): 463-475, spécialement 465, fig. 3. L'une des empreintes de sceau ayant retenu l'attention de Beyer est reproduite par Charpin dans *"Tu es de mon sang,"* 59. Pour la scène représentée sur le "bassin rituel" du temple de Shamash à Ebla, contemporaine elle aussi de nos textes et de ces sceaux, voir Paolo Matthiae, *Ebla: Archaeology and History* (New York, NY/London: Routledge, 2021), 247 et 249, fig. 11.32.

Fig. 2 – Dessin de l'empreinte du cylindre TH.90. 129
(D. Beyer). Échelle 2:1.

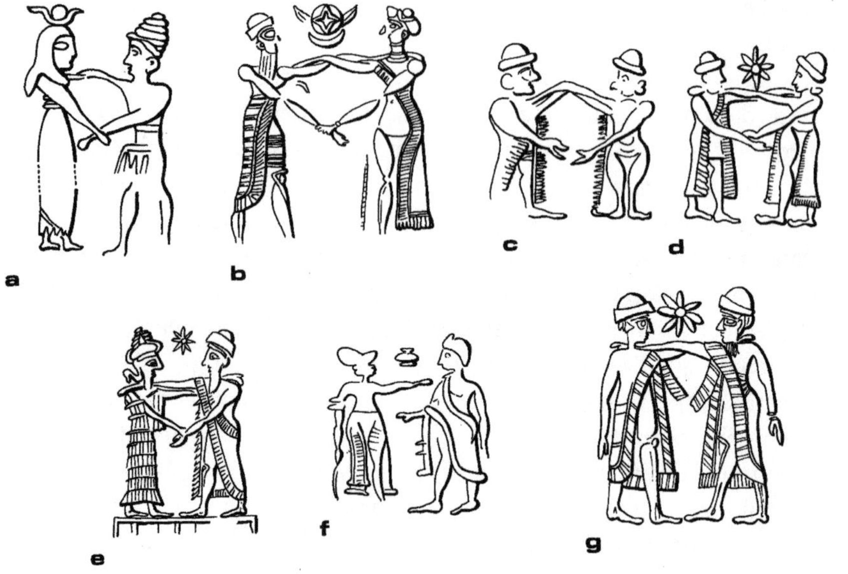

Fig. 3 – Scènes d'embrassade (échelles diverses).
a – Alalah (d'après Collon 1975, n° 147) ; b – Louvre A.934 (d'après Safadi 1974, n° 3) ;
c – Yale (d'après Buchanan 1981, n° 1269) ; d – Marcopoli (d'après Teissier 1984, n° 445) ;
e – Bruxelles O.1448 (d'après Safadi 1974, n° 104) ; f – Tell Ledîs (d'après Collon 1982, n° 16) ;
g – de Clercq 390 ter (d'après Safadi 1974, n° 76).

FIGURE 11.1 Empreintes de sceau d'époque amorrite représentant des "scènes d'embrassade"
Dominique Beyer, "Deux nouveaux sceaux de style syrien provenant de Mari," *MARI* 8 (1997) : 468, fig. 3.

FIGURE 11.2 "Officials embracing each other." Bassin rituel du temple de Shamash à Ebla (XVIIIe siècle avant notre ère)
Paolo Matthiae, *Ebla: Archaeology and History* (New York, NY/London: Routledge, 2021), 249.

Mari, mais aussi dans celle d'Uruk, de Shemshara[16] et dorénavant de Tell Leilan, cette dernière documentant l'usage de ce rituel jusqu'à Alep. C'est donc clairement l'ensemble du Proche-Orient amorritisé qui, d'est en ouest, a eu recours à cette pratique.

Face à cela, l'autre rite utilisé pour s'allier consistait à immoler un ou plusieurs ânon(s) (*ḫayāram qaṭālum*). En la matière, le texte le plus intéressant, désormais souvent cité, est la lettre de Mari ARM 26/2 404 qui est un rapport fait au roi de Mari à propos d'une alliance conclue entre Atamrum d'Andarig et Ashkur-Addu de Karana:

> [9] Atamrum, avec son armée de renfort et les rois qui sont avec lui, est allé à Ṣidqum au-devant d'Ashkur-Addu. Ils se sont tous rejoints à Ṣidqum, ils ont entrepris de discuter de l'affaire entre eux et ils ont immolé un ânon-*ḫayārum*. Avant de tuer l'ânon-*ḫayārum*, lors de leur discussion, Atamrum en présence des gens de Babylone, d'Eshnunna, des Turuk-

16 Cf. Lafont, *Relations internationales*, 271-274, liste B, à laquelle il convient désormais d'ajouter le texte PIHANS 117 54.

> kéens, et des sept rois qui se tiennent à son service, et devant toutes les troupes de renfort, a parlé en ces termes: "Il n'y a pas d'autre roi que Zimri-Lim, notre père, notre frère aîné, et celui qui nous ouvre la marche."
>
> (*S'ensuivent des négociations à la suite d'exigences exprimées par plusieurs des parties en présence*)
>
> 60 Après qu'ils se furent concertés et eurent fait alliance, l'ânon-*ḫayārum* fut immolé; ils se prêtèrent mutuellement serment par le dieu et ils prirent place pour (le rituel de) la coupe. Après être allé boire la coupe, chacun gratifia l'autre d'un présent. Puis Ashkur-Addu repartit pour son pays et Atamrum repartit pour Andarig[17].

Il y a clairement ici un rituel d'alliance qui associe cette fois de *nombreux partenaires* présents à la cérémonie: les sept rois qui "suivent" Atamrum, les représentants de Babylone, Eshnunna et des Turukkéens, ainsi que Haqba-Hammu et les anciens de Numhâ. Avec chacun d'entre eux, il convient de discuter et négocier (l. 18-60 du texte); la prestation de serment par les dieux des deux principaux protagonistes n'intervient qu'à l'issue de ces discussions et du sacrifice d'un ânon.

Quel rapport existe alors entre ces deux rites? L'idée de Jesper Eidem de voir les deux cérémonies du toucher de gorge et du sacrifice de l'ânon comme structurellement équivalentes est séduisante et il me semble qu'il convient de la suivre[18]. Dominique Charpin s'interroge pourtant: "Si les deux cérémonies étaient équivalentes comme le prétend Jesper Eidem, il faudrait trouver dans quel contexte on aurait eu recours à l'une et pas à l'autre."[19]

La réponse pourrait être celle-ci: dans tous les exemples dont on dispose, le "toucher de gorge" n'implique que *deux rois* qui s'engagent l'un envers l'autre,

---

17 ^{I}*a-tam-rum qa-du-um ṣa-ab til-la-ti-šu ù* LUGAL.MEŠ *ša it-ti-šu a-na* [*ṣí*]*-id-qí-im*^{ki} *a-na pa-an aš-kur-*^{d}IŠKUR *il-li-ik i-na ṣí-id-qí-im*^{ki} [*k*]*a-lu-šu-nu in-ne-em-du-ma a-wa-at bi-ri-šu-nu ir-ṭú-bu da-ba-ba-am ù* A[NŠE *ḫa*]*-a-*[*ra-am iq-ṭú-lu*] *la-ma da-ak* ANŠE *ḫa-a-ri-im i-na di-bi-šu-nu* [*a-tam-rum*] *mé-eḫ-re-et* LU$_2$ KA$_2$.DINGIR.RA^{ki} LU$_2$ EŠ$_3$.NUN.NA^{ki} LU$_2$ *tu-r*[*u-ki-im ù*] 7 LUGAL.MEŠ *ša ma-aḫ-ri-šu i-za-az-zu ù ma-ḫar ṣa-ab til-la-t*[*im*] *ka-li-ši-na ú-še-ši-ir-ma a-wa-tam ki-a-am iq-bi um-ma-a-mi ul-la-nu-um zi-im-ri-li-im a-bi-ni a-ḫi-ni* GAL *ù a-li-ik pa-ni-ne* LUGAL *ša-nu-um ú-ul i-ba-aš-ši* (…). *iš-tu ṭe$_4$-em-šu-nu uš-ta-di-nu ù ri-ik-sa-*[*tim ir-ku-s*]*ú-ma* ANŠE *ḫa-a-ru-um iq-qa-ṭì-il a-ḫu-um a-ḫa-a*[*m*] *ni-*[*iš*] DINGIR*-lim* [*ú*]*-ša-àz-ki-ir-ma a-na ka-si-im úš-bu iš-tu ig-ru-šu ù ka-sa-am iš-*[*tu*]*-ú a-ḫu-um a-na a-ḫi-im qí-iš-tam iš-ši-ma aš-kur-*^{d}IŠKUR *a-na ma-a-ti-šu ú-ra-am-mi ù a-tam-rum a-na li-ib-bi* [*an*]*-da-ri-ig*^{ki} *ú-ra-am-mi.* Voir Charpin, *"Tu es de mon sang,"* 55-60 et 188-189.

18 Eidem, *Royal Archives*, 311-312 et 321.

19 Charpin, *Chroniques bibliographiques*, 182, repris dans *"Tu es de mon sang,"* 73.

soit au cours d'une rencontre en tête-à-tête, soit en exécutant la procédure à distance devant leurs témoins respectifs. Au contraire, le sacrifice d'un ânon est un rituel *collectif* engageant de nombreux participants présents à la réunion organisée pour la cérémonie d'alliance.

On notera par ailleurs que, le plus souvent, l'immolation d'ânons implique clairement des populations d'origine bédouine dont il convient sans doute de rappeler les liens tribaux qui les unissent en faisant couler le sang de cet animal, à l'inverse du "toucher de gorge" qui ne concerne que deux monarques en leurs royaumes, lors de leur face-à-face ou bien à l'issue des négociations distantes qu'ils ont entreprises.

Au total, chacun des protocoles se déroule ainsi autour d'étapes similaires associant gestes rituels et paroles prononcées. L'opposition entre "ânon" et "gorge" ne serait donc pas entre un rituel effectué *en présentiel* (pour prendre une expression devenue d'actualité…) par rapport à un autre qui serait utilisé *à distance*, mais plutôt en réalité entre un rite n'impliquant principalement que deux partenaires (le plus souvent des rois [LUGAL]) et un autre, d'origine tribale, engageant collectivement de nombreux participants réunis au cours d'une cérémonie, avec souvent parmi eux des chefs ou représentants de tribus bédouines.

2 Le rôle du sang (*dāmum*)

Dans ce contexte, on voit bien le rôle central joué par le sang, tant dans le rite de l'ânon (*ḫayārum*) que dans celui du "toucher de gorge" (*lipit napištim*), même si cela n'apparaît pas d'emblée dans le second cas. Trois lettres provenant de Mari et deux autres de Tell Leilan[20] apportent désormais des informations essentielles à son sujet.

Le contenu de l'une de celles trouvées à Tell Leilan (PIHANS 117 185) est assez spectaculaire. Il décrit pour la première fois et de façon explicite une véritable transaction sanguine engagée entre les deux partenaires qui devaient s'échanger leur propre sang:

20 Je les avais déjà rassemblées dans Lafont, *Relations internationales*, 260 ("Le rôle fondamental du sang"): il s'agit des lettres de Mari A.2730, A.4350, A.1265+ et des lettres de Tell Leilan devenues PIHANS 117 89 et 185. Elles ont fait l'objet d'importants commentaires, tant par Eidem (*Royal Archives*, 315-317) que par Charpin (*Chroniques bibliographiques*, 182, et *"Tu es de mon sang,"* 74-78). L'injonction contenue dans A.2730 et qu'il a commentée p. 76 a été choisie par Charpin comme titre de son ouvrage.

5' J'ai fait apporter du sang de Till-Abnu. Avant que nous fassions partir (notre) expédition, touchons son sang et prononçons un serment par les dieux. Lorsque nous aurons touché son sang et prononcé un serment par les dieux, que Yahil-pi-[…], Belshunu et Yasrah-Dagan fassent route la nuit même, de sorte que, dès le lendemain, Till-Abnu, ses fils et les Anciens de son district qui marchent à sa suite touchent mon sang et prononcent le serment par les dieux, et que la nuit même ils reviennent ici[21].

On comprend de cette lettre qu'un roi, sans doute Halu-rabi, a souhaité s'assurer formellement de son alliance avec Till-Abnu d'Apum, avant de partir en guerre. Il décide pour cela de procéder au rituel consistant à "toucher le/du sang" (*dāmam lapātum*) de Till-Abnu, qu'il a fait spécialement apporter, et de s'engager envers lui par serment. Afin de ne pas retarder l'expédition militaire prévue, Halu-rabi exprime le souhait que trois émissaires fassent un aller et retour exprès dans la nuit même pour apporter son propre sang jusqu'à Apum, afin que Till-Abnu accomplisse symétriquement et à son tour le même rituel. Les messagers devront être revenus avant l'aube afin de témoigner que le rite a été correctement accompli. Le cadre est donc celui d'une alliance à distance, pour une affaire qui est au fond assez similaire à celle évoquée dans la lettre PIHANS 117 54 ci-dessus. Mais un élément apparaît ici de façon très nouvelle: on apprend que du sang des deux protagonistes est manipulé au cours du rituel d'alliance[22].

Pour explicite que soit ce texte, il suscite cependant bien des interrogations: comment était transporté le sang et quel procédé éventuel utilisait-on pour qu'il demeure à l'état liquide ou sous une autre forme utilisable? Diverses propositions ont été émises à ce sujet[23], mais qui demeurent très hypothétiques et débattues.

---

21 *d[a]-mi ti-la-ab-nu-ú ú-ša-bi-l[am] la-ma a-na* KASKAL *nu-še-ṣú-ú da-mi-šu i nu-la-ap-pí-it ù ni-[i]š* DINGIR.[ME]Š *i ni-ì[z]-k[u-ur i-nu-ma da]-mi-šu [n]u-la-ap-pa-tu ù n[i-iš* DINGIR.MEŠ] *ni-iz-za-ak-ru* [I]*ia-ḫi-il-pí-*[d][x] [I]*be-el-šu-nu ù* [I]*ia-as-ra-aḫ-*[d]*da-g[an nu-b]a-at-ta-šu-nu l[i-li-k]u-ma [ki]-ma ur-ra-am [ti-la-ab-nu]-ú* DUMU.MEŠ-*šu ù* LU_2 ŠU.GI.[MEŠ] *ša ḫa-al-ṣí-šu [š]a wa-a[r-ki-šu] i-la-ku da-mi ú-la-a[p-pa-tu-ma] ni-iš* DINGIR.MEŠ *i-za-ak-ka-ru-ma nu-ba-at-ta-šu-nu [ki]-i li-it-ru-nim-ma.*

22 On notera que Halu-rabi n'est pas le seul à "toucher le sang" qu'il a fait apporter de Till-Abnu ni le seul à prêter serment, étant donné l'emploi des verbes à la première personne du pluriel. Symétriquement, on voit que plusieurs membres de l'entourage proche de Till-Abnu devront "toucher le sang" avec lui.

23 Voir notamment Eidem, *Royal Archives*, 320, et Charpin, *Chroniques bibliographiques*, 183-184, repris en partie dans *"Tu es de mon sang,"* 76.

Sous quelle forme et de quelle manière le sang était-il utilisé lors de la cérémonie d'alliance et quels gestes étaient accomplis lors de ce "toucher de sang"? Du fait du parallélisme des tournures, il est en réalité très tentant de rapprocher les expressions *dāmam lapātum* et *napištam lapātum* et de mettre en rapport "toucher de sang" et "toucher de gorge."[24] On proposera donc ici qu'il s'agisse en fait de deux façons différentes de désigner un seul et même rituel, accompli soit en présence des deux partenaires, soit à distance.

Si c'est bien le cas, il est intéressant d'en revenir alors aux représentations figurées contemporaines évoquées ci-dessus (fig. 11.1 et 11.2): de préférence à une "embrassade," ne mettent-elles pas plutôt en scène ce rituel du "toucher de gorge/sang," avec chacun des protagonistes en train d'enduire de son propre sang la gorge de l'autre? Textes et images doivent-ils finalement pousser à envisager que, lors d'une procédure à distance, on touchait sa propre gorge, mais que chacun touchait la gorge de son partenaire dans les situations en face à face?

Quoi qu'il en soit, ces éléments nouveaux amènent à modifier l'interprétation qui prévalait jusqu'alors et qui voyait dans ce "toucher de gorge" un geste d'auto-malédiction. Le rite dont on a désormais une description précise montre qu'il s'agit plutôt de transmuer les protagonistes en parents par alliance, le rituel créant une forme de consanguinité entre les partenaires. Par le partage du sang, c'est une allégorie de la famille qui était ainsi mise en scène: ce type d'alliance devait manifester une forme de parenté nouvelle, satisfaisant aux règles et contraintes touchant aux relations familiales et tribales caractéristiques de ce temps.

Un extrait de lettre de Mari (A.1265+) donne, pour sa part, une information assez similaire, qui est donc à replacer dans le cadre de ce rituel d'échange sanguin. On y conseille au destinataire de la missive de s'allier en effectuant le même geste que dans le texte de Tell Leilan, même si cela est exprimé ici de façon légèrement différente (*ina dāmim lapātum* au lieu de *dāmam lapātum*): "Touche-toi avec son sang afin qu'il voie la confiance qu'il peut t'accorder."[25]

---

24 L'équation entre *dāmum* et *napištum* pour signifier le "sang" a d'ailleurs été proposée, sur d'autres bases, par Jean-Marie Durand, "Remarques sur le vocabulaire de quelques parties du corps," in *Médecine et médecins au Proche-Orient ancien: Actes du Colloque international organisé à Lyon les 8 et 9 novembre 2002, Maison de l'Orient et de la Méditerranée*, ed. L. Battini et P. Villard, BARIS 1528 (Oxford: BAR Publishing, 2006), 65-71, spécialement 69-70. Par ailleurs, Dylan Johnson attire mon attention, et je l'en remercie, sur le fait que "biblical tradition supports this equation in the prohibition on eating flesh with its *nefesh*/its blood (Gen 9:4; Lev 17:12-14; Deut 12:23)."

25 *i-na da-me-šu li-it-pa-at-ma qí-pu-ut-ka li-na-me-er* (Eidem, *Royal Archives*, 315, et Charpin, *"Tu es de mon sang,"* 75).

Par ailleurs, dans la lettre de Tell Leilan ci-dessus concernant Till-Abnu (PIHANS 117 185), on constate que le rituel du "toucher de sang" est explicitement lié à la prestation de serment par les dieux, ce qui se retrouve également dans l'extrait de lettre de Mari A.4350: "Le sang et un serment par les dieux sont placés entre nous."[26] Mais en réalité, dans ce dernier cas, on ne sait pas très bien si le sang dont il est question est celui d'un ânon immolé ou celui provenant des protagonistes eux-mêmes. Même incertitude avec la lettre de Tell Leilan PIHANS 117 89, où le rituel du sang et le serment se déroulent en outre clairement lors d'une rencontre entre rois:

> Jusqu'à ce que tu sois monté, que toi et moi nous nous soyons vus, que nous ayons prononcé le serment par les dieux et que des liens de sang aient été placés entre nous[27].

On notera avec intérêt le mot *dāmuttum* ("liens de sang") utilisé dans ce texte: il ne se retrouve nulle part ailleurs dans notre dossier. Une dernière lettre de Mari (A.2730), confirme cependant clairement que l'on a bien affaire ici à des rites établissant une consanguinité symbolique entre les partenaires:

> [7] Entre Sharraya et moi, il y a du sang (*dāmum*) et un engagement solennel (*dannātum*) est établi (entre nous). Cent Bédouins et cent de mes sujets des Bords-de-l'Euphrate avec moi, soit deux cents de mes sujets de confiance, notables de mon pays, se sont "tenus dans le sang" et je lui ai prêté serment par le dieu. (...) [17] En outre, j'ai écrit à Sharraya en lui disant: "Tu es de mon sang, donne-moi des troupes!"[28]

Cette lettre utilise elle aussi une expression inédite: "se tenir dans le sang" (*ina dāmim izuzzum*). On aimerait savoir ce qu'elle recouvre exactement. Elle peut faire allusion au "toucher de gorge/de sang," au rituel collectif de l'ânon (d'autant que des centaines d'individus semblent concernées) ou à tout autre

---

26 *da-mu-ú ù ni-iš* DINGIR.MEŠ *bi-ri-ni ša-ak-nu* (Dominique Charpin and Nele Ziegler, *Mari et le Proche-Orient à l'époque amorrite: Essai d'histoire politique*, FM 5 [Paris: SEPOA, 2003], 51 n. 191). Voir Charpin, *"Tu es de mon sang,"* 74.

27 *a-di te-le-em-ma a-na-ku ù at-ta ni-in-na-ma-ru ni-iš* DINGIR.MEŠ *i-na bi-ri-ni ni-za-ka-ru da-mu-ut-tum i-na [b]i-ri-ni iš-ša-ka-na*. Voir Charpin, *"Tu es de mon sang,"* 74-75.

28 *bi-ri-ti-ia ù bi-ri-it* [I]*šar-ra-ia da-mu ù dan-na-tum ša-ak-na* 1 ME ḪA.NA.MEŠ ù 1 ME IR_3*-du-ia ša a-aḫ pu-ra-an-tim it-ti-ia* 2 *me-tim* IR_3*-du-ia ta-ak-lu-tum qa-qa-[d]a-at ma-ti-ia i-na da-mi iz-zi-zu ù ni-iš* DINGIR-*lim [l]u-ú za-ak-ra-ak-šum* (...) *ù a-na šar-ra-ia aš-pu-ur-ma um-ma a-na-ku-ma [ša da-mi]-ia at-ta ṣa-ba-ka id-nam-ma*. Voir Eidem, *Royal Archives*, 315 et Charpin, *Chroniques bibliographiques*, 185, repris dans *"Tu es de mon sang,"* 76-77.

chose encore: on ne sait finalement pas de quelle façon concrète toutes ces personnes “se sont tenues dans le sang.” Cependant, la métaphore semble demeurer la même: le rituel consistait à établir des liens symboliques de consanguinité et à se prêter serment[29]. Ainsi, le mot *dannātum* (“engagement solennel”) de ce texte fait assez clairement écho au *dāmuttum* (“liens de sang”) du texte de Tell Leilan ci-dessus (PIHANS 117 89).

En définitive, force est de reconnaître que la complexité anthropologique de la symbolique attachée au sang, à laquelle s’ajoutent le trop petit nombre d’attestations contextualisées et l’absence de description concrète de tous ces gestes et expressions, font qu’il demeure beaucoup d’incertitudes et de questions sans réponse dans ce dossier.

3 Petite tablette (*ṭuppum ṣeḫrum*) et grande tablette (*ṭuppum rabûm*)

Un dernier point de discussion reste ouvert: il concerne le recours aux documents écrits et leur rôle dans ces procédures. Il s’agit d’une question cruciale qui est au cœur même des diverses études récentes sur le thème considéré.

Il semble pourtant désormais qu’il convient de “déconnecter” cette question de tout ce qui vient d’être précédemment exposé. Car pour conclure une alliance à cette époque, les étapes que nous avons décrites (gestes et paroles) se suffisaient à elles-mêmes et la place de l’écrit dans cette affaire est, en quelque sorte, une “autre” question. Ainsi, comme le rappelle Jesper Eidem, “the available evidence for international agreements in this period could be understood as largely oral procedures which did not involve the use of written documents.”[30] La nécessité de s’écrire intervenait surtout lorsque les négociations et engagements subséquents ne pouvaient avoir lieu qu’à distance. Mais pas seulement! Et il semble que des tablettes étaient aussi utilisées lors de cérémonies d’alliance se déroulant *en présence* des protagonistes[31].

---

29 Je maintiens donc ce que j’ai écrit dans Bertrand Lafont, “Sacrifices et rituels à Mari et dans la Bible,” *RA* 93 (1999): 74, malgré Charpin, *“Tu es de mon sang,”* 53.

30 Eidem, *Royal Archives*, 310. Ce qui fait écho à ce que j’avais moi-même écrit dans Lafont, *Relations internationales*, 280-281: “Un texte n’est pas toujours indispensable pour s’allier (…) il existe de nombreux témoignages de prestation de serment d’alliance où il n’y a pas la moindre allusion à une mise par écrit des termes du traité. (…) Ce sont, après accord des parties, les *verba solemnia* prononcées sous la garantie des dieux, ainsi que les gestes solennels effectués devant témoins, qui comptent par dessus tout.”

31 Eidem, *Royal Archives*, 321-322 et voir ci-dessus n. 9 à propos du traité de Tell Leilan LT3.

Dans la documentation de Mari, l'exemple le plus significatif de négociation à distance est la lettre de Yarim-Addu ARM 26/2 372 (à compléter par la fin d'ARM 26/2 373), relative aux tractations entre les rois d'Eshnunna et de Babylone qui souhaitaient faire alliance. Dans leurs échanges, il est question de recourir à une "petite tablette" (*ṭuppum ṣeḫrum*), associée à la cérémonie du "toucher de gorge" (*lipit napištim*), puis à une "grande tablette" (*ṭuppum rabûm*) utilisée ensuite lors du "serment par les dieux" (*nīš ilī*). De cette lettre qu'il a éditée, Dominique Charpin a proposé le commentaire suivant:

> *Ṭuppum ṣeḫrum* fonctionne manifestement, par opposition à *ṭuppum rabûm*, comme le projet de traité par rapport au traité définitif. Dans le scénario décrit ici, l'envoi d'une "petite tablette" (*ṭuppum ṣeḫrum*) est mis en rapport avec l'engagement par geste symbolique (*napištašu lapâtum* = "se toucher la gorge"), alors que l'envoi de la "grande tablette" (*ṭuppum rabûm*) requiert un engagement verbal (*nîš ilî zakârum* = "prêter serment par les dieux"). L'association faite ici entre le format de la tablette et le type d'engagement est remarquable: on voit donc que la "petite tablette" correspond à ce qui est ailleurs décrit comme une *ṭuppi lipit napištim*, alors que la "grande tablette" est manifestement identique à une *ṭuppi nîš ilî*[32].

C'est à partir de cette intéressante lettre de Mari que toute la procédure d'alliance a été reconstruite, avec une mise en parallèle entre les gestes accomplis et le type de tablette utilisé, en deux étapes successives. Soit le tableau suivant:

ARM 26/2 372	Gestes symboliques	Tablette associée
Étape 1	*lipit napištim* "toucher de gorge"	*ṭuppum ṣeḫrum* "petite tablette" = *ṭuppi lipit napištim*
Étape 2	*nīš ilī* "serment par les dieux"	*ṭuppum rabûm* "grande tablette" = *ṭuppi nīš ilī*

Il apparaît cependant que l'on ne sait en réalité toujours pas très bien ce que sont ces "petites" et "grandes" tablettes: leur forme, leur contenu, leur usage ne

32 Charpin, *Archives Épistolaires*, 144.

sont explicités nulle part. D'un autre côté, l'association qui est faite dans ce texte entre format de tablette et type d'engagement est très inhabituelle. Ce qui suscite l'interrogation de Dominique Charpin:

> Cette lettre de Yarim-Addu, avec son luxe de détails, pose un problème de méthode: décrit-elle la façon de faire habituelle, ou s'agit-il d'une procédure exceptionnelle – et pour cette raison détaillée par le menu? Pour trancher, il faut voir si les différentes étapes ici indiquées sont attestées ailleurs[33].

En réalité, on ne retrouve cela nulle part ailleurs dans la documentation de cette époque. Et les exemples sont au contraire nombreux désormais, où l'on voit la procédure associant gestes et serment être accomplie en une seule fois. Il existe même un texte de Mari (A.1289+) qui associe clairement "tablette du serment par le dieu" (*ṭuppi nīš ilī*) et rituel du *lipit napištim*. Dans cette longue lettre que le roi d'Eshnunna écrivit au roi de Mari, on peut ainsi lire:

> iii18 À présent, sur la *tablette du serment par le dieu* que tu dois me faire porter, fixe ma frontière à partir de Harradum et explicite cette clause par écrit, sans me faire d'objection, et alors je *toucherai ma gorge* pour toi[34].

Mieux vaut donc considérer que la procédure décrite par la lettre de Yarim-Addu ARM 26/2 372 a été très atypique, et que:

> Le plus souvent, les rois se mettaient d'accord au préalable de manière informelle, par des échanges de messagers et de lettres. Une seule cérémonie avait lieu: le roi s'engageait par le geste du "toucher de la gorge" et prêtait un serment correspondant aux engagements que son homologue lui avait fait parvenir par écrit, qui est généralement désignée comme "tablette de serment par les dieux" (*ṭuppi nîš ilî*)[35].

---

33 Charpin, *"Tu es de mon sang,"* 98. Voir aussi *Chroniques bibliographiques*, 183.

34 *i-[na-an-n]a i-na* DUB *ni-iš* DINGIR *ša tu-ša-ab-ba-lam iš-tu ḫa-ra-di-im pa-ṭì-ia ki-in-na ši-iṭ-ra-am ša-tu mu-[ul]-la-a-am-ma pa-ri-ik-tam la tu-ša-ar-ša-am na-[p]í-iš-ti lu-ul-pu-ta-kum*. Voir Dominique Charpin, "Un traité entre Zimri-Lim de Mari et Ibal-pi-El II d'Ešnunna," in *Marchands, diplomates et empereurs: Études sur la civilisation mésopotamienne offertes à Paul Garelli*, ed. D. Charpin and F. Joannès (Paris: Éditions Recherche sur les Civilisations, 1991), 139-166, et Jean-Marie Durand, *Documents épistolaires du Palais de Mari, tome 1*, LAPO 16 (Paris: Éditions du Cerf, 1997), nº 281.

35 Charpin, *"Tu es de mon sang,"* 99-100.

Dès lors, on pourrait envisager que, dans la plupart des cas, une équation soit à établir entre *ṭuppi lipit napištim* et *ṭuppi nīš ilī*, utilisées indifféremment selon que l'on souhaitait mettre en avant le geste symbolique accompli ou le serment prononcé. Soit le schéma suivant:

	Gestes symboliques	**Tablette associée**
Étape unique	*lipit napištim* "toucher de gorge" + *nīš ilī* "serment par les dieux"	*ṭuppi lipit napištim* = *ṭuppi nīš ilī*

L'utilisation des tablettes *ṭuppum ṣeḫrum* et *ṭuppum rabûm* dans ARM 26/2 372, avec les deux étapes successives qui y sont décrites, relève donc pour l'heure d'une procédure tout à fait singulière.

Quel était donc le contenu de ces tablettes? On a raisonnablement supposé qu'il s'agissait sans doute dans le premier cas d'un brouillon (on parlerait aujourd'hui d'"éléments de langage" ou de négociation) et dans l'autre du texte définitif de l'accord tel qu'il était prononcé lors du serment[36], mais on ne sait en réalité pas grand-chose, finalement, de ces documents et de la façon dont ils étaient utilisés.

À leur sujet, Jesper Eidem a d'ailleurs fait des propositions complémentaires[37], remarquant notamment le rôle très concret que semble avoir joué la *ṭuppi lipit napištim* durant la cérémonie d'alliance. Il relève ainsi au moins deux textes (ARM 26/2 372 et 469) qui précisent qu'une partie du rituel avait lieu "dans/sur/avec" la tablette d'engagement (***ina*** *ṭuppi lipit napištim*).

Difficile de savoir à quoi cela fait référence, mais dans le cadre des parallélismes que nous avons essayé d'établir ici, on pourrait peut-être trouver une nouvelle analogie avec ce qui est dit du rituel de l'ânon immolé dans ARM 26/2 404. On y lit en effet (l. 32): "dans leurs paroles et ***dans leur ânon*** ils ont placé mon seigneur comme étant leur père" (***ina*** *dibbišunu u ḫayārišunu bēlī ana abišunu iškunū*). Mais on n'en sait pas davantage sur les gestes, actions ou situations qu'une telle phrase permettrait de supposer.

Il reste donc en définitive encore beaucoup à comprendre sur ces affaires. Mais on constate aussi quelles avancées significatives ont déjà été réalisées, grâce en particulier aux travaux récents des éditeurs des textes de Mari et de Tell Leilan.

36 Charpin, *"Tu es de mon sang,"* 99.
37 Eidem, *Royal Archives*, 319-320.

Bibliographie

Beyer, Dominique. "Deux nouveaux sceaux de style syrien provenant de Mari." *MARI* 8 (1997): 463-475.

Charpin, Dominique. *Archives Épistolaires de Mari 1/2*. ARM 26/2. Paris: Éditions Recherche sur les Civilisations, 1988.

Charpin, Dominique. "Une alliance contre l'Elam et le rituel du *lipit napištim*." Pages 109-118 in *Contribution à l'histoire de l'Iran: Mélanges offerts à Jean Perrot*. Edited by F. Vallat. Paris: Éditions Recherche sur les Civilisations, 1990.

Charpin, Dominique. "Un traité entre Zimri-Lim de Mari et Ibal-pi-El II d'Ešnunna." Pages 139-166 in *Marchands, diplomates et empereurs: Études sur la civilisation mésopotamienne offertes à Paul Garelli*. Edited by D. Charpin and F. Joannès. Paris: Éditions Recherche sur les Civilisations, 1991.

Charpin, Dominique. "Chroniques bibliographiques 18: Les débuts des relations diplomatiques au Proche-Orient ancien." *RA* 110 (2016): 127-186.

Charpin, Dominique. "Les alliances au Proche-Orient ancien, entre diplomatie et religion." *Annuaire du Collège de France* 116 (2018): 229-242.

Charpin, Dominique. *"Tu es de mon sang": Les alliances dans le Proche-Orient ancien*. Paris: Collège de France – Les Belles Lettres, 2019.

Charpin, Dominique, and Nele Ziegler. *Mari et le Proche-Orient à l'époque amorrite: Essai d'histoire politique*. FM 5. Paris: SEPOA, 2003.

Durand, Jean-Marie. *Documents épistolaires du Palais de Mari, tome 1*. LAPO 16. Paris: Éditions du Cerf, 1997.

Durand, Jean-Marie. "Remarques sur le vocabulaire de quelques parties du corps." Pages 65-71 in *Médecine et médecins au Proche-Orient ancien: Actes du Colloque international organisé à Lyon les 8 et 9 novembre 2002, Maison de l'Orient et de la Méditerranée*. Edited by L. Battini and P. Villard. BARIS 1528. Oxford: BAR Publishing, 2006.

Eidem, Jesper. *The Royal Archives from Tell Leilan: Old Babylonian Letters and Treaties from the Lower Town Palace East*. PIHANS 117. Leiden: Brill, 2011.

Fleming, Daniel. *Democracy's Ancient Ancestors: Mari and Early Collective Governance*. Cambridge: Cambridge University Press, 2004.

Lafont, Bertrand. "Sacrifices et rituels à Mari et dans la Bible." *RA* 93 (1999): 57-77.

Lafont, Bertrand. "Relations internationales, alliances et diplomatie au temps des royaumes amorrites: Essai de synthèse." Pages 213-328 in *Mari, Ebla et les Hourrites, dix ans de travaux*. Edited by J.-M. Durand and D. Charpin. Amurru 2. Paris: Éditions Recherche sur les Civilisations, 2001.

Matthiae, Paolo. *Ebla: Archaeology and History*. New York, NY/London: Routledge, 2021.

Munn-Rankin, Joan Margaret. "Diplomacy in Western Asia in the Early Second Millennium B.C." *Iraq* 18 (1956): 68-110.

12

Kings, Peoples, and Their Gods: Bar Rakib's Political Portrayal of Divinity

Theodore J. Lewis

Introduction[1]

Successful kings are skilled in the use of political and religious language—both visual and textual narratives—to shape the perceptions of their constituents and external powers. The present endeavor is a study of how the Sam'alian King Bar Rakib (ca. 733–713/711 BCE) employed various narratives of divinity in ways that were tailored to different audiences. It hopes to show how his different portrayals of divinity (both traditional and innovative) were socially, culturally and politically astute. In particular, it will focus on Bar Rakib's portrayals as the last ruler of ancient Yadiya/Sam'al, a polity marked for its hybridity as it blended Anatolian and West Semitic cultural traditions while at the same time navigating the power dynamics of the Neo-Assyrian empire.

1 Bar Rakib's Portrayal of Divinity in *KAI* 215 (Panamuwa II Inscription)

Bar Rakib left behind orthostats, inscriptions, and seals that give us direct windows into his portrayal of divinity. Though scholars label *KAI* 215 as "the Panamuwa Inscription," unlike many other royal inscriptions this is not a text written by the king (in the first person) to celebrate his accomplishments. A tragedy has occurred. King Panamuwa II has unexpectedly been killed on the Damascus battlefield fighting on behalf of Tiglath-pileser III. So it is that Bar Rakib, his son and heir, sets up a twice life-sized statue of his father (**Figure 12.1**) at the very beginning of his reign.[2]

---

1 Daniel Fleming is exceptional—as a scholar and as an interlocutor devoted to colleagues and students alike. It is a pleasure celebrating his many contributions to our field and the many ways in which he has improved our work on a personal level.

2 Originally the statue would have stood at ca. 3.5 m. high (ca. 11.4 feet). As we now have it, only the bottom half of the dolerite statue is preserved, measuring 1.54 m. high with King Panamuwa II's upper torso and head missing.

 | DOI:10.1163/9789004511538_013

FIGURE 12.1
The statue of King Panamuwa II erected by his son Bar Rakib containing an inscription written in Sam'alian Aramaic (KAI 215)
COURTESY OF THE ORIENTAL INSTITUTE OF THE UNIVERSITY OF CHICAGO. ILLUSTRATION RECONSTRUCTING PANAMUWA II'S UPPER TORSO AND HEAD BY KAREN RECZUCH, USED BY PERMISSION

1.1 *The Visual Narrative of Divinity*

Visually, Bar Rakib's sole focus is on his deceased father's image.[3] No deity is portrayed, as the statue functions on a funerary level for the benefit of his postmortem existence. Due to the benevolence of Tiglath-pileser III in providing his father with a prestigious (state-sponsored) burial in far off Assyria, Bar Rakib is deprived of using the symbolism of his father's funeral to legitimize his claim to the throne.[4] But he wisely sets up a stele—engraved with his father's image and name—in which his father's disembodied essence (*nabš*) can reside and receive cult. As we clearly see in the Katumuwa Stele, local belief (of Anatolian influence) held that one's post-mortem *nabš*-essence could indeed reside apart from one's body. Moreover, as with the Katumuwa Stele, the stele of Panamuwa II can be the location of ongoing funerary cult. As regular offerings are prescribed in the Katumuwa Stele (*ywmn lywmn*, line 10), so too Bar Rakib demonstrates his loyalty to his father by offering ongoing funerary cult—and in Yadiya in full view of his local constituency.[5] There is an equally important communicative function of the stele and Bar Rakib's ritual performance. Both serve to legitimize Bar Rakib's claim to the throne and the ongoing dynasty with the message: "The King is dead; Long live the King!"

1.2 *The Textual Narrative of Divinity*

In contrast to the lack of divine portrayals in the visual narrative, Bar Rakib portrays a cluster of divinity in his textual narrative. In every case, his textual portrayal of divinity (and the portrayal of Tiglath-pileser III) is tied to legitimizing his role in carrying on the dynastic house of his ancestors—specifically mentioning Kings Qarali, Panamuwa I, Bar Sur, and Panamuwa II. Bar Rakib's first mention of divinity is a local reference to how "the gods of Yadiya" delivered his father Panamuwa II from an unnamed usurper, whose violent massacre could easily have wiped out the entire ruling dynasty (*plṭwh ʾlh yʾdy mn šḥth ʾzh hwt bbyt ʾbwh*; KAI 215.2). The consistent use of the toponym Yadiya (six times in KAI 215) is telling, as it is a Luwian-derived indigenous name that speaks of his local

3 The image is dressed in what Schloen refers to as a "distinctive court dress": "a fringed mantle" with a "hanging hem" as well as an "ankle-length tunic with tasseled hem" and "another garment worn over the tunic." See J. David Schloen, "Statue of Panamuwa II of Samʾal," in *In Remembrance of Me: Feasting with the Dead in the Ancient Middle East*, ed. Virginia R. Hermann and J. David Schloen (Chicago, IL: Oriental Institute Museum Publications, University of Chicago, 2014), 120.

4 See Theodore J. Lewis, "Bar Rakib's Legitimation and the Problem of a Missing Corpse: The End of the Panamuwa Inscription in Light of the Katumuwa Inscription," *ARAM Periodical* 31/2 (2019): 349–374.

5 See Lewis, "Bar Rakib's Legitimation," 362–371.

constituency as opposed to the toponym Sam'al that is preferred in Akkadian sources as well as in Old Aramaic sources that reflect Neo-Assyrian influence (see below).[6] In the same breath, Bar Rakib also highlights how the premier Aramean god Hadad stood by his father Panamuwa II during this crisis (*wqm ʿmh hdd*; KAI 215.2). Near the end of the inscription, Bar Rakib makes reference to his father's post-mortem *nabš*-essence eating and drinking in the afterlife, an imagined banquet that would be consumed along with the god Hadad (as noted in KAI 214.17–18a).

The final reference to divinity occurs in the closing lines of the inscription:

> *wzkr . znh . hʾ . pʾ . hdd . wʾl . ⸢wr⸣kb⸢ʾl⸣ . bʿ⸢l⸣ . byt . wšmš . wkl . ʾlhy . yʾdy* [. *yrqw. wty. br. pnmw*] [*wytn rkbʾl ḥn*]*y . qdm . ʾlhy . wqdm . ʾnš .*
>
> The (stele) constitutes a *ḏikr*-memorial.[7] Thus may Hadad, El, Rakib-El, the lord of the dynastic house, and Shamash, and all the gods of Yadiya [have favor upon me, the son of Panamuwa]. [And may Rakib-El show favor] to me before the gods and before men.
>
> KAI 215.22–23[8]

Bar Rakib's closing lines are telling. His ancestor, Panamuwa I (ca. 790–750 BCE), included four occurrences of a fivefold pantheon in what scholars have labeled the "Hadad Inscription" (KAI 214), a reference to the inscription being written on a colossal statue of the god Hadad, whose original height would have been approximately 4 m. [**Figure 12.2**]. Its 34-line inscription was written on the lower torso in Sam'alian Aramaic, and carved (not incised) in bas-

6 See Younger for the three different toponyms (Bīt-Gabbāri, Yadiya, Sam'al) that were used by different parties based on their relation to the city-state especially with its hybrid Luwian-Aramean character. K. Lawson Younger, *A Political History of the Arameans: From Their Origins to the End of Their Polities* (Atlanta, GA: SBL Press, 2016), 378–384.

7 Tropper suggests that *zkr* here is elliptical for *nṣb zkr*. Josef Tropper, *Die Inschriften von Zincirli: Neue Edition und vergleichende Grammatik des phönizischen, sam'alischen und aramäischen Textkorpus* (Münster: Ugarit-Verlag, 1993), 130. We agree that the stele is in focus here as it functions as a place of remembering and invoking the dead. On the importance of the latter, see Lewis, "Bar Rakib's Legitimation," 371.

8 The two restorations are based respectively on KAI 214.13 and on KAI 217.7–9. For those favoring such restorations, see Tropper, *Die Inschriften von Zincirli*, 133; K. Lawson Younger, "The Panamuwa Inscription," in COS 2.37 (pp. 158–160); and A. Lemaire, "Rites des vivants pour les morts dans le royaume de Sam'al (VIIIe siècle av. n. è.)," in *Les vivants et leurs morts: Actes du colloque organisé par le Collège de France, Paris, les 14–15 avril 2010*, ed. Jean-Marie Durand, Thomas Römer and Jürg Hutzli (Fribourg: Academic Press, 2012), here 133.

FIGURE 12.2
A colossal statue of the god Hadad erected by King Panamuwa I containing an inscription written in Sam'alian Aramaic (KAI 214)
PHOTO COURTESY VIRGINIA HERRMANN

relief.[9] Though Panamuwa I's unified visual and textual presentation is Hadad-centric, the king's clear devotion to Hadad works in concert with a fivefold group of deities who occur four times in this single inscription, in an ordered (hierarchical?) fashion with minor variation as to the placement or alternative name of the god Rashap/ʾArqû-Rashap:

KAI 214.2a	Hadad, El, Rashap, Rakib-El, and Shamsh
KAI 214.2b–3a	Hadad, El, Rakib-El, Shamsh, and Rashap
KAI 214.11	Hadad, El, Rakib-El, Shamsh, ʾArqû-Rashap
KAI 214.18b–19a	Hadad, El, Rakib-El, Shamsh, [Rashap].

In *KAI* 215, Bar Rakib omits the god Rashap altogether (he could have used a sixfold list) in favor of again listing "all the gods of Yadiya" (*wkl ʾlhy yʾdy*), whom he praised at the outset of the inscription.[10] This is intentional. If the above reconstruction is correct, Bar Rakib's final words highlight the role of Rakib-El, the dynastic god, after whom he is named. The petition is twofold: to give him favor among the gods (*qdm ʾlhy*)—revealing the perceived/imputed influence and standing of Rakib-El within the pantheon—as well as with his local constituency at Yadiya (*qdm ʾnš*).

2 Bar Rakib's Portrayal of Divinity on Palace Orthostats

We have four contemporary orthostats depicting King Bar Rakib, all of which come from his palace complex designated as Hilani IV in the archaeological

9 The older King Kulamuwa's royal inscription (*KAI* 24), written in north Phoenician, is also carved (not incised) in hieroglyphic Luwian-inspired raised script using a Phoenician (or Aramaic) ductus. See Eudora J. Struble and Virginia R. Herrmann. "An Eternal Feast at Samʾal: The New Iron Age Mortuary Stele from Zincirli in Context," *BASOR* 356 (2009): 20. For a thorough study of ninth-century BCE Phoenician and Aramaic scripts and how they pertain to the Kulamuwa inscription, see Heather Dana Davis Parker, "The Levant Comes of Age: The Ninth Century BCE Through Script Traditions," (Ph.D. diss., Johns Hopkins University, 2013), 65–78, esp. 66–67 n. 255.

Most scholars assume that Kulamuwa's use of Phoenician must be due to its status as a prestige language, especially in trade. See Herbert Niehr, "The Power of Language: Language Situation and Language Policy in Samʾal," in *In Search for Aram and Israel: Politics, Culture, and Identity*, ed. Omer Sergi, Manfred Oeming, and Izaak J. de Hulster (Tübingen: Mohr Siebeck, 2016), 305–332 (here 311–314, 318–321); and Frederick Mario Fales, "Phoenicia in the Neo-Assyrian Period: An Updated Overview," *SAAB* 23 (2017): 181–295. Cf. too the lengthy Azitawada/Karatepe Phoenician-Hieroglyphic Luwian bilingual inscription (*KAI* 26). Note though that when king Kulamuwa refers to himself as "son" (*KAI* 24.1, 4, 9) he uses the Aramaic *bar* and not the Phoenician *bin*.

10 Note how *KAI* 215.22–23 distinguishes "the gods of Yadiya" from the fivefold cluster.

reports.[11] Three of the four bear inscriptions. The various sigla used for these four orthostats is as follows:

- BR1/*KAI* 216/Tropper B1/TSSI 2.15/Schwiderski BarRak:1/Gilibert Zinjirli 74
- BR2/*KAI* 217/Tropper B2/TSSI 2.16/Schwiderski BarRak:8/Gilibert Zinjirli 75
- BR3/*KAI* 218/Tropper B3/TSSI 2.17/Schwiderski BarRak:2/Gilibert Zinjirli 66
- Gilibert Zinjirli 69 (= Voos's reconstruction of Bar Rakib banqueting[12])

In BR1/*KAI* 216, Bar Rakib refers to his illustrious building of Hilani IV that surpassed the royal palace of his predecessor King Kulamuwa who reigned a hundred years earlier from 840–815/810 BCE. As many have acknowledged, Bar Rakib consciously frames his inscriptions, his iconography, and his building programs in conversation with Kulamuwa. In his lengthiest extant inscription (*KAI* 216.12–20), Bar Rakib refers to "the house/dynasty of Kulamuwa" (*byt klmw*), which he brags about expanding with the same play on the word *byt* as used in 2 Samuel 7.[13] Archaeologically, this "house" refers to the palatial complex of Kulamuwa located in the northwestern half of the citadel, especially buildings J and K [**Figure 12.3**].[14] Gilibert's description deserves to be quoted in full:

> [T]he southern façade and entrance of the "palace of Barrakib" is a conscious architectural replica of the "palace of Kulamuwa," with a larger, three-columns-portico at the west side and a smaller, single-column portico at the east side, each leading into separate functional units. In this perspective, the rich decoration of Hilani IV and the inscribed orthostats Zinjirli 74–75 [= our BR1, BR2], may be considered an enlarged, inflated version of Kulamuwa's orthostat which, of course, was still standing in

11 For locations of these four orthostats, see Alessandra Gilibert, *Syro-Hittite Monumental Art and the Archaeology of Performance: The Stone Reliefs at Carchemish and Zincirli in the Earlier First Millennium BCE* (Berlin: de Gruyter, 2011), 84–88.

12 Joachim Voos, "Zu einigen späthethitischen Reliefs aus den Beständen des Vorderasiatischen Museums Berlin," *AoF* 12 (1985): 65–86.

13 This was astutely pointed out by K. Lawson Younger, "Panammuwa and Bar-Rakib: Two Structural Analyses," *JANES* 18 (1986): 102; Younger, "The Bar-Rakib Inscription," *COS* 2.38 (p. 161 n. 8); and Younger, "Gods at the Gates: A Study of the Identification of the Deities Represented at the Gates of Ancient Sam'al (Zincirli) with Possible Historical Implications," *ARAM Periodical* 31/2 (2019): 318 n. 5.

14 For Figure 12.3, see Gilibert, *Syro-Hittite Monumental Art*, 81 fig. 4, and Marina Pucci, *Functional Analysis of Space in Syro-Hittite Architecture* (Oxford: Archaeopress, 2008), pl. 11–12.

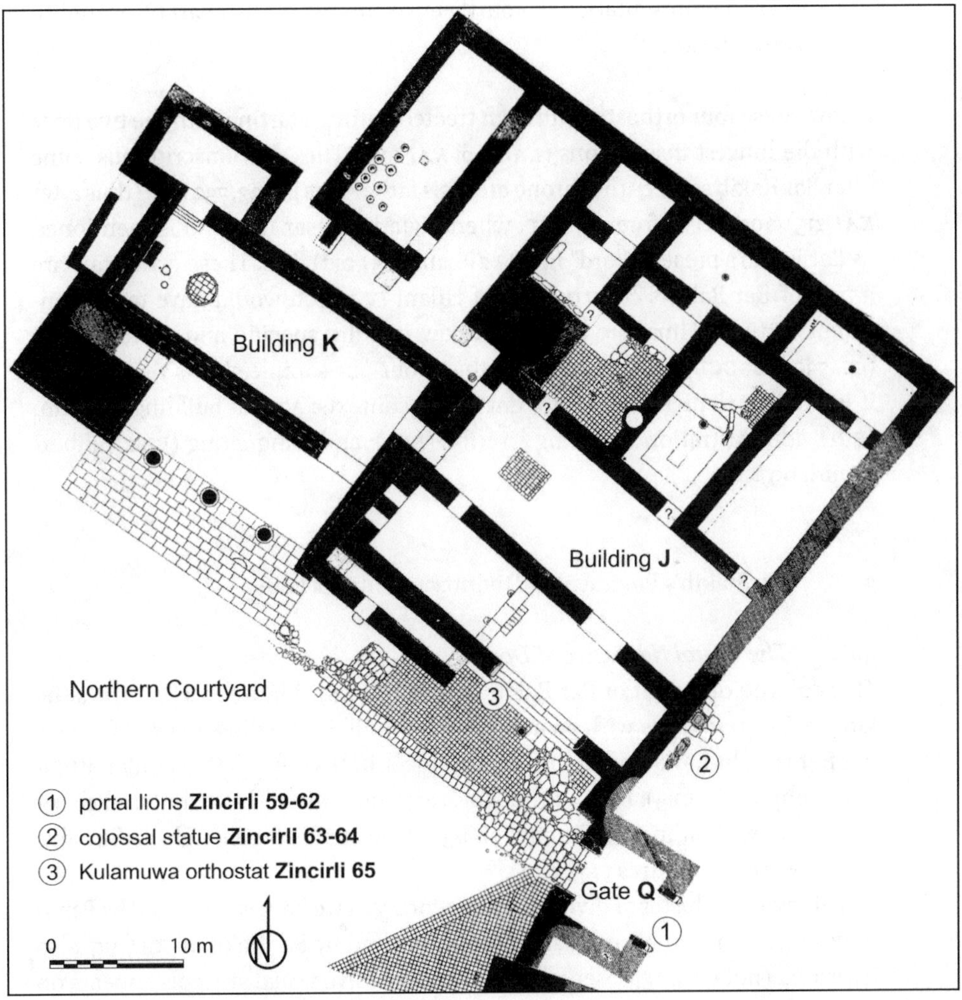

FIGURE 12.3 The north-western area of the citadel at Zincirli with Bar Rakib's palatial complex (esp. building J and K) and the position of various orthostats. Alessandra Gilibert, *Syro-Hittite Monumental Art and the Archaeology of Performance: The Stone Reliefs at Carchemish and Zincirli in the Earlier First Millennium* BCE (Berlin: De Gruyter, 2011), 81 fig. 4

Barrakib's time. In fact, the explicit mention of Kulamuwa and [his] palace in Barrakib's inscriptions as well as the reprise of the literary topos on the king's amity with Assyria testify to a conscious reception and a will to elaborate on Kulamuwa's heritage. The sculptural program at Hilani IV also shows how the elite figurative discourse that had just begun to be developed in Kulamuwa's time is seen in Barrakib's time, one hundred years later, in its full-blown form, with a cycle of orthostats giving a

> detailed representation of courtly environment at the heart of the political institutions.[15]

Below, these four orthostats are each treated in turn, starting with the two texts with the longest inscriptions (*KAI* 216, *KAI* 217). These two inscriptions come after Bar Rakib secures the throne after his father dies in 733/732 BCE (thus after *KAI* 215) and yet before 727 BCE, when Tiglath-pileser III (who is mentioned as Bar Rakib's present "lord" in *KAI* 216 and *KAI* 217) dies. These orthostats are a part of Bar Rakib's construction of Hilani IV which would have taken considerable time. Thus, the dating window is quite specific and quite narrow (ca. 730–727 BCE). What is noteworthy about our sample size is that, though it is small, it depicts three different social contexts: a royal building program (BR1); administration involving a scribe (BR3); and banqueting (BR2; Gilibert Zinjirli 69).

3 Bar Rakib's Portrayal of Divinity on BR1/*KAI* 216

3.1 *The Visual Narrative of Divinity*

This dolerite orthostat of Bar Rakib (1.3 m. × .62 m.) [**Figure 12.4**] portrays the king in Assyrian dress with an attendant behind him holding a raised feather-fan in his right hand and an unknown object in his left (cf. the similar attendant's objects in BR3). Both of the king's arms are raised (his right hand close-fisted, his left holding a palmette; cf. B3) as he stands facing right before five divine symbols [**Figures 12.5, 12.6**].[16]

This fivefold cluster of divinity is noteworthy as we have seen it used by Panamuwa I (*KAI* 214) in his textual presentation, and by Bar Rakib in *KAI* 215, also in textual (not visual) presentation. A cluster of five visual symbols appears on

15 Gilibert, *Syro-Hittite Monumental Art*, 88.

16 Compare the difference with the Kulamuwa image, which depicts an upward gesture of the king pointing with his finger to four divine symbols (a horned helmet, a yoke-bar, a winged sun disk, and a lunar symbol), thereby promoting his allegiance to four specific deities (Hadad, Rakib-El, the Aramean Shamsh or the Neo-Assyrian god Shamash, and the local Aramean moon god Śahr or the Neo-Assyrian Sin). The four divine symbols could very well represent local Sam'alian representations and/or a hybrid of Aramean/Assyrian divinity. Ornan nuances such portrayals suggesting that "iconographic borrowings were inspired by local features, embedded in Assyrian imagery," and this certainly makes sense due to the king being indebted to Shalmaneser III to secure his reign against the powerful Danunian threat (*KAI* 24.7b–8a). See Tallay Ornan, *The Triumph of the Symbol: Pictorial Representation of Deities in Mesopotamia and the Biblical Image Ban* (Fribourg: Academic Press, 2005), 139.

FIGURE 12.4 An orthostat of Bar Rakib portraying the king in Assyrian dress together with five symbols of divinity (BR1) and a lengthy inscription written in Old Aramaic (KAI 216)

COURTESY MARK AHSMANN (CC BY-SA 3.0) WIKIMEDIA COMMONS FILE:20131205 ISTANBUL 067.JPG

FIGURE 12.5 A close-up of Figure 12.4 showing the five divine symbols on Bar Rakib's orthostat BR1

FIGURE 12.6 A line drawing of the five divine symbols on Bar Rakib's orthostat BR1. Figure from Yigael Yadin, "Symbols of Deities at Zinjirli, Carthage and Hazor" in *Near Eastern Archaeology in the Twentieth Century: Essays in Honor of Nelson Glueck*, ed. James A. Sanders, 206, fig. 4

BR2 (*KAI* 217), unless there are more in the breakage.[17] The divine symbols here are exactly the same as those of Kulamuwa (and in the same order), except for the addition of a double-circled star located underneath the winged sun disk. Thus with regard to divinity, Gilibert's comments about Bar Rakib consciously echoing and elaborating on Kulamuwa's century-old heritage ring true.

Scholars are divided about the identity of the deity symbolized by the elaboration of the double-circled star, and often note how the symbol is without par-

17 Cf. Yigael Yadin, "Symbols of Deities at Zinjirli, Carthage and Hazor," in *Near Eastern Archaeology in the Twentieth Century*, ed. James A. Sanders (Garden City, NY: Doubleday, 1970), here 209, fig. 6.

allel.[18] Nominations include Rakib-El,[19] Rashap,[20] and Ishtar.[21] The correlation with Rakib-El is unlikely and has few if any modern advocates. It was based on a false premise that visual portrayals must align with textual portrayals. Tropper nominated Rashap due to how Venus was personified by the North-Arabian-Palmyrene god Ruḍâ/ʾArṣu (cf. ʾArqû-Rashap in *KAI* 214.11[22]), an identification that Novak finds unconvincing.[23] In contrast to those who bemoan any parallels, an iconographic analogue is found on an Egyptian cylinder seal depicting a militarized anthropomorphic Reshep with his shield and spear together with a double-circled five-pointed star [**Figure 12.7**].[24]

Ishtar is especially attractive for a deity represented by a star symbol. There is overwhelming evidence of Neo-Assyrian Ishtar portrayed with star symbols (with six or eight points), notably on royal stelae in conjunction with other divine symbols, three of which are common at Zincirli (horned helmet, winged disk, lunar symbol) [**Figure 12.8**].[25] Neo-Assyrian imagery also includes the so-called "encircled Ishtar" motif where an anthropomorphic Ishtar (surrounded

---

18 See Tropper, *Die Inschriften von Zincirli*, 26. Marian Feldman (personal communication) has astutely pointed out how the double circled star is not carved in as high a relief as the rest of the symbols, and it appears squished in its placement, unlike the other symbols. She wonders if this symbol is a later addition. The ramifications of this probing are tantalizing. If the star is secondary, then we have an even gnarlier situation that mimics similar dilemmas with secondary additions in textual criticism: Who added it and why? Could it be the sculptor who is self-correcting his mistake in omitting it the first time around? A supervisor who noticed the error? Or is it ideological in nature, added by either Bar Rakib or someone else who wanted it there for a particular emphasis?

19 See R.D. Barnett, "The Gods of Zincirli," *Compte Rendu de l'Onzième Rencontre Assyriologique Internationale* 11 (1964): 68, 76–79; Yadin, "Symbols of Deities at Zinjirli," 207, 212.

20 See Tropper, *Die Inschriften von Zincirli*, 26; Dominik Bonatz, "The Iconography of Religion in the Hittite, Luwian, and Aramaean Kingdoms," in *Iconography of Deities and Demons in the Ancient Near East* (2007), http://www.religionswissenschaft.uzh.ch/idd/prepublication.php; and Younger, "Gods at the Gates," 334.

21 See Mirko Novak, "Die Religionspolitik der aramäischen Fürstentümer im 1. Jahrtausend v. Chr.," in *Offizielle Religion, lokale Kulte und individuelle Religiosität*, ed. Manfred Hutter and Sylvia Hutter-Braunsar (Münster: Ugarit-Verlag, 2004), 331 n. 29; Herbert Niehr, "Rakib-El," in *Iconography of Deities and Demons in the Ancient Near East* (2008), http://www.religionswissenschaft.uzh.ch/idd/prepublication.php; and Bonatz, "The Iconography of Religion in the Hittite, Luwian, and Aramaean Kingdoms," 15.

22 See Edward Lipiński, *The Aramaeans: Their Ancient History, Culture, Religion* (Leuven: Peeters, 2000), 617–620; William J. Fulco, *The Canaanite God Rešep* (New Haven, CT: American Oriental Society, 1976), 45–46.

23 See Tropper, *Die Inschriften von Zincirli*, 26; and Novak, "Die Religionspolitik," 331 n. 29.

24 See Othmar Keel, Menakhem Shuval, and Christoph Uehlinger, *Studien zu den Stempelsiegeln aus Palästina/Israel III* (Fribourg: Universitätsverlag, 1990), 302–303, fig. 65; Izak Cornelius, *The Iconography of the Canaanite Gods Reshef and Baal: Late Bronze and Iron Age I Periods (c. 1500–1000 BCE)* (Fribourg: Academic Press, 1994), 94–95, fig. RM6.

25 See Ornan, *The Triumph of the Symbol*, 271–273, 277.

FIGURE 12.7 An Egyptian cylinder seal depicting a militarized anthropomorphic Reshep with his shield and spear together with a double circled five-pointed star. Hugo Prinz, *Altorientalische Symbolik* (Berlin: K. Curtius, 1915), 130; Taf. 12,2

by multiple stars) is shown sometimes standing and other times riding on a lion [**Figure 12.9**].[26] Such portrayals of the latter include seven silver medallions of Ishtar (/Astarte?) found at Zincirli [**Figure 12.10**].[27] Of particular note for the

26 Othmar Keel and Christoph Uehlinger, *Gods, Goddesses, and Images of God in Ancient Israel* (Minneapolis, MN: Fortress, 1998), 294–297, 320–323; Tallay Ornan, "The Bull and Its Two Masters: Moon and Storm Deities in Relation to the Bull in Ancient Near Eastern Art," *IEJ* 51 (2001): 1–26; Ornan, *The Triumph of the Symbol*, 151–152 and *passim*; Tallay Ornan, "The Lady and the Bull: Remarks on the Bronze Plaque from Tel Dan," in *Essays on Ancient Israel in Its Near Eastern Context: A Tribute to Nadav Na'aman*, ed. Yairah Amit, Ehud Ben Zvi, Israel Finkelstein, and Oded Lipschits (Winona Lake, IN: Eisenbrauns, 2006), 302.

27 See Felix von Luschan, *Die Kleinfunde von Sendschirli in Ausgrabungen in Sendschirli V*, ed. Walter Andrae, Mitteilungen aus den Orientalischen Sammlungen 15 (Berlin: de Gruyter, 1943), Tafel figs. 44a–e, 46 a–e; Herbert Niehr, "The Religion of the Aramaeans in the West: The Case of Sam'al," in *Arameans, Chaldeans, and Arabs in Babylonia and Palestine in the First Millennium B.C.*, ed. Angelika Berlejung and Michael P. Streck (Wiesbaden: Harrassowitz, 2013), 198 fig. 5; Herbert Niehr, "Religion," in *The Aramaeans in Ancient Syria*, ed. Herbert Niehr (Leiden: Brill, 2014), 164; Izak Cornelius, "In Search of the Goddesses of Zincirli (Sam'al)," *ZDPV* 128 (2012): 19–21.

FIGURE 12.8 An eight-pointed star symbol on a royal stele from Assurnaṣirpal II's stele from Nimrud in conjunction with other divine symbols, three of which are common at Zincirli (horned helmet, winged disk, lunar symbol). D.J. Wiseman, "A New Stela of Aššur-naṣir-pal II," *Iraq* 14.1 (1952) Plate VII
REPRODUCED WITH PERMISSION

FIGURE 12.9 An anthropomorphic Ishtar (surrounded by multiple stars) known as the "encircled Ishtar" motif. Jeremy Black, Anthony Green and Tessa Rickards, *Gods, Demons and Symbols of Ancient Mesopotamia: An Illustrated Dictionary* (London: British Museum Press, 1992), 108, fig. 87
COURTESY THE TRUSTEES OF THE BRITISH MUSEUM AND THE BRITISH MUSEUM PRESS

present study is that Ishtar is almost never associated with a five-pointed star within our comprehensive dataset.[28] Thus of these two nominees, one would lean toward the encircled five-pointed star as a symbol of Rashap. Yet the dominant Neo-Assyrian motif of an Ishtar star together with the horned helmet, winged disk, lunar symbol begs for a more nuanced assessment of what is going

28 Ornan notes a single example of a "provincial" five-pointed star from Hasanlu in northwest Iran described by Marcus as "irregular." See Ornan, *The Triumph of the Symbol*, 151 n. 459; Michelle I. Marcus, "Centre, Province and Periphery: A New Paradigm from Iron-Age Iran," *Art History* 13/2 (1990): 136–137, fig. 4.

FIGURE 12.10 One of seven silver medallions of Ishtar (/Astarte?) found at Zincirli
COURTESY OSAMA SHUKIR MUHAMMEDAMIN FRCP (GLASGOW) (CC BY-SA 4.0) WIKIMEDIA COMMONS FILE: SILVER PENDANT, DEVOTEE BEFORE ISHTAR, WORSHIP SCENE. 9TH–7TH CENTURY BCE. FROM SAM'AL, TURKEY. PERGAMON MUSEUM.JPG

on at Zincirli. Perhaps we should posit that our creative Zincirlian artist is morphing a well-known Ishtar motif into one of Rashap. To balance this, perhaps the addition of a rosette inside the winged sun disk could be "alluding to a female deity" (i.e., Ishtar).[29]

29 Ornan, *The Triumph of the Symbol*, 152.

The five-pointed star draws the ancient and modern viewer's attention precisely because of its rarity. Is it a coincidence that Zincirli has several fivefold representations of divinity, itself a rarity in the ancient Near East?[30] Rashap is among the fivefold presentation of divinity depicted by Bar Rakib's great grandfather, Panamuwa I in *KAI* 214. Bar Rakib with his five symbols would be following in this local tradition—though with a noticeable change: the swapping out of the Aramean god El in favor of the Neo-Assyrian god Sin (or his local representation Śahr). Here he would be following in the footsteps of Kulamuwa who also portrays the moon symbol. As noted above, Bar Rakib's visual presentation of divinity in BR1 is exactly the same as Kulamuwa's apart from the addition of Rashap/the encircled star.

3.2 *The Textual Narrative of Divinity*

In contrast to the five divine symbols, the textual portrayal of divinity in BR1 (*KAI* 216) is remarkable for its minimalism. The only deity mentioned is the dynastic god (*bʿl byt*) Rakib-El, whom Bar Rakib refers to as "my lord" (*mrʾy rkbʾl*; *KAI* 216.5). The mention of Rakib-El correlates with his divine symbol of a yoke-bar, on display in (its characteristic?) second position, but there is no attempt textually to give even a nod to the other four deities represented visually. Visual and textual narratives have diverse functions and/or audiences and reflect different kinds of literacies. The text narrows the effectual power of divinity to the local god so that Bar Rakib can accentuate the agency of Tiglath-pileser III whom he also calls "my lord" (*mrʾy tgltplysr*). The royal legitimation function is blatant, as Bar Rakib mentions both his dynastic god and the Neo-Assyrian king as his "lords" who are responsible for putting him on the throne of his father (*hwšbny mrʾy rkbʾl wmrʾy tgltplysr ʿl krsʾ ʾby*; lines 5–7). In so doing, Bar Rakib is following the precedent he set at the outset of his reign in *KAI* 215, when he praised Tiglath-pileser III for putting his father Panamuwa II on his grandfather Bar Sur's throne (*mlk ʾšwr wmlkh ʿl byt ʾbh*, *KAI* 215.7) and then doing the very same for himself (*hwšbny mrʾ[y tgltplsr mlk ʾš̌r ʿl mwṯb] ʾby pnmw br brṣr*; *KAI* 215.19b–20). Clearly, Bar Rakib frames his two lords, Rakib-El and Tiglath-pileser III, as working in tandem to secure and promote the dynasty.

30 Exceptions include the Tel Dan clusters of five standing stones that could betray Aramean influence. See Theodore J. Lewis, *The Origin and Character of God: Ancient Israelite Religion through the Lens of Divinity* (New York, NY: Oxford University Press, 2020), 187–192.

4 Bar Rakib's Portrayal of Divinity on BR2/*KAI* 217

BR2 [**Figure 12.11**] is a fragment of a much larger banquet scene. Joachim Voos's reconstruction of yet another banquet scene (**Figure 12.12**; Gilibert Zinjirli 69)[31] helps us to imagine the grandeur of the originals and the underlying elaborate royal occasions where, according to Gilibert, "the king was at the centre of the activities taking place ... [which] had an official character that was governed by court protocol. In fact, the scenes depicted on the orthostats may very well be a concrete representation of what occurred in the portico of Hilani IV, where the enthroned king [Bar Rakib] may have dealt with royal affairs and staged ceremonial banquets."[32]

4.1 *The Visual Narrative of Divinity*

Once again, it is likely that we have a fivefold representation of divinity [**Figure 12.13**], though Yadin reconstructs a sixth (lunar) symbol.[33] Three of the five symbols (Hadad's horned helmet, Rakib-El's yoke-bar, and likely the Aramean Shamsh's winged disk) are what we would expect from what we have seen above. Yet two differences are striking: an additional, slightly variant portrayal of the yoke-bar (underscoring the prominence of Rakib-El yet again); and a double-faced symbol (with the two faces facing in opposite directions) that is regularly referred to anachronistically as a "Janus" symbol known from Roman religion.[34] The long-standing consensus is that the janiform symbol represents the deity El. No other deity has found support apart from Usmu (Isimud), a lesser deity who functioned as a minister of Enki/Ea and who is attested, according to Lambert, "from late Early Dynastic to Late Assyrian times."[35] Bossert sees his presence at Zincirli due to Hittite mediation.[36]

The strength of the El nomination lies in large part due to his presence in Panamuwa I's inscription (*KAI* 214), where El is attested four times within a five-

---

31 See Voos, "Zu einigen späthethitischen Reliefs."

32 Gilibert, *Syro-Hittite Monumental Art*, 87.

33 Yadin, "Symbols of Deities at Zinjirli," 209 fig. 6.

34 Brandl reconstructs a janiform head on the Ördekburnu inscription, though this is quite uncertain. See Baruch Brandl, "Rakib ʾil and 'Kubaba of Aram' at Ördekburnu and Zincirli and New Observations on Kubaba at Zincirli, Carchemish and Ugarit," in *Alphabets, Texts and Artifacts in the Ancient Near East: Studies Presented to Benjamin Sass*, ed. I. Finkelstein, C. Robin, and T. Römer (Paris: Van Dieren, 2016), 47–61.

35 W.G. Lambert, "Isimu (Philologish)," *RlA* 5 (1976–1980): 179. See too R.M. Boehmer, "Isimu (In der Bildkunst)," *RlA* 5 (1976–1980): 179–181.

36 Helmuth Th. Bossert, *Janus und der Mann mit der Adler- oder Greifenmaske* (Istanbul: Nederlands Historisch-Archaeologisch Instituut in het Nabije Oosten, 1959), 103.

FIGURE 12.11 A fragment depicting Bar Rakib in a banquet context together with 5 divine symbols (BR2), and an inscription written in Old Aramaic (KAI 217) and carved in raised script
COURTESY RICHARD MORTEL (CC BY-SA 2.0) WIKIMEDIA COMMONS FILE: RELIEF FROM THE CITADEL OF SAM'AL (ZINCIRLI) IN TURKEY, CA. 730 BCE; PERGAMON MUSEUM, BERLIN (3) (40208720312).JPG

fold group of deities: Hadad, El, Rakib-El, Shamash, and Rashap. The order here is the preferred order in three of the four occurrences (see above). In all four references, El is always in the second position, as he is in the iconography here with the janiform head following after Hadad's horned helmet (reading right to left, proceeding away from the king's image). Indeed, if the janiform head depicts El, the visual narrative here (Hadad's horned helmet, El's double face, Rakib-El's yoke-bar, Shamash's winged disk, and Rakib-El's yoke-bar) exactly matches the preferred order of Panamuwa I's inscription apart from the last symbol, where the second yoke-bar reemphasizes Rakib-El in place of Rashap. A second datum used to support the janiform head symbolizing El is a reference to Kronos (El) in Philo of Byblos (Eusebius, *Preparatio Evangelica*, 36c).[37] Philo

37 See H. Donner, "Ein Orthostatenfragment des König Barrakab von Sam'al," *MIOF* 3 (1955): 81–82; R.D. Barnett, "The Gods of Zincirli," 72–73.

FIGURE 12.12 Joachim Voos's reconstruction of yet another Bar Rakib banquet scene at Zincirli. Joachim Voos, "Zu einigen späthethitischen Reliefs aus den Beständen des Vorderasiatischen Museums Berlin," *Altorientalische Forschungen* 12 (1985): 65–86

mentions that the god Taautos (Egyptian Thoth) "invented as royal emblems for Kronos [El] four eyes, on the front and in the rear, ⟨two awake,⟩ and two closed restfully; and upon the shoulders, four wings, two as if fluttering and two as relaxed. This a symbol, since Kronos [El] was watchful even when in repose, and was in repose even when awake … in addition, he also had two wings on his head, one for the mind, which is the supreme authority, and one for the faculty of perception."[38] Using Philo of Byblos presents notorious methodological problems.[39] Scholars understandably turn to this reference out of desperation and it may offer some qualified support.

38 Harold W. Attridge and Robert A. Oden, *Philo of Byblos: The Phoenician History*. (Washington, DC: The Catholic Biblical Association of America, 1981), 56–59.

39 See Lewis, *The Origin and Character of God*, 87, 255–256.

FIGURE 12.13 A close-up of Figure 12.11 showing the five divine symbols represented on the fragmentary Bar Rakib orthostat (BR2)

4.2 *The Textual Narrative of Divinity*

The textual portrayal of divinity in BR2 is similar to that of BR1, in that Bar Rakib highlights the dynastic god Rakib-El and the Neo-Assyrian monarch Tiglath-pileser III. Here he draws attention to his role as their "servant" (*ʿbd,* lines 1–2). Rakib-El's presence is certain in lines 7b–8a and restored by most scholars in line 2.[40] As with BR1, the text mentions no other individual deity besides Rakib-El. Bar Rakib frequently calls Tiglath-pileser III "my lord" (*mrʾy,* lines 4, [4], [5], 8; cf. *mrʾ* in line 2), though not Rakib-El (as he does in BR1). Consider, too, how he notes his "right conduct" (*ṣdq*) with Tiglath-pileser III and his imperial representatives (⌜*ṣ*⌝[*dq . ʾnh . ʿm . m*] *rʾy . wʿm . ʿbdy . by*⌜*t*⌝ [*. mrʾy . mlk . ʾšwr*]; lines 3b–4). Such behavior, together with that of his sons, mark their superior fidelity in comparison with other vassal kings. Dual dynasties are in focus with Bar Rakib's closing line where he appeals to his dynastic god (Rakib-El) for favor not only with Tiglath-pileser III but also with his sons.[41]

The only other mention of divinity is the corporate "the gods of the house of my father" (*ʾlhy byt ʾby*) that occurs in line 3 immediately after the likely restoration of Rakib-El, known elsewhere as the god of the dynastic house (*bʿl byt*). The plural expression here is reminiscent of the singular *ʾlh ʾbh* "the god of his father" in *KAI* 214.29. In that text, the referent could be either one's deified ancestor or the patron god of one's ancestor. In the present text with its plurality and (dynastic) house (*ʾlhy byt ʾby*), the latter is more likely. Bar Rakib does not articulate the gods' names, assuming perhaps that they were well known

40 This is much more likely than other options. For example, Donner ("Ein Orthostatenfragment," 87) prefers Assur and Gibson prefers Hadad. For the latter, see John C.L. Gibson, *Textbook of Syrian Semitic Inscriptions, Volume II: Aramaic Inscriptions including inscriptions in the dialect of Zenjirli* (Oxford: Clarendon, 1975), 92, text number 2.16.

41 Lines 7b–9 read: [*wytn . r*]*kbʾl . ḥny . qd*[*m . mrʾy . tgltplysr . mlk*] *ʾšwr . wqdm . b*[]. Tropper (*Die Inschriften von Zincirli,* 144) presents the following possible reconstructions for the end of this line: *bnwh,* "his sons"; *bny mrʾy,* "the sons of my lord"; *bny mrʾy mlk ʾšwr,* "the sons of my lord, the king of Assyria"; *br mrʾy,* "the son of my lord"; *bʿly mrʾy,* "the ministers of my lord."

(cf. the standard five in *KAI* 214) or that his audience would easily see here a reference to local deities termed elsewhere "the gods of Yadiya" (*ʾlhy yʾdy*) or simply "the gods" (*ʾlhy*; *KAI* 215.22–23).

5 Bar Rakib's Portrayal of Divinity on BR3/*KAI* 218

Gilibert describes Bar Rakib's Hilani IV palace as "lavishly decorated" with its multiple orthostats "distinctly cut in a refined style" and originally "painted in strong colours."[42] Of these orthostats, BR3 [**Figure 12.14**] is well known due to its administrative subject matter. Here we have a scribe (sometimes referred to as a "state secretary") with writing tools presenting himself before the enthroned monarch. Behind the king stands an attendant holding a raised feather-fan in his right hand and an unknown object in his left (cf. the similar attendant's objects in BR1). This impressive dolerite orthostat of the enthroned monarch (113 cm high × 115 cm wide) is paired with the banqueting orthostat reconstructed by Voos (see above) that may have originally portrayed divine symbols.[43] Gilibert describes the powerful mirroring scene: "Zinjirli 66 shows the king sitting on an Assyrian-style throne while in Zinjirli 69, Barrakib sits on a more elaborated throne of Western Syrian manufacture. These are conspicuous details conveying a subtext about Barrakib's royalty that for the contemporary beholder would resonate with meaning."[44]

The visual and textual narratives offer a unified representation of divinity celebrating a single deity. Surprisingly, the deity in focus is not Bar Rakib's dynastic god Rakib-El (a constant in all his other inscriptions) but rather the moon god, here specifically called Baal Harran (*bʿlḥrn*).

The tightly focused, intentional construction is powerfully communicative [**Figure 12.15**]. The raised hands of king and scribe direct the viewer's attention to a lunar symbol that resides in the center top of the overall scene. The lunar symbol is elaborate—a large crescent wrapped around the lower two thirds of a moon disk, situated on a pole with two hanging tassels on each side—not the simpler crescent moon disk we saw above. The image is also centered in the middle of the inscription with the text to the right proclaiming the king's religious allegiance ("My lord is Baal Harran," *mrʾy bʿlḥrn*) and the one on the left his ancestry ("I am Bar Rakib, the son of Panamu[wa]," *ʾnh brrkb. br pnm*[*w*]).

42 Gilibert, *Syro-Hittite Monumental Art*, 87; Zinjirli 66.

43 See Voos, "Zu einigen späthethitischen Reliefs," 84 n. 50; Gilibert, *Syro-Hittite Monumental Art*, Zinjirli 69.

44 Gilibert, *Syro-Hittite Monumental Art*, 86–87.

FIGURE 12.14 An orthostat of an enthroned Bar Rakib that is administrative in nature (note the presence of a scribe before the king) and focuses on the moon god, here specifically called Baal-Harran

COURTESY GARY TODD (CC0 1.0) WIKIMEDIA COMMONS FILE: BASALT STELE BAS-RELIEF OF KING BAR-RAKIB AND HIS SCRIBE, SAM'AL, ANATOLIA, C. 730 BC.JPG

A great deal has been written on the moon god of Harran and the "crescent-on-a-pole" imagery [**Figure 12.16**].[45] Holloway summarizes:

45 See especially Othmar Keel, "Das Mondemblem von Harran auf Stelen und Siegelamuletten und der Kult der nächtlichen Gestirne bei den Aramäern," in *Studien zu den Stempelsiegeln aus Palästina/Israel IV* (Fribourg: Universitätsverlag, 1994), 135–202; Ornan, *The Triumph of the Symbol*, 163–167; Thomas Staubli, "Sin von Harran und seine Verbreitung im Westen," in *Werbung für die Götter*, ed. Thomas Staubli (Fribourg: Universitätsver-

FIGURE 12.15 A close up of Figure 12.14 that shows the centered icon and inscription, both focusing on the mood god of Harran

> The enduring root of the international fame of the cult of the moon god of Ḫarrān, stretching back into the Bronze Age, remains enigmatic. By the Iron Age, Sin of Ḫarrān was singled out for explicit mention in royal Neo-Luwian, Aramaean, and Assyrian inscriptions erected across hundreds of kilometers in Anatolia and North Syria; clearly, all of these kings aggressively sought to capitalize on the power of this local moon god for their own political magnification. The Neo-Assyrians won this contest, and from the time of Sargon II at the latest, Ḫarrān's pantheon assumed a highly visible role in the ideological architecture of Assyrian imperialism in the West.[46]

With regard to iconography, Ornan concludes that "crescents-on-a-pole are age-old religious icons distributed throughout the ancient Near East ... known in the region of Harran in northern Syria during the second millennium ... (becoming) more common at the end of the second millennium, reaching its peak with Assyrian expansion westward, particularly from the second half of the eighth century onwards."[47]

We noted the identity of the moon god at Zincirli above regarding the lunar symbol appearing on the Kulamuwa orthostat and on BR1 (*KAI* 216).[48] Cres-

lag, 2003), 65–90; Steven W. Holloway, *Aššur is King! Aššur is King! Religion in the Exercise of Power in the Neo-Assyrian Empire* (Leiden: Brill, 2002), 388–425, esp. 398 n. 439; Tamara M. Green, *The City of the Moon God: Religious Traditions of Harran* (Leiden: Brill, 1992).

46 Holloway, *Aššur is King! Aššur is King!*, 416–417.

47 Ornan, *The Triumph of the Symbol*, 164–165.

48 See perhaps two flanking moon symbols on the Ördekburnu stele. Yadin also recon-

FIGURE 12.16
An elaborate symbol of the moon god of Harran with a large crescent wrapped around the lower two thirds of a moon disk, situated on a pole with two hanging tassels on each side

cent moon symbols appear as a regular motif on "encircled Ishtar" representations (see **Figure 12.9** above[49]). A crescent standard-top or finial (16 cm wide, 1 m. thick; S 3902) with a long tab, representing some type of ritual performance related to the deity, was found in an indefinite location at Zincirli [**Figure 12.17**].[50]

With regard to our orthostat, we have no way of knowing for certain whether local viewers who could not read the inscription saw the lunar symbol here as a representation of the local Aramean moon god Śahr or the Neo-Assyrian Sin of Harran, or most likely, one and the same as at Nerab.[51] Yet with his inscription, Bar Rakib makes a bold declaration that the moon god to whom he shows allegiance is not a local moon god tied to Yadiya (cf. the "gods of Yadiya" in *KAI* 215), but the moon god of Harran with all of its Neo-Assyrian connections. Niehr perceptively notes how, apart from our inscription, "the moon-god of Harran is never mentioned" in the entire corpus of inscriptions from Zincirli, currently twenty-three in number.[52] Thus Bar Rakib's usage is telling.

structed a lunar symbol for BR2 (*KAI* 217). See Yadin, "Symbols of Deities at Zinjirli," 209 fig. 6.

49 See above n. 26.

50 See Luschan, *Die Kleinfunde von Sendschirli*, 105, Tafel fig. 48z.

51 The two early seventh-century BCE Nerab mortuary stelae describe two priests who bear the Neo-Assyrian moon god Sin in their names (Sinzeribni, Si'gabbar) but who each self-identify as "priest of (the local Aramean) Śahr" (*KAI* 225.1–2; 226.1). Elsewhere, in the curse sections of their inscriptions, Sinzeribni refers to a quartet of deities (Śahr, Shamash, Nikkal, and Nusk) where Si'gabbar mentions a triad (Śahr, Nikkal, and Nusk), though with Śahr in the lead position. Clearly, these presentations present divinity on a continuum that equates and blends ethnic parameters for sociological and political reasons.

52 Herbert Niehr, "Questions of Text and Image in Ancient Sam'al (Zincirli)," in *Text and Image: Proceedings of the 61e Rencontre Assyriologique Internationale, Geneva and Bern, 22–26 June 2015*, ed. Pascal Attinger, Antoine Cavigneaux, Catherine Mittermayer, and Mirko Novàk (Leuven: Peeters, 2018), 314.

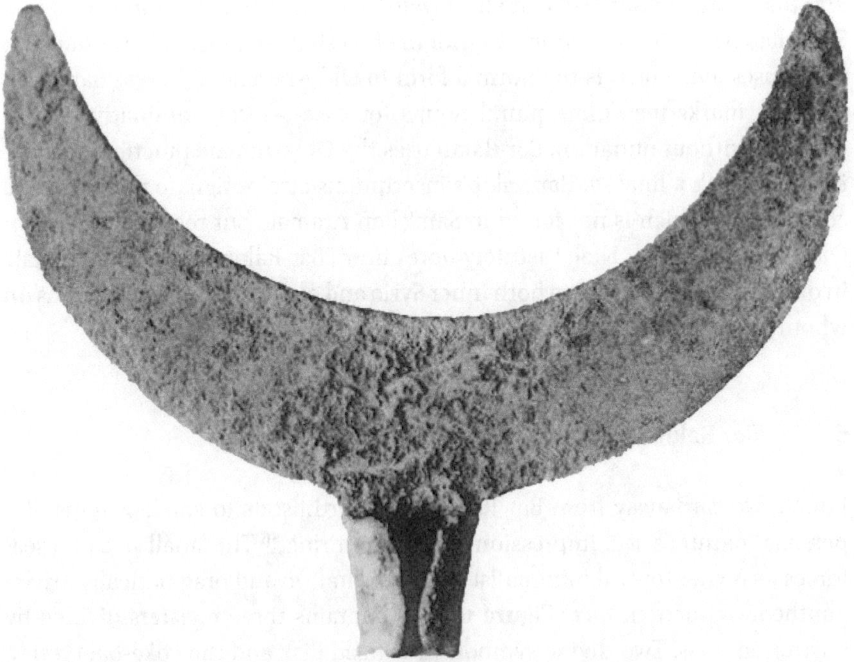

FIGURE 12.17 A crescent standard-top or finial found at Zincirli that represents some type of ritual performance dedicated to the moon god. Felix von Luschan, *Die Kleinfunde von Sendschirli* in *Ausgrabungen in Sendschirli V* (Berlin: de Gruyter, 1943), 105; Tafel fig. 48z

Here Bar Rakib is ideologically embracing Neo-Assyrian divinity. A pro-Assyrian ideology is also behind Bar Rakib's nomenclature where he turns from previously referring to his city as Yadiya, a local preference dating back to Kulamuwa (*KAI* 24.2) to consistently using the toponym Sam'al that is preferred in Akkadian sources.[53] For the former, see Bar Rakib's older inscription linked to his father where he uses Yadiya (*KAI* 215.1, 2, 7, 8, 12, 22) in contrast to his consistent use of the toponym Sam'al in his later inscriptions (*KAI* 216.2–3, 17; 217.1). Noting how Sam'al is not used at Zincirli prior to Bar Rakib, Niehr refers to "the renaming of Yadiya to Sam'al" at this time as a "simultaneous orientation" toward not only the Assyrians but also local Aramean populations.[54]

There are similar political motivations behind Bar Rakib abandoning his local Sam'alian Aramaic dialect (*KAI* 215) in favor of Old Aramaic (*KAI* 216;

53 Younger, *A Political History of the Arameans*, 379.

54 Niehr ("The Power of Language," 325) notes the use of Sam'al in the inscription of Zakkur, King of Hamath and Luʿash (*KAI* 202.7).

217) that would better articulate his loyalty to his Assyrian overlords. Whereas Sam'alian Aramaic uses *ʾnk* and *ʾnky* for the first singular personal pronoun, Bar Rakib uses *ʾnh*, which is the normal form in Old Aramaic. Whereas Sam'alian Aramaic marks masculine plural nouns for case (*-w* for nominative, *-y* for oblique) without nunation, Bar Rakib uses the Old Aramaic practice of marking them with a final *-n*. Bar Rakib's inscriptions also designate the emphatic state with -ʾ, which is not found in Sam'alian Aramaic but regularly occurs in Old Aramaic. Again, Niehr astutely notes how "Bar-Rakib chose Old Aramaic in order to open up a way to both inner Syria and also towards the Assyrians on whom he depended."[55]

6 Bar Rakib's Portrayal of Divinity on His Royal Seals

Finally, we turn away from Bar Rakib's large orthostats to smaller items of a personal nature: a seal impression and a signet ring.[56] The small size of a seal forces its owner toward minimalist self-presentation and pragmatically driven pantheon reduction. BR7 (**Figure 12.18**[57]) contains three registers divided by horizontal lines. Two divine symbols (a winged disk and the yoke-bar) reside in the top register, while the king's name resides underneath in the bottom two registers. The juxtaposition of divinity and monarchy on the same authoritative and administrative seal is telling. When Bar Rakib chose to limit his divine portrayal to two, naturally he would privilege the yoke-bar symbol of his dynastic god Rakib-El. Apart from the ideologically driven BR3/*KAI* 218, Rakib-El is the one constant in all of Bar Rakib's visual and textual presentations. The larger question is, why the sun disk?

Yigael Yadin has suggested that the sun disk here (as a symbol of El) works in tandem with the yoke-bar (as a symbol of Rakkab, the charioteer) to represent Rakib-El.[58] But why would the monarch need two symbols to represent the

55 Niehr, "The Power of Language," 327.

56 Bar Rakib's name appears on three silver ingots but I have left them out of the present study due to no mention of divinity. The ingots and the seal impression all contain the monarch's full name (Bar Rakib, son of Panamuwa) showing the importance of his father's lineage, and an indication of personal ownership.

57 Luschan, *Die Kleinfunde von Sendschirli*, 73–74, 159, Tafel 38b. A photograph can be found in Nahman Avigad and Benjamin Sass, *Corpus of West Semitic Stamp Seals* (Jerusalem: Israel Exploration Society, 1997), 280 #750.

58 Yadin, "Symbols of Deities at Zinjirli," 202–203, 209; cf. Tallay Ornan, "A Complex System of Religious Symbols: The Case of the Winged-Disc in Near Eastern Imagery of the First Millennium BCE," in *Crafts and Images in Contact: Studies on Eastern Mediterranean Art of the*

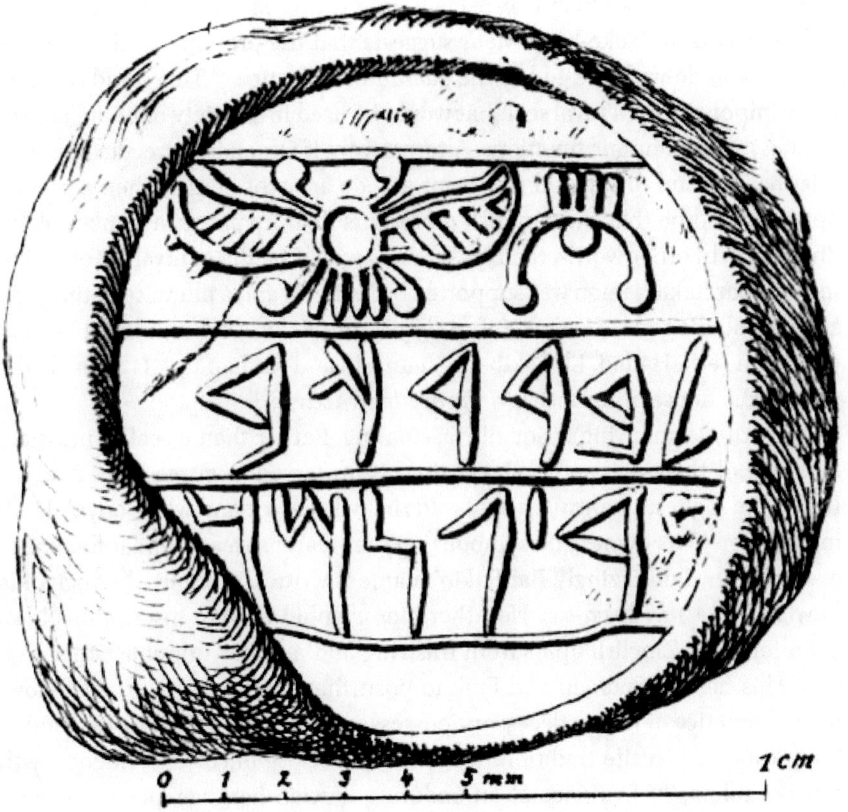

FIGURE 12.18 A seal impression (BR7) mentioning "Bar Rakib, the son of Panamuwa" and two divine symbols. Felix von Luschan, *Die Kleinfunde von Sendschirli* in *Ausgrabungen in Sendschirli V* (Berlin: de Gruyter, 1943), 73–74 159, Tafel 38b

same deity where he uses only one elsewhere? The yoke-bar is the dominant symbol of Rakib-El and its presence alone on Bar Rakib's signet ring is all that would be needed to underscore the king's allegiance to Rakib-El, who stood behind his authority to rule. The presence of the sun disk on BR7 must have an additional function. Two strong options present themselves. The most straightforward would be simply to see Shamsh here. Textually, the god is not privileged elsewhere at Zincirli other than as one of the fivefold pantheon in Panamuwa I's inscription—and even there he is consistently listed in the fourth (even fifth) slot. Visually, two of Bar Rakib's orthostats portray the sun disk (BR1/*KAI* 216;

First Millennium BCE, ed. Claudia E. Suter and Christoph Uehlinger (Fribourg: Academic Press, 2005), 230.

BR2/*KAI* 217). BR2/*KAI* 217 is especially interesting in how it frames the sun disk between two yoke-bars. Niehr suggests that the presence of the sun disk may have to do with the god as the guarantor of justice.[59] This could be especially important for a royal seal that would be used in a variety of political (e.g., treaties) and economic functions. Alternatively, if Ornan is correct in her analysis that the sun disk could represent a wide array of deities, then a second option would be that the sun disk represents divinity per se, a symbol of "all divinity."[60] In other words, the two symbols would be the equivalent of claiming that Bar Rakib's reign was supported by Rakib-El and a plurality of the gods, such as: "all the gods of Yadiya" (cf. *kl ʾlhy yʾdy* in *KAI* 215.2, 22–23); or the fivefold pantheon (e.g., Hadad, El, Rakib-El, Shamash, and Rashap in *KAI* 214); or "the gods of the house of my father" (*ʾlhy byt ʾby*; *KAI* 217).[61]

The other signet ring is equally fascinating. Rather than a seal impression, here one of the king's actual signet rings is preserved (**Figures 12.19–12.20**).[62] It is of the highest quality (a heavy gold ring with black and white onyx), lending prestige to its owner and symbolizing the wearer's wealth and influence to every viewer. Tantalizingly, Bar Rakib's name is written in cursive hieroglyphic Luwian (*pa + ra/i-ki-pa-sa*). No other hieroglyphic Luwian inscriptions have been found at Zinclirli apart from this ring and another unpublished stamp seal. This has led Schloen and Fink to posit that "Barrakib, no doubt following the practice of his predecessors, possessed a Luwian signet ring in a nod to the prestigious Hittite tradition (and perhaps for use in correspondence with Luwian rulers)."[63] Evidence of an enduring Luwian heritage, preserved onomastically and locally, suggests that the king could have worn the ring for a variety of local occasions including ceremonial rituals as well as legal and economic transactions.[64]

59 Niehr, "Questions of Text and Image," 312–313.

60 See Ornan, "A Complex System of Religious Symbols," 227–235.

61 A third less likely option, again building on Ornan's research, would be to see the sun disk here representing yet another major god. If Bar Rakib were to choose a second major god in addition to the dynastic god Rakib-El, surely Hadad would be the obvious choice from what we have seen above. Yet the enduring and consistent use of the horned helmet for Hadad at Zincilri (a century-long tradition) is secure and thus he cannot be in mind.

62 J.D. Hawkins, *Inscriptions of the Iron Age*, vol. 1 of *Corpus of Hieroglyphic Luwian Inscriptions* (Berlin: de Gruyter, 2000), 576, pl. 329 = Luschan, *Die Kleinfunde von Sendschirli*, Plate 45l (drawing) and Plate 47i (photograph).

63 J. David Schloen and Amir S. Fink, "New Excavations at Zincirli Höyük in Turkey (Ancient Sam'al) and the Discovery of an Inscribed Mortuary Stele," *BASOR* 356 (2009): 10.

64 Cf. Virginia R. Herrmann, "Cosmopolitan Politics in the Neo-Assyrian Empire: Local Elite Identity at Zincirli-Sam'al," *Sem* 60 (2018): 517. For onomastica, we have the names Kula-

7 Summary

During a very brief period (ca. 733–727 BCE), Bar Rakib marshalled political and economic resources, first to secure the throne against a backdrop of regicide, usurpation, economic devastation, the death of his father on the battlefield, and Assyrian vassalage;[65] and then to cement his reign that would continue for two decades. His visual and textual portrayals of divinity reveal how the gods were perceived as actively engaging in every aspect of royal life: installing the king on the throne; preserving an ongoing dynasty from internal and external threats; rebuilding a shattered economy; building a magnificent palace; administering with justice; securing favor with local constituencies and foreign powers; and banqueting, both in this life and the hereafter.

Bar Rakib's portrayals of divinity also provide windows into his art of persuasion and manipulation for a variety of audiences. Overall, Bar Rakib presents a fluid portrayal of divinity that changes depending on his audience. This in itself is quite telling. Though he shows a strong allegiance to Rakib-El, the dynastic deity, he is not wedded solely to this deity if the pragmatics of a situation demand otherwise. He is respectful of inherited traditions, though at the same time can break quite radically from these traditions.

For visual representation, Bar Rakib always uses symbols to represent divinity, and here he follows in the footsteps of Kulamuwa, who preceded him by

---

muwa, Qarali, Panamuwa I, Panamuwa II, and Katumuwa. For local presence, see Hermann's urban social network theory and the divine profile of the Katumuwa Stele.

Three of the five deities mentioned in the Katumuwa Stele are Luwian, not Semitic. These include Hadad Qarpatalli, Hadad of the Vineyards, and Kubaba (spelled curiously with a final *w*). On Hadad Qarpatalli, see Herrmann, "Cosmopolitan Politics," 515; Dennis Pardee, "The KTMW Inscription," *COS* 4.23 (95 n. 6); and Seth L. Sanders, "The Appetites of the Dead: West Semitic Linguistic and Ritual Aspects of the Katumuwa Stele," *BASOR* 369 (2013): 35–55 (here 44–45). Several scholars posit that Hadad of the Vineyards is the local equivalent of "Tarhunza of the Vineyards"; see, for example, Dennis Pardee "A New Aramaic Inscription from Zincirli," *BASOR* 356 (2009): 62; Younger, "Gods at the Gates," 321.

The nature of the god *ngd/r ṣwd/rn* is complicated due to epigraphically ambiguous readings of either *d* or *r*. See Pardee, "A New Aramaic Inscription," 54–56. Several scholars see a reference to a local (West Semitic) deity, "he who is in charge of provisions" (*ngd ṣwd/rn*). See Pardee "A New Aramaic Inscription," 61; Sanders, "The Appetites of the Dead," 45. In contrast, Fales and Grassi translate "l'Ufficiale (?) della cacce" (*ngd ṣwdn*) with Runtiya/Runzas in mind. See Frederick Mario Fales and Giulia Francesca Grassi, *L'aramaico antico: Storia, grammatica, testi commentate* (Udine: Forum, 2016), 205, 208; cf. Younger, "Gods at the Gates," 332–333. See too Émilia Masson ("La stèle mortuaire de Kuttamuwa [Zincirli]: Comment l'appréhender," *Semitica et Classica* 3 [2010]: 52–53) who sees a reference to Nikarawas/Nikaruhas of hunters (reading *ngr ṣwdn*).

65 See Lewis, "Bar Rakib's Legitimation and the Problem of a Missing Corpse."

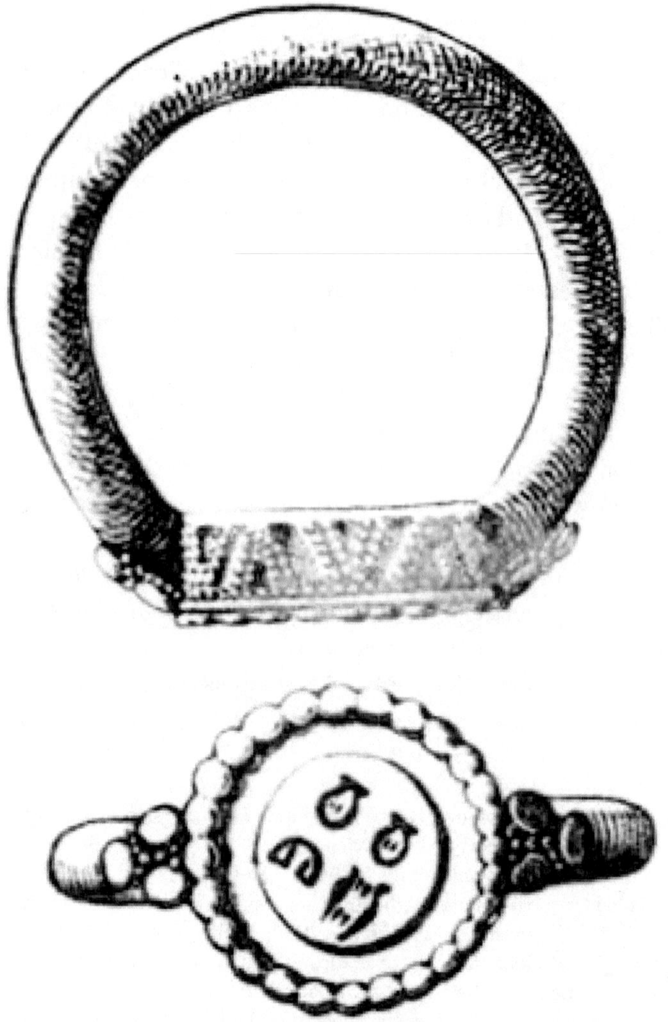

FIGURE 12.19 A gold signet ring with black and white onyx containing Bar Rakib's name written in cursive hieroglyphic Luwian. Felix von Luschan, *Die Kleinfunde von Sendschirli* in *Ausgrabungen in Sendschirli V* (Berlin: de Gruyter, 1943), Plate 45l

FIGURE 12.20 A photograph of Bar Rakib's signet ring depicted in the line drawing of Figure 12.19. Felix von Luschan, *Die Kleinfunde von Sendschirli in Ausgrabungen in Sendschirli* V (Berlin: de Gruyter, 1943), Plate 47i.

more than a century and who himself was indebted to Neo-Assyrian models. Of these symbols, three show a preference toward an astralization of divinity (winged sun disk, lunar symbol, encircled star) to which one could add the multiple stars encircling Ishtar on the various pendants found at Zincirli. For a contrast to Bar Rakib's preference for symbols, elsewhere at Zincirli we have the following anthropomorphic images: (a) the anthropomorphic Hadad Inscription of Bar Rakib's great grandfather Panamuwa I; (b) the many anthropomorphic figures found at the Southern City Gate and the Outer Citadel Gate (D); (c) the anthropomorphic "encircled Ishtar" pendants; (d) the bronze fan/crescent shaped object (of a chariot pole?) with a nude "mistress of animals";[66] and (e) the naked female on a horse frontlet.[67] Bar Rakib's only concession to anthropomorphism is the two-faced janiform symbol in BR2.

Theriomorphic representations of divinity are also nonexistent in Bar Rakib's portrayal of divinity, apart from the bull horns on the helmet, symbols for the god Hadad that could be some type of a concession to a theriomorphic heritage. This rarity stands in contrast to plethora of theriomorphic images elsewhere at Zincirli, including: (a) the attendant lion on which the "encir-

66 See Cornelius, "In Search of the Goddesses," 19–20, fig. 3.
67 See Cornelius, "In Search of the Goddesses," 17–18, fig. 2.

cled Ishtar" rides; (b) the lions associated with the (divine?) ancestor Gabbar;[68] (c) the numerous theriomorphic images (especially portal lions and hunting scenes) of the Southern City Gate, the Outer Citadel Gate, the Lion's Pit and Gate Q;[69] and again (d) the "mistress of animals" noted above.

As for quantity, at times Bar Rakib displays a preference for divine singularity. He consistently shows a strong allegiance to the dynastic god Rakib-El (*bʿl byt*) in both visual (the yoke-bar in BR1, and twice in BR2) and textual representations (*KAI* 215.22–23; BR1/*KAI* 216.5; BR2/*KAI* 217.[1,] 7–9). With this allegiance to the god of his fathers (*ʾlh ʾbh, ʾlhy byt ʾby*) he honors the Rakib-El worship of his royal predecessors Kulamuwa, Panamuwa I, and Panamuwa II. At the same time, Bar Rakib can highlight a single local Aramean god (Hadad) for standing with his father Panamuwa II (*KAI* 215.2) in line with the Hadad-centrism of Panamuwa I. At yet other times, Bar Rakib looks politically to the east with his singular focus on Baal Harran, whom he highlights materially by erecting the impressive orthostat BR3 in his royal palace (Hilani IV).

Bar Rakib is henotheistic, as his allegiance to a single deity is not threatened by expressing homage to other deities. When it comes to divine plurality, Bar Rakib's seal impression shows the monarch's use of a dual image, either combining his dynastic god with Shamsh, the guarantor of justice, or with a symbol for all divinity. Several scholars feel the data may point to a triad of divinity, though the constituent members differ among scholars. For example, Lipiński has El, Rakib-El, and Shamsh whereas Ornan prefers Hadad, El, and Rakib-El.[70] In the end, there is no explicit evidence of a divine triad either textually or visually apart from King Kulamwua's curse that involves Baal Semed, Baal Hammon, and Rakib-El (*KAI* 24). There is but one example of a fourfold cluster (Kulamuwa's visual display). Noticeably, there is repeated evidence of a fivefold cluster of divinity at Zincirli including King Panamuwa I's textual expression of an Aramean cluster (Hadad, El, Rakib-El, Shamsh, and Rashap in *KAI* 214) that should be juxtaposed with the nonroyal Luwian-dominant cluster of Kutamuwa's inscription (Hadad Qarpatalli, *ngd/r ṣwd/rn*, Shamash, Hadad of the Vineyards, and Kubaba).

Here, Bar Rakib demonstrates both his respect for tradition and his political savviness in breaking from it. As we saw with BR1/*KAI* 216, Bar Rakib's fivefold visual cluster of images contains the exact four of Kulamuwa (and in the same order) to which he adds a rare double-circled five-pointed star, highlighting, seemingly, Rashap. It is of some note that Panamuwa I also singled out Rashap

68 See Gilibert, *Syro-Hittite Monumental Art*, 76–79, 211, fig. 63.

69 See Gilibert, *Syro-Hittite Monumental Art*, 58–79.

70 Lipiński, *The Aramaeans*, 614–615; Ornan, "A Complex System of Religious Symbols," 231.

for attention in his Hadad-centric inscription (*KAI* 214.3). In BR2 Bar Rakib has yet another fivefold visual cluster, this time breaking with tradition by adding in a dual symbol for his preferred Rakib-El as well as a unique janiform double-face symbol, probably of the god El. Textually, Bar Rakib has a fivefold cluster in his inscription for his father, and here too he innovates with the addition of "all the gods of Yadiya" (*wkl ʾlhy yʾdy*) in slot number 5—seemingly replacing Rashap (if *KAI* 214 is used as a model).

As for gendering divinity, Bar Rakib is male-centric if we consider Zincirlian Shamsh as masculine.[71] Apart from two possible visuals in BR1—the double-circled five-pointed star if Ishtar and not Rashap, and the rosette with the sun disk—Bar Rakib only references male divinity in his visuals and his textual representations. Had the king wanted explicitly to invoke Ishtar, he could have used her dominant six or eight-pointed star. Note how his personal seal does not contain the rosette within its sun disk. All of this is surprising when we know definitively of the cult of Ishtar, Kubaba, and the "mistress of animals" elsewhere at the site. Yet here too with his male-centrism, Bar Rakib seems to be following his predecessors, Kulamuwa, Panamuwa I, and Panamuwa II. Goddesses must have been included in the generic references to the "gods" or "all the gods" or "the gods of Yadiya." And perhaps Bar Rakib wore an "encircled Ishtar" medallion around his neck. Yet the explicit data we have to work with is that of a male-gendered portrayal of divinity.

We come now to Bar Rakib's internal and external audiences. The ability to read Bar Rakib's Sam'alian Aramaic (*KAI* 215) and Old Aramaic (*KAI* 216–221) inscriptions would be restricted to a small but prestigious class of local and Neo-Assyrian scribes and educated officials including kings, viziers, and ambassadors, with whom they worked. Bar Rakib explicitly refers to his proper conduct with the imperial representatives, or "servants of the house" (*ʿbdy byt*) of Tiglath-pileser III in *KAI* 217.4. The palace context would imply that the majority of viewers of his visual narrative would be elite officials and visiting dignitaries, though open reception/ceremonial spaces could entertain groups from Yadiya/Sam'al at large. We see from the Katumuwa Stele that an elite official from a social class with a differing cultural matrix worked within his father's

71 Cf. masculine Mesopotamian Shamash and Hebrew Shemesh in contrast to the feminine Shapshu at Ugarit. See Edward Lipiński, *Studies in Aramaic Inscriptions and Onomastics II* (Leuven: Peeters, 1994), 207. Ornan ("A Complex System of Religious Symbols," 227) considers "the possibility that the [winged sun disk] symbol transcended gender boundaries and could have referred to both male and female deities." Note how there is a much larger presentation of male figures (23) over female figures (3) among the images attested at Zincirli's Outer Citadel Gate. See Gilibert, *Syro-Hittite Monumental Art*, 65.

administration. Certain legal and economic functions could also bring members of the society at large into royal space.

For local consumption, Bar Rakib astutely includes an overwhelming representation of both the dynastic god Rakib-El and a good assortment of Aramean gods, five of whom are named (Hadad, El, Shamsh, Śahr, Rashap) and others who are explicitly referred to as "the gods of Yadiya" (*ʾlhy yʾdy*; note: *not* the gods of Samʾal) or as ancestral gods (*ʾlh ʾbh, ʾlhy byt ʾby*). Ethnically, though "the art and pantheon of Samʾal exhibit numerous Luwian links,"[72] Bar Rakib shows a clear preference for Aramean over Luwian. His Aramean name contrasts with the Luwian names of Kulamuwa, his great grandfather Panamuwa I, and his father Panamuwa II. Bar Rakib did possess an expensive signet with his name carved in hieroglyphic Luwian, perhaps as a purely antiquarian prestige item but more likely for transactional purposes with those constituents, at Zincirli and regional polities, with a Luwian heritage. Despite this, he felt no need to include Luwian divinity on this signet ring nor on any of his orthostats. Compare the Aramean divine symbols on his other seal, and contrast the way in which Katumuwa inscribes four Luwian deities on his stela, not to mention the numerous Luwian divine portrayals at the Outer Citadel Gate.[73]

For external consumption, Bar Rakib goes out of his way to use his portrayal of divinity to ingratiate favor with the Neo-Assyrians—in particular Tiglath-pileser III but also his sons and his imperial officials (*KAI* 217.3–4, 9)—and to show himself to be a most loyal vassal. For the relevant backstory, Younger sees the year 858 BCE as "a watershed in Samʾal's history" when it "first encountered the expanding Assyrian Empire" in the person of Shalmaneser III. The following years 857 and 853 find records of tribute to the king from "Ḫayānu, the Samʾalian."[74] The next relevant datum comes with Kulamuwa who actively seeks out ("hires") the king of Assyria to fend off the Danunians (*KAI* 24.7b–8a) around the year 839 BCE. Thus, there is little wonder why Kulamuwa wears Assyrian attire and showcases the four divine symbols with their Aramean/Assyrian divinity hybridity. Though Bar Rakib's great-grandfather Panamuwa I reigned over Samʾal during a period of local autonomy, once again his father Panamuwa II had to send tribute to the Assyrian empire for help. It was Tiglath-pileser III who destroyed a violent usurper around the year 743 BCE and placed Panamuwa II on his father's throne (*KAI* 215.6b–7).[75] A decade

72 Younger, *A Political History of the Arameans*, 394.

73 See Gilibert, *Syro-Hittite Monumental Art*, 61–67; Younger, "Gods at the Gates."

74 Younger, *A Political History of the Arameans*, 401.

75 Younger, (*A Political History of the Arameans*, 416) suggests that Tiglath-pileser's intervention on behalf of Panamuwa II in 743 BCE "was likely coordinated" with his putting down the revolt by Mati'-el King of Arpad at the same time.

later, Bar Rakib likewise turned to the Neo-Assyrians to secure his throne in 733/732 BCE, and it was his vassalage to the Neo-Assyrians that allowed him to reign and prosper for the next two decades (to 713/711 BCE).

Bar Rakib uses Neo-Assyrian textual rhetoric to describe Tiglath-pileser III as "lord of the four quarters of the earth" (*mrʾ rbʿy ʾrqʾ*; *KAI* 216.3b–4a; 217.2) and to boast of how he, like his father, "ran at the wheel" of the king (*rṣt bglgl mrʾy mlk ʾšwr*; *KAI* 216.8b–9a; 215.[12–]13). Like his father, Bar Rakib behaved with "right conduct" (*ṣdq*) toward his Assyrian overload (*KAI* 216.4–7; 217.3b–7; 215.11, 19; cf. *KAI* 219.4–5). Bar Rakib speaks of his patron Neo-Assyrian monarch with the same language he uses of his patron deity Rakib-El. They are both termed "lord" (*mrʾ*) and they both are responsible for putting Bar Rakib on the throne (*KAI* 216.4b–7a; cf. *KAI* 219.4–5; 215.7, 19). Bar Rakib is a "servant" (*ʿbd*) of Tiglath-pileser III as he is a servant of Rakib-El and his ancestral gods (*KAI* 216.1–4; 217.[1–3]). Bar Rakib ends one of his inscriptions with a special request of Rakib-El: to grant him favor with Tiglath-pileser III and his sons (*KAI* 217.7b–9).

Visually, many scholars have pointed out how Bar Rakib employs Neo-Assyrian stylistic features as did Kulamuwa, especially in his attire. We have already noted Bar Rakib's close copying of Kulamuwa's four divine symbols. Yet Bar Rakib outdoes all previous kings with his bold portrayal of BR3. Here with prominent royal display—correlating the textual and the visual portrayals which are of little or no concern on his other orthostats—he sheds any notion of local divinity in order to favor the moon god of Harran. In his bid to underscore his status as a loyal vassal, he removes any question of Aramean/Assyrian hybridity with his singular devotion toward the moon god of Harran, knowing how this would appeal to Assyrian emissaries who would carry this report of his fidelity back to Tiglath-pileser III.

8 Conclusion: Conservative/Traditional and Innovative Approaches

Bar Rakib is a consummate politician who covers all his bases, locally and abroad. Learning from his predecessors, he knows how to employ both visual and textual narratives of divinity to convey different messages in order to manipulate different audiences. Yet he out-performs his predecessors with what on the surface appears to be the most inconsistent of portrayals. A closer look at the diversity of his approaches shows an unmatched diplomatic skill where his portrayals of divinity are socially, culturally, and politically contingent.

In some ways Bar Rakib is very conservative with the traditions he inherits. He consistently underscores his allegiance to the local god Rakib-El (with textual praise and with the ever-present yoke-bar symbol) knowing that the century-long tradition of this god's support is foundational to his dynastic success. Similarly, he knows the value of showing allegiance to the local "gods of Yadiya" and the god(s) of his ancestors. Third, he knows how the Assyrianization of divinity can work to his favor, especially with the longstanding tradition of using divine symbols that allow for an Aramean/Assyrian syncretism, for example the horned helmet (Hadad-Assur), winged sun disk (Shamsh/Shamash), and lunar symbol (Śahr/Sin) that can allow his constituents to read what they want to see.

At other times, he is boldly innovative. If there was indeed a fivefold fixed canon of divinity, he feels free to adjust it to meet particular needs, especially for local consumption. He boldly uses symbols such as the double-circled star and the janiform head, which are so rare that they must point to particular functions. Though we are hard pressed to articulate what these functions were, they seem to be focused locally (Rashap and El worship). At other times, his bold new moves are externally focused, such as his use of elaborate royal display to embrace Baal Harran alone for when Neo-Assyrian emissaries would visit. At every turn we see in Bar Rakib's diverse portrayal of divinity a monarch's finessing of multiple religious narratives to satisfy the complex demands of his various audiences.

Bibliography

Attridge, Harold W., and Robert A. Oden. *Philo of Byblos: The Phoenician History*. Washington, DC: The Catholic Biblical Association of America, 1981.

Avigad, Nahman, and Benjamin Sass. *Corpus of West Semitic Stamp Seals*. Jerusalem: Israel Exploration Society, 1997.

Barnett, R.D. "The Gods of Zincirli." *Compte Rendu de l'Onzième Rencontre Assyriologique Internationale* 11 (1964): 59–87.

Black, Jeremy, Anthony Green, and Tessa Rickards. *Gods, Demons and Symbols of Ancient Mesopotamia: An Illustrated Dictionary*. London: British Museum Press, 1992.

Boehmer, R.M. "Isimu (In der Bildkunst)." *RlA* 5 (1976–1980): 179–181.

Bonatz, Dominik. "The Iconography of Religion in the Hittite, Luwian, and Aramaean Kingdoms." In *Iconography of Deities and Demons in the Ancient Near East*. 2007. Electronic pre-publication. http://www.religionswissenschaft.uzh.ch/idd/prepublication.php

Bossert, Helmuth Th. *Janus und der Mann mit der Adler- oder Greifenmaske*. Istanbul: Nederlands Historisch-Archaeologisch Instituut in het Nabije Oosten, 1959.

Brandl, Baruch. "Rakib'il and 'Kubaba of Aram' at Ördekburnu and Zincirli and New

Observations on Kubaba at Zincirli, Carchemish and Ugarit." Pages 47–61 in *Alphabets, Texts and Artifacts in the Ancient Near East: Studies Presented to Benjamin Sass*. Edited by I. Finkelstein, C. Robin, and T. Römer. Paris: Van Dieren, 2016.

Cornelius, Izak. *The Iconography of the Canaanite Gods Reshef and Baal: Late Bronze and Iron Age I Periods (c. 1500–1000 BCE)*. Fribourg: Academic Press, 1994.

Cornelius, Izak. "In Search of the Goddesses of Zincirli (Sam'al)." *ZDPV* 128 (2012): 15–25.

Donner, H. "Ein Orthostatenfragment des König Barrakab von Sam'al." *MIOF* 3 (1955): 73–98.

Donner, Herbert, and Wolfgang Röllig. *Kanaanäische und aramäische Inschriften*. 5th ed. Wiesbaden: Harrassowitz, 2002.

Fales, Frederick Mario. "Phoenicia in the Neo-Assyrian Period: An Updated Overview." *SAAB* 23 (2017): 181–295.

Fales, Frederick Mario, and Giulia Francesca Grassi. *L'aramaico antico: Storia, grammatica, testi commentate*. Udine: Forum, 2016.

Fulco, William J. *The Canaanite God Rešep*. New Haven, CT: American Oriental Society, 1976.

Gilibert, Alessandra. *Syro-Hittite Monumental Art and the Archaeology of Performance: The Stone Reliefs at Carchemish and Zincirli in the Earlier First Millennium BCE*. Berlin: de Gruyter, 2011.

Green, Tamara M. *The City of the Moon God: Religious Traditions of Harran*. Leiden: Brill, 1992.

Hawkins, J.D. *Inscriptions of the Iron Age*. Vol. 1 of *Corpus of Hieroglyphic Luwian Inscriptions*. Berlin: de Gruyter, 2000.

Herrmann, Virginia R. "Cosmopolitan Politics in the Neo-Assyrian Empire: Local Elite Identity at Zincirli-Sam'al." *Sem* 60 (2018): 493–535.

Holloway, Steven W. *Aššur is King! Aššur is King! Religion in the Exercise of Power in the Neo-Assyrian Empire*. Leiden: Brill, 2002.

Keel, Othmar. "Das Mondemblem von Harran auf Stelen und Siegelamuletten und der Kult der nächtlichen Gestirne bei den Aramäern." Pages 135–202 in *Studien zu den Stempelsiegeln aus Palästina/Israel IV*. OBO 135. Fribourg: Universitätsverlag, 1994.

Keel, Othmar, Menakhem Shuval, and Christoph Uehlinger. *Studien zu den Stempelsiegeln aus Palästina/Israel III*. Fribourg: Universitätsverlag, 1990.

Keel, Othmar, and Christoph Uehlinger. *Gods, Goddesses, and Images of God in Ancient Israel*. Minneapolis, MN: Fortress, 1998.

Lambert, W.G. "Isimu (Philologish)." *RlA* 5 (1976–1980): 179.

Lemaire, André. "Rites des vivants pour les morts dans le royaume de Sam'al (VIIIe siècle av. n. è.)." Pages 129–137 in *Les vivants et leurs morts: Actes du colloque organisé par le Collège de France, Paris, les 14–15 avril 2010*. Edited by Jean-Marie Durand, Thomas Römer, and Jürg Hutzli. Fribourg: Academic Press, 2012.

Lewis, Theodore J. "Bar-Rakib's Legitimation and the Problem of a Missing Corpse: The End of the Panamuwa Inscription in Light of the Katumuwa Inscription." *ARAM Periodical* 31/2 (2019): 349–374.

Lewis, Theodore J. *The Origin and Character of God: Ancient Israelite Religion through the Lens of Divinity*. New York, NY: Oxford University Press, 2020.

Lipiński, Edward. *Studies in Aramaic Inscriptions and Onomastics II*. Leuven: Peeters, 1994.

Lipiński, Edward. *The Aramaeans: Their Ancient History, Culture, Religion*. Leuven: Peeters, 2000.

Luschan, Felix von. *Die Kleinfunde von Sendschirli in Ausgrabungen in Sendschirli V*. Edited by Walter Andrae. Mitteilungen aus den Orientalischen Sammlungen 15. Berlin: de Gruyter, 1943.

Marcus, Michelle I. "Centre, Province and Periphery: A New Paradigm from Iron-Age Iran." *Art History* 13/2 (1990): 129–150.

Masson, Émilia. "La stèle mortuaire de Kuttamuwa (Zincirli): Comment l'appréhender." *Semitica et Classica* 3 (2010): 47–58.

Niehr, Herbert. "Rakib-El." In *Iconography of Deities and Demons in the Ancient Near East*. 2008. Electronic pre-publication. http://www.religionswissenschaft.uzh.ch/idd/prepublication.php

Niehr, Herbert. "The Religion of the Aramaeans in the West: The Case of Sam'al." Pages 183–221 in *Arameans, Chaldeans, and Arabs in Babylonia and Palestine in the First Millennium B.C.* Edited by Angelika Berlejung and Michael P. Streck. Wiesbaden: Harrassowitz, 2013.

Niehr, Herbert. "Religion." Pages 127–303 in *The Aramaeans in Ancient Syria*. Edited by Herbert Niehr. Leiden: Brill, 2014.

Niehr, Herbert. "The Power of Language: Language Situation and Language Policy in Sam'al." Pages 305–332 in *In Search for Aram and Israel: Politics, Culture, and Identity*. Edited by Omer Sergi, Manfred Oeming, and Izaak J. de Hulster. Tübingen: Mohr Siebeck, 2016.

Niehr, Herbert. "Questions of Text and Image in Ancient Sam'al (Zincirli)." Pages 309–319 in *Text and Image: Proceedings of the 61e Rencontre Assyriologique Internationale, Geneva and Bern, 22–26 June 2015*. Edited by Pascal Attinger, Antoine Cavigneaux, Catherine Mittermayer, and Mirko Novàk. Leuven: Peeters, 2018.

Novak, Mirko. "Die Religionspolitik der aramäischen Fürstentümer im 1. Jahrtausend v. Chr." Pages 319–346 in *Offizielle Religion, lokale Kulte und individuelle Religiosität*. Edited by Manfred Hutter and Sylvia Hutter-Braunsar. Münster: Ugarit-Verlag, 2004.

Ornan, Tallay. "The Bull and Its Two Masters: Moon and Storm Deities in Relation to the Bull in Ancient Near Eastern Art." *IEJ* 1 (2001): 1–26.

Ornan, Tallay. "A Complex System of Religious Symbols: The Case of the Winged-Disc in Near Eastern Imagery of the First Millennium BCE." Pages 207–241 in *Crafts and*

Images in Contact: Studies on Eastern Mediterranean Art of the First Millennium BCE. Edited by Claudia E. Suter and Christoph Uehlinger. Fribourg: Academic Press, 2005.

Ornan, Tallay. *The Triumph of the Symbol: Pictorial Representation of Deities in Mesopotamia and the Biblical Image Ban*. Fribourg: Academic Press, 2005.

Ornan, Talay. "The Lady and the Bull: Remarks on the Bronze Plaque from Tel Dan." Pages 297–312 in *Essays on Ancient Israel in Its Near Eastern Context: A Tribute to Nadav Na'aman*. Edited by Yairah Amit, Ehud Ben Zvi, Israel Finkelstein, and Oded Lipschits. Winona Lake, IN: Eisenbrauns, 2006.

Pardee, Dennis. "A New Aramaic Inscription from Zincirli." *BASOR* 356 (2009): 51–71.

Pardee, Dennis. "The KTMW Inscription." Pages 95–96 in *The Context of Scripture 4: Supplements*. Edited by K. Lawson Younger, Jr. (Leiden: Brill, 2017), 95–96.

Parker, Heather Dana Davis. "The Levant Comes of Age: The Ninth Century BCE Through Script Traditions." Ph.D. diss., Johns Hopkins University, 2013.

Prinz, Hugo. *Altorientalische Symbolik*. Berlin: K. Curtius, 1915.

Pucci, Marina. *Functional Analysis of Space in Syro-Hittite Architecture*. BAR International Series 1738. Oxford: Archaeopress, 2008.

Sanders, Seth L. "The Appetites of the Dead: West Semitic Linguistic and Ritual Aspects of the Katumuwa Stele." *BASOR* 369 (2013): 35–55.

Scholen, J. David. "Statue of Panamuwa II of Sam'al." Pages 120–121 in *In Remembrance of Me: Feasting with the Dead in the Ancient Middle East*. Edited by Virginia R. Herrmann and J. David Schloen. Chicago, IL: Oriental Institute Museum Publications, University of Chicago, 2014.

Schloen, J. David, and Amir S. Fink. "New Excavations at Zincirli Höyük in Turkey (Ancient Sam'al) and the Discovery of an Inscribed Mortuary Stele." *BASOR* 356 (2009): 1–13.

Schwiderski, Dirk. *Die alt- und reichsaramäischen Inschriften*. Vol. 2. Berlin: de Gruyter, 2004.

Staubli, Thomas. "Sin von Harran und seine Verbreitung im Westen." Pages 65–90 in *Werbung für die Götter*. Edited by Thomas Staubli. Fribourg: Universitätsverlag, 2003.

Struble, Eudora J., and Virginia R. Herrmann. "An Eternal Feast at Sam'al: The New Iron Age Mortuary Stele from Zincirli in Context." *BASOR* 356 (2009): 15–49.

Tropper, Josef. *Die Inschriften von Zincirli: Neue Edition und vergleichende Grammatik des phönizischen, sam'alischen und aramäischen Textkorpus*. Münster: Ugarit-Verlag, 1993.

Gibson, John C.L. *Textbook of Syrian Semitic Inscriptions, Volume II: Aramaic Inscriptions including Inscriptions in the Dialect of Zenjirli*. Oxford: Clarendon Press, 1975.

Voos, Joachim. "Zu einigen späthethitischen Reliefs aus den Beständen des Vorderasiatischen Museums Berlin." *AoF* 12 (1985): 65–86.

Wiseman, D.J. "A New Stela of Aššur-naṣir-pal II." *Iraq* 14/1 (1952): 24–44.

Yadin, Yigael. "Symbols of Deities at Zinjirli, Carthage and Hazor." Pages 199–231 in *Near Eastern Archaeology in the Twentieth Century*. Edited by James A. Sanders. Garden City, NY: Doubleday, 1970.

Younger, K. Lawson, "Panammuwa and Bar-Rakib: Two Structural Analyses," *JANES* 18 (1986): 91–103.

Younger, K. Lawson, Jr. "The Panamuwa Inscription." Pages 158–160 in *The Context of Scripture 2: Monumental Inscriptions from the Biblical World*. Edited by William W. Hallo and K. Lawson Younger, Jr. Leiden: Brill, 2000.

Younger, K. Lawson, Jr. "The Bar-Rakib Inscription." Pages 160–161 in *The Context of Scripture 2: Monumental Inscriptions from the Biblical World*. Edited by William W. Hallo and K. Lawson Younger, Jr. Leiden: Brill, 2000.

Younger, K. Lawson, Jr. *A Political History of the Arameans: From Their Origins to the End of Their Polities*. ABS 13. Atlanta, GA: SBL Press, 2016.

Younger, K. Lawson, Jr. "Gods at the Gates: A Study of the Identification of the Deities Represented at the Gates of Ancient Sam'al (Zincirli) with Possible Historical Implications." *ARAM Periodical* 31/2 (2019): 317–348.

13

Teaching with a Dose of Humor in the Mesopotamian *Unica*

Sara J. Milstein

1 Notes on Dan

New York City, 2004. Dan was offering a course on Amos and Hosea, and although I wasn't a Hebrew Bible student, I decided to enroll. On the first day, Dan stated that our final papers had to be grounded in New Ideas. Each week, he would model for us what it was like to have New Ideas. He would come to class with a single sheet of lined paper, neatly inscribed in printing on both sides, bursting with insights. Most of it went over my head. But I knew that it was new, for the room would buzz with electricity. A few weeks in, I shared with Dan a preliminary idea I had for my paper on Amos 3:3–8, the famous interrogative sequence that illustrates Amos' irrepressible call to prophesy. The following day, he handed me a carefully inscribed page, filled with notes on lions roaring from a mysterious volume called *CAD* L. He was showing me a path down the rabbit hole, one that involved a detour to Babylon. A month later, he handed back our rough drafts, drenched in red, but cheering us on in the name of New Ideas. By the year's end, I had switched into biblical studies. *Who can but prophesy?*

2 Not I: The Power of Collective Authorship

Lay down your weary tune, lay down
Lay down the song you strum
And rest yourself 'neath the strength of strings
No voice can hope to hum.

BOB DYLAN

∵

 | DOI:10.1163/9789004511538_014

In 2000, at the age of twenty-one, I was convinced that poetry had the power to save the world. I was teaching poetry-writing at the juvenile psychiatric unit at St. Mary's Hospital in Lewiston, a dilapidated mill-town in southern Maine that had seen its share of heartache. The unit was for teenagers who had attempted suicide. Shoelaces were confiscated at the door. I never knew their stories, but their faces were already etched with their weight. The director, Ron, would escort me past security after each session, lamenting the world for exactly the length of one cigarette before heading back inside. Group exercises always worked best. I would bring a stack of sheets with a line of poetry inscribed at the top of each one. Each student got a piece. All they had to do was add a line and pass it to someone else. Ron would warn them not to write anything vulgar. There would be a few snickers. But then, heads bent in concentration, they would lay down their verses, and poems would emerge. Whoever was holding the poem at the end would read it aloud. Shielded by anonymity, and buoyed by the power of the group, they would read. And then: silence in the room as the punch of the poem sunk in. *The crying rain like a trumpet sang and asked for no applause*. And then: the poets would shuffle back to their rooms—always in socks—and Ron would smoke me to the end of the block.

3 Scribes, Not Authors

> [*An author is*] *a fool who, not content with boring everyone around him during his lifetime, insists on boring generations yet to come.*
>
> MONTESQUIEU

∵

In *Scribal Culture and the Making of the Hebrew Bible*, Karel van der Toorn warns the reader not to impose modern concepts of authorship on the ancients. Authorship as we know it is bound up with individualism, van der Toorn reminds us, a concept that was all but nonexistent in the ancient Near East.[1] Although many works were credited to specific individuals, the actual composers remained anonymous. There were, of course, a few exceptions to the

1 Karel van der Toorn, *Scribal Culture and the Making of the Hebrew Bible* (Cambridge, MA: Harvard University Press, 2009).

rule. Saggil-kīnam-ubbib cleverly "signed" the Babylonian Theodicy with an acrostic that spelled out his name; and Kabti-ilāni-Marduk, son of Dabibi, claimed that Erra himself had revealed the *Erra Epic* to him in the middle of the night. Most works, though, whether Mesopotamian or biblical, were not signed by their actual authors but instead attributed to gods, legendary figures, or famous scholars of yore: a clever way of imbuing these works with antiquity and authority. Instead of authors, then, we should speak of *scribes*. The distinction is not merely semantic. These were not tortured poets, Amos-like, who had no choice but to write. Rather, they were skilled craftsmen who belonged to societal systems; were often commissioned by others to write; and who copied, revised, and collected far more than they invented from scratch. Anonymity was not a reflection of modesty but a natural by-product of collective, multigenerational systems of literature production. The key, then, is to read these works in the context of scribal culture.

4 Teacher-Authors, One-Offs, and a Few Jokes

> *A scribe who does not know Sumerian, what kind of scribe is he?*
> Sumerian proverb

It's hard to argue with van der Toorn, but I want to see if I can complicate the picture a bit. It is well known that excavations from Mesopotamia have yielded hundreds of school-texts of various types: hymns and myths, proverbs, sign lists and word lists, sample contracts, and mathematics problems, to name a few. Many of these texts were preserved accidentally, in that the clay tablets were simply used as filler for building foundations. The bulk of the texts are written in Sumerian, a language that by the early second millennium BCE (Old Babylonian period) was no longer spoken but remained essential to scribal training. The number of copies of any given school-text range; some are only attested in ten copies or so, while others, particularly those integral to the curriculum, number as many as two hundred.

A small subset of these pedagogical texts, however, are *unica*, or texts that are attested in only a single copy. In certain cases, scholars have surmised that the texts were written by teachers or perhaps advanced students.[2] One intrigu-

2 See, e.g., Jacob Klein and Tonia Sharlach's discussion of CBS 11324, a tablet with three model

ing example is the text known alternatively as "Why Do You Curse Me?" or "The Illiterate Doctor of Isin."[3] The single attested copy is from Uruk and dates to 818 BCE. A certain Ninurta-sagentarbi-zaemen from Nippur gets bitten by a dog. The guy heads to Isin to see a doctor, Amēl-ba'u, who heals him by reciting Sumerian incantations. The grateful Ninurta-sagentarbi-zaemen tells Amēl-ba'u to come to Nippur, promising to treat him to a wonderful feast. He gives the doctor directions for most of the way, then instructs him to ask Nin-lugal-apsu, an elderly vegetable seller, for help with the last stretch.[4]

So Amēl-ba'u heads to Nippur, follows his patient's instructions, and sure enough comes upon Nin-lugal-apsu, selling her fruits and veggies. It's here where the story picks up. When the doctor addresses Nin-lugal-apsu, she responds politely in Sumerian: *anni lugalmu* ("Yes, sir"). (The implication appears to be that in the scholastic town of Nippur, even the vegetable sellers know the long-dead language of Sumerian.) What follows is a classic case of Script Opposition, to borrow a term from humor theory: the doctor repeatedly assumes that the woman is cursing him, when she is merely answering his questions ("Why would I curse you?!" I said, "He is not at home"). The implication seems to be that the doctor only knows academic Sumerian, and cannot decipher the "everyday Sumerian" of a Nippurean peasant.[5] After a series of such misunder-

cases from Nippur, attested in a single copy. They suggest that the tablet may have been written by an advanced student, practicing his legal formulae, but alternatively consider that the tablet was composed by a teacher, given the organized way in which the compositions are arranged, from shortest to longest and from simplest to most complicated ("A Collection of Model Court Cases from Old Babylonian Nippur [CBS 11324]," *ZA* 97/1 [2007]: 3). Martha Roth similarly suggests that CBS 10467, a colorful text that she describes as a "comic morality tale," is either "tongue-in-cheek," mimicking a legal document, or was written by a clever student scribe ("The Slave and the Scoundrel: CBS 10467, A Sumerian Morality Tale?" *JAOS* 103/1 [1983]: 279). As I discuss below, Franco D'Agostino suggests that "Why Do You Curse Me?" was likely written by a teacher, or *ummānu*, as a pedagogical aid for his students ("Some Considerations on Humour in Mesopotamia," *RSO* 72 [1998]: 276).

3 The text was first published by Antoine Cavigneaux, "Texts und Fragmente aus Warka (32. Kampagne)," *BaM* 10 (1979): 111–142. See the translation in Benjamin Foster, *Before the Muses: An Anthology of Akkadian Literature* (Bethesda, MD: CDL Press, 2005), 936–938; see also Erica Reiner, "Why Do You Cuss Me?," *Proceedings of the American Philosophical Society* 130/1 (1986): 1–6; D'Agostino, "Some Considerations on Humour"; and Andrew George, "Ninurta-Pāqidāt's Dog Bite, and Notes on Other Comic Tales," *Iraq* 55 (1993): 63–75 (with a new edition).

4 The scene reminds me of what happens in Israel when you ask for directions: someone will navigate you up until a certain point, and then conclude with, אז תשאל ("Then ask!").

5 I follow here Reiner's interpretation of the situation ("Why Do You Cuss Me?," 4–5; see also D'Agostino, "Some Considerations on Humour"). For George, however, the humor is more targeted, and instead revolves around the fact that a learned man from Isin cannot comprehend the dialect of Akkadian spoken at Nippur ("Ninurta-Pāqidāt's Dog Bite," 66). He notes that the

standings, with the doctor repeatedly thinking that the woman is cursing him, the playful story concludes with a dash of mockery for the so-called expert: "What a fool he is! The students ought to get together and chase him out of the Grand Gate with their practice tablets!"

As Franco D'Agostino explains, there are two main indicators that the text is pedagogical. Most explicit is the colophon: "Text written for the recitation of young scribes." In addition, all of the personal names in the text—Ninurta-sagentarbi-zaemen, Amēl-ba'u, Nin-lugal-apsu, and so on—are known from a bilingual lexical list; and as Andrew George observes, the text also appears to quote from a topographical lexical list.[6] D'Agostino concludes that the text must have been written by a teacher who aimed to help his students master the unwieldy Sumerian names and their Akkadian equivalents.[7] This proposal is intriguing for two reasons. First of all, if D'Agostino is correct, we have here an *author*, at least in the most basic sense. This person may not be a named author and he may not have composed multiple works, but he was nonetheless an individual who created a particular piece for a particular audience. And second, as D'Agostino acknowledges, the teacher uses humor in his composition.[8] From the perspective of humor theory, there are a number of explicitly humorous elements at work in this composition.[9] As alluded to earlier, having two "scripts" that operate simultaneously, with one figure perpetually misunderstanding the situation, is a standard humor trope.[10] It is, moreover, common

vegetable seller (or gardener, in his reading) initially responds either in a mixture of Akkadian and Kassite-period Sumerian or solely in Sumerian (65). Either way, however, the text exhibits "Script Opposition," and the doctor's inability to understand the woman can be understood as humorous.

6 George, "Ninurta-Pāqidāt's Dog Bite," 64.

7 D'Agostino, "Some Considerations on Humour," 276. George instead sees the Sumerian names as invented backward from the Akkadian as a way for the scribe to "show off his scholarship" and "render his work inaccessible to those of lesser learning" ("Ninurta-Pāqidāt's Dog Bite," 63–64).

8 D'Agostino, "Some Considerations on Humour," 276–278.

9 For a helpful overview of the three dominant theories of humor (superiority theory, relief theory, and incongruity theory), see Lauren Olin, "Questions for a Theory of Humor," *Philosophy Compass* 11/6 (2016): 338–350. Humor theorists recognize that certain features recur in jokes across cultures, even as cultures naturally display variation in what they consider humorous. Thus, for example, the practice of ridiculing out-group members is ubiquitous (Christie Davies, *Ethnic Humor Around the World: A Comparative Analysis* [Indianapolis, IN: Indiana University Press, 1990]); and sexual and hostile themes are also prevalent in humor across cultures and over time (Olin, "Questions for a Theory of Humor," 341).

10 On "Script Opposition," also known as "script-switching," see Victor Raskin, *Semantic Mechanisms of Humor* (Dordrecht, Netherlands: D. Reidel, 1985). The idea, still relevant

for jokes to lampoon authority figures and experts, with doctors a frequent target.[11] Incongruity has been proven to be central to humor across cultures, and it is thus not surprising that the one person who speaks Sumerian is both female and non-elite.[12] Repetition is yet another standard ingredient in humor, and it is clear that the story becomes funnier and funnier with each "Why do you curse me?!"[13] The closing line, finally, is a classic case of what humor theorists call "superiority humor": the budding scribes are implicitly smarter than a doctor! And who could help but laugh at the image of students chasing the doctor out of Nippur, tablets raised as weapons? This guy was not only a good teacher but a decent humorist, too.

5 Looking for Laughs

Take my wife—please![14]

HENNY YOUNGMAN

∵

in humor theory, is that humor arises when two opposed scripts are "running" simultaneously. One of these scripts must be explicit and the other one can be either direct or at least inferable from the text. In "Why Do You Curse Me?" the explicit script is that of the vegetable seller, who simply answers the doctor in Sumerian. When the doctor reacts in horror, the reader (or better, the students) must search for "another" script that accounts for his response, namely, that to the doctor's untrained ear, the woman is cursing him. Humor emerges at the incompatibility of the two scripts.

11 This lampooning of authority figures reminds me of one of my favorite old-time Jewish jokes. Ruthie, Mabel, and Dolores are out for their weekly lunch, and before long, the subject turns to their favorite topic: their sons. "Oh, girls, I have to tell you about David," Ruthie brags. "He just made partner at the firm!" "Oh, Ruthie, you must be *kvelling*," the ladies gush. "How wonderful!" Then Mabel speaks up. "I also have some news to share. My Stevie is now the head surgeon at General! Oy, it's such a big responsibility!" "Mabel," the others exclaim, "Mazel tov! You must be so proud." A few minutes pass by, and the ladies notice that Dolores is quiet, looking down at her soup. "Dolores," they prod, "how about you? How's Alan? What does he do for a living again?" "Well," Dolores stammers, "He's—he's a rabbi." "A rabbi?" say Ruthie and Mabel. "What kind of a job is that for a Jewish boy?"

12 D'Agostino points to the paradoxical nature of the vegetable seller knowing Sumerian, a language that not only reflects elevated knowledge but also would have died out 1500 years prior ("Some Considerations on Humour," 277).

13 Or, alternatively, in George's translation, "Why are you being rude to me?" ("Ninurta-Pāqidāt's Dog Bite," 67). As Lauren Olin notes, stock characters in comedy engage in "routinized, almost mechanical patterns of behavior" ("The Comic Stance," *The Philosophy of Humor Yearbook* 1/1 [2020]: 51).

14 The original utterance of this famous line was actually a misunderstanding. Apparently

It stands to reason that "Why Do You Curse Me?" might not be the only humorous pedagogical *unicum* out there. So let's turn to a different text-type, what scholars call "model (court) cases," or what I refer to as "fictional cases."[15] These Sumerian texts are apparently pedagogical but are attested in limited numbers, with most represented only by a single copy.[16] The limited "corpus" includes a homicide case, two cases of adultery, a few inheritance disputes, a case regarding the assault of a slave-girl, a dispute over heirs to a slave-girl, a dispute over office, two cases about a barley loan, two cases concerning burglary, and a case of slander.[17] The texts purport to report cases, but lack witnesses, dates, and seals, a telltale sign that they are not actual records. Scholars have generally assumed, however, that the "model cases" were based on actual court cases that were adapted for use in pedagogical contexts, most likely in order to expose scribes to the form of actual trial records.[18] As such, the model cases are likened to the well-attested genre of "model contracts," sample contracts of various types that prepared students for the composition of actual contracts.[19]

Youngman took his wife to a radio show and asked a stagehand to escort her to her seat. The guy thought Youngman was kidding, prompting the "King of One-Liners" to reuse the line as a joke after that (Mervyn Rothstein, "Henny Youngman, 'King of the One-Liners,' Is Dead at 91 After 6 Decades of Laughter," *The New York Times*, p. B9, Feb. 25, 1998).

15 Martha T. Roth initially referred to these texts as model court records (Roth, "Slave and the Scoundrel," 279); she then shifts to "model court cases" in "'She Will Die by the Iron Dagger': Adultery and Neo-Babylonian Marriage," *JESHO* 31 (1988): 196–197.

16 The one exception is the text known as the Nippur Homicide Trial. See Thorkild Jacobsen, "An Ancient Mesopotamian Trial for Homicide," in *Toward the Image of Tammuz and Other Essays on Mesopotamian History and Culture*, ed. William Moran, HSS 21 (Cambridge, MA: Harvard University Press, 1970), 193–215; and Martha T. Roth, "Gender and Law: A Case Study from Ancient Mesopotamia," in *Gender and Law in the Hebrew Bible and the Ancient Near East*, ed. Bernard Levinson, Tikva Frymer-Kensky, and Victor H. Matthews, JSOTSup 262 (Sheffield: Sheffield Academic Press, 1998), 173–184.

17 Those that are published include Samuel Greengus, "A Textbook Case of Adultery in Ancient Mesopotamia," *HUCA* 40/41 (1969–1970): 33–44; Raymond Westbrook, *Old Babylonian Marriage Law*, AfOB 23 (Horn: Verlag Ferdinand Berger & Söhne, 1988), 133; William Hallo, "A Model Court Case Concerning Inheritance," in *Riches Hidden in Secret Places: Ancient Near Eastern Studies in Memory of Thorkild Jacobsen*, ed. Tzvi Abusch (Winona Lake, IN: Eisenbrauns, 2002), 141–154; Jacob Klein and Tonia Sharlach, "A Collection of Model Court Cases from Old Babylonian Nippur (CBS 11324)," *ZA* 97/1 (2007): 1–25; J.J. Finkelstein, "Sex Offenses in Sumerian Laws," *JAOS* 86/4 (1966): 359–360; and Gabriella Spada, "Old Babylonian Model Contracts and Related Texts," in *Old Babylonian Texts in the Schøyen Collection, Part Two: School Letters, Model Contracts, and Related Texts*, ed. Andrew R. George and Gabriella Spada, CUSAS 43 (University Park, PA: Eisenbrauns, 2019), 100–101.

18 See Roth, "Slave and the Scoundrel," 279.

19 Hallo, "A Model Court Case Concerning Inheritance," 142–144.

Unlike contracts, however, the trial records of this time do not follow a template. It is thus less apparent how the model cases would have served a comparable practical end. The fictional cases are also attested in far fewer numbers than the model contracts, which were integral to the elementary Old Babylonian curriculum.[20] The question of purpose is even more perplexing for the *unica*, for even if these texts are demonstrably "pedagogical," there is no proof that they were ever recopied by students.

One of the *unica* is particularly colorful. The text was reedited by Samuel Greengus, and appears in a perfectly titled article: "A Textbook Case of Adultery in Ancient Mesopotamia." The reediting is significant. When the text was first edited, Jan van Dijk presented it as a married man whose wife catches him *in flagrante* with another man.[21] In Greengus's reading, however, it's the wife who is the adulterer: a more likely scenario, given that in Mesopotamia, adultery was strictly regarded as an offense against a husband. As the case unfolds, we learn that Eshtar-ummī committed a series of three offenses against her husband, Irra-malik. First, she burglarized his storeroom. Second, she pilfered from his oil jar and covered up her tracks. And third—the real kicker—she got caught in bed with another man. This last offense is reported with elaborate detail. When Irra-malik catches his wife in the act, he ties her "to the body of the man on the bed … and carried her (or it?) to the assembly." As Greengus points out, the scene parallels the Greek tradition of Hephaestus trapping his wife Aphrodite in bed with Ares.[22] Though anachronistic, the comparison illuminates the degree to which this detail is a literary flourish, not a judicial one. Based on the evidence, the assembly decides that the woman's pudendum is to be shaved and she is to be paraded around the city, her nose pierced with an arrow. There also appears to be some sort of reference to "divorce money," and given the circumstances, it is likely that the assembly also freed the man of all financial obligations.

Although at first glance this *unicum* has little in common with the previous one, a second look reveals that they may have more in common than meets the eye. As discussed above, in "Why Do You Curse Me?," a teacher appar-

20 On the model contracts, see Gabriella Spada, *Sumerian Model Contracts from the Old Babylonian Period in the Hilprecht Collection Jena*, Texte und Materialien der Frau Professor Hilprecht Collection of Babylonian Antiquities im Eigentum der Friedrich-Schiller-Universität Jena XI (Wiesbaden: Harrassowitz, 2018); and Walter Bodine, *How Mesopotamian Scribes Learned to Write Legal Documents: A Study of the Sumerian Model Contracts in the Babylonian Collection at Yale University* (Lewiston, NY: Mellen Press, 2015).

21 Jan Van Dijk, "Neusumerische Gerichtsurkunden in Bagdad," *ZA* 55 (1963): 70–77.

22 The story is recounted in the *Odyssey* and again by Ovid in *Ars Amatoria* (Greengus, "Textbook Case," 37).

ently embedded names from a lexical series in the text in order to help his students learn them. The beginning of this text—"Eshtar-ummī, daughter of Ilī-asû, did Irra-malik take in marriage"—may reflect something similar. The formula is nearly identical to the opening formulas of some contemporaneous marriage contracts. A contract from Nippur, for example, reads, "Awilia, son of Warad-Sin, has taken Naramtum, daughter of Sinatum, for marriage." Another reads, "Warad-Shamash has taken Taram-Sagila and Iltani, daughter of Sin-abushu, for marriage."[23] Although the fictional case fronts the woman's name—anticipating, perhaps, the crucial role she will play in the "plotline"—the wording is virtually the same, and its inclusion likewise appears to have served a pedagogical purpose, namely, to teach students the contract formula.[24]

It appears, then, that this *unicum* had some sort of pedagogical aim. But is there any indication that it was meant to be humorous? After all, didn't the Mesopotamians frown upon adultery, to say the least? Indeed, a number of laws address adultery, with penalties that are no joke. The Laws of Hammurabi (LH) § 129 likewise deals with a man who catches his wife with another man, and if the husband so chooses, the two are to be bound and drowned.[25] In LH § 133b, if a woman whose husband is captured "enters another man's house," she, too, is to be drowned if there are sufficient provisions in her house. Even if someone accuses a woman of having committed adultery without proof, as in LH § 132,

23 Westbrook, *Old Babylonian Marriage Law*, 115–116.

24 It is worth noting a Latin parallel to this phenomenon that takes the combination of humor and pedagogy to a new level. The text is known as "Testamentum Porcelli," or "Testament of the Piglet," and is delivered in the first-person voice of a piglet on the brink of death. To an even greater extent than the Mesopotamian examples, "Testamentum Porcelli" makes ample, playful use of contract formulas, in this case, those from wills: "To my father Verrinus Lardinus I give and bequeath thirty measures of acorns, and to my mother Veturina Scrofa I give and bequeath forty measures of Laconian white wheat.… And from my body I shall give and contribute to the cobblers my bristles, to quarrelers my head-parts, to the deaf my ears, to lawyers and the wordy my tongue, to sausage-makers my intestines.…" (Terrence Lockyer, "Testamentum Porcelli: A Little Pig's Will" [2012], https://tlockyer.wordpress.com/2012/04/20/testamentum-porcelli-a-little-pigs-will/). Edward Champlin treated this text as "a parody of legal form," noting that it is the first in a long line of satirical animal testaments. Most intriguingly for our purposes, however, Saint Jerome reports—much to his disdain—that the text was chanted by schoolboys. As such, Champlin suggests that its author may have been "an anonymous schoolmaster of genius" ("The Testament of the Piglet," *Phoenix* 41/2 [1987]: 175–176, 183). I thank my student Thomas Ellison for alerting me to this text.

25 Alternatively, however, if the husband wishes for his wife to be released, the king will allow the man to live as well (Martha Roth, *Law Collections from Mesopotamia and Asia Minor*, WAW 6 [Atlanta, GA: SBL Press, 1997], 105). All references to the laws rely on Roth's collection.

she still has to undergo the divine River Ordeal to prove her innocence. LH §141 then deals with the other offenses that are represented in this fictional case, and again, there are grave consequences. If a woman decides to leave her husband and "appropriates goods, squanders her household possessions, or disparages him," the man can divorce her with no financial consequences: he need not pay her travel expenses, divorce money, or anything else. He also is entitled to marry another woman and turn his first wife into a slave. The fictional case thus appears to combine a number of the elements that are present in these laws: theft of household goods, adultery *in flagrante delicto*, binding, no divorce payment, and possibly, the rendering of the wife as a slave, as suggested by the nose-piercing. Given these parallels, it is even possible that the case is related to the laws in some way, whether as their source or as a creative expression that had the laws as its starting point.

All that said, is the text actually *funny*? I would say yes, on several counts. First of all, the style used to recount the sequence of transgressions is humorous, in a deadpan sort of way. The text begins with two counts of theft of household goods ("In the first place ... In the second place ..."). These crimes surely pale in comparison to being caught with another man, and yet the adulterous act is simply prefaced with the same banal formula: "In the third place...." Moreover, the fact that the text stays in its detached legal register ("The assembly, because she was caught with a man upon her ..."), despite the absurdity of the situation (the assembly is literally making their judgment in front of a bed to which a naked couple is tied), enhances the humor further. Second, and more explicitly, the text employs a hyper-literal image of *in flagrante delicto*. In "real life," we can presume that a cuckolded husband would merely need to testify that he had caught his wife in the act. The notion that someone would tie his wife and her paramour together and haul the entire bed to the assembly as "evidence" is thus preposterous—and hence, hilarious. Finally, as humor theorists have shown, one of the main functions of humor is tied to social management; jokes often serve to reinforce social norms by highlighting the violation of rules and deviant behavior.[26] In this case, the depiction of the wife's crime and humiliation—especially when set in an imaginary legal context—would have worked inversely to enforce the norm of marital fidelity.[27]

---

26 Annarita Guidi, "Humor Universals," *The Routledge Handbook of Language and Humor*, ed. Salvatore Attardo (New York, NY: Routledge, 2017), 18–19.

27 One other *unicum* may reflect a similar phenomenon: the aforementioned CBS 11324. The text, edited by Klein and Sharlach, preserves a series of three model cases. The first case pertains to a foundling who is adopted by a woman—itself an unusual scenario—and starts out with a string of legal formulae known from *Ana ittišu* that pertain to adoption

6 Socializing with the Mesopotamians

And I knew it was going to be a terrible, horrible, no good, very bad day.

JUDITH VIORST, *Alexander and the Terrible, Horrible, No Good, Very Bad Day*

Humor theorists assert that humor is fundamentally a social phenomenon: other people provide the context in which we experience humor.[28] Humor is also, of course, highly culture-bound, both in terms of space and time.[29] The notion that humor is a good coping strategy, for example, is strictly a Western belief.[30] In a major study on cross-cultural humor conducted by Israeli and Singaporean scholars, striking differences were observed regarding the content of jokes told in North America and Singapore.[31] This combination of factors would appear to make it difficult to identify humorous texts from the ancient Near East. Without knowing how these works would have been received, and without the insider knowledge needed to appreciate humor in

("A suckling male child, found in a well, saved from the mouth of a dog, having no mother, having no sister, having no brother, and having no stepbrother ..."). In classic legal form, the text then outlines consequences if someone should make a claim on the baby. The stipulation, however, is utterly "bizarre," as Klein and Sharlach observe: the biological parent is to bring the foster parent a twenty-liter jar of human milk as compensation! They suggest that the fanciful detail might be used to indicate that the claimant is supposed to cover all the expenses of the foster mother, down to "the last penny" ("A Collection of Model Court Cases," 9). The specification is nonetheless strange and also illogical—what would a new ex-foster parent do with twenty liters of breastmilk?—and it is thus possible that it, too, was composed with humorous intent. Even if this demand is used to prove that the biological mother is indeed the mother, twenty liters is an absurdly enormous quantity to expect.

28 Rod Martin and Thomas Ford, *The Psychology of Humor*, 2nd ed. (Cambridge, MA: Academic Press, 2008), 3.

29 See Tonglin Jiang, Hao Li, and Yubo Hou, "Cultural Differences in Humor Perception, Usage, and Implications," *Frontier Psychology* (2019), https://www.frontiersin.org/articles/10.3389/fpsyg.2019.00123/full; see also Guidi, "Humor Universals," 19.

30 As Jiang, Li, and Hou point out, humor is not as an important coping device in Japan as it is in the United States. Chinese and Singaporean students are less likely to use humor as a coping strategy with stress than their American and Canadian counterparts ("Cultural Differences").

31 Among other findings, the study revealed that North Americans were more apt to tell

full, how can we conclude that any of these texts were intentionally funny? These challenges are compounded by the fact that unlike the Greeks, the Mesopotamians had no distinct genre of comedy, no named comic authors, no comedy competitions, no amphitheaters or masks or props. One might conclude, then, that to label anything from Mesopotamia a "humorous text" is not only impossible but also anachronistic. But that would also be evaluating Mesopotamia on nonnative terms, something any serious Assyriologist would advise against.

If we start with a different notion of "author" and "audience," however, then we might start to get somewhere. Education in Mesopotamia, like education today, involved teachers and students. And there is decent evidence that there were at least a few chuckles to be had in Mesopotamian school settings. The Mesopotamians had a particular category of texts that had school as their subject, called "*edubba* literature." In a recent article, Andrew George makes reference to the "witty insights" into scribal learning in the *edubba* texts known as "Schooldays" and "Edubba D."[32] The first composition gleefully details a poor kid's terrible day, in which he does everything wrong—leaves the room without permission, takes water (or beer?) without asking the jug monitor, speaks Akkadian instead of Sumerian, and has awful penmanship—each of which earns him a beating. George observes that the passage demonstrates that instruction took place in Sumerian, and one could also conclude that corporal punishment was used liberally. But there may be more to glean. Just as Viorst's 1972 classic is hilarious precisely because Alexander's bad day is so over the top, so too is "Schooldays" funny because the speaker's day is a series of mishaps, one after the other in rapid succession. And with both, we can laugh because in the end, no lasting harm ensues. Before bed, Alexander's mom assures him simply that "some days are like that," telling the reader implicitly that the next day will be a better one. "Schooldays" is even more explicit. That evening, the boy's father invites the teacher to their house and bribes him with beer. The teacher does a total about-face, and the student becomes his prized pupil. Both plots

---

sex jokes than Singaporeans, while Singaporeans were more apt than North Americans to tell jokes with violence (Steven Jackson, "What's Funny? It Depends Where You're From," *Psychology Today*, https://www.psychologytoday.com/ca/blog/culture-conscious/201205/whats-funny).

32 Andrew George, "In Search of the é.dub.ba.a: The Ancient Mesopotamian School in Literature and Reality," in *An Experienced Scribe Who Neglects Nothing: Ancient Near Eastern Studies in Honor of Jacob Klein*, ed. Yitschak Sefati et al. (Bethesda, MD: CDL Press, 2005), 128.

thus sail along on a "U-shaped curve," having their protagonists hit rock bottom before swinging upward toward a happy ending. Put simply, this is how humor works.[33]

It can be highly problematic to assume that the Mesopotamians were always serious, interested only in plucking out eyes for eyes or wailing laments. After all, "the oldest joke in the world" comes from these guys.[34] The form is proverbial, another text-type that was part and parcel of early scribal education. The joke goes like this: "What has never happened since time immemorial? A woman did not break wind in her husband's lap." Laughing yet? The joke is built on incongruity: one would expect something profound or mythical to have "never happened" since the beginning of time, but instead the punchline is purely human, even crass. The double negative ("What has never happened … a woman did not break wind …") serves to enhance the humor, for in order to get the joke, one must revisit the riddle and do the math: "Since the beginning of time, women … *always* break wind in their husbands' laps!" In Mesopotamia, moreover, the "husband's lap" is a euphemism for sex, and thus, the joke is perfect for teenage boys: a bathroom joke and a sex joke wrapped up into one—and all this several millennia before Judd Apatow came on the scene. This is hardly the only zinger among the proverbs ("For his pleasure he got married. On his thinking it over he got divorced." "The fox, having urinated into the sea, said: 'The depths of the sea are my urine!'"), suggesting again that teachers occasionally used humor as a pedagogical strategy: a way to get the students to learn (Sumerian) without realizing they were learning.[35] And while their humor surely differed from "ours," in some ways, for better or worse, it seems that not much has really changed.

The *unica* profiled earlier, however, reveal not merely the *use* of humor in pedagogical contexts, but also the creation of humorous, pedagogical pieces

33 Northrop Frye introduced the influential notion of the "U-shaped plot" as a defining structural device of comic work. After a typically harmonious exposition, the "action sink[s] into deep and often potentially tragic complications" but then "suddenly turn[s] upward into a happy ending" (*Fables of Identity: Studies in Poetic Mythology* [New York, NY: Harcourt, Brace & World, 1963], 25). Tragic plots, in contrast, are characterized by an inverted "U."

34 See Paul McDonald, "Heard the One About the Oldest Joke in the World? It's a Cracker!," *The Independent* (2010), https://www.independent.co.uk/voices/commentators/paul-mcdonald-heard-one-about-oldest-joke-world-it-s-cracker-2164293.html. McDonald's characterization is an exaggeration, of course: this "joke" is just one among a number of humorous proverbs that are preserved in the collections.

35 These proverbs are available at https://etcsl.orinst.ox.ac.uk/catalogue/catalogue6.htm.

from scratch by teachers. The humor in these texts—like good humor today—was, of course, extremely niche: funny only to the limited circle of scribes under the teacher's wing. It was utilized, moreover, toward a practical end: namely, to aid in the process of memorization. But it was still funny, with a discernible relationship between "author" and "audience." In studying the ancients, Dan used to say that his goal was simply to enter into their worlds, and I have often heard him speak of the Emarites as if they were his own kin. With this modest offering in his honor, I hope that he (and also you, dear reader) might be able to hear some distant peals of laughter, reverberating across time and space all the way from ancient Nippur: just a teacher and his students, sharing a few laughs in the name of education.

Bibliography

Bodine, Walter. *How Mesopotamian Scribes Learned to Write Legal Documents: A Study of the Sumerian Model Contracts in the Babylonian Collection at Yale University*. Lewiston, NY: Mellen Press, 2015.

Cavigneaux, Antoine. "Texts und Fragmente aus Warka (32. Kampagne)." *BaM* 10 (1979): 111–142.

Champlin, Edward. "The Testament of the Piglet." *Phoenix* 41/2 (1987): 174–183.

D'Agostino, Franco. "Some Considerations on Humour in Mesopotamia." *RSO* 72 (1998): 273–278.

Davies, Christie. *Ethnic Humor Around the World: A Comparative Analysis*. Indianapolis, IN: Indiana University Press, 1990.

Finkelstein, J.J. "Sex Offenses in Sumerian Laws." *JAOS* 86/4 (1966): 355–372.

Foster, Benjamin R. *Before the Muses: An Anthology of Akkadian Literature*. Bethesda, MD: CDL Press, 2005.

Foster, Benjamin R. "Humor and Cuneiform Literature." *JANES* 6 (1974): 69–85.

Frye, Northrop. *Fables of Identity: Studies in Poetic Mythology*. New York, NY: Harcourt, Brace & World, 1963.

George, Andrew. "In Search of the é.dub.ba.a: The Ancient Mesopotamian School in Literature and Reality." Pages 127–137 in *An Experienced Scribe Who Neglects Nothing: Ancient Near Eastern Studies in Honor of Jacob Klein*. Edited by Yitschak Sefati, Pinhas Artzi, Chaim Cohen, Barry L. Eichler, and Victor Avigdor Hurowitz. Bethesda, MD: CDL Press, 2005.

George, Andrew. "Ninurta-Pāqidāt's Dog Bite, and Notes on Other Comic Tales." *Iraq* 55 (1993): 63–75.

Greengus, Samuel. "A Textbook Case of Adultery in Ancient Mesopotamia." *HUCA* 40/41 (1969–1970): 33–44.

Guidi, Annarita. "Humor Universals." Pages 17–33 in *The Routledge Handbook of Language and Humor*. Edited by Salvatore Attardo. New York, NY: Routledge, 2017.

Hallo, William. "A Model Court Case Concerning Inheritance." Pages 141–154 in *Riches Hidden in Secret Places: Ancient Near Eastern Studies in Memory of Thorkild Jacobsen*. Edited by Tzvi Abusch. Winona Lake, IN: Eisenbrauns, 2002.

Jackson, Steven. "What's Funny? It Depends Where You're From." *Psychology Today* (2012), https://www.psychologytoday.com/ca/blog/culture-conscious/201205/whats-funny.

Jacobsen, Thorkild. "An Ancient Mesopotamian Trial for Homicide." Pages 193–215 in *Toward the Image of Tammuz and Other Essays on Mesopotamian History and Culture*. Edited by William Moran. HSS 21. Cambridge, MA: Harvard University Press, 1970.

Jiang, Tonglin, Hao Li, and Yubo Hou. "Cultural Differences in Humor Perception, Usage, and Implications." *Frontier Psychology* 29 (Jan. 2019), https://doi.org/10.3389/fpsyg.2019.00123.

Klein, Jacob, and Tonia Sharlach. "A Collection of Model Court Cases from Old Babylonian Nippur (CBS 11324)." *ZA* 97/1 (2007): 1–25.

Lockyer, Terrence. "Testamentum Porcelli: A Little Pig's Will" (2012). https://tlockyer.wordpress.com/2012/04/20/testamentum-porcelli-a-little-pigs-will/.

Martin, Rod, and Thomas Ford. *The Psychology of Humor*. 2nd ed. Cambridge, MA: Academic Press, 2008.

McDonald, Paul. "Heard the One About the Oldest Joke in the World? It's a Cracker!" *The Independent* (2010), at https://www.independent.co.uk/voices/commentators/paul-mcdonald-heard-one-about-oldest-joke-world-it-s-cracker-2164293.html.

Olin, Lauren. "Questions for a Theory of Humor." *Philosophy Compass* 11/6 (2016): 338–350.

Olin, Lauren. "The Comic Stance." *The Philosophy of Humor Yearbook* 1/1 (2020): 49–71.

Raskin, Victor. *Semantic Mechanisms of Humor*. Dordrecht, Netherlands: D. Reidel, 1985.

Reiner, Erica. "Why Do You Cuss Me?" *Proceedings of the American Philosophical Society* 130/1 (1986): 1–6.

Rothstein, Mervyn. "Henny Youngman, 'King of the One-Liners,' Is Dead at 91 After 6 Decades of Laughter." *The New York Times*, p. B9, Feb. 25, 1998.

Roth, Martha T. "Gender and Law: A Case Study from Ancient Mesopotamia." Pages 173–184 in *Gender and Law in the Hebrew Bible and the Ancient Near East*. Edited by Bernard Levinson, Tikva Frymer-Kensky, and Victor H. Matthews. JSOTSup 262. Sheffield: Sheffield Academic Press, 1998.

Roth, Martha T. *Law Collections from Mesopotamia and Asia Minor*. 2nd ed. WAW 6. Atlanta, GA: SBL Press, 1997.

Roth, Martha T. "'She Will Die by the Iron Dagger': Adultery and Neo-Babylonian Marriage." *JESHO* 31 (1988): 186–206.

Roth, Martha T. "The Slave and the Scoundrel: CBS 10467, A Sumerian Morality Tale?" *JAOS* 103/1 (1983): 275–282.

Spada, Gabriella. "Old Babylonian Model Contracts and Related Texts." Pages 73–145 in *Old Babylonian Texts in the Schøyen Collection, Part Two: School Letters, Model Contracts, and Related Texts*. Edited by Andrew R. George and Gabriella Spada. CUSAS 43. University Park, PA: Eisenbrauns, 2019.

Spada, Gabriella. *Sumerian Model Contracts from the Old Babylonian Period in the Hilprecht Collection Jena*. Texte und Materialien der Frau Professor Hilprecht Collection of Babylonian Antiquities im Eigentum der Friedrich-Schiller-Universität Jena XI. Wiesbaden: Harrassowitz, 2018.

Van der Toorn, Karel. *Scribal Culture and the Making of the Hebrew Bible*. Cambridge, MA: Harvard University Press, 2009.

Van Dijk, Jan. "Neusumerische Gerichtsurkunden in Bagdad." *ZA* 55 (1963): 70–77.

Westbrook, Raymond. *Old Babylonian Marriage Law*. AfOB 23. Horn: Verlag Ferdinand Berger & Söhne, 1988.

14

The Sociomorphic Structure of the Polytheistic Pantheon in Mesopotamia and Its Meaning for Divine Agency and Mentalization

Beate Pongratz-Leisten

It gives me the greatest pleasure to dedicate this article to Daniel Fleming, with whom I share a longstanding friendship, going back to our days as students at Harvard and our studies under Bill Moran.[1,2] Over the years, Bill became a dear friend to both Daniel and me and generated the scholarly and intellectual bond between us. Today, I am moved by, grateful for, and continue to be nurtured by this intellectual bond with Daniel, which has carried us from Boston to our shared academic home at New York University.[3]

1 Cosmic Order and Human-divine Interdependency

In ancient Mesopotamia, cosmic order was equated with cosmic stability (*kittu*), which was decreed by the gods, while civic order, or "straightness" (*mīšaru*) was maintained by the king through the passing of judgments (*dīnu dânu; purussâ parāsu*). In other words, the act of judgment readjusted and

1 Wilfred G. Lambert, "Gott: Nach akkadischen Texten," *RlA* 3/7 (1971): 543–546; Gebhard Selz, "Götter der Gesellschaft—Gesellschaft der Götter: Zur Dialektik von Abbildung und Ordnung," in *Wissenskultur im Alten Orient: Weltanschauung, Wissenschaften, Techniken, Technologien. 4. Internationales Colloquium der Deutschen Orient-Gesellschaft 20.–22. Februar* 2002, ed. Hans Neumann (Wiesbaden: Harrassowitz, 2012), 61–85.

2 On the notion of conceptual metaphor, see George Lakoff and Mark Johnson, *Metaphors We Live By* (Chicago, IL: Chicago University Press, 1980); on its applicability to the textual and pictorial material in Mesopotamia, see Ludovico Portuese, "Metaphorical Allusions to Life-Giving Plants in Neo-Assyrian Texts and Images," *Antiguo Oriente* 16 (2018): 93–116; and Marta Pallavidini and Ludovico Portuese, ed., *Researching Metaphor in the Ancient Near East* (Wiesbaden: Harrassowitz, 2020).

3 The topic for this article was inspired by my intense discussions with Anastasia Amrhein on the nature of divinity while supervising her dissertation on "Multimedia Image-Making in Assyria and Babylonia: Visualizations of the Numinous in Political Contexts" (Ph.D. diss., University of Pennsylvania, forthcoming). I would like to thank Liat Naeh and Irina Oryshkevich for editing my article.

 | DOI:10.1163/9789004511538_015

restored civic order to comply with the cosmic order. Humans' sociomorphic understanding of the divine was a further reflection of such interdependence. Mortals and divinities cooperated to maintain order, and it was within this framework that the gods were perceived as mentalized agents. The gods therefore manifested their intentionality through natural phenomena—celestial, atmospheric, and seismic events such as eclipses, earthquakes, floods, and storms, as well as terrestrial omens in town and country.[4] In particular contexts and under particular circumstances, they could turn all things—animate and inanimate—into conduits for expressing their decisions regarding human life, which then had to be decoded by divinatory experts.[5] As discussed first by Thorkild Jacobsen and later by Gebhard Selz, the use of priestly and royal titles such as EN, NIN, and LUGAL to define not only human rulers but also divinities, as well as divine and human assemblies, is further reflected in this modeling of heavenly conditions along the lines of sociopolitical structures in the human world.[6] Not only was the polytheistic pantheon perceived in sociomorphic terms, but it also operated as an integrated network.

4 Leo A. Oppenheim, "Divination and Celestial Observation in the Last Assyrian Empire," *Centaurus* 14 (1969): 97–135.

5 Beate Pongratz-Leisten, "The King at the Crossroads Between Divination and Cosmology," in *Divination, Politics, and Ancient Near Eastern Empires*, ed. Alan Lenzi and Jonathan Stökl (Atlanta, GA: Society of Biblical Literature, 2014), 33–48.

6 See Thorkild Jacobsen, "Primitive Democracy in Ancient Mesopotamia," *JNES* 2 (1943): 159–172; and Selz, "Götter der Gesellschaft," 68 and 74. In the beginning, the term NIN was sex- and gender-neutral and was used for female as well as male divinities. However, in my view, this does not imply that gendering of divinities took place only in the third and second millennia BCE. Julia Asher-Greve and Joan Goodnick Westenholz claim that divinity became anthropomorphized during the third and second millennia BCE; *Goddesses in Context: On Divine Powers, Roles, Relationships and Gender* (Fribourg: Academic Press; Göttingen: Vandenhoeck & Ruprecht, 2013), 18–59, 133. However, what appears ambiguous to us may not have necessarily been deemed ambiguous in the eyes of the ancients. Already during the Old Babylonian period, the use of the term *ilu* "god" was a deliberate expression of the close relationship between an individual and his or her god or goddess. In contexts such as theophoric personal names—such as "Mercy is God" (Ḥinn-el) or "Unique is God" (Yaḥad-ʾelum)—the personal god was known to the individual, and was by no means ambiguous; Michael Streck, "Die Amurriter der altbabylonischen Zeit im Spiegel des Onomastikons: Eine ethnische Evaluierung," in *2000 v. Chr. Politische, wirtschaftliche und kulturelle Entwicklung im Zeichen einer Jahrtausendwende: 3. Internationales Colloquium der Deutschen Orient-Gesellschaft*, ed. Jan-Waalke Meyer and Walter Sommerfeld (Saarbrücken: Saarbrücker Druckerei und Verlag, 2004), 313–355. This practice continued into the first millennium BCE; Beate Pongratz-Leisten, "A New Agenda for the Study of the Rise of Monotheism" and "Divine Agency and Astralization of the Gods in Ancient Mesopotamia," in *Reconsidering the Concept of Revolutionary Monotheism*, ed. Beate Pongratz-Leisten (Winona Lake, IN: Eisenbrauns, 2011), 31–34 and 137–187. The use of the term *ilu* in the omen series *šumma ālu* of the first millennium BCE,

2 Assyriological Approaches to the Polytheistic Pantheon

Approaches to the Mesopotamian polytheistic pantheon range from the evolutionary, for example, that of Thorkild Jacobsen, who was influenced by Rudolf Otto's phenomenological works and their focus on the mysterious numinous,[7] to the more functionalist and role-oriented, for example, the work of Jean Bottéro,[8] to the more contextualized approach of Wilfred Lambert. While taking into consideration different levels of theological sophistication, the last of these three still maintains that before the systematization of Sumerian and Babylonian religions, the gods were believed to be "archaic matter," bound to natural phenomena.[9] More recently, the focus of the debate has moved on to the question of the anthropomorphic and nonanthropomorphic shape of divinity,[10] as well as the anthropomorphizing qualities or agency of what was generally perceived as inanimate matter.[11] In some cases, however, con-

---

on the other hand, reflects another scribal convention, namely, leaving the applicability of the omen open to any kind of concrete context or situation, rather than reflecting a "new emphasis on disembodied powers" or a notion of disenchantment, as argued by Seth Richardson, "The Hypercoherent Icon: Knowledge, Rationalization, and Disenchantment at Nineveh," in *Iconoclasm and Text Destruction in the Ancient Near East and Beyond*, ed. Natalie Naomi May (Chicago, IL: The Oriental Institute, 2012), 231–258. For further discussion on the concept of anthropomorphizing, see below.

7 See Thorkild Jacobsen, *Toward the Image of Tammuz and Other Essays on Mesopotamian History and Culture*, ed. William L. Moran (Cambridge, MA: Harvard University Press, 1970); Thorkild Jacobsen, *The Treasures of Darkness: A History of Mesopotamian Religion* (New Haven, CT: Yale University Press, 1976); and the review by Walther Sallaberger, "Zur Genese der Mesopotamischen Götterwelt: Eine Auseinandersetzung mit Thorkild Jacobsens *Central Concerns*," in *mu-zu an-za3-še3 kur-ur2-še3 ḫe2-ĝal2: Altorientalistische Studien zu Ehren von Konrad Volk*, ed. Jessica Baldwin, Jana Matuszak, and Manuel Ceccarelli, Dubsar 17 (Münster: Zaphon, 2020), 391–412.

8 Jean Bottéro, *Religion in Ancient Mesopotamia*, trans. Teresa Lavender Fagan (Chicago, IL: University of Chicago Press, 2001).

9 Lambert, "Götterlisten"; Lambert, "Gott"; Lambert, "Ancient Mesopotamian Gods: Superstition, Philosophy, Theology," *Revue de l'histoire des religions* 207/2 (1990): 115–130.

10 Gebhard Selz, "'The Holy Drum, the Spear, and the Harp': Toward an Understanding of the Problems of Deification in Third Millennium Mesopotamia," in *Sumerian Gods and Their Representations*, ed. I.J. Finkel and M.J. Geller (Groningen: Styx, 1997), 167–209; Barbara Nevling Porter, ed., *What Is a God? Anthropomorphic and Non-Anthropomorphic Aspects of Deity in Ancient Mesopotamia*, Transactions of the Casco Bay Assyriological Institute 2 (Winona Lake, IN: Casco Bay Assyriological Institute, 2009); Tallay Ornan, *The Triumph of the Symbol: Pictorial Representation of Deities in Mesopotamia and the Biblical Image Ban* (Fribourg: Academic Press; Göttingen: Vandenhoeck & Ruprecht, 2005); Tallay Ornan, "In the Likeness of Man: Reflections on the Anthropocentric Perception of the Divine in Mesopotamian Art," in Porter, *What is a God?*, 93–151.

11 Francesca Rochberg, "Personifications and Metaphors in Babylonian Celestial *Omina*,"

fusion has arisen from the conflation of the human form with the anthropomorphizing capabilities of interaction and communication. Such conflation is illustrated, for example, by Wolfram von Soden's claim that: "the terrestrial world was carried over to the primarily heavenly world of the gods .... All Mesopotamian deities had a human form,"[12] and by a question posed by Barbara Nevling Porter in the title of one of her articles: "Blessings from a Crown, Offerings to a Drum: Were There Non-Anthropomorphic Deities in Mesopotamia?"[13]

Porter's article brings me to the matter of agency, a notion crucial to our understanding of the divine world in Mesopotamia. Quoting from the instructions of a Seleucid ritual for daily offerings performed at the temple of Anu, which lists offerings to the gods of the temple as well as the seat of Anu—the household of his consort Antu, Anu's two tiaras, the ziggurat, etc.,[14] Porter concludes that these objects "were considered to be *gods*,"[15] because they received offerings in the same manner as the deities populating the temple. She goes on to argue that the ancient concept of divinity differed from the modern one in that objects and nouns, including diseases, could be written with the determinative DINGIR. Accordingly, this qualified them as "gods" even though our modern categorization of "gods" suggests "a degree of uniformity in their form and nature."[16] Porter places much weight on the fact that in certain contexts the ancients chose to put the determinative DINGIR before the respective object and concludes that "although Mesopotamian gods were often represented as beings with fully developed personalities, the writing of epilepsy [for example] with the label used for gods' names in itself suggests *that personality was not considered an essential quality* of DINGIRs and *ilus*."[17] Her list of "non-anthropomorphic gods" includes natural phenomena, with a particular focus on mountains; objects, including chariots and boats of gods; musical instru-

---

JAOS 116/3 (1996): 475–485; Pongratz-Leisten, "Divine Agency"; Beate Pongratz-Leisten and Karen Sonik, "Between Cognition and Culture: Theorizing the Materiality of Divine Agency in Cross-Cultural Perspective," in *The Materiality of Divine Agency*, ed., Beate Pongratz-Leisten and Karen Sonik (Boston, MA and Berlin: de Gruyter, 2015), 3–69.

12 Wolfram von Soden, *The Ancient Orient: An Introduction to the Study of the Ancient Near East*, trans., Donald G. Schley (Grand Rapids, MI: Eerdmans, 1994), 175.

13 Barbara Nevling Porter, "Blessings from a Crown, Offerings to a Drum: Were There Non-Anthropomorphic Deities in Ancient Mesopotamia?," in Porter, *What is a God?*, 153–194.

14 François Thureau-Dangin, *Rituels Accadiens* (Paris: Editions Ernest Leroux, 1921), 61–86 ll. I 21–33 = Marc J.H. Linssen, *The Cults of Uruk and Babylon: The Temple Ritual Texts as Evidence for Hellenistic Cult Practice* (Boston, MA/Leiden: Brill, 2004), 172–183 ll. 21–33.

15 Porter, "Blessings of a Crown," 157, italics mine.

16 Porter, "Blessings of a Crown," 158.

17 Porter, "Blessings of a Crown," 158; italics mine.

ments; weapons, including Ningirsu's/Ninurta's weapons Shargaz and Sharur; and crowns, especially Assur's crown "Lord-Tiara" (Bēl-Agû). Porter's exhaustive and minute discussion of all these various entities reveals the complexity of the conceptualization of the divine in ancient Mesopotamia, and demonstrates that, depending on the period, even these nonanthropomorphic entities were regarded "as having a variety of different natures, functions, and behaviors,"[18] with some being passive and others actively involved in the human sphere. Nonetheless, Porter does not engage with Jacobsen's idea of *metaphor*, which holds that the experience of the numinous may only be grasped through metaphor, and that "the situationally determined, nonhuman, forms ... are all original or old forms or ... survivals into a later stage. They appear to have had their floruit in Protoliterate or earlier periods."[19] According to Jacobsen's evolutionary approach, the notion of the divine as metaphor lies at the origin of religion in Mesopotamia.

The idea of metaphor was reintroduced by Francesca Rochberg in her discussion of the Babylonian celestial omina in which she explored "the conception of the relation of the divine to the celestial bodies and their phenomena, the signs."[20] Rochberg explicitly states that while most omens do not reveal any explicit concept of the involvement of deities in natural phenomena (e.g., an eclipse), the language used to describe these phenomena may be anthropomorphizing. So, for example, the moon "mourns" or "feels distress" during an eclipse, which indicates that the ancients regarded planets as giving perceptible form to deities and therefore as manifesting divine agency.[21] Yet I would like to stress that the pervasiveness of metaphor, as posited by George Lakoff and Mark Johnson as well as Christopher Tilley,[22] is no indication of an archaic state of thought, but rather a characteristic of human thought and language.[23] "[W]ithout metaphor human communication would be nigh impossible ... metaphors provide the basis for an interpretative understanding of the world."[24] A beautiful example of this human manner lies in the introductory

18 Porter, "Blessings of a Crown," 187.

19 Jacobsen, *The Treasures of Darkness*, 9.

20 Rochberg, "Personifications and Metaphors," 475.

21 Rochberg, "Personifications and Metaphors."

22 George Lakoff and Mark Johnson, *Metaphors We Live By* (Chicago, IL: Chicago University Press, 1980); Christopher Tilley, *Metaphor and Material Culture* (Oxford: Blackwell Publishing, 1999).

23 Beate Pongratz-Leisten, "Seeing and Knowing: Cultural Concepts and the Deictic Power of the Image in Mesopotamia," in *Artifacts and Art/Works in the Ancient World*, ed. Karen Sonik (Philadelphia, PA: University of Pennsylvania Museum Press, forthcoming).

24 Tilley, *Metaphor and Material Culture*, 4.

lines of *Lugal-e*, also known as *Ninurta's Exploits*, which conjure the devastating forces of the warrior god Ninurta in powerful, figurative language:

> An, king of the gods, majestic one: O king, storm of majestic splendor, peerless Ninurta, possessing superior strength; who pillages the mountains all alone; deluge, indefatigable serpent hurling yourself at the rebel land, hero striding formidably into battle; lord whose powerful arm is fit to bear the mace, reaping like barley the necks of the insubordinate: Ninurta, king, son in whose strength his father rejoices; hero whose awesomeness covers the mountains like a south storm; Ninurta, who makes the good tiara, the rainbow (?), flash like lightning; grandly begotten by him who wears the princely beard; dragon who turns on himself, strength of a lion snarling at a snake, roaring hurricane; Ninurta, king, whom Enlil has exalted above himself; hero, great battle-net flung over the foe: Ninurta, with the awesomeness of your shadow extending over the Land; releasing fury on the rebel lands, overwhelming their assemblies! Ninurta, king, son who has forced homage to his father far and wide!
>
> Inspiring great numinous power, he had taken his place on the throne, the august dais, and was sitting gladly at his ease at the festival celebrated in his honor, rivalling An and Enlil in drinking his fill, while Bau was pleading petitions in a prayer for the king, and he, Ninurta, Enlil's son, was handing down decisions. At that moment the lord's battle-mace looked towards the mountains, the Šar-ur cried out aloud to its master.[25]

While Ninurta's actions assume a human form, their effect is described in figurative language with a host of metaphors that evoke his devastating force and superiority in battle. These metaphors make the destructive force of battle no less real. On the contrary, thanks to their colorful and vibrant rhetoric they go far beyond being mere literary devices or ornamental analogies to evoke the agonizing experience of war in a highly intense and incisive way, while still focusing on the agency of the warrior god Ninurta.[26] In other words, myth and the metaphorical description of Ninurta's agency serve as a cloak for capturing the human physical experience of the horrors of war. Thus, as Lakoff and Johnson suggest in their notion of the conceptual metaphor, myth emerges as a

25 ETCSL 1.6.2:1–23.

26 Jacobsen, *The Treasures of Darkness*, 5, described the use of religious metaphor as follows: "The whole purpose of the metaphor is a leap from that level (the literal), and a religious metaphor is not truly understood until it is experienced as a means of suggesting the Numinous."

tool of thought.[27] Building on Rochberg's points, we ought therefore to consider what kind of textual genre we are dealing with as the intensity of metaphorical language differs according to genre.

3 Agency and Mentalization

I have previously pursued Rochberg's approach further by drawing inspiration from the fields of cognitive religion and anthropology.[28] In its nascent years, cognitive religion focused on the *anthropomorphizing* aspects in descriptions of divine agency.[29] More recently, however, it has turned to the mentalizing aspects by emphasizing mind perception and assuming that supernatural beings, like humans, are "guided by a variety of mental states—attitudes, desires, motivations, knowledge, and preferences."[30] The scholarly progress of this approach lies in the fact that it shifts the focus from anthropomorphism to mentalization, and so relinquishes the idea of anthropomorphic form. Karen Sonik and I have made the essential point that the new perspectives offered by the cognitive sciences of religion, neuroaesthetics, and neuroarthistory must be applied in a nuanced way, and, above all, the cultural-historical context in which the manifestation of the divine was mediated must always be taken into account.[31]

Arguing from the perspective of cognitive sciences, I understand the conceptualization of the divine world as the religious expression of social and cultural learning, whereby cultural learning includes "imitative learning, instructed

27 Palladivini and Portuese, *Researching Metaphor*, 4.

28 Pongratz-Leisten, "Divine Agency and Astralization."

29 Stewart Elliott Guthrie, *Faces in the Clouds: A New Theory of Religion* (New York, NY: Oxford University Press, 1993); Justin L. Barrett, "Exploring the Natural Foundations of Religious Belief," *Trends in Cognitive Sciences* 4 (2000): 29–34; Barrett, "Cognitive Science of Religion: What Is It and Why Is It?" *RC* 1/6 (2007): 768–786; Pascal Boyer, *The Naturalness of Religious Ideas: A Cognitive Theory of Religion* (Berkeley, CA: University of California Press, 1994); Boyer, *Religion Explained: The Evolutionary Origins of Religious Thought* (New York, NY: Basic Books, 2001); and Scott Atran, *In Gods We Trust: The Evolutionary Landscape of Religion* (Oxford: Oxford University Press, 2002).

30 Will M. Gervais, "Perceiving Minds and Gods: How Mind Perception Enables, Constrains, and is Triggered by Belief in Gods," *Perspectives on Psychological Science* 8/4 (2013): 380–394; see further Illka Pyysiänen, *How Religion Works* (Leiden: Brill, 2001); Pyysiänen, *Supernatural Agents: Why We Believe in Souls, Gods and Buddhas* (Oxford: Oxford University Press, 2009).

31 Pongratz-Leisten and Sonik, "Between Cognition and Culture."

learning, and collaborative learning" based primarily on reconstruction.[32] The learning process should never be understood as passive reception, but rather as a local and situational response "contingent on context, resources, instructional sets, authority relations, framing devices, and modes of construal."[33] While investigating the ancient construction of a protective social network that ultimately reaches into the divine world, I draw on aspects of current models of culture in the cognitive sciences as developed by Atran and others,[34] who consider culture as the result of concatenated individual interactions at the level of individual decisions that generate macrostructural norms from the bottom up, rather than as a set of ideas and beliefs imposed from the top down. I will therefore focus here on religious expression as something constructed through group interaction within particular forms of social organizations that evolved in the ancient Near East over time—from small group units based primarily on the nuclear family,[35] to larger settlements and city states.[36] I will demonstrate that particular relational constructs with the divine world do not necessarily replace each other over time. Rather, those developed by more mobile groups live on in the societies of urban cultures as they construct authority, inheritance rights, and the identity of individuals. An approach to religion that views it as something relational rather than as a form of emotional expression is supported by Atran's argument that "worship" involves an "authoritarian ranking relationship" based on social interaction characterized by "gifts, petitions, thanks [and] submission of the body" rather than emotional attachment.[37]

From an anthropological perspective, Alfred Gell's notion of distributed personhood with its distinction between primary and secondary agents provides a framework for determining the difference between the immaterial and invisi-

---

32 Michael Tomasello, *The Cultural Origins of Human Cognition* (Cambridge, MA: Harvard University Press, 2000). See, however, recent approaches showing that memory and communication "involve reconstruction rather than copying of the material remembered or communicated"; Dan Sperber and Lawrence A. Hirschfeld, "The Cognitive Foundations of Cultural Stability and Diversity," *Trends in Cognitive Science* 8/1 (2004): 40–46.

33 R. Shweder, "Cultural Psychology: What Is It?," in *Cultural Psychology*, ed. J. Stigler, R. Shweder, and G. Herdt (New York, NY: Cambridge University Press, 1990), 13; and Scott Atran, Douglas L. Medin, and N.O. Ross, "The Cultural Mind: Environmental Decision Making and Cultural Modeling Within and Across Populations," *Psychological Review* 112 (2005): 744–776.

34 Atran, Medin, and Ross, "The Cultural Mind," 749.

35 Petr Charvát, *Mesopotamia before History*, 2nd ed. (London and New York, NY: Routledge, 2002).

36 Norman Yoffee, *Myths of the Archaic State* (New York, NY and Cambridge: Cambridge University Press, 2005).

37 Atran, *In Gods We Trust*, 71–73.

ble divinity of the primary agent and referent, and its manifestation in a host of referees, including astral bodies, statues, standards, emblematic animals, etc., that serve as secondary agents.[38] In Mesopotamia, in other words, a divinity, always thought of as an intentional agent, could adopt a multitude of modes dependent on particular settings. Thus, in the context of the cult, interaction with the divinity occurred primarily through the media of the statue and the cultic symbol; in the context of prayer, which plays a part not only in the cult, but also in rituals, such as those of purification performed on the roof of a house, the divinity to whom it is addressed often assumes the form of a celestial body. This same mode of agency occurred in the context of divination since prayer and divination were preferably performed at night.[39] Notably, even stars, which did not serve as a secondary mode of any divinity, could have agency, as shown by the particular address directed at them, which includes the verb "to enter" (*erēbu*) or to "stand by" (*uzuzzu*): "Enter, gods of the night, great stars!"[40] Due to their mobility, standards and weapons were brought out from the temple for the performance of oath-taking during judicial procedures. Objects in their artifactual and astrophysical nature thus mediated between the divinity and the worshiper and provided a spatiotemporal context of divine presence. Serving as material carriers of divinities, they extended their social agency beyond the confines of the "divine body." Albeit ontologically distinct from the deities they signified, all these animate and inanimate objects were still regarded as divine or were granted divine status due to their potential capability to exert agency and intentionality.[41]

In their function as icon, index, or symbol, these referees could *act* for and interact with the divine referent,[42] as we can see in another passage in *Lugal-e*:

---

38 Alfred Gell, *Art and Agency: An Anthropological Theory* (Oxford: Clarendon Press; New York: Oxford University Press, 1998); Lambert, "Gott"; Pongratz-Leisten, "Divine Agency and Astralization."

39 Piotr Steinkeller, "Of Stars and Men: The Conceptual and Mythological Setup of Babylonian Extispicy," in *Biblical and Oriental Essays in Memoriam of William Moran*, ed. Augustinus Gianto, BibOr 48 (Rome: Pontifical Institute, 2005) 11–47.

40 *erbānim ilāni mušīti kakkabū ra*[*bûtu*], OECT 6 pl. XII 12.

41 Gell, *Art and Agency*, 121 with reference to Guthrie, *Faces in the Crowd*; Robin Osborne and Jeremy Tanner, *Art's Agency and Art History* (Malden, MA and Oxford: Blackwell Publishing, 2007); Atran, *In Gods We Trust*; Boyer, *Religion Explained*; Pascal Boyer, "Religious Thought and Behaviour as By-Products of Brain Function," *Trends in Cognitive Science* 7/3 (2003): 119–124. On the very materiality of divine agency, see David Wengrow, *The Archaeology of Early Egypt: Social Transformations in North-East Africa, 10,000–2650 BC* (Cambridge: Cambridge University Press, 2006).

42 Caroline Walker Bynum, "The Sacrality of Things: An Inquiry into Divine Materiality in the Christian Middle Ages," *Irish Theological Quarterly* 78 (2013): 3–18, 10 and n. 29 referencing

> In his heart, [Ninurta] beamed at his lion-headed weapon, as it flew up like a bird, trampling the mountains for him. It raised itself on its wings to take away prisoner the disobedient, it spun around the horizon of heaven to find out what was happening. Someone from afar came to meet it, brought news for the tireless one, the one who never rests, whose wings near the deluge, the Šar-ur. What did it gather there … for Lord Ninurta? It reported the deliberations of the mountains, it explained their intentions to Lord Ninurta, it outlined what people were saying about the Asag.[43]

Here, initially pictured as a lion-headed weapon, Sharur's agency, though described in theriomorphic terms, mirrors the martial and devastating force of the warrior god Ninurta. Yet it also advises its lord not to wage battle against Asag any longer, and so, in its deliberations, displays the full cognitive range of agency normally ascribed to personified beings. However, the interest of the author is not to personify Sharur, but rather, through a mentalization process, provide it with the potential power to complement or even counteract the warrior god in his field of action through the performance of a speech act, thus putting the power of language at center stage. For us modern scholars the important thing is that the ancient author had no problem shifting between the weapon as an extension of Ninurta's physical body and agency, and the concept of Sharur as an independent agent.

Unlike Porter, I posit that cultic paraphernalia, including the pedestal, bed, or boat of a divinity, do not operate on the same level as the aforementioned referees, including weapons such as Sharur. While certain cultic paraphernalia could be treated as if they were divinities through the presentation of offerings during cultic performances, and though they could be declared to possess a divine quality through a written sign such as DINGIR, the use of the determinative simply indicated that they belonged to the divine sphere of the respective divinity. Despite such honors, they remained passive. In other words, the scribal convention of combining either a divinity's name or paraphernalia with DINGIR is very much in line with the practice of conceiving lexical lists of categories, such as wood, stone, metal, etc., all of which are organized through the use of the respective determinative. Moreover, the sacred status of any kind of object pertaining to the divine sphere could be enhanced by its fabrication out of precious materials that were regarded as possessing pure

---

Peircian sign theory; Cynthia Hahn, "Objects of Devotion and Desire: Relics, Reliquaries, Relation, and Response," in *Objects of Devotion and Desire: Medieval Relic to Contemporary Art*, curated by Cynthia Hahn (New York, NY: Hunter College, 2011), 13.

43 ETCSL 1.6.2, 109–118.

or even sacred qualities. Research into the materiality of divine agency has emphasized that particular stones, metals, etc., were chosen because of their inherent purity, shininess and lustrous appearance, and/or their color, all of which were integral to the efficacy of the divine, the sacredness of the divine abode, and cultic ritual.[44] It is the *inherent physical property* of purity that exists in these materials and properties (e.g., sparkle, shine) that may have activated a sense of sacredness and, consequently, would have sacralized objects so that the assignment of sacred *quality* in cultural conceptualization, in some cases, would not even have required ritual performance.[45] There is, however, no context in which cultic paraphernalia *acted* as independent agents on behalf of the divinity, or interacted with the human world as if "responding" to prayers, as icons or symbols do. In other words, Mesopotamian religion operated with a multilayered spectrum of primary agents who possessed divine agency, secondary agents who could extend their scope of action in a particular context such as a cult, divination, legislation, war, etc., and objects that belonged to the divine sphere and therefore permeated and imbued the entire space of the temple with sacredness while reinforcing the divine presence of the temple's owners along with their divine retinue.

Such conceptualization of hierarchical and contextualized divinity and divine agency constantly oscillated between the materialized, local aspect of limited agency, and its divine referent, which was omnipotent and interactive. Future discussion must therefore combine the spatial dimensions and

44 David Freedberg, *The Power of Images: Studies in the History and Theory of Response* (Chicago, IL: The University of Chicago Press, 1989), 66–74; Irene J. Winter, "Agency Marked, Agency Ascribed: The Affective Object in Ancient Mesopotamia," in *Art's Agency and Art History*, ed. Robin Osborne and Jeremy Tanner (Malden, MA: Blackwell Publishing, 2007), 73–98; Winter, "Gold! Light and Lustre in Ancient Mesopotamia," in *Ancient and Modern Issues in Cultural Heritage: Colour and Light in Architecture, Art and Material Culture. Islamic Archaeology*, ed. Roger Matthews and John Curtis, Proceedings of the Seventh International Congress on the Archaeology of the Ancient Near East 2 (Wiesbaden: Harrassowitz Verlag, 2012), 153–171; Anais Schuster-Brandis, *Steine als Schutz- und Heilmittel: Untersuchung zu ihrer Verwendung in der Beschwörungskunst Mesopotamiens im 1 Jt. v. Chr* (Münster: Ugarit-Verlag, 2008); Beate Pongratz-Leisten, "Reflections on the Translatability of Holiness," in *Of God(s), Trees, Kings, and Scholars: Neo-Assyrian and Related Studies in Honour of Simo Parpola*, ed. Mikko Luukko, Saana Svärd, and Raija Mattila (Helsinki: Finnish Oriental Society, 2009), 409–428; Kim Benzel, "'What Goes In Is What Comes Out'—But What Was Already There? Divine Materials and Materiality in Ancient Mesopotamia," in Pongratz-Leisten and Sonik, *Materiality of Divine Agency*, 89–118.

45 Tim Ingold, *Being Alive: Essays on Movement, Knowledge and Description* (London and New York, NY: Routledge, 2011), 29–30; Benzel, "What Goes In," 104.

materialized presencing of the divine in a variety of contexts while taking into account the scope of agency and the notion of a divine referent.[46]

There is also a kind of animation of matter that must be distinguished from agency. Agency emerges from the mentalization of the nonhuman other and the assignment of goal-oriented behavior to it. Such agency is associated with interaction and may be categorized as anthropomorphizing agency. Animation, however, implies that things come alive, and not necessarily through consecration or interaction with a human being. Caroline Bynum, in particular, in discussing the aspect of transubstantiation has stressed the animated nature of bread and wine used for the Eucharist in the Middle Ages: through the performance of the sacrament of the Eucharist, both were believed to come alive and to change into corporeal matter, i.e., bread into flesh and wine into blood, converting these substances into freshly bleeding flesh with their original appearance remaining. This kind of animism, as she argues, was neither simple anthropomorphism, nor perceived as a "likeness" of God. Statues, relics, paintings, and other matter provided access to the divine by coming alive, by serving as a venue for communicating with the divine through acts such as blessings, bleeding, weeping, glowing, winking at viewers, or even descending from their pedestals and walking around.[47] Animism, it seems, encompassed the entire range of having affect, coming alive, and interacting with the human world. What needs to be clarified in our modern scholarly discussion then is the use of the terms "anthropomorphism" and "animism." Both have been used to describe the divine in a statue, relief, or painting, and to define agency as mentalized, decisive behavior, which has resulted in the blurring of the two.

It is important to bear in mind that though the entire universe was considered animate in both the ancient Near East and the Middle Ages, the forces of nature and/or certain substances were not divine by virtue of the way in which their presence materialized itself. The ancients were highly capable of distinguishing the thunderstorm as meteorological phenomenon from the "voice" of

46 Beate, Pongatz-Leisten, "Conceptualizing Divinity Between Cult and Theology in the Ancient Near East," in *Dieux, rois et capitales dans le Proche-Orient ancien: Compte rendu de la LXVe Rencontre Assyriologique Internationale (Paris, 8–12 juillet 2019)*, ed. Marine Béranger, Francesca Nebiolo and Nele Ziegler (Leuven: Peeters, forthcoming); Pongratz-Leisten, "Assyriological Approaches towards a History of Religion in Mesopotamia," in *The Intellectual Heritage of the Ancient Near East: Proceedings of the 64th Rencontre Assyriologique Internationale in Innsbruck*, ed. Robert Rollinger, Irene Madreiter, and Martin Lang, Melammu Symposia 12 (Vienna: Austria Academy of Sciences Press, 2021), in press.

47 Caroline Walker Bynum, "The Animation and Agency of Holy Food," in *The Materiality of Divine Agency*, ed. Beate Pongratz-Leisten and Karen Sonik (Boston, MA and Berlin: de Gruyter, 2015), 70–85, 78.

the storm god. This kind of distinction goes beyond what Rudolf Otto defined as the "numinous," as the indexing of some impersonal divine power experienced as an irrational-emotional mysterium, which he considered to lie at the origin of religion.[48] In the early twentieth century, Otto's notion of religious experience was established as a methodological element and prerequisite for any scholarly inquiry into religion and was adopted by a host of scholars including Gerd van der Leeuw, Joachim Wach, Friedrich Heiler, and Mircea Eliade, to name but a few, all of whom were striving to prove that congenial empathy stood at the *origin* of religion.[49] Needless to say, "religion" as an object of scholarly inquiry cannot be grasped from a person's feelings toward religion; it can only be grasped as lived in and practiced by communities and their institutions within the context of a theological discourse.[50]

4 Complexity in the Materialization of the Divine

I now return to the distinctions already made by the ancients when they conceived of natural phenomena as manifestations of divinities. The archaeological record of the fourth millennium BCE clearly illustrates their complex and highly sophisticated concept of the divine. Two objects evincing such complexity are the Uruk seal from the Erlenmeyer Collection, and the famous Uruk Vase. The sealing contains various representations of, or referents to, the goddess Inanna, the patron deity of the city. It includes an image of Inanna's symbol, the reed bundle, and a star representing either the divine determinative or her astral aspect, the pictograph UD, i.e., the sun rising between two mountains, and the mirror image SIG designating its setting. To the right of Inanna's symbol is a drum representing the sign EZEN or "festival." To the right of this sign is the bull, the emblematic animal of Inanna. The group can thus be read as a "festival of the rising and setting star."[51] With the added pictorial evidence of the famous Uruk Vase, which also dates to around 3200 BCE, we get the full

48 Rudolf Otto, *Das Heilige: Über das Irrationale in der Idee des Heiligen und sein Verhältnis zum Rationalen* (Breslau: Trewendt und Granier, 1917).

49 Rainer Flasche, "Numinos," in *Handbuch religionswissenschaftlicher Grundbegriffe*, ed. Hubert Cancik, Burkhard Gladigow, and Karl-Heinz Kohl, vol. 4 (Stuttgart: Kohlhammer, 1998), 252–255.

50 Pongratz-Leisten, "Assyriological Approaches."

51 Christopher Woods, "The Earliest Mesopotamian Writing," in *Visible Language: Inventions of Writing in the Ancient Middle East and Beyond*, ed. Christopher Woods, Oriental Institute Museum Publications 32 (Chicago, IL: The Oriental Institute of Chicago University, 2010), 50.

range of divine representation.[52] In its upper register, the Uruk Vase shows the king before a priestess, who is once again standing in front of two reed bundles that symbolically mark the entrance to her temple.[53] In its inner sanctum we see a ram carrying two pedestals with two goddesses and a reed bundle. One of these female figures holds what has been interpreted as the sign EN, standing for the En-priest. It could well be that one or both of the female figures repre-

52 Although it was found in a temple treasury hoard dating to level III around 3000 BCE. Nonetheless, as Zainab Bahrani points out, it shows repairs that already date to antiquity, thereby suggesting that it was carved in some earlier period; Zainab Bahrani, "Performativity and the Image: Narrative, Representation, and the Uruk Vase," in *Leaving No Stones Unturned: Essays on the Ancient Near East and Egypt in Honor of Donald P. Hansen*, ed. Erica Ehrenberg (Winona Lake, IN: Eisenbrauns, 2002), 16.

53 The scholars arguing for ambiguity and deliberate blending of the human with the divine include Donald Hansen, "Art of the Early City States," in *Art of the First Cities: The Third Millennium BC from the Mediterranean to the Indus*, ed. Joan Aruz with Ronald Wallenfels (New York, NY: The Metropolitan Museum of Art and Yale University Press, 2003), 24; Marian H. Feldman, "Mesopotamian Art," in *A Companion to the Ancient Near East*, ed. Daniel C. Snell (Malden, MA and Oxford: Blackwell, 2005), 286; Gianni Marchesi and Nicolò Marchetti, *Royal Statuary of Early Dynastic Mesopotamia* (Winona Lake, IN: Eisenbrauns, 2011), 190–191. Others, like Wiggermann, took the female figure for Inanna; Frans A.M. Wiggermann, "Agriculture as Civilization: Sages, Farmers, and Barbarians," in *The Oxford Handbook of Cuneiform Culture*, ed. Karen Radner and Eleanor Robson (Oxford: Oxford University Press, 2011), 663. Suter, by contrast, persuasively argued for identifying her with a human priestess, as both she and the nude carrier in front of her are depicted smaller than the ruler approaching the temple; Claudia E. Suter, "Human, Divine or Both? The Uruk Vase and the Problem of Ambiguity in Early Mesopotamian Visual Arts," in *Critical Approaches to Ancient Near Eastern Art*, ed. Brian A. Brown and Marian H. Feldman (Boston, MA and Berlin: de Gruyter, 2014), 545–568. On the problem of identifying the scene with the Sacred Marriage rite, see Suter, "Human, Divine or Both?," 556–560. As observed by Bahrani, "Performativity and the Image," 17, the headdress is damaged, so it is impossible to know whether or not the figure wore a horned crown as marker of divinity. In light of the representation of Ningirsu on the tablet known as "Figure aux Plumes," it might be worth considering that at this time the horned crown had not yet been introduced as a marker of divinity; Ignace Gelb, Piotr Steinkeller, and Robert D. Whiting, *Earliest Land Tenure Systems in the Ancient Near East: Ancient Kudurrus*, 2 vols., University of Chicago Oriental Institute Publications 104 (Chicago, IL: The Oriental Institute, 1991), no. 18; Claus Wilcke, "Die Inschrift der 'Figure aux plumes'—ein frühes Werk sumerischer Dichtkunst," in *Beiträge zur Kulturgeschichte Vorderasiens: Festschrift für Rainer Michael Boehmer*, ed. Uwe Finkbeiner, Reinhard Dittmann, and Harald Hauptmann (Mainz: Philipp von Zabern, 1995), 669–674. Rather than wearing a horned crown, Ningirsu is depicted wearing a feathered headdress. Moreover, whether the ambiguity of the figures (Dumuzi and Inanna or the Priest King and the Priestess?) in the uppermost register of the Uruk Vase was intentional (Bahrani, "Performativity and the Image," 21), and whether this scene was supposed to represent the ritual of the Sacred Marriage, as suggested by Hansen and Bahrani, is hard to determine.

sent Ishtar in the anthropomorphic shape that she assumes in archaic offering lists as Inanna-morning star, Inanna-evening star, and Inanna-prince. In addition, the four registers of the Uruk Vase that depict the marshes, husbandry and the bearers of offerings reveal that Inanna was imagined in sociomorphic terms as the owner of the temple and head of the temple household.

The textual and archaeological evidence, which includes the sealing that displays the reed bundle as Inanna's symbol, the rising and setting of Venus as Inanna's astral aspect, the bull as her emblematic animal, and finally the vase, not only depict her anthropomorphically but also insinuate her role as owner of the temple, thereby revealing the full range of ways in which divinity could materialize itself and be referenced and imagined in its scope of agency in the ancient Near East. The decision by image-producers to depict all possible variants of divine presence was guided precisely by their desire to activate their performative force and effectively generate their full range of action. To this discussion, I believe, one could add the famous head of the Lady of Uruk, which is yet another anthropomorphic representation of the goddess. Although scholars have been cautious about identifying it as a representation of the goddess, it is striking that the head not only contains a hole at the top to accommodate a headdress or wig,[54] but is also flattened at the back, thereby suggesting that it belonged to a statue mounted on the wall. No such mounting has ever been attested in statues of human figures in Mesopotamia. However, similar archaeological evidence of the representation of Ishtar has been found in the form of a wall-mounted relief plaque in the Early Dynastic strata of the Ishtar temple in the city of Assur.[55]

Archaeological and textual evidence of the late fourth millennium BCE from archaic Uruk thus points to a concept of divinity that reveals all the aforementioned ways of materializing the divine and imagining its agency, and which, in terms of complexity, did not change until the decline of ancient Near Eastern civilization.[56] What did change, geographically and chronologically, were the

54 In his discussion of the female figure on the Burney Relief, Thorkild Jacobsen, "Pictures and Pictorial Language (The Burney Relief)," in *Figurative Language in the Ancient Near East*, ed. M. Mindlin, Mark J. Geller, and J. Wansbrough (London: School of Oriental and African Studies, University of London, 1987), 3, mentions a stone wig in the British Museum (probably BM 91075 as Michael Seymour suggested to me), which, in his view, may resemble the wigs worn by statues in the round, such as the one in the Metropolitan Museum (62.70.2), for instance.

55 Jürgen Bär, *Die ältesten Ischtar-Tempel in Assur* (Saarbrücken: Saarbrücker Druckerei und Verlag, 2003), 164 and pl. 62.

56 Richardson, "The Hypercoherent Icon." The large number of divinatory texts concerned with the agency of demons or other forces imposing diseases on human beings assembled

cultural decisions to emphasize particular forms within the pictorial repertoire based on the textual genre and the context of the interaction with the divine.

5 Ancient Scholars Conceptualizing Divinity

While the records of Mesopotamia do not amount to a treatise on divinity comparable to Cicero's *On the Nature of Gods*, various genres, including god lists, myths, and prayers, hint at the analytical, explanatory, and classificatory endeavors of scholarly authorities. While these genres belong to the scribal world, they do reflect real-life experience, as I shall discuss in greater depth below.[57] Administrative texts, such as lists of offerings and ritual texts pertaining to local cults, may also reflect the order in which divinities were ranked. In addition, the so-called divine directories, such as the *Assur Directory*, attest to an arrangement of divinities and groupings within various rooms and spaces in temples that were informed by existing ideas about the divine world. As Gonzalo Rubio observes, not all the divine names in the early lists of gods appear in the administrative texts, and there may be similar discrepancies among theophoric names that reflect the popular cult and the lists of gods.[58] However, all the aforementioned textual genres exhibit either the operations of the daily cult or an attempt to construct a coherent view of reality, albeit not conceived in abstract terms, and are thus instructive with regard to the pragmatics of polytheism in the ancient world.

It is also important to bear in mind that divinity was understood not simply as a composite assemblage of parts comparable to the ancient notion of a per-

in the libraries of Nineveh do not reflect a change in the conceptualization of divinity. Rather, the fact that divine punishment could be meted out by the "Hand of DN" or the "hand of a demon" (*qāt DN*, etc.) due to the violation of a taboo (Nils Heeßel, "Identifying Divine Agency: The Hands of the Gods in Context," in *Sources of Evil: Studies in Mesopotamian Exorcistic Lore*, ed. G. van Buylaere et al. [Boston, MA/Leiden: Brill, 2018], 133–149) reflects another interesting development at the end of the second millennium BCE regarding the conceptualization of retributive divine agency and an explanatory pattern for a disturbed divine-human relationship; Erica Couto-Ferreira, "From Head to Toe: Listing the Body in Cuneiform Texts," in *The Comparable Body: Analogy and Metaphor in Ancient Mesopotamian, Egyptian, and Graeco-Roman Medicine*, ed. J.Z. Wee (Boston, MA/Leiden: Brill, 2017), 43–71.

57 Gonzalo Rubio, "Gods and Scholars: Mapping the Pantheon in Early Mesopotamia," in *Reconsidering the Concept of Revolutionary Monotheism*, ed. Beate Pongratz-Leisten (Winona Lake, IN: Eisenbrauns, 2011), 91–116. See also Geza Komoróczy, "Das Pantheon im Kult, in den Götterlisten und in der Mythologie," *Orientalia Nova Series* 45 (1976): 80–86.

58 Rubio, "Gods and Scholars," 106–107.

son as body, body parts, name, and representative trappings and clothes. Just as a person was viewed as an integral part of a family, clan, city, and embedded in a protective network that extended from the world of the living to that of the divine through a chain of intermediaries that included the protective genius, personal god, city god, local and regional pantheon, all the way up to the supreme god, so too the polytheistic pantheon was perceived in sociomorphic and interdependent terms. In other words, polytheism in ancient Mesopotamia should not be regarded as the random divinization of natural, nonorganic or other phenomena. On the contrary, modeled on social real-life experience, it was perceived as a sophisticated network, in which every member of the pantheon had an assigned place with a particular set of roles and functions that guaranteed the smooth operation of the cosmic order. Divine and human worlds were viewed as interconnected in their respective relationship to the particular role assigned to the king, whose duty it was to mediate between the two worlds.

6 Conceptualizing an Integrated Network in Myth as an Analytical Tool and Metaphor

The cultural endeavor to shape human society into an integrated whole and structure the pantheon as its divine counterpart is reflected in two Sumerian myths: *Enki and Ninmah* and *Enki and the World Order*. *Enki and Ninmah* is an etiological tale about the crippled and handicapped individuals in society who, despite their afflictions, play a role in the functioning of society. It tells the story of how two gods first created humankind in order to alleviate the toil required for their subsistence and the provisions of their cult. As they banquet and carouse, they create incapacitated mortals and challenge each other to assign them specific roles in society. These include: a man with crippled hands who is turned into a servant of the king; a blind man who is allotted the musical arts; persons with broken or paralyzed feet who are assigned the job of the silversmith; an idiot who is put into the service of the king; an infertile woman who becomes a weaver in the queen's household; and a eunuch who is assigned an equally close position to the king. The list of these individuals reveals the social attempt to integrate every human being into the larger societal network without leaving anyone at the margins.

This cultural interest in conceiving the community as a functioning, interdependent and interrelated societal body is equally characteristic of the ancient construction of the pantheon. Nowhere is the idea of a synergetic divine collective better expressed than in the Sumerian poem *Enki and the World Order*.

The work begins with high praise of the creator god Enki in his role as patron of the fresh-water ocean and guarantor of the prosperity of nature, agriculture, and husbandry. It goes on to extol his ability to secure subsistence not only in the regions of the southern city states, but also in Meluhha and Dilmun, to vanquish Elam and Marhashi, to secure silver and lapis lazuli, and to create the two lifelines, the Euphrates and the Tigris. The poem then recounts how Enki proceeds to assign roles and functions to a host of divinities: Nanshe is charged with flooding, the storm god with filling canals with water, Ashnan with grain, Shakkan with husbandry, Dumuzi with fertile plains, and the sun god Utu with the verdicts on heaven and earth, while the brick god Kulla and his companion Mushdama become the master builders, and Uttu the weaver. All of these gods represent the division of labor that made civilized life in the southern plain possible and, indeed, promoted the growth of the urban centers into powerful city states during the fourth and third millennium BCE. The author, seemingly aware of the cultural and political potential of coordinated synergistic cooperation to generate a vigorously productive and dynamic urban life that meets the expansionist ambitions of the various city states, introduces the notion of conflict by having the goddess Inanna enter the scene and, enumerating various female goddesses and their responsibilities, complain bitterly to her father Enki that he has left her without any responsibility or role: "But why did you treat me, the woman, in an exceptional manner? I am Holy Inanna—where are my functions?"[59]

Heeding her plea, Enki grants her a sphere of agency that encompasses all the ambiguities, inconsistencies, and contradictions that define her character, which has beneficial as well as detrimental effects on humanity, as is evident in Sumero-Babylonian literature, which turned warfare into one of her major spheres of action. It is interesting that when requesting a "function," Inanna uses the Sumerian term GARZA, the meaning of which, when used as a logogram for *parṣu* in later Akkadian literature, can be narrowed down to the "offices" and "regulations" that define the operation of cultic life in temples. Originally associated with the ME, it represents the principles that make the cosmos and society run smoothly,[60] as indicated by the long list of MEs in the

59 *Enki and the World Order*, ll. 422–423: ^{422}munus-me-en dili-gu$_{10}$-ne a-na bi$_{2}$-ak ^{423}kug ^{d}inana-me-en mar-za-gu$_{10}$ me-a.

60 Jean-Jacques Glassner, "Inanna et les ME," in *Nippur at the Centennial : Papers Read at the 3e Rencontre Assyriologique Internationale, 1988*, ed. Maria de Jong Ellis (Philadelphia, PA: Distributed by the S.N. Kramer Fund, Babylonian Section, University Museum, 1992), 55–86.

Sumerian myth *Inanna and Enki*, which relates the story of how Inanna stole the MEs from her father Enki in order to move them from Eridu to the city of Uruk.

Despite their various plots and characters, all these mythical narratives share a common worldview that brings into high relief the ancient concern for assigning everybody his or her appropriate place in society so that all can help maintain an integrated community and keep society and the cosmos functioning. Beyond its concern for establishing a network that guarantees a civilized life, *Enki and the World Order* reveals an attempt to control disruptive elements by having them incorporated and played out by the goddess Inanna/Ishtar. This quest for control over the negative aspects of human society is equally reflected in the list of ME in *Inanna and Enki*, which, in addition to institutions, professions, and positive social behavior, includes things such as slander and defamation (nam-eme-sig), flattery (nam-še-er-ka-an), dishonorable behavior (nam-nì-ne-ru), the pillage of cities (uru-lah_x-lah_x), and the rebellious land (kur-ki-bala). By entrusting these disruptive elements to a divine authority—to Inanna in *Enki and the World Order*, and initially to Enki, but afterwards to Inanna in *Inanna and Enki*—the ancients seem to have believed that divine control would ultimately turn these to the benefit of society.

As revealed by the *Stoff*[61] of all three of these Sumerian poems, myth served as a *Denkform*,[62] as an analytical tool and conceptual metaphor[63] that provided a space for negotiating real-life experiences in explanatory, interpretative, and even legitimizing patterns. Its power thus lay in its construction and interpretation of social or other phenomena. As a sense-making instrument, it offered a way of structuring and understanding particular situations and events, and, indeed, provided a scaffold for consciousness itself.[64] In fulfilling these functions, myth constantly adapted to new contexts or circumstances and operated effectively only in the historically defined space and time of a particular com-

---

61 Fritz Graf, *Griechische Mythologie: Eine Einführung* (München and Zürich: Artemis and Winkler, 1991), 8: "Der Mythos ist nicht der aktuelle Dichtertext, sondern transzendiert ihn: er ist der Stoff, ein in großen Zügen festgelegter Handlungsablauf mit ebenso festen Personen, den der individuelle Dichter nur in Grenzen variieren kann."

62 Hans Blumenberg, *Work on Myth*, trans. R.M. Wallace (Cambridge, MA: MIT Press, 1985).

63 Lakoff and Johnson, *Metaphors We Live By*; for a recent discussion on metaphor, see the volume of collected articles edited by Pallavidini and Portuese, *Researching Metaphor*.

64 Jerome Bruner, *Acts of Meaning: Four Lectures on Mind and Culture* (Cambridge, MA: Harvard University Press, 1990); David Herman, "Cognitive Narratology," in *Handbook of Narratology*, ed. Peter Hühn, Jan Christoph Meier, John Pier, and Wolf Schmid, vol. 1 (Boston, MA/Berlin: de Gruyter, 2014), 30–43.

munity. Although the *emplotment*[65] of certain categories of myth may have evolved along similar lines, as in the case of combat myths, for instance,[66] and certain narratives were transmitted over centuries in Mesopotamian history, it is important to take account of their original or later embeddedness within a particular local tradition. Any innovative features or additions tell us something about their adaptation to new contexts. Rather than being purely imaginary tales, mythic narratives are anchored in real-life experiences[67]—i.e., not only those of the senses, but also those of the mind—which the audience can share through past experience or accept as an explanatory pattern for present or future experiences. In this context, as Hans Blumenberg points out, the "status of reality does not mean empirical demonstrability; the place of the latter can be filled by taken-for-grantedness, familiarity, having been part of the world from the beginning,"[68] and a familiar pattern of explanation.

In addition to conveying the ancient perspective of the pantheon as an integrated network, myth may also reflect cultic realities by indicating a particular city's patronage of a deity and thus declaring itself as his or her cultic center. Such information has been incorporated into the Sumerian poem *Inanna's Descent*, the Akkadian *Anzû Myth*, *Enuma elish*, and the *Erra Epic*. And it might explain certain cultic practices, such as the offerings to the gods as recounted in *Lugalbanda and the Mountain Cave* or in *Atrahasis*, for example; or divine names, such as Ninurta's renaming of his mother in *Lugal-e*; or situations entailing conflict or cooperation; as well as ones that offer potentialities and alternatives. All these aspects turn mythic narrative into an analytical tool that offers insight into life experiences, conveys cultural knowledge, and provides potential models for decision-making, behavior, etc., and/or explains existing cultic realities as well as political and social structures and hierarchies.[69]

---

65 Hayden White, *Metahistory: The Historical Imagination in Nineteenth-Century Europe* (Baltimore, MD: Johns Hopkins University Press, 1973).

66 Beate Pongratz-Leisten, *Religion and Ideology in Assyria* (Boston, MA/Berlin: de Gruyter, 2015), 232–238; Karen Sonik, "One or Many? Characterization and Identity in the *Gilgamesh Epic* and Other Mesopotamian Narratives," in *How to Tell a Story: Approaches to Mesopotamian Literature*, ed. Dahlia Shehata, Karen Sonik, and Frauke Weiershäuser (Leiden: Brill, forthcoming).

67 Christian Zgoll, "Myths as Polymorphous and Polystratic Erzählstoffe," in *Mythische Sphärenwechsel: Methodisch Neue Zugänge zu antiken Mythen in Orient und Okzident*, ed. Annette Zgoll and Christian Zgoll (Boston, MA/Berlin: de Gruyter, 2020), 61.

68 Blumenberg, *Work on Myth*, 68.

69 Burkhard Gladigow, "Mythische Experimente—experimentelle Mythen," in *Faszination des Mythos*, ed. Renate Schlesie (Basel and Frankfurt: Suhrkamp, 1985) 61–82; Burkhard Gladigow, "Mythenzensur und Symbolkontrolle," in *Kanon und Zensur*, ed. Aleida and Jan Assann (München: Wilhelm Fink Verlag, 1986), 158–168; Burkhard Gladigow, "Mytholo-

7 God Lists as a Reflection of a Divine Integrated Network

The idea of a network that ties together members of human society with the pantheon further characterizes the systematic work reflected in ancient god lists. While these lists were productions of the scholarly world and to some degree share organizational principles—e.g., grouping names by graphic signs—with the lexical lists, they may also reflect the mythographic knowledge used to construct divine hierarchies through genealogies, as seen in mythic literature. For this reason, they go beyond operating as mere "reproductive organs of the notational system" or as "basic learning tools."[70] Although Early Dynastic lists from Fara and Abu Salabikh already display the divine hierarchy, with the heaven god Anu, Enlil, and Ea heading the pantheon as we know from later lists,[71] these early god lists are not informed by mythographic knowledge. Instead, they contain sections dedicated to the administration and kitchen personnel of the city of Uruk and thus bear witness not only to the local character of god lists, but also to the fact that these texts probably originated in the experience of the Eanna temple, which served as an administrative center in archaic Uruk.[72] Like the lexical lists, they stick to organizational patterns that follow the phonetic or graphic resemblances of signs and semantic associations. Furthermore, they display a range of deified objects.[73] If one follows Gebhard Selz's proposal that the double entries x–^{d}x in the archaic metal list represent deified

gie und Theologie: Aussagestufen im griechischen Mythos," in *Theologien und Theologen in verschiedenen Kulturkreisen*, ed. Heinrich von Stietencron (Düsseldorf: Patmos Verlag, 1988), 77–88.

70 Piotr Michalowski, "Literacy, Schooling and the Transmission of Knowledge in Early Mesopotamian Culture," in *Theory and Practice of Knowledge Transfer: Studies in School Education in the Ancient Near East and Beyond. Papers Read at the Symposium in Leiden, 17–19 December 2008*, ed. W.S. van Egmond and W.S.H. van Soldt (Leiden: Nederlands Insitituut voor het Nabije Oosten, 2012), 39–57.

71 Inanna, here figuring right after Ea, will later be relegated to a position further down in the divine hierarchy.

72 Manfred Krebernik, "Die Götterlisten aus Fāra," *ZA* 76 (1986): 161–204; Pietro Mander, *Il pantheon di Abu-Ṣālabīkh* (Naples: Istituto Universitario Orientale, 1986); Selz, "The Holy Drum."

73 Gebhard Selz, "The Divine Prototypes," in *Religion and Power: Divine Kingship in the Ancient World and Beyond*, ed. Nicole Brisch, OIS 4 (Chicago, IL: The Oriental Institute of the University of Chicago, 2008), 13–31; Gebhard Selz, "Vergöttlichung," *RlA* 14 (2016): 545–548; and Selz, "Who Is a God? A Note on the Evolution of Divine Classifiers in a Multilingual Environment," in *Libiamo ne' lieti calici: Ancient Near Eastern Studies Presented to Lucio Milano on the Occasion of his 65th Birthday by Pupils, Colleagues and Friends*, ed. Paola Corò, Elena Devecchi, Nicla De Zorzi, and Masimmo Maiocchi, with the collaboration of Stefania Ermidoro and Erica Scapra (Münster: Ugarit-Verlag, 2016), 605–614.

objects,[74] then the deification of objects can be dated as early as these lists, that is, between 3200 and 2900 BCE. It should be noted that the earliest known god lists can be properly dated only several hundred years later, when they appear in the Early Dynastic III period (2600–2340 BCE). Written testimony cannot, of course, be taken as definitive proof for the conceptualization of the supernatural world, but it is noteworthy that in addition to the names of deities, Selz's provisional survey of the god lists includes deified entities that can be classified as (1) divine emblems and paraphernalia, (2) deified professions/offices, (3) cultural achievements or properties, (4) musical instruments, (5) deified animals, and (6) varia such as "Lord: Statue" or the deified "Radiance."[75] In other words, a significant number of the entries represent a divine agency that is imagined in forms other than the anthropomorphic and can at best be only partially understood as representing the extended agency of a deity. Beyond that, the ancients deemed certain cultural achievements important enough to merit deification.

The Early Dynastic god lists from Farah and Abu Salabikh already reflect a supraregional approach to organizing the pantheon according to both theological hierarchical principles (placing the god of heaven Anu first, followed by Enlil) and lexical principles (i.e., grouping together all deities whose names begin with NIN). Mythographic knowledge would likewise have an impact somewhat later, as attested by the *Weidner God List*, originally a single-column god list documented as early as the Ur III period and again in several Old Babylonian manuscripts from Babylon and Ṭabētum on the Habur River. Later Middle Babylonian evidence includes manuscripts from Nippur and peripheral regions such as Emar, Ugarit, and Tell el-Amarna, while Middle Assyrian and Neo-Assyrian manuscripts come from Assur, and Neo-Babylonian manuscripts from Babylon, Kish, Nippur and Uruk. Although the *Weidner God List* usually appears written in a single column, the Neo-Assyrian manuscripts feature sub-columns alongside each god's name. These sub-columns record the pronunciation of each name, the names of the signs used in each name, and explanatory equivalents such as other names of deities or explanatory phrases.[76] The sub-columns also reveal a concern for translating or equating divinities on the basis of their status, functions, and role—features that characterize the *Weidner God List* as a forerunner to the god list AN : *Anum*, which, in its canonized form, contained nearly two thousand divine names. Two Middle Assyrian exemplars

74 Selz, "The Holy Drum," 170, with reference to Robert K. Englund and Hans J. Nissen, *Lexikalische Listen der archaischen Texte aus Uruk* (Berlin: Gebr. Mann, 1993).

75 Selz, "Divine Prototypes," 13–31.

76 Daisuke Shibata, "An Old Babylonian Manuscript of the Weidner God List from Tell Taban," *Iraq* 71 (2009): 33–42.

survive from Assur, as do Neo-Assyrian manuscripts from Assur and Nineveh and late Babylonian ones from Uruk and Nippur.[77] The very arrangement of the names—divinity, spouse of the divinity, children, family and courtiers, including the wet nurse,[78] and finally household servants—indicates part of the list's explanatory purpose[79] as being based on the institutional experience of the royal court. This principle was not always followed strictly, as the pair Enlil and Ninlil can be separated by the section dedicated to Ninurta, the warrior god and son of Enlil. Short descriptive elements often establish kinship ties between deities and so "constitute organizational devices that draw genealogies within the Mesopotamian pantheon"[80] that may be equally reflected in myth.[81]

To some degree, such an entourage of a divinity may be reflected in the assemblage of divinities in the temple, as suggested by topographical compendia, such as the *Assur Directory* or *Tintir*^{ki}.[82] In addition, a number of entries offer a host of names for one and the same deity. Rather than indicating any kind of cultic reality, these lists are the product of a scholarly endeavor aimed at systematization and completeness.

The reason why I include these god lists in the discussion of the sociomorphic nature of the Sumero-Babylonian pantheon is because their organizing principles—grouping divinities by genealogical and kinship relations and according to the institutional models of the royal court and household—once again testifies to a concept that, anchored in real-life experience, regarded the members of the pantheon as an integrated network modeled upon human institutions and relations that complemented each other in terms of functions and roles in order to guarantee the integrity of the cosmic totality. Within the cultural context of Mesopotamia, therefore, and in addition to the somatic

---

77 Richard Litke, *A Reconstruction of the Assyro-Babylonian God Lists* AN: *^{d}A-nu-um and* AN: *Anu ša amēli*, Texts from the Babylonian Collection 3 (New Haven, CT: Yale Babylonian Collection, 1998).

78 This entry indicates once more the high-ranking position of the wet nurse at the royal court. Beate Pongratz-Leisten, "When the Gods are Speaking: Toward Defining the Interface Between Polytheism and Monotheism," in *Propheten in Mari, Assyrien und Israel*, ed. Matthias Köckert and Martti Nissinen (Göttingen: Vandenhoeck & Ruprecht, 2003), 132–169; Beate Pongratz-Leisten and Elizabeth Knott, "The Old Babylonian Ritual Text BM 29638, Enūma eliš, and Developments in Marduk's Cult," *NABU* 1/13 (2020): 27–33.

79 Lambert, "Götterlisten."

80 Rubio, "Gods and Scholars," 98.

81 Manfred Krebernik, "Vielzahl und Einheit im altmesopotamischen Pantheon," in *Polytheismus und Monotheismus in den Religionen des Vorderen Orients*, ed. Manfred Krebernik and Jürgen von Oorshot (Münster: Ugarit-Verlag, 2002), 38–39.

82 Andrew R. George, *Babylonian Topographical Texts* (Leuven: Peeters, 1992).

experience of ritual and the iconic experience, myth and god lists represent two discursive means of conceptualizing the agency and mentalization of otherworldly beings by envisaging them in sociomorphic terms.

Bibliography

Amrhein, Anastasia. "Multimedia Image-Making in Assyria and Babylonia: Visualizations of the Numinous in Political Contexts." Ph.D. diss., University of Pennsylvania, forthcoming.

Asher-Greve, Julia, and Joan Goodnick Westenholz. *Goddesses in Context: On Divine Powers, Roles, Relationships and Gender*. Fribourg: Academic Press; Göttingen: Vandenhoeck & Ruprecht, 2013.

Atran, Scott. *In Gods We Trust: The Evolutionary Landscape of Religion*. Oxford: Oxford University Press, 2002.

Atran, Scott, Douglas L. Medin, and N.O. Ross. "The Cultural Mind: Environmental Decision Making and Cultural Modeling Within and Across Populations." *Psychological Review* 112 (2005): 744–776.

Bahrani, Zainab. "Performativity and the Image: Narrative, Representation, and the Uruk Vase." Pages 15–22 in *Leaving No Stones Unturned: Essays on the Ancient Near East and Egypt in Honor of Donald P. Hansen*. Edited by Erica Ehrenberg. Winona Lake, IN: Eisenbrauns, 2002.

Bär, Jürgen. *Die ältesten Ischtar-Tempel in Assur*. Saarbrücken: Saarbrücker Druckerei und Verlag, 2003.

Barrett, Justin L. "Exploring the Natural Foundations of Religious Belief." *Trends in Cognitive Sciences* 4 (2000): 29–34.

Barrett, Justin L. "Cognitive Science of Religion: What Is It and Why Is It?" *RC* 1/6 (2007): 768–786.

Benzel, Kim. "'What Goes In Is What Comes Out'—But What Was Already There? Divine Materials and Materiality in Ancient Mesopotamia." Pages 89–118 in *The Materiality of Divine Agency*. Edited by Beate Pongratz-Leisten and Karen Sonik. Boston, MA/Berlin: de Gruyter, 2015.

Blumenberg, Hans. *Work on Myth*. Translated by R.M. Wallace. Cambridge, MA: MIT Press, 1985.

Bottéro, Jean. *Religion in Ancient Mesopotamia*. Translated by Teresa Lavender Fagan. Chicago, IL/London: University of Chicago Press, 2001.

Boyer, Pascal. *The Naturalness of Religious Ideas: A Cognitive Theory of Religion*. Berkeley, CA: University of California Press, 1994.

Boyer, Pascal. *Religion Explained: The Evolutionary Origins of Religious Thought*. New York, NY: Basic Books, 2001.

Boyer, Pascal. "Religious Thought and Behaviour as By-Products of Brain Function." *Trends in Cognitive Science* 7/3 (2003): 119–124.

Braun-Holzinger, Eva A. *Das Herrscherbild in Mesopotamien und Elam Spätes 4. Bis frühes 2. Jt. v. Chr.* Münster: Ugarit-Verlag, 2007.

Bruner, Jerome. *Acts of Meaning: Four Lectures on Mind and Culture*. Cambridge, MA: Harvard University Press, 1990.

Bynum, Caroline Walker. "The Sacrality of Things: An Inquiry into Divine Materiality in the Christian Middle Ages." *Irish Theological Quarterly* 78 (2013): 3–18.

Bynum, Caroline Walker. "The Animation and Agency of Holy Food." Pages 70–85 in *The Materiality of Divine Agency*. Edited by Beate Pongratz-Leisten and Karen Sonik. Boston, MA/Berlin: de Gruyter, 2015.

Charvát, Petr. *Mesopotamia before History*. 2nd ed. New York, NY/London: Routledge, 2002.

Couto-Ferreira, Erica. "From Head to Toe: Listing the Body in Cuneiform Texts." Pages 43–71 in *The Comparable Body: Analogy and Metaphor in Ancient Mesopotamian, Egyptian, and Graeco-Roman Medicine*. Edited by J.Z. Wee. Boston, MA/Leiden: Brill, 2017.

Englund, Robert K., and Hans J. Nissen. *Lexikalische Listen der archaischen Texte aus Uruk*. Berlin: Gebr. Mann, 1993.

Black, Jeremy A., Graham Cunningham, Jarle Ebeling, Esther Flückiger-Hawker, Eleanor Robson, Jon Taylor, and Gabor Zólyomi. *The Electronic Text Corpus of Sumerian Literature*. Oxford, 1998–2006. http://etcsl.orinst.ox.ac.uk/.

Feldman, Marian H. "Mesopotamian Art." Pages 281–301 in *A Companion to the Ancient Near East*. Edited by Daniel C. Snell. Malden/Oxford: Blackwell, 2005.

Flasche, Rainer. "Numinos." Pages 252–255 in *Handbuch religionswissenschaftlicher Grundbegriffe*. Edited by Hubert Cancik, Burkhard Gladigow, and Karl-Heinz Kohl. Vol. 4. Stuttgart: Kohlhammer, 1998.

Freedberg, David. *The Power of Images: Studies in the History and Theory of Response*. Chicago, IL: University of Chicago Press, 1989.

Gelb, Ignace, J., Piotr Steinkeller, and Robert D. Whiting. *Earliest Land Tenure Systems in the Ancient Near East: Ancient Kudurrus*. 2 vols. University of Chicago Oriental Institute Publications 104. Chicago, IL: The Oriental Institute, 1991.

Gell, Alfred. *Art and Agency: An Anthropological Theory*. Oxford: Clarendon Press; New York: Oxford University Press, 1998.

George, Andrew, R. *Babylonian Topographical Texts*. Leuven: Peeters, 1992.

Gervais, Will M. "Perceiving Minds and Gods: How Mind Perception Enables, Constrains, and Is Triggered by Belief in Gods." *Perspectives on Psychological Science* 8/4 (2013): 380–394.

Gladigow, Burkhard. "Mythische Experimente—experimentelle Mythen." Pages 61–82 in *Faszination des Mythos*. Edited by Renate Schlesier. Basel and Frankfurt: Suhrkamp, 1985.

Gladigow, Burkhard. "Mythenzensur und Symbolkontrolle." Pages 158–168 in *Kanon und Zensur*. Edited by Aleida and Jan Assann. München: Wilhelm Fink Verlag, 1986.

Gladigow, Burkhard. "Mythologie und Theologie: Aussagestufen im griechischen Mythos." Pages 77–88 in *Theologien und Theologen in verschiedenen Kulturkreisen*. Edited by Heinrich von Stietencron. Düsseldorf: Patmos Verlag, 1988.

Glassner, Jean-Jacques. "Inanna et les ME." Pages 55–86 in *Nippur at the Centennial: Papers Read at the 3e Rencontre Assyriologique Internationale, 1988*. Edited by Maria de Jong Ellis. Philadelphia, PA: Distributed by the S.N. Kramer Fund, Babylonian Section, University Museum, 1992.

Graf, Fritz. *Griechische Mythologie: Eine Einführung*. München and Zürich: Artemis and Winkler, 1991.

Guthrie, Stewart Elliott. *Faces in the Clouds: A New Theory of Religion*. New York, NY: Oxford University Press, 1993.

Hahn, Cynthia. "Objects of Devotion and Desire: Relics, Reliquaries, Relation, and Response." Pages 8–20 in *Objects of Devotion and Desire: Medieval Relic to Contemporary Art*. Curated by Cynthia Hahn. New York, NY: Hunter College, 2011.

Hansen, Donald P. "Art of the Early City States." Pages 21–37 in *Art of the First Cities. The Third Millennium BC from the Mediterranean to the Indus*. Edited by Joan Aruz with Ronald Wallenfels. New York, NY: The Metropolitan Museum of Art and Yale University Press, 2003.

Heeßel, Nils. "Identifying Divine Agency: The Hands of the Gods in Context." Pages 133–149 in *Sources of Evil: Studies in Mesopotamian Exorcistic Lore*. Edited by G. van Buylaere, Mikko Luukko, Daniel Schwemer, and Avigail Mertens-Wagschal. Boston, MA/Leiden: Brill, 2018.

Herman, David. "Cognitive Narratology." Pages 30–43 in *Handbook of Narratology* 1. Edited by Peter Hühn, Jan Christoph Meier, John Pier, and Wolf Schmid. Boston, MA/Berlin: de Gruyter, 2014.

Ingold, Tim. *Being Alive: Essays on Movement, Knowledge and Description*. New York, NY/London: Routledge, 2011.

Jacobsen, Thorkild. "Primitive Democracy in Ancient Mesopotamia." *JNES* 2 (1943): 159–172.

Jacobsen, Thorkild. *Toward the Image of Tammuz and Other Essays On Mesopotamian History and Culture*. Edited by William L. Moran. Cambridge, MA: Harvard University Press, 1970.

Jacobsen, Thorkild. *The Treasures of Darkness: A History of Mesopotamian Religion*. New Haven, CT/London: Yale University Press, 1976.

Jacobsen, Thorkild. "Pictures and Pictorial Language (The Burney Relief)." Pages 1–11 in *Figurative Language in the Ancient Near East*. Edited by M. Mindlin, Mark J. Geller, and J. Wansbrough. London: School of Oriental and African Studies, University of London, 1987.

Komoróczy, Geza. "Das Pantheon im Kult, in den Götterlisten und in der Mythologie." *Orientalia Nova Series* 45 (1976): 80–86.

Krebernik, Manfred. "Die Götterlisten aus Fāra." ZA 76 (1986): 161–204.

Krebernik, Manfred. "Vielzahl und Einheit im altmesopotamischen Pantheon." Pages 33–51 in *Polytheismus und Monotheismus in den Religionen des Vorderen Orients*. Edited by Manfred Krebernik and Jürgen von Oorshot. Münster: Ugarit-Verlag, 2002.

Lakoff, George and Mark Johnson. *Metaphors We Live By*. Chicago, IL: Chicago University Press, 1980.

Lambert, Wilfred G. "Gott: Nach akkadischen Texten." *RlA* 3 (1971): 543–546.

Lambert, Wilfred G. "Götterlisten." *RlA* 3 (1971): 473–479.

Lambert, Wilfred G. "The Historical Development of the Mesopotamian Pantheon: A Study in Sophisticated Polytheism." Pages 191–200 in *Unity and Diversity: Essays in the History, Literature, and Religion of the Ancient Near East*. Edited by H. Goedicke and J.J.M. Roberts. Baltimore, MD/London: Johns Hopkins University Press, 1975.

Lambert, Wilfred G. "Ancient Mesopotamian Gods: Superstition, Philosophy, Theology." *Revue de l'histoire des religions* 207/ 2 (1990): 115–130.

Linssen, Marc J.H. *The Cults of Uruk and Babylon: The Temple Ritual Texts as Evidence for Hellenistic Cult Practice*. Boston, MA/Leiden: Brill, 2004.

Litke, Richard, L. *A Reconstruction of the Assyro-Babylonian God Lists, AN: ^{d}A-nu-um and AN: Anu ša amēli*. Texts from the Babylonian Collection 3. New Haven, CT: Yale Babylonian Collection, 1998.

Mander, Pietro. *Il pantheon di Abu-Ṣālabīkh*. Naples: Istituto Universitario Orientale, 1986.

Marchesi, Gianni, and Nicolò Marchetti. *Royal Statuary of Early Dynastic Mesopotamia*. Winona Lake, IN: Eisenbrauns, 2011.

Michalowski, Piotr. "Literacy, Schooling and the Transmission of Knowledge in Early Mesopotamian Culture." Pages 39–57 in *Theory and Practice of Knowledge Transfer: Studies in School Education in the Ancient Near East and Beyond. Papers Read at the Symposium in Leiden, 17–19 December 2008*. Edited by W.S. van Egmond and W.S.H. van Soldt. Leiden: Nederlands Insitituut voor het Nabije Oosten, 2012.

Mindlin, M., Mark J. Geller, and J. Wansbrough. *Figurative Language in the Ancient Near East*. London: Taylor and Francis, 2005.

Oppenheim, A. Leo. "Divination and Celestial Observation in the Last Assyrian Empire." *Centaurus* 14 (1969): 97–135.

Ornan, Tallay. *The Triumph of the Symbol: Pictorial Representation of Deities in Mesopotamia and the Biblical Image Ban*. Fribourg: Academic Press; Göttingen: Vandenhoeck & Ruprecht, 2005.

Ornan, Tallay. "In the Likeness of Man: Reflections on the Anthropocentric Perception of the Divine in Mesopotamian Art." Pages 93–151 in *What Is a God? Anthropomorphic and Non-Anthropomorphic Aspects of Deity in Ancient Mesopotamia*. Edited by

Barbara Nevling Porter. Vol. 2. Winona Lake, IN: Casco Bay Assyriological Institute, 2009.

Osborne, Robin, and Jeremy Tanner. *Art's Agency and Art History*. Malden, MA/Oxford: Blackwell Publishing, 2007.

Otto, Rudolf. *Das Heilige: Über das Irrationale in der Idee des Heiligen und sein Verhältnis zum Rationalen*. Breslau: Trewendt und Granier, 1917.

Pallavidini, Marta, and Ludovico Portuese, ed. *Researching Metaphor in the Ancient Near East*. Wiesbaden: Harrassowitz, 2020.

Pongratz-Leisten, Beate. "When the Gods are Speaking: Toward Defining the Interface Between Polytheism and Monotheism." Pages 132–169 in *Propheten in Mari, Assyrien und Israel*. Edited by Matthias Köckert and Martti Nissinen. Göttingen: Vandenhoeck & Ruprecht, 2003.

Pongratz-Leisten, Beate. "Reflections on the Translatability of Holiness." Pages 409–428 in *Of God(s), Trees, Kings, and Scholars: Neo-Assyrian and Related Studies in Honour of Simo Parpola*. Edited by Mikko Luukko, Saana Svärd, and Raija Mattila. Helsinki: Finnish Oriental Society, 2009.

Pongratz-Leisten, Beate. "Divine Agency and Astralization of the Gods in Ancient Mesopotamia." Pages 137–187 in *Reconsidering the Concept of Revolutionary Monotheism*. Edited by Beate Pongratz-Leisten. Winona Lake, IN: Eisenbrauns, 2011.

Pongratz-Leisten, Beate. "The King at the Crossroads Between Divination and Cosmology." Pages 33–48 in *Divination, Politics, and Ancient Near Eastern Empires*. Edited by Alan Lenzi and Jonathan Stökl. Atlanta, GA: Society of Biblical Literature, 2014.

Pongratz-Leisten, Beate. *Religion and Ideology in Assyria*. Boston, MA/Berlin: de Gruyter, 2015.

Pongratz-Leisten, Beate. "Seeing and Knowing: Cultural Concepts and the Deictic Power of the Image in Mesopotamia." Forthcoming in *Artifacts and Art/Works in the Ancient World*. Edited by Karen Sonik. Philadelphia, PA: University of Pennsylvania Museum Press.

Pongratz-Leisten, Beate. "Conceptualizing Divinity Between Cult and Theology in the Ancient Near East." Forthcoming in *Dieux, rois et capitales dans le Proche-Orient ancien: Compte rendu de la LXVe Rencontre Assyriologique Internationale (Paris, 8–12 juillet 2019)*. Edited by Marine Béranger, Francesca Nebiolo and Nele Ziegler. Leuven: Peeters.

Pongratz-Leisten, Beate. "Assyriological Approaches Towards a History of Religion in Mesopotamia." Forthcoming in *The Intellectual Heritage of the Ancient Near East: Proceedings of the 64th Rencontre Assyriologique Internationale in Innsbruck*. Melammu Symposia 12. Edited by Robert Rollinger, Irene Madreiter, and Martin Lang, Vienna: Austria Academy of Sciences Press.

Pongratz-Leisten, Beate. "The Old Babylonian Ritual Text BM 29638, Enūma eliš, and Developments in Marduk's Cult." *NABU* 1/13 (2020): 27–33.

Pongratz-Leisten, Beate. "Between Cognition and Culture: Theorizing the Materiality of Divine Agency in Cross-Cultural Perspective." Pages 3–69 in *The Materiality of Divine Agency*. Edited by Beate Pongratz-Leisten and Karen Sonik. Boston, MA/Berlin: de Gruyter, 2015.

Porter, Barbara Nevling. "Blessings from a Crown, Offerings to a Drum: Were There Non-Anthropomorphic Deities in Ancient Mesopotamia?" Pages 153–194 in *What Is a God? Anthropomorphic and Non-Anthropomorphic Aspects of Deity in Ancient Mesopotamia*. Edited by Barbara Nevling Porter. Vol. 2. Transactions of the Casco Bay Assyriological Institute 2. Winona Lake, IN: Casco Bay Assyriological Institute, 2009.

Porter, Barbara Nevling, ed. *What Is a God? Anthropomorphic and Non-Anthropomorphic Aspects of Deity in Ancient Mesopotamia*. Transactions of the Casco Bay Assyriological Institute 2. Winona Lake, IN: Casco Bay Assyriological Institute, 2009.

Portuese, Ludovico. "Metaphorical Allusions to Life-Giving Plants in Neo-Assyrian Texts and Images." *Antiguo Oriente* 16 (2018): 93–116.

Pyysiänen, Illka. *How Religion Works*. Leiden: Brill, 2001.

Pyysiänen, Illka. *Supernatural Agents: Why We Believe in Souls, Gods and Buddhas*. Oxford: Oxford University Press, 2009.

Richardson, Seth. "The Hypercoherent Icon: Knowledge, Rationalization, and Disenchantment at Nineveh." Pages 231–258 in *Iconoclasm and Text Destruction in the Ancient Near East and Beyond*. Edited by Natalie Naomi May. Chicago, IL: The Oriental Institute, 2012.

Rochberg, Francesca. "Personifications and Metaphors in Babylonian Celestial *Omina*." *JAOS* 116/3 (1996): 475–485.

Rochberg, Francesca. "'The Stars Their Likeness': Perspectives on the Relation Between Celestial Bodies and Gods in Ancient Mesopotamia." Pages 41–91 in *What Is a God? Anthropomorphic and Non-Anthropomorphic Aspects of Deity in Ancient Mesopotamia*. Edited by Barbara Nevling Porter. Transactions of the Casco Bay Assyriological Institute 2. Winona Lake, IN: Casco Bay Assyriological Institute, 2009.

Rubio, Gonzalo. "Gods and Scholars: Mapping the Pantheon in Early Mesopotamia." Pages 91–116 in *Reconsidering the Concept of Revolutionary Monotheism*. Edited by Beate Pongratz-Leisten. Winona Lake, IN: Eisenbrauns, 2011.

Sallaberger, Walther. "Zur Genese der Mesopotamischen Götterwelt: Eine Auseinandersetzung mit Thorkild Jacobsens *Central Concerns*." Pages 391–412 in *mu-zu an-za3-še3 kur-ur2-še3 ḫe2-ĝal2 : altorientalistische Studien zu Ehren von Konrad Volk*. Edited by Jessica Baldwin, Jana Matuszak, and Manuel Ceccarelli. Dubsar 17. Münster: Zaphon, 2020.

Schuster-Brandis, Anais. *Steine als Schutz- und Heilmittel: Untersuchung zu ihrer Verwendung in der Beschwörungskunst Mesopotamiens im 1 Jt. v. Chr.* Münster: Ugarit-Verlag, 2008.

Selz, Gebhard. "'The Holy Drum, the Spear, and the Harp: Toward an Understanding of the Problems of Deification in Third Millennium Mesopotamia." Pages 167–209 in *Sumerian Gods and Their Representations*. Edited by I.J. Finkel and M.J. Geller. Groningen: Styx, 1997.

Selz, Gebhard. "The Divine Prototypes." Pages 13–31 in *Religion and Power: Divine Kingship in the Ancient World and Beyond*. Edited by Nicole Brisch. Oriental Institute Seminars 4. Chicago, IL: The Oriental Institute of the University of Chicago, 2008.

Selz, Gebhard. "Götter der Gesellschaft, Gesellschaft der Götter: Zur Dialektik von Abbildung und Ordnung." Pages 61–85 in *Wissenskultur im Alten Orient: Weltanschauung, Wissenschaften, Techniken, Technologien. 4. Internationales Colloquium der Deutschen Orient-Gesellschaft 20.–22. Februar 2002*. Edited by Hans Neumann. Münster and Wiesbaden: Harrassowitz, 2012.

Selz, Gebhard. "Vergöttlichung." *RlA* 14 (2016): 545–548.

Selz, Gebhard. "Who Is a God? A Note on the Evolution of Divine Classifiers in a Multilingual Environment." Pages 605–614 In *Libiamo ne' lieti calici: Ancient Near Eastern Studies Presented to Lucio Milano on the Occasion of his 65th Birthday by Pupils, Colleagues and Friends*. Edited by Paola Corò, Elena Devecchi, Nicla De Zorzi, and Masimmo Maiocchi, with the collaboration of Stefania Ermidoro and Erica Scapra. Münster: Ugarit-Verlag, 2016.

Shibata, Daisuke. "An Old Babylonian Manuscript of the Weidner God List from Tell Taban." *Iraq* 71 (2009): 33–42.

Shweder, R. "Cultural Psychology: What Is It?" Pages 1–43 in *Cultural Psychology*. Edited by J. Stigler, R. Shweder, and G. Herdt. New York, NY: Cambridge University Press, 1990.

Soden, Wolfram von. *The Ancient Orient: An Introduction to the Study of the Ancient Near East*. Translated by Donald G. Schley. Grand Rapids, MI: Eerdmans, 1994.

Sonik, Karen. "One or Many? Characterization and Identity in the *Gilgamesh Epic* and Other Mesopotamian Narratives." Forthcoming in *How to Tell a Story: Approaches to Mesopotamian Literature*. Edited by Dahlia Shehata, Karen Sonik, and Frauke Weiershäuser. Leiden: Brill.

Sperber, Dan, and Lawrence A. Hirschfeld. "The Cognitive Foundations of Cultural Stability and Diversity." *Trends in Cognitive Science* 8/1 (2004): 40–46.

Steinkeller, Piotr. "Of Stars and Men: The Conceptual and Mythological Setup of Babylonian Extispicy." Pages 11–47 in *Biblical and Oriental Essays in Memoriam of William Moran*. Edited by Augustinus Gianto. BibOr 48. Rome: Pontifical Institute, 2005.

Streck, Michael. "Die Amurriter der altbabylonischen Zeit im Spiegel des Onomastikons: Eine ethnische Evaluierung." Pages 313–355 in *2000 v. Chr. Politische, wirtschaftliche und kulturelle Entwicklung im Zeichen einer Jahrtausendwende: 3. Internationales Colloquium der Deutschen Orient-Gesellschaft*. Edited by Jan-Waalke Meyer and Walter Sommerfeld. Saarbrücken: Saarbrücker Druckerei und Verlag, 2004.

Suter, Claudia E. "Human, Divine or Both? The Uruk Vase and the Problem of Ambiguity in Early Mesopotamian Visual Arts." Pages 545–568 in *Critical Approaches to Ancient Near Eastern Art*. Edited by Brian A. Brown and Marian H. Feldman. Boston, MA/Berlin: de Gruyter, 2014.

Thureau-Dangin, François. *Rituels Accadiens*. Paris: Editions Ernest Leroux, 1921.

Tilley, Christopher. *Metaphor and Material Culture*. Oxford: Blackwell Publishing, 1999.

Tomasello, Michael. *The Cultural Origins of Human Cognition*. Cambridge, MA: Harvard University Press, 2000.

Wengrow, David. *The Archaeology of Early Egypt: Social Transformations in North-East Africa, 10,000–2650 BC*. Cambridge: Cambridge University Press, 2006.

White, Hayden. *Metahistory: The Historical Imagination in Nineteenth-Century Europe*. Baltimore, MD: Johns Hopkins University Press, 1973.

Wiggermann, Frans A.M. "Agriculture as Civilization: Sages, Farmers, and Barbarians." Pages 663–689 in *The Oxford Handbook of Cuneiform Culture*. Edited by Karen Radner and Eleanor Robson. Oxford: Oxford University Press, 2011.

Wilcke, Claus. "Die Inschrift der 'Figure aux plumes'—ein frühes Werk sumerischer Dichtkunst." Pages 669–674 in *Beiträge zur Kulturgeschichte Vorderasiens. Festschrift für Rainer Michael Boehmer*. Edited by Uwe Finkbeiner, Reinhard Dittmann, and Harald Hauptmann. Mainz: Philipp von Zabern, 1995.

Winter, Irene J. "Agency Marked, Agency Ascribed: The Affective Object in Ancient Mesopotamia." Pages 73–98 in *Art's Agency and Art History*. Edited by Robin Osborne and Jeremy Tanner. Malden, MA: Blackwell Publishing, 2007.

Winter, Irene J. "Gold! Light and Lustre in Ancient Mesopotamia." Pages 153–171 in *Ancient and Modern Issues in Cultural Heritage: Colour and Light in Architecture, Art and Material Culture. Islamic Archaeology*. Edited by Roger Matthews and John Curtis. Proceedings of the Seventh International Congress on the Archaeology of the Ancient Near East 2. Wiesbaden: Harrassowitz Verlag, 2012.

Woods, Christopher. "The Earliest Mesopotamian Writing." Pages 33–50 in *Visible Language: Inventions of Writing in the Ancient Middle East and Beyond*. Edited by Christopher Woods. Oriental Institute Museum Publications 32. Chicago, IL: The Oriental Institute of Chicago University, 2010.

Yoffee, Norman. *Myths of the Archaic State*. New York, NY/Cambridge: Cambridge University Press, 2005.

Zgoll, Christian. "Myths as Polymorphous and Polystratic Erzählstoffe." Pages 9–82 in *Mythische Sphärenwechsel: Methodisch Neue Zugänge zu antiken Mythen in Orient und Okzident*. Edited by Annette Zgoll and Christian Zgoll. Boston, MA/Berlin: de Gruyter, 2020.

15

Unpopulated and Underpoliticized: Reconsidering Exterior Spaces in the Practice of Politics in Northern Mesopotamia

Anne Porter

It is with great pleasure (and a deep sense of passing time) that I commemorate my professional and personal friendship with Daniel Fleming in this paper. Dan and I were first brought together in 1998 over our shared interests in Mari and mobile pastoralism, but I wish here to explore the impact for archaeology of his work on the rituals of Emar. For those of us embedded in a field where class divisions and elite paradigms are the rule, the evidence of a community where the citizenry had a major role in politics and decision-making—kings and councils notwithstanding—was revelatory. From the high priestess's job open to all daughters of citizens of Emar,[1] to the *zukru* festival where every member of the town, from divinity to ditch-digger, came together at a feast seven years in the making,[2] to the removal of the king by the people,[3] it is clear that communal ritual acts in this Late Bronze Age town countered the potential for destructive social divisions, at the same time as those divisions were subtly, and perhaps unintentionally, reinforced by the contributions each participant brought to the table.

On a macroscale, the Emar rituals should make us think more closely about the agented participation of the general public in rituals we usually attribute to the ideological manipulations of the elite. On a microscale, there is another aspect of the Emar material that is eye-opening—the significance of outside spaces in the life of the citizenry. Example after example shows us that such spaces were socially and politically integrative. Streets were not mere ways to get from A to B, but routes for the specialized intersection of different elements of society in the ritualized progression of gods, their functionaries, and their

---

1 Daniel Fleming, *The Installation of Baal's High Priestess at Emar*, HSS 42 (Atlanta: Scholars Press, 1992).

2 Daniel Fleming, *Time at Emar: The Cultic Calendar and the Rituals from the Diviner's Archive* (Winona Lake, IN: Eisenbrauns, 2000).

3 Sophie Démare-Lafont and Daniel Fleming, "Emar Chronology and Scribal Streams: Cosmopolitanism and Legal diversity," *RA* 109/1 (2015): 45–77.

 | DOI:10.1163/9789004511538_016

followers. Spaces outside the temple were no doubt used for the usual gathering of congregants, some of whom may have been permitted inside, as well as rarer ceremonies where the whole population was observer/participant, including those who would not normally have access to the interior mysteries. It is at the gate of the god's temple that tables covered in food were erected for the key participants[4] and that items taken out from both temple and palace were poured over the priestess-in-becoming's head in the installation ritual.[5] The many steps of ceremony weave inside and outside spaces, institutional and public places, and the people who occupy them, into a tightly woven social, as well as religious, fabric.

So too do the various passageways of the *zukru* festival. In both rituals, that weaving is accomplished by very specific conjunctions of movement and food: who provides what, and who consumes what, from which provider, and where. Sharing of food is, as I have often noted, a critical aspect of not just social communing, but social incorporation, and the offerings to gods and to people serve to tie each to the other ever more tightly. But it is the evidence for the use of spaces outside the town itself in the *zukru* that most powerfully drew my attention to the possibilities for other times and places. By their very nature, outside, unenclosed spaces offer the possibility of unconstrained and nonhierarchical interaction. This possibility, it may be understood from the *zukru* rites, is the very reason everyone progresses outside the town to conduct this feast. It is not just because there would not be enough space within the town for the whole town to come together there. As shown by Augusta McMahon,[6] even in the highly urbanized cities of southern Mesopotamia there was enough space around the main temples that all the adult male inhabitants could congregate. Little of Emar has been excavated, so it is impossible to judge the full potential for open space there. However, the installation ritual was a public performance,

4 Including, I would propose, the deceased priestess in the flesh. Evidence for the prolonged presence of certain deceased individuals in ritual performance is provided by the selective heating of some bodies as a form of preservation. This has been recognized in the third millennium at Ur (Aubrey Baadsgaard, Janet Monge, and Richard L. Zettler, "Bludgeoned, Burned, and Beautified: Reevaluating Mortuary Practices in the Royal Cemetery of Ur," in *Sacred Killing: The Archaeology of Sacrifice in the Ancient Near East*, ed. Anne Porter and Glenn Schwartz [Winona Lake, IN: Eisenbrauns, 2012], 125–158) and at Tell Banat (Anne Porter, "The Materiality of Mourning," in *How to Cope with Death: Mourning and Funerary Practices in the Ancient Near East*, ed. Candida Felli [Pisa: ETS, 2016], 157–188).

5 Fleming, *Installation*, 51, lines 15–20.

6 Augusta McMahon, "Spacious or Empty: Making Courtyards in Mesopotamia," in *Pomp, Circumstance, and the Performance of Politics: Acting Politically Correct in the Ancient World*, ed. Kathryn Morgan, OIS 15 (Chicago, IL: The Oriental Institute of the University of Chicago, forthcoming).

and the area in which its main elements were enacted has been excavated,[7] so that we may follow step by step the actors as they traversed the ritual's spatial dimensions. In Phase 1, the temple of Baal, a classic temple *in antis*, is 95.48 square meters, while the open porch is 21 square meters.[8] At 2–3 persons per square meter, considered optimal for both use of space and safety,[9] this allows for a combined 350 persons inside the actual building, possibly enough for the male heads of the town's families. Yet this ritual was conducted outside, "at the opening of the courtyard gate,"[10] because the priestess-to-be cannot enter the temple precincts until she has been transformed into the appropriate persona.

That choice of location for ritual performance is governed not by practicality but by the intent of the ritual is clearly the case for the *zukru*, where adult male citizens were also the focus of the ceremony.[11] Although just because the texts do not specify whether women and children also participated, we cannot assume that they did not.[12] The *zukru* involves all the town, regardless of class or profession. Whether or not universal participation makes it a functional necessity to conduct large-scale rituals outside of the town, there are outcomes to this situation, unintended or otherwise. We have to visualize the statues of seventy gods processing out of the town as well as hundreds, if not thousands of people. Gods, life-sized, or miniature, require transport and attendants. For the god Dagan to come out of the temple for the *zukru*, for the veil to be lifted from his face, is to make him accessible not just to the select few, but to everyone—those permitted and those not. The uninitiated, the underage, the unqualified of gender, are all potentially able to peer around corners, view from rooftops, or wrap themselves around the legs of actors as the procession passes. But once Dagan leaves the town, the only way to prevent people even from beyond Emar from seeing him, is via the veil. This alone undermines the mystique, if not the power, of the god. It democratizes the religious experience. It is not the only relationship that is democratized, though, when all the people of the town leave its confines to join with all the gods. Everyone in town is brought in some intrinsic way to the same level, even if the trappings of their

7 Uwe Finkbeiner, and Ferhan Sakal, "Emar 2002: Bericht über die 5. Kampagne der syrisch-deutschen Ausgrabungen," *BaM* 34 (2003): 9–117.

8 The temple of Baal in Phase 2 is quite a bit smaller: 47.5 square meters for the interior of the building, while the porch is 13 square meters.

9 McMahon, "Spacious."

10 Fleming, *Installation*, 50, line 9.

11 Fleming, *Time*, 249, line 169.

12 Even if not official participants, it is impossible to imagine such scenes without onlookers, especially children, following on or racing ahead of the procession.

normal positions are still in evidence. They are no longer segregated one from the other by walls and gates, as they share a common experience.

Despite frequent claims that a landscape archaeology brings into the light ordinary people in contrast to the picture of top-down power derived from texts,[13] it is nevertheless in texts such as these that we see the actuality of ordinary people involved in common efforts and joint experiences in outside spaces, the things they did and who they did them with in a way rarely addressed in archaeological research. This is not to say that kings and elites were not part of the process at Emar, but that they were certainly not the focus of these events. Indeed, at these particular moments they were in essence at one with the citizenry.[14]

At the same time, the significance of these texts is often quite different for archaeologists than Assyriologists, and so I am certainly not suggesting that Assyriologists have a monopoly on this kind of insight. Yet, ironically, it is all too often archaeologists that, one way or another, focus on elite constructs at the expense of the nonelite, in the very studies that incorporate a trans-site-specific approach. Ömür Harmanşah claims that "If landscapes are fluid and intractable, richly textured and layered, as most thinkers of landscape and place would argue today, limiting the agency to transform landscapes solely to political actors needs to be questioned."[15] He is right, but underlying this statement seems to be the understanding that only rulers and elites are political actors, while underlying *that* perspective is the fact that Near Eastern constructs of power are still dominantly top-down whether derived from text or material culture.[16] This idea in turn is based on the assumption, firmly in place since the mid-twentieth century, that only a centralized administration can produce monumental structures. And that is because it is somehow inconceivable that communities can marshal a large workforce or act cooperatively without both direction and some means of enforcing compliance. Yet all members of society are political actors whether they claim to be apolitical or not. All members of society create the political worlds in which they live,[17] whether

---

13 Ömür Harmanşah, *Cities and the Shaping of Memory in the Ancient Near East* (Cambridge: Cambridge University Press, 2013), 15, and the quotes gathered there.

14 Fleming, *Time*, 56. John Tracy Thames, Jr., *The Politics of Ritual Change: The* zukru *Festival in the Political History of Late Bronze Age Emar*, HSM 65 (Leiden: Brill, 2020).

15 Harmanşah, *Cities*, 16.

16 Cf. Brendon C. Benz, *The Land Before the Kingdom of Israel: A History of the Southern Levant and the People Who Populated It*, HACL 7 (Winona Lake, IN: Eisenbrauns, 2016).

17 Adam T. Smith, "The Limitations of Doxa: Agency and Subjectivity from an Archaeological Point of View," *Journal of Social Archaeology* 1/2 (2001): 155–171.

through action, silence, rejection, compliance, collaboration, or rebellion, and no matter how oppressed. Moreover, societies based on kinship have structural mechanisms that foster consensus and cooperation, while compliance is ensured by subtle group pressures rather than by force or the edicts of a single authoritarian figure.

Because of these texts, Emar is judged by some to have weak kingship, rather than limited kingship as described by Fleming.[18] From this perspective, evidence of collective politics is considered indicative of a less complex polity than the supposedly autocratic systems of the third millennium, and is, moreover, thought to be a feature particular to the second millennium BCE.[19] There are indications, however, that such community-wide political practices existed in the third millennium within those polities cited as examples of a developed complexity. Those practices might have been integrative or sectarian, but in either case, they were not restricted to the elite. To explore this, I examine the political possibilities of the extramural spaces of two third-millennium sites, the period in which autocracy is thought to be at its peak. Those sites are Tell Chuera and Tell Banat, each quite distinctive in their spatial morphologies, each with archaeological evidence of descent systems and kin groups as the basis of social structure, and each with monumentalized spaces external to the town, albeit in very different ways. The very natures of Chuera and Banat allow for a reconsideration of these issues, beginning with the question of who could build certain monuments and ending with the possibility of participatory political practices in the spaces around these settlements.

Language here is a problem though. Traditional archaeological discourse focuses on "elites." Those who do not fall into this category are "nonelite," or "ordinary." Such terms perpetuate a binary opposition that is at the root of our conceptions of the past—one group of people is important and has power—important *because* it has power—while the other does not, and therefore *is* not. One group of people is treated as disconnected from the other in any socially meaningful way. These features are the hallmarks of "complexity." Yet the true complexity of ancient societies lies not in their divisions, but in the myriad ways they are interconnected, and in the often-unseen ways power and agency are enacted in some capacity by everyone. For these reasons I use "community"

18 Daniel E. Fleming, "A Limited Kingship: Late Bronze Emar in Ancient Syria," *UF* 24 (1992): 59–71.

19 Adelheid Otto, "Archaeological Evidence for Collective Governance along the Upper Syrian Euphrates during the Late and Middle Bronze Age," in *Organization, Representation, and Symbols of Power in the Ancient Near East*, ed. Gernot Wilhelm (Winona Lake, IN: Eisenbrauns, 2012), 87–99.

to refer to all the constituents of a settlement/polity, "institutional" to refer to those who populate the administrative offices of temple and palace and who are thereby defined by profession rather than class, and "public" to denote the myriad other professions, functions, and relationships members of a community may hold.

1 Tell Chuera

It is community, rather than only institution, that occupies the physical and ideological center of Tell Chuera. Established on an abandoned Late Chalcolithic III–IV site "designed as a circular, proto-urban settlement" according to Jan-Waalke Meyer,[20] the Early Bronze Age town seems also to have been planned.[21] If so, then the arrangement of the site is not an ad hoc growth from a small undifferentiated village, but a conscious representation of how society was supposed to be. For unlike the classic model of the Mesopotamian town, where the center of the site is dominated by institutional buildings such as temple and palace, the initial Bronze Age settlement of Chuera, now dated to ca. 3100 BCE, begins with the core elements that were to define the site throughout its history: a public square at the center of the tell, surrounded by residential buildings[22] and approached on the northwest and southeast by a wide thoroughfare that bisected the settlement.[23] Access to this public square eventually became restricted,[24] and it was perhaps then only used on special occasions.[25]

---

20 Jan-Waalke Meyer, "The Birth of the Circular Cities," in *Circular Cities of Early Bronze Age Syria*, ed. Corinne Castel, Jan-Waalke Meyer, and Philippe Quenet, Subartu 42 (Turnhout: Brepols, 2020), 38.

21 Henrike Backhaus and Tobias Helms, "Decentralized Decision-Making Processes in Third Millennium Syro-Mesopotamian City Planning: The Example of Tell Chuera," in *Urban Practices: Repopulating the Ancient City*, ed. Annette Haug and Stephanie Merten (Turnhout: Brepols, 2020), 18; Meyer, "Birth," 38. Compare Andrew Creekmore, "The Social Production of Space in Third-Millennium Cities of Upper Mesopotamia," in *Making Ancient Cities: Space and Place in Early Urban Societies*, ed. Andrew Creekmore and Kevin Fisher (Cambridge: Cambridge University Press, 2014), 59.

22 Ralph Hempelmann, "The Origin and Early Development of Tell Chuēra and Neighbouring Settlements," in Castel, Meyer, and Quenet, *Circular Cities*, 49.

23 Meyer, "Birth," 38. In addition, there are hints that the radial street pattern that characterizes the site was also established in this initial occupation (Ralph Hempelmann, *Tell Chuēra, Kharab Sayyar und die Urbanisierung der Westlichen Ǧazīra* [Wiesbaden: Harrassowitz, 2013], 42).

24 Hempelmann, "Origin," 52.

25 Backhaus and Helms, "Decentralized," 18.

This may have occurred as part of changes to the thoroughfare, which was monumentalized in the middle of the third millennium by the addition of a series of stone buildings raised high above the street.[26] Traditionally interpreted as religious structures—temples and their ancillary buildings—the layout of the *Steinbauten*, as they are known, and their relationship to the residential areas, tells a complex social story.

Firstly, the primacy of community is marked by the centrality of the residential quarter. If there was an emerging institutional body responsible for the planning of the settlement, it did not foreground itself in that plan. The earliest date for the presence of an administrative structure at Chuera—or for that matter, any institutional building that might be understood as encompassing in its purview the whole town—is the mid-third millennium.[27] But there is no reason why there should have been such a body. Although it is usually claimed that the fortification of this, and any other, settlement is in itself evidence of a central authority that could amass the required workforce and resources,[28] this is simply not necessary. Kin-groups may marshal considerable numbers of laborers for large-scale projects. Multiple kin-groups resident in a single settlement may reach agreement by negotiated community consensus.[29] At Chuera, the details of how the second phase of fortifications (around the lower town) were built show "decentralized, bottom-up decision-making processes."[30] These details include varied construction materials and techniques such as different kinds of bricks, disjointed sections of connecting wall, and unevenly spaced bastions.[31] The lower town wall dates to around the end of the second phase of occupation (1B), ca. 2500 BCE,[32] as the settlement reached its floruit. So even at this late stage of political formation, when large-scale institutions are present not just here (Palace, Area F), but across northern Mesopotamia, "it is possible that representatives of lineages or neighborhood organizations still held influence on

26 Olesia Kromberg, "Creating the Urban Landscape: the Emergence of Monumentality in Third Millennium Chuēra," in Castel, Meyer, and Quenet, *Circular Cities*, 101.

27 Alexander Tamm, "The Early Bronze Age Palace at Chuēra and the Decline of the Settlement," in Castel, Meyer, and Quenet, *Circular Cities*, 112.

28 See Backhaus and Helms, "Decentralized," 16–17 for references.

29 The deep-seated belief in archaeology that a central authority with some form of coercive power was required to accomplish any large-scale project may be traced ultimately to a very basic theoretical conviction: the fundamentally self-serving nature of humankind and its inability to cooperate.

30 Backhaus and Helms, "Decentralized," 14.

31 Tobias Helms and Philippe Quenet, "The Fortifiction of Circular Cities: The Examples of Tell Chuēra and Tell al-Rawda," in Castel, Meyer, and Quenet, *Circular Cities*, 77–99.

32 See Hempelmann, "Origin," 48 for dating.

the highest decision-making level during the later third millennium."[33] In the early third millennium, these groups *were* the highest decision-making level.

That there was more than one kin-group living in the heart of the settlement around the public square in the early life of Chuera may be indicated by the development of two temples *in antis* in this area located just off to the sides of the public square, one on the south side of the thoroughfare, one on the north,[34] both of which were associated with residential quarters.[35] These are the *Kleiner Antentempel* (31.96 m^2) and *Steinbau* VI (173 m^2) respectively. Despite the differences in size, these buildings have many features in common. Both evolved over a considerable period of time, beginning very early in the history of the site. Although usually considered part of the institutional complex because it is made of stone and becomes part of the later *Steinbauten* lining the thoroughfare, *Steinbau* VI had its origins in a mudbrick *in antis* structure at least as early as 2800 BCE.[36] Both *Steinbau* VI and the *Kleiner Antentempel* have bench-like platforms distinct from the traditional podium on the backwall of the cella, most likely for the placement of objects or statues.[37] Traces of a copper-clad wooden statue were found in *Steinbau* VI, while the well-known "Mesilim" statues recovered from rooms around the last phases of the *Kleiner Antentempel* (EB IVA, ca. 2450 BCE)[38] point to the history of that structure. The Mesilim statues date stylistically to a period well before the date of the level in which they were found (ED II/ED III, ca. 2700–2500),[39] occasioning much debate over chronology. However, subsequent excavations revealed the *Kleiner Antentempel* to have grown out of a sequence of houses beginning in the earliest levels of the Bronze Age settlement. Beneath the floor of the first house were two graves, raising the possibility that the occupants of those graves had, over time, become ancestors, memorialized in statues curated level after level and culminating in a shrine for their continued commemoration.[40]

33 Backhaus and Helms, "Decentralized," 19; see also Hempelmann, *Tell Chuēra*, 232–234.

34 See Hempelmann, "Origin," for an alternative path to the same conclusion.

35 See Creekmore, "Social," fig. 2.3, for a helpful plan of these relationships.

36 Kromberg, "Creating," 103–104. Details of this earlier building are not yet published.

37 Corinne Castel, "The First Temples *in antis*: The Sanctuary of Tell Al-Rawda in the Context of 3rd Millennium Syria," in *Kulturlandschaft Syrien: Zentrum und Peripherie, Festschrift für Jan-Waalke Meyer*, ed. Jorg Becker, Ralph Hempelmann, and Ellen Rehm (Münster: Ugarit-Verlag, 2010), 135–136. Compare to Jean Evans, *The Lives of Sumerian Sculpture: An Archaeology of the Early Dynastic Temple* (Cambridge: Cambridge University Press, 2012).

38 Castel, "First Temples," 146.

39 Max Mallowan, "Tell Chuēra in Nordost Syrien," *Iraq* 28/1 (1966): 92–93.

40 Ralph Hempelmann, "Die Ausgrabungen in Bereich K," in *Tell Chuera: Vorberichte zu den Grabungskampagnen 1998 bis 2005*, ed. Jan-Waalke Meyer (Wiesbaden: Harrassowitz, 2010), 35–81.

Although *Steinbau* VI seems to have maintained the same features since its foundation,[41] it too may have evolved to house a different set of practices from those associated with its original incarnation, for, over time, the monumental set of *Steinbauten* lining the central thoroughfare grew up to incorporate this square temple *in antis* in their midst, just as the structure itself was transformed from mudbrick to stone. Usually considered an integral part of the *Steinbauten* is an extramural complex. Located in what appears to be a direct line with the thoroughfare, and approximately 350 meters as the crow flies from *Steinbau* III, is the *Aussenbau*. Consisting of a temple *in antis* and parts of another structure, with several pebbled open areas in between, traces of a wall to the rear of the temple suggest the area was enclosed. Anton Moortgat[42] interpreted the second structure to the south of the *in antis* building as a gateway to the complex, with steps leading up to it, but this edifice does not align with either the temple, or what is perhaps the most extraordinary feature of the *Aussenbau*: the *Stelenstrasse*. The *Stelenstrasse* is a paved street running 70 m. northwest/southeast[43] flanked by standing stones ranging from two to three meters high on either side of its entire length.[44] Severely weathered, little trace of any modification of these stones has survived, but one, clearly modeled, triangular stone indicates these were not only once stelae, but were possibly anthropomorphic in nature.

It is not clear how the *Stelenstrasse* begins or ends, but it seems likely the gateway east of the temple opens on to this street via a pebbled square.[45] The date of the *Stelenstrasse* is equally unclear—it is presumed to correspond to the stone structures of the *Aussenbau*, that is, ca. 2450,[46] the date of both the *Kleiner Antentempel* and *Steinbau* VI. However, like *Steinbau* VI, mudbrick walls underlie the *Aussenbau*'s temple. Moortgat[47] understood this mudbrick structure to be the foundations of the stone *Aussenbau*, but the sequence he describes warrants reconsideration. First, a natural rock outcrop was manually leveled, then covered with a layer of "fine" gravel followed by a layer of clay. The mudbrick structure was placed on this clay layer, with a sloping plastered

41 Kromberg, "Creating," 104.

42 Anton Moortgat, *Tell Chuēra in Nordost-Syrien: Vorläufiger Bericht über die Grabung 1958* (Köln und Opladen: Westdeutscher Verlag, 1960), 19.

43 The directions given are confusing as they seem to be the same orientation as the thoroughfare. However, examination of the plan (Moortgat, *Tell Chuēra*, figs. 4, 9) makes the differences very clear.

44 Moortgat, *Tell Chuēra*, 9–12.

45 Moortgat, *Tell Chuēra*, 13.

46 Castel, "First Temples," 146.

47 Moortgat, *Tell Chuēra*, 13, 18–19.

screed all around it. This was then covered with a thick plaster layer. Subsequently the foundations of the *Aussenbau* were laid. There is no dating material provided for the layers beneath the stone structure, but it is quite possible that they represent an earlier building dating to the first half of the third millennium.[48]

The orientation of these structures in regard to each other, and to Chuera's central thoroughfare, raises questions about their relationship in both ritual and chronological terms. The presumed gateway to the complex lies 50 m. away from, and is oriented at right angles to, the *Stelenstrasse*, which heads slightly northwest in the direction of the lower town wall, not toward the thoroughfare. *Steinbauten* I–IV form an organized complex, understood now to be a monumentalized entranceway leading into the town from the south-east side. And while the *Aussenbau* complex does lie in what appears at first glance to be a direct line with thoroughfare, which is oriented southeast to northwest, the entrance to the *Aussenbau* is open to the east, away from the settlement.[49] People therefore did not travel directly from the thoroughfare to either the temple precinct or the *Stelenstrasse*, but rather must have made some significant turns: One, at an oblique angle, to enter the *Stelenstrasse* coming from the town, the next, a right angle, to leave the *Stelenstrasse* to enter the temple gate. Such turns have a significant impact on the experience of not just the spatial relationship between monumental structures such as these, but the ideological one too, as the traveler is consciously turned away from whence they came.

What is more, once in the temple, the view to the rear *cella* and whatever was on the podium there, aligns the audience to the open country outside the settlement, whether they would have been aware of this or not. This difference is rather fundamental. It certainly challenges the idea that the *Aussenbau* is an integral part of the *Steinbauten* system—part of the settlement's "armature."[50] Instead, we must consider multiple possibilities: that the *Aussenbau* exists in a dialogic relationship with the settlement *Steinbauten*; that it is a deliberate rejection of them; and that the *Aussenbau* is not intended first and foremost to serve the settlement, but to "capture" people from outside it, or coming to it. And if it *was* built by the same sector of society that built the *Steinbauten*, it would not seem to serve the same function as those intramural buildings.

Here chronological refinement is essential for adjudicating between the possibilities listed above, a refinement that is unfortunately lacking for the outer

---

48 Moreover, this sequence is tantalizingly like the construction techniques used in one of the monumental mortuary mounds at Banat, discussed below.

49 Moortgat, *Tell Chuēra*, figs. 4, 9.

50 Creekmore, "Social," 56.

complex. The *Steinbauten* were built around 2450 BCE, the thoroughfare monumentalized, after the construction of the outer town wall around 2550 BCE. But the thoroughfare extended beyond the confines of even the earliest settlement,[51] dated to 3100–2850 BCE.[52] The thoroughfare then, from this time, links inside and outside space, and—given that a mudbrick structure underlies *Steinbau* VI, and a mudbrick structure underlies the *Aussenbau*, perhaps residential and ritual space. That is to say, there may have been a connection here from the beginning of the settlement, but that connection changed when the thoroughfare was institutionalized.[53]

That the *Aussenbau* is the same style of structure, built in the same way, does not automatically render it part of the same institutional system though. Because we have long been locked into the idea that all monuments must be state-sponsored, we have paid insufficient attention to this possibility. Today, counter-monuments have become increasingly visible in public spaces as the hegemony of the establishment is increasingly challenged by those excluded from it.[54] The counter-monument may emphasize that which the establishment monument omits,[55] but it may also take the form of that with which it engages, expressing its distinction from the establishment monument by some kind of inversion. Well-known is Horst Hoheisel's *Negative Form: Memorial to the Aschrottbrunnen Fountain* in Kassel, Germany, where the original fountain, destroyed by the Nazis, was commemorated by inserting its replica upside-down into the ground.[56] In one kind of counter monument, the "anti-monument," the original monument itself is destabilized. It is re-inscribed[57]

51 Meyer, "Birth," fig. 3.1.

52 Hempelmann, "Origin," 48.

53 And contra Creekmore, "Social," 56.

54 Paul Ashton, Paula Hamilton, and Rose Searby, *Places of the Heart: Memorials in Australia* (North Melbourne: Australian Scholarly Publishing, 2012); Quentin Stevens, Karen Franck, and Ruth Fazakerley, "Counter-monuments: The Anti-Monumental and the Dialogic," *The Journal of Architecture* 17/6 (2012): 951–972; Ágnes Erőss, "'In Memory of Victims': Monument and Counter-Monument in Liberty Square, Budapest," *Hungarian Geographical Bulletin* 65/3 (2016): 237–254; Kristine Nielsen, "Monumental Attack: The Visual Tools of the German Counter-Monument in Two Works by Jochen Gerz and Esther Shalev-Gerz, and Horst Hoheisel," *Images* 9/1 (2016): 122–139; Malcom Angelucci and Stefano Kerschbamer, "One Monument, One Town, Two Ideologies: The Monument to the Victory of Bolzano—Bozen," *Public History Review* 24 (2017): 54–75; James Osborne, "Counter-Monumentality and the Vulnerability of Memory," *Journal of Social Archaeology* 17/2 (2017): 163–187.

55 Such as Marc Quinn's sculpture, *Alison Lapper Pregnant* erected in Trafalgar Square, London (Stevens, Franck, and Fazakerley, "Counter-monuments," fig. 3).

56 James Young, "The Counter-Monument: Memory Against Itself in Germany Today," *Critical Inquiry* 18/2 (1992): 267–296.

57 Sarah Demoiny and Stewart Waters, "Remembering What We Would Rather Forget," in

or re-dressed, becoming a locus of contested power.[58] In another, the "dialogic monument," structures are paired so that their individual significance is transformed when juxtaposed with one another.[59]

We need not think that this materialization of a social and/or political contestation is restricted to the modern world. In the third millennium, inversion may consist of outside versus in, while replication of form establishes the dialogic relationship. It may be that institutionalization was resented, if not resisted, by the public who had long been at the literal and figurative center of the community, and the *Aussenbau* repurposed to enact that resistance.

On the other hand, it is just too simplistic to assume that all power, be it heterarchical or hierarchical, comes from within a site and disseminates outward. The countryside around any settlement could not be under the exclusive and policed control of the polity. There are two basic populations that need to be taken into consideration in addition to the inhabitants of the town. One is the inhabitants of smaller settlements in the vicinity of Tell Chuera. The three-tiered settlement model is fundamentally an economic construct and does not account for the great variety of relationships and attitudes implicit in rural/urban relationships. An external site of ritual/political practice might form a neutral place for the meeting of both sectors; it might also form a locus of resistance. While gates and walls might be intended to control who accesses a space, they do not in and of themselves tell us who was allowed and who was not.

The second population is comprised of mobile pastoralists, whether attached or unattached to the settlement.[60] This seems to have become an increasingly contentious, and increasingly misunderstood, issue. Meyer, for example, writes that "we no longer consider that nomadic groups took part in their (circular cities) foundation; such planned, partly urban settlements and settle-

---

Democracy at a Crossroads: Reconceptualizing Socio-Political Issues in Schools and Society, ed. Gregory Samuels and Amy Samuels (Charlotte, NC: Information Age Publishing, 2019), 98.

58 Stevens, Franck, and Fazakerley, "Counter-monuments," 954.

59 Anne Porter, "The Power of the Populace: Politics and the Mortuary Monuments of Tell Banat," in *Pomp, Circumstance, and the Performance of Politics: Acting "Politically Correct" in the Ancient World*, ed. Kathryn Morgan, OIS (Chicago, IL: The Oriental Institute of the University of Chicago), forthcoming.

60 See Anne Porter, "Isotopes and Ideograms: Bio-archaeological and Theoretical Approaches to Pastoralism in Light of the Mari (and Other) Texts," *Clarascuro* 20 (2019): 1–34; Anne Porter, "Mobile Pastoralism in the Ancient Near East," in *A Companion to the Ancient Near East*, ed. Daniel C. Snell (Hoboken, NJ: Wiley-Blackwell, 2020), 125–143, for discussions of the many misapprehensions underpinning this issue.

ment systems would not correspond to the way of thinking of nomadic populations."[61] Whatever one thinks of the relationship between mobile pastoralists and the settlement of Tell Chuera, it is certainly presumptuous to claim that we know the way of thinking now, let alone then, of "nomadic populations"—itself a commonly employed, but meaningless phrase, laden with outdated prejudice. Mobility is not an immutable state. It does not require an absence of affective ties with sedentary populations.[62] It is not a default choice employed when there is no better option.[63] Nor, by the same token, is it a heroic anti-settlement, anti-civilization sentiment embedded in the DNA of certain groups. Whatever the climatic conditions at the time, whatever the agricultural regime, this landscape, like most of northern Syria, was exploited for animal husbandry in a variety of socioeconomic constructs.[64] As I have repeatedly discussed, mobile pastoralism does not necessitate politically independent or unattached pastoralists. The seasonal presence of such an additional population and their animals may have put pressure on the settlement's facilities so that an external temple was built to accommodate them. Or it may have been built by them, as an expression of a relationship that might be hostile, strained, convivial, or familial—or all of the above at different times.

2 Tell Banat

In contrast to the community that lies at the heart of Tell Chuera, it is the dead that occupy the physical and conceptual center of Tell Banat. The appropriation of two (putative) burials and their consequent expansion into major monuments mark two distinct spaces in this complex of sites.[65] One, Mortuary Mound II, is situated in the heart of what would become the main settlement of

61 Meyer, "Birth," 38.

62 An understanding put forward in Susan Lees and Daniel Bates, "The Origins of Specialized Nomadic Pastoralism: A Systemic Model," *American Antiquity* (1974): 191, and widely perpetuated in archaeology. See Anne Porter, "Beyond Dimorphism: Ideologies and Materialities of Kinship as Time-Space Distanciation," in *Nomads, Tribes, and the State in the Ancient Near East: Cross-disciplinary Perspectives*, ed. Jeffrey Szuchman (Chicago, IL: the Oriental Institute of the University of Chicago, 2009), 201–225.

63 Contra Hempelmann, "Origin," 50.

64 Porter, "Isotopes."

65 See Anne Porter, "The Tell Banat Settlement Complex during the Third and Second Millennia BCE," in *From Pottery to Chronology: The Middle Euphrates Region in Late Bronze Age Syria*, ed. Adelheid Otto, Münchener Abhandlungen zum Alten Orient Band 1 (Gladbeck: PeWe-Verlag2018), 195–224.

Tell Banat, the other at Tell Banat North, is the White Monument, located about 200 m. (as the crow flies) from the outer edge of the main settlement. Having discussed the latest phase of both mortuary monuments elsewhere,[66] I confine the discussion here to the earlier one. The similarities in concept, and in some instances execution, show that these two monuments were constructed in reference to each other, yet the divergences between them manifest considerable ideological differences. These differences in turn suggest a dialogic, if not outright conflictual, relationship between those who built the structures.

We cannot determine which burial sparked the building process, but I will start with the one in the center of the settlement of Tell Banat, Mortuary Mound II. Here a circular tumulus coated in a dense gypsum surface, modelled in bands, constituted the beginning of the sequence. As far as exposed, the tumulus was 7 m. in diameter and 3 m. deep. Subsequently, a deposit of sterile gravel some 60 m. in diameter was placed over this tumulus to form a shallow mound. Geomagnetic surveys show it to have been somewhat irregular in shape.[67] The spoil heap of a pit dug through this gravel mound revealed the probable mortuary nature of the underlying tumulus, as it included objects known only as burial goods in Banat's assemblage. Also found were a few randomly sized rocks, typical of the interiors of the tumuli within the other monumental mortuary mound at Tell Banat North.

This pit was dug prior to the enhancement of the gravel mound by the placement of two stone columns, 1 m. in diameter, on its apex, and the construction of a major entranceway leading from the street in the east to the columns in the west. The entrance was flanked by a series of rooms built around the sloping sides of the mound and terraced over three levels,[68] labelled Building 7. Building 7 may have wrapped around the mound on all sides, but because of the constraints entailed by excavating in an inhabited village this was not definitively established.

Dug into the southern side of the gravel mound was a monumental tomb, Tomb 7. It is not clear if Tomb 7 would have been incorporated within the walls of Building 7 or not, but its roof was part of the surface of a large open area, suggesting, perhaps, that it was not. Eventually the gravel mound, Building 7, and Tomb 7 were all submerged beneath a later structure, Building 6.

66 For White Monument A, see Anne Porter et al., "Their Corpses Shall Reach the Base of Heaven: A Third-Millennium BC War Memorial in Northern Mesopotamia?," *Antiquity* 95 (2021): 1–19; for Mortuary Mound IIA, see Porter, "Power," forthcoming.

67 See Porter, "Power," fig. 4, for a schematic rendering.

68 Anne Porter, "Communities in Conflict: Death and the Contest for Social Order in the Euphrates River Valley," *NEA* 65/3 (2002): 157.

The earliest phase of Tell Banat North is unknown, but traces of a series of small circles of low conductivity suggest that it began as one of a series of small earthen tumuli that was subsequently enhanced by the construction of a larger mound over it.[69] This second phase, White Monument C, was smooth-surfaced and somewhat angular. The nature of its interior is unknown. But placed on its exterior was a series of small earthen and stone tumuli in which human skeletal remains and some few objects had been placed. Four were excavated, labelled Inner Tumulus (IT) 1–4. A thick white band of marl and gypsum, that served both to stabilize the cairns and to separate them, was interleaved with the right edges of IT4, and the left edges of IT1 and IT3, demonstrating that they were compiled as a single construction event. Nevertheless, each inner tumulus was a discrete entity. The human constituents within them varied in number, age range, and gender distribution. IT1 housed a minimum number of five individuals, IT2 a minimum number of three. IT3 also contained a minimum number of three individuals, one of whom suffered perimortem trauma with a sharp object, while a minimum number of two adults were found in IT4. Soon after compilation these individual but interconnected tumuli were unified within a casing composed of a clean, very white, packed earth built up in bands and resulting in a corrugated effect. This is White Monument B, a constructed dome-like mound that literally shone, giving rise to its label, on the plain outside the settlement.

Seams in this corrugated surface indicate different groups of workers simultaneously building up the surface. This construction pattern of "together but separate" is very eloquent. It speaks of individual families collaborating in maintaining the identity of community as much as it does state-sponsored work gangs.[70] While it might be tempting, given the size and visibility of the monument, to see these individual tumuli as belonging to the elite, comparison with other contemporaneous tombs at Tell Banat negates this idea. Like the inner tumuli of White Monument B, Banat shaft and chamber tombs 1 and 2 contained a minimum number of five and three individuals respectively. Unlike the inner tumuli of White Monument B, tombs 1 and 2 also contained approximately two hundred and one hundred pots, respectively, as well as multiple metals, beads, and other objects.

69 Porter, "Power," fig. 3. At least two meters of alluviation had deposited since the foundation of Tell Banat North, further obscuring its origins.

70 See for example, Jordan Pickett et al., "Architectural Energetics for Tumuli Construction: The Case of the Medieval Chungul Kurgan on the Eurasian Steppe," *Journal of Archaeological Science* 75 (2016): 101–114.

Nevertheless, discussions of the White Monument focus on its size as obvious indicators of power and prestige. For some, the monumentality of both Tomb 7 and the White Monument render them the same, on the assumption that deep beneath the latter mound must lie a rich royal burial. For this audience, either both belong to kings of different generations, or one belongs to the king, one the queen. For others, it is the assumption that monumentality is the exclusive province of the state. Without defining the nature of the White Monument, Lauren Ristvet describes it as a destination of a royal ritual progression, whereby the White Monument was incorporated into the rhetoric of the polity.[71] This idea is similar to that of the Ebla Royal Ritual, in which the king and queen, their gods, and various members of their retinue progress out of the town into the countryside to visit the burials of previous rulers.[72] A fundamental understanding of royal processions as elite manipulation of ideology and display is widespread; its purpose is seen as a means of integrating the components of the state that live at a remove from its everyday demonstrations of authority, thereby reminding them of who is in charge and why. The audience may be impressed, awed, resentful of the munificence of the state, or indifferent. But this is a momentary awareness at best. Once the procession passes, everyone returns to their normal routine.

But these understandings of the White Monument and Tomb 7 are focused on the finished product, rather than the sequences that gave rise to them, and they fail to consider the combined effect of the many differences between them. How the mounds were enlarged, and where they were enlarged, does not just reflect two separate constituencies for each, two separate visions of society, but creates them.[73] Whichever location began this push and pull, both monuments should be understood as the appropriation of an earlier burial that through expansion became the ancestral legitimation of this vision. Open, enclosed; high, low; outside the settlement, within it; inclusionary, exclusionary: community, institution. These aspects of Tell Banat North and Mortuary Mound II shape the experience and awareness of those who live in their vicinity. They position the person relative to society to the degree the person is relative to the monuments themselves. This works in two ways. One, as ancestral

71 Lauren Ristvet, *Ritual, Performance, and Politics in the Ancient Near East* (Cambridge: Cambridge University Press, 2014).

72 If any connection between the actions of the Ebla Royal Ritual and Banat is to be made, it is with Tomb 7—the largest tomb known in northern Mesopotamia, with five rooms, ceilings of standing height, and plenty of space for sojourning overnight as the Ebla king and queen do.

73 Christopher Gosden, "What Do Objects Want?," *Journal of Archaeological Method and Theory* 12 (2005): 196.

appropriations the monuments are descent systems manifest. They automatically invoke a constituency of those who claim a connection to said ancestor. Even if the intent is to submerge the original burial in a bigger, grander structure with stated affiliations to a different body altogether, genealogical memories are long. The imposing presence of the White Monument and the mystique of Mortuary Mound II are, each in their own way, constant calls to rehearse those memories and the ways they may have been subverted. They are, therefore, potentially places of simmering resentments.

Two, Banat is a small site. It is difficult to find a place within the town where one would be oblivious to the presence of either monument. What one sees and what one does not see, what one has access to and what one does not, is a daily reminder of where one fits in the scheme of things. This is not a simple matter. The monuments invoke the simultaneous relationships of class, kinship, professional connections, religious affiliations, and even cosmological constructs, as one moves about the settlement in quotidian actions. These relationships may cut across each other or they may be congruent. In either case, they form a particular sociopolitical network in which each individual is situated. The monuments are, therefore, potentially places of incorporation too.

These are not necessarily two mutually exclusive conditions, but ones that may be enacted to varying outcomes. Evidence of ritual performance is found at both places,[74] but the nature of those performances is inevitably differentiated by the constraints and affordances of the structures themselves. Mortuary Mound II is enclosed, Tomb 7 semi-subterranean. Placed on the open plain, the White Monument is an unpoliceable place of assembly, constructing its own public, a public that may consist of anyone, of any class, of any ethnicity, from near or from far.

At the same time, though, as the *Steinbauten* and stone version of the *Aussenbau* were constructed, the White Monument underwent another expansion, this time in a very different, and rather specific way. Secondary burials were incorporated within the undifferentiated matrix of a new expansion phase, White Monument A, in a manner that depicts the organization of an army. While this could as well have been constructed by the public as was the earlier phase, White Monument B, one of the aspects that speaks to an organized army, rather than an ad hoc public caught up in battle, is the fact that one section of the cemetery portrays battle-cart teams: driver, jumper, and the equids that pulled the vehicle.[75] These elements are the purview of the state.

74 Porter et al., "Corpses"; Porter, "Power."

75 As portrayed on the standard of Ur; see Porter et al., "Corpses," for further details.

The institutional sector at both sites would *appear* therefore to have emerged as the dominant force in society early in the second half of the third millennium. But appearances can be deceiving. Appropriating a symbol of the public sector does not necessarily mean that sector was successfully subordinated, nor that the mound no longer held its previous symbolic value for that group.

3 Interpretation

Thus far I have explored a construct whereby institutional power is in tension with the power of the public. But rather than assume that the balance automatically shifts in favor of the institutional over time, we should better understand it as always in flux—and always requiring negotiation. And this is the point: there are many ways the data can be interpreted, but we are locked into a monolithic way of looking at it, because in large part we do not include a broad enough range of data, and we do not experiment with a broad enough range of theoretical considerations. Although different in form, both Tell Banat and Tell Chuera may be understood to express the same social and cosmological situation: communities structured through descent systems that are entwined with religious precepts, rather than necessarily under the power of religious institutions. Kin groups may be defined by the smaller temples situated in residential sectors at Chuera, while ancestral appropriations mark the emergence of two such groups at Banat. Intramural monumental structures denote institutional sectors of the society, extramural ones, the public. Concomitantly, the White Monument and the *Aussenbau* stand as beacons of resistance, Mortuary Mound II and the *Steinbauten* as assertions of dominance. The outcome of this is that the power of the public—unconstrained by walls, visible for miles around, and ultimately unpoliceable—reaches farther in the consciousness of various populations than the power of the institutions enclosed by walls in their own, segregated quarter, and visible only to those permitted through the gates. It may be argued that this presents a defensive posture, one uncertain of its own control.

But what of the collective identity of the polity? A conception of society whereby the individual networks of every member of society may be dissolved or reworked into a single entity? It is the *zukru* festival that points to another interpretation of this material: rituals that effect a transcendence of such divisions—institution and public—to create a moment of community. It might be claimed that all rituals of the state do this, but the *zukru* is different from those we think seduce an unagented public to accept the rhetoric of an institutional ideology. In this kind of ritual, the event is held within the confines of institutional power. Leaving the town, leaving those confines behind, effectively negates that institutional power. Institutions, especially religious ones, may certainly assert their power over the landscape in all sorts of ways, but the public is free to see the impossibility of such a situation. It would take little for participants to realize the vulnerability of institutional actors in a structure that could easily be overwhelmed by that population. The inviolability of such a ritual depends then on the concurrence of the people.

So for example, even if the institutional sector built the *Aussenbau*, and even if the gods, the priests, or the ruler, in some combination, process out from the town to the *Aussenbau*, by leaving the town they are placing themselves in a space where they have no real, effective control; where people who may come under their dominion can escape it, and where people who are not under their dominion can challenge them. Then they approach a structure with its back turned to the town, its entrance open to the countryside, where no narrow streets, walls or gateways can be manned to constrain the movements of the population. All these features are a negation of the hierarchical reality of the settlement. All participants are on a common footing.

It is not necessary for the exterior spaces where this other kind of ritual happens, the communal kind, to be marked. Yet in the case of the *zukru* it *is* marked, by standing stones. Or at least the transition from spaces where the social realities of everyday life are enacted to spaces where those realities may be negated is marked. Passing through the stone is, in the case of Dagan as he returns to the town, transformative in some way. Standing stones, while prominent in the second millennium, should also be considered a feature of Syrian religious practices from the third millennium onward.[76] They seem closely associated with the temple *in-antis* style. One example is the betyl in its own enclosure within the temenos of the temple *in antis* at late third-millennium al-Rawda.[77] But the earliest example of which I am aware is Chuera's *Stelenstrasse*. Corinne Castel's discussion of standing stones does not mention the *Stelenstrasse*, despite the associations she draws between Chuera and al-Rawda, perhaps because the *Stelenstrasse* does not consist of an individual stone, and perhaps because the stones are assumed to be anthropomorphized. Nevertheless, the seventy-meter-long road that is the *Stelenstrasse* does more than just accentuate the

---

76 Jean-Marie Durand, *Le culte des pierres et les monuments commémoratifs en Syrie amorrite*, FM 8 (Paris: Société pour l'Étude du Proche-Orient Ancien, 2005).

77 Corinne Castel, "Al-Rawda et le culte des pierres dressées en Syrie à l'âge du Bronze," in *Pierres levées, stèles anthropomorphes et dolmens*, ed. Tara Steimer-Herbet (Oxford: British Archaeological Reports, 2011), 69–88.

Aussenbau. For those who passed along it, this space outside the town is marked as different in some way. No such indicators were in evidence at Banat, but, given the two meters of alluviation that has accumulated over this landscape since the third millennium, this is hardly surprising. The White Monument itself, though, stands as the mesmerizing draw of anyone moving toward it. That passage is itself transitional for those coming from the town, whose field of sight incorporates fields, water, and the hills that ring this small part of the river valley. Landscape embodies the network of social relationships that extend far beyond the confines of the town. Networks can be activated to challenge the limited powers of the institutional sector.

Through the lens of the Emar rituals, then, we can see not only that all actors are political, whatever their station in life, but that all spaces may be politicized too. They require us to think far more deeply about the relationship of monumentality and landscape. The *zukru* festival in particular shows us just how significant exterior spaces may be to the negotiation of the tensions between institution and public in the production of community.

Bibliography

Angelucci, Malcom, and Stefano Kerschbamer. "One Monument, One Town, Two Ideologies: The Monument to the Victory of Bolzano—Bozen." *Public History Review* 24 (2017): 54–75.

Ashton, Paul, Paula Hamilton, and Rose Searby. *Places of the Heart: Memorials in Australia*. North Melbourne: Australian Scholarly Publishing, 2012.

Backhaus, Henrike, and Tobias Helms. "Decentralized Decision-Making Processes in Third Millennium Syro-Mesopotamian City Planning: The Example of Tell Chuera." Pages 13–32 in *Urban Practices: Repopulating the Ancient City*. Edited by Annette Haug and Stephanie Merten. Turnhout: Brepols, 2020.

Baadsgaard, Aubrey, Janet Monge, and Richard L. Zettler. "Bludgeoned, Burned, and Beautified: Reevaluating Mortuary Practices in the Royal Cemetery of Ur." Pages 125–158 in *Sacred Killing: The Archaeology of Sacrifice in the Ancient Near East*. Edited by Anne Porter and Glenn Schwartz. Winona Lake, IN: Eisenbrauns, 2012.

Benz, Brendon C. *The Land Before the Kingdom of Israel: A History of the Southern Levant and the People who Populated it*. HACL 7. Winona Lake, IN: Eisenbrauns, 2016.

Biga, Maria-Giovanna. "Buried Among the Living at Ebla? Funerary Practices and Rites in a XXIV cent. BC Syrian Kingdom." Pages 249–275 in *Sepolti tra i vivi: Evidenza ed interpretazione di contesti funerari in abitato. Atti del Convegno Internazionale*. Edited by Gilda Bartoloni and M.-Gilda Benedettini. Scienze dell'Antichità 15. Rome: Edizione Quasar, 2007/8.

Castel, Corinne. "Al-Rawda et le culte des pierres dressées en Syrie à l'âge du Bronze." Pages 69–88 in *Pierres levées, stèles anthropomorphes et dolmens/Standing Stones, Anthropomorphic Stelae and Dolmens*. Edited by Tara Steimer-Herbet. Oxford: British Archaeological Reports, 2011.

Castel, Corinne. "The First Temples *in antis*: The Sanctuary of Tell Al-Rawda in the Context of 3rd Millennium Syria." Pages 123–164 in *Kulturlandschaft Syrien: Zentrum und Peripherie, Festschrift für Jan-Waalke Meyer*. Edited by Jorg Becker, Ralph Hempelmann, and Ellen Rehm. AOAT 371. Münster: Ugarit-Verlag, 2010.

Creekmore III, Andrew T. "The Social Production of Space in Third-Millennium Cities of Upper Mesopotamia." Pages 32–73 in *Making Ancient Cities: Space and Place in Early Urban Societies*. Edited by Andrew Creekmore and Kevin Fisher. Cambridge: Cambridge University Press, 2014.

Démare-Lafont, Sophie, and Daniel Fleming. "Emar Chronology and Scribal Streams: Cosmopolitanism and Legal Diversity." *RA* 109/1 (2015): 45–77.

Demoiny, Sarah, and Stewart Waters. "Remembering What We Would Rather Forget." Pages 95–112 in *Democracy at a Crossroads: Reconceptualizing Socio-Political Issues in Schools and Society*. Edited by Gregory Samuels and Amy Samuels. Charlotte, NC: Information Age Publishing, 2019.

Durand, Jean-Marie. *Le culte des pierres et les monuments commémoratifs en Syrie amorrite*. FM 8. Paris: Société pour l'Étude du Proche-Orient Ancien, 2005.

Erőss, Ágnes. "'In Memory of Victims': Monument and Counter-Monument in Liberty Square, Budapest." *Hungarian Geographical Bulletin* 65/3 (2016): 237–254.

Evans, Jean M. *The Lives of Sumerian Sculpture: An Archaeology of the Early Dynastic Temple*. Cambridge: Cambridge University Press, 2012.

Finkbeiner, Uwe, and Ferhan Sakal. "Emar 2002: Bericht über die 5. Kampagne der syrisch-deutschen Ausgrabungen." *BaM* 34 (2003): 9–117.

Fleming, Daniel E. "A Limited Kingship: Late Bronze Emar in Ancient Syria." *UF* 24 (1992): 59–71.

Fleming, Daniel E. *The Installation of Baal's High Priestess at Emar*. HSS 42. Atlanta, GA: Scholars Press, 1992.

Fleming, Daniel E. *Time at Emar: The Cultic Calendar and the Rituals from the Diviner's Archive*. Winona Lake, IN: Eisenbrauns, 2000.

Fleming, Daniel E. *Democracy's Ancient Ancestors*. Cambridge: Cambridge University Press, 2004.

Fleming, Daniel E. "Seeing and Socializing with Dagan at Emar's *zukru* Festival." Pages 197–210 in *The Materiality of Divine Agency*. Edited by Beate Pongratz-Leisten and Karen Sonik. SANER 8. Boston, MA/Berlin: de Gruyter, 2015.

Fronzaroli, Pelio. "The Ritual Texts of Ebla." Pages 163–185 in *Literature and Literary Language at Ebla*. Edited by Pelio Fronzaroli. Quaderni di Semitistica 18. Firenze: Università di Firenze, 1992.

Gosden, Christopher. "What Do Objects Want?" *Journal of Archaeological Method and Theory* 12 (2005): 193–211.

Harmanşah, Ömür. *Cities and the Shaping of Memory in the Ancient Near East*. Cambridge: Cambridge University Press, 2013.

Helms, Tobias, and Philippe Quenet. "The Fortifiction of Circular Cities: The Examples of Tell Chuēra and Tell al-Rawda." Pages 77–99 in *Circular Cities of Early Bronze Age Syria*. Edited by Corinne Castel, Jan-Waalke Meyer, and Philippe Quenet. Subartu 42. Turnhout: Brepols, 2020.

Hempelmann, Ralph. "Die Ausgrabungen in Bereich K." Pages 35–81 in *Tell Chuera: Vorberichte zu den Grabungskampagnen 1998 bis 2005*. Edited by Jan-Waalke Meyer. Wiesbaden: Harrassowitz, 2010.

Hempelmann, Ralph. *Tell Chuēra, Kharab Sayyar und die Urbanisierung der Westlichen Ğazīra*. Wiesbaden: Harrassowitz, 2013.

Hempelmann, Ralph. "The Origin and Early Development of Tell Chuēra and Neighbouring Settlements." Pages 47–59 in *Circular Cities of Early Bronze Age Syria*. Edited by Corinne Castel, Jan-Waalke Meyer, and Philippe Quenet. Subartu 42. Turnhout: Brepols, 2020.

Kromberg, Olesia. "Creating the Urban Landscape: The Emergence of Monumentality in Third Millennium Chuēra." Pages 101–107 in *Circular Cities of Early Bronze Age Syria*. Edited by Corinne Castel, Jan-Waalke Meyer, and Philippe Quenet. Subartu 42. Turnhout: Brepols, 2020.

Lees, Susan, and Daniel Bates. "The Origins of Specialized Nomadic Pastoralism: A Systemic Model." *American Antiquity* (1974): 187–193.

Mallowan Max. "Tell Chuēra in Nordost Syrien." *Iraq* 28/1 (1966): 89–95.

McMahon, Augusta. "Spacious or Empty: Making Courtyards in Mesopotamia." Forthcoming in *Pomp, Circumstance, and the Performance of Politics: Acting "Politically Correct" in the Ancient World*. Edited by Kathryn Morgan. OIS 15. Chicago, IL: The Oriental Institute of the University of Chicago.

Meyer, Jan-Waalke. "The Birth of the Circular Cities." Pages 37–44 in *Circular Cities of Early Bronze Age Syria*. Edited by Corinne Castel, Jan-Waalke Meyer, and Philippe Quenet. Subartu 42. Turnhout: Brepols, 2020.

Moortgat, Anton. *Tell Chuera in Nordost-Syrien: Vorläufiger Bericht über die Grabung 1958*. Wissenschaftliche Abhandlungen der Arbeitsgemeinschaft für Forschung des Landes Nordrhein—Westfalen. Köln und Opladen: Westdeutscher Verlag, 1960.

Nielsen, Kristine. "Monumental Attack: The Visual Tools of the German Counter-Monument in Two Works by Jochen Gerz and Esther Shalev-Gerz, and Horst Hoheisel." *Images* 9/1 (2016): 122–139.

Osborne, James. "Counter-Monumentality and the Vulnerability of Memory." *Journal of Social Archaeology* 17/2 (2017): 163–187.

Otto, Adelheid. "Archaeological Evidence for Collective Governance along the Upper Syrian Euphrates during the Late and Middle Bronze Age." Pages 87–99 in *Organization, Representation, and Symbols of Power in the Ancient Near East: Proceedings of the 54th Rencontre Assyriologique Internationale at Würzburg 20–25 July*. Edited by Gernot Wilhelm. Winona Lake, IN: Eisenbrauns, 2012.

Pickett, Jordan, John S. Schreck, Renata Holod, Yuriy Rassamakin, Oleksandr Halenko, and Warren Woodfin. "Architectural Energetics for Tumuli Construction: The Case of the Medieval Chungul Kurgan on the Eurasian Steppe." *Journal of Archaeological Science* 75 (2016): 101–114.

Porter, Anne. "Communities in Conflict: Death and the Contest for Social Order in the Euphrates River Valley." *NEA* 65/3 (2002): 156–173.

Porter, Anne. "Beyond Dimorphism: Ideologies and Materialities of Kinship as Time-Space Distanciation." Pages 201–225 in *Nomads, Tribes, and the State in the Ancient Near East: Cross-disciplinary Perspectives*. Edited by Jeffrey Szuchman. Oriental Institute Seminars 5. Chicago, IL: the Oriental Institute of the University of Chicago, 2009.

Porter, Anne. "The Materiality of Mourning." Pages 157–188 in *How to Cope with Death: Mourning and Funerary Practices in the Ancient Near East. Proceedings of the International Workshop held at the University of Firenze, December 5–6, 2013*. Edited by Candida Felli. Pisa: ETS, 2016.

Porter, Anne. "The Tell Banat Settlement Complex during the Third and Second Millennia BCE." Pages 195–224 in *From Pottery to Chronology: The Middle Euphrates Region in Late Bronze Age Syria Proceedings of the International Workshop in Mainz (Germany), May 5–7, 2012*. Edited by Adelheid Otto. Münchener Abhandlungen zum Alten Orient Band 1. Gladbeck: PeWe-Verlag, 2018.

Porter, Anne. "Isotopes and Ideograms: Bio-archaeological and Theoretical Approaches to Pastoralism in Light of the Mari (and Other) Texts." *Clarascuro* 20 (2019): 1–34.

Porter, Anne. "Mobile Pastoralism in the Ancient Near East." Pages 125–143 in *A Companion to the Ancient Near East*. Edited by Daniel C. Snell. Hoboken, NJ: Wiley-Blackwell, 2020.

Porter, Anne, Thomas McClellan, Susanne Wilhelm, Jill Weber, Alexandra Baldwin, Jean Colley, Brittany Enriquez, Meagan Jahrles, Bridget Lanois, Vladislav Malinov, Sumedh Ragavan, Alexandra Robins, and Zarhuna Safi. "Their Corpses Shall Reach the Base of Heaven: A Third-Millennium War BC Memorial in Northern Mesopotamia?" *Antiquity* 95 (2021): 1–19.

Porter, Anne. "The Power of the Populace: Politics and the Mortuary Monuments of Tell Banat." Forthcoming in *Pomp, Circumstance, and the Performance of Politics: Acting "Politically Correct" in the Ancient World*. Edited by Kathryn Morgan. OIS 15. Chicago, IL: The Oriental Institute of the University of Chicago.

Ristvet, Lauren. *Ritual, Performance, and Politics in the Ancient Near East*. Cambridge: Cambridge University Press, 2014.

Smith, Adam T. "The Limitations of Doxa: Agency and Subjectivity from an Archaeological Point of View." *Journal of Social Archaeology* 1/2 (2001): 155–171.

Stevens, Quentin, Karen Franck, and Ruth Fazakerley. "Counter-monuments: The Anti-Monumental and the Dialogic." *The Journal of Architecture* 17/6 (2012): 951–972.

Tamm, Alexander. "The Early Bronze Age Palace at Chuēra and the Decline of the Settlement." Pages 109–123 in *Circular Cities of Early Bronze Age Syria*. Edited by Corinne Castel, Jan-Waalke Meyer, and Philippe Quenet. Subartu 42. Turnhout: Brepols, 2020.

Thames Jr., John Tracy. *The Politics of Ritual Change: The* zukru *Festival in the Political History of Late Bronze Age Emar*. HSM 65. Leiden: Brill, 2020.

Young, James. "The Counter-Monument: Memory Against Itself in Germany Today." *Critical Inquiry* 18/2 (1992): 267–296.

16

From Babylon to Jerusalem: Water Ordeals in the Ancient World

Jack M. Sasson

Hilary Mantel, the superb confectioner of historical fiction, has defined history as "What's left in the sieve when the centuries have run through it—a few stones, scraps of writing, scraps of cloth."[1] In this presentation, I will retrieve from that sieve a few bones and sort them into a time continuum to flesh out arcane judicial practices that sought to achieve justice. In turn, I will chart a transfiguration of the practice as it moves from one orbit to another. I offer these pages to Dan Fleming, a master of scholarship on several archives from antiquity. Dan had already penetrated the culture of Late Bronze Age Emar when an urge for new challenges brought him to a world with which we are both now hopelessly in love. I could easily be alluding to Israel and its richest intellectual contribution, the Hebrew Bible; but in this case, the successful seducer was Mari, with records of unprecedented density of action and actors. Dan and I bonded in the twilights of our second millennium CE, when I was privileged to recommend his work on our shared addiction to professional organizations. It is therefore a delight for me to offer him these few pages that try to bridge evidence from the two cultures that continue to absorb us over so many years. Dan once told me that he liked the way I weave ancient records into stories. May these pages succeed in pleasing him, even if they will hardly expand the breadth of his knowledge.[2]

---

1 From one of her 2017 BBC-sponsored Reith lectures; summary and access are via https://www.bbc.co.uk/programmes/articles/2WroW91d332q5mk8FwySysb/what-we-learnt-from-hilary-mantel-s-reith-lectures.

2 An aurally accessible version of this paper was Zoomed to a wider public toward the end of May, 2021. I have largely kept the format of addressing a larger audience rather than one that engages scholars exclusively.

The literature on ordeals is enormous. It includes overviews on Mesopotamia by Wilfred van Soldt ("Ordal A. Mesopotamien," *RlA* 10 [2003]: 124–129); on Hatti by Theo van den Hout ("Ordal B. Bei der Hethitern," *RlA* 10 [2003]: 129–130); on Elam by Joseph Klíma ("L'ordalie par le fleuve en Elam [d'après les documents akkadiens de Suse et de Ḫuḫnur-Mālamir]," *RA* 66 [1972], 39–59); on Israel by Karel van der Toorn ("Ordeal," *ABD* 5:40–42); and comparatively by Tikva Frymer-Kensky ("Suprarational Legal Procedures in Elam and Nuzi," in *Studies on*

 | DOI:10.1163/9789004511538_017

We are around 1770 BCE, plus or minus a few years. Hammurabi commissioned his scribes to glorify him with multiple copies of an eye-catching stone monument. They did so by sandwiching almost 300 case-laws between hymnic tributes to him as a promoter of justice. Breaking precedents, the scribes opened their collection with basic rules of judicial conduct: no witness is to bear false testimony on pain of death if in a capital case (¶3–4); no judge is to reverse a decision, on the suspicion of a bribe (¶5); no individual may charge another with homicide without demonstrable proof (¶1). However, when witchcraft is charged without adequate confirmation, rather than summary execution of the malicious accuser, an extrajudicial procedure takes over (¶2): "If a man charges another person with witchcraft but cannot bring proof against him, he on whom witchcraft is charged must go to (divine) River and plunge into (divine) River. If (divine) River overwhelms him, his accuser will take away his estate; but if (divine) River clears him so that he survives, whoever charged him with witchcraft will be killed and he who plunged into (divine) River will take over his estate."

Details in this law as drafted are few, thus allowing the application of broad analogies. We do not know, for example, whether the parties were neighbors or strangers, young or old; only that they are owners of property that they might hope to enlarge or risk losing. The reference to men is purely stylistic in this literature; for, then as now, women were targets of most of the sorcery accusations. We may surmise, however, that the charge of witchcraft does not concern benign magical acts to mend broken bodies, spirits, marriages, or even hearts; rather, it is about the deployment of black arts that potentially affect a community rather than only those involved.[3] The presumption here too is that experienced witches or warlocks might successfully cover their tracks. Under such circumstances, therefore, higher powers must enter the dispute, for as Ray

the Civilization and Culture of Nuzi and the Hurrians, 1: In Honor of Ernest R. Lacheman on His Seventy-fifth Birthday, April 29, 1981, ed. Martha A. Morrison and David I. Owen [Winona Lake, IN: Eisenbrauns, 1981], 115–131); Sophie Démare-Lafont (*Femmes, droit et justice dans l'Antiquité orientale: contribution à l'étude du droit pénal au Proche-Orient ancient*, OBO 165 [Fribourg: Editions universitaires], 269–274); and Bruce Wells ("The Cultic Versus the Forensic: Judahite and Mesopotamian Judicial Procedures in the First Millennium B.C.E," *JAOS* 128 [2008]: 205–232). The legal dimension of ordeals is discussed in many pages of Raymond Westbrook's magisterial reference volume (*A History of Ancient Near Eastern Law*, HOS 1, The Near and Middle East 72. [Leiden: Brill, 2003], esp. 155, 196–197, 375–376, 495–496, 529, 575–576, 891, and 925).

3 On differentiating between kinds of witchcraft, see R. Westbrook, "Witchcraft and the Law in the Ancient Near East," in *Recht Gestern und Heute: Festschrift zum 85. Geburtstag von Richard Haase*, ed. Joachim Hengstl and Ulrich Sick (Wiesbaden: Harrassowitz, 2006), 45–51.

Westbrook stated it, "If retribution from human justice was uncertain, there was no doubt in the mind of ancient litigants as to the inevitability of divine retribution."[4]

The accused, therefore, must "go to ^{d}ÍD," ÍD being Sumerian for river, in Akkadian *nāru*, Hebrew *nāhār*, with the superscript "d" indicating that a deity (DINGIR) is in control.[5] I therefore give the word "River" with an initial capital "R." The process required the accused to plunge in River. The verb *šalûm*, "to plunge or submerge oneself," hardly tells us where or how deep are the waters; but the verbs for the potential results give us hints. River could "defeat" or "conquer" (*kašādum*) the guilty, resulting in his death. Consequently, his family will lose his home. Should River "clear" him (*ubbubum*), his accuser would suffer that outcome. Some documents even suggest that those falsely accused receive gifts.[6] A neat solution, all around.

This is what happens on earth. A literary text from about the same period, however, reveals a simultaneous unfolding drama On High. A deity grabs those about to drown, dragging them before the goddess Nungal for judgment and sentencing.[7] Yet, while this brief law captures the essence of the procedure, to

4 R. Westbrook, "Judges in the Cuneiform Sources," *Maarav* 12 (2005), 39.

5 In Akkadian, *nārum* is feminine; but in personal names, it designates a male deity. King Zimri-Lim of Mari addresses him as such in a profoundly touching appeal with sentiments that remind of the biblical priestly blessings of Num 6:24–26, "I am herewith dispatching a gold vessel to my Lord. When in the past I sent tidings to my Lord, my Lord showed me a sign. May my Lord fulfill the sign he showed me; may my Lord not fail to protect me; may my Lord not turn his attention elsewhere; may my Lord not favor anyone else but me" (ARM 26 191); translation from J.M. Sasson, *From the Mari Archives: An Anthology of Old Babylonian Letters* (University Park, PA: PSU Press, 2017), 23–39 (hereafter abbreviated *FMA*). Sumerian ÍD is commonly (but with a few objections) treated as the basis for Hebrew *ʾēd*, the primordial gush of waters mentioned in Gen 2:6 and Job 36:27.

6 W. Heimpel, "The Location of Madga," *JCS* 61 (2009): 58–59.

7 The Hymn to Nungal is available online at https://etcsl.orinst.ox.ac.uk/cgi-bin/etcsl.cgi?text=t.4.28.1&charenc=j#; printed version is in Jeremy Black, Graham Cunningham, Eleanor Robson, and Gábor Zólyomi, *The Literature of Ancient Sumer* (Oxford: Oxford University Press, 2004), 339–342. See especially lines 55–62 and 95–105. For further studies, see Tikva Frymer-Kensky, "The Nungal-Hymn and the Ekur-Prison," *JESHO* 20 (1977): 78–89; and Miguel Civil, "On Mesopotamian Jails and Their Lady Wardens," in *The Tablet and the Scroll: Near Eastern Studies in Honor of William W. Hallo*, ed. Mark E. Cohen, Daniel C. Snell, and David B. Weisberg (Bethesda, MD: Capital Decisions Ltd, 1993), 72–78. An Old Babylonian hymn to Bazi alludes (l. 33) to the "Shamash of blood and Great River of sorcery (^{d}ÍD.GAL *ša kišpi*)," in a context suggesting punishment or penitence for the killing of Shakkan, Shamash's son. Perhaps a river ordeal is at stake. The full text is published by Andrew George, *Babylonian Literary Texts in the Schøyen Collection*, CUSAS 10 (Bethesda, MD: CDL Press, 2009), 1–15. It received full treatment in Anette Zgoll and B. Cuperly ("Mythos als rituell aufgeführtes Drama: Inthronisation, Tempelschöpfung und Stadtgründung im altbabylonischen Lied auf Bazi," in *De l'argile au*

fill its many gaps requires living testimony as conveyed in contemporaneous documents. With actual verdicts on obdurate disputes rarely delivering much information on the process, details from the actual practice are embedded in letters. As it happens, the most revealing and detailed contributions on the actual practice come from the letters in the Mari archives, from where I will draw illustrations.[8] Here are issues that I cover briefly below:

1. What does "going to River" mean?
2. Who is tested at River?
3. What happens at River?
4. Where does one go to River?
5. What kind of disputes are resolved by River?
6. What happens to River at Jerusalem's gates?

1 What Does "Going to River" Mean?

When we encounter it in Hammurabi's laws, the river procedure is already centuries old, practiced in many moments and corners of antiquity, ancient Egypt possibly excepted.[9] Terse evocations of it are already in third-millennium Sumerian documents.[10] From court procedures in living legal documents since then, we know that in many cases it was common for litigants and witnesses to take oaths, inviting otherworldly powers to retaliate against deceit and deception. So ominous were the threats that some litigants and witnesses refused to perjure themselves, especially after manipulating symbols or emblems of the

numérique: Mélanges assyriologiques en l'honneur de Dominique Charpin, ed. Gregory Chambon, Michaël Guichard, and Anne-Isabelle Langlois, PIPOAC 3 [Leuven: Peeters], 1209–1242), who consider River to be the spouse of Bazi.

8 Fundamental for the Mari corpus on ordeals is Jean-Marie Durand, "L'ordalie," in ARM 26/1, pp. 509–539. Aside from editing the relevant documents, Durand practically reconstructs the process in detail. An overview on ordeals may be found in Jean-Marie Durand, *Documents épistolaires du palais de Mari*, vol. 3, LAPO 18 (Paris: Cerf, 2000), 150–160. See also his, "La Religion amorrite en Syrie à l'époque des archives de Mari," in *Mythologie et Religion des Sémites Occidentaux*, ed. Gregorio del Olmo Lete, vol. 1, OLA 162 (Leuven: Peeters, 2008), 539–546. Another splendid overview is by Antoine Jacquet, "L'Ordalie," *Supplément au Dictionnaire de la Bible* 77–78 (2008): 379–388.

9 Some Egyptologists consider an episode in the mythological "The Contending of Horus and Seth" to be an ordeal; see Marcelo Campagno, "'Ordalías,' parentesco y estado en la contienda entre Horus y Seth," *Antiguo Oriente* 3 (2005): 89–103.

10 See Cristina Simonetti, "The River Ordeal in the Third Millennium BC," in *^{d}Nisaba za$_3$-mi$_2$: Ancient Near Eastern Studies in Honor of Francesco Pomponio*, ed. Palmiro Notizia, Annunziata Rositani, and Lorenzo Verderame, Dubsar 19 (Münster: Zaphon, 2021), 277–282. In

gods to substantiate their pronouncements.[11] It must have occurred to folks in antiquity, however, that deities operated on their own timeline. To elicit more timely resolutions, and perhaps also to lessen reliance on witnesses or evade verdicts by potentially prejudiced judges, Mesopotamians developed adaptable protocols for tests in which the gods mediated obstinate cases. By far the most conclusive method was to engage the River god, and the phrase "going to River" is figurative for such an occasion.[12] In English, we call the process an "ordeal." Our term is derived from Indo-European, as is the German "Urteil," having to do with "apportioning" or "dealing out" judgments. We must beware, however, not to lump Hammurabi's "ordeals" with the metaphoric sense we apply to our usage, that of "being severely tested," such as we face now under Covid 19.[13] God may well have put a Jonah or a Job through harrowing "ordeals," but this is not what Hammurabi had in mind. For him, a judicial "ordeal" required deities to arbitrate between disputing parties.

Sumerian archives, a register gives a slew of protocols for river ordeals mostly for civil disputes. One Sargonic text speaks of someone returning from a river ordeal; see C. Wilcke, *Early Ancient Near Eastern Law: A History of Its Beginnings. The Early Dynastic and Sargonic Periods* (Munich: Bayerische Akademie der Wissenschaften, 2003), 46 and n. 119. M. Roth's volume (*Law Collections from Mesopotamia and Asia Minor*, 2nd ed., WAW 6 [Atlanta, GA: Scholars Press, 1997]) includes several river ordeal case-laws: Laws of Ur Namma ¶13 (false accusation, p. 18); same ¶14 (wife's promiscuity, p. 18); Laws of Hammurabi ¶132 (unwitnessed wife's promiscuity, p. 106); Middle Assyrian Laws ¶A17 (slander on wife, p. 159); same ¶A22 (rape of woman, p. 160), ¶A24 (abuse of married woman, 161–162). For an expansive application of river ordeals in the Laws of Hammurabi, see Sophie Démare-Lafont, *Femmes, droit et justice dans l'Antiquité orientale*, OBO 165 (Fribourg: Editions universitaires, 1999), 48–55. Paola Negri Scafa's study gives a broad review of the material, with special attention to the Nuzi material, in "L'acqua come 'fonte' di giustitia: La cd. ordalia fluviale in ambito mesopotamico," in *Terre, acque, diritto: Forme delle società antiche. Convegno di studi Università di Salerno* (Fisciano SA, Italy: Centro Studi sui Fondamenti del Diritto Antico, forthcoming), 213–245.

11 Several articles are of interest in Sophie Démare-Lafont, ed., *Jurer et maudire: pratiques politiques et usages juridiques du serment dans le Proche-Orient ancient*, Méditerranées: Revue de l'association Méditerranées 10–11 (Paris: L'Harmattan, 1997). We have dramatic settings for such procedures in ARM 33 98 and 99, two recently published tablets in Jean-Marie Durand, *Les premières années du roi Zimrî-Lîm de Mari: Première partie*, ARM 33 (Leuven: Peeters, 2019).

12 The phrase remains in full use for a few more centuries until a more specific term, *ḫuršān* (Neo-Assyrian *ḫursan*; both possibly from Sumerian ḫur.sag), begins to compete with it.

13 See https://www.etymonline.com/word/ordeal.

2 Who Is Tested at River?

To broach the matter of who gets tested at River, I cite an event recalled by Mari scribes years after it happened. The occasion is recorded in a document about a land dispute in the days of Yaḫdun-Lim (ca. 1800 BCE).[14] The relevant passage reads:

> About this property, Abimatar and Alpan went to court. Abimatar came to Yaḫdun-Lim, bringing to him 10 pounds of silver and 1,000 sheep. He said, "Help me! If it is Alpan's property, a servant of Alpan should lift a millstone and transport (it) across the river (*nārum*)." The servant of Alpan lifted a millstone, but during his crossing, he sank. A servant of Abimatar lifted a millstone and transported (it) across the river. Abimatar took the property and Yaḫdun-Lim sustained him (lit., "held his hand").

Two individuals had probably gone to court and, as their dispute could not be settled there, an appeal was made to higher powers. Here the word for river, *nārum*, is not preceded by a symbol for divinity, likely because this trial occurred by a canal or watercourse near the several acres of disputed bottomlands. One of the contenders brought a substantial tribute to the king—we might label it a bribe. However, as we know that royal officials proctored ordeals (ARM 26 253; *FMA* 292), let us be charitable and declare it a fee or a tariff.

Several issues arise from this event. I address just two of them: the use of surrogates and the staging of the ordeal.

3 What Happens at River?

3.1 *Surrogates*

In antiquity, reliance on proxies covered a whole range of actions, including military replacements for those evading the draft, substitute wombs for childless women, and scapegoats for kings fated to die.[15] In the Yaḫdun-Lim era document, neither the litigants nor any witnesses were tested. Instead, they

14 The text is published in Dominique Charpin, "Les champions, la meule et le fleuve, ou le rachat du terroir de Puzurran au roi d'Ešnunna par le roi de Mari Yaḫdun-Lim," *FM* 1 (1992): 29–38. The relevant segment is translated in *FMA* 291.

15 To judge from its terse lines, one of our earliest ordeal texts may have involved a surrogate; see David I. Owen, "A Unique Late Sargonic River Ordeal in the John Frederick Lewis

were represented by surrogates, one of whom died when transporting millstones across the waters. The inference here is that gods were to judge the merit of the case brought to them rather than to expose the guilty. From On High, therefore, it would not matter who actually was representing the contending sides. With Heaven in judgment, whether individuals knew how to swim well or not could not have mattered, for humans were but puppets for the gods.[16] Both this text and the Hammurabi law encourage us to imagine that the outcome was either survival or death for at least one of the surrogates. In this case, River settled the problem and all but one servant (and one millstone) went back home. We may wonder: what if both surrogates had survived instead of one of them drowning? One conjecture is that the test might be renewed after altering the criteria or after selecting a more dangerous spot.[17] We shall soon see, however, that a third option was available.

3.2 *Staging*

From other Mari letters, we learn something about the choice of substitutes. They may include brothers, wives, daughters, and even mothers. Litigators evidently had substantial authority over their kin and could force them into unhappy situations. Yet, a Mari ordeal that decided a territorial dispute between vassals suggests that, in fact, the choice of participants was likely decided on the spur of the moment. Meptum, a *merḫûm* (military leader of tribal troops) reports to Zimri-Lim on two vassals seeking to resolve differences (ARM 26 249; *FMA* 290–291):

Collection," in *A Scientific Humanist: Studies in Memory of Abraham Sachs*, ed. Erle Leichty, Maria deJ. Ellis, and Pamela Gerardi (Philadelphia, PA: The University Museum, 1988), 307.

16 Whether or not in antiquity people had perfected the art of swimming is debated. A succinct statement is in Michael P. Streck, "Schwimmen," *RlA* 12 (2010): 339. A broader overview that cites previous studies and features Mari ordeals is Silvia Festuccia, "Un tuffo nell'Eufrate: le attività natatorie nella Mesopotamia antica," in *Studî di storia, archeologia e antropologia "in acqua" dedicati a Claudio Moccheggiani Carpano*, ed. Massimiliano Marazzi, Germana Pecoraro, and Sebastiano Tusa, Ricerche di storia, epigrafia e archeologia mediterranea 5 (Rome: Bagatto, 2016), 163–176, especially 171–173. Wolfgang Heimpel gives a dramatic reading for the event in which those undergoing ordeals at Ḫ/Ḫīt not only had to withstand bitumen-heated waters at local springs but also survive noxious sulfuric gases that emanated from them; see his "The River Ordeal in Hit," *RA* 90 (1996): 8–10.

17 This was standard practice in omen takings when they proved inconsistent or ambiguous. Antoine Cavigneaux edits a (damaged) *šakkanakkum*-period text that (possibly) instructs on how to assess the results of an ordeal. It involves five persons under test, the result considered conclusive only if one of them survives; see his "Nouveaux cas d'ordalie à Mari," in 'ina ^{d}marri u qan ṭuppi.' *Par la bêche et le stylet! Cultures et sociétés syro-mésopotamiennes: Mélanges offerts à Olivier Rouault*, ed. Philipe Abrahami and Laura Battini (Oxford: Archaeopress, 2019), 23–37.

> About the group that my lord sent to plunge (in the River) for (King) Šubram and (King) Ḫaya-sumu—I sent trustworthy examiners along with this group of plungers. First, a woman from Ḫaya-sumu was made to plunge. She came out (safely). After her, a (town's) elder was made to plunge. He was absolved by moving a (distance of) about 80 "measures" (lit., fields) into (the River) God and coming out (safely). After him, a second woman was led (into the water) and she came out. After her, a third woman; but (divine) River overcame (her).

A euphemism reveals the fate of the unfortunate third woman. River is said to "pour into" (*irtaḫi*, from *reḫûm*) the victim, as in "possessing, inseminating" her. Here it obviously means to "overpower," and can refer also to diseases and to sleep; in effect, she drowned.[18] It is difficult to estimate how many feet within River the plungers had to negotiate. The "measure" here may be a cubit, each about 1½ feet, so in total 120 feet or 40 yards. The danger would have been intensified by the depth or turbulence in the water at that spot, and possibly its toxicity if close to sulfuric pits.[19] The text continues:

> Because the elder had established a (distance) of 80 "measures," but (divine) River overwhelmed the third woman, the men of Ḫaya-sumu did not agree for 3 more women to plunge. They affirmed the following, "Town and land are not ours!" The elder fell at the feet of the men of Šubram, saying, "You must not make other women die by taking the plunge. We will produce a document of non-contest for the town and territory. In the future, no one will contest (over them), for the town and the territory are Šubram's!" In the presence of examiners, Babylonian palace functionaries and (elders) of the town had a no-contest document drawn up.
>
> I am now sending to my lord the group of plungers so that my lord could question them. [...]

Šubram could have forced tests on several other of Ḫaya-sumu's substitutes; but he did not, for revenge was not a primary motivation of these proceedings. From this letter, we gather that fear of further human loss may stop an ordeal, that scribes were at the ready to draft a document of concession, and that in a political contest, the decision of River was final and accepted by all parties. From other cases, we also learn that tests took place early in the day, that

18 This metaphor for bodily penetration will resurface later.

19 On the estimate, see Jean-Marie Durand, ARM 26/1, pp. 519–520; but see also Marvin A. Powell, "Masse und Gewichte," *RlA* 7 (1987–1990): 477.

water was poured over the hands of the plungers, and that they were made to recite the charges at stake in the contest. Whether or not Judge River was only open for consultation on specific days of the year is not clear. Still, the question remains: Where does one experience the judgment of River?

4 Where Does One Go to River?

While a few Sumerian administrative texts suggest that river ordeals could occur at several sanctified sites, the cases in the Mari archives largely favored the town of Ḫīt (Īdu, modern Ḥīt), between Mari and Babylon, on the Euphrates in today's Iraq.[20] The area was so rich in bitumen reserves that its control was bitterly contested by both powers, contributing to much tension between them. But in that period and centuries afterwards, its fame rested on its temple complex for the River god; so much so that people east and west brought their disputes there from distant corners. Even from culturally distinct Elam in the Iranian plateau, an Elamite ruler sent two men to be tested, but we do not know why (ARM 26 255:23–39).

Very informative is a note from Yatar-Ami, who ruled Carchemish about four hundred miles from Ḫ/Ḥīt, so over a month of travel on foot. A man in his court accuses two others of spilling state secrets. The king keeps the accuser under his control, but the alleged offenders are to be tested. He writes to Zimri-Lim (ARM 28 20; *FMA* 291–292): "Together with my servant [Napsuna-Addu], one of your trustworthy servants ought to lead these (two) men to (the god) River. If these men survive the ordeal, I shall burn their challenger; but if these men die, right here I shall give their house(hold) and their servants to their accuser." We are not told what would happen if only one of the accused survived. This is by no means the only kind of dispute that brings people to River.

20 In Mari we find [d]ÍD[ki], *i-da*[ki], *i-ta-i*, among many spellings; see Nele Ziegler and Anne-Isabelle Langlois, *Les toponymes paléo-babyloniens de la Haute-Mésopotamie: La Haute-Mésopotamie au IIe millénaire av. J.-C.*, MTT I/1 (Paris: SEPOA, 2016), 157–158. Several other sites for ordeals are cited in Heimpel, "The Location of Madga," 56–57. He also suggests that Madga may have been another (real?) name of Ḫ/Ḥīt, at least in the days of Gudea, because Madga was also known for its bitumen reserves.

5 What Kind of Disputes Are Resolved by River?

Beyond territorial and land quarrels, the Mari archives contain diverse calls for river ordeals to resolve accusations, among them theft, be it of military spoils (ARM 26 254; *FMA* 293) or sacred objects (ARM 26 256), as well as treason, witchcraft, and adultery. Here are samples from these categories.

5.1 *Witchcraft*

I opened with a Hammurabi directive for witchcraft cases that was very short on details. A Mari letter tells us about an actual event. Meptum, the same *merḫûm* featured above, confronted a detachment that had come all the way from Aleppo in Syria, almost four hundred miles away. The group was leading a woman, her daughter, and a boy, to River (ARM 26 253; *FMA* 292). Apparently, the women had been accused of conniving against the boy, and the mother sought absolution for themselves. Before plunging into River, the mother took this oath: "[I swear] that my daughter Marat-Ištar performed no witchcraft against Ḫammi-epuḫ, son of Dadiya; that this woman nowhere within the (city) gate or elsewhere has given me sticks (for) sorcery; that she (or I) never fed Ḫammi-epuḫ, son of Dadiya, (bewitched) food, solid, liquid, or whatever." Alas, the mother did not survive. I do not know what happened to the daughter. But the boy was cleared, presumably of any false accusation. It seems likely that his parents had lodged the complaint, probably alleging seduction.

5.2 *Multiple Charges*

From the letter Meptum posted to Zimri-Lim about a dispute between two vassals (ARM 26 249; *FMA* 290–291), we learn about a king (Yarkab-Addu of Ḫanzat) who leveled almost all these charges against his wife at the same occasion, leading us to suspect that he was simply trying to get rid of her. Worth noting here is that Meptum is reporting on behalf of the priest of River and of the governor of Ḫīt, high officials who obviously played a role in the matter. They reveal that Yarkab-Addu's queen had designated a servant with a prestigious blood line (kin to Samsi-Addu, a tribal leader) to take the test. Before plunging, the servant had to defend against the following accusations: "(May River decide) (if) your mistress has not transgressed against her lord." I do not know whether each of these charges—treason, witchcraft, adultery, *lèse-majesté*—required its own test. At any rate, the substitute did not survive; but only River knew which of these accusations had stuck.

5.3 *Promiscuity*

One might imagine that the future of Yarkab-Addu's queen was sealed. Yet, our next documents suggest that the elite rarely pay the ultimate price. A spicy allegation is contained in the following novel justification as delivered by the wife of a prominent vassal. In ancient Israel, according to Deuteronomy 22, parents of a bride were expected to keep the marital bedding used during consummation to prove their daughter's virginity.[21] In our case, the wife of another ruler, Sin-iddinam, made this confession by alluding to premarital hanky-panky, likely before she or a substitute took the plunge (ARM 26 488:29–41; *FMA* 293): "Before Sin-iddinam could marry me, I agreed with father and son, so that whenever Sin-iddinam left his home (on a trip), the son of Asqudum (the diviner?) would notify me, 'I want to have you!' He kissed my lips and touched my vagina; but his penis did not penetrate my vagina, for I thought, I will not sin against Sin-iddinam who has not sinned against me. I have not done in my own house what I am not to do."[22] The report continues, "The wife is safe." We do not know too much about the circumstances, but the final line suggests that either she or her surrogate must have been cleared, likely through a river ordeal.

As it happens, another text (ARM 26 252 = *FMA* 292–293) reveals that the concubine ("travel-mate") of a Sin-iddinam was designated to take the plunge. Should the two texts be sharing the same cuckold, the accused queen may have found a way to rid herself of her husband's companion, likely her personal servant. In yet another twist, the companion was nowhere to be found. Evidently, this drama had other volleys yet in play.

5.4 *Ordeal among the Gods*

A fragment of a letter tells us that even gods may be subjected to an ordeal. When her husband Zimri-Lim was set to battle mighty Elam, Queen Shiptu reassures her husband by citing a vision attributable to a divine mouthpiece

---

21 An enormous scholarly literature is available on this subject; see Aaron Koller, who discusses it as an issue of failed parental control and provides a nice bibliography, "Sex or Power? The Crime of the Bride in Deuteronomy 22," *ZABR* 16 (2010): 279–296.

22 In a trial before her beheading, Catherine Howard, fifth wife of Henry VIII, admitted to the same intimate premarital foreplay with her one-time music teacher, "At the flattering and fair persuasions of [Henry] Mannox, being but a young girl, I suffered him at sundry times to handle and touch the secret parts of my body, which neither became me with honesty to permit nor him to require." This admission is widely reported online, among them at https://englishhistory.net/tudor/monarchs/catherine-howard/.

(*āpilum*). The passage is damaged, but I pick it up with the challenge Ea, a god in full command of words and oaths, is making to the gods (ARM 26 208:11′–26′; *FMA* 282):

> Ea proceeded by saying, "Because we shall take [an oath], dirt from the doorpost of Mari's gate has to be taken for us to conform to the oath ("dirt *and* doorpost"; *rûšam u sippam ... lilqûnimma*)." Doorpost dirt from Mari's gate was taken and soaked in water and the gods and goddesses drank (it). Said Ea to the gods, "*Stand up*, those who would do harm to Mari's brickwork or to its protective guardian!" The gods and goddesses [said], "We will do no harm to Mari's brickwork or to its (protective) guardian."[23]

In this apocalypticizing vision, the gods stake their own eternity to secure the future of Mari. They do so by symbolically dissolving an essence of the city in consecrated water. When drunk, the potion carried a curse with the potential of inciting a Wagnerian *Twilight of the Gods* (*Götterdämmerung*). We are obviously not dealing with an ordeal adjudicated by River, as it might be potentially demeaning for one deity to pass judgment on equals. Rather, a liquid potion carries a potent instrument that invades, tracks down, and punishes those who transgress against commitments or evade honesty. This is a useful scene to keep in mind as river ordeals morphed when moving toward the gates of Jerusalem.

---

23 The exact kind of material to be taken from the door jamb is debated, but I think that the *CAD*'s collection of references confirms this choice; see volume *CAD* R 432 sub *rūšu* A. I have studied this text on two occasions, the last in "Mari Apocalypticism Revisited," in *Immigration and Emigration within the Ancient Near East: Festschrift E. Lipiński*, ed. Karel van Lerberghe and Anton Schoors (Leuven: Peeters, 1995), 285–295.

Imbibing words to involve the divine or to achieve inspiration occurs widely in antiquity. An interesting variation in purpose occurs in a Demotic tale known as Setne. Aspiring to absorb the secrets of the gods, Setne, (fabled) son of Rameses II, "had a sheet of new papyrus brought to him. He wrote on it every word that was in the book before him. He burnt it with fire, he dissolved it in water. When he knew it had dissolved, he drank it and knew what had been in it." I cite this passage from Miriam Lichtheim, *Ancient Egyptian Literature, Vol. 3: The Late Period* (Berkeley, CA: University of California Press, 1980), 131 as emended by Robert K. Ritner, *The Mechanics of Ancient Egyptian Magical Practice*, Studies in Ancient Oriental Civilization 54 (Chicago, IL: Oriental Institute of the University of Chicago, 1993), 108. The third chapter of Ritner's book (73–110) is a rich storehouse of lore on the magical power behind "spitting, licking, and swallowing" liquids.

6 What Happens to River at Jerusalem's Gates?

Rivers have a way of streaming in and out of our consciousness. In the remaining centuries of the second millennium, the justice they dispensed was trusted in Elam to the west, Assyria to the north, and Nuzi in Kurdistan.[24] Closer to the Mediterranean coast where rivers were not as central ecologically, commercially, or intellectually as in Mesopotamia, we miss clear references to river ordeals. Among the Hittites of Anatolia of a somewhat similar period, testing via running waters came to be supplanted by imbibing a potion, the act cited as "drinking the cup of the deity, that is, of life."[25] How the verdict was decided is not detailed. As we saw earlier, this shift from surviving a river plunge to oath-taking while absorbing a potion is not new; but it invites inspection of the West Semitic world, to which ancient Israel famously belonged.

In late second-millennium lore from Ugarit, the god Yammu is occasionally cited with the epithet, "Prince Sea, Judge River" (*zbl ym ṯpṭ nhr*), suggesting to some that the river ordeal was vestigial there.[26] I cannot find any evidence that Phoenicians or Arameans knew this or any other form of water ordeal to resolve disputes; but Hebrew scripture, as rich a repository of ancient Near Eastern

24 In second-millennium Mesopotamia, ordeals designed for instant decision were always staged at rivers, but not necessarily at Ḫ/Ḫīt or even the Euphrates. In reviewing some Elamite Susa references to (river) ordeals under the sponsorship of Shazi, son of River, Hossein Badamchi (incongruously) equates the experience with unleashing a curse ("The Care of the Elderly in Susa: A Study in the Akkadian Documents from the Sukkalmah Period," *Akkadica* 139 [2018]: 164–166). Assyrians of the late second millennium codified instruction on river ordeals, especially when dealing with a married woman's accusation of sexual promiscuity; but the locality is not stated. In Nuzi of around 1400 BCE, contradictory testimony is resolved by "undergoing a river ordeal," with the term (I$_7$) *ḫuršan* attached to the process; see Brigitte Lion, "Les textes judiciaires du royaume d'Arrapha," in *Rendre la justice en Mésopotamie: Archives judiciaires du Proche-Orient ancien*, ed. Francis Joannès (Vincennes: Presses Universitaires, 2000), 151–153; Frymer-Kensky, "Suprarational Legal Procedures in Elam and Nuzi"; and now especially Scafa, "La cd. ordalia fluviale in ambito mesopotamico." The procedure was done locally and failure did not involve death, for the relevant texts define the expected punishments. From around the same period and area (Suḫu), rulers from Emar in Upper Syria resolved a dispute over a slave; see Yoram Cohen, "A Letter from the Governor of Emar to the Governor of Suḫu Concerning a River Ordeal," *JA* 303 (2015): 175–180.

25 van den Hout, "Ordal B. Bei der Hethitern," 129–130; Cahit Günbattı, "The River Ordeal in Ancient Anatolia," in *Veenhof Anniversary Volume: Studies Presented to Klaas R. Veenhof on the Occasion of his Sixty-Fifth Birthday*, ed. Wilfred H. van Soldt (Leiden: Brill, 2001), 151–160.

26 Wilfred G.E. Watson, "Ugaritic 'Judge River' and the River Ordeal," *NABU* (1993–1995): 80–81.

practices as we might wish to have, has indeed kept memory of it. As in Hatti, we find in it several passages in which God forces Israel to drink a "cup of poison" (*kôs ḥēmâ*; Isa 51:17, Jer 25:15), a "cup of stagger" (*kôs tarʿēlâ*; Isa 51:22), as well as their opposite, a "cup of salvation" (*kôs yəšûʿôt*; Ps 116:13). These are obviously evocative of a divine judgment, on Israel's guilt as on its redemption, activated through a truth-seeking potion. In its legal compilations, Israel features a couple of injunctions (as in Exod 21:6; 22:8–9) that likewise bring God into direct judgment to resolve disputes.[27] Intriguing is the notice in Exodus 22:8 where the dispute is set before God himself (*ʿad hāʾəlōhîm yābōʾ dəbar-šənêhem*). When it controls a verb in the singular, the subject *ʾelōhîm*, although plural in construction, is the Hebrew God. What is striking here, however, is that the verbal form for imposing penalty (*yaršîʿûn*) is plural, thus favoring a plural subject. Traditional exegeses, based on Rashi, simply glide over the oddity, likely because in parallel language, such as in Deuteronomy 25:1, judges (and not God) are contextually the subject. This subject/verb discord is not unique in the Hebrew Bible, but it invites speculation that the language is invoking an appeal to divine decisions, likely with cultic paraphernalia as witness, paralleling neighboring legal practices. A grammatically correct translation of the final clause, therefore, could be, "the case of both parties will come before the gods and on whom they impose guilt shall pay double to the other." Water is not an instrument here; still, the potential direct involvement of divinity in adjudicating conflict moves us to two more fully articulated passages that add details to the process.

6.1 *Suspect Wife and Jealous Husband*

Biblical law occasionally reports on how disputes are settled by bringing contenders before God without clarifying whether before a statue or emblem. More commonly, however, such matters are resolved through an intermediary, be it Moses or a priest. The last includes a case law to which the book of Numbers allots almost an entire chapter (5:11–31). The context itself is ambiguous, as the case concerns adultery kept successfully secret (5:13, 29) and/or jealousy, baseless or otherwise (5:14, 29). The wording of the case is prolix, but its gist is in the coda to the proceedings (5:29–31):

---

27 Scholars have long debated whether the process involved an oracle, an oath, or some form of ordeal. A brief review of opinions is in Bernard S. Jackson, *Wisdom-Laws: A Study of the Mishpatim of Exodus 21:1–22:16* (Oxford: Oxford University Press, 2006), 338–344. Samuel Greengus (*Laws in the Bible and in Early Rabbinic Collections: The Legal Legacy of the Ancient Near East* [Eugene, OR.: Cascade, 2011], 188–193) turns to Lev 5:20–24 to argue that an oath was likely at stake in all these passages.

> This is the ritual in cases of jealousy, when a woman goes astray while married to her husband and defiles herself, or when a fit of jealousy comes over a man and he despises his wife: He will have his wife stand before the Lord for the priest to carry out all this ritual with her. The man will be clear of guilt; but that woman will suffer for her guilt.

An accusation uncorroborated by witnesses is normally dismissed in Hebraic jurisprudence; but as family cohesion is at stake, a kind of ordeal takes place. In the order Nashim, the Talmud has consecrated an elaborate tractate to the episode, titling it "Sotah" (*sôṭâ* or *śôṭâ*, "errant spouse"). Frankly, its contents are heavily voyeuristic if not also misogynist. In modern scholarship, there are streams of monographs and articles devoted to the subject, to defend the accused woman, to excoriate the jealous husband, or to assess the action of the priest.[28] For us, the focus is on the process as it unfolds.

Already in the Hammurabi Code (¶131) a millennium earlier, a wife is to take an oath specifically in a similar situation; but she must undergo a River ordeal if a third party accuses her of unwitnessed promiscuity (¶132). In the biblical account, with a meal offering in hand ("of remembrance," *zikkārôn*, in Num 5:18, glossed as *mazkeret ʿāvôn*, "recalling transgression"), the suspicious husband leads his wife before the priest. There, the woman loosens her hair—normally a mourning sign, possibly also of submission before God—and accepts an oath mouthed for her by the priest, invoking dire consequences should she fail the text.

---

28 See Ishay Rosen-Zvi's excellent book and large bibliography on the rabbinic readings of the law, *The Mishnaic Sotah Ritual: Temple, Gender and Midrash*, JSJSup 160 (Leiden: Brill, 2012). His thumbnail overview (2015) of rabbinic alterations is at https://thegemara.com/article/the-sotah-spectacle. The Rabbis attributed—who knows how reliably?—the abolition of the ritual to Johanan ben Zakkai, so already before the destruction of the Second Temple. Aside from his notes to the relevant verses, in his JPS commentary Jacob Milgrom devotes three valuable excurses (#8–10) to the subject, *Numbers* (Philadelphia, PA: Jewish Publication Society, 1990), 346–352. For comparative Semitic lore on ordeal, see Julius Morgenstern, "Trial by Ordeal among the Semites and in Ancient Israel," *HUC Jubilee Volume, 1875–1925* (1925): 13–43.

Alice Bach assembled several published essays on the Sotah ordeal in her *Women in the Hebrew Bible: A Reader* (New York, NY: Routledge, 1999). Among these articles are Tikvah Frymer-Kensky, "The Strange Case of the Suspected Sotah (Numbers V 11–31)," 463–474; Jacob Milgrom, "The Case of the Suspected Adulteress, Numbers 5:11–31: Redaction and Meaning," 475–482; Jack M. Sasson, "Numbers 5 and the 'Waters of Judgement'," 483–486; Michael Fishbane, "Accusation of Adultery: A Study of Law and Scribal Practice in Numbers 5:11–31," 487–502; and Alice Bach's own, "Good to the Last Drop: Viewing the Sotah (Numbers 5:11–31) as the Glass Half Empty and Wondering How to View It Half Full," 503–522.

The priest prepares a potion termed *mê hammārîm hammə'ārărîm* (5:18), a phrase whose exact translation is not yet secure, something like "The waters of *bitterness* that cause a curse."[29] The consecrated water (*mayim qədōšîm*; 5:17) comes in an earthen jar.[30] In it, the priest drops a pinch of earth taken from a special spot at the floor of the tabernacle, possibly one not trampled by priestly movement.[31] The next step is what brings God into judgment: The curse invoking God's punishment is committed to leather or papyrus, the consecrated words dissolving into the potion. Drunk, the powerful combination of temple ingredient and divine essence enters the belly of the woman to decide her fate.[32] Admittedly, what we have here is not quite the river ordeal from Mari, but its congener, also attested there: integrity is confirmed when truth fulfills its potential deep within the human body. In essence, whereas in

29 In Bach's *Women in the Hebrew Bible*, I proposed that the phrase is a *merismus*, composed of blessing and cursing, so "waters of judgment."

30 Normally it is "fresh water" (*mayim ḥayyîm*) that is brought in such jars to receive the blood of sacrificed birds (Lev 14:5, 50) when ministering to a healed leper. The jar was likely destroyed on termination of employment; see Lev 6:21; 11:33. In a somewhat related procedure, a person defiled by contact with the dead is sprinkled with a mixture of dirt (*'āfār*) from a fire of purification in fresh water.

31 The Mishna (*mSotah* 2.2) is precise on its location: "[Then the priest] enters the temple and turns to his right and there was a place there [on the floor] that was a cubit by a cubit, and a marble tablet, to which a ring was attached. When he would lift this up, he would take some dust from beneath it which he puts [into the bowl] so that it would be seen on top of the water" (https://www.sefaria.org/Mishnah_Sotah.2.2-3?lang=bi).

32 Aside from shunning by the community, the negative consequences of the woman's guilt are stated as "her belly will swell while her thigh will sag" (*ṣāvətâ biṭnāh wənāpəlâ yərēkāh*; Num 5:27). Many explanations are offered in the literature, my own being thrombophlebitis in the genitalia that causes swelling of genitals and edema in the thighs. Frymer-Kenski proposes "uterine prolapse." Or it may be that the guilt itself induces psychosomatic symptoms, possibly false pregnancy. These and other explanations are in Frymer-Kensky's article, which is republished in Bach's *Women in the Hebrew Bible*. If innocent, the woman will be able to conceive (*nizrə'â zāra'* in 5:28). The last may seem an odd reward, but it implies reconciliation with her husband, resumption of cohabitation, and marital harmony, so *šəlôm bayit*, as it is termed in the Talmud.

Note, however, Richard Friedman's thesis: "The purpose of the priest's procedure is to administer a potion that, if she is pregnant, will produce a curse. The water's function is not to make her womb swell. Its function is ... to cause a curse. She becomes a curse among her community, and she will bear her sin, which is to say it is between her and God; there is no punishment from humans" ("The Sotah: Why Is This Case Different from All Other Cases?," in *Let Us Go Up to Zion: Essays in Honour of H.G.M. Williamson on the Occasion of his Sixty-Fifth Birthday*, ed. Iain Provan and Mark Boda, VTSup 153 [Leiden: Brill, 2012], 376). This notion is far-fetched, as it totally ignores the bodily changes that the curse induces. Friedman also clears the potential adulterer (who, in his reading, may not have existed) rather than the husband.

Mesopotamia divine waters swallow those guilty, here those guilty swallow the instrument of their conviction.[33] Our final biblical illustration might bridge the gap between the two processes. Before we turn to it, however, a mythological scene from Ugarit of a few centuries earlier will sharpen the relevant issues.

6.2 *Imbibing the Enemy*

In one myth (the *Baal Cycle*), the goddess Anat had defeated Môtu, the nemesis of her brother/lover Baal. This is what she does to him, "She seizes Môt … / with a knife she splits him, / with a winnowing-fork she winnows him, / with fire she burns him, / with grindstones she pulverizes him, / in the field she sows him; / The birds eat his flesh, / the fowl finish off his body parts, / flesh(-eaters) grow fat on flesh."[34] There is no river to surmount or potion to imbibe. Yet, when the god Môtu resurrects (as gods are wont to do) and recounts what Anat had done to him, he adds that she sowed his pulverized remains on the Sea (*yammu*).[35] As noted earlier, that Sea god was also called "Judge River." Water, possibly riverine, had thus become an element in Môtu's travail. When first published almost a century ago, these Canaanite scenes were promptly connected with a very striking biblical episode—the last example to which we now turn.[36]

6.3 *The Golden Calf*

Coming down the slopes of Mount Sinai and chock full of divine instruction, Moses confronts a people raucously worshiping a golden calf. Outraged by this sacrilege, "[Moses] seized the calf that the people had made. He set it to fire, ground it into powder, and scattered (it) on the water. Then [Moses] forced the

33 In Mesopotamia, too, individuals placed themselves at risk by partaking of the divine, in most cases, as *asakkum* (taboo, sacrality), possibly a sanctified herb. The language (among other formulae) included *asakkam* (SAR.MEŠ)/*nīšam akālum* "partaking of taboo/oath," and *asakkam ina pī* PN *šakānum*, "setting the taboo in someone's mouth"; see Dominique Charpin, "Manger un serment," in Lafont, *Jurer et maudire*, 85–96. Sophie Démare-Lafont reviews the subject in "Manger un tabou: sacrilège ou parjure? Une relecture des procès de Lugal-giškim-zi," in *Tabous et transgressions: Actes du colloque organisé par le Collège de France, Paris, les 11 et 12 avril 2012*, ed. Jean-Marie Durand, Michaël Guichard, and Thomas Römer, OBO 274 (Fribourg: Academic Press, 2015), 19–30.

34 CTA 6[= *KTU*³ 1.6 = UT 49].ii.30–37. The tablet is assigned to the *Baal Cycle*. I cite it from Dennis Pardee's translation in *COS* 1.86 (p. 270).

35 CTA 6.v.19, cited from *COS* 1.86 (p. 272).

36 Comments and bibliography in Samuel E. Loewenstamm, "The Making and Destruction of the Golden Calf," *Bib* 48 (1967): 481–490.

people of Israel to drink it" (Exod 32:20).[37] The test resulted in the massacre of three thousand implicated idolaters (32:28), presumably of those linked to the sacrilege.

Since Talmudic times, the incident was cast as an ordeal, in tandem with Sotah (*bAvodah Zarah* 44a, *bYomah* 66b), but its obscurity has also elicited many questions.[38] Here are several: If the calf (*ʿēgel*) is molten (*massēkâ*; Exod 32:4, 8; Deut 9:16) or golden (*zāhāb*), how could it be ground into powder when fire likely melted it?[39] How could imbibing the residue of a bogus deity be as effective in deciding truth as absorbing the essence of the true God? What about the water that received the pulverized calf? Was the concoction drunk from cups or lapped up from some pool as would Gideon's warriors who failed God's own test (Judg 7:4–7)? As in the Ugaritic lore we just sampled, another report on this event gives us an intriguing answer. It is embedded in Deuteronomy.

When, accepting his impending death, Moses reviewed Israel's past deeds and misdeeds, he recalled this about the golden calf incident: "As to the abomination that you have made—that calf I seized and set it to fire. I crushed it to the smallest specks, as fine as dust. I then threw its dust to the stream coming down the mountain" (Deut 9:21). In this account, there is nothing about forcing a potion on the sinful and nothing about consequent punishment.[40] In fact, in Moses's telling, no ordeal was necessary; responsibility for generating the calf

---

37 The bibliography on the golden calf episode is long and diverse. A brief listing is in John R. Spencer, "Golden Calf," *ABD* 2:1065–1069; but see also the pages of the more scholarly commentaries on Exodus 32 and to a lesser extent Deuteronomy 9. A good overview of the exegetical tradition across cultures and times is in Michael Pregill, *The Golden Calf between Bible and Qur'an* (Oxford: Oxford University Press, 2020).

38 Nahmanides (comments on Exod 32:20) claimed that the incident exposed the humiliation of the calf.

39 The suggestions (none without challenge) are that the calf was wooden but plated with gold (since J.D. Michaelis), that it was charred before grinding (since Ibn Ezra), or that it sat on a wooden pedestal (since Abravanel). Nahmanides sharply opposed any practical solution to the process, judging it a divinely controlled act; on this, see David Frankel, "The Destruction of the Golden Calf: A New Solution," *VT* 44 (1994): 330–339.

40 Jeffrey H. Tigay references 2 Kgs 23:12, where King Josiah dumped shattered pagan altars into the Kidron Valley (*naḥal*), in *Deuteronomy: The Traditional Hebrew Text with the New JPS Translation* (Philadelphia, PA: Jewish Publication Society, 1996), 101–102. He also allows that it may be a metaphoric allusion, as in God hurling sins into the sea (Mic 7:19). P. Kyle McCarter, "The River Ordeal in Israelite Literature," *HTR* 66 (1973): 403–412, finds echoes of river ordeals whenever poets speak about their rescues from overwhelming waters (as in Jonah and Psalm 18). He also thinks the metaphor had no basis in actual legal practices. Karel van der Toorn adopts an expansive usage of the term "ordeal" in applying it to Psalm 23, "Ordeal Procedures in the Psalms and the Passover Meal," *VT* 38 (1988): 441.

was clearly Aaron's, his guilt absolved through Moses's plea on his behalf.[41] As a result, the mention of a stream may seem superfluous, especially when in Sinai only a fortuitous flashflood could have produced it.[42] Historicizing or justifying the event would hardly be useful in this context. Rather, in concluding, we might wonder why in Late Bronze Ugarit and Iron Age Israel, narratives that echo ordeals would embed memories of water judgments and streams in which to accomplish them.

If we return to Mesopotamia and continue into its first-millennium culture, we find that attestations of river ordeals peter out, with an occasional spike here and there.[43] In imperial Assyria, where court intrigues and defamations were rife, two individuals accused of naming their sons after Assyrian kings undergo ordeals.[44] Accused of treason by an individual he ruled, a governor failed to submit to an ordeal.[45] A man who took an oath in a "reservoir or wadi" (*nadabaktu*/*natbaktu*) was to pay a fine on failing a test in a god's presence.[46] Increasingly, however, it seems adversaries in a dispute relied on divine oracles by the god Adad to settle accounts, probably by drawing lots—in Israel related to the Urim and Thummim, or by manipulating ancestral idols—in Israel called

---

41 An interesting take on the discrepancies between the Exodus and Deuteronomy accounts is Philippe Guillaume, "Drinking Golden Bull: The Erased Ordeal in Exodus 32," in *Studies in Magic and Divination*, ed. Helen R. Jacobus, Anne Katrine de Hemmer Gudme, and Philippe Guillaume (Piscataway, NJ: Gorgias Press, 2013), 135–147; on Aaron's role, see 137–139.

42 No rivers are in Sinai where the alleged incident occurred; but wadis are there that transform into raging torrents after rainstorms. Wadi Feiran, among the largest of such occasional surges, lies near St. Catherine Monastery by Mt. Sinai, that since the fourth century CE has been claimed as the spot where God and Moses met; see Gamal El Afandi, Mostafa Morsy, and Fathy El Hussieny, "Heavy Rainfall Simulation over Sinai Peninsula Using the Weather Research and Forecasting Model," *International Journal of Atmospheric Sciences* (2013): https://www.hindawi.com/journals/ijas/2013/241050/.

43 This is shown for the Middle Babylonian period by Susanne Paulus in "Ordal statt Eid—Das Beweisverfahren in mittelbabylonischer Zeit," in *Prozessrecht und Eid: Recht und Rechtsfindung in antiken Kulturen*, ed. Heinz Barta, Martin Lang, and Robert Rollinger (Wiesbaden: Harrassowitz, 2015), 207–226.

44 Text in Laura Kataja, "A Neo-Assyrian Document on Two Cases of River Ordeal," *SAAB* 2 (1987): 65–68. See Betina Faist's fine essay, "The Ordeal in the Neo-Assyrian Legal Procedure," in *From Source to History: Studies on Ancient Near Eastern Worlds and Beyond Dedicated to Giovanni Battista Lanfranchi on the Occasion of His 65th Birthday on June 23, 2014*, ed. Salvatore Gaspa, Alessandro Greco, Daniel Morandi Bonacossi, Simonetta Ponchia, and Robert Rollinger, AOAT 41 (Münster: Ugarit-Verlag, 2014), 196–198.

45 Frances Reynold, *The Babylonian Correspondence of Esarhaddon*, SAA 18 (Helsinki: Helsinki University Press, 2003), 102–103 (#125).

46 Karen Radner, "Vier neuassyrische Privatrechtsurkunden aus dem vorderasiatischen Museum, Berlin," *AfO* 24 (1997): 121–123.

teraphim.[47] By the time the biblical episodes that I have cited were set, say, around the Babylonian exile in the sixth century BCE, river ordeals had sunk into memory. Only a compendium of anecdotes in praise of either Nebuchadnezzar or Nabonidus of Neo-Babylonian times seems to evoke the practice, consciously attributing its inspiration to a forgotten practice.[48] I would therefore not be shocked if the biblical examples that include imbibing water or cite streams to bolster divine resolutions of knotty cases were themselves moribund, clues to forgotten settings that no longer had much meaning in actual life but were likely perpetuated in scribal curricula.

Bits of history may remain after the scraps drain their liquid through the sieves of the centuries. Over time, therefore, water trials seeped out of our memory. We might celebrate their disappearance, especially since ordeals have morphed into such horrors as the staging of mortal combats, the manipulation of red-hot objects, the dunking of body parts into boiling water, and the forced ingestion of poison.[49] Thankfully, oaths on sacred objects or threats of perjury have replaced such tests. Yet, as reported in the media, government units are not beyond adopting brutal techniques to elicit confessions. Among the more notorious of current practices is waterboarding, certainly an ordeal in our sense

---

47 Remko Jas, *Neo-Assyrian Judicial Procedures*, SAAS 5 (Helsinki: Neo-Assyrian Text Corpus Project, 1996), 17–19 [#7] and 21–24 [#10, 11]. Several nonlegal texts are judged to refer to ordeals, occasionally involving (streams) of water but not always suggesting judgment or consequent punishment; see Klíma, "L'ordalie par le fleuve en Elam," 41 n. 1. Clearest among these pseudo-ordeals involves the god Marduk himself; see T. Frymer-Kensky, "The Tribulations of Marduk: The So-Called 'Marduk Ordeal Text'," *JAOS* 103 (1983): 131–141; A. Livingstone, *Court Poetry and Literary Miscellanea*, SAA 3 (Helsinki: Helsinki University Press, 1989), 82–91 [#34, 35].

48 W.G. Lambert, "Nebuchadnezzar King of Justice," *Iraq* 27 (1965): 9; text in Benjamin R. Foster, *Before the Muses: An Anthology of Akkadian Literature* (Bethesda, MD: CDL Press, 2005), 870–874. The ordeal is said to occur "upstream from Sippar," so likely thinking of Ḫ/Ḥīt where most Mari examples are set. In the NB period, there was a move toward oath-taking and away from performed ordeals; nonetheless, occasionally, we read of oaths taken within magic circles (*gišḫurru*), presumably shaped by a ring of flour; See *CAD* G 102, citing *Šurpu* III:127 and YOS 7 61 (on the latter, see Wells, "The Cultic Versus the Forensic," 210.)

Late (Neo-Babylonian) commentaries to Tablet I of the Diagnostic Handbook (*sakikkū*) connect the fate of patients to the observations of physicians making their way to them. "The patients will die" is the prognosis, assumed to occur because they turned away from a river (ordeal); see Andrew R. George, "Babylonian Texts from the Folios of Sidney Smith. Part Two: Prognostic and Diagnostic Omens, Tablet I," *RA* 85 (1991): 147, 149 (reference, courtesy of Mark Geller).

49 Many interesting tidbits on medieval avatars of ordeals in Europe, including among Jews there, can be found in Shlomo Eidelberg's "Trial by Ordeal in Medieval Jewish History: Laws, Customs and Attitudes," *Proceedings of the American Academy for Jewish Research* 46/47 (1979–1980): 105–120.

of the word. Ironically, waterboarding seeks to trigger the sensation of drowning that, as we saw, had stopped Mesopotamians from advancing defiantly into River. In their days, when truth wore a stubborn veil and when Heaven was there to judge, gods buttressed the cause of justice. Who can say what—or who—might be standing in the breach today?

Bibliography

Bach, Alice. *Women in the Hebrew Bible: A Reader*. New York, NY: Routledge, 1999.

Badamchi, Hossein. "The Care of the Elderly in Susa: A Study in the Akkadian Documents from the Sukkalmah Period." *Akkadica* 139 (2018): 159–178.

Black, Jeremy, Graham Cunningham, Eleanor Robson, and Gábor Zólyomi. *The Literature of Ancient Sumer*. Oxford: Oxford University Press, 2004.

Campagno, Marcelo. "'Ordalías,' parentesco y estado en la contienda entre Horus y Seth." *Antiguo Oriente* 3 (2005): 89–103.

Cavigneaux, Antoine. "Nouveaux cas d'ordalie à Mari." Pages 23–37 in 'ina ^{d}marri u qan ṭuppi.' *Par la bêche et le stylet! Cultures et sociétés syro-mésopotamiennes: Mélanges offerts à Olivier Rouault*. Edited by Philippe Abrahami and Laura Battini. Oxford: Archaeopress, 2019.

Charpin, Dominique. "Les champions, la meule et le fleuve, ou le rachat du terroir de Puzurran au roi d'Ešnunna par le roi de Mari Yaḫdun-Lim." *FM* 1 (1992): 29–38.

Charpin, Dominique. "Manger un serment." Pages 85–96 in *Jurer et maudire: pratiques politiques et usages juridiques du serment dans le Proche-Orient ancien*. Edited by Sophie Lafont. Méditerranées: Revue de l'association Méditerranées 10–11. Paris: L'Harmattan, 1997.

Civil, Miguel. "On Mesopotamian Jails and Their Lady Wardens." Pages 72–78 in *The Tablet and the Scroll: Near Eastern Studies in Honor of William W. Hallo*. Edited by Mark E. Cohen, Daniel C. Snell, and David B. Weisberg. Bethesda, MD: Capital Decisions, 1993.

Cohen, Yoram. "A Letter from the Governor of Emar to the Governor of Suḫu Concerning a River Ordeal." *Journal Asiatique* 303 (2015): 175–180.

Durand, Jean-Marie. *Archives épistolaires de Mari*. Vol. 1/1. ARM 26/1. Paris: Éditions Recherche sur les Civilisations, 1988.

Durand, Jean-Marie. *Documents épistolaires du palais de Mari*. Vol. 3. LAPO 18. Paris: Cerf, 2000.

Durand, Jean-Marie. "La Religion amorrite en Syrie à l'époque des archives de Mari." Pages 163–715 in *Mythologie et Religion des Sémites Occidentaux*. Edited by Gregorio del Olmo Lete. Vol. 1: Ebla, Mari. Orientalia Lovaniensia Analecta 162. Leuven: Peeters, 2008.

Durand, Jean-Marie. *Les premières années du roi Zimrî-Lîm de Mari: Première partie.* ARM 33. Leuven: Peeters, 2019.

Durand, Jean-Marie, Michaël Guichard, and Thomas Römer. *Tabous et transgressions: Actes du colloque organisé par le Collège de France, Paris, les 11 et 12 avril 2012.* OBO 274. Fribourg: Academic Press, 2015.

Eidelberg, Shlomo. "Trial by Ordeal in Medieval Jewish History: Laws, Customs and Attitudes." *Proceedings of the American Academy for Jewish Research* 46/47 (1979–1980): 105–120.

El Afandi, Gamal, Mostafa Morsy, and Fathy El Hussieny. "Heavy Rainfall Simulation over Sinai Peninsula Using the Weather Research and Forecasting Model." *International Journal of Atmospheric Sciences* (2013): https://www.hindawi.com/journals/ijas/2013/241050/.

Faist, Betina. "The Ordeal in the Neo-Assyrian Legal Procedure." Pages 189–200 in *From Source to History: Studies on Ancient Near Eastern Worlds and Beyond Dedicated to Giovanni Battista Lanfranchi on the Occasion of His 65th Birthday on June 23, 2014.* Edited by Salvatore Gaspa, Alessandro Greco, Daniel Morandi Bonacossi, Simonetta Ponchia, and Robert Rollinger. AOAT 412. Münster: Ugarit-Verlag, 2014.

Festuccia, Silvia. "Un tuffo nell'Eufrate: le attività natatorie nella Mesopotamia antica." Pages 163–176 in *Studî di storia, archeologia e antropologia "in acqua" dedicati a Claudio Moccheggiani Carpano.* Edited by Massimiliano Marazzi, Germana Pecoraro, and Sebastiano Tusa. Ricerche di storia, epigrafia e archeologia mediterranea 5. Rome: Bagatto, 2016.

Foster, Benjamin R. *Before the Muses. An Anthology of Akkadian Literature.* 3rd ed. Bethesda, MD: CDL Press, 2005.

Frankel, David. "The Destruction of the Golden Calf: A New Solution." *VT* 44 (1994): 330–339.

Friedman, Richard Elliott. "The Sotah: Why Is This Case Different from All Other Cases?" Pages 371–382 in *Let Us Go Up to Zion: Essays in Honour of H.G.M. Williamson on the Occasion of his Sixty-Fifth Birthday.* Edited by Iain Provan and Mark Boda. VTSup 153. Leiden: Brill 2012.

Frymer-Kensky, Tikva Simone. "The Nungal-Hymn and the Ekur-Prison." *JESHO* 20 (1977): 78–89.

Frymer-Kensky, Tikva Simone. "Suprarational Legal Procedures in Elam and Nuzi." Pages 115–131 in *Studies on the Civilization and Culture of Nuzi and the Hurrians, 1: In Honor of Ernest R. Lacheman on His Seventy-fifth Birthday, April 29, 1981.* Edited by Martha A. Morrison and David I. Owen. Winona Lake, IN: Eisenbrauns, 1981.

Frymer-Kensky, Tikva Simone. "The Tribulations of Marduk: The So-Called 'Marduk Ordeal Text'." *JAOS* 103 (1983): 131–141.

George, Andrew. "Babylonian Texts from the Folios of Sidney Smith. Part Two: Prognostic and Diagnostic Omens, Tablet I." *RA* 85 (1991): 137–163.

George, Andrew. *Babylonian Literary Texts in the Schøyen Collection*. CUSAS 10. Bethesda, MD: CDL Press, 2009.

Greengus, Samuel. *Laws in the Bible and in Early Rabbinic Collections: The Legal Legacy of the Ancient Near East*. Eugene, OR: Cascade, 2011.

Guillaume, Philippe. "Drinking Golden Bull: The Erased Ordeal in Exodus 32." Pages 135–147 in *Studies in Magic and Divination*. Edited by Helen R. Jacobus, Anne Katrine de Hemmer Gudme, and Philippe Guillaume. Piscataway, NJ: Gorgias, 2013.

Günbattı, Cahit. "The River Ordeal in Ancient Anatolia." Pages 151–160 in *Veenhof Anniversary Volume: Studies Presented to Klaas R. Veenhof on the Occasion of his Sixty-Fifth Birthday*. Edited by Wilfred H. van Soldt. Leiden: Brill, 2001.

Heimpel, Wolfgang. "The River Ordeal in Hit." *RA* 90 (1996): 7–18.

Heimpel, Wolfgang. "The Location of Madga." *JCS* 61 (2009): 25–61.

Hout, Theo van den. "Ordal B. Bei der Hethitern." *RlA* 10 (2003): 129–130.

Jackson, Bernard S. *Wisdom-Laws: A Study of the Mishpatim of Exodus 21:1–22:16*. Oxford: Oxford University Press, 2006.

Jacquet, Antoine. "L'Ordalie." *Supplément au Dictionnaire de la Bible* 77–78 (2008): 379–388.

Jas, Remko. *Neo-Assyrian Judicial Procedures*. SAAS 5. Helsinki: Neo-Assyrian Text Corpus Project, 1996.

Kataja, Laura. "A Neo-Assyrian Document on Two Cases of River Ordeal." *SAAB* 2 (1987): 65–68.

Klíma, Joseph. "L'ordalie par le fleuve en Elam (d'après les documents akkadiens de Suse et de Ḫuḫnur-Mālamir)." *RA* 66 (1972): 39–59.

Koller, Aaron. "Sex or Power? The Crime of the Bride in Deuteronomy 22." *ZABR* 16 (2010): 279–296.

Démare-Lafont, Sophie. *Jurer et maudire: pratiques politiques et usages juridiques du serment dans le Proche-Orient ancien*. Méditerranées: Revue de l'association Méditerranées 10–11. Paris: L'Harmattan, 1997.

Démare-Lafont, Sophie. *Femmes, droit et justice dans l'Antiquité orientale: contribution à l'étude du droit pénal au Proche-Orient ancien*. OBO 165. Fribourg: Editions universitaires, 1999.

Démare-Lafont, Sophie. "Manger un tabou: sacrilège ou parjure? Une relecture des procès de Lugal-giškim-zi." Pages 19–30 in *Tabous et transgressions: Actes du colloque organisé par le Collège de France, Paris, les 11 et 12 avril 2012*. Edited by Jean-Marie Durand, Michaël Guichard, and Thomas Römer. OBO 274. Fribourg: Academic Press, 2015.

Lambert, Wilfred G. "Nebuchadnezzar King of Justice." *Iraq* 27 (1965): 1–11.

Lichtheim, Miriam. *Ancient Egyptian Literature, Vol. 3: The Late Period*. Berkeley, CA: University of California Press, 1980.

Lion, Brigitte. "Les textes judiciaires du royaume d'Arrapha." Pages 151–162 in *Rendre la justice en Mésopotamie: Archives judiciaires du Proche-Orient ancien* (IIIe–Ier millénaires avant J.-C.). Edited by Francis Joannès. Vincennes: Presses Universitaires, 2000.

Livingstone, Alasdair. *Court Poetry and Literary Miscellanea*. SAA 3. Helsinki: Helsinki University Press, 1989.

Loewenstamm, Samuel E. "The Making and Destruction of the Golden Calf." *Bib* 48 (1967): 481–490.

McCarter, P. Kyle, Jr. "The River Ordeal in Israelite Literature." *HTR* 66 (1973): 403–412.

Milgrom, Jacob. *Numbers*. The JPS Torah Commentary: The Traditional Hebrew Text with the New JPS Translation. Philadelphia, PA: Jewish Publication Society, 1990.

Morgenstern, Julian. "Trial by Ordeal among the Semites and in Ancient Israel." *Hebrew Union College Jubilee Volume, 1875–1925* (1925): 13–43.

Owen, David I. "A Unique Late Sargonic River Ordeal in the John Frederick Lewis Collection." Pages 305–311 in *A Scientific Humanist: Studies in Memory of Abraham Sachs*. Edited by Erle Leichty, Maria deJ. Ellis, and Pamela Gerardi. Philadelphia, PA: The University Museum, 1988.

Paulus, Susanne. "Ordal statt Eid—Das Beweisverfahren in mittelbabylonischer Zeit." Pages 207–226 in *Prozessrecht und Eid: Recht und Rechtsfindung in antiken Kulturen*. Edited by Heinz Barta, Martin Lang, and Robert Rollinger. Wiesbaden: Harrassowitz, 2015.

Powell, Marvin A. "Masse und Gewichte." *RlA* 7 (1987–1990): 457–517.

Pregill, Michael. *The Golden Calf between Bible and Qur'an: Scripture, Polemic, and Exegesis from Late Antiquity to Islam*. Oxford: Oxford University Press, 2020.

Radner, Karen. "Vier neuassyrische Privatrechtsurkunden aus dem vorderasiatischen Museum, Berlin." *AoF* 24 (1997): 115–134.

Reynold, Frances. *The Babylonian Correspondence of Esarhaddon*. SAA 18. Helsinki: Helsinki University Press, 2003.

Ritner, Robert Kriech. *The Mechanics of Ancient Egyptian Magical Practice*. Studies in Ancient Oriental Civilization 54. Chicago, IL: Oriental Institute of the University of Chicago, 1993.

Rosen-Zvi, Ishay. *The Mishnaic Sotah Ritual: Temple, Gender and Midrash*. JSJSup 160. Leiden: Brill, 2012.

Roth, Martha T. *Law Collections from Mesopotamia and Asia Minor*. 2nd ed. WAW 6. Atlanta, GA: Scholars Press, 1997.

Sasson, Jack M. "Mari Apocalypticism Revisited." Pages 285–295 in *Immigration and Emigration within the Ancient Near East: Festschrift E. Lipiński*. Edited by K. van Lerberghe and A. Schoors. Leuven: Peeters, 1995.

Sasson, Jack M. *From the Mari Archives: An Anthology of Old Babylonian Letters*. University Park, PA: Penn State University Press, 2017.

Scafa, Paola Negri. "L'acqua come 'fonte' di giustitia: La cd. ordalia fluviale in ambito mesopotamico." Pages 213–245 in *Terre, acque, diritto: Forme delle società antiche*. Convegno di studi Università di Salerno. Fisciano SA, Italy: Centro Studi sui Fondamenti del Diritto Antico, forthcoming.

Simonetti, Cristina. "The River Ordeal in the Third Millennium BC." Pages 277–282 in *^{d}Nisaba za$_3$-mi$_2$: Ancient Near Eastern Studies in Honor of Francesco Pomponio*. Edited by Palmiro Notizia, Annunziata Rositani, and Lorenzo Verderame. Dubsar 19. Münster: Zaphon, 2021.

Soldt, Wilfred van. "Ordal A. Mesopotamien." *RlA* 10 (2003): 124–129.

Spencer, John R. "Golden Calf." *ABD* 2:1065–1069.

Streck, Michael P. "Schwimmen." *RlA* 12 (2010): 339.

Tigay, Jeffrey H. *Deuteronomy*. The JPS Torah Commentary: The Traditional Hebrew Text with the New JPS Translation. Philadelphia, PA: Jewish Publication Society, 1996.

Toorn, Karel van der. *Sin and Sanction in Israel and Mesopotamia: A Comparative Study*. Assen: Van Gorcum, 1985.

Toorn, Karel van der. "Ordeal Procedures in the Psalms and the Passover Meal." *VT* 38 (1988): 427–445.

Toorn, Karel van der. "Ordeal." *ABD* 5:40–42.

Watson, Wilfred G.E. "Ugaritic 'Judge River' and the River Ordeal." *NABU* (1993–1995): 80–81.

Wells, Bruce. "The Cultic Versus the Forensic: Judahite and Mesopotamian Judicial Procedures in the First Millennium B.C.E." *JAOS* 128 (2008): 205–232.

Westbrook, Raymond. *A History of Ancient Near Eastern Law*. 2 vols. HOS 1. The Near and Middle East 72. Leiden. Brill, 2003.

Westbrook, Raymond. "Judges in the Cuneiform Sources." *Maarav* 12 (2005): 27–39.

Westbrook, Raymond. "Witchcraft and the Law in the Ancient Near East." Pages 45–51 in *Recht Gestern und Heute: Festschrift zum 85. Geburtstag von Richard Haase*. Edited by Joachim Hengstl and Ulrich Sick. Wiesbaden: Harrassowitz, 2006.

Wilcke, Claus. *Early Ancient Near Eastern Law: A History of Its Beginnings. The Early Dynastic and Sargonic Periods*. Bayerische Akademie der Wissenschaften Philosophisch-Historische Klasse Sitzungsberichte 2003/2. Munich: Bayerische Akademie der Wissenschaften, 2003.

Zgoll, Annete, and B. Cuperly. "Mythos als rituell aufgeführtes Drama: Inthronisation, Tempelschöpfung und Stadtgründung im altbabylonischen Lied auf Bazi." Pages 1209–1242 in *De l'argile au numérique: Mélanges assyriologiques en l'honneur de Dominique Charpin*. Edited by Grégory Chambon, Michaël Guichard, and Anne-Isabelle Langlois. PIPOAC 3. Leuven: Peeters, 2019.

Ziegler, Nele, and Anne-Isabelle Langlois. *Les toponymes paléo-babyloniens de la Haute-Mésopotamie: La Haute-Mésopotamie au IIe millénaire av. J.-C.* MTT I/1. Paris: SEPOA, 2016.

17

"People" between Liturgical Experience and Political Imagination: Preliminary Observations on *ʿām* in the Psalms

Mark S. Smith

1 Appreciation and Introduction

The essays in this volume, written in honor of my dear friend and longtime colleague Dan Fleming, echo his important work on "people" and other terms denoting sociopolitical collectives.[1] In his *The Legacy of Israel in Judah's Bible*,[2] Dan probes passages in Genesis—Kings for ongoing and shifting identities and definitions of Israel and Judah, as well as tribal units and other groups. With his additional goal "to disentangle Israelite content from the constant company of additions and alterations,"[3] Dan has brought a powerful lens to the study of biblical texts, showing how they embed a variety of sociopolitical identities, which in turn provide some index for their backgrounds.

As a result, both the shifting landscape of ancient Israel's sociopolitics and the Bible's literary history are being rethought in tandem, as seen in several of the dissertations conducted under Dan's direction. With the aid of its sociopolitical focus, this research is highly attuned to the literary history of texts as well as their larger ancient Near Eastern contexts. Several of these dissertations have appeared as books, indicative of Dan's cutting-edge scholarship and surpassed only by the kindness and generosity that he brings to the scholarly endeavors and lives of his students, colleagues and friends alike. For me, Dan has been not only an excellent friend; I have also learned tremendously from him. For these reasons, it is with gratitude and joy that I offer this essay in his honor.

1 Biblical references are given according to the MT (as in NJPS). The siglum // denotes either poetic parallelism or parallel passages. An asterisk marks a hypothetical form, including roots. This discussion focuses on the MT Psalter, without reference to Psalms 151–155.

2 Fleming, *The Legacy of Israel in Judah's Bible: History, Politics, and the Reinscribing of Tradition* (Cambridge/New York, NY: Cambridge University Press, 2012).

3 Fleming, *Legacy*, xiii.

 | DOI:10.1163/9789004511538_018

In keeping with this volume's theme, my subject is *ʿām* in the book of Psalms. Commonly translated "people,"[4] the noun has been the subject of many studies. Over the twentieth century, the noun's original meaning pursued via a comparative etymological approach was a significant concern. The culmination of this approach was perhaps Robert McClive Good's 1986 monograph, *The Sheep of His Pasture*, which posited that the noun's original meaning was "flock" and thus "a nomadic group," derived onomatopoetically from the sound of bleating sheep.[5] Somewhat illogically, Good locates this semantic development in "the world of the pastoral nomad"[6] in two different periods, once in the "prehistory" of "the historical Semitic languages,"[7] and again at "the threshold of Israelite history."[8]

More constructively, I think, Good underscores that it would be misplaced to think that the word *ʿām* "carries overtones of ethnicity."[9] Good's overlooked reevaluation of the traditional view of the noun putatively denoting ethnicity anticipates current research dismantling long-reigning assumptions about biblical representations of ethnicity. This trend is reflected not only by Dan Fleming's own book, which retells the story of Israel and Judah and unpacks the notions of ethnicity and "people."[10] More recently, Brian Rainey has pub-

4 For a survey of this geminate *qatl* noun, see Robert McClive Good, *The Sheep of His Pasture: A Study of the Hebrew Noun ʿAm(m) and Its Semitic Cognates*, HSM 29 (Chico, CA: Scholars Press, 1983); and Edward Lipiński, "*ʿam*," *TDOT* 11:163–177. This noun is generally regarded as a geminate, e.g., Lipiński, "*ʿam*," 164; and John Huehnergard, "Biblical Hebrew Noun Patterns," in *Epigraphy, Philology, and the Hebrew Bible: Methodological Perspectives on Philological and Comparative Study of the Hebrew Bible in Honor of Jo Ann Hackett*, ed. Jeremy M. Hutton and Aaron D. Rubin, ANEM 12 (Atlanta, GA: SBL Press, 2015), 35. For Good (*Sheep*, 41), the noun was originally "biliteral *ʿm*" and subsequently developed as a geminate. This reconstruction is also important for the etymology that Good proposed for the noun; see below.

5 Good, *Sheep*, 41, 42, 53, 56–57, 62, 84–85, 93, and 141–146.

6 Good, *Sheep*, 55.

7 Good, *Sheep*, 42.

8 Good, *Sheep*, 56.

9 Good, *Sheep*, 62.

10 For the latter subjects, see especially Fleming, *Legacy*, 239–255, esp. 252; and Lauren A.S. Monroe and Daniel E. Fleming, "Earliest Israel in Highland Company," *NEA* 82/1 (2019): 16–23. See also Lauren A.S. Monroe and Daniel E. Fleming, "Israel before the Omrides," *HeBAI* 10/2 (2021): 97–105; as well as Lauren Monroe, "On the Origins and Development of Greater Israel," *HeBAI* 10/2 (2021): 187–227; cf. the response in the same issue by Aren C. Maeir, "On Defining Israel: Or, Let's do the *Kulturkreislehre* again!," *HeBAI* 10/2 (2021): 106–148. The studies of Fleming and Monroe are in conversation with the work of Israel Finkelstein represented by his article, "First Israel, Core Israel, United (Northern) Israel," *NEA* 82 (2019): 8–15.

lished a book on ancient ethnicity, and Ki-Eun Jang completed an important dissertation on gentilics directed by Dan Fleming.[11] Dan's own research marks a decided shift in the sociopolitical role that the term plays in denoting "bodies of people" (or one might say, bodies consisting of persons) with its usage sometimes denoting their polity.[12] Apart from some well-known phrases using the noun *ʿām*, the Psalms play a relatively minor role in this discussion.[13] Still, no single scholarly work could treat every biblical book, and it is under the inspiration of Dan's work that I would like to focus on the singular forms of *ʿām* in the Psalms. This piece, too, can hardly be comprehensive, with each psalm attesting this noun deserving its own treatment. Still, I hope to intimate some ways in which Dan's intellectual project applies to the Psalms. The discussion that follows in this section offers some introductory observations; this essay then considers *ʿām*'s first attestation in the book in Psalm 3 and also in older psalms, briefly notes two further developments, and finally ends with the noun's last appearance in Psalm 149 and in the Psalms' so-called doxologies.

To anticipate, the story of *ʿām* in the Psalms entails the story of the Psalter itself.[14] Synchronically, this "story" has been read based on the critical place-

11 Rainey, *Religion, Ethnicity and Xenophobia in the Bible: A Theoretical, Exegetical and Theological Survey* (London/New York, NY: Routledge, 2019); Jang, "The Sociology of 'Gentilics' in Biblical and Northwest Semitic Literature" (Ph.D. diss., New York University, 2021), with prior literature on ethnicity listed on pp. 25–26 n. 64. For the question of ethnicity in the Greco-Roman context, see Erich S. Gruen, "Did Ancient Identity Depend on Ethnicity? A Preliminary Probe," *Phoenix* 67 (2013): 1–22, and Gruen, *Ethnicity in the Ancient World—Did It Matter?* (Berlin: de Gruyter, 2020). Lipiński ("*ʿam*," 170) offers a complex view of the BH noun in relation to the West Semitic evidence (as well as Arabic *ʿāmma*): "The collective sense includes the totality of agnates, a clan, but also the people as a whole, a multitude, or a religious assembly. The biblical usage of *ʿam* appropriates this double meaning without any difficulty." Contradictory to this approach is the separately authored comment by W. von Soden inserted into Lipiński's presentation (p. 173): "It should be noted that outside of Israel the concept of a 'people' is totally absent from the ancient Near East. Groups of human beings are distinguished by their dwelling places, geographical regions, and social classes, as well as by their various languages, a distinction that sometimes results in different groupings." The categories listed by von Soden apply also to the BH noun, which also seems to be used similarly in Aramaic and Phoenician (see Lipiński, "*ʿam*," 169; *DNWSI* 865–866; and the discussion below).

12 Fleming, *Legacy*, 61–69, 95–96, 103–105, 140, 142, 182 and 232.

13 Good, *Sheep*, confined to Pss 14:7 (pp. 126–128), 45:11 (p. 61), 78:52 and 70–71 (pp. 57, 159), 95:7 and 100:3 (p. 53).

14 For two discussions of "the story" "told" by the Psalms in their overarching configuration, see Nancy L. DeClaissé-Walford, "The Meta-Narrative of the Psalter," in *The Oxford Handbook of the Psalms*, ed. William P. Brown (Oxford/New York, NY: Oxford University Press, 2014), 363–376, and in the same volume J. Clinton McCann, Jr., "The Shape and Shaping of the Psalter: Psalms in Their Literary Context," 350–362. Note also Mark S. Smith, "The

ment of psalms concerned with the human king (Psalms 2, 72 and 89) in conjunction with the superscriptions about David in the two books (Psalms 3–72), with the collection of hymns to the deity as divine king (see Psalms 95–100) marking a major transition between its first three books (Psalms 1–89) and the last two (Psalms 90–100).[15] In short, the religio-political order under the figure of David and ending with Solomon in Psalm 72 seemed to work for a time, as particularly celebrated in Psalms 2 and 72 (Psalms 3–72); afterward the monar-

---

Theology of the Redaction of the Psalter: Some Observations," *ZAW* 104 (1992): 408–412. These studies benefitted greatly from the "canonical approach" of my teacher Brevard S. Childs, *Introduction to the Old Testament as Scripture* (Philadelphia, PA: Fortress, 1979). My usage of the "story told" by the Psalms is not an oblique means for introducing this approach into this discussion. While there is very much that is highly valuable for the Psalms in the canonical approach, arguably it can be overweighted to some of its practitioners' theological perspectives or concerns (see below). In my view, the fundamental distrust of diachronic development and historical context manifest by some practitioners of the "canonical approach" abstracts Scripture from its time and place and thus in effect lifts Scripture out of history. "The story" of the Psalter as contained in its formal, textual character is to be understood and sketched out no less as a historical and cultural matter located in time and place; both dimensions are core to its theological purposes. Otherwise, the approach would run the risk of diminishing one of the Psalter's fundamental theological dimensions, namely what might be called its "incarnational" dimension as human words that "the people" came to understand as God's own word to them, as recognized by Childs, 513. For a useful "incarnational" corrective to the canonical approach, see James B. Prothro, "Theories of Inspiration and Catholic Exegesis: Scripture and Criticism in Dialogue with Denis Farkasfalvy," *CBQ* 83 (2021): 294–314, drawing substantially on *Dei Verbum* para. 11.

15 See DeClaissé-Walford, "The Meta-Narrative of the Psalter," 363–376; McCann, "The Shape and Shaping of the Psalter," 350–362; and Smith, "The Theology of the Redaction of the Psalter," 408–412. The discussion also assumes many of the details discussed in detail by David Willgren, *The Formation of the 'Book' of Psalms: Reconsidering the Transmission and Canonization of Psalmody in Light of Material Culture and the Poetic Anthologies*, FAT 2/88 (Tübingen: Mohr Siebeck, 2016). I prescind from a diachronic classification and consideration of *ʿām* according to different collections of the Psalms (e.g., Korahite psalms, Asaphite psalms, and Davidic psalms), in view of the issues in using superscriptions for historical reconstruction raised by David W. Davage, "Why Davidic Superscriptions Do Not Demarcate Earlier Collections of Psalms," *JBL* 139 (2020): 67–86. See also the essays in *David, Messianism, and Eschatology: Ambiguity in the Reception History of the Book of Psalms in Judaism and Christianity*, ed. E. Koskenniemi and D.W. Davage, Studies in the Reception History of the Bible 10 (Abo: Abo Akademi University, 2021). In addition, because of scholarly disputes over the classifications of Psalms by genres, this study does not divide the uses of *ʿām* according to putative form-critical categories. For some of the issues, see William H. Bellinger, Jr., "Psalms and the Question of Genre," in *The Oxford Handbook of the Psalms*, ed. William P. Brown (Oxford/New York, NY: Oxford University Press, 2014), 313–325. For further reflections, see Hindy Najman, "The Idea of Biblical Genre," in *Prayer and*

chy fell, as lamented in Psalm 89 (Psalms 73–89); this situation gave way to the religio-political order of the divine king, remarkably celebrated in Psalms 95–100 and extended into the rest of the Psalter, in which "Israel" is restored from exile in the world and this "people" is restored to the proper religious service of the divine king (Psalms 90–150).[16]

The "people" plays a central role in the Psalter's story. The earliest expression of *ʿām*, both from synchronic and diachronic perspectives, is a "liturgical people," in other words a "people" formed and informed by ritual practice and traditions. At times, it also shows a capacity to engage military enemies in concert with its human king and supported, it is hoped, by a divine king. This people would also become transregional as Israelite identity of the northern kingdom would be subsumed into Judean identity. As the books of the Psalms develop from the Iron Age into the Persian and Hellenistic periods, this "people" on the one hand maintains its liturgical character and sociopolitical collective sense, and on the other hand shifts out of its military function headed by both human and divine kings to a reliance on the divine king, both at home and abroad. In the later context, this "people" both broadens into a transregional identity and deepens its sense of transgenerational identity.

The comments made below about specific psalms may benefit first from some framing and perspective. Of the 1869 occurrences of the BH word *ʿām*,[17] about 120 are found in the Psalms. In a number of cases, the singular represents a liturgical body, as marked by parallelism or collocation with terms such as *qāhāl* (see Pss 35:18; 107:32). In Ps 116:12–15 and 17–19, the first-person speaker locates "the people" in the context of liturgical ritual of the Jerusalem temple, specifically "all his people" in vv. 14 and 18, the only verses in the Psalms that use this expression (cf. the liturgical usage of the same expression in 1 Kgs 8:38//2 Chr 6:29). Sometimes *ʿām* corresponds to "Israel" more broadly, as in the parallelism of "Israel" and "people" (Pss 14:7, 50:7, 53:7, 78:71, 81:12, 14), in other forms of collocation (e.g., Pss 68:35; 106:48; 135:12; see also "his people" in Ps 125:2 and Israel in Ps 125:5), or both "his people" and "the people of Israel" (Ps 148:14). The "people" and "Israel" together may denote "the gathered people at worship," a characterization that Dan Fleming uses for the representation in

---

Poetry in the Dead Sea Scrolls and Related Literature: Essays in Honor of Eileen Schuller on the Occasion of Her 65th Birthday, ed. Jeremy Penner, Ken M. Penner, and Cecilia Wassen, STDJ 98 (Leiden/Boston: Brill, 2012), 307–321.

16 See Martin Leuenberger, *Konzeptionen des Königtums Gottes in Psalter: Untersuchungen zu Komposition Bücher IV–V im Psalter*, ATANT 83 (Zürich: Theologischer Verlag Zurich, 2004).

17 *DCH* 6:431.

1 Chr 32:5.[18] Papyrus Amherst 63 expresses a partially analogous identity for this "liturgical people."[19] Its five, mostly liturgical, collections arguably show it to be the closest extrabiblical analogue to the Psalter before 11QPs^{a}.[20] While the fifth collection's story departs from the liturgical character of the rest of the text, the initial three collections are markedly liturgical, with several references to "people" (see col. ii 3; col. v 5, 8; col. ix 2; col. xiii 2, 3, 4, 13, 17; col. xv 2; and xvi 5).[21]

The BH singular *ʿām* not uncommonly denotes speakers' perceptions of their own religious polity or social body, the one to which they belong and with which they identify. Many psalms constitute rhetorical discourse between (at least) two parties involving a represented first-person speaker (whether singular or plural) and a second-person addressee (again, whether singular or plural) often concerning a third party. Even sections of psalms cast in third-person narration are embedded in larger rhetorical frameworks of speaker and addressee. Expressions about "people" (*ʿām*) in the Psalms may serve in negotiating this relationship. The use of *ʿām* in the Psalms may be both descriptive and prescriptive of this relationship: it often signals to the addressee the speaker's view of her or his relationship to this collective identity, but it often serves further to express to the addressee the identity that the speaker seeks in relation to that addressee. Thus, *ʿām* may serve as an indexical marker for speakers' senses of the collective and its identity as well as their place in relation to it, whether actual or aspirational. This noun thereby forms one strand in the web of rela-

18 Fleming, *Legacy*, 54. Good (*Sheep*, 146) similarly emphasizes that "Israel as a people was a worshipping community."

19 See Richard S. Steiner, "The Aramaic Text in Demotic Script (1.99)," *COS* 1:309–328; and Karel van der Toorn, *Papyrus Amherst 63*, AOAT 448 (Münster: Ugarit-Verlag, 2018). The text is cited according to van der Toorn's edition.

20 Papyrus Amherst 63 also shows heavy usage of *sp*, "end," for ending compositions especially in its first three major sections and then only once in the fourth section, in its last line (as in Aramaic *sôpāʾ* in Dan 7:28 closing the section; cf. Eccl 12:13); the fifth section is a narrative appendix without such a liturgical textual marker. Papyrus Amherst 63 is not included in the comparison of the Psalter with extrabiblical anthological collections made by Willgren, *The Formation of the 'Book' of Psalms*, 39–79. With its variant version of Psalm 20, Papyrus Amherst 63 stands closer in time and perhaps in space to the Psalter, compared to the other extrabiblical anthological collections in Willgren's survey, ten from Mesopotamia, and two others being the Homeric Hymns and the Hodayot texts from Qumran.

21 A further identity marker for "people" in this papyrus occurs in xvii 3, which according to van der Toorn (*Papyrus Amherst 63*, 75) is direct discourse asking, "from where are the [pe]ople of your dialect?" (cf. Steiner, "The Aramaic Text in Demotic Script," 321). Two lines later (in xvii 5), that "people" is identified as liturgical. As this case (and others) suggest, the identities entailed in this work are complex. See further below.

tional identities, locating individual and groups within the collective landscape and situating them between a wider collectively remembered past and hoped-for futures.

"The people" is further an important dramatis persona for the imagined "stage-performance" on rhetorical display in several psalms.[22] The overarching context for these expressions in the Psalms is not uncommonly represented as a liturgical communication system combining the stage (often identified as the temple), its various actors, and the sacrificial and/or musical script that they play out. Other psalms that play out against other settings apparently know these liturgical conventions and use several of their tropes. This assumed cultural knowledge carries over to the Psalms' liturgical-scribal production,[23] which represents a further *Sitz im Leben*[24] that identifiably left its mark on the

---

22 For liturgical psalms as verbal elements within a larger communication system also involving body language as well as sacrifices, see Mark S. Smith, with contributions by Elizabeth M. Bloch-Smith, *The Pilgrimage Pattern in Exodus*, JSOTSup 239 (Sheffield: Sheffield Academic Press, 1997), 118–126. For the representation of the temple as the stage for that communication, see Smith, *The Pilgrimage Pattern*, 81–109. Critiques of a performance approach to ritual have been voiced, for example by Catherine Bell, *Ritual Theory, Ritual Practice* (Oxford: Oxford University Press, 1992), 42–43. Clearly, rituals are not merely the performance or dramatization of a priori thought and beliefs, per Bell's critique; ritual is not even simply a potential generator or modifier of worldview. Unlike Bell's critique of some performance theorists, I take seriously indigenous claims made in ancient texts about rituals, especially how they provide a space and means for the potential meeting and interaction of deities and humans, as emphasized by David P. Wright, *Ritual in Narrative: The Dynamics of Feasting, Mourning, and Retaliation Rites in the Ugaritic Tale of Aqhat* (Winona Lake, IN: Eisenbrauns, 2001). Indeed, in any number of ritual contexts, deities and human are actors and agents together. Such ritual interaction "primarily acts to restructure bodies in the very doing of the acts themselves" (Bell, *Ritual Theory*, 100). Accordingly, for many of the ritual expressions represented in Psalms, a performance perspective may remain useful.

23 See Susan E. Gillingham, "The Levites and the Editorial Composition of the Psalms," in *The Oxford Handbook of the Psalms*, ed. William P. Brown (Oxford/New York, NY: Oxford University Press, 2014), 201–213. See also Mark S. Smith, "The Levitical Compilation of the Psalter," *ZAW* 103 (1991): 258–263.

24 The reformulation of this aspect of the form-critical agenda reflects what may be called "the scribal turn" in Hebrew Bible studies. The issue was lifted up for biblical studies initially by William M. Schniedewind, *How the Bible Became a Book* (Cambridge: Cambridge University Press, 2004). The "scribal turn" was largely due to two rather different works on the topic: David M. Carr, *Writing on the Tablet of the Heart: Origins of Scripture and Literature* (Oxford/New York, NY: Oxford University Press, 2005); and Karel van der Toorn, *Scribal Culture and the Making of the Hebrew Bible* (Cambridge, MA/London: Harvard University Press, 2007). Other important works include Christopher A. Rollston, *Writing and*

poetic psalms with their prose superscriptions[25] and perhaps contributed the composition of Psalm 1 as well.[26] Informed with this background, the singular use of *ʿām* in the Psalms is generally a representation of a "liturgical people." The noun may also be expressive of political identity in the face of political pressures on the part of other polities sometimes characterized as "people" or "peoples."

Literacy in the World of Ancient Israel: Epigraphic Evidence from the Iron Age, SBLABS 11 (Leiden: Brill, 2010); Seth L. Sanders, *The Invention of Hebrew* (Urbana/Chicago, IL: University of Illinois Press, 2009); Brian B. Schmidt, ed., *Contextualizing Israel's Sacred Writings: Ancient Literary, Orality, and Literary Production*, AIL 22 (Atlanta, GA: SBL Press, 2015). The topic continues to make an impact; see Andrew R. Burlington, "Writing and Literacy in the World of Ancient Israel: Recent Developments and Future Directions," *BO* 76/1–2 (2019): 46–74; William M. Schniedewind, *The Finger of the Scribe: How Scribes Learned to Write the Bible* (New York, NY: Oxford University Press, 2019); and Omer Sergi, "On Scribal Tradition in Israel and Judah and the Antiquity of the Historiographical Narratives in the Hebrew Bible," in *Eigensinn und Entstehung der Hebräischen Bibel: Erhard Blum zum siebzigsten Geburtstag*, ed. J.J. Krause, W. Oswald, and K. Weingart (Tübingen: Mohr Siebeck, 2020), 275–299.

25 The prose superscriptions are secondary elaborations to the poetic psalms; as such they are also valuable indications of many psalms' "inner biblical interpretation," as discussed by Brevard S. Childs, "Psalm Titles and Midrashic Exegesis," *JSS* 16 (1971): 137–150; and Michael Fishbane, *Biblical Interpretation in Ancient Israel* (Oxford: Clarendon Press, 1985), 403–407. For a more recent and detailed discussion of the superscriptions, see Willgren, *The Formation of the 'Book' of Psalms*, 172–201. Cf. what *bT. Shabbat* 115b calls "the targum in the Torah" in reference to *yəgar śāhădûtāʾ* in Gen 31:47.

26 Psalm 1 contains a density of particles particularly at home in prose (what may be loosely called "prose particles," which do not appear to be elements in the repertoire of traditional poetry). These may be an indicator of this psalm's origins as a scribal production. Psalm 1 contains two compound particles that appear only here in the Psalter: *kî ʾim* in vv. 2 and 4; and *lōʾ-kēn* in v. 4. A third particle is particularly prominent in Psalm 1, namely *ʾăšer*, in v. 1, 3 [2×], and 4. Particles additionally appear with *kə-* in vv. 3 and 4, *ʿal-kēn* in v. 5, and *kî* in v. 6. While such particles appear broadly in Psalms, several stand in high relief in Psalm 1, and they are critical to the psalm's structure and progression. That the high use of *ʾăšer* in Psalm 1, especially in v. 1, may reflect a scribal innovation might also be indicated by the inclusion that it would form with Ps 2:12, perhaps signaling the "introductory role" that the two psalms jointly are to serve for the book. For "prose particles" in Hebrew poetry as a possible reflection of scribal production, I am indebted to Frederick W. Dobbs-Allsopp, *On Biblical Poetry* (New York, NY/Oxford: Oxford University Press, 2015), 343, 507 n. 21, and 520 n. 105; and "A Song of Love: Isaiah 5:1–7," in *Some Wine and Honey for Simon: Biblical and Ugaritic Aperitifs in Memory of Simon B. Parker*, ed. A.J. Ferrera and H.B. Huffmon, with the assistance of S. Kozin (Eugene, OR: Pickwick, 2020), 228 and 234.

2 In the Beginning: The Liturgical-Political People in Psalm 3 and in Older Psalms

In the book of Psalms, the singular noun *ʿām* first appears in Psalm 3 as a "liturgical people" entangled in the political and military situation. From the perspective of the synchronic "story of the Psalms," it might be understood that the first two psalms set the frame for the references to "people" from Psalm 3 onward. The contrast between the righteous versus the wicked opens the book in Psalm 1 (notably in vv. 1–3 versus vv. 4–5, echoed within v. 6).[27] It is followed by Psalm 2's disquisition on the king against the "nations"//"peoples" (*gôyīm* //*lǝʾummîm* in 2:1), commanded to submit to the divine, royal order of reality. As indicated by vv. 10–12, Psalm 2 is a royal psalm of instruction[28] to those "peoples." Thus Psalms 1–2 introduce important dramatis personae for the book's "story."[29]

The addition of *ʿām* in Ps 3:7 and 3:9 provides an additional delineation of the Psalter's dramatis personae. On the one side is "the people" in 3:9 implicitly aligned with the deity and the righteous (as aligned in Psalm 1) and with the deity and the king (as aligned in Psalm 2). On the other side are "the myriad forces" (NJPS), literally "myriads of people" (*mēribǝbôt ʿām*), arrayed against

27 The construction of contrast between the types of persons in Psalm 1 operates at its overarching structure (its "macrostructure"), in vv. 1–3 versus vv. 4–5 and then within v. 6 itself. The psalm's basic contrast is also represented by "microlevel" elements, beginning with the alliterative *ʾašrê* and *ʾăšer* generating sonant parallelism in reverse order of consonants with *rǝšāʿîm* throughout the psalm (vv. 1, 4, 5, 6). (For *ʾašrê* as a third-weak root elative adjective "most happy" and not construct, see Aaron D. Rubin, "The Form and Meaning of Hebrew *ʾašrê*," *VT* 60 [2010]: 366–372.) In other words, this sonant parallelism in the psalm corresponds to its semantic contrast between the types of persons; as a form of contrast, it also marks the contrast drawn at the level of the psalm's two major sections, in vv. 1–3 and 4–5, as well as its coda in v. 6. For the definition of a "sound pair" as two parallel words sharing two consonants and a third similar consonant, see Adele Berlin, *The Dynamics of Biblical Parallelism*, rev. and exp. ed., BRS (Grand Rapids, MI: Eerdmans; Dearborn, MI: Dove Booksellers, 2008), 104. This phenomenon, which may be called "sonant parallelism," extends in Psalm 1 (and elsewhere) beyond contiguous parallel lines.

28 See below on the problem of "royal psalms" as a genre classification.

29 Childs (*Introduction*, 513–514) emphasizes the "new theocentric understanding of the psalms" introduced by Psalm 1. For Psalm 2, Childs (*Introduction*, 516) stresses its putatively eschatological dimension, a sensibility that permeates Childs' canonical reading of the Psalter (the future arrival of "God's coming kingship," p. 518), which turns to the present of every audience ("a personal word from God in each individual situation," p. 521; see also p. 523). A further formulation for the Psalter appears in Childs, *Old Testament Theology in a Canonical Context* (Philadelphia, PA: Fortress, 1986), 231: "the believing and suffering community stands in between the forces of life and death."

the first-person speaker. The speaker's own "people" in Ps 3:9, it is hoped, will receive "your blessing." Implicitly then Psalm 3 contributes to the construction of the series of binaries beginning in Psalms 1–2 and appearing elsewhere in the book, including "peoples" and "people" (e.g., Ps 47:10; see also "peoples" in Ps 33:10 vs. "people" in Ps 33:12; cf. Ps 18:28, 44–45, 48; and in Ps 68:8, 31 and 36). No less important for the book's dramatis personae, Psalm 3 elaborates on the first-person speaker initially introduced in Ps 2:7a (framed by the quoted first-person divine speech in 2:6 and 7b–9). The "I-voice" locates and identifies with the "people" (*ʿām*) first in 3:9 in contrast to *gôyīm*// *ləʾummîm* in 2:1 and in contrast to *mēribəbôt ʿām* in 3:7. This oppositional construction is but one of several binaries laid out over the course of the Psalms.

From a historical perspective, the beginnings of *ʿām* in the Psalter may be examined through the lens of some of its earlier psalms and their "inner biblical" development. Arguably containing some of the oldest BH liturgical material is Psalm 68, which uses *ʿām* in vv. 8 and 36. The date of this psalm is unclear; it refers to a world of "kings" in vv. 15 and 30, and it refers to "your temple over Jerusalem" in v. 30, a reflection of its adoption and adaptation in the Judean monarchic context, perhaps in the Neo-Assyrian period.[30] In v. 8 the patron warrior-deity is represented as going out "before your people" (*ʿamməkā*).[31] Here the noun may bear a military sense as "your army" (so NJPS),[32] which

30 Linguistic evidence may be helpful for situating some of the psalm's later additions: *qərāb* in v. 31 is an Aramaic loan, according to Paul V. Mankowski, S.J., *Akkadian Loanwords in Biblical Hebrew*, HSS 47 (Winona Lake, IN: Eisenbrauns, 2000), 133–134; and the phrase *tārîṣ yādāyw* in v. 32 looks like a possible calque on Akkadian *qāta tarāṣu*, "to entreat" (*CAD* T 211); see David M. Goldenberg, *The Curse of Ham: Race and Slavery in Early Judaism, Christianity and Islam* (Princeton, NJ/London: Princeton University Press, 2003), 222 n. 45 with prior scholarship.

31 For Frank-Lothar Hossfeld, v. 8 belongs to an "inner ring" surrounding the poem's core. At the same time, Hossfeld sees "a self-contained basic psalm in vv. 8–32, melding Yahwist-oriented traditions from the Northern Kingdom with Jerusalem Temple theology." See Frank-Lothar Hossfeld and Erich Zenger, *Psalms 2: A Commentary on Psalms 51–100*, ed. Klaus Baltzer, trans. Linda M. Maloney, Hermeneia (Minneapolis, MN: Fortress Press, 2005), 163. Hossfeld (*Psalms 2*, 165) also sees Judg 5:4–5 as the model for vv. 8–11. For vv. 5–34 as the poem's core, see Israel Knohl, "Psalm 68: Structure, Composition and Geography," *JHS* 12, article 5 (2012) (DOI: 10.5508/jhs.2012.v.12.a15).

32 For this usage, see Good, *Sheep*, 27–28, 32, 124–126, cited by Frank Moore Cross, *From Epic to Canon: History and Literature in Ancient Israel* (Baltimore, MD/London: The Johns Hopkins University Press, 1998), 12. Note also Lawrence Kutler, "A Structural Semantic Approach to Israelite Communal Terminology," *JANES* 14 (1982): 69–77, here 71–72; and Klaus Koch, *Der Gott Israels und die Götter des Orients: Religionsgeschichtliche Studien II. zum 80. Geburstag von Klaus Koch*, ed. Friedhelm Hartenstein and Martin Rösel, FRLANT 216 (Göttingen: Vandenhoeck & Ruprecht, 2007), 190–192.

appears to be traditional usage.[33] In the larger context of the psalm's core, this "people" is also centrally a liturgical one that blesses the deity (see vv. 25–27). Verse 36, part of the psalm's later frame,[34] does not interpret the people as part of the deity's military forces as much as the beneficiary of that warrior-deity's might and power (as seen also in v. 11 of the arguably early and northern Psalm 29).[35] The combination of the people's military synergy with the deity and its status as the deity's beneficiary marks the word's usage in Psalm 68, as seen above also in Psalm 3. Furthermore, Ps 68:8–9 may witness to what appears to be a northern sense of "people" and "Israel" (in "god of Israel")[36] incorporated into a southern context (see Jerusalem in v. 30).[37] In this case, the liturgical-political "people" would be expressive of a northern-southern transregional identity emergent in the preexilic context, a development paralleled by the incorporation of the northern Psalm 29 into "Judah's Bible" (see the "people"

33 According to Fleming (*Legacy*, 62), the usage of "people" for fighting forces is a secondary development from the notion that "people" may refer to communities gathered for battle. Note also Abraham Malamat's comment in this vein: "armies in their earliest stages were formed on the basis of actual families." See Malamat, "*Ummatum* in Old Babylonian Texts and Its Ugaritic and Biblical Counterparts," *UF* 11 (1979 = Festschrift für C.F.A. Schaeffer): 528.

34 For Hossfeld (*Psalms* 2, 163), v. 36 is part of an outer ring consisting of vv. 5–7 and 33–36.

35 For Psalm 29, see Lowell K. Handy, ed., *Psalm 29 through Time and Tradition* (Eugene, OR: Pickwick, 2009); and for an argument for its literary integrity, see Gianni Barbiero, "The Two Structures of Psalm 29," *VT* 66 (2016): 378–392. The theme in v. 11 is traditional. The name of the Jerusalem temple column *yākîn* (1 Kgs 7:21) was taken by William Foxwell Albright as a clause, "[the deity] will establish [your throne] forever or the like"; see Albright, *Archaeology and the Religion of Israel*, 5th ed., republ. OTL (Louisville, KY/London: Westminster John Knox, 2006), 139. The two columns' names taken together as wishes as in Ps 29:11 might be understood as, "may [the deity] establish the people in strength," as suggested in Smith, *The Pilgrimage Pattern in Exodus*, 81–83. Cf. "Erra and Naram-Sin," lines 50–51, in Joan Goodnick Westenholz, *The Legends of the Kings of Akkade: The Texts*, MC 7 (Winona Lake, IN: Eisenbrauns, 1997), 198–199: "and the name of Erra « and of Naram-Sin » was inscribed on them [on 'the fixed double doors,' mentioned in the preceding line]: 'Battle.' Affixed was the name of the king, inscribed on them: 'Prosperity'."

36 For different views of the literary relationship between Ps 68:8–9 and Judg 5:4–5, see Mark S. Smith, *Poetic Heroes: The Literary Commemoration of Warriors and Warrior Culture in the Early Biblical World* (Grand Rapids, MI/Cambridge: Eerdmans, 2014), 235–237. Whichever view is correct, the attestations are suggestive of a northern monarchic literary context.

37 See Michael J. Stahl, "The 'God of Israel' in Judah's Bible: Problems and Prospects," *JBL* 139 (2020): 741–742, for this transregional shift as marked by the BH distribution of this divine title. A northern sense of difference from the south is reflected in a human title in Samaria Ostracon 51.3, "Aha the Judah[ite]," in F.W. Dobbs-Allsopp, J.J.M. Roberts, C.L. Seow and R.E. Whitaker, *Hebrew Inscriptions: Texts from the Biblical Period of the Monarchy with Concordance* (New Haven, CT/London: Yale University Press, 2005), 471.

in v. 11). Finally, Psalm 68 constructs its sense of "people" ultimately in contrast to "peoples" represented as foreign (v. 31), likely as a result of its royal reception and adaptation in the south.

The same political construction of "people" and "peoples" figure in psalms with the king as their central topic and/or voice (commonly called "royal psalms").[38] While such psalms show signs of additions, most of them reflect a grounding in a monarchical worldview. Psalm 18 (//2 Samuel 22) is a royal psalm of thanksgiving evidently from the southern monarchy,[39] apparently set with a liturgical framing (see vv. 2–4 and 47–51). It contrasts God's people and other peoples in political, even military, terms. In v. 28, the warrior deity is praised for delivering "a lowly people (*ʿam*)" (ultimately through the king), while in v. 44 the speaker (the king) thanks the deity for rescuing "me" from "the strife of people" (*ʿām*), with the result that "peoples (*ʿammîm*) I did not know serve me"; this is a trope of royal discourse (cf. Ps 72:11). Finally, Psalm 18 thanks the deity for subduing "peoples (*ʿammîm*) under me" in v. 48.

The opening of the prayer for the king in Psalm 72[40] refers to the "people" three times. Verses 1–2 request that the king and his successor "judge your people rightly." Verse 3 adds a wish of blessing of wellbeing "to the people," and v. 4 asks the deity "to champion the lowly ones of the people." Thus, this psalm begins by giving a prominent place to the *ʿām* in its universal, political vision of the powerful and enriched monarch compassionately helping the lowly of the "people" (see v. 4, expanded in vv. 12–14). Psalm 72 seems to combine royal pro-

38 Royal psalms belong to different genres, with the king as their subject or addressee. On this point, see Mark S. Smith, "Taking Inspiration: Authorship, Revelation, and the Book of Psalms," in *Psalms and Practice: Worship, Virtue, and Authority*, ed. Stephen Breck Reid (Collegeville, MN: Liturgical Press, 2001), 244–273; and Norman K. Gottwald, "Kingship in the Book of Psalms," in *The Oxford Handbook of the Psalms*, ed. William P. Brown (New York, NY/Oxford: Oxford University Press, 2014), 437–444.

39 See variously Hans-Joachim Kraus, *Psalms 1–59: A Commentary*, trans. Hilton C. Oswald (Minneapolis, MN: Augsburg, 1988), 257–258; and Fleming, *Legacy*, 23.

40 The psalm's core dates to the later part of the monarchy under Neo-Assyrian influence according to commentators such as Hossfeld, in Hossfeld and Zenger, *Psalms* 2, 205. One of the pertinent pieces of evidence is the Akkadian loan *iškāru* in BH *ʾiskār* in v. 10, in Mankowski, *Akkadian Loanwords in Biblical Hebrew*, 42. Jessie DeGrado also notes that *ʾiškāru* was a special tax levied only in the Neo-Assyrian period. In addition, he points to the geographical horizon "from sea to sea" (v. 8) as a Mesopotamian royal motif, as well as the picture of tribute received from faraway kingdoms such Tarshish and Sheba/Saba (v. 10). Accordingly, he reads Psalm 72 "as a piece of monarchic propaganda that appropriates Assyrian rhetoric to characterize an extant Judean monarch." See DeGrado, *Authoring Empire: Assyria, Judah, and the Dynamics of Imperial Exchange* (in preparation; cited by gracious permission of the author).

pagandistic ideology of the "people" as recipients of divine blessing[41] thanks to the king (v. 3), with the traditional ancient Near Eastern theme of the king helping the poor among the "people" (vv. 2–4), along with the place of kings and their nations subservient to the king (vv. 9–11).[42] The references to "people" and "peoples" in Psalms 18 and 68 noted above show a similar concern, though with fewer overt signs of Neo-Assyrian political ideology at least in their older, core material. In Psalm 110, the "people" appears at first glance in a series of assurances addressed to the king (notably embedding two oracles),[43] specifically in

41 The theme is evident in Neo-Assyrian royal rhetoric as well. Jessie DeGrado (personal communication) points out to me that the "people" (written logographically UN.ME for *nišī*) of Assyria is a collective whose fate is tied to the king, for example in Assurbanipal's Coronation Hymn, obv., lines 9–12, while line 17 expresses a wish for the gods to give the king "a straight sceptre to extend the land and the peoples." For the text, see Alasdair Livingstone, *Court Poetry and Literary Miscellanea*, SAA 3 (Helsinki: Helsinki University Press, 1989), 27. For "the people of Assyria," see Shalmaneser III's campaign to Urartu, obv., line 26, in Livingstone, *Court Poetry*, 45. In contrast is the expression, "the land and the peoples (UN.MEŠ)," also in Assurbanipal's Hymn to Assur, rev., line 13, in Livingstone, *Court Poetry*, 6. In the Underworld Vision of the Assyrian Prince, obv., line 27, there is also the title, "shepherd of the multitudinous peoples," in Livingstone, *Court Poetry*, 70. Thus not entirely unlike biblical rhetoric, this royal ideology dwells on the place of both "the people" and "the peoples" within its universal order, in Sargon's terms (in line 43), "the lands from sunri[se] to sunset, the sum total of all the lands," along with their peoples (some named in the text); see Wayne Horowitz, *Mesopotamian Cosmic Geography*, 2nd printing with corrections and addenda, MC 8 (Winona Lake, IN: Eisenbrauns, 2008), 72–77. My thanks go to Jessie DeGrado, who is not responsible for any of the comments in this note. A comparative study of "people" and "peoples" in biblical and Neo-Assyrian royal rhetoric remains a desideratum.

42 See the older survey of the latter theme by F.C. Fensham, "Widow, Orphan, and the Poor in Ancient Near Eastern Legal and Wisdom Literature," *JNES* 21/2 (1962): 129–139, plus the parade examples in poetic narrative in *KTU*[3] 1.16.vi.45–50 and in Ugaritic ritual in *KTU*[3] 1.40.21, 29–30, and 38. Note also *Social Justice in the Ancient World*, ed. K.D. Irani and Morris Silver (Westport, CT: Greenwood, 1995); and Raymond Westbrook, "The Character of Ancient Near Eastern Law," in *A History of Ancient Near Eastern Law*, ed. Raymond Westbrook, vol. 1, HdO I/72:1 (Leiden/Boston: Brill, 2003), 26. For a series of Akkadian passages reflecting concern for "the feeble, the weak, the oppressed and the poor," see *CAD* U/W 70 under *ulālu*.

43 The combination of two oracles in a single psalm such as Ps 110:1 and 4 and also in Ps 89:4–5 and 20–38 suggests the availability of collected royal oracles that could be recycled in other textual genres. For the recontextualization of royal oracles, see Scott R.A. Starbuck, *Court Oracles in the Psalms: The So-Called Royal Psalms in their Ancient Near Eastern Context*, SBLDS 172 (Atlanta, GA: Society of Biblical Literature, 1999), 121–204. The Zakkur Stele inscription (*KAI* 202), a royal thanksgiving text devoted to deity Iluwer and crediting the help of Baal-shamayn, likewise cites two oracles from the latter deity (ll. 13–17); see C. Leong Seow, "The Zakkur Inscription," in Martti Nissinen, *Prophets and Prophecy in the Ancient Near East*, ed. Peter Machinist, 2nd ed., SBLWAW 41 (Atlanta, GA: SBL Press,

the apparently ungrammatical and textually difficult MT v. 3, "your people are willing on the day of your power (?)." However, the textual reading may be secondary and late.[44] Setting Psalm 110 aside for this discussion, the "people" as a central concern in these "royal psalms" contrasts with the common figuring of "peoples" as potentially subjugated populations or vassals.

Before addressing *ʿām* at the end of the Psalter, there is an important development to note in its rhetorical representation. Over the unfolding of the Psalter, the "people" is figured as the deity's "flock," which in some psalms is given its own voice in the form of first-person plural direct discourse. For example, the communal lament of Psalm 44, arguably anchored in the late monarchic period,[45] begins with the "we-voice" recounting the aid that their ancestors

---

2019), 253–257. Note also the two oracles embedded together in prose narrative in Gen 35:10–12 (considered priestly), with a reference to kings in v. 11; cf. the parallel material in Gen 17:4–8 represented in a single divine speech, which is subsequently elaborated in two more divine speeches in Gen 17:9–14 and 15–21 (all three considered priestly). Such royal oracles may also be embedded in other media, such as temple architecture given names (see note 35 above), or the inscriptions on the statuary of Rameses II with Anat and on a stele inscription of Anat presenting what they call "words spoken by Anat" that look like oracles to this king; see Keiko Tazawa, *Syro-Palestinian Deities in New Kingdom Egypt: The Hermeneutics of Their Existence*, BAR International Series 1965 (Oxford: BAR Publishing, 2009), 74 #4 and 5, and 75 #9. Whether composed for the occasion of each inscription or not, these "words spoken by Anat" represent a fund of royal oracular discourse. See also such "words spoken by Astarte" in Tazawa, *Syro-Palestinian Deities*, 86 #9. First-person speech evidently on the part of a deity to the king appears also on a statue of a god; Tazawa, *Syro-Palestinian Deities*, 19 #14. More complex analogies are furnished by four Neo-Assyrian oracle collections from Nineveh dating to ca. 681–679, in Simo Parpola, *Assyrian Prophecies*, SAA 9 (Helsinki: Helsinki University Press, 1997), lxviii–lxx, 1–30; and Nissinen, *Prophets and Prophecy*, 107–144. Though not specifically royal in character, the Deir ʿAllā inscription contains a narrative with quotations of multiple oracles (see Seow, "Deir ʿAlla Plaster Texts," in Nissinen, *Prophets and Prophecy*, 258–263); for a consideration of the oral dimension of the text, see Gareth Wearne, "The Second Rubric in the Deir ʿAlla Plaster Texts as an Instruction for the Oral Performance of the Narrative," in *Registers and Modes of Communication in the Ancient Near East: Getting the Message Across*, ed. Kyle H. Keimer and Gillan Davis (London/New York, NY: Routledge, 2018), 125–142.

44 See Erich Zenger, in Frank-Lothar Hossfeld and Erich Zenger, *Psalms 3: A Commentary on Psalms 101–150*, ed. Klaus Baltzer, trans. Linda M. Maloney, Hermeneia (Minneapolis: Fortress Press, 2011), 142–144 and 149, noting LXX *meta sou* and Vulgate *tecum*, "with you," apparently assuming a Hebrew *Vorlage* **ʿimməkā* for MT *ʿamməkā*. For further discussion of the textual witnesses, see Dominique Barthélemy, *Critique textuelle de l'ancient Testament: Tome 4. Psaumes*, ed. Stephen D. Ryan and Adrian Schenker, OBO 50/4 (Fribourg: Academic Press; Göttingen: Vandenhoeck & Ruprecht, 2005), 736–744. Zenger (p. 141) regards the MT version as one of the psalm's "interpretive relectures."

45 A postexilic date is preferred by Erhard S. Gerstenberger, *Psalms: Part 1 with an Introduction to Cultic Poetry*, FOTL 14 (Grand Rapids, MI: Eerdmans, 1988), 186.

had received from the deity (vv. 2–4, 6–9, with first-person singular voice in v. 5). It further complains that "you do not go out with our armies" (v. 10), and "you sold your people for a trifle" (v. 13). This psalm twice figures the people as "your sheep" (vv. 11, 23), a traditional metaphor of royal responsibility. A number of other communal psalms similarly figure "your people" as the sheep of the deity. In the wake of the destruction of the Jerusalem temple,[46] the first-person plural community voice of Psalm 79 claims, "we are your people, the sheep of your pasture" (v. 13). Ps 95:7 and 100:3 show late use of this metaphor for the people of the deity.[47] Arguably situated after the fall of Jerusalem, the speakers of Psalm 95 would place their first-person plural identity under the protection of the divine king,[48] while the speakers of Psalm 100 proclaim the deity before "all the earth" (v. 1).[49] Across Psalms 95–100, the looming loss of political identity marked by the demise of the human monarchy perhaps foregrounds not only the people's vulnerability, but also the divine king's central importance in the people's liturgical-political identity.[50] In this context, the image of the people as sheep evokes the deity's capacity to provide political protection or the lament that the deity does not do so. It is this particular intersection of the "we"-speakers figuring themselves as the deity's "people" and specifically as the deity's "sheep" that is one of the notable political uses of "people" in the Psalms. In these psalms, "we the people," one might say, is a powerful political expression.

3 Toward the Psalter's End: The Liturgical-Political *ʿām* of the Persian Period

The last attestation *ʿām* in the MT 150 psalm-Psalter appears in Ps 149:4. Yahweh's "people" is the culmination of a series of linked identities beginning with "the congregation of the faithful" (v. 1; see also v. 9) followed by "Israel" and "the children of Zion" (v. 2). This identity stands in contrast with the "nations" and

46 For a defense of this setting, see Zenger, in Hossfeld and Zenger, *Psalms* 2, 305. Note the metaphor of sheep also in Jer 13:18–20 in the context of exile.

47 Good, *Sheep*, 53.

48 For Hossfeld (Hossfeld and Zenger, *Psalms* 2, 460), this psalm entails a "late-exilic or postexilic positioning," although he also notes claims for older formulary.

49 For a Second Temple dating, see Zenger in Hossfeld and Zenger, *Psalms* 2, 495. Zenger proposes that Psalm 100 was composed to serve as the final summarizing psalm for Psalms 95–100.

50 See Marc Z. Brettler, *God is King: Understanding an Israelite Metaphor*, JSOTSup 76 (Sheffield: Sheffield Academic Press, 1989).

"peoples" (v. 7). This contrast echoes the first reference to the people and peoples in Psalm 3. Both cast and celebrated in terms of its religious identity, the people in Psalm 149 is geographically centered on Zion, and also evokes the old identity of Israel (see also Ps 148:14). Psalm 148 likewise ends with a number of the same identity markers, with "his people," and "the people close to Him" framing "his faithful ones," and "Israel."

The representation of the people in Psalms 148 and 149 belongs to the Psalter's late formation and temporal context, marked also by the four doxologies (Pss 41:14; 72:18–19; 89:53; 106:48); Psalm 150 or Psalms 146–150 might be regarded as the book's substitute for a final doxology. The noun's liturgical identity informs the Psalter's four explicit doxologies. These final MT psalms picture *ʿām* as a "liturgical people," amplified not only by "people" used twice in Ps 148:14, but also by a series of corresponding terms: "Zion" in Ps 146:10; "Jacob"//"Israel" in Ps 147:19–20; "faithful ones" in Ps 149:1 and 9, and "Israel" and "the children of Zion" in Ps 149:2. Among the doxologies, "all the people" responding with its "Amen" is explicit only in Ps 106:48 = 1 Chr 16:36 (Neh 8:6; cf. the response of Amen to the curses in Deut 27:15–26). The qualifier "all" (*kol*) suggests a corporate body. The people may also be implicit to the blessing formulary plus the "double-Amen" in the doxologies in Pss 41:14; 72:19; and 89:53.[51] Taken collectively, the doxologies suggest that "the people" are a collective, liturgical body that responds "Amen" to the blessing pronounced.[52] The divine title "the god of Israel," which appears in three of the doxologies (Pss 41:14; 72:18; and 106:48; cf. the blessing formulary following the reference to "the god of Israel" and "the people" in Ps 68:36), additionally marks this "people" in

51 See Willgren, *The Formation of the 'Book' of Psalms*, 216–222. The oldest use of double *ʾmn in West Semitic literature is Ugaritic *ʾimt ʾimt*, "truly, truly," also in direct discourse, in the *Baal Cycle* (*KTU*³ 1.5.i.18). Biblical doxologies continued to be models for later Jewish expressions, for example, 1QS 1:20 and 2:10 and 18. See also "Let all the people say: 'Amen amen! Selah'," in an En-Gedi Synagogue inscription (line 8), possibly dating to the sixth century CE, in Joseph A. Fitzmyer, S.J. and Daniel J. Harrington, S.J., *A Manual of Palestinian Aramaic Texts (Second Century B.C.—Second Century A.D.)*, BibOr 34, 3rd repr. (Rome: Pontificio Istituto Biblico, 2002), 260–261, 288–289, #A22. Note also "Amen" spoken by the good angel and by the bad angel in *bT. Shabbat* 119b.

52 See K. Seybold, "Zur Vorgeschichte der liturgischen Formel 'Amen'," *ThZ* 48 (1992): 114–115, cited by Zenger (Hossfeld and Zenger, *Psalms* 2, 218–219). Double-Amen's appear four times in the second major section of Papyrus Amherst 63, col. x lines 17 and 24 and xi 8 and 16, all concluding compositions: "let the throng (or crowd) say, 'Amen, amen'." See Steiner, "The Aramaic Text in Demotic Script," 316–318; and van der Toorn, *Papyrus Amherst 63*, 60–63.

the doxologies as "Israel."[53] "Israel" is also not uncommon in the Psalter's final psalms (147:2, 19; 148:14; 149:2).

The doxologies representing the "liturgical people of Israel" were at home in its postexilic cult, as reflected by the *qāhāl* and *ʿām* together in Neh 5:13 responding "Amen" and by its response "Amen, Amen" to Ezra's blessing of the deity in Neh 8:6. This liturgical identity for the "people" intersects in the literary projects of the Psalter and 1–2 Chronicles, most explicitly in the citation of Ps 106:47 in 1 Chr 16:35 followed by "all the people" responding with its "Amen" in both Ps 106:48 and 1 Chr 16:36. The blessing entailed by the doxologies may have been imagined to be spoken to the people by priestly leadership (cf. "we bless you by the name of Yahweh," in Ps 129:8). Such a picture informs the priestly blessings of the people in Lev 9:22–23, Num 6:24, and Sir 50:1–21, as well the covenant curses spoken by the Levites and the people's answer of "Amen" in Deut 27:14–26 and the covenant curse met with "Amen" in Jer 11:1–5 (cf. the accused woman's double-Amen in Num 5:22).

This liturgical "people" constitutes the Persian-period collective ideal of "the people of Israel" (Ezra 9:2; Neh 1:6; 7:7), centered in Jerusalem or "Zion" (e.g., Ezra 1:3; 2:2, 70; 3:1; 8:29; 10:5; Neh 1:6; 7:72–73; 8:17; 10:34; 11:19–21). Ezra 3:10 captures this ideal's seminal elements: "the temple of Yahweh, the priests in their vestments," with liturgical praise directed by "the Levites, the sons of Asaph, with cymbals, according to the directions of King David of Israel." In Ezra 3:11 this description is followed by all this leadership singing a psalmic verse, such as Pss 106:1 or 136:1 (Ezra 3:11 seems to evoke both in combining **hll* as in Ps 136:1 and **ydh* in the C-stem, as in Ps 106:1); it is followed by the response of "all the people." As these verses evidence (see also Ps 135:19–21; Ezra 8:29), this "liturgical people" is a priestly (or perhaps more precisely Levitical) construction and ideal,[54] suggested also by the references to priests in reference to these blessings of the Psalter's doxologies. The scope of this vision of Israel is extraordinarily expanded in the 198 references to Israel in 1–2 Chronicles, suggesting a massive historiographic project, serving to fold the past, remembered preexilic "Israel" of Judean southern memory into the current religious praxis of postexilic "Israel" based in Jerusalem, as signaled also by Psalm 149 (as noted above; see also Pss 146:10; 147:2, 12).

53 See recently the publication of the revised dissertation (directed by Dan Fleming) by Michael J. Stahl, *The "God of Israel" in History and Tradition*, VTSup 187 (Leiden: Brill, 2021); Stahl, "The 'God of Israel'," 721–745.

54 For this perspective, see Smith, "The Levitical Compilation of the Psalter," 258–263; Gillingham, "The Levites and the Editorial Composition of the Psalms," 201–213; and Willgren, *The Formation of the 'Book' of Psalms*, 237, 304–309, 314, and 380.

In Persian-period Yehud, the name of Israel came to stand for the memory of a transregional identity entailing both the northern kingdom of Israel and the southern kingdom of Judah. The memory of Israel was captured in Ezekiel's expression of hope for "the whole house of Israel" (Ezek 37:11), including those in exile brought to the land of Israel (37:12, 21). In Ezek 37:15–23 the prophet announces the reunification of the "two kingdoms," beginning with the instruction: "and write on it, 'Of (*lə-*) Judah and the Israelites his associates'," balanced by "Of Joseph, the stick of Ephraim, and all the House of Israel associated with him" (v. 16). Together these units constitute "the sons of your people" (v. 18) and "the sons of Israel" (v. 21). In this passage the remembered northern kingdom and southern kingdom are to constitute a single people of Israel, whom the deity "will take from the nations among whom they have gone" (v. 21), and thus will be "re-membered" as "one nation in the land, on the mountains of Israel" (v. 22). Hardly a political reality on the ground in the Persian period, "Israel" here serves as a sort of ideal term for the single and singular identity of the descendants of the old preexilic kingdoms, wherever they may be. Indeed, Israel as well as "people" is expressed sometimes in contrast to the political reality in the Persian period. For example, "Judah and Benjamin" and "the returned exiles" build a "temple for Yahweh the god of Israel" in Ezra 4:1. Similarly, the "people of Judah" in Neh 12:44 is hardly distinguished from "all Israel" that supports the religious personnel of the Jerusalem temple in Neh 12:47.

As reflected in the reference to David as "king of Israel" in Ezra 3:10 (cf. "Solomon king of Israel" over "all Israel" in Neh 13:26), "Israel" as a political term in the Persian period was a matter of collective imagination and memory retrieved from the preexilic period; indeed, that very polity name had already been repurposed for Judean national identity in the wake of Israel's own fall.[55] In the postexilic period, this sense of ancient memory would be traced back to "Joshua" and "the sons of Israel" (Neh 8:14), while the recitation of past events of the "people of Israel" in Nehemiah 9 extends even further back, to Abram, in v. 7 following the reference to creation in v. 6. This ancient memory was imprinted on postexilic priestly genealogies, e.g., "the descendants of Mahli son of Levi son of Israel" (Ezra 8:18; cf. Neh 11:22; 12:45–47) or in the recollection of putative religious celebration (e.g., Booths not celebrated since Joshua, in Neh 8:17).

55 See Jean Louis Ska, "Why is the Chosen People Called Israel and Not Judah?," in *Yahwistic Diversity and the Hebrew Bible: Tracing Perspectives on Group Identity from Judah, Samaria, and the Diaspora in Biblical Traditions*, ed. Benedikt Hensel, Dany Nocquet, and Bartosz Adamczewski, FAT 2/120 (Tübingen: Mohr Siebeck, 2020), 151–167.

In postexilic liturgy, this "people" was understood to go back to an ancient political past, which was thought to have been carried forward by and considered to inhere in those who "praise Yahweh" (so the command at the opening of both Psalms 105 and 106, both referring later to the "people" in 105:24, 43; 106:4, 40, 48). Thus "generation to generation shall praise your works" (Ps 145:4), corresponding to the praise of divine rule "in each and every generation" (Ps 145:13; see also Pss 71:18; 135:13; Esth 9:28).[56] This representation of the transgenerational people is also constituted and maintained by means of the covenant, divinely "commanded for a thousand generations" (Ps 105:8//1 Chr 16:15; cf. Ezra 7:10, 11).[57] Notably, in Ezra 7:10 the expression "in Israel" may sound like the old geographical polity, yet here it stands for the socioreligious entity that undertakes the study of "the law of Yahweh" and the teaching of "the statutes and ordinances in Israel" (see also Neh 8:1, 14, 18).

Like Israel in Ezra 7:28, this postexilic "people" also includes an extended spatial reality. It crosses regions in what was considered to constitute Israel in the preexilic period (see Psalms 122 and 133), but it is also "transnational";[58] it is both in Jerusalem and in Babylon (Psalm 137),[59] in both Meshech and Kedar

---

56 The basic model of transgenerational praise may correspond to the transgenerational ideal of family perduring (see also Deut 32:7; cf. the opposite of which is expressed in terms of a curse in Ps 109:13). This transgenerational ideal is expressed at the royal level in the transgenerational "eternity" of the royal dynasty and its praise (see Ps 72:5 and 17; cf. Ps 45:18).

57 Cf. the temporal expression in the prayer in Papyrus Amherst 63 col. xiii 17 referring to the "people" devoted to Yaho: "Arise Yaho! Do protect, As you have been protecting Your people since olden times" (van der Toorn, *Papyrus Amherst 63*, 173).

58 For "transnational identity," see Robin D.G. Kelley, "'But a Local Phase of a World Problem': Black History's Global Vision, 1883–1950," *Journal of American History* 86/3 (1999): 1045–1077. To the degree that "transnational" may imply nations or nation-states, it is not a particularly fitting label for the ancient context; see *Nationalism*, ed. John Hutchinson and Anthony D. Smith (New York, NY/Oxford: Oxford University Press, 1994). The term is modern verbiage, as would be "international." Kelley (p. 1051) sounds a cautionary note for study of colonial and postcolonial contexts that is no less applicable to the ancient context: "We must proceed with caution when comparing diasporas and diasporic identities with nations and nationalisms." Still, Kelley (p. 1077) asks in the end: "how could anyone not write histories that are transnational?" Perhaps "transcolonial" (p. 1067) might be helpful, as it could apply to persons self-perceived as members of a "people" and either remaining in conquered and/or occupied homelands, or displaced and/or forced from them. Below "transregional" is used; it seems less freighted.

59 See Anja Klein, "Sehnsucht nach Zion und Wunsch nach Vergeltung: Theologien des Exils in Psalms 137," in *Fromme und Frevler: Studien zu Psalmen und Weisheit: Festschrift für Hermann Spieckermann zum 70. Geburstag*, ed. Corinna Körting and Reinhard Gregor Kratz (Tübingen: Mohr Siebeck, 2020), 159–172. Klein notes that the singers mentioned in vv. 3–4 and the bodily deficit to be suffered in vv. 5–6 may point to the Jerusalem temple's Levit-

(Ps 120:5).[60] This imagined, transregional "people" includes, liturgically, persons not necessarily present in Jerusalem; ideally, they too keep this central site in their heart (Ps 137:7; see also Psalms 122, 125, 126; note also the Passover celebration in Ezra 6:21–22 and the offering for "all of Israel" in Ezra 8:35).[61] As the focus of Ezra–Nehemiah and 1–2 Chronicles remained fixed on Jerusalem, so too this transregional reality is imagined as ultimately grounded in Jerusalem, the perspective reflected also in the final reference to the people in Psalm 149 (as noted above). "Transregional identity" linked to "the Judean homeland" is known also from the Mesopotamian place name, *āl-Yāḫūdu* (URU *ia-ḫu-du*, "Judah-town"), attested in Akkadian documents dating from ca. 587 through 477.[62]

Such transregional "Judah" identity continued to be expressed down through the turn of the era, for example in an Aramaic funerary inscription from Giv'at Ha-Mivtar in Jerusalem witnessing to a man named Abba representing himself as "son of the priest of Eleaz⟨ar⟩, son of Aaron the elder."[63] He says that he was born in "Jerusalem and went into exile to Babylon, brought (back to Jerusalem),

---

ical singers in exile; she takes vv. 7–9 as "prophetische Fortschreibung." Arguably fitting with Klein's theory about vv. 1–6, vv. 7–9 are regarded as critically encoded song sung to the captors, in Rodney S. Sadler, "Singing a Subversive Song: Psalm 137 and 'Colored Pompey'," in *The Oxford Handbook of the Psalms*, ed. William P. Brown (New York, NY/Oxford: Oxford University Press, 2014), 447–458.

60 A transregional liturgical sensibility is expressed also in invocations of "all you peoples" (Pss 47:1; 49:2; 97:6; see also 1 Kgs 22:28//2 Chr 18:27 compared with Mic 1:2) and in commands for "the peoples" to praise (e.g., Ps 67:4 and 6). Note also the intention to praise the deity "among the nations" (2 Sam 22:50//Ps 18:50).

61 It is also an "epistolary" transregional "people," as reflected in correspondences between Yehudian communities in Egypt and Jerusalem and Samaria, as attested in the Elephantine letters (see the works cited in the following note), and between Jerusalem and Babylon (as reflected in Jeremiah 29). This corresponds to the biblical representation of Persian epistolary practice (e.g., Ezra 1–6, more specifically Ezra 1:2–4, further summarized in 5:13–15 and putatively quoted in 6:3–5; see also Neh 2:7, 8, 9; 6:5, 17, 19; Esth 8:9–13; 9:20, 26, 29; 10:29–30). On such documents in the literary world of Ezra 1–6, see Tamara Eskenazi, *In an Age of Prose: A Literary Approach to Ezra–Nehemiah*, SBLMS 36 (Atlanta, GA: Scholars Press, 1988) 59, 73. Note further Laura Carlson Hasler, *Archival Historiography in Jewish Antiquity* (New York, NY: Oxford University Press, 2020).

62 See Laurie E. Pearce and Cornelia Wunsch, *Documents of Judean Exiles and West Semites in Babylonia in the Collection of David Sofer*, CUSAS 28 (Bethesda, MD: CDL Press, 2014), xxxiv–xxxv, 14–15, and 98–188. Dates in the range 572–400 are given by Pearce, "Continuity and Normality in Sources Relating to the Judean Exile," *HeBAI* 3/2 (2014): 163–184, here 167. See additionally the essays in *HeBAI* 3/2 (2014) and 9/1 (2020) for various expressions of "transregional identity" between Judah and Judeans in Mesopotamia.

63 See Fitzmyer and Harrington, *A Manual of Palestinian Aramaic Texts*, 168–169, 221–222, #68.

Mattathi(ah), son of Jud(ah); and I buried him in the cave which I had acquired by the writ." The inscription's Paleo-Hebrew script may also evoke an old identity.

The usages of identity markers varied in the Greco-Roman period. "Jewish" transregional identity was common, as expressed by "Jew" (*Ioudaios*) or "Jews" (*Ioudaoi*).[64] Yet transregional identity could also be expressed in terms of "Israel" and "Israelite(s)," thereby connoting ancient origins. For example, the book of Tobit represents a transregional identity of "people" (*laos* in Tobit 4:13) and "all Israel" (1:6; see also 5:5, 13:3, 14:5, 7) that includes "all the Jews that were in Nineveh" (11:17); it further retained a devotion to Jerusalem (Tobit 1:4, 6, 13:9, 17, 14:5). This identity is not simply Yehudian or Judean (cf. "Samaria and Jerusalem" in 14:5).[65] Similarly, "Israel" is very common in the Dead Sea Scrolls notably as "your people Israel" in 1QM col. x lines 9–10.[66] The term "Israelites"

64 Combined the forms occur 195 times in the NT. For the term in the Greco-Roman period, see Shaye J.D. Cohen, *The Beginnings of Jewishness: Boundaries, Varieties, Uncertainties* (Berkeley, CA: University of California Press, 1999). For homeland and diaspora in the Greco-Roman period, see Eric S. Gruen, *The Construct of Identity in Hellenistic Judaism: Essays on Early Jewish Literature and History*, DCLS 29 (Boston, MA/Berlin: de Gruyter, 2020), 283–312.

65 The book of Judith offers a comparable set of identities for the people of Israel in both Judah and Samaria. Set largely around Bethulia to the north of Jerusalem, Judith refers to "the Israelites living in Judea" (4:1; for Israelites, see also 4:8, 9, 11; 5:23; 6:10, 14; 15:7, 8; 16:25; see also Judea in 1:12; 3:9; 11:19) and "the house of Israel" (8:6; 13:4), little distinguished from "all the people of Judea" (4:3) or "the people of Israel" (6:2; 9:14; 10:8); its people's devotion too is centered in Jerusalem (4:2, 6, 13; 5:19; 9:13; 11:13, 19; 15:8, 9; 16:18, 20) and reveres "the God of Israel" (6:19; 10:1; 14:10; see also 12:8; 13:7), the "God of the heritage of Israel" (9:12). This collective is also called a "people" (*laos*, 5:5, 6, 20, 22, 23; 6:16, 18; 7:23, 26, 32; 8:9, 29; 10:19; 11:2, 13, 22; 12:8; 13:17; 14:6, 8, 9; 15:10, 11, 13; 16:3, 18, 19, 20; *ethnos*, 9:14). See van der Toorn, *Becoming Diaspora Jews*, 17, also noting that this identity in Judith is not limited to Yehud but includes relations with Samaria. For van der Toorn, *laos* in Judith is not premised primarily on a geographical identity related specifically to Yehud (and thus "Yehudians"). Instead, it refers more broadly to a religious-ethnic identity ("Jews"), a point that he claims also for *yhwdy*ʾ (e.g., *TADAE* A4.7/Cowley 30, line 16) in the Elephantine community; see further below.

66 See Lawrence H. Schiffman, "Israel," in *Encyclopedia of the Dead Sea Scrolls*, ed. Lawrence H. Schiffman and James C. VanderKam, vol. 1 (New York, NY/Oxford: Oxford University Press, 2000), 388–391, here 389–390. The noun is not used in a gentilic form in the Dead Sea Scrolls. Judah is used in the Dead Sea Scrolls, including for "the house of Judah" (e.g., CD IV, 11; 1QpHab VIII, 1), "sons of Judah" (1QM I, 2), and for the land by that name ("the exiles of Israel that went out from the land of Judah," in CD IV, 3; see also VI, 5), again without any corresponding gentilic form except perhaps for what seems to be the PN in 4Q333 2, 1.

(*andres Israēlitai*, literally "Israelite men") refers in Acts 2:22 to pilgrims from around the world (2:5–11), as well as "men of Judea" and "Galileans" (see 2:14).[67]

Signs of such transregional identity in this period are discernible in other groups. For example, Phoenician inscriptions point to webs of identity between the Phoenician "homeland" and various sites in the wider Mediterranean basin, for example "the people of Sidon" (*ʿm ṣdn*) in an inscription from Piraeus dating to the Greco-Roman period (*KAI* 60.1),[68] identified in the same inscription by the so-called "gentilic" adjective, "the Sidonians" (line 7).[69] This "people of Sidon" constituted the "community," *gw* (lines 2, 5, 7, and 8).[70] The inscription's six references to the temple (*bt ʾlm* in lines 2 [2×], 3, 4–5, 5 and *ʾlm* in line 6) are indicative of the religious identity of this "people of Sidon." Evidence of transregional identity is similarly provided by a "Sidonian" named in a Phoenician-Greek bilingual inscription on what the Phoenician text calls "a pillar of remembrance" (*mṣbt skr*) from Athens (*KAI* 53).[71] In addition, the label "son of Carthage" applies to two figures mentioned in funerary inscriptions from the region of Tyre,[72] while conversely "the inhabitants of Carthage

67 See *andres Israēlitai* also in Acts 3:12, 5:35, 13:16, 21:28, and *Israēlitai* in John 1:47, Rom 9:4, 11:1 and 2 Cor 11:22. Note also "the god of this people Israel" in Acts 13:17. For the use of "Israel" in a more restricted geographical scope, see 1 Macc 1:43, 53, 58, 3:46, 5:9, 45, 6:18 and 7:23.

68 See John C.L. Gibson, *Textbook of Syrian Semitic Inscriptions: Volume III. Phoenician Inscriptions* (Oxford: Clarendon Press, 1982), 148–149; Vadim S. Jigoulov, *The Social History of Achaemenid Phoenicia: Being a Phoenician, Negotiating Empires* (London: Equinox, 2010), 63–65; and J. Brian Peckham, *Phoenicia: Episodes and Anecdotes from the Ancient Mediterranean* (Winona Lake, IN: Eisenbrauns, 2014), 489–491. The usage of *ʿm* here is not exceptional, as seen by the parallel expressions listed by Charles Krahmalkov, *Phoenician-Punic Dictionary*, OLA 90, Studia Phoenicia 15 (Leuven: Peeters, 2000), 376.

69 For a thorough examination as well as a useful critique of this category, see Jang, "The Sociology of 'Gentilics' in Biblical and Northwest Semitic Literature."

70 For this meaning for *gw*, see *DNWSI* 215; Krahmalkov, *Phoenician-Punic Dictionary*, 137–138; and Giovanni Mazzini, *The Ancient South Arabian Royal Edicts from the Southern Gate of Timnaʿ and the Ǧabal Labaḫ: A New Edition with Philological and Historical Commentary*, Epigraphische Forschungen auf der Arabischen Halbinsel 8 (Wiesbaden: Ludwig Reichert, 2020), 289–290; cf. *KAI* 17.1 in Gibson, *Textbook*, 117. This entity could also meet as an "assembly," according to the interpretation of *ʾspt* in line 1 given by Gibson, *Textbook*, 149; the reading is debated.

71 See Gibson, *Textbook*, 148.

72 Hélène Sader, *Iron Age Funerary Stelae from Lebanon*, Cuadernos de Arqueología Mediterránea 11 (Barcelona: Edicions Bellaterra, 2005), 82–84. Another notable inscription was discovered in the locality of al-Maʿmura southeast of Tyre, according to Sader, *Iron Age Funerary Stelae*, 80–81. "The stela" (*hmnṣbt*) is in memory of a person named *špṭ* (line 1), with a lineage of five generations including his great-grandfather *ʿzrbʿl* bearing the title *hšpṭ* (lines 2–3). The inscription's Carthaginian script, to be dated to the fourth or third

always considered themselves *bn Ṣr*, sons of Tyre, or *ḥ ṣry*, Tyrians, as can be deduced from their epigraphs."[73]

Other sources, such as Aramaic documents from Egypt in the Persian and Hellenistic periods, are replete with gentilics denoting peoples from outside of Egypt, including Sidon and Judah.[74] The transmission of the liturgical-literary

century, points to a Carthaginian apparently buried in the Phoenician homeland. (It is also to be noted that this inscription lists five generations, suggestive of "transgenerational identity" as well.) However these Carthaginians came to be buried in the environs of Tyre, their "inscriptional identity" includes indications of transregional cultural ties between Phoenicia proper and communities in the wider Mediterranean basin, just one element in the larger pattern of relations detailed by Ahmed Ferjaoui, *Recherches sur les relations entre l'Orient phénicien et Carthage*, OBO 124 (Göttingen: Vandenhoeck & Ruprecht, 1993). For the well-known relations also between Tyre and Carthage (including the latter's annual delegation to the former for a festival devoted to Melqart), see Josette Elayi, "The Relations between Tyre and Carthage during the Persian Period," *JANES* 13 (1981): 15–29; Corinne Bonnet, *Melqart: Cultes et mythes de l'Héraclès tyrien en Méditerranée*, Studia Phoenicia 8 (Leuven: Peeters; Namur: Presses universitaires de Namur, 1988), 166–167; and Peckham, *Phoenicia*, 466–468.

73 Maria Eugenia Aubet, *The Phoenicians and the West: Politics, Colonies, and Trade*, trans. Mary Turton, 2nd ed. (Cambridge: Cambridge University Press, 2001), 227. For presentation and discussion of votive inscriptions from Carthage with "son of Tyre" (CIS I 617, 913, 1477, 2020, 3968, 5526, 5826, 5970, and 6051), see Brett Kaufman, "A Citizen of Tyre in Sabatha: Colonial Identity in Punic North Africa," *Maarav* 16/1 (2009): 39–48. See further Pierre Bordreuil and Ahmed Ferjaoui, "À propose des «fils de Tyr» et des «fils de Carthage»," in *Studia Phoenicia VI*, ed. Edward Lipiński, OLA 26 (Leuven: Peeters, 1988), 137–142. Cf. the gentilic *ḥṣry* attached to a PN from Delos, in Frank L. Benz, *Personal Names in the Phoenician and Punic Inscriptions*, Studia Pohl 8 (Rome: Biblical Institute Press, 1972), 402 and 404.

74 See the listings of gentilics compiled by Bezalel Porten and Jerome A. Lund, *Aramaic Documents from Egypt: A Key-Word-in-Context Concordance*, The Comprehensive Aramaic Lexicon Project Texts and Studies 1 (Winona Lake, IN: Eisenbrauns, 2002), 439–441. For various gentilics in the Elephantine texts, see also Bob Becking, *Identity in Persian Egypt: The Fate of the Yehudite Community of Elephantine* (University Park, PA: Eisenbrauns, 2020), 18–77. The gentilic *yhwdy'* at Elephantine has been understood as "Judeans" (or Yehudians); see Cohen, *The Beginnings of Jewishness*, 83–84. Alternatively, it has been rendered as "Jews" already by A.E. Cowley, *Aramaic Papyri of the Fifth Century B.C.* (Oxford: Clarendon Press, 1923), 113–114. It is arguably problematic to characterize the community at Elephantine as "Yehudian," given the community's appeal to both Samaria and Judah (*TADAE* A4.7/Cowley 30). Moreover, against the common view that the roots of the Elephantine community go back to Judah, a northern background has been reconstructed by Karel van der Toorn, "Anat-Yahu, Some Other Deities, and the Jews at Elephantine," *Numen* 39 (1992): 80–101, here 95–97. The position as expressed there is rejected by André Lemaire, *Levantine Epigraphy and History of the Achaemenid Period (539–332 BCE)*, The Schweich Lectures of the British Academy 2013 (Oxford: Oxford University Press, 2015), 65. Van der Toorn has since defended and amplified this view in *Becoming Diaspora Jews: Behind the Story of Elephan-*

text of Papyrus Amherst 63 and the literary text of Ahiqar in Egypt suggests communities that wished to preserve traditions from their "homelands." The variety of these ancient diasporas, whether Judean, Phoenician or otherwise,[75] could use more study of their ancient sources (textual, iconographic and archaeological), put in dialogue with the burgeoning literature on modern diasporic identities.[76]

As these sources suggest, transregional identities in the Persian and Hellenistic periods were operative in a wide array of ancient Near Eastern and Mediterranean communities. At the same time, the varying "transregional identities" in different communities and in various locales entailed different configurations. On the one hand, some types of transregional features were shared by different communities. For example, the gentilics appear somewhat comparable to one another in marking identities linked in some way to various "homelands." The same point may be applicable to some geographical labels. The use of "Judah-town" for the community in Mesopotamia noted above seems somewhat analogous to the use of "Sidon" in the Piraeus inscription also noted above. The preservation of liturgical or literary texts in new lands, such as Amherst Papyrus 63 and Ahiqar in Egypt, is also suggestive for the transmission in Babylon of what would become biblical works, with the imprint of Babylon highlighted in some cases (e.g., 2 Kings 23//Jeremiah 52; Jeremiah 29; 50–51; Ezekiel 10; and Psalm 137). Likewise, the funerary inscriptions from the environs of Tyre and of Jerusalem speak to comparable transregional identification made in the same genre.

On the other hand, there seem to be important differences. For example, old city names in Phoenicia continued to serve as markers of transregional Phoenician identity, while the old label "Lebanon" used for themselves appears rarely

---

tine, AYBRL (New Haven, CT/London: Yale University Press, 2019), 15–18, 115–142. Accordingly, van der Toorn prefers to call this identity "Jewish."

75 So the main title of Philip C. Schmitz, *The Phoenician Diaspora: Epigraphic and Historical Studies* (Winona Lake, IN: Eisenbrauns, 2012).

76 A classic work in this area is Paul Gilroy, *The Black Atlantic* (Cambridge, MA: Harvard University Press, 1993). Note what is called "the practice of peoplehood" in novels addressing diaspora identity, in Stefano Harney, *Nationalism and Identity: Culture and the Imagination in a Caribbean Diaspora* (Atlantic Highlands, NJ/London: Zed Books, 1996; repr., Kingston: University Press of the West Indies, 2006), 48–49. See further Bettina Schmidt, *Caribbean Diaspora in the USA: Diversity of Caribbean Religions in New York City* (London: Routledge, 2008). Such works are suggestive of the potential for a study of "diasporic historiography" in late biblical books and other works of the Persian and Hellenistic periods. In terms of postexilic diasporic experience of Yehudians/Jews, it is arguably echoed in some respects by Palestinian diasporic experience; see H. Lindholm Shulz, *The Palestinian Diaspora: Formation of Identities and Politics of Homeland* (London: Routledge, 2003).

at best (possibly in *bn lbnn*, "son of Lebanon" in an "early linear Phoenician" inscription on a jar discovered in a tomb at Tekke in Crete).[77] The name of Lebanon "serving to denote the Phoenician motherland"[78] is expressed, however, via divine names, for example Baal of Lebanon in a Phoenician inscription of the governor of Carthage in Cyprus (*KAI* 31.1) and Tnt in Lebanon in a Punic inscription from Carthage (*KAI* 81.1).[79] In these cases, deities carried the memory of an older homeland identity,[80] perhaps like Yahweh as the "god of Israel" in the postexilic period, for example in the doxologies in Pss 41:14, 72:18 and 106:48 (with other instances including Ezra 1:3; 3:2; 4:1, 3; 6:21; 7:6; 8:35; 9:4, 15; and Mal 2:16).[81]

The use of "Israel" in postexilic contexts varied considerably. It is not entirely clear that "Israel" was an assumed transregional identity in some communities involving persons that would be called Yehudian or Jewish. As indicated by the famous petition from the community in Elephantine to rebuild its temple (*TADAE* A4.7/Cowley 30), it was connected to authorities in both Jerusalem and Samaria. At the same time, the community did not (as far as is known) represent itself as a "people" or as members of the "Israel"[82] that some Persian-period biblical books apply to persons in Yehud. The terminological lack of "Israel" extends also to some postexilic works of the Hebrew Bible. This absence may be of little import in some Persian-period works, such as Haggai; it is also absent from the preexilic book of Habakkuk. However, it seems that a book like Esther might have used "Israel," as it famously evokes the figure of Saul (via Mordecai's genealogy in 2:5) and that king's ancient enemy (via Haman's genealogy in 3:1, 10; 9:24), as well as the last king of "Judah" (2:6). It is the "people

---

77 Frank Moore Cross, *Leaves from an Epigrapher's Notebook: Collected Papers in Hebrew and West Semitic Palaeography and Epigraphy*, HSS 51 (Winona Lake, IN: Eisenbrauns, 2003), 227 and 255.

78 Krahmalkov, *Phoenician-Punic Dictionary*, 253.

79 These titles are examples of DN in GN, as discussed in Mark S. Smith, *Where the Gods Are: Spatial Dimensions of Anthropomorphism in the Biblical World*, AYBRL (New Haven, CT/London: Yale University Press, 2016), 89–90.

80 Note also the PN *ʾmtbʿlḥṣry*, "handmaiden of the Tyrian Baal," in an inscription from Lepcis Magna, in Karel Jongeling and Robert M. Kerr, *Late Punic Epigraphy* (Tübingen: Mohr Siebeck, 2005), 22.

81 For the distribution of this divine title in the HB, see Stahl, "The 'God of Israel'," 728–737, with the general conclusion (p. 728): "the vast majority of attestations belong to Judahite writing dating to the late monarchic and, especially, postmonarchic periods."

82 Stahl, "The 'God of Israel'," 726. Not unlike the Elephantine papyri (*TADAE* A4.7/Cowley 30), Papyrus Amherst 63 refers to Judah as well as Samaria, but not to Israel. See col. xvii 3 according to Steiner, "The Aramaic Text in Demotic Script," 321; and van der Toorn, *Papyrus Amherst 63*, 75.

of Mordecai," specifically "all the Yehudians," whom Haman seeks to kill (3:6). "Israel" does not appear on the radar of the book of Esther. The terms Israel and Judah are absent from Jonah, though perhaps largely for literary reasons.[83] It may be that "Israel" as an identity marker may have differed among and perhaps even within the communities that produced the Persian- and Hellenistic-period works that became books of the Hebrew Bible.

Transgenerational and transregional in the Persian and Hellenistic periods, the people that could represent itself as "Israel" constituted an "imagined community,"[84] or perhaps better, an imagined community of communities. In any given liturgical act, its members may be collectively present either in person or not. In this sense, the absent may also be present, including those present and past as well as potentially future (see Pss 102:19; 128:6). This identity is not reducible to a single political reality, and it might not be restricted to a single "people" or "ethnicity" (note Isa 56:6–8). Indeed, the boundaries of this iden-

83 The book of Jonah focuses instead on the presence of the prophet's deity to the west in chapters 1–2 and then to the east in chapters 3–4. It also does not use "Judah," only "my land" (4:2, "my own country," in NJPS). When asked "where have you come from? what is your land?" (1:8), Jonah does not identify it (cf. "Canaan" in the same question in Gen 42:7, "Bethlehem of Judah" in Judg 17:9, and "Judah" in Papyrus Amherst 63, col. xvii 3, in van der Toorn, *Papyrus Amherst 63*, 75; cf. Steiner, "The Aramaic Text in Demotic Script," 321). Jonah's answer is, "I am an *ʿibrî*" (1:9), evidently denoting his foreignness relative to the unidentified sailors, presumably Phoenician. They are specifically Tyrians according to Peckham (*Phoenicia*, 372), as suggested by the reference to Tarshish in both Jonah 1.3 and the oracle against Tyre in Ezek 27:13. Sidonians also seem possible, given the association of Jaffa with Sidonian and Tyrian shippers in Ezra 3:7, along with the connection made between Jaffa and Lebanon in 2 Chr 2:15. The extrabiblical evidence allows for a fairly wide range of dates. Phoenician shipping in the area of Jaffa is known thanks to the two eighth-century shipwrecks off the coast of Ashkelon, discussed by Robert D. Ballard and Lawrence E. Stager, "Iron Age Shipwrecks in Deep Water off Ashkelon, Israel," *AJA* 106/2 (2002): 151–168. The Treaty of Esarhaddon with Baal of Tyre is likewise indicative (*ANET* 534): "May Baal-sameme, Baal-malaga and Baal-saphon raise an evil wind against your ships." A Persian-period Tyrian inscription engraved on the outside rim of a stone model of a boat sounds like a testimonial to the Phoenician storm god at sea ("[he has b]lessed Tyre and saved Sidonians from thick clouds" in Lemaire, *Levantine Epigraphy*, 23), not unlike Jonah's god in Jonah 1:4, 14–15. The sarcophagus inscription of Eshmunazor, king of Sidon, claims dominion over Jaffa (*KAI* 14.19; Lemaire, *Levantine Epigraphy*, 17). Cf. archaeological evidence of Phoenician influence in Persian-period Philistia, in Ephraim Stern, "The Phoenician Architectural Elements in Palestine during the Late Iron Age and the Persian Period," in *The Architecture of Ancient Israel: From the Prehistoric to the Persian Periods*, ed. Aharon Kempinski and Ronny Reich (Jerusalem: Israel Exploration Society, 1992), 302–309.

84 Cf. Benedict Anderson, *Imagined Communities: Reflections on the Origin and Spread of Nationalism* (London: Verso, 2006).

tity in the postexilic context could also be regarded in expansive terms: Egypt, too, is "my people," Assyria "my handiwork," and Israel "my inheritance" (Isa 19:25); Israel will be a "third" to Egypt and Assyria as a "blessing in the midst of the earth" (Isa 19:24).[85] This "imagined community" does not engage in a single religious praxis, as reflected by the diverse, multiple identities and practices of the community at Elephantine (cf. Isa 19:17–19)[86] and within the Hebrew Bible itself.[87] In sum, in several if not most postexilic books of the Hebrew Bible, the terms "people" and "Israel" express various dimensions of identity whether at home or abroad, while other works biblical and otherwise know such a transregional identity without reference to either term.

As evoked by the title of this volume in honor of Dan Fleming, *ʿām* in the Persian and Hellenistic periods may denote "a community of peoples," or perhaps for the noun's singular use "a people of communities," entailing a complex and shifting constellation of identities.[88] For the Psalter, the "liturgical people" represents one of the threads running through it as well as its "last word." These tentative remarks indicate the need for further study of *ʿām* in the Psalms and in other sources. For the moment, I conclude by expressing my great gratitude to Dan Fleming.[89]

---

85 See Bernd Schipper, "'The City by the Sea Will Be a Drying Place': Isaiah 19.1–25 in Light of Prophetic Texts from Ptolemaic Egypt," in *Monotheism in Late Prophetic and Early Apocalyptic Literature: Studies of the Sofja Kovalevskaja Research Group on Early Jewish Monotheism. Vol. III*, ed. Nathan MacDonald and Kenneth Brown, FAT 2/72 (Tübingen: Mohr Siebeck, 2014), 25–56.

86 See van der Toorn, *Becoming Diaspora Jews*; and Becking, *Identity in Persian Egypt*. According to Schipper ("'The City by the Sea'," 46), the community at Elephantine may be recalled in Isa 19:17.

87 For a recent discussion, see Benedikt Hensel, "Yahwistic Diversity and the Hebrew Bible: State of the Field, Desiderata, and Research Perspectives in a Necessary Debate on the Formative Period of Judaism(s)," in *Yahwistic Diversity and the Hebrew Bible: Tracing Perspectives on Group Identity from Judah, Samaria, and the Diaspora in Biblical Traditions*, ed. Benedikt Hensel, Dany Nocquet, and Bartosz Adamczewski, FAT 2/120 (Tübingen: Mohr Siebeck, 2020), 1–44. See also the essays in *Monotheism in Late Prophetic and Early Apocalyptic Literature: Studies of the Sofja Kovalevskaja Research Group on Early Jewish Monotheism. Vol. III*, ed. Nathan MacDonald and Ken Brown, FAT 2/72 (Tübingen: Mohr Siebeck, 2014).

88 Whether and/or how such identity anticipates the Jewish notion of *klal Yisrael* or Christian notions of "the (mystical) body of Christ" and the "universal Church" lies beyond the scope of this discussion.

89 And for their aid with various aspects of this piece, I thank the editors of this volume and the series editor, as well as Liz Bloch-Smith, Rachel Smith, and Karel van der Toorn.

Bibliography

Albright, William Foxwell. *Archaeology and the Religion of Israel*. 5th ed. Louisville, KY/London: Westminster John Knox, 2006.

Aubet, Maria Eugenia. *The Phoenicians and the West: Politics, Colonies, and Trade*. 2nd ed. Translated by Mary Turton. Cambridge: Cambridge University Press, 2001.

Anderson, Benedict. *Imagined Communities: Reflections on the Origin and Spread of Nationalism*. London: Verso, 2006.

Ballard, Robert D., and Lawrence E. Stager. "Iron Age Shipwrecks in Deep Water off Ashkelon, Israel." *AJA* 106/2 (2002): 151–168.

Barbiero, Gianni. "The Two Structures of Psalm 29." *VT* 66 (2016): 378–392.

Barthélemy, Dominique. *Critique textuelle de l'ancient Testament: Tome 4. Psaumes*. Edited by Stephen D. Ryan and Adrian Schenker. OBO 50/4. Fribourg: Academic Press; Göttingen: Vandenhoeck & Ruprecht, 2005.

Becking, Bob. *Identity in Persian Egypt: The Fate of the Yehudite Community of Elephantine*. University Park, PA: Eisenbrauns, 2020.

Bell, Catherine. *Ritual Theory, Ritual Practice*. Oxford: Oxford University Press, 1992.

Bellinger, William H., Jr. "Psalms and the Question of Genre." Pages 313–325 in *The Oxford Handbook of the Psalms*. Edited by William P. Brown. New York, NY/Oxford: Oxford University Press, 2014.

Benz, Frank L. *Personal Names in the Phoenician and Punic Inscriptions*. Studia Pohl 8. Rome: Biblical Institute Press, 1972.

Berlin, Adele. *The Dynamics of Biblical Parallelism*. Rev. and exp. ed. BRS. Grand Rapids, MI: Eerdmans; Dearborn, MI: Dove Booksellers, 2008.

Bonnet, Corinne. *Melqart: Cultes et mythes de l'Héraclès tyrien en Méditerranée*. Studia Phoenicia 8. Leuven: Peeters; Namur: Presses universitaires de Namur, 1988.

Bordreuil, Pierre, and Ahmed Ferjaoui. "À propose des « fils de Tyr» et des « fils de Carthage »." Pages 137–142 in *Studia Phoenicia VI*. Edited by Edward Lipiński. OLA 26. Leuven: Peeters, 1988.

Brettler, Marc Z. *God is King: Understanding an Israelite Metaphor*. JSOTSup 76. Sheffield: Sheffield Academic Press, 1989.

Burlington, Andrew R. "Writing and Literacy in the World of Ancient Israel: Recent Developments and Future Directions." *BO* 76/1–2 (2019): 46–74.

Carr, David M. *Writing on the Tablet of the Heart: Origins of Scripture and Literature*. New York, NY/Oxford: Oxford University Press, 2005.

Childs, Brevard S. *Introduction to the Old Testament as Scripture*. Philadelphia, PA: Fortress, 1979.

Childs, Brevard S. *Old Testament Theology in a Canonical Context*. Philadelphia, PA: Fortress, 1986.

Childs, Brevard S. "Psalm Titles and Midrashic Exegesis." *JSS* 16 (1971): 137–150.

Cohen, Shaye J.D. *The Beginnings of Jewishness: Boundaries, Varieties, Uncertainties*. Berkeley, CA: University of California Press, 1999.

Cowley, A.E. *Aramaic Papyri of the Fifth Century B.C.* Oxford: Clarendon Press, 1923.

Cross, Frank Moore. *From Epic to Canon: History and Literature in Ancient Israel*. Baltimore, MD/London: The Johns Hopkins University Press, 1998.

Cross, Frank Moore. *Leaves from an Epigrapher's Notebook: Collected Papers in Hebrew and West Semitic Palaeography and Epigraphy*. HSS 51. Winona Lake, IN: Eisenbrauns, 2003.

Davage, David W. "Why Davidic Superscriptions Do Not Demarcate Earlier Collections of Psalms." *JBL* 139 (2020): 67–86.

DeClaissé-Walford, Nancy L. "The Meta-Narrative of the Psalter." Pages 363–376 in *The Oxford Handbook of the Psalms*. Edited by William P. Brown. New York, NY/Oxford: Oxford University Press, 2014.

DeGrado, Jessie. *Authoring Empire: Assyria, Judah, and the Dynamics of Imperial Exchange*. In preparation.

Dobbs-Allsopp, Frederick W. *On Biblical Poetry*. New York, NY/Oxford: Oxford University Press, 2015.

Dobbs-Allsopp, Frederick W. "A Song of Love: Isaiah 5:1–7." Pages 218–251 in *Some Wine and Honey for Simon: Biblical and Ugaritic Aperitifs in Memory of Simon B. Parker*. Edited by A.J. Ferrera and H.B. Huffmon, with the assistance of S. Kozin. Eugene, OR: Pickwick, 2020.

Dobbs-Allsopp, F.W., J.J.M. Roberts, C.L. Seow, and R.E. Whitaker. *Hebrew Inscriptions: Texts from the Biblical Period of the Monarchy with Concordance*. New Haven, CT/London: Yale University Press, 2005.

Elayi, Josette. "The Relations between Tyre and Carthage during the Persian Period." *JANES* 13 (1981): 15–29.

Eskenazi, Tamara. *In an Age of Prose: A Literary Approach to Ezra–Nehemiah*. SBLMS 36. Atlanta, GA: Scholars Press, 1988.

Fensham, F.C. "Widow, Orphan, and the Poor in Ancient Near Eastern Legal and Wisdom Literature." *JNES* 21/2 (1962): 129–139.

Ferjaoui, Ahmed. *Recherches sur les relations entre l'Orient phénicien et Carthage*. OBO 124. Göttingen: Vandenhoeck & Ruprecht, 1993.

Finkelstein, Israel. "First Israel, Core Israel, United (Northern) Israel." *NEA* 82 (2019): 8–15.

Fishbane, Michael. *Biblical Interpretation in Ancient Israel*. Oxford: Clarendon Press, 1985.

Fitzmyer, Joseph A.S.J., and Daniel J. Harrington, S.J. *A Manual of Palestinian Aramaic Texts (Second Century B.C.—Second Century A.D.)*. BibOr 34. Third reprint. Rome: Pontificio Istituto Biblico, 2002.

Fleming, Daniel E. *The Legacy of Israel in Judah's Bible: History, Politics, and the Reinscribing of Tradition*. New York, NY/Cambridge: Cambridge University Press, 2012.

Gerstenberger, Erhard S. *Psalms: Part 1 with an Introduction to Cultic Poetry*. FOTL XIV. Grand Rapids, MI: Eerdmans, 1988.

Gibson, John C.L. *Textbook of Syrian Semitic Inscriptions: Volume III. Phoenician Inscriptions*. Oxford: Clarendon Press, 1982.

Gillingham, Susan E. "The Levites and the Editorial Composition of the Psalms." Pages 201–213 in *The Oxford Handbook of the Psalms*. Edited by William P. Brown. New York, NY/Oxford: Oxford University Press, 2014.

Gilroy, Paul. *The Black Atlantic*. Cambridge, MA: Harvard University Press, 1993.

Goldenberg, David M. *The Curse of Ham: Race and Slavery in Early Judaism, Christianity and Islam*. Princeton, NJ/London: Princeton University Press, 2003.

Good, Robert McClive. *The Sheep of His Pasture: A Study of the Hebrew Noun 'Am(m) and Its Semitic Cognates*. HSM 29. Chico, CA: Scholars Press, 1983.

Gottwald, Norman K. "Kingship in the Book of Psalms." Pages 437–444 in *The Oxford Handbook of the Psalms*. Edited by William P. Brown. New York, NY/Oxford: Oxford University Press, 2014.

Gruen, Erich S. "Did Ancient Identity Depend on Ethnicity? A Preliminary Probe." *Phoenix* 67 (2013): 1–22.

Gruen, Erich S. *Ethnicity in the Ancient World—Did It Matter?* Berlin: de Gruyter, 2020.

Gruen, Erich S. *The Construct of Identity in Hellenistic Judaism: Essays on Early Jewish Literature and History*. DCLS 29. Boston, MA/Berlin: de Gruyter, 2020.

Handy, Lowell K., ed. *Psalm 29 through Time and Tradition*. Eugene, OR: Pickwick, 2009.

Harney, Stefano. *Nationalism and Identity: Culture and the Imagination in a Caribbean Diaspora*. Atlantic Highlands, NJ/London: Zed Books, 1996. Repr., Kingston: University Press of the West Indies, 2006.

Hasler, Laura Carlson. *Archival Historiography in Jewish Antiquity*. New York, NY: Oxford University Press, 2020.

Hensel, Benedikt. "Yahwistic Diversity and the Hebrew Bible: State of the Field, Desiderata, and Research Perspectives in a Necessary Debate on the Formative Period of Judaism(s)." Pages 1–44 in *Yahwistic Diversity and the Hebrew Bible: Tracing Perspectives on Group Identity from Judah, Samaria, and the Diaspora in Biblical Traditions*. Edited by Benedikt Hensel, Dany Nocquet, and Bartosz Adamczewski. FAT 2/120. Tübingen: Mohr Siebeck, 2020.

Hossfeld, Frank-Lothar, and Erich Zenger. *Psalms 2: A Commentary on Psalms 51–100*. Edited by Klaus Baltzer. Translated by Linda M. Maloney. Hermeneia. Minneapolis, MN: Fortress Press, 2005.

Hossfeld, Frank-Lothar, and Erich Zenger. *Psalms 3: A Commentary on Psalms 101–150*. Edited by Klaus Baltzer. Translated by Linda M. Maloney. Hermeneia. Minneapolis, MN: Fortress Press, 2011.

John Huehnergard. "Biblical Hebrew Noun Patterns." Pages 25–64 in *Epigraphy, Philology, and the Hebrew Bible: Methodological Perspectives on Philological and Compara-*

tive Study of the Hebrew Bible in Honor of Jo Ann Hackett. Edited by Jeremy M. Hutton and Aaron D. Rubin. ANEM 12. Atlanta, GA: SBL Press, 2015.

Hurowitz, Wayne. *Mesopotamian Cosmic Geography*. 2nd printing with corrections and addenda. MC 8. Winona Lake, IN: Eisenbrauns, 2008.

K.D. Irani and Morris Silver, ed. *Social Justice in the Ancient World*. Westport, CT: Greenwood, 1995.

Jang, Ki-Eun. "The Sociology of 'Gentilics' in Biblical and Northwest Semitic Literature." Ph.D. diss., New York University, 2021.

Jigoulov, Vadim S. *The Social History of Achaemenid Phoenicia: Being a Phoenician, Negotiating Empires*. London: Equinox, 2010.

Jongeling, Karel, and Robert M. Kerr. *Late Punic Epigraphy*. Tübingen: Mohr Siebeck, 2005.

Kaufman, Brett. "A Citizen of Tyre in Sabatha: Colonial Identity in Punic North Africa." *Maarav* 16/1 (2009): 39–48.

Kelley, Robin D.G. "'But a Local Phase of a World Problem': Black History's Global Vision, 1883–1950." *Journal of American History* 86/3 (1999): 1045–1077.

Klein, Anja. "Sehnsucht nach Zion und Wunsch nach Vergeltung: Theologien des Exils in Psalms 137." Pages 159–172 in *Fromme und Frevler: Studien zu Psalmen und Weisheit: Festschrift für Hermann Spieckermann zum 70. Geburstag*. Edited by Corinna Körting and Reinhard Gregor Kratz. Tübingen: Mohr Siebeck, 2020.

Knohl, Israel. "Psalm 68: Structure, Composition and Geography." *JHS* 12, article 5 (2012). DOI:10.5508/jhs.2012.v.12.a15.

Koch, Klaus. *Der Gott Israels und die Götter des Orients: Religionsgeschichtliche Studien II. zum 80. Geburstag von Klaus Koch*. Edited by Friedhelm Hartenstein and Martin Rösel. FRLANT 216. Göttingen: Vandenhoeck & Ruprecht, 2007.

Krahmalkov, Charles. *Phoenician-Punic Dictionary*. OLA 90. Studia Phoenicia 15. Leuven: Peeters, 2000.

Kraus, Hans-Joachim. *Psalms 1–59: A Commentary*. Translated by Hilton C. Oswald. Minneapolis, MN: Augsburg, 1988.

Kutler, Lawrence. "A Structural Semantic Approach to Israelite Communal Terminology." *JANES* 14 (1982): 69–77.

Lemaire, André. *Levantine Epigraphy and History of the Achaemenid Period (539–332 BCE)*. The Schweich Lectures of the British Academy 2013. Oxford: Oxford University Press, 2015.

Leuenberger, Martin. *Konzeptionen des Königtums Gottes in Psalter: Untersuchungen zu Komposition Bücher IV–V im Psalter*. ATANT 83. Zürich: Theologischer Verlag Zurich, 2004.

Lipiński, Edward. "*ʿam*." *TDOT* 11:163–177.

Livingstone, Alasdair. *Court Poetry and Literary Miscellanea*. SAA 3. Helsinki: Helsinki University Press, 1989.

MacDonald, Nathan, and Ken Brown, ed. *Monotheism in Late Prophetic and Early Apocalyptic Literature: Studies of the Sofja Kovalevskaja Research Group on Early Jewish Monotheism. Vol. III*. FAT 2/72. Tübingen: Mohr Siebeck, 2014.

Maeir, Aren C. "On Defining Israel: Or, Let's do the *Kulturkreislehre* again!" *HeBAI* 10/2 (2021): 106–148.

Malamat, Abraham. "*Ummatum* in Old Babylonian Texts and Its Ugaritic and Biblical Counterparts." Festschrift für C.F.A. Schaeffer. *UF* 11 (1979): 527–536.

Mankowski, Paul V., S.J. *Akkadian Loanwords in Biblical Hebrew*. HSS 47. Winona Lake, IN: Eisenbrauns, 2000.

Mazzini, Giovanni. *The Ancient South Arabian Royal Edicts from the Southern Gate of Timnaʿ and the Ǧabal Labaḫ: A New Edition with Philological and Historical Commentary*. Epigraphische Forschungen auf der Arabischen Halbinsel 8. Wiesbaden: Ludwig Reichert, 2020.

Monroe, Lauren. "On the Origins and Development of Greater Israel." *HeBAI* 10/2 (2021): 187–227.

Monroe, Lauren, and Daniel E. Fleming. "Earliest Israel in Highland Company." *NEA* 82/1 (2019): 16–23.

Monroe, Lauren, and Daniel E. Fleming. "Israel before the Omrides." *HeBAI* 10/2 (2021): 97–105.

Najman, Hindy. "The Idea of Biblical Genre." Pages 307–321 in *Prayer and Poetry in the Dead Sea Scrolls and Related Literature: Essays in Honor of Eileen Schuller on the Occasion of Her 65th Birthday*. Edited by Jeremy Penner, Ken M. Penner, and Cecilia Wassen. STDJ 98. Boston, MA/Leiden: Brill, 2012.

Nissinen, Martti. *Prophets and Prophecy in the Ancient Near East*. Edited by Peter Machinist. 2nd ed. SBLWAW 41. Atlanta, GA: SBL, 2019.

Pearce, Laurie E. "Continuity and Normality in Sources Relating to the Judean Exile." *HeBAI* 3/2 (2014): 163–184.

Pearce, Laurie E., and Cornelia Wunsch. *Documents of Judean Exiles and West Semites in Babylonia in the Collection of David Sofer*. CUSAS 28. Bethesda, MD: CDL Press, 2014.

Peckham, J. Brian. *Phoenicia: Episodes and Anecdotes from the Ancient Mediterranean*. Winona Lake, IN: Eisenbrauns, 2014.

Porten, Bezalel, and Jerome A. Lund. *Aramaic Documents from Egypt: A-Key-Word-in-Context Concordance*. The Comprehensive Aramaic Lexicon Project Texts and Studies 1. Winona Lake, IN: Eisenbrauns, 2002.

Rainey, Brian. *Religion, Ethnicity and Xenophobia in the Bible: A Theoretical, Exegetical and Theological Survey*. New York, NY/London: Routledge, 2019.

Rubin, Aaron D. "The Form and Meaning of Hebrew *ʾašrê*." *VT* 60 (2010): 366–372.

Koskenniemi, E., and D.W. Davage, ed. *David, Messianism, and Eschatology: Ambiguity in the Reception History of the Book of Psalms in Judaism and Christianity*. Studies in the Reception History of the Bible 10. Abo: Abo Akademi University, 2021.

McCann, J. Clinton, Jr. "The Shape and Shaping of the Psalter: Psalms in Their Literary Context." Pages 350–362 in *The Oxford Handbook of the Psalms*. Edited by William P. Brown. New York, NY/Oxford: Oxford University Press, 2014.

Nissinen, Martti. *Prophets and Prophecy in the Ancient Near East*. Edited by Peter Machinist. 2nd ed. SBLWAW 41. Atlanta, GA: SBL, 2019.

Parpola, Simo. *Assyrian Prophecies*. SAA 9. Helsinki: Helsinki University Press, 1997.

Prothro, James B. "Theories of Inspiration and Catholic Exegesis: Scripture and Criticism in Dialogue with Denis Farkasfalvy." *CBQ* 83 (2021): 294–314.

Rollston, Christopher A. *Writing and Literacy in the World of Ancient Israel: Epigraphic Evidence from the Iron Age*. SBLABS 11. Atlanta, GA: SBL, 2010.

Sader, Hélène. *Iron Age Funerary Stelae from Lebanon*. Cuadernos de Arqueología Mediterránea 11. Barcelona: Edicions Bellaterra, 2005.

Sadler, Rodney S. "Singing a Subversive Song: Psalm 137 and 'Colored Pompey'." Pages 447–458 in *The Oxford Handbook of the Psalms*. Edited by William P. Brown. New York, NY/Oxford: Oxford University Press, 2014.

Sanders, Seth L. *The Invention of Hebrew*. Urbana/Chicago, IL: University of Illinois Press, 2009.

Schiffman, Lawrence H. "Israel." Pages 388–391 in *Encyclopedia of the Dead Sea Scrolls*. Edited by Lawrence H. Schiffman and James C. VanderKam. Vol. 1. New York, NY/Oxford: Oxford University Press, 2000.

Schipper, Bernd. "'The City by the Sea Will Be a Drying Place': Isaiah 19.1–25 in Light of Prophetic Texts from Ptolemaic Egypt." Pages 25–56 in *Monotheism in Late Prophetic and Early Apocalyptic Literature: Studies of the Sofja Kovalevskaja Research Group on Early Jewish Monotheism. Vol. III*. Edited by Nathan MacDonald and Ken Brown. FAT 2/72. Tübingen: Mohr Siebeck, 2014.

Schmidt, Bettina. *Caribbean Diaspora in the USA: Diversity of Caribbean Religions in New York City*. London: Routledge, 2008.

Schmidt, Brian B., ed. *Contextualizing Israel's Sacred Writings: Ancient Literary, Orality, and Literary Production*. AIL 22. Atlanta, GA: SBL Press, 2015.

Seybold, Klaus. "Zur Vorgeschichte der liturgischen Formel 'Amen'." *ThZ* 48 (1992): 109–117.

Schmitz, Philip C. *The Phoenician Diaspora: Epigraphic and Historical Studies*. Winona Lake, IN: Eisenbrauns, 2012.

Seow, C. Leong. "The Zakkur Inscription." Pages 253–257 in Martti Nissinen, *Prophets and Prophecy in the Ancient Near East*. Edited by Peter Machinist. 2nd ed. SBLWAW 41. Atlanta, GA: SBL, 2019.

Sergi, Omer. "On Scribal Tradition in Israel and Judah and the Antiquity of the Historiographical Narratives in the Hebrew Bible." Pages 275–299 in *Eigensinn und Entstehung der Hebräischen Bibel: Erhard Blum zum siebzigsten Geburtstag*. Edited by J.J. Krause, W. Oswald, and K. Weingart. Tübingen: Mohr Siebeck, 2020.

Shulz, H. Lindholm. *The Palestinian Diaspora: Formation of Identities and Politics of Homeland*. London: Routledge, 2003.

Ska, Jean Louis. "Why is the Chosen People Called Israel and Not Judah?" Pages 151–167 in *Yahwistic Diversity and the Hebrew Bible: Tracing Perspectives on Group Identity from Judah, Samaria, and the Diaspora in Biblical Traditions*. Edited by Benedikt Hensel, Dany Nocquet, and Bartosz Adamczewski. FAT 2/120. Tübingen: Mohr Siebeck, 2020.

Smith, Mark S. *Poetic Heroes: The Literary Commemoration of Warriors and Warrior Culture in the Early Biblical World*. Grand Rapids, MI/Cambridge: Eerdmans, 2014.

Smith, Mark S. "Taking Inspiration: Authorship, Revelation, and the Book of Psalms." Pages 244–273 in *Psalms and Practice: Worship, Virtue, and Authority*. Edited by Stephen Breck Reid. Collegeville, MN: Liturgical Press, 2001.

Smith, Mark S. "The Levitical Compilation of the Psalter." *ZAW* 103 (1991): 258–263.

Smith, Mark S. "The Theology of the Redaction of the Psalter: Some Observations." *ZAW* 104 (1992): 408–412.

Smith, Mark S. *Where the Gods Are: Spatial Dimensions of Anthropomorphism in the Biblical World*. AYBRL. New Haven, CT/London: Yale University Press, 2016.

Smith, Mark S., with contributions by Elizabeth M. Bloch-Smith. *The Pilgrimage Pattern in Exodus*. JSOTSup 239. Sheffield: Sheffield Academic Press, 1997.

Stahl, Michael J. *The "God of Israel" in History and Tradition*. VTSup 187. Leiden: Brill, 2021.

Stahl, Michael J. "The 'God of Israel' in Judah's Bible: Problems and Prospects." *JBL* 139 (2020): 721–745.

Steiner, Richard S. "The Aramaic Text in Demotic Script (1.99)." *COS* 1:309–328.

Stern, Ephraim. "The Phoenician Architectural Elements in Palestine during the Late Iron Age and the Persian Period." Pages 302–309 in *The Architecture of Ancient Israel: From the Prehistoric to the Persian Periods*. Edited by Aharon Kempinski and Ronny Reich. Jerusalem: Israel Exploration Society, 1992.

Schniedewind, William M. *How the Bible Became a Book*. Cambridge: Cambridge University Press, 2004.

Schniedewind, William M. *The Finger of the Scribe: How Scribes Learned to Write the Bible*. New York, NY: Oxford University Press, 2019.

Starbuck, Scott R.A. *Court Oracles in the Psalms: The So-Called Royal Psalms in their Ancient Near Eastern Context*. SBLDS 172. Atlanta, GA: Society of Biblical Literature, 1999.

Tazawa, Keiko. *Syro-Palestinian Deities in New Kingdom Egypt: The Hermeneutics of Their Existence*. BAR International Series 1965. Oxford: BAR Publishing, 2009.

van der Toorn, Karel. "Anat-Yahu, Some Other Deities, and the Jews at Elephantine." *Numen* 39 (1992): 80–101.

van der Toorn, Karel. *Becoming Diaspora Jews: Behind the Story of Elephantine*. AYBRL. New Haven/London: Yale University Press, 2019.

van der Toorn, Karel. *Papyrus Amherst 63*. AOAT 448. Münster: Ugarit-Verlag, 2018.

van der Toorn, Karel. *Scribal Culture and the Making of the Hebrew Bible*. Cambridge, MA/London: Harvard University Press, 2007.

Wearne, Gareth. "The Second Rubric in the Deir ʿAlla Plaster Texts as an Instruction for the Oral Performance of the Narrative." Pages 125–142 in *Registers and Modes of Communication in the Ancient Near East: Getting the Message Across*. Edited by Kyle H. Keimer and Gillan Davis. New York, NY/London: Routledge, 2018.

Westbrook, Raymond. "The Character of Ancient Near Eastern Law." Pages 1–90 in *A History of Ancient Near Eastern Law*. Edited by Raymond Westbrook. Vol. 1. HdO I/72:1. Boston, MA/Leiden: Brill, 2003.

Westenholz, Joan Goodnick. *The Legends of the Kings of Akkade: The Texts*. MC 7. Winona Lake, IN: Eisenbrauns, 1997.

Willgren, David. *The Formation of the 'Book' of Psalms: Reconsidering the Transmission and Canonization of Psalmody in Light of Material Culture and the Poetic Anthologies*. FAT 2/88. Tübingen: Mohr Siebeck, 2016.

Wright, David P. *Ritual in Narrative: The Dynamics of Feasting, Mourning, and Retaliation Rites in the Ugaritic Tale of Aqhat*. Winona Lake, IN: Eisenbrauns, 2001.

18

Pregnant with Meaning: The Politics of Gender Violence in the Mesha Stele's *Ḥērem*-List (KAI 181.16–17)

Michael J. Stahl

1 Introduction

The Louvre's Mesha Stele (*KAI* 181) is the longest extant Northwest Semitic inscription from the Iron Age southern Levant, and its contents and materiality have been the subject of numerous scholarly studies since its discovery in 1868 CE.[1] An unparalleled source of information about the political, social, and religious history of the region during the ninth century, the Mesha Stele further offers numerous points of comparison for the study of the Hebrew Bible and ancient Israel.[2] Indeed, the Mesha Stele is the earliest local nonbiblical source to mention Israel and the god YHWH, the people and deity whose story dominates the Hebrew Bible.[3] In particular, many scholars—including the honoree of this volume, Daniel Fleming[4]—have compared the Mesha Stele's reference to the practice of *ḥērem*-warfare against the Israelite town of Nebo (ll. 14–18) to the biblical tradition(s) of *ḥērem*-warfare in the account of Israel's conquest of the land of "Canaan" and the extermination of its indigenous peoples in the

1 For an entry point, see John Andrew Dearman, ed., *Studies in the Mesha Inscription and Moab*, ABS 2 (Atlanta, GA: Scholars Press, 1989); Bruce Routledge, "The Politics of Mesha: Segmented Identities and State Formation in Iron Age Moab," *JESHO* 43/3 (2000): 221–256; Routledge, *Moab in the Iron Age: Hegemony, Polity, Archaeology*, ACS (Philadelphia: University of Pennsylvania Press, 2004), 133–153; Bob Becking, "A Voice from across the Jordan: Royal Ideology as Implied in the Moabite Stela," in *Herrschaftslegitimation in vorderorientalischen Reichen der Eisenzeit*, ed. Christoph Levin and Reinhard Müller, ORA 21 (Tübingen: Mohr Siebeck, 2017), 125–145.

2 See, e.g., Nadav Na'aman, "Royal Inscription versus Prophetic Story: Mesha's Rebellion according to Biblical and Moabite Historiography," in *Ahab Agonistes: The Rise and Fall of the Omri Dynasty*, ed. Lester L. Grabbe, LHBOTS 421 (London: T&T Clark, 2007), 145–183; André Lemaire, "The Mesha Stele and the Omri Dynasty," in Grabbe, *Ahab Agonistes*, 135–144.

3 Karel Van der Toorn, "Yahweh," *DDD*: 910; Michael J. Stahl, "The Historical Origins of the Biblical God Yahweh," *RC* 14/11 (2020): e12378 (pp. 4–5).

4 Daniel E. Fleming, *The Legacy of Israel in Judah's Bible: History, Politics, and the Reinscribing of Tradition* (Cambridge: Cambridge University Press, 2012), 125–128, 137–143.

 | DOI:10.1163/9789004511538_019

books of Deuteronomy and Joshua (see Deut 7:1–6; 13:12–18; 20:16–18; Josh 6:20–21; 8:24–29; 10:1, 28, 34–42; 11:10–23; cf. also Num 21:1–3; Deut 2:31–37; 3:1–7; Josh 2:10; Judg 1:17; 1 Sam 15; 1 Kgs 9:20–21).[5] Both the Mesha Stele and the biblical texts, as well as Sabean sources from South Arabia (RES 3945; DAI Ṣirwāḥ),[6] present *ḥērem*-warfare as a religiously inflected political act in which an invading people targeted an enemy town, annihilated (some significant portion of) its population, and consecrated the slaughter to the attacking group's deity.[7] As a political-religious custom historically localized to the Iron Age southern Levant and South Arabia,[8] *ḥērem*-warfare—whether in actual practice or

---

5 S.-M. Kang, *Divine War in the Old Testament and in the Ancient Near East*, BZAW 177 (Berlin: de Gruyter, 1989), 80–84; Lauren A.S. Monroe, "Israelite, Moabite and Sabaean War-*ḥērem* Traditions and the Forging of National Identity: Reconsidering the Sabaean Text RES 3945 in Light of Biblical and Moabite Evidence," *VT* 57 (2007): 318–341; Reinhard Achenbach, "Divine Warfare and YHWH's Wars: Religious Ideologies of War in the Ancient Near East and in the Old Testament," in *The Ancient Near East in the 12th–10th Centuries BCE*, ed. Gershon Galil et al., AOAT 392 (Münster: Ugarit-Verlag, 2012), 1–16.

6 Monroe, "Israelite, Moabite and Sabaean War-*ḥērem* Traditions," 318–341; George Hatke, "For 'Īlmuquh and for Saba': The *Res Gestae* of Karib'īl Bin Ḏhamar'alī from Ṣirwāḥ in Context," *Wiener Zeitschrift für die Kunde des Morgenlandes* 105 (2015): 87–133; cf. Alessandra Avanzini, "Review of Norbert Nebes, *Der Tatenbericht des Yiṯaʿʾamar Watar Bin Yakrubmalik aus Ṣirwāḥ (Jemen): Zur Geschichte Südarabiens im frühen 1. Jahrtausend vor Christus*," *JSS* 63 (2018): 532–543.

7 On the concept of *ḥērem*-warfare in the Hebrew Bible, see C.H.W. Brekelmans, *De Ḥerem in het Oude Testament* (Nijmegen: Centrale Drukkerij, 1959); Moshe Weinfeld, "The Conquest of Canaan Land and the Native Ḥerem," *Beth Mikra* 12 (1967): 123–124 (in Hebrew); Weinfeld, "The Ban on the Canaanites in the Biblical Codes," in *History and Traditions of Early Israel*, ed. André Lemaire and Benedikt Otzen, VTSup 50 (Leiden: Brill, 1993), 142–160; Weinfeld, *The Promise of the Land: The Inheritance of the Land of Canaan by the Israelites* (Berkeley, CA: University of California Press, 1993), 76–120; Philip D. Stern, "1 Samuel 15: Towards an Ancient View of the War-Ḥerem," *UF* 21 (1989): 414–444; Stern, *The Biblical* Ḥerem: *A Window on Israel's Religious Experience* (Atlanta, GA: Scholars Press, 1991); Susan Niditch, *War in the Hebrew Bible: A Study in the Ethics of Violence* (Oxford: Oxford University Press, 1993), 28–77; Walter Dietrich, "The 'Ban' in the Age of Israel's Early Kings," in *The Origins of the Ancient Israelite State*, ed. Volkmar Fritz and Philip R. Davies, JSOTSup 228 (Sheffield: Sheffield Academic Press, 1996), 196–210; Richard Nelson, "*Ḥerem* and the Deuteronomic Social Conscience," in *Deuteronomy and Deuteronomic Literature: Festschrift for C.H.W. Brekelmans*, ed. Marc Vervenne and Johan Lust (Leuven: Leuven University Press/Peeters, 1997), 39–54; Frank Crüsemann, "Gewaltimagination als Teil der Ursprungsgeschichte: Banngebot und Rechtsordnung im Deuteronomium," in *Religion, Politik, und Gewalt: Kongressband des XII. Europäischen Kongresses für Theologie, 18.–22. September 2005 in Berlin*, ed. Friedrich Schweitzer (Gütersloh: Gütersloher Verlagshaus, 2006), 343–360; Rüdiger Schmitt, *Der "Heilige Krieg" im Pentateuch und im deuteronomistischen Geschichtswerk: Studien zur Forschungs-, Rezeptions- und Religionsgeschichte von Krieg und Bann im Alten Testament*, AOAT 381 (Münster: Ugarit-Verlag, 2011).

8 See further Michael J. Stahl, "*Ḥērem*-Warfare at Ugarit? Reevaluating *KTU* 1.13 and *KTU* 1.3 II," *UF* (2016): 287–291.

in its literary presentation—functioned to replace the indigenous population of a defeated town with that of the conquerors. Ideologically, the practice or literary representation of *ḥērem*-warfare served to assert the victor's political rights over the conquered land, guaranteed on the divine level by the victorious group's deity.[9]

While scholarship often focuses on the historical dimensions of *ḥērem*-warfare, some scholars emphasize the ethical problems it raises.[10] Joining concern for both the historical and the ethical, this study combines philology with postcolonial and critical feminist theoretical tools to offer a fresh historical interpretation of the religious politics of King Mesha's literary portrayal of *ḥērem*-warfare by analyzing the gendered dimensions of the Mesha Stele's *ḥērem*-list (ll. 16–17), which specifies five gendered subgroups within Nebo's slaughtered population.[11] In particular, I argue on contextual, etymo-

9 Monroe, "Israelite, Moabite and Sabaean War-*ḥērem* Traditions," 318–341.

10 Hubert Junker, "Der alttestamentliche Bann geben heidnische Völker als moraltheologisches und offenbarungsgeschichtliches Problem," *TTZ* 3/4 (1947): 74–89; Peter Craigie, *The Problem of War in the Old Testament* (Grand Rapids, MI: Eerdmans, 1978); Edward Said, "Michael Walzer's 'Exodus and Revolution: A Canaanite Reading'," *Grand Street* 5/2 (1986): 86–106; Robert A. Warrior, "Canaanites, Cowboys, and Indians," *Christianity and Crisis* 49 (1989): 261–265; Lawson Stone, "Ethical and Apologetic Tendencies in the Redaction of the Book of Joshua," *CBQ* 53 (1991): 25–36; Andreas Ruffing, *Jahwekrieg als Weltmetapher: Studien zu Jahwekriegstexten des chronistischen Sondergutes*, SBB 24 (Stuttgart: Katholisches Bibelwerk, 1992); Rannfrid I. Thelle, "The Biblical Conquest Account and Its Modern Hermeneutical Challenges," *ST* 61 (2007): 61–81; Ziony Zevit, "The Search for Violence in Israelite Culture and in the Bible," in *Religion and Violence: The Biblical Heritage*, David A. Bernat and Jonathan Klawans, RRBS 2 (Sheffield: Sheffield Phoenix, 2007), 16–37; R.W.L. Moberly, "Is Election Bad for You?," in *The Centre and the Periphery: A European Tribute to Walter Brueggemann*, ed. Jill Middlemas, David J.A. Clines, and Else K. Holt, HBM 27 (Sheffield: Sheffield Phoenix Press, 2010), 95–111; David Frankel, *The Land of Canaan and the Destiny of Israel: Theologies of Territory in the Hebrew Bible* (Winona Lake, IN: Eisenbrauns, 2011); Wes Morriston, "Ethical Criticism of the Bible: The Case of Divinely Mandated Genocide," *Sophia* 51 (2012): 117–135; Mary Crist, "Frybread in Canaan," *First Peoples Theology Journal* 7 (2014): 2–15; Pekka Pitkänen, "Ancient Israel and Settler Colonialism," *Settler Colonial Studies* 4 (2014): 64–81; Isaac S.D. Sassoon, "Obliterating Cherem," *TheTorah.com* (2015) https://thetorah.com/article/obliterating-cherem; Christian Hofreiter, *Making Sense of Old Testament Genocide: Christian Interpretations of Herem Passages*, Oxford Theology and Religion Monographs (Oxford: Oxford University Press, 2018); Mark R. Glanville, "Ethics of Reading Unethical Texts Ethically: A Fresh Reading of *ḤEREM* in Deuteronomy and Joshua" (paper presented at the annual meeting of the Society of Biblical Literature, 7 December, 2020).

11 Cf. the combination of historical/philological and ethical analysis in Carly L. Crouch, *War and Ethics in the Ancient Near East: Military Violence in Light of Cosmology and History*, BZAW 40 (Berlin: de Gruyter, 2009), 174–189; Seth Sanders, "The Referent of West Semitic

logical, literary, and conceptual grounds that the *ḥērem*-inventory's final term, *rḥmt* (l. 17)—commonly translated by scholars as "female slaves," "maidservants," "concubines," or the like—most likely refers to "pregnant women." In its culmination with pregnant women, the Mesha Stele's *ḥērem*-list rhetorically demonstrates the king's complete fulfillment of his religious obligations to the Moabite god Kemosh, as well as Moab and Kemosh's political dominance over Israel and its god YHWH. Pregnant women (and their fetuses) were highly vulnerable members of ancient society whose continued existence harbored the potentiality for the social and political rebirth of the Israelite "Other." Religiously sanctioning violence against the bodies of "foreign" pregnant women thus serves as a special point of emphasis in the construction of the boundaries of an independent Moabite political identity ideologically centered on the institution of divine kingship.

I originally proposed the idea that the noun *rḥmt* might actually refer to pregnant women when I first read the Mesha Stele in full under Dan's tutelage as a first-year doctoral student in his seminar on "Northwest Semitic Inscriptions" at New York University (Spring 2013). To this day, I can still remember timidly raising my hand in class to propose the idea. I can also recall Dan's face lighting up at the suggestion, along with his enthusiastic response: "You know, I like that!" It is therefore a pleasure to offer this article in honor of Dan, whose enduring contributions to the study of the peoples of the Hebrew Bible and ancient Near East comprise not only his own ground-breaking scholarship, but also the community of rising scholars—including many of the contributors in this volume, such as myself—whose intellectual formation is indebted to Dan's teaching, mentorship, and friendship.

2 Mesha's Campaigns against Ataroth and Nebo: Text and Translation

At the oracular command of the Moabite god Kemosh, King Mesha of Moab recounts in *KAI* 181.14–18a his successful imposition of *ḥērem* on Nebo, an Israelite town east of the Jordan River that maintained a cult to Israel's god YHWH during the Omride period. The account of Mesha's attack on Nebo, in turn, belongs to a larger textual unit with its own literary and conceptual integrity that begins in l. 10b with Mesha's assault on the town of Ataroth.[12] As

**ḥrm*: Ancient Genocide and the Ethics of Philology" (unpublished paper). I wish to thank Seth for providing me with a pre-publication version of his paper.

12 Max Miller, "The Moabite Stone as a Memorial Stela," *PEQ* 106 (1974): 17; Alviero Niccacci, "The Stele of Mesha and the Bible: Verbal System and Narrativity," *Or* 63 (1994): 226–

Bruce Routledge and other scholars point out, the ancient equivalent to paragraphs in the Mesha Stele are introduced by a noun phrase plus finite verb (ll. 5, 7b, 10b, 19, and 31b), a construction that frames ll. 10b–18a.[13] The two campaigns are further connected through shared thematic and linguistic elements, such as the total slaughtering of the enemy, the removal of important objects, etc.[14] In what follows, I provide a transliteration and translation of these lines, with critical notes that inform the historical interpretation to follow.[15]

10b	Now the people of Gad lived in the land of Ataroth[16] from time immemorial, and the king of	*|wʾš.gd.yšb.bʾrṣ.ʿṭrt.mʿlm.wybn.lh. mlk.y*

248; Simon Parker, *Stories in Scripture and Inscriptions: Comparative Studies on Narratives in Northwest Semitic Inscriptions and the Hebrew Bible* (Oxford: Oxford University Press, 1997), 44–58; Anson F. Rainey, "Syntax, Hermeneutics and History," *IEJ* 48 (1998): 239–251; Routledge, "Politics of Mesha," 227–231; Routledge, *Moab*, 141–143; cf. J.C.L. Gibson, *Syrian Semitic Inscriptions, Vol. 1: Hebrew and Moabite* (Oxford: Clarendon Press, 1971), 74.

13 Routledge, *Moab*, 143; cf. Shmuel Aḥituv, *Echoes from the Past: Hebrew and Cognate Inscriptions from the Biblical Period* (Jerusalem: Carta, 2008), 403.

14 Parker, *Stories*, 51.

15 I have reproduced the text as it appears in the latest edition of Herbert Donner and Wolfgang Röllig's standard reference work (*KAI* 181). Textual-critical matters, including any preferred readings that deviate from this edition, are discussed in the footnotes to the translation.

16 Many scholars identify the "people (lit. 'man') of Gad" who inhabit the "land of Ataroth" as an Israelite tribe that Mesha slaughters in his attack on the fortified town of Ataroth (e.g., J. Liver, "The Wars of Mesha, King of Moab," *PEQ* 99 [1967]: 16; Gibson, *Syriac Semitic Inscriptions*, 79; Gary Rendsburg, "A Reconstruction of Moabite-Israelite History," *JANES* 13 [1981]: 68; Gerald L. Mattingly, "Moabite Religion and the Meshaʿ Inscription," in Dearman, *Studies in the Mesha Inscription*, 235; Rainey, "Syntax," 244–245; Routledge, "Politics of Mesha," 238 and n. 48; Eveline J. Van der Steen and Klaas A.D. Smelik, "King Mesha and the Tribe of Dibon," *JSOT* 32 [2007]: 152; contrast Nadav Na'aman, "King Mesha and the Foundation of the Moabite Monarchy," *IEJ* 47 [1997]: 83–92, who understands the people of Gad to be Moabite). However, Daniel Fleming observes (*Legacy*, 245) that "Gad is not called a 'tribe,' but it is defined as more than the town that Israel's king had built (or rebuilt), and not defined by any town. Interestingly, the Mesha text mentions Gad more by way of commentary than as an object of royal ire. Israel's fortified city of Aṭarot is the target, identified by its longstanding location among the Gad people, and only the townspeople are slaughtered *ḥērem*-style with no further reference to Gad. It is as if they were not even considered part of Israel, and one could conclude that with Aṭarot now in Mesha's hands, the Gad population was his as well, not by forced submission but simply as a transfer from one outside royal power to another." I agree with Fleming that the "people of Gad" cannot be identified in this early period as either Moabite or Israelite—let alone as an Israelite "tribe"—and that the Mesha Stele does not claim that Mesha slaughtered this population (though, *pace* Fleming, the text does not state that the inhabitants of the town of Ataroth were slaugh-

11	Israel fortified Ataroth for himself/ them.[17] I fought against the town and seized it. I killed all the people.	*śrʾl.ʾt.ʿṭrt|wʾltḥm.bqr.wʾḥzh|wʾhrg.ʾt. kl.hʿm.*
12	The city became the possession of[18] Kemosh and Moab. I captured from there the *ʾr-ʾl*(-statue)[19] of its *dwd*[20] and	*hqr.hyt.lkmš.wlmʾb|wʾšb.mšm.ʾt.ʾrʾl. dwdh.wʾ*[*s*]

---

tered in conjunction with *ḥērem*). Rather, the text identifies this collective entity only as the "people of Gad" in connection with the "land"—not the town—of Ataroth. Cf. Parker, *Stories*, 49–50.

17 The question here is whether the preposition *lh* refers to the "people of Gad" or the king of Israel. Routledge ("The Politics of Mesha," 248 and n. 89), following Rainey ("Syntax," 244–245), argues for the former. Aḥituv also prefers this option (*Echoes*, 404). Rainey's argument is syntactical-rhetorical: Mesha contrasts the people's fate with the fact that the town itself was turned over to the deity. He highlights the fact that *hqr* is topicalized with a following suffix-conjugation verb and notes that this type of syntactical construction can be used as a mechanism for contrast ("Syntax," 245 n. 26). However, Liver ("Wars of Mesha," 24) understands this preposition as referring to the king of Israel, as does Walter Dietrich ("The 'Ban'," 202), Gibson (*Syrian Semitic Inscriptions*, 76), André Lemaire ("'House of David' Restored in Moabite Inscription," *BAR* 20/3 [1994]: 30–37), A.H. Van Zyl (*The Moabites*, Pretoria Oriental Series 3 [Leiden: Brill, 1960], 190), A.F.L. Beeston ("Mesha and Ataroth," *JRAS* [1985]: 143), and Kent P. Jackson ("The Language of the Meshaʿ Inscription," in Dearman, *Studies in the Mesha Inscription and Moab*, 97). Parker (*Stories*, 45) provides translations for both options, as I do here.

18 For the translation "became the possession of," reading *hyt* for the old reading *ryt*, see André Lemaire, "Notes d'épigraphie nord-ouest Semitique," *Syria* 64 (1987): 205–214; Lemaire, "New Photographs and *ryt* or *hyt* in Mesha, Line 12," *IEJ* 57 (2007): 204–207 (contra Aaron Schade, "New Photographs Supporting the Reading *ryt* in Line 12 of the Mesha Inscription," *IEJ* 55 [2005]: 205–208); H. An, "Some Additional Epigraphic Comments on the Mesha Stele: The Case for Reading *hyt* in Line 12," *Maarav* 17 (2010): 149–172. This reconstruction has become standard in recent scholarship; see Routledge, "The Politics of Mesha," 248 n. 90; Routledge, *Moab*, 135; Rainey, "Syntax," 244; Parker, *Stories*, 45; Aḥituv, *Echoes*, 405. Thus, this new reading renders older discussions about the difficult term *ryt* unnecessary (cf. Liver, "Wars of Mesha," 24–25 and n. 33; Van Zyl, *Moabites*, 141, 175, 190; Susan Niditch, *War in the Hebrew Bible*, 39; Nelson, "*Ḥerem* and the Deuteronomic Social Conscience," 47; Gibson, *Syrian Semitic Inscriptions*, 79–80; Gary Rendsburg, "ואשב in the Mesha Stele, Line 12," *Maarav* 14 [2007]: 9, 24–25; Mattingly, "Moabite Religion," 235; Beeston, "Mesha and Ataroth," 143; Jackson, "Language," 98, 111–112).

19 Scholars have offered numerous possibilities for the difficult term *ʾr-ʾl*, which Mesha captures and drags before Kemosh in Qirioth. For some of the options, see Beeston, "Mesha and Ataroth," 144–145; Jackson, "Language," 98, 112–113; Aḥituv, *Echoes*, 405–406. Religious-comparative evidence and the partial analogy with l. 17 suggests that the *ʾr-ʾl* should refer to a cult item, probably a divine statue (Ryan Thomas, p.c.). Thus, Routledge writes ("The Politics of Mesha," 248 n. 91) that the *ʾr-ʾl* "should be some sort of cultic object, favoring the translation 'the altar-hearth of its beloved (i.e., city-god)' … or 'the lion-statue of its beloved (i.e., city-god)'." Cf. Gibson, *Syrian Semitic Inscriptions*, 76; Mattingly, "Moabite

<table>
<tr><td>13</td><td>[dra]gged it before Kemosh in Qirioth. I settled in it the people of Sharon and the people of</td><td>ḥbh.lpny.kmš.bqryt|wʾšb.bh.ʾt.ʾš.šrn. wʾt.ʾš.</td></tr>
<tr><td>14</td><td>Maharoth. (Then) Kemosh said to me: “Go! Seize Nebo from Israel!”[21] I</td><td>mḥrt|wyʾmr.ly.kmš.lk.ʾḥz.ʾt.nbh.ʿl. yśrʾl|wʾ</td></tr>
<tr><td>15</td><td>went in the night and fought against it from the breaking of dawn until noon.</td><td>hlk.bllh.wʾltḥmbh.mbqʿ.hšḥrt.ʿd. hṣhrn|wʾḥ</td></tr>
<tr><td>16</td><td>I seized it and slew all [of it]: seven thousand men and boys, women and girls,[22]</td><td>zh.wʾhrg.kl[h].šbʿt.ʾlpn[.]g[b]rn. wgrn|wgbrt.wg[r]</td></tr>
</table>

Religion,” 235; Nadav Na’aman, “The Campaign of Mesha against Horonaim,” *BN* 73 (1994): 27–28; Dietrich, “The ‘Ban’,” 202–203; Rainey, “Syntax,” 244; Rendsburg, “ואשב in the Mesha Stele,” 21 n. 21. On the politics of godnapping in the ancient Near East, see Steven W. Cole and Peter Machinist, ed., *Letters from Priests to the Kings Esarhaddon and Assurbanipal*, SAA 13 (Helsinki: Helsinki University Press, 1998), esp. 11–13, 134–153; Kathryn F. Kravitz, “Divine Trophies of War in Assyria and Ancient Israel: Case Studies in Political Theology” (Ph.D. diss., Brandeis University, 1999); Barbara N. Porter, “Gods’ Statues as a Tool of Assyrian Political Policy: Esarhaddon’s Return of Marduk to Babylon,” in *Religious Transformations and Socio-Political Change: Eastern Europe and Latin America*, ed. Luther Martin, RelSoc 33 (Berlin: de Gruyter, 1999), 9–24; Erika D. Johnson, “Stealing the Enemy’s Gods: An Exploration of the Phenomenon of Godnap in Ancient Western Asia” (Ph.D. diss., University of Birmingham, 2011); Hanspeter Schaudig, “Death of Statues and Rebirth of Gods,” in *Iconoclasm and Text: Destruction in the Ancient Near East and Beyond*, ed. Natalie N. May, OIS 8 (Chicago, IL: Oriental Institute, 2012), 123–149; Shana Zaia, “State-Sponsored Sacrilege: ‘Godnapping’ and Omission in Neo-Assyrian Inscriptions,” *JANEH* 2 (2015): 19–54; Becking, “A Voice from across the Jordan,” 131–135.

20 For the interpretive possibilities of this difficult term, see Gibson, *Syrian Semitic Inscriptions*, 80; Beeston, “Mesha and Ataroth,” 145; Mattingly, “Moabite Religion,” 236; Jackson, “Language,” 112–113; Aḥituv, *Echoes*, 405–407.

21 As Parker observes (*Stories*, 50), the means of communication for this oracle are left unstated, and the text never claims that Mesha promised to “devote” (**ḥrm*) the town to the deity. This fact is “disclosed as an analepsis or flashback only after he has carried it out (see l. 17)” (Parker, *Stories*, 51). Cf. Num 21:2; Josh 6:16–17.

22 For the translation/interpretation of the terms *g*[*b*]*rn*, *grn*, *gbrt*, and *g*[*r*]*t* as “men,” “boys,” “women,” and “girls,” respectively, see further Liver, “Wars of Mesha,” 25; William F. Albright, “The Moabite Stone,” *ANET* 320; Lemaire, “Notes,” 207–208; Na’aman, “Royal Inscription,” 147; Aḥituv, *Echoes*, 394, 409; cf. Mark Lidzbarski, *Ephemeris für semitische Epigraphik* (Giessen: Töpelmann, 1902), 7; Lidzbarski, *Kanaanäische Inschriften* (*Moabitisch, Althebräisch, Phönizisch, Punisch*) (Giessen: Töpelmann, 1907), 7; van Zyl, *Moabites*, 141. Contrast Gibson, *Syrian Semitic Inscriptions*, 76 (“men and women, both natives and aliens” [but cf. p. 80]); Niditch, *War*, 31 (“native men, foreign men, native women, foreign women”); Routledge, “Politics of Mesha,” 248; Routledge, *Moab*, 136 (“male citizens and foreign men / female citizens, foreign women”); Parker, *Stories*, 45 (“men and male aliens, and women and female aliens”); cf. Pierre Bordreuil, “A propos de l’inscription de Meshaʿ: deux

<table>
<tr><td>17</td><td>and pregnant women. It was to Ashtar-Kemosh[23] (that) I devoted it to destruction. I took from there</td><td>t.wrḥmt|ky.lʿštr.kmš.hḥrmth|wʾqḥ.
mšmʾ[t.k]</td></tr>
<tr><td>18a</td><td>YHWH's [ves]sels[24] and I dragged them before Kemosh.</td><td>ly.yhwh.wʾsḥb.hm.lpny.kmš|</td></tr>
</table>

3 *Rḥmt*: "Pregnant Women"?

Mesha's campaigns against Ataroth and Nebo have received much attention from biblical scholars on account of their importance for elucidating the bib-

---

notes," in *The World of the Aramaeans, III: Studies in Language and Literature in Honour of Paul-Eugène Dion*, ed. P.M. Michèle Daviau, John W. Wevers, and Michael Weigl, JSOTSup 326 (Sheffield: Sheffield Academic Press, 2001), 158–162.

23 Some scholars have suggested that Ashtar-Kemosh may be the Moabite god Kemosh's consort (Van Zyl, *Moabites*, 196–197, 199; Kang, *Divine War*, 77; Thomas Römer, *The Invention of God*, trans. Raymond Guess [Cambridge, MA: Harvard University Press, 2015], 160; Römer, "L'énigme de 'Ashtar-Kemosh dans la stèle de Mésha," in *Alphabets, Texts and Artifacts in the Ancient Near East: Studies presented to Benjamin Sass*, ed. Israel Finkelstein, Christian J. Robin, and Thomas Römer [Paris: Van Dieren, 2016], 385–394). This seems unlikely since both Ashtar and Kemosh were male deities (Josey Bridges Snyder, "Chemosh Looks Like YHWH, but That's Okay," in Collin Cornell, ed., *Divine Doppelgängers: YHWH's Ancient Look-Alikes* [University Park, PA: Eisenbrauns—PSU Press, 2020]), 120–121; Josey Bridges Snyder and Brent A. Strawn, "Reading (in) Moabite Patterns: 'Parallelism' in the Mesha Inscription and Its Implications for Understanding Three Cruxes (*ʿštr kmš*, line 17; *h/ryt*, line 12; and *ʾrʾl dwdh*, line 12)," forthcoming; cf. Gibson, *Syrian Semitic Inscriptions*, 81. Snyder ("Chemosh Looks Like YHWH," 120–121) also argues that it is likely Ashtar-Kemosh "is used as an alternative name for Chemosh," since "[i]t would not make sense for Mesha to devote the city to a deity other than the one who commanded him to conquer it, especially when the Mesha Inscription never refers to a deity other than Chemosh." Instead, "the name Ashtar-Chemosh might reflect the assimilation of characteristics of a deity Ashtar into the deity Chemosh" (Snyder, "Chemosh Looks Like YHWH," 121).

24 For the traditional restoration [*k*]*ly*, "vessels," see further van Zyl, *Moabites*, 191 and n. 6; Liver, "Wars of Mesha," 25; Dietrich, "The 'Ban'," 203; Routledge, "Politics of Mesha," 248 n. 91; Na'aman, "Royal Inscription," 148 and n. 7; Aḥituv, *Echoes*, 410; cf. Jackson, "Language," 98, 116; Kent P. Jackson and J. Andrew Dearman, "The Text of the Meshaʿ Inscription," in Dearman, *Studies in the Mesha Inscription*, 94 and n. 5; Rendsburg, "ואשב in the Mesha Stele," 22 and n. 58. Other proposals include: ʾ[*y*]*ly*, "leaders" (lit. "rams") (so Edward Lipiński, "Etymological and Exegetical Notes on the Mešaʿ Inscription," *Or* 40 [1971]: 335; cf. Mattingly, "Moabite Religion," 237); and ʾ[*ry*]*ly*, "prophets" (see Gösta W. Ahlström, *Royal Administration and National Religion in Ancient Palestine*, SHANE 1 [Leiden: Brill, 1982], 14; Beeston, "Mesha and Ataroth," 146–148; Lemaire, "Notes," 208–209; Rainey, "Syntax," 249; Parker, *Stories*, 45).

lical *ḥērem*, often translated "ban, devoted to destruction," or the like.[25] My present concern is with clarifying the meaning and significance of one difficult term in this text: *rḥmt* in l. 17.

Scholars typically translate *rḥmt* in *KAI* 181.17 as "female slaves," "maidservants," "concubines," etc.[26] In proposing this translation, scholars often cite Judg 5:30 for comparative purposes: "Are (Sisera and his soldiers) not finding and distributing the spoil—a girl? or two? for each man?" (הלא ימצאו יחלקו שלל לראש גבר רַחַם רַחֲמָתַיִם). However, the translation of this passage is difficult. The Hebrew feminine (dual) nominal form רַחֲמָתַיִם occurs only here. *HALOT* provides רַחֲמָתַיִם with its own entry, *רַחֲמָה, an unattested feminine singular noun said to be derived from רַחַם, evidently a biform of the well-attested noun רֶחֶם.[27] Comparing the Moabite noun *rḥmt* in *KAI* 181.17, Koehler and Baumgartner interpret רַחַם רַחֲמָתַיִם as follows: "one or two laps, a euphemism for vaginas, meaning one or two women as spoils of war, bed-mates, in vulgar conversation of soldiers."[28] However, there are no other instances in the Hebrew Bible where the noun רֶחֶם, by metonymy, means "maiden, girl," let alone "slave girl, maidservant, concubine," etc. Rather, as with its cognates in Akkadian (*rēmu*), Arabic (*raḥim, riḥm*), Aramaic (רַחְמָא), and Syriac (*raḥmā*), the Hebrew noun's primary meaning is "womb" (see Gen 20:18, 29:31, 30:22, 49:25; Num 12:12; 1Sam 1:5; Isa 46:3; Jer 1:5, 20:17–18; Hos 9:14; Pss 22:11, 58:4, 110:3; Prov 30:16; Job 3:11, 10:18, 31:15, 38:8; cf. Job 24:20).[29]

HALOT further compares רַחֲמָתַיִם in Judg 5:30 and *rḥmt* in *KAI* 181.17 with the rare use of the Ugaritic noun *rḥm* as a title for the goddess Anat at Late Bronze Ugarit (*KTU*³ 1.6.ii.27; cf. *KTU*³ 1.5.iv.3 [reconstructed], 1.13.2?, 1.17.ii.47?).[30] Gregorio del Olmo Lete and Joaquín Sanmartín gloss Ugaritic *rḥm* as, "'vientre' por metonima: 'muchacha núbil, doncella', dicho de la diosa *'nt*," although they

25 Friedrich Schwally, *Semitische Kriegsaltertümer* (Leipzig: Dieterich'sche Verlagsbuchhandlung, Theodor Weicher, 1901), 29–44; Brekelmans, *Ḥerem*, 29–33; Stern, *The Biblical* Ḥerem; Niditch, *War*, 28–77; Dietrich, "The 'Ban'," 196–210; Nelson, "*Ḥerem* and the Deuteronomic Social Conscience," 39–54; Monroe, "Israelite, Moabite and Sabaean War-*ḥērem* Traditions," 318–341; Fleming, *Legacy*, 125–131, 137–143, 244–245, 278.

26 E.g., Van Zyl, *Moabites*, 191 and n. 5; Liver, "Wars of Mesha," 25; Albright, "Moabite Stone," 320; Gibson, *Syrian Semitic Inscriptions*, 76; Jackson, "Language," 98; Parker, *Stories*, 45; Routledge, "Politics of Mesha," 248; Routledge, *Moab*, 136; K.A.D. Smelik, "The Inscription of King Mesha," *COS* 2:138; Snyder, "Chemosh Looks Like YHWH," 121.

27 *HALOT* 2:1217–1218.

28 *HALOT* 2:1218.

29 *HALOT* 2:1217–1218. One might also compare Hebrew רַחֲמָתַיִם and Moabite *rḥmt* with the rare Akkadian noun *rēmtu*, which also means "womb" (*CAD* R 259 [*rēmtu*]).

30 *HALOT* 2:1217–1218.

note that the basic meaning of this word at Ugarit is also "womb."[31] Similarly, *DULAT* gives the primary meaning of Ugaritic *rḥm* as "womb" and notes its evidently secondary, metonymic usage as an epithet for Anat, meaning "nubile girl, damsel."[32] As Philip Stern observes, the use of the *rḥm* as an epithet for the goddess Anat at Ugarit likely speaks against the alleged meaning "female slave, maidservant."[33]

Lacking clear parallels in other Northwest Semitic inscriptions, Hoftijzer and Jongeling list the term *rḥmt* in the Mesha Stele under its own entry, *rḥmh*$_2$, which they interpret as a feminine absolute noun meaning "female slave."[34] However, they also cite a second, frequently overlooked option originally put forward by André Lemaire: a G-stem active feminine plural participle of "*rḥm*$_2$ (= to be pregnant) = pregnant woman."[35] For this possibility, I quote Lemaire at length:

> De même, la traduction *rḥmt*, « servant » ou « concubine », paraît quelque peu étrange dans ce contexte et la référence à l'hébreu, en particulier à *Juges* 5, 30 ne justifie probablement pas cette traduction car le passage du sens bien attesté *raḥam*, « matrice », « sein maternel » d'où « jeune femme » à celui de « servante » ou « concubine » paraît bien hypothétique. En fait, le sens de l'hébreu *raḥam* suggérerait plutôt ici une traduction telle que « femme enceinte », *rḥmt* étant peut-être une forme participiale d'un verbe dénominatif *rḥm*, « concevoir », « être enceinte ». De fait, le massacre des femmes enceintes était alors, au IXe–VIIIe s. av. J.-C., un cliché littéraire pour exprimer une guerre sans pitié. Ainsi, par exemple, *2 Rois* 8, 12, à propos du roi araméen Hazael contemporain de Mésha: « Tu tueras par l'épée leurs jeunes gens; tu écraseras leurs petits enfants; tu fendras leurs femmes enceintes » (cf. aussi *2 Rois* 15, 16; *Os.* 14, 1 et surtout *Amos* 1, 13 faisant allusion à des événements survenus en Transjordanie).[36]

Lemaire observes that the translation of *rḥmt* in *KAI* 181.17 as "female slave, concubine" based on a comparison with רַחֲמָתַיִם in Judg 5:30 remains uncertain, since one would have to posit several hypothetical stages of semantic drift—

---

31 Gregorio del Olmo Lete and Joaquín Sanmartín, *Diccionario de la Lengua Ugarítica*, vol. 2 (Barcelona: Editorial AUSA, 1996), 388.

32 *DULAT* 737.

33 Stern, *The Biblical* Ḥerem, 33.

34 *DNWSI* 2:1071.

35 *DNWSI* 2:1071.

36 Lemaire, "Notes," 208.

from "womb," to "young woman," to "female slave, concubine." Moreover, the translation "female slave, concubine" does not appear to suit the logic of the text. The context of the Mesha Stele clearly indicates a group of persons, but as Lemaire notes, the specification of "female slaves" seems "quelque peu étrange." How would Mesha have distinguished between "women" (*gbrt*), "girls" (*g*[*r*]*t*), and "female slaves" (*rḥmt*)?[37] Moreover, why would Mesha single out female slaves, but not male slaves? The two gendered classes of persons listed just before *rḥmt* in ll. 16–17 are set in parallel in the pattern male—male, female—female (*g*[*b*]*rn.wgrn*|*wgbrt.wg*[*r*]*t*, "men and boys, women and girls"), but there is no parallel male counterpart to accompany *rḥmt*. I therefore concur with Lemaire that the meaning of *rḥmt* probably lies closer to the basic meaning of the root *rḥm*, "womb,"[38] which specifies a part of the female body whose reproductive capacities could be visually perceived during the later stages of pregnancy.[39]

Furthermore, Lemaire notes that the slaughter of pregnant women was a common literary motif to express the cruelty of a war in ancient Near Eastern battle accounts.[40] For instance, the prophet Elisha laments in 2 Kgs 8:12 that King Hazael of Aram will "raze (the Israelites') fortresses with fire, slay their young men with the sword, smash their children, and rip open their pregnant women" (מבצריהם תשלח באש ובחריהם בחרב תהרג ועלליהם תרטש והרתיהם תבקע; cf. also 2 Kgs 15:16; Hos 13:16; Amos 1:13).[41] While Lemaire is correct that the slaughter of pregnant women and infants appears to have been a literary trope in ancient Near Eastern battle accounts, the reference to "pregnant women" in the

37 Cf. Stern, *The Biblical* Ḥerem, 33.

38 If Lemaire is correct that *rḥmt* is a participle of a denominative verb *rḥm*, it would have to be a G-stem denominative. Although the D-stem is more common for denominative verbs, the participle in the D-stem would require a prefixed *m*-.

39 Alongside my preferred interpretation of "pregnant women," one could also interpret *rḥmt* as referring to "women of reproductive age" more broadly (cf. Stern, *The Biblical* Ḥerem, 33–34 ["young" or "nubile women"]; Na'aman, "Royal Inscription," 147 and n. 6 ["maidens," citing Bordreuil, "A propos," 158–161]; Aḥituv, *Echoes*, 409 ["maidens"]). If so, then the previous term *g*[*r*]*t*, "girls," would probably have to be understood as specifically referring to prepubescent girls. However, the comparative evidence indicates that the killing of pregnant women and their fetuses was a common literary trope in ancient Near Eastern war accounts (see below). Regardless, Mesha's use of the term *rḥmt*—whether understood as pregnant women or women of reproductive age—emphasizes the complete destruction of the female reproductive potential of the conquered population.

40 See also Mordechai Cogan, "'Ripping open Pregnant Women' in Light of an Assyrian Analogue," *JAOS* 103 (1983): 755–757; Niditch, *War*, 129ff. Cf. the Deir ʿAllā inscription's emphatic use of the phrase *ʾl rḥm* (2.13)—perhaps meaning either "fetus of the womb" or "newborn child" (*DNWSI* 2:844)—to portend utter devastation.

41 Note that this passage does not explicitly mention *ḥērem*-warfare.

Mesha Stele may have a further, more specific rationale within its literary context. As Gary Rendsburg observes, the appearance of the term *rḥmt* in *KAI* 181.17 looks to be connected to the use of the verb *hḥrmth*, "I devoted it to destruction," in the same line, with which the noun *rḥmt* alliterates nicely.[42] Thus, the reference to "pregnant women" is linked literarily to the description of Mesha's use of *ḥērem*-warfare against Nebo.

From a religious-historical perspective, Mesha's listing of several different gendered classes of persons whom he killed using *ḥērem*-warfare, ultimately culminating with pregnant women, further emphasizes the complete fulfillment of his obligations to the Moabite god Kemosh. Richard Nelson terms comparable biblical lists in the implementation of *ḥērem*-warfare a "'*ḥerem* inventory,' an all-inclusive list of the classes of people or domestic animals treated as *ḥerem*. This emphasized the comprehensive nature of the proceeding."[43] The biblical *ḥērem*-lists often include the slaughtering of women, children, and/or infants (Deut 2:34, 3:6, Josh 6:21, Judg 21:10, 1 Sam 15:3)—although such lists never mention slaves, whether male or female.[44] Mesha's specification of "pregnant women" among the other classes of persons killed ("men and boys, women and girls") in his *ḥērem*-attack on Nebo rhetorically demonstrates that all persons in the town were put to death in fulfillment of the requirements of *ḥērem*-warfare. Not even the most vulnerable of the enemy population—pregnant women (and by implication their fetuses)—were spared.

4 The Rhetoric and Ideology of *Ḥērem*-Warfare: Ataroth versus Nebo

Mesha's campaigns against the towns of Ataroth and Nebo belong to a section of the Mesha Stele with its own literary and conceptual integrity.[45] Moreover, the descriptions of Mesha's attacks on Ataroth and Nebo are connected through important thematic elements (e.g., the killing of both towns' populations [ll. 11, 16–17], the Moabite deity's possession of both Ataroth and Nebo [ll. 12, 17], the placement of cultic objects from both locations before Kemosh [ll. 12–13, 17–18], etc.). For these reasons, some scholars have proposed that Mesha implemented *ḥērem*-warfare against both towns.[46]

42 Stern, *The Biblical* Ḥerem, 34 n. 37; Rendsburg, "ואשב in the Mesha Stele," 24.
43 Nelson, "*Ḥerem* and the Deuteronomic Social Conscience," 47.
44 Stern, *The Biblical* Ḥerem, 33.
45 Routledge, *Moab*, 143; Aḥituv, *Echoes*, 403.
46 Liver, "Wars of Mesha," 24–25; Dietrich, "The 'Ban'," 202; cf. Van Zyl, *Moabites*, 201; Mattingly, "Moabite Religion," 234–235; Routledge, *Moab*, 149.

However, my analysis of the term *rḥmt* supports the conclusion that these two towns did not receive the same treatment (at least as portrayed in the text). Mesha's listing of the categories of inhabitants that he kills in his *ḥērem*-attack on Nebo—culminating with pregnant women—exceeds in intensity the inscription's prior description of the slaughter of the people of Ataroth (ll. 10b–14). While Mesha claims that he "killed all the people" (*wʾhrg.ʾt.kl.hʿm*) of Ataroth (l. 11), the text does not provide an itemized list of the different classes of persons killed as in the *ḥērem*-attack on Nebo (ll. 16–17), nor does the Mesha Stele give a symbolic number ("seven thousand") representing the totality of those killed at Ataroth, as with Nebo (see l. 16). Moreover, only the attack on Nebo explicitly states that the population was "devoted to destruction" (*hḥrmth*, l. 17); the verb **ḥrm* is not used in the attack on the town of Ataroth, which is only said to have been "seized" (*wʾḥzh*, l. 11; cf. ll. 15–16).[47] Furthermore, Nebo is the only city which Mesha sacks that is not said to have been rebuilt or resettled.[48] Such differences indicate that Nebo represented a special situation for Mesha,[49] reflected in the campaign's emphatic placement at the literary center of the inscription.[50]

Whatever the practical differences may have been, the Mesha Stele appears to draw an ideological distinction between the wholesale slaughter of an enemy people during war (i.e., Ataroth) and the extermination of the population of an enemy town because one has "devoted" (C-stem **ḥrm*) it to the deity (i.e., Nebo).[51] Parker thus observes that Mesha devotes Nebo to the deity alone (l. 17),

---

47 Nelson, "*Ḥerem* and the Deuteronomic Social Conscience," 47; Monroe, "Israelite, Moabite and Sabaean War-*ḥērem* Traditions," 324 n. 13.

48 Liver, "Wars of Mesha," 25; Parker, *Stories*, 51; Aḥituv, *Echoes*, 410.

49 Nelson, "*Ḥerem* and the Deuteronomic Social Conscience," 47.

50 Observed in Stern, *The Biblical* Ḥerem, 34; Monroe, "Israelite, Moabite and Sabaean War-*ḥērem* Traditions," 325 n. 14.

51 Scholars disagree as to the distinct conceptual logic of *ḥērem*-warfare. Stern argues (*The Biblical* ḤEREM, 41, 47, 50, 80, 83, 85, 86, *passim*) that *ḥērem*-warfare represents an expression of the defeat of chaos (i.e., enemies conceptually represent the forces of chaos) and the creation of order. Kang (*Divine War*, 80) understands *ḥērem*-warfare in terms of "consecration" or "taboo," denoting "the status of being prohibited from common use or contact either because of proscription as an abomination to god or because of consecration to god"; cf. Abraham Malamat, *Mari and the Early Israelite Experience*, The Schweich Lectures 1984 (Oxford: Oxford University Press, 1989), 70–79; Mattingly, "Moabite Religion," 235; M. Malul, "Taboo," *DDD*: 824–825. Susan Niditch (*War*, 28–55) and Mark Smith and Wayne Pitard (*The Ugaritic Baal Cycle, Vol. 2: Introduction with Text, Translation and Commentary of KTU 1.3–1.4*, VTSup 114 [Leiden: Brill, 2009], 180, 182–183) consider sacrifice to be the conceptual key to understanding the nature of *ḥērem*-warfare. Nelson ("*Ḥerem* and the Deuteronomic Social Conscience," 41–44), Routledge (*Moab*, 150), and Monroe ("Israelite, Moabite, and Sabaean War-*ḥērem*," 321) understand the concept of *ḥērem*-warfare concep-

whereas Ataroth becomes the property of both the deity and Moab (l. 12).[52] Furthermore, the attack on Nebo is initiated by an oracle from the deity ("Kemosh said to me: 'Go! Seize Nebo from Israel'!"; l. 14), whereas the assault on Ataroth is not. It may be that such differences between the treatment of Ataroth and Nebo should be connected with Nebo's sanctuary and cult center to YHWH, who only is referred to in the attack on Nebo and who may have been understood—at least from the Moabite perspective—to be Israel's royal patron god (see further below). In any case, the Mesha Stele's use of the term *rḥmt*, "pregnant women," belongs rhetorically to the language/ideology of *ḥērem*-warfare, which the inscription applies only to Nebo.[53]

5 Pregnant with Meaning

The interpretation of *rḥmt* as "pregnant women" is not simply a philological and/or historical issue—it is also an ethical one. Mesha's emphatic placement of pregnant women at the end of his *ḥērem*-inventory has important political implications tied to the ideological significance of *ḥērem*-warfare. Recent scholarship situates the politics of *ḥērem*-warfare in general, and in the Mesha Stele in particular, in "tribal contexts during the early stages of state formation," "associated with assertions of collective identity and emergent political authority."[54] The collective politics of *ḥērem*-warfare ideology and Mesha's gendered rhetoric for its implementation against Nebo thus calls for consideration from a postcolonial feminist perspective, which joins the analysis of polity and gender to deconstruct the sexual politics of "nationalist" discourses.[55]

---

tually as having "its basis in gift exchange as the foundation of non-kin based human sociability ... the key to invoking *ḥērem* is the prevention of exchange through the insertion of the deity who holds booty and captives as inalienable possessions" (Monroe, "Israelite, Moabite, and Sabaean War-*ḥērem*," 321); cf. Ziony Zevit, "Mesha's *Ryt* in the Context of Moabite and Israelite Bloodletting," in *Puzzling out the Past: Studies in Northwest Semitic Languages and Literatures in Honor of Bruce Zuckerman*, ed. Marilyn J. Lundberg, Steven Fine, and Wayne T. Pitard (Leiden: Brill, 2012), 236.

52 Parker, *Stories*, 51–52.

53 Note again the alliteration in l. 17 between *rḥmt*, "pregnant women," and the verb *hḥrmth*, "I devoted it to destruction."

54 Monroe, "Israelite, Moabite, and Sabaean War-*ḥērem*," 339, 341; see also Routledge, *Moab*, 141.

55 Such "nationalist" discourses "produce, construct, inscribe, question, revise, and rewrite collective identities across gender, class, and ethnic difference" (Esther Fuchs, *Feminist Theory and the Bible: Interrogating the Sources*, Feminist Studies and Sacred Texts [New York, NY: Lexington Books, 2016], 71).

While the interventions of postcolonial literary critics cannot be said to represent a unified theory, there are certain common issues that repeatedly emerge in postcolonial studies. Of particular relevance to this study, Jane Webster observes that postcolonial discourse analyses often serve to deconstruct "the relationship between power and knowledge in the production of the colonial Other."[56] Political identities are inherently unstable ideological constructions produced through discursive practices located in particular social-historical contexts—they are "imagined communities," to use Benedict Anderson's famous phrase.[57] Such identities are relational, forged through interaction with "Other"/"foreign" collective identities that are equally unstable and relational.[58] The understanding of political communities as discursively constructed, historically contingent bodies (re)produced in relation to other "foreign" communal identities provides a fruitful theoretical framework for analyzing the literary-ideological character of the Mesha Stele, which constitutes "Moabite" identity in relation to "Israelite" identity through its narrative account of Mesha's military conflict with Israel—including the special use of *ḥērem*-warfare against Nebo.

Furthermore, feminist critics informed by postcolonial theorizing, such as Esther Fuchs, highlight how narratives of war often serve to publicly legitimize violence against (enemy) women, constituting masculinity as violent and dominant and femininity as vulnerable and subordinate.[59] Fuchs observes: "Militarization, as the site of homosocial (male only) bonding and as the institutional legitimization of collective violence, is constitutive of the definition of mas-

56 Jane Webster, "Roman Imperialism and the 'Post Imperial Age'," in *Roman Imperialism: Post-Colonial Perspectives*, ed. Jane Webster and Nicholas J. Cooper, Leicester Archaeology Monographs 3 (Leicester: School of Archaeological Studies University of Leicester, 1996), 7. See also Patrick Williams and Laura Chrisman, "Colonial Discourse and Post-Colonial Theory: An Introduction," in *Colonial Discourse and Post-Colonial Theory: A Reader*, ed. Patrick Williams and Laura Chrisman (New York, NY: Columbia University Press, 1994), 8. For the value of postcolonial perspectives in the historical study of ancient literary texts and their politics, see Elizabeth A. Clark, *History, Theory, Text: Historians and the "Linguistic Turn"* (Cambridge, MA: Harvard University Press, 2004), 181–185.

57 Homi Bhabha, "Dissemination: Time, Narrative, and the Margins of the Modern Nation," in *Nation and Narration*, ed. Homi Bhabha (London: Routledge, 1990), 291–322; Bhabha, *The Location of Culture* (London: Routledge, 1994), 199–244; Benedict Anderson, *Imagined Communities: Reflections on the Origin and Spread of Nationalism* (London: Verso, 2006); Fuchs, *Feminist Theory and the Bible*, 83.

58 Esther Fuchs writes (*Feminist Theory and the Bible*, 82–83): "As a coherent imagined community, the nation requires an 'Other,' an imagined collective opponent who threatens its survival and cultural ideals."

59 Fuchs, *Feminist Theory and the Bible*, 79–80.

culinity as such. The authorization of masculine hegemony in the definition of the nation is contingent on military activity and participation. Warfare thus constructs both masculine and national identity."[60] Fuchs, among others, interrogates how "nationalist" narratives of violence against the bodies of women serve to rhetorically construct the body politic. To my knowledge, this type of analysis has never been applied to the Mesha Stele generally, or to its portrayal of *ḥērem*-warfare specifically.

As a royal literary text, the Mesha Stele represents a concerted intellectual effort to construct a distinctively Moabite collective political identity ideologically centered on the institution of divine kingship through its narration of Mesha and Moab's conflict with Omri and Israel.[61] In this way, the Mesha Stele serves to legitimize Mesha's rightful rule as king of Moab, with Kemosh as his royal patron god.[62] Although the Mesha Stele presents Mesha's role as Moab's dynastic king and Kemosh's function as Mesha and Moab's divine patron as hearkening back to earlier times, recent studies suggest that the Mesha Stele's constitution of "Moab as a politically unified territory under the dynastic rule of Mesha and his god Chemosh" represents a historical innovation.[63] In other words, the Mesha Stele witnesses to Mesha's attempt to create a new Moabite political identity centered around deity, king, and people.

The rhetoric of *ḥērem*-warfare in the Mesha Stele—with its particular emphasis on the slaying of pregnant women, who occupy the final position of Mesha's *ḥērem*-inventory—belongs to this broader effort to construct an independent Moabite political identity ideologically centered on the institution of divine kingship. As historiographical literature, the Mesha Stele narrates the process of Moab's collective identity formation by deliberately contrasting

60 Fuchs, *Feminist Theory and the Bible*, 79–80.

61 Omer Sergi, "State Formation, Religion and 'Collective Identity' in the Southern Levant," *HeBAI* 4 (2015): 56–77; Becking, "A Voice from across the Jordan," 125–145; Michael J. Stahl, *The "God of Israel" in History and Tradition*, VTSup 187 (Leiden: Brill, 2021), 121–124.

62 Mattingly, "Moabite Religion," 44–60; Miller, "Moabite Stone," 9–18; Joel F. Drinkard, "The Literary Genre of the Mesha' Inscription," in Dearman, *Studies in the Mesha Inscription*, 131–154; Klaas A.D. Smelik, "King Mesha's Inscription between History and Fiction," in *Converting the Past: Studies in Ancient Israelite and Moabite Historiography*, OtSt 28 (Leiden: Brill, 1992), 59–92; Niccacci, "Stela of Mesha," 226–248; Parker, *Stories*, 47–53; Christian Molke, *Der Text der Mescha-Stele und die biblische Geschichtschreibung*, Beiträge zur Erforschung der antiken Moabitis (Arḍ el-Kerak) 5 (Frankfurt am Main: Peter Lang, 2006), 26–28, 48–49; Sergi, "State Formation," 60–61, 73–75; Becking, "Voice from across the Jordan," 125–145; Stahl, *"God of Israel" in History and Tradition*, 121–124.

63 Routledge, "Politics of Mesha," 221–256; Routledge, *Moab*, 139–150; van der Steen and Smelik, "King Mesha," 139–162; Sergi, "State Formation," 60–61, 73–75 (the quote is from p. 60).

Moab, led by Mesha as king and Kemosh as divine patron, with the "foreign Other" of Israel, ruled by Omri (and his son) and divinely protected by YHWH. Within this context, I suggest that the *ḥerem*-list's stress on pregnant women: (1) masculinizes Moabite political identity and feminizes Israelite identity; and (2) reflects the ideological threat that "foreign" Israelite pregnant women (and their implied fetuses) represent to the new Moabite political order that King Mesha sought to create, in part, through the use of *ḥērem*-warfare.[64] In the first instance, Mesha's representation of his successful implementation of *ḥērem*-warfare on the Israelite population of Nebo serves to construct Moabite collective identity in masculine terms as powerful, victorious, and appropriately violent. In necessary contrast, Israelite identity is thereby feminized as weak/vulnerable, submissive, and inappropriately aggressive. Thus, the Mesha Stele portrays Israel as the violent aggressor, having transgressively "violated" (***ʿ*nh*; cf. this verb's use in sexual contexts in Gen 34:2; Deut 22:24, 29; Judg 19:24, 20:5; 2 Sam 13:12, 14, 22, 32; Ezek 22:10; Lam 5:11) the "land" (*ʾrṣ*, a grammatically feminine noun) of Moab in the time of Omri (ll. 5–7). However, Omride Israel's pretension to act as Moab's lord or master do not match reality. Ultimately, Israel cannot even protect its most vulnerable members—women, children, and pregnant women—or its god YHWH from Moabite retribution under the leadership of Mesha and Kemosh. In this way, Mesha emasculates both Israel and YHWH, while also using the Israelite threat as a foil to authorize his "patriarchal protection and justif[y] hierarchical arrangements" in the new Moabite polity.[65]

Finally, the placement of pregnant women at the end of the Mesha Stele's *ḥērem*-inventory—which, in turn, stands at the literary center of the text as part of the campaign against Nebo—signals their special importance within Mesha's larger political-ideological program. Although some of the most vulnerable members of ancient society, pregnant women harbor the powerful potential for the social and political rebirth of the Israelite "Other." In its culmination with pregnant women, the Mesha Stele's *ḥērem*-list thus demonstrates the king's complete fulfillment of his religious obligations to the Moabite god Kemosh, as well as Moab and Kemosh's political dominance over Israel and YHWH. In this way, ritually sanctioned violence against the bodies of

64 Contrast Stern, *The Biblical* Ḥerem, 34. Stern proposes that the word *rḥmt* at the end of Mesha's *ḥērem*-list emphasizes the social and economic value of "nubile women" as "the most desirable booty of all" (cf. Deut 21:10–14; Judg 5:30), thereby earning the Moabite king "maximum credit from his god" since he devoted them to destruction.

65 This phraseology, used in a different context, comes from Fuchs, *Feminist Theory and the Bible*, 84.

"foreign"/"Israelite" pregnant women serves as a distinct point of emphasis in the construction of the boundaries of an independent Moabite political body, ideologically centered on the institution of divine kingship.

Bibliography

Achenbach, Reinhard. "Divine Warfare and YHWH's Wars: Religious Ideologies of War in the Ancient Near East and in the Old Testament." Pages 1–16 in *The Ancient Near East in the 12th–10th Centuries BCE*. Edited by Gershon Galil et al. AOAT 392. Münster: Ugarit-Verlag, 2012.

Aḥituv, Shmuel. *Echoes from the Past: Hebrew and Cognate Inscriptions from the Biblical Period*. Jerusalem: Carta, 2008.

Ahlström, Gösta W. *Royal Administration and National Religion in Ancient Palestine*. SHANE 1. Leiden: Brill, 1982.

Albright, William F. "The Moabite Stone." *ANET* 320.

An, H. "Some Additional Epigraphic Comments on the Mesha Stele: The Case for Reading *hyt* in Line 12." *Maarav* 17 (2010): 149–172.

Anderson, Benedict. *Imagined Communities: Reflections on the Origin and Spread of Nationalism*. London: Verso, 2006.

Avanzini, Alessandra. "Review of Norbert Nebes, *Der Tatenbericht des Yiṯaʿʾamar Watar Bin Yakrubmalik aus Ṣirwāḥ (Jemen): Zur Geschichte Südarabiens im frühen 1. Jahrtausend vor Christus*." *JSS* 63 (2018): 532–543.

Bhabha, Homi. "Dissemination: Time, Narrative, and the Margins of the Modern Nation." Pages 291–322 in *Nation and Narration*. Edited by Homi Bhabha. London: Routledge, 1990.

Bhabha, Homi. *The Location of Culture*. London: Routledge, 1994.

Becking, Bob. "A Voice from across the Jordan: Royal Ideology as Implied in the Moabite Stela." Pages 125–145 in *Herrschaftslegitimation in vorderorientalischen Reichen der Eisenzeit*. Edited by Christoph Levin and Reinhard Müller. ORA 21. Tübingen: Mohr Siebeck, 2017.

Beeston, A.F.L. "Mesha and Ataroth." *JRAS* (1985): 143–148.

Bordreuil, Pierre. "A propos de l'inscription de Meshaʿ: deux notes." Pages 158–167 in *The World of the Aramaeans, III: Studies in Language and Literature in Honour of Paul-Eugène Dion*. Edited by P.M. Michèle Daviau, John W. Wevers, and Michael Weigl. JSOTSup 326. Sheffield: Sheffield Academic Press, 2001.

Brekelmans, C.H.W. *De Ḥerem in het Oude Testament*. Nijmegen: Centrale Drukkerij, 1959.

Clark, Elizabeth A. *History, Theory, Text: Historians and the "Linguistic Turn"*. Cambridge, MA: Harvard University Press, 2004.

Cogan, Mordechai. "'Ripping open Pregnant Women' in Light of an Assyrian Analogue." *JAOS* 103/4 (1983): 755–757.

Cole, Steven W., and Peter Machinist, ed. *Letters from Priests to the Kings Esarhaddon and Assurbanipal.* SAA 13. Helsinki: Helsinki University Press, 1998.

Craigie, Peter. *The Problem of War in the Old Testament.* Grand Rapids, MI: Eerdmans, 1978.

Crist, Mary. "Frybread in Canaan." *First Peoples Theology Journal* 7 (2014): 2–15.

Crouch, Carly L. *War and Ethics in the Ancient Near East: Military Violence in Light of Cosmology and History.* BZAW 40. Berlin: de Gruyter, 2009.

Crüsemann, Frank. "Gewaltimagination als Teil der Ursprungsgeschichte: Banngebot und Rechtsordnung im Deuteronomium." Pages 343–360 in *Religion, Politik, und Gewalt: Kongressband des XII. Europäischen Kongresses für Theologie, 18.–22. September 2005 in Berlin.* Edited by Friedrich Schweitzer. Gütersloh: Gütersloher Verlagshaus, 2006.

Dearman, John Andrew, ed. *Studies in the Mesha Inscription and Moab.* ABS 2. Atlanta, GA: Scholars Press, 1989.

Dietrich, Walter. "The 'Ban' in the Age of Israel's Early Kings." Pages 196–210 in *The Origins of the Ancient Israelite State.* Edited by Volkmar Fritz and Philip R. Davies. JSOTSup 228. Sheffield: Sheffield Academic Press, 1996.

Drinkard, Joel F. "The Literary Genre of the Meshaʿ Inscription." Pages 131–154 in *Studies in the Mesha Inscription and Moab.* Edited by John Andrew Dearman. ABS 2. Atlanta, GA: Scholars Press, 1989.

Fleming, Daniel E. *The Legacy of Israel in Judah's Bible: History, Politics, and the Reinscribing of Tradition.* Cambridge: Cambridge University Press, 2012.

Frankel, David. *The Land of Canaan and the Destiny of Israel: Theologies of Territory in the Hebrew Bible.* Winona Lake, IN: Eisenbrauns, 2011.

Fuchs, Esther. *Feminist Theory and the Bible: Interrogating the Sources.* Feminist Studies and Sacred Texts. New York, NY: Lexington Books, 2016.

Gibson, J.C.L. *Syrian Semitic Inscriptions, Vol. 1: Hebrew and Moabite.* Oxford: Clarendon Press, 1971.

Glanville, Mark R. "Ethics of Reading Unethical Texts Ethically: A Fresh Reading of *Ḥerem* in Deuteronomy and Joshua." Paper presented at the annual meeting of the Society of Biblical Literature, 7 December, 2020.

Hatke, George. "For ʾĪlmuquh and for Saba': The *Res Gestae* of Karibʾīl Bin Ḏamarʿalī from Ṣirwāḥ in Context." *Wiener Zeitschrift für die Kunde des Morgenlandes* 105 (2015): 87–133.

Hofreiter, Christian. *Making Sense of Old Testament Genocide: Christian Interpretations of Herem Passages.* Oxford Theology and Religion Monographs. Oxford: Oxford University Press, 2018.

Jackson, Kent P. "The Language of the Meshaʿ Inscription." Pages 96–130 in *Studies in the Mesha Inscription and Moab*. Edited by John Andrew Dearman. ABS 2. Atlanta, GA: Scholars Press, 1989.

Jackson, Kent P., and John Andrew Dearman, "The Text of the Meshaʿ Inscription." Pages 93–95 in *Studies in the Mesha Inscription and Moab*. Edited by John Andrew Dearman. ABS 2. Atlanta, GA: Scholars Press, 1989.

Johnson, Erika D. "Stealing the Enemy's Gods: An Exploration of the Phenomenon of Godnap in Ancient Western Asia." Ph.D. diss., University of Birmingham, 2011.

Junker, Hubert. "Der alttestamentliche Bann geben heidnische Völker als moraltheologisches und offenbarungsgeschichtliches Problem." *TTZ* 3/4 (1947): 74–89.

Kang, S.-M. *Divine War in the Old Testament and in the Ancient Near East*. BZAW 177. Berlin: de Gruyter, 1989.

Kravitz, Kathryn F. "Divine Trophies of War in Assyria and Ancient Israel: Case Studies in Political Theology." Ph.D. diss., Brandeis University, 1999.

Lemaire, André. "Notes d'épigraphie nord-ouest Semitique." *Syria* 64 (1987): 205–214.

Lemaire, André. "'House of David' Restored in Moabite Inscription." *BAR* 20/3 (1994): 30–37.

Lemaire, André. "New Photographs and *ryt* or *hyt* in Mesha, Line 12." *IEJ* 57 (2007): 204–207.

Lemaire, André. "The Mesha Stele and the Omri Dynasty." Pages 135–144 in *Ahab Agonistes: The Rise and Fall of the Omri Dynasty*. Edited by Lester L. Grabbe. LHBOTS 421. London: T&T Clark, 2007.

Lidzbarski, Mark. *Ephemeris für semitische Epigraphik*. Giessen: Töpelmann, 1902.

Lidzbarski, Mark. *Kanaanäische Inschriften* (*Moabitisch, Althebräisch, Phönizisch, Punisch*). Giessen: Töpelmann, 1907.

Lipiński, Edward. "Etymological and Exegetical Notes on the Mešaʿ Inscription." *Or* 40 (1971): 325–340.

Liver, J. "The Wars of Mesha, King of Moab." *PEQ* 99 (1967): 14–31.

Malamat, Abraham. *Mari and the Early Israelite Experience*. The Schweich Lectures 1984. Oxford: Oxford University Press, 1989.

Malul, M. "Taboo." *DDD* 824–827.

Mattingly, Gerald L. "Moabite Religion and the Meshaʿ Inscription." Pages 211–238 in *Studies in the Mesha Inscription and Moab*. Edited by John Andrew Dearman. ABS 2. Atlanta, GA: Scholars Press, 1989.

Miller, Max. "The Moabite Stone as a Memorial Stela." *PEQ* 106 (1974): 9–18.

Moberly, R.W.L. "Is Election Bad for You?" Pages 95–111 in *The Centre and the Periphery: A European Tribute to Walter Brueggemann*. Edited by Jill Middlemas, David J.A. Clines, and Else K. Holt. HBM 27. Sheffield: Sheffield Phoenix Press, 2010.

Molke, Christian. *Der Text der Mescha-Stele und die biblische Geschichtschreibung*. Beiträge zur Erforschung der antiken Moabitis (Arḍ el-Kerak) 5. Frankfurt am Main: Peter Lang, 2006.

Monroe, Lauren A.S. "Israelite, Moabite and Sabaean War-*ḥērem* Traditions and the Forging of National Identity: Reconsidering the Sabaean Text RES 3945 in Light of Biblical and Moabite Evidence." *VT* 57 (2007): 318–341.

Morriston, Wes. "Ethical Criticism of the Bible: The Case of Divinely Mandated Genocide." *Sophia* 51 (2012): 117–135.

Na'aman, Nadav. "The Campaign of Mesha against Horonaim." *BN* 73 (1994): 27–30.

Na'aman, Nadav. "King Mesha and the Foundation of the Moabite Monarchy." *IEJ* 47 (1997): 83–92.

Na'aman, Nadav. "Royal Inscription versus Prophetic Story: Mesha's Rebellion according to Biblical and Moabite Historiography." Pages 145–183 in *Ahab Agonistes: The Rise and Fall of the Omri Dynasty*. Edited by Lester L. Grabbe. LHBOTS 421. London: T&T Clark, 2007.

Nelson, Richard. "*Ḥerem* and the Deuteronomic Social Conscience." Pages 39–54 in *Deuteronomy and Deuteronomic Literature: Festschrift for C.H.W. Brekelmans*. Edited by Marc Vervenne and Johan Lust. Leuven: Leuven University Press/Peeters, 1997.

Niccacci, Alviero. "The Stele of Mesha and the Bible: Verbal System and Narrativity." *Or* 63 (1994): 226–248.

Niditch, Susan. *War in the Hebrew Bible: A Study in the Ethics of Violence*. Oxford: Oxford University Press, 1993.

Olmo Lete, Gregorio del, and Joaquín Sanmartín. *Diccionario de la Lengua Ugarítica*. Vol. 2. Barcelona: Editorial AUSA, 1996.

Parker, Simon. *Stories in Scripture and Inscriptions: Comparative Studies on Narratives in Northwest Semitic Inscriptions and the Hebrew Bible*. Oxford: Oxford University Press, 1997.

Pitkänen, Pekka. "Ancient Israel and Settler Colonialism." *Settler Colonial Studies* 4 (2014): 64–81.

Porter, Barbara N. "Gods' Statues as a Tool of Assyrian Political Policy: Esarhaddon's Return of Marduk to Babylon." Pages 9–24 in *Religious Transformations and Socio-Political Change: Eastern Europe and Latin America*. Edited by Luther Martin. RelSoc 33. Berlin: de Gruyter, 1999.

Rainey, Anson F. "Syntax, Hermeneutics and History." *IEJ* 48 (1998): 239–251.

Rendsburg, Gary. "A Reconstruction of Moabite-Israelite History." *JANES* 13 (1981): 67–73.

Rendsburg, Gary. "ואשב in the Mesha Stele, Line 12." *Maarav* 14 (2007): 9–25.

Römer, Thomas. *The Invention of God*. Trans. Raymond Guess. Cambridge, MA: Harvard University Press, 2015.

Römer, Thomas. "L'énigme de 'Ashtar-Kemosh dans la stèle de Mésha." Pages 385–394 in *Alphabets, Texts and Artifacts in the Ancient Near East: Studies presented to Ben-*

jamin Sass. Edited by Israel Finkelstein, Christian J. Robin, and Thomas Römer. Paris: Van Dieren, 2016.

Routledge, Bruce. "The Politics of Mesha: Segmented Identities and State Formation in Iron Age Moab." *JESHO* 43/3 (2000): 221–256.

Routledge, Bruce. *Moab in the Iron Age: Hegemony, Polity, Archaeology*. ACS. Philadelphia: University of Pennsylvania Press, 2004.

Ruffing, Andreas. *Jahwekrieg als Weltmetapher: Studien zu Jahwekriegstexten des chronistischen Sondergutes*. SBB 24. Stuttgart: Katholisches Bibelwerk, 1992.

Said, Edward. "Michael Walzer's 'Exodus and Revolution: A Canaanite Reading'." *Grand Street* 5/2 (1986): 86–106.

Sanders, Seth. "The Referent of West Semitic **ḥrm*: Ancient Genocide and the Ethics of Philology." Unpublished paper.

Sassoon, Isaac S.D. "Obliterating Cherem." *TheTorah.com*. 2015. https://thetorah.com/article/obliterating-cherem.

Schade, Aaron. "New Photographs Supporting the Reading *ryt* in Line 12 of the Mesha Inscription." *IEJ* 55 (2005): 205–208.

Schaudig, Hanspeter. "Death of Statues and Rebirth of Gods." Pages 123–149 in *Iconoclasm and Text: Destruction in the Ancient Near East and Beyond*. Edited by Natalie N. May. OIS 8. Chicago: Oriental Institute, 2012.

Schmitt, Rüdiger. *Der "Heilige Krieg" im Pentateuch und im deuteronomistischen Geschichtswerk: Studien zur Forschungs-, Rezeptions- und Religionsgeschichte von Krieg und Bann im Alten Testament*. AOAT 381. Münster: Ugarit-Verlag, 2011.

Schwally, Friedrich. *Semitische Kriegsaltertümer*. Leipzig: Dieterich'sche Verlagsbuchhandlung, Theodor Weicher, 1901.

Sergi, Omer. "State Formation, Religion and 'Collective Identity' in the Southern Levant." *HeBAI* 4 (2015): 56–77.

Smelik, Klaas A.D. "King Mesha's Inscription between History and Fiction." Pages 59–92 in *Converting the Past: Studies in Ancient Israelite and Moabite Historiography*. OtSt 28. Leiden: Brill, 1992.

Smelik, Klaas A.D. "The Inscription of King Mesha." *COS* 2:138.

Smith, Mark S., and Wayne Pitard. *The Ugaritic Baal Cycle, Vol. 2: Introduction with Text, Translation and Commentary of KTU 1.3–1.4*. VTSup 114. Leiden: Brill, 2009.

Snyder, Josey Bridges. "Chemosh Looks Like YHWH, but That's Okay." Pages 115–125 in *Divine Doppelgängers: YHWH's Ancient Look-Alikes*. Edited by Collin Cornell. University Park, PA: Eisenbrauns—PSU Press, 2020.

Snyder, Josey Bridges, and Brent A. Strawn. "Reading (in) Moabite Patterns: 'Parallelism' in the Mesha Inscription and Its Implications for Understanding Three Cruxes (*ʿštr kmš*, line 17; *h/ryt*, line 12; and *ʾrʾl dwdh*, line 12)." Forthcoming.

Stahl, Michael J. "*Ḥērem*-Warfare at Ugarit? Reevaluating *KTU* 1.13 and *KTU* 1.3 II." *UF* (2016): 265–299.

Stahl, Michael J. "The Historical Origins of the Biblical God Yahweh." *RC* 14/11 (2020): e12378 (pp. 1–14).
Stahl, Michael J. *The "God of Israel" in History and Tradition*. VTSup 187. Leiden: Brill, 2021.
Stern, Philip D. "1Samuel 15: Towards an Ancient View of the War-Ḥerem." *UF* 21 (1989): 414–444.
Stern, Philip D. *The Biblical* Ḥerem: *A Window on Israel's Religious Experience*. Atlanta, GA: Scholars Press, 1991.
Stone, G. Lawson. "Ethical and Apologetic Tendencies in the Redaction of the Book of Joshua." *CBQ* 53 (1991): 25–36.
Thelle, Rannfrid I. "The Biblical Conquest Account and Its Modern Hermeneutical Challenges." *ST* 61 (2007): 61–81.
Van der Steen, Eveline J., and Klaas A.D. Smelik. "King Mesha and the Tribe of Dibon." *JSOT* 32 (2007): 139–162.
Van der Toorn, Karel. "Yahweh." *DDD*: 910–919.
Van Zyl, A.H. *The Moabites*. Pretoria Oriental Series 3. Leiden: Brill, 1960.
Warrior, Robert A. "Canaanites, Cowboys, and Indians." *Christianity and Crisis* 49 (1989): 261–265.
Webster, Jane. "Roman Imperialism and the 'Post Imperial Age'." Pages 1–17 in *Roman Imperialism: Post-Colonial Perspectives*. Edited by Jane Webster and Nicholas J. Cooper. Leicester Archaeology Monographs 3. Leicester: School of Archaeological Studies University of Leicester, 1996.
Weinfeld, Moshe. "The Conquest of Canaan Land and the Native Ḥerem." *Beth Mikra* 12 (1967): 121–127 (in Hebrew).
Weinfeld, Moshe. "The Ban on the Canaanites in the Biblical Codes." Pages 142–160 in *History and Traditions of Early Israel*. Edited by André Lemaire and Benedikt Otzen. VTSup 50. Leiden: Brill, 1993.
Weinfeld, Moshe. *The Promise of the Land: The Inheritance of the Land of Canaan by the Israelites*. Berkeley, CA: University of California Press, 1993.
Williams, Patrick, and Laura Chrisman. "Colonial Discourse and Post-Colonial Theory: An Introduction." Pages 1–20 in *Colonial Discourse and Post-Colonial Theory: A Reader*. Edited by Patrick Williams and Laura Chrisman. New York, NY: Columbia University Press, 1994.
Zaia, Shana. "State-Sponsored Sacrilege: 'Godnapping' and Omission in Neo-Assyrian Inscriptions." *JANEH* 2 (2015): 19–54.
Zevit, Ziony. "The Search for Violence in Israelite Culture and in the Bible." Pages 16–37 in *Religion and Violence: The Biblical Heritage*. Edited by David A. Bernat and Jonathan Klawans. Recent Research in Biblical Studies 2. Sheffield: Sheffield Phoenix, 2007.
Zevit, Ziony. "Mesha's *Ryt* in the Context of Moabite and Israelite Bloodletting." Pages

235–238 in *Puzzling out the Past: Studies in Northwest Semitic Languages and Literatures in Honor of Bruce Zuckerman*. Edited by Marilyn J. Lundberg, Steven Fine, and Wayne T. Pitard. Leiden: Brill, 2012.

Index

West Semitic sources

Aegean/Greek sources

Roman/Latin sources